Lecture Notes in Computer Science 12884

Founding Editors

Gerhard Goos
Karlsruhe Institute of Technology, Karlsruhe, Germany

Juris Hartmanis
Cornell University, Ithaca, NY, USA

Editorial Board Members

Elisa Bertino
Purdue University, West Lafayette, IN, USA

Wen Gao
Peking University, Beijing, China

Bernhard Steffen
TU Dortmund University, Dortmund, Germany

Gerhard Woeginger
RWTH Aachen, Aachen, Germany

Moti Yung
Columbia University, New York, NY, USA

More information about this subseries at http://www.springer.com/series/7409

Tinne De Laet · Roland Klemke ·
Carlos Alario-Hoyos · Isabel Hilliger ·
Alejandro Ortega-Arranz (Eds.)

Technology-Enhanced Learning for a Free, Safe, and Sustainable World

16th European Conference
on Technology Enhanced Learning, EC-TEL 2021
Bolzano, Italy, September 20–24, 2021
Proceedings

Editors
Tinne De Laet
KU Leuven
Leuven, Belgium

Carlos Alario-Hoyos
Universidad Carlos III de Madrid
Leganés, Spain

Alejandro Ortega-Arranz
Universidad de Valladolid
Valladolid, Spain

Roland Klemke
Open University of the Netherlands
Heerlen, The Netherlands

Isabel Hilliger
Pontificia Universidad Católica de Chile
Santiago, Chile

ISSN 0302-9743　　　　　　ISSN 1611-3349　(electronic)
Lecture Notes in Computer Science
ISBN 978-3-030-86435-4　　　ISBN 978-3-030-86436-1　(eBook)
https://doi.org/10.1007/978-3-030-86436-1

LNCS Sublibrary: SL3 – Information Systems and Applications, incl. Internet/Web, and HCI

© Springer Nature Switzerland AG 2021
Chapter "From Paper to Online: Digitizing Card Based Co-creation of Games for Privacy Education" is licensed under the terms of the Creative Commons Attribution 4.0 International License (http://creativecommons.org/licenses/by/4.0/). For further details see license information in the chapter.

This work is subject to copyright. All rights are reserved by the Publisher, whether the whole or part of the material is concerned, specifically the rights of translation, reprinting, reuse of illustrations, recitation, broadcasting, reproduction on microfilms or in any other physical way, and transmission or information storage and retrieval, electronic adaptation, computer software, or by similar or dissimilar methodology now known or hereafter developed.
The use of general descriptive names, registered names, trademarks, service marks, etc. in this publication does not imply, even in the absence of a specific statement, that such names are exempt from the relevant protective laws and regulations and therefore free for general use.
The publisher, the authors and the editors are safe to assume that the advice and information in this book are believed to be true and accurate at the date of publication. Neither the publisher nor the authors or the editors give a warranty, expressed or implied, with respect to the material contained herein or for any errors or omissions that may have been made. The publisher remains neutral with regard to jurisdictional claims in published maps and institutional affiliations.

This Springer imprint is published by the registered company Springer Nature Switzerland AG
The registered company address is: Gewerbestrasse 11, 6330 Cham, Switzerland

Preface

Welcome to the proceedings of the 16th European Conference on Technology Enhanced Learning (EC-TEL 2021), one of the flagship events of the European Association of Technology Enhanced Learning (EATEL).

The world faces challenges, which require strong educational responses: globalized economies undermine achievements of democratic societies; tendencies towards totalitarian regimes put freedom at risk; the distribution of fake news and conspiracy theories destroy trust in scientific processes and results; growing global populations and demographic changes in developed countries hinder the fair distribution of opportunities; and environmental consequences of human activity, such as climate change, lead to consequences for humanity as a whole. At the same time, new opportunities arise due to technological developments, increased computational power, the availability of technological and computational resources worldwide, and new research results and discoveries.

In response to these tendencies and newly available opportunities, education needs to outreach to global communities of learners, connect people worldwide, and strengthen learners in their understanding of science, democracy, economy, ecology, and freedom. Education needs to help learners, regardless of their individual situation, to stay involved in continuous learning, in active involvement in learning communities, and in supporting the transfer of skills, knowledge, and insights into daily activities.

Technological trends can support these needs but also impose challenges on their own: we observe that the increasingly fast technological developments impact many aspects of our daily lives and challenge educational routines. Digitalization as one of the key trends at global scale only very abstractly describes the consequences and changes routines and processes undergo. Artificial intelligence, increasing computer power, immersive interactive environments, fast internet everywhere, and synchronous and asynchronous ways of communication and collaboration enable new work situations and professional careers.

Likewise, educational technologies emerge in a plethora of forms supporting new forms of learning, teaching, tutoring, supervising, and collaboration. These technologies allow us to scale up learning processes, to individualize learning paths, to support remote, face to face, and hybrid forms of learning, or to better analyze learning progress and success. They promise to support all stakeholders of the educational ecosystems (learners, teachers, educational institutions, employers, and whole societies).

How do these technologies help to address the global challenges? Which benefits do they offer to whom? Which new risks do they impose, and how do we handle these risks? Addressing questions like these, the European Conference on Technology Enhanced Learning (EC-TEL) targets the intersection of technological innovation, educational challenges, and global impact. The EC-TEL 2021 theme of "Technology-enhanced Learning for a Free, Safe, and Sustainable World" addressed how emerging and future learning technologies can be used in a meaningful way to address the global challenges in an increasingly digitized world.

Due to the ongoing COVID-19 pandemic, EC-TEL 2021, while originally planned to take place in Bolzano, Italy, was held online. As with the online conference of last year, we embraced this as an opportunity to continue learning and evolving as a community in the digital era. The committee worked hard to ensure a powerful conference experience where researchers and practitioners could share their knowledge and experiences.

For EC-TEL 2021, 74 research paper contributions were received. All of these contributions were reviewed by three members of the TEL community, who also had follow-up discussions to agree on a meta-review. As a result, 21 research papers (28%) were accepted and presented at the conference. This shows the high level of competitiveness and the quality of this conference year after year. In addition, 18 posters and 10 demos were presented during the conference to fuel the discussions among the researchers. Research, poster, and demo papers can be found in this volume. In addition, the conference offered 12 workshops over two days and a doctoral consortium.

The last words are words of gratitude. Thanks to the researchers who sent their contributions to EC-TEL 2021. Thanks to the members of the Program Committee who devoted their time to give feedback to authors and supported decision making on paper acceptance. We are grateful to the workshop chairs, Ioana Jivet and Jan Schneider; the practice chairs, Tracie Farrell and Emmanuel Guardiola; the doctorial consortium chairs, Mikhail Fominykh and Maria Aristeidou; and the steering committee representative, Ralf Klamma. Finally, deep thanks to the local organizers, Claus Pahl and Ilenia Fronza, who worked very hard to make the second online EC-TEL conference a success.

July 2021

Tinne De Laet
Roland Klemke
Carlos Alario-Hoyos
Isabel Hilliger
Alejandro Ortega-Arranz

Organization

General Chair

Carlos Alario-Hoyos   Universidad Carlos III de Madrid, Spain

Program Chairs

Tinne De Laet   Katholieke Universiteit Leuven, Belgium
Roland Klemke   Open University of the Netherlands, The Netherlands

Poster and Demo Chairs

Isabel Hilliger   Pontificia Universidad Católica de Chile, Chile
Alejandro Ortega-Arranz   Universidad de Valladolid, Spain

Program Committee

Mohsin Abbas	The Open University, The Netherlands
Marie-Helene Abel	Université de Technologie de Compiègne, France
Andrea Adamoli	Università della Svizzera italiana, Switzerland
Gokce Akcayir	University of Alberta, Canada
Patricia Albacete	University of Pittsburgh, USA
Laia Albó	Universitat Pompeu Fabra, Spain
Vincent Aleven	Carnegie Mellon University
Liaqat Ali	Simon Fraser University, Canada
Hector R. Amado-Salvatierra	Universidad Galileo, Guatemala
Ishari Amarasinghe	Universitat Pompeu Fabra, Spain
Muhammad Naveed Anwar	Northumbria University, UK
Roberto Araya	Universidad de Chile, Chile
Maria Aristeidou	The Open University, UK
Juan I. Asensio-Pérez	Universidad de Valladolid, Spain
Soumela Atmatzidou	Aristotle University of Thessaloniki, Greece
Antonio Balderas	University of Cádiz, Spain
Nicolas Ballier	Université de Paris, France
Jordan Barria-Pineda	University of Pittsburgh, USA
Jason Bernard	McMaster University, Canada
Geoffray Bonnin	Université de Lorraine, France
Miguel L. Bote-Lorenzo	Universidad de Valladolid, Spain
François Bouchet	Sorbonne Université, France
Yolaine Bourda	CentraleSupélec - LRI, France
Andreas Breiter	Universität Bremen, Germany

Julien Broisin	Université Toulouse 3 Paul Sabatier, France
Manuel Caeiro Rodríguez	University of Vigo, Spain
Pankaj Chejara	Tallinn University, Estonia
Henrique Chevreux	Universidad Austral de Chile, Chile
Irene-Angelica Chounta	University of Duisburg-Essen, Germany
Ruth Cobos	Universidad Autónoma de Madrid, Spain
John Cook	University of the West of England, UK
Audrey Cooke	Curtin University, Australia
Alessia Eletta Coppi	Swiss Federal Institute for Vocational Education and Training, Switzerland
Ulrike Cress	Knowledge Media Research Center, Germany
Mutlu Cukurova	University College London, UK
Peter de Lange	RWTH Aachen University, Germany
Felipe de Morais	Universidade do Vale do Rio dos Sinos, Brazil
Inge de Waard	EIT InnoEnergy, Belgium
Carlos Delgado Kloos	Universidad Carlos III de Madrid, Spain
Stavros Demetriadis	Aristotle University of Thessaloniki, Greece
Carrie Demmans Epp	University of Alberta, Canada
Michael Derntl	University of Tübingen, Germany
Philippe Dessus	University Grenoble Alpes, France
Stefan Dietze	GESIS - Leibniz Institute for the Social Sciences, Germany
Yannis Dimitriadis	University of Valladolid, Spain
Monica Divitini	Norwegian University of Science and Technology, Norway
Juan Manuel Dodero	Universidad de Cádiz, Spain
Hendrik Drachsler	DIPF - Leibniz Institute for Research and Information in Education, Germany
Erkan Er	Middle East Technical University, Turkey
Maka Eradze	University of Modena and Reggio Emilia, Italy
Iria Estévez-Ayres	Universidad Carlos III de Madrid, Spain
Tracie Farrell	The Open University, UK
Baltasar Fernandez-Manjon	Universidad Complutense de Madrid, Spain
Carmen Fernández-Panadero	Universidad Carlos III de Madrid, Spain
Rafael Ferreira	Federal Rural Univerisity of Pernambuco, Spain
Angela Fessl	Know-Center, Austria
Anna Filighera	Technical University of Darmstadt, Germany
Olga Firssova	The Open University, The Netherlands
Mikhail Fominykh	Norwegian University of Science and Technology, Norway
Thomas Gaillat	Université de Rennes 2, France
Felix J. Garcia Clemente	Universidad de Murcia, Spain
Dragan Gasevic	Monash University, Australia
Sébastien George	Le Mans Université, France
Carlo Giovannella	Tor Vergata University of Rome, Italy

Sabine Graf	Athabasca University, Canada
Monique Grandbastien	Université de Lorraine, France
Andrina Granić	University of Split, Croatia
Wolfgang Greller	Vienna University of Education, Austria
Dai Griffiths	iTED - UNIR, Spain
Emmanuel Guardiola	TH Köln, Germany
Julio Guerra	University of Pittsburgh, USA
Nathalie Guin	Université de Lyon - LIRIS, France
Eduardo Gómez-Sánchez	Universidad de Valladolid, Spain
Bernhard Göschlberger	Research Studios Austria, Austria
Franziska Günther	TU Dresden, Germany
Christian Gütl	Graz University of Technology, Austria
Stuart Hallifax	Université Jean Moulin Lyon 3, France
Eelco Herder	Radboud University, The Netherlands
Josefina Hernandez	Universidad de Chile, Chile
Ángel Hernández-García	Universidad Politécnica de Madrid, Spain
Tore Hoel	Oslo Metropolitan University, Norway
Adrian Holzer	University of Neuchâtel, Switzerland
Sharon Hsiao	Arizona State University, Spain
Pasquale Iero	The Open University, UK
Francisco Iniesto	The Open University, UK
Patricia Jaques	Universidade do Vale do Rio dos Sinos, Brazil
Johan Jeuring	Utrecht University and Open University, The Netherlands
Ioana Jivet	TU Delft, The Netherlands
Srecko Joksimovic	University of South Australia, Australia
Jelena Jovanovic	University of Belgrade, Serbia
Rogers Kaliisa	University of Oslo, Norway
Reet Kasepalu	Tallinn University, Estonia
Mohammad Khalil	University of Bergen
Michael Kickmeier-Rust	Graz University of Technology, Austria
Andrea Kienle	University of Applied Sciences Dortmund, Germany
Ralf Klamma	RWTH Aachen University, Germany
Styliani Kleanthous	Open University of Cyprus and Research Centre on Interactive Media, Smart Systems and Emerging Technologies, Cyprus
Tomaž Klobučar	Jozef Stefan Institute, Slovenia
Anders Kluge	University of Oslo, Norway
Simone Kopeinik	Graz University of Technology, Austria
Külli Kori	Tallinn University, Estonia
Panagiotis Kosmas	Cyprus University of Technology, Cyprus
Vitomir Kovanovic	University of South Australia, Australia
Dominik Kowald	Know-Center, Austria
Milos Kravcik	DFKI GmbH, Germany
Karel Kreijns	Open Universiteit and Fontys University of Applied Sciences, The Netherlands

Birgit Krogstie	Norwegian University of Science and Technology, Norway
Mart Laanpere	Tallinn University, Estonia
Elise Lavoué	Université Jean Moulin Lyon 3, France
Marie Lefevre	Université Lyon 1, France
Dominique Lenne	Université de Technologie de Compiègne, France
Marina Lepp	University of Tartu, Estonia
Tobias Ley	Tallinn University, Estonia
Amna Liaqat	University of Toronto, Canada
Paul Libbrecht	IUBH Fernstudium, Germany
Lisa Lim	University of Technology Sydney, Australia
Andreas Lingnau	Ruhr West University of Applied Sciences, Germany
Martin Llamas-Nistal	University of Vigo, Spain
Aurelio Lopez-Lopez	INAOE, Mexico
Domitile Lourdeaux	CNRS, France
Vanda Luengo	Sorbonne Université, France
Piret Luik	University of Tartu, Finland
Kris Luyten	Hasselt University, Belgium
George Magoulas	Birkbeck College, University of London, UK
Nils Malzahn	Rhine-Ruhr Institute for Applied System Innovation e. V., Germany
Estefania Martin	Universidad Rey Juan Carlos, Spain
Carlos Martínez-Gaitero	Pompeu Fabra University, Spain
Alejandra Martínez-Monés	Universidad de Valladolid, Spain
Agathe Merceron	Beuth University of Applied Sciences Berlin, Germany
Vasileios Mezaris	Centre for Research and Technology Hellas, Greece
Christine Michel	Université de Poitiers, France
Konstantinos Michos	University of Zurich, Switzerland
Alexander Mikroyannidis	The Open University, UK
Martijn Millecamp	Katholieke Universiteit Leuven, Belgium
Constanza Miranda	Johns Hopkins University, USA
Tanja Mitrovic	University of Canterbury, New Zealand
Riichiro Mizoguchi	Japan Advanced Institute of Science and Technology, Japan
Inge Molenaar	Radboud University, The Netherlands
Miguel Morales	Universidad Galileo, Ecuador
Anders Morch	University of Oslo, Norway
Pedro Manuel Moreno-Marcos	Universidad Carlos III de Madrid, Spain
Mathieu Muratet	Sorbonne University - LIP6, France
Jorge Muñoz Gama	Pontificia Universidad Católica de Chile, Chile
Juan A. Muñoz-Cristóbal	Universidad de Valladolid, Spain
Pedro J. Muñoz-Merino	Universidad Carlos III de Madrid, Spain
Rob Nadolski	The Open University, The Netherlands
Stavros Nikou	University of Strathclyde, UK

Alexander Nussbaumer	Graz University of Technology, Austria
Alejandro Ortega-Arranz	Universidad de Valladolid, Spain
Julia Othlinghaus-Wulhorst	University of Duisburg-Essen
Lahcen Oubahssi	Le Mans Université - LIUM, France
Viktoria Pammer-Schindler	Graz University of Technology, Austria
Abelardo Pardo	University of South Australia, Australia
Mar Perez-Sanagustin	Université Paul Sabatier Toulouse III, France
Maria Perifanou	University of Macedonia, Aristotle University of Thessaloniki, and Hellenic Open University, Greece
Yvan Peter	Université de Lille, France
Niels Pinkwart	Humboldt-Universität zu Berlin, Germany
Gerti Pishtari	Tallinn University, Estonia
Elvira Popescu	University of Craiova, Romania
Francesca Pozzi	Istituto Tecnologie Didattiche - CNR, Italy
Luis P. Prieto	Tallinn University, Estonia
Ronald Pérez Álvarez	Universidad de Costa Rica, Costa Rica
Mar Pérez-Sanagustín	Pontificia Universidad Católica de Chile, Chile
Hans Põldoja	Tallinn University, Estonia
Eyal Rabin	The Open University of Israel, Israel, and The Open University of the Netherlands, The Netherlands
Juliana Elisa Raffaghelli	University of Florence, Italy
Symeon Retalis	University of Piraeus, Greece
Marc Rittberger	DIPF - Leibniz Institute for Researach and Information in Education, Germany
Tiago Roberto Kautzmann	Universidade do Vale do Rio dos Sinos, Brazil
M. Cristina Rodriguez-Sanchez	Rey Juan Carlos University, Spain
María Jesús Rodríguez-Triana	Tallinn University, Estonia
José A. Ruipérez-Valiente	Universidad de Murcia, Spain
Adolfo Ruiz-Calleja	Universidad de Valladolid, Spain
Merike Saar	Tallinn University, Estonia
Demetrios Sampson	Curtin University, Australia
Eric Sanchez	University of Geneva
Olga C. Santos	Universidad Nacional de Educación a Distancia, Spain
Patricia Santos	Universitat Pompeu Fabra, Spain
Mohammed Saqr	University of Eastern Finland, Finland
Petra Sauer	Beuth University of Applied Sciences Berlin, Germany
Maren Scheffel	Ruhr-Universität Bochum, Germany
Daniel Schiffner	DIPF - Leibniz Institute for Research and Information in Education, Germany
Andreas Schmidt	Karlsruhe University of Applied Sciences, Germany
Marcel Schmitz	Zuyd Hogeschoo Zuydl, The Netherlands
Jan Schneider	DIPF - Leibniz Institute for Research and Information in Education, Germany

Yann Secq	Université de Lille, France
Karim Sehaba	Université Lumière Lyon 2 - LIRIS, France
Paul Seitlinger	Tallinn University, Estonia
Audrey Serna	Institut National Des Sciences Appliquées Lyon, France
Sergio Serrano-Iglesias	Universidad de Valladolid, Spain
Shashi Kant Shankar	Tallinn University, Estonia
Mike Sharples	The Open University, UK
Bernd Simon	Knowledge Markets Consulting, Austria
Tanmay Sinha	ETH Zurich, Switzerland
Andrzej M. J. Skulimowski	AGH University of Science and Technology, Poland
Alan Smeaton	Dublin City University, Ireland
Sergey Sosnovsky	Utrecht University, The Netherlands
Srinath Srinivasa	International Institute of Information Technology, Bangalore, India
Tim Steuer	Technical University of Darmstadt, Germany
Slavi Stoyanov	The Open University The Netherlands
Alexander Streicher	Fraunhofer IOSB, Germany
Bernardo Tabuenca	Universidad Politécnica de Madrid, Spain
Esther Tan	Delft University of Technology, The Netherlands
Stefano Tardini	Università della Svizzera italiana, Switzerland
Stefan Thalmann	University of Graz, Austria
Sverrir Thorgeirsson	ETH Zurich, Switzerland
Paraskevi Topali	Universidad de Valladolid, Spain
Richard Tortorella	University of North Texas, USA
Stefan Trausan-Matu	University Politehnica of Bucharest, Romania
Yi-Shan Tsai	Monash University, Australia
Peter Van Rosmalen	Maastricht University, The Netherlands
Guillermo Vega-Gorgojo	Universidad de Valladolid, Spain
Olga Viberg	KTH Royal Institute of Technology, Sweden
Markel Vigo	University of Manchester, UK
Joshua Weidlich	Leibniz Institute for Research and Information in Education, Germany
Armin Weinberger	Saarland University, Germany
Nikoletta Xenofontos	University of Cyprus, Cyprus
Jane Yau	University of Mannheim, Germany
Amel Yessad	Sorbonne Université - LIP6, France
Tanja Zdolsek Draksler	Jožef Stefan Institute, Slovenia
Raphael Zender	University of Potsdam, Germany

Contents

The Impact of Explicating Learning Goals on Teaching and Learning
in Higher Education: Evaluating a Learning Goal Visualization 1
   *Angela Fessl, Katharina Maitz, Sebastian Dennerlein,
and Viktoria Pammer-Schindler*

Catching Group Criteria Semantic Information When Forming
Collaborative Learning Groups 16
   *Yongchao Wu, Jalal Nouri, Xiu Li, Rebecka Weegar, Muhammad Afzaal,
and Aayesha Zia*

The Role of Social Practices of Knowledge Appropriation for Sustaining
TEL Innovations in the Classroom 28
   Janika Leoste, Tobias Ley, Mati Heidmets, and Jelena Stepanova

Visual Aids for Teaching Piano to Students with Autism: Designing
a Web App Through Practice 37
   *Caterina Senette, Maria Claudia Buzzi, Marina Buzzi,
and Amaury Trujillo*

Interactive and Explainable Advising Dashboard Opens the Black Box
of Student Success Prediction 52
   Hanne Scheers and Tinne De Laet

Investigating the Role of Educational Robotics in Formal Mathematics
Education: The Case of Geometry for 15-Year-Old Students 67
   *Jérôme Brender, Laila El-Hamamsy, Barbara Bruno,
Frédérique Chessel-Lazzarotto, Jessica Dehler Zufferey,
and Francesco Mondada*

Analysing Peer Assessment Interactions and Their Temporal Dynamics
Using a Graphlet-Based Method 82
   *Fahima Djelil, Laurent Brisson, Raphaël Charbey, Cecile Bothorel,
Jean-Marie Gilliot, and Philippe Ruffieux*

VLE Limits and Perspectives for Digital Integration in Teaching Practices:
Lessons Learned from the French Basic Education Teachers' Experience
During the COVID-19 Pandemic 96
   Christine Michel, Laëtitia Pierrot, and Melina Solari-Landa

First-Year University Students in Distance Learning: Motivations
and Early Experiences 110
   Maria Aristeidou

The Dire Cost of Early Disengagement: A Four-Year Learning Analytics
Study over a Full Program... 122
  Mohammed Saqr and Sonsoles López-Pernas

Analysis of the "D'oh!" Moments. Physiological Markers of Performance
in Cognitive Switching Tasks....................................... 137
  Tetiana Buraha, Jan Schneider, Daniele Di Mitri, and Daniel Schiffner

Examining the Effect of Self-explanations in Distributed Self-assessment.... 149
  Cheng-Yu Chung and I-Han Hsiao

Examining the Relationship Between Reflective Writing Behaviour
and Self-regulated Learning Competence: A Time-Series Analysis 163
  Wannapon Suraworachet, Cristina Villa-Torrano, Qi Zhou,
  Juan I. Asensio-Pérez, Yannis Dimitriadis, and Mutlu Cukurova

From Paper to Online: Digitizing Card Based Co-creation of Games
for Privacy Education 178
  Patrick Jost and Monica Divitini

An In-Depth Methodology to Predict At-Risk Learners 193
  Amal Ben Soussia, Azim Roussanaly, and Anne Boyer

A Framework to Guide Educational Technology Studies in the Evolving
Classroom Research Environment 207
  Tomohiro Nagashima, Gautam Yadav, and Vincent Aleven

Using Prompts and Remediation to Improve Primary School Students
Self-evaluation and Self-efficacy in a Literacy Web Application 221
  Thomas Sergent, François Bouchet, Morgane Daniel,
  and Thibault Carron

Harnessing Student Creativity to Design Fake News Literacy Training:
An Overview of Twelve Graduate Student Projects 235
  Christian Scheibenzuber, Marvin Fendt, and Nicolae Nistor

Recommendations for Orchestration of Formative Assessment Sequences:
A Data-Driven Approach 245
  Rialy Andriamiseza, Franck Silvestre, Jean-François Parmentier,
  and Julien Broisin

Surveying Teachers' Preferences and Boundaries Regarding Human-AI
Control in Dynamic Pairing of Students for Collaborative Learning........ 260
  Kexin Bella Yang, LuEttaMae Lawrence, Vanessa Echeverria,
  Boyuan Guo, Nikol Rummel, and Vincent Aleven

What Do Learning Designs Show About Pedagogical Adoption?
An Analysis Approach and a Case Study on Inquiry-Based Learning....... 275
   María Jesús Rodríguez-Triana, Luis P. Prieto, and Gerti Pishtari

On the Linguistic and Pedagogical Quality of Automatic Question
Generation via Neural Machine Translation 289
   Tim Steuer, Leonard Bongard, Jan Uhlig, and Gianluca Zimmer

Developing a Prototype of an Open Educational Resource on Research
Methods for PhD Candidates in Technology-Enhanced Learning.......... 295
   Lorena Sousa, Luís Pedro, and Carlos Santos

Comparing Usage in and Between Primary and Secondary Schools
for a Blended TEL Portal.. 300
   Sohum Mandar Bhatt, Lien De Bie, and Wim Van Den Noortgate

Investigating the Associations Between Emotion, Cognitive Load
and Personal Learning Goals: The Case for MOOCs.................... 305
   Maartje Henderikx, Karel Kreijns, and Kate M. Xu

"I Need More Motivation": Engaging Students in the Gamification
Design Process.. 310
   *Valeria Barzola, Harlyn Pichardo, Julio Macías, Dick Zambrano,
   and Vanessa Echeverria*

Augmented Reality as Educational Tool: Perceptions, Challenges,
and Requirements from Teachers 315
   Matthias Heintz, Effie Lai-Chong Law, and Pamela Andrade

Towards a Self-assessment Tool for Teachers to Improve LMS Mastery
Based on Teaching Analytics 320
   Ibtissem Bennacer, Rémi Venant, and Sébastien Iksal

Uncovering Latent Profiles Based on How Students Review
Paper-Based Assessments... 326
   Yancy Vance Paredes and I-Han Hsiao

Orchestrating an Ubiquitous Learning Situation About Cultural Heritage
with Casual Learn... 332
   *Adolfo Ruiz-Calleja, Sara Lorena Villagrá Sobrino,
   Miguel L. Bote-Lorenzo, Sergio Serrano-Iglesias, Pablo García-Zarza,
   Víctor Alonso-Prieto, and Juan I. Asensio-Pérez*

Bibliometric Analysis of the Last Ten Years of the European Conference
on Technology-Enhanced Learning 337
   *Manuel J. Gomez, José A. Ruipérez-Valiente,
   and Félix J. García Clemente*

Interactive Screencasts as Learning Tools in Introductory Programming 342
  Kristina Litherland, Anders Kluge, and Anders I. Mørch

Teachers' Orchestration Needs During the Shift to Remote Learning 347
  *LuEttaMae Lawrence, Kenneth Holstein, Susan R. Berman,
  Stephen Fancsali, Bruce M. McLaren, Steven Ritter, and Vincent Aleven*

Designing a Pre-service Teacher Community Platform: A Focus
on Participants' Motivations 352
  *Nicolas Felipe Gutiérrez-Páez, Patricia Santos,
  Davinia Hernández-Leo, and Mar Carrió*

Exploring Teachers' Needs for Guidance While Designing
for Technology-Enhanced Learning with Digital Tools 358
  *Eleni Zalavra, Kyparisia Papanikolaou, Yannis Dimitriadis,
  and Cleo Sgouropoulou*

Measuring and Predicting Students' Effort: A Study on the Feasibility
of Cognitive Load Measures to Real-Life Scenarios 363
  Barbara Moissa, Geoffray Bonnin, and Anne Boyer

Educawood: A Socio-semantic Annotation System
for Environmental Education 368
  *Jimena Andrade-Hoz, Guillermo Vega-Gorgojo, Irene Ruano,
  Miguel L. Bote-Lorenzo, Juan I. Asensio-Pérez, Felipe Bravo,
  and Cristóbal Ordóñez*

Understanding the Well-Being Impact of a Computer-Supported
Collaborative Learning Tool: The Case of PyramidApp 373
  Eyad Hakami, Davinia Hernández-Leo, and Ishari Amarasinghe

Atelier – Tutor Moderated Comments in Programming Education 379
  Ansgar Fehnker, Angelika Mader, and Arthur Rump

Smart Groups: A Tool for Group Orchestration in Synchronous Hybrid
Learning Environments 384
  *Adrián Carruana Martín, Carlos Alario-Hoyos,
  and Carlos Delgado Kloos*

Awareness Tools for Monitoring Socio-emotional Regulation During
Collaboration in Settings Outside School Without Teacher Supervision 389
  Mariano Velamazán, Patricia Santos, and Davinia Hernández-Leo

Narrative Scripts Embedded in Social Media Towards Empowering Digital
and Self-protection Skills 394
  *Davinia Hernández-Leo, Emily Theophilou, René Lobo,
  Roberto Sánchez-Reina, and Dimitri Ognibene*

Conceptual Checks for Programming Teachers 399
   Luca Chiodini, Matthias Hauswirth, and Andrea Gallidabino

Demonstration of SCARLETT: A Smart Learning Environment
to Support Learners Across Formal and Informal Contexts 404
   *Sergio Serrano-Iglesias, Eduardo Gómez-Sánchez,
Miguel L. Bote-Lorenzo, Juan I. Asensio-Pérez, Adolfo Ruiz-Calleja,
and Guillermo Vega-Gorgojo*

The L2L System for Second Language Learning Using Visualised Zoom
Calls Among Students 409
   *Aparajita Dey-Plissonneau, Hyowon Lee, Vincent Pradier,
Michael Scriney, and Alan F. Smeaton*

Usage-Based Summaries of Learning Videos 414
   Hyowon Lee, Mingming Liu, Michael Scriney, and Alan F. Smeaton

Including Students' Voices in the Design of Blended Learning
Lesson Plans 419
   *Laia Albó, Nayia Stylianidou, Xenofon Chalatsis, Max Dieckmann,
and Davinia Hernández-Leo*

EvaWeb: A Web App for Simulating the Evacuation of Buildings
with a Grid Automaton 424
   André Greubel, Hans-Stefan Siller, and Martin Hennecke

Self-tracking Time-On-Task: Web-Based Weekly Timesheets for Higher
Education Students 430
   *Isabel Hilliger, Constanza Miranda, Gregory Schuit,
and Mar Pérez-Sanagustín*

Author Index 435

The Impact of Explicating Learning Goals on Teaching and Learning in Higher Education: Evaluating a Learning Goal Visualization

Angela Fessl[1,2](✉), Katharina Maitz[1], Sebastian Dennerlein[3], and Viktoria Pammer-Schindler[1,2]

[1] Know-Center GmbH, Inffledgasse 13/6, 8010 Graz, Austria
{afessl,kmaitz}@know-center.at
[2] Institute for Interactive Systems and Data Science, Graz University of Technology, Graz, Austria
vpammer@tugraz.at
[3] Haus der Digitalisierung, Graz University of Technology, 8010 Graz, Austria
sdennerlein@tugraz.at

Abstract. Clear formulation and communication of learning goals is an acknowledged best practice in instruction at all levels. Typically, in curricula and course management systems, dedicated places for specifying learning goals at course-level exist. However, even in higher education, learning goals are typically formulated in a very heterogeneous manner. They are often not concrete enough to serve as guidance for students to master a lecture or to foster self-regulated learning. In this paper, we present a systematics for formulating learning goals for university courses, and a web-based widget that visualises these learning goals within a university's learning management system. The systematics is based on the revised version of Bloom's taxonomy of educational objectives by Anderson and Krathwohl. We evaluated both the learning goal systematics and the web-based widget in three lectures at our university. The participating lecturers perceived the systematics as easy-to-use and as helpful to structure their course and the learning content. Students' perceived benefits lay in getting a quick overview of the lecture and its content as well as clear information regarding the requirements for passing the exam. By analysing the widget's activity log data, we could show that the widget helps students to track their learning progress and supports them in planning and conducting their learning in a self-regulated way. This work highlights how theory-based best practice in teaching can be transferred into a digital learning environment; at the same time it highlights that good non-technical systematics for formulating learning goals positively impacts on teaching and learning.

Keywords: Learning goals · Learning goal systematics · Self-regulated learning · Learning goal widget · User study

1 Introduction

Teaching and learning in higher education benefit from well-designed learning experiences based on clearly communicated learning goals. From the instructors' perspective, defining and setting learning goals is commonly seen as a key factor for effective and successful teaching [20,23] as learning goals describe what a learner should be able to do after a specific learning experience. From the learners' perspective, pre-defined learning goals can serve as a guideline or focal point of what to learn in order to complete a course and, if applicable, pass the upcoming exam [1,18,19].

Most universities recognised the crucial role of learning goals for successful teaching and learning by requiring instructors to state learning goals in the course description. Although universities usually provide guidelines on how to formulate clear learning goals, the learning goals available in the course descriptions are often formulated in a very heterogeneous way. This also applies to the representation of learning goals (when they are explicated at all) in learning management systems (LMS) of universities. LMS typically present the learning content in a conventional hierarchical order, but there is a lack in providing students with sufficient guidance for self-directed learning along learning goals. To the best of our knowledge, LMS do not provide the possibility of visualising learning goals of a course or allowing students' to easily track their own learning progress.

To address these challenges, we will present in this work a systematics supporting instructors to systematically formulate learning goals. And, we will introduce a widget called "Learning Goal Widget" that visualises the learning goals of a course in a sophisticated way to support students during their self-regulated learning journey. In this regard, we investigate the usefulness of the learning goal systematics and the learning goal widget in an university context. For three different lectures at the Graz University of Technology, we formulated learning goals together with the lecturers using the learning goal systematics. Through the widget, these learning goals were made available for student in the summer semester 2020 and data regarding students' usage of the widget as well as their feedback on the widget were collected and analysed.

2 Related Work

Learning Goals. Providing guidance by thoroughly planning instructional processes, assigning relevant learning resources, allowing for meaningful learning experiences, and monitoring their efficacy is called 'instructional design' and strongly depends on the definition of learning objectives, also known as learning goals [11,12,20,23]. Learning goals describe what a learner should be able to do after a specific learning experience (e.g., a university course) [1,18,19].

In higher education, learning goals frequently are a key component of curricula and serve as basis for assessment and as a facilitator for the application of technologies for learning and assessing [10,24]. There are plenty of taxonomies and guides addressing the definition and/or classification of learning goals (e.g.[1,6,18,19]). However, the quality of learning goals in higher education is often poor, particularly in terms of measurability and a common structure [10,14]. One reason for this could be the relative complexity of most guides that makes them difficult to handle for instructors with little to no knowledge about instructional design and didactics. Thus, formulating learning goals in an effective and efficient way is difficult and requires instructors to invest a significant amount of effort and time during the planning of a course [6]. Nevertheless, defining and setting learning goals is commonly seen as a key factor for effective and successful teaching in higher education [4,20,23].

For learners, pre-defined learning goals provide orientation regarding what is expected from them and what they can expect to learn [7]. Learning goals are supposed to help self-regulated learners achieve the required knowledge of a lecture by approaching their academic tasks in a strategic way and applying changes in their strategy if it is necessary for succeeding ([21] based on [25]). Thus, learning goals may serve as a critical focal point of the regulatory learning process and hence, play a central role in self-regulated learning (ibid). This is also in line with [14], who state that learning goals may serve as individual standards upon which students' make self-judgements and self-evaluations to pursue their own successive cycles of studying. Goal orientation, often associated with (self-set) achievement goals, is a significant facilitator for successful self-regulated learning and academic achievement [27].

Additionally, there are some general relevant advantages of well- and pre-defined learning goals and why learning goals should be given special consideration. First, learning goals are said to lead to *"direct planning, strategy choice and flexible task engagement"* [21], thus providing guidance or serving as a blueprint for learning. Second, learning goals are a good starting point for *monitoring and evaluating one's own learning performance* and enable timely interventions when there is risk that a goal might not be achieved, when, for instance, sticking to the current learning strategy [26]. Third, it is important that learning goals are of certain quality, i.e. that they are precise, clear and achievable. They must be defined and formulated thoroughly, but simultaneously kept rather universal in order to be adoptable by all students in a course.

Learning Goals in Technology Enhanced Learning. In the area of Technology-Enhanced Learning (TEL), there exists a plethora of educational technologies that support various forms of learning, teaching, tutoring, aiming at scaling up, scaffolding, structuring etc. the learning process and supporting different types of instructional settings (face-to-face, remote, blended) and addressing different types of stakeholders (teachers, learners etc.) in various educational ecosystems [5,17]. Several research areas such as didactics, learning sciences or educational technologies investigate theoretical and practical applications of technology-enhanced teaching and learning. Although in these research fields learning goals are theoretically and practically well investigated (e.g.[1,7,18,19]), most research on TEL in higher education does not specifically include learning goals and how they can be explicated with the help of technology.

In higher education, technology enhanced teaching and learning is often mediated with the help of learning management systems LMS [15,16,22]. Popular LMS for universities such as Moodle[1], ATutor[2], and OLAT[3] are rather limited with regard to how learning goals can be represented. Moodle as a far-spread open-source LMS only allows to include learning goals in textual format[4] or as part of learning plans[5]. Additionally, LMS typically present the learning content in a conventional hierarchical order, but there is a lack in providing students with systematic guidance for self-directed learning along learning goals.

Other approaches aiming at visualising the students' learning progress are related to adaptive hypermedia systems (AHS) based upon user models. Tools like Quizguide [3], QuizMap[2] or the Mastery Grids system [13] adapt automatically to the users' learning progress by changing the content of the visualisations on the fly, however, without taking learning goals into account.

To the best of our knowledge, neither LMS nor AHS do provide the possibility of visualising learning goals of a course and the students' own learning progress in a simple but comprehensive way.

3 Contribution and Research Questions

For evaluating our learning goal systematics as well as our Learning Goal Widget, we have defined the following research questions:

- RQ1: To what extend does the engagement with learning goals impact teaching and learning?
- RQ1a: How did the instructors perceive the applicability of the learning goal systematics?
- RQ1b: How did the students assess the usefulness of the visualisation of the learning goals through the widget?
- RQ1c: How did the students use and assess the possibility to track their own learning progress in a self-regulated way along learning goals?

The contribution of our work lies in i) presenting how theory-based best practice in teaching can be transferred into a digital learning environment, ii) showing that good non-technical systematics for formulating learning goals can positively impact teaching and consequently learning. Moreover, our work is kept domain-independent, so that the sytematics and the widget can be applied to any course or lecture independent of the content.

---

[1] https://moodle.com/de/.
[2] https://atutor.github.io/.
[3] https://olat.org/.
[4] https://docs.moodle.org/310/en/Outcomes.
[5] https://moodle.org/plugins/block_learning_plan.

4 Learning Goals in Lecture Descriptions - An Exemplary Analysis at Two Universities

According to Bloom et al.'s definition, learning goals should clearly state the *"student behaviours that represent the intended outcomes of the educational process"* [1]. Based on this definition, we investigated for two faculties, namely one faculty at Graz University of Technology (U1) and one faculty from the University of Graz (U2), the formulation of learning goals available in the generic description of the courses. To do so, we extracted for all lectures of type "VO - Vorlesung" (lecture) the learning goal descriptions available in the winter semester 2020 and the summer semester 2021 and categorised them according to Bloom et al.s' definition. Altogether, we analysed learning goals from 109 lectures at U1 and 136 lectures from U2. From these learning goals at U1, 52 (48%) were not aligned with Bloom's definition. These learning goal formulations were very short such as *"Basic theoretical and practical understanding of important aspects of [the subject]"* or just summarised major topics of the lecture. In contrast, 56 (51%) learning goal descriptions did somehow follow the definition of Bloom like for example *"Students should be able to implement a classical [topic] system themselves"*. For 1 (1%) lecture no learning goals were defined. The analysis at U2 revealed similar results: for 64 (47%) lectures the learning goals were not described in line with Bloom's definition like *"Bringing closer the problem of [the subject]"*, while 68 (50%) learning goal descriptions were well formulated, like for example *"The students are able to structure Europe based on different geographic and economic characteristics"*. For 4 (3%) lectures no learning goals were defined. These results show that there is a need to support instructors in systematically defining learning goals for their lectures.

5 The Learning Goal Systematics

We have developed a learning goal systematics (see Table 1) that serves as instructional guidance for lecturers to formulate learning goals.

The systematics is roughly based on the revised version by Anderson and Krathwohl [18] of Bloom et al.'s [1] taxonomy of educational objectives for the cognitive domain of learning, which distinguishes six, hierarchically structured, levels of performance - Remember, Understand, Apply, Analyse, Evaluate, Create (see Table 1, col. 2). For our systematics the goal was to create a simple version of the taxonomy which is easy to apply even with little knowledge about didactics. Our approach was to combine certain levels of performance and distinguish between three types of learning goals: i) *knowledge/comprehension-oriented learning goals* that address the levels Remember and Understand; ii) *application/competence-oriented learning goals* that target the levels Apply, Analyse, Evaluate and Create; iii) *transfer-oriented learning goals* which describe the demonstration of an application/competence oriented learning goal in a specific context or for a specific use case. For each of the three categories, we provide the instructors with a list of verbs - so-called action-components - for constructing the learning goal. For example, to formulate a knowledge/comprehension

Table 1. Learning goal systematics based on Bloom's revised taxonomy.

Meta-categories	Bloom's revised taxonomy	Action components	Context
Knowledge/ Comprehension	Remember	Define, describe, recognise, list, name, select, recall, tabulate, enumerate, locate, quote...	
	Understand	Explain, interpret, paraphrase, summarise, compare, differentiate, discuss...	
Application/ competence-oriented	Apply	Apply, solve, demonstrate, use, sketch, calculate, modify, show, discover, paint...	
	Analyse	Analyse, interpret, contrast, categorise, discriminate, prioritise, survey...	
	Evaluate	Reframe, criticise, evaluate, appraise, judge, decide, recommend...	
	Create	Design, produce, compose, create, plan, construct, develop, integrate, modify...	
Transfer-oriented	Apply, Analyse, Evaluate, Create	Solve, demonstrate, use, sketch, calculate, modify, show, discover, paint, illustrate, complete, analyse, interpret, contrast, categorise, discriminate...	...for their project work., ...in their research., ...in their thesis., etc.

oriented learning goal the following verbs can be used "define, describe, explain, compare ..." (see Table 1, col. 3).

For formulating learning goals, we propose a two-step approach. Step 1: The instructor needs to identify/isolate the main subjects (e.g. theories, concepts, action fields ...) of the course and representative subtopics - the so-called learning components. Step 2: The instructor defines what the students should be able to do with regard to the selected (sub-)topics after s/he has attended the lecture. This means that the instructor should select a verb (action-component) that describes best the desired action from the systematics (see Table 1, col. 3). The workflow of how to develop learning goals is presented exemplary for the lecture called "Introduction to Interactive Systems and Artificial Intelligence (IDSAI)". First, the lecturer defines a list of main subjects s/he wants to introduce in the lecture e.g. "Data science, rules, logic, graphs, ...". Then, the lecturer lists learning components for each of the subjects. For example for "Data science", learning components could be "building blocks of intelligent systems" or "definitions of intelligence". Next, the lecturer selects verbs as measurable action component to define what a student should be able to do at the end of a lecture e.g. "describe, explain, ...". Finally, the lecturer brings together the learning components with the action component and creates a set of learning goals for each subject, e.g. "At the end of the lecture, students should be able to explain building blocks of intelligent systems." (Knowledge) or "At the end of the lecture, students should be able to apply different definitions of intelligence." (Application).

6 The Learning Goal Widget

The Learning Goal Widget (see Fig. 1) is a small application that presents main subjects/topics (inner circle) and learning goals (outer circle) of a course in an easy-to-grasp way. The widget consists of two views: The "Lernziele"-view (engl.: learning goal view) presents the learning goals in a grey sunburst visualisation (not depicted in Fig. 1) and the list of learning goals (see Fig. 1, point 2). When clicking on one single learning goal either in the visualisation or in the list, a user is directly navigated to the corresponding learning content (e.g. slides) - provided that the instructor linked content to the learning goal in the widget. The "Mein Lernfortschritt"-view (engl.: learning progress view) presents the same subjects/topics and learning goals but highlighted with different colours (see Fig. 1, point 1). When clicking on a learning goal in this visualisation, a student can select and record the own estimated learning progress (options between 0%, 50% or 100% are available). The learning goal arcs in the visualisation get a colour corresponding to the self-estimated learning progress - from red (0%) over yellow (50%) to green (100%) - while the colour of the subjects/topics are automatically calculated based on the average learning goal progress.

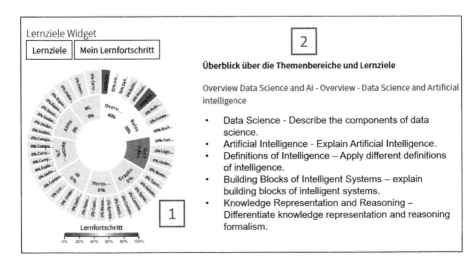

Fig. 1. Learning goal widget: coloured sunburst visualisation indicating progress in the 'Mein Lernfortschritt'-view (1) with the list of learning goals (2)

7 Methodology

Procedure. The study is set up at our university and applied to students attending one of the three courses: "Fundamentals of Electric Drives" (L1), "Introduction to Data Science and Artificial Intelligence" (L2) and "Construction Chemistry" (L3) in the summer semester, lasting from March to June 2020.

Before the semester started, the lecturers were asked to prepare learning goals for their lecture. The lecturers from L1 and L3 met several times with one of the authors to formulate high quality learning goals. Lecturer of L2 defined the learning goals herself using the learning goal systematics. The learning goals were made available for the students by integrating them into the widget when entering the corresponding course in the LMS of our university. In the first unit of each lecture, the researchers together with the lecturers introduced the widget and its purpose to the students and the students were asked to use the widget during the course of the respective lectures. At the end of the semester, in L1 a focus group was conducted in the context of a preparation session before the exam. After the exam (19th May 2020) a general questionnaire was sent out to collect feedback from the students of L1 and the same questionnaire was also sent out after the exam (17th of June 2020) for students of L2. In L3, we used a more widget-specific questionnaire, which was sent out in autumn 2020.

Evaluation Tools. One author of this paper held the coaching sessions together with the lecturers of L1 and L3 before the semester started. In these sessions, they discussed the learning goals of each lecture and the researcher collected oral feedback about the systematics. The focus group held in L1 (7th May 2020) was conducted online via the video-conferencing tool WebEx as part of the last lecture unit. The participants were asked to give feedback about the lecture in general, the learning goals, and their experiences with the widget. The general questionnaire consisted of a large section regarding the general quality of the lecture and a short section with widget-specific questions mostly related to the usability and perceived usefulness of the widget. Due to the CoVid-19 pandemic the response rate was extremely low ($n = 8$), thus, we have to exclude the questionnaire and its results from our reporting and discuss only the caused implications in Sect. 10. The widget specific questionnaire consisted of 16 questions in total, including statements regarding the usefulness of the widget (rated on a 5-point Likert scale from "disagree = 1" to "agree = 5") in terms of getting an overview of the lecture, navigating the lectures content in the LMS, tracking the own learning progress, etc. Additionally, the students were asked to indicate the perceived ease-of-use of the widget, how frequently they used the widget, whether they would like to have access to the widget in their other courses and whether they would recommend using the widget to fellow students. Additionally, the questionnaire included two open questions regarding positive and improvable aspects of the widget. The link to the questionnaire was sent out via email by the lecturer. Finally, we used activity log data for descriptive statistics about the widget's usage during the semester. For each interaction with the widget, we captured the timestamp as well as the activity: click on "Lernziele"-view, click on the widget to open the learning content, click on "Mein Lernfortschritt"-view, or saving the own learning progress.

Participants. Our participants consist of students and lecturers of Graz University of Technology. The Learning Goal Widget was used by three lecturers and available to 150–200 undergraduate students studying Electrical Engineering who attended L1, 400–500 students of computer science or software development and economics who attended L2, and about 150 students enrolled from civil engineering who attended L3.

8 Results

8.1 Coaching Session

One of the authors met two times each with the lecturers of L1 and L3 to support the formulation of learning goals for both lectures. After the sessions, both lecturers had formulated measurable learning goals for each subject/topic of their courses. The oral feedback we received was that they were happy with the systematics in that it helped them to focus on the most relevant subjects/topics and made them aware of unnecessary learning content that was thereupon removed. As a result they decided to rethink and restructure the lecture. However, both admitted that they had to invest some extra hours not so much for formulating the learning goals but rather for adapting the course structure and the learning content accordingly.

8.2 Focus Group

The online focus group ($n = 25$) conducted in L1 was held to collect general feedback about the lecture and to get deeper insights about the learning goals and the usefulness of the widget. Only a few students stated that they have used the widget. One student clearly highlighted the value of the learning goals: *"Pretty much one of the only courses where I know exactly what I have to be able to do to finish positively"*, which was agreed to by other students. Furthermore, we also received some feedback for improving the widget such as relating the widget with a lecture related quiz, so that the quiz results can be directly integrated as learning progress into the widget. On the other hand, students admitted to not have used the widget due to time reasons or individual preferences: *"I have - 'old school' like - printed out the script and study with it"*.

8.3 Widget Specific Questionnaire

The widget specific questionnaire was only distributed in L3 and we received 22 complete answers. As a first step we examined the internal consistency of the set of eight statements regarding the usefulness of the widget. The reliability analysis yielded a Cronbach's alpha of .923 which indicates high internal consistency of the scale. Subsequently, we computed the mean score of the scale to depict the overall perceived usefulness of the widget. On average ($M = 3.55, SD = 0.98$) the perceived usefulness of the widget was high. The most important benefit the widget provides to the students concerns the overview about the lecture content. 95.5% of the users agreed or slightly agreed that the widget allowed them to quickly get an overview about the lecture content. Regarding the ease-of-use of the widget, 86.3% agreed or slightly agreed that the widget was easy to use, while 59.1% agreed or slightly agreed that they liked to use the widget. In addition, 63.6% of the students agreed or slightly agreed that they would like to have the widget available also in other lectures.

Regarding how often the students used the widget per week, 5 (22.7%) students indicated to use the widget more than 2 times a week, 9 (40.9%) students reported to use the widget 1–2 times a week, while 8 (36.4%) students used the widget less than once a week. Relating the frequency of usage with the perceived usefulness we see a linear relation. This means that those students who perceived the widget as useful also used it more often, however, this relation is not statistically significant, partly due to the low number of participants.

The loyalty metric ($n = 21$) describes how likely it is that the students would recommend the widget to others, with a scale from 10 (absolutely) to 0 (not at all). The widget would be actively promoted by 14,4% (promoters scale: 9–10), passively recommended by another 38% (passives scale: 7–8) and not recommended by 47.6% (distractors scale: 0–6).

We got valuable feedback from 8 students of what they like w.r.t the widget such as "*Good overview about the subject areas*". or "*Learning Goals*". One student highlighted the value of the widget as follows: "*Visualises well where you stand and what comes to the exam [...] You can easily see what is still missing until you have everything through and thus divide the time accordingly*".

Additionally we asked the students ($n = 12$) how the widget could be improved, resulting in two major suggestions. First, the selection of the own learning progress ($n = 3$) was mentioned as too limited with the three options available (e.g. 0%, 50% and 100%). A more fine-grained functionality would be preferable to track the own learning progress in more detail. In this regard, they also stated that it is not so easy to estimate the own learning status "*Presentation of the assessment of learning progress, as it is often difficult to assess how well one has already mastered the respective subject area*". Second, linking the learning material within the widget ($n = 12$) should be done during course and not shortly before the exam and should be tailored to the learning goals and not to the overall lecture topic. However, not all students saw a benefit in linking smaller chunks of learning material to the widget: "*It is actually quite cumbersome if you have to download the documents for each topic separately. I find a complete script clearer and more practical*".

8.4 Widget Usage and Log Data

The user interactions we stored consist of the following four interaction possibilities: click on "Lernziele"-view, click on the widget to open the learning content, click on "Mein Lernfortschritt"-view, and saving the own learning progress.

Table 2 summarises the interactions registered. Overall, the widget logged 9647 user interactions across the three lectures. Altogether the "Lernziele"-view was clicked on 2701 (28%) times and in this view 860 (9%) clicks were counted to open a course content. The click on the "Mein Lernfortschritt"-view was done 3183 (33%) times, while 2903 (30%) times a learning progress was saved. A detailed look at the distribution per course shows that there are some differences between the three courses. For L1, 504 (29%) interactions were clicks to open a document, while this activity was much rarer for the other two courses. The least popular feature of the widget in L1 was saving one's own learning progress (13%). In contrast, in L2 this was the most frequently used feature (38%).

Table 2. Interactions with the widget per lecture and activities

Lecture	No. of students	Overall activities	Lernziele view	Lernfort-schritt view	Open Content	Save learning progress
L1, L2, L3	About 775	9647	2701 (28%)	3183 (33%)	860 (9%)	2903 (30%)
L1	About 175	1756	523 (30%)	504 (29%)	504 (29%)	225 (13%)
L2	About 450	6244	1595 (26%)	2116 (34%)	180 (3%)	2353 (38%)
L3	About 150	1647	583 (35%)	563 (34%)	176 (11%)	325 (20%)

9 Discussion

RQ1: The Impact of Learning Goals. The quality of learning goals in today's higher education is often poor in terms of measurability and a common structure [14]. This is in-line with our findings of the analysis of the learning goal descriptions of two different faculties, where the learning goals are formulated very heterogeneous and where around 50% are not measurable. Learning goals can be seen as equally supportive for lecturers and students. When supporting lecturers to formulate their learning goals for their lecture, they informally gave us feedback that the formulation alone stimulated them to rethink, restructure and streamline the content of their lecture. This is in line especially with [21,23], who see learning goals as a key factor for effective and successful teaching. Also, the feedback we received from the students clearly showed that the learning goals could be very helpful. Especially the answer given in the focus group, namely that L1 is one of those lectures where students exactly know what they need to be able to do to pass the exam, shows the value of learning goals. This is exactly what [21] stated, saying that learning goals can provide guidance or serve as a blueprint for learning.

RQ1a: Applicability of the Learning Goal Systematics. Both lecturers with whom we applied the learning goal systematics during coaching sessions, confirmed the applicability of the systematics, and indicated that the engagement with learning goals helped them to re-structure their courses and putting more focus on the relevant topics. This led to the removal of unnecessary learning material and simultaneously to focus on relevant learning topic. Both of them teach technical subjects and did not have any formal education in didactics or similar. However, they are very motivated lecturers and they invested more time to prepare the lecture in the summer semester 2020 than usual, for which they received some very positive feedback from their students.

RQ1b: Usefulness of Visualising Learning Goals through the Widget. The widget-specific questionnaire distributed in L3 confirmed the usefulness of the widget. The respondents indicated that the widget is useful for getting an overview of the lecture and that it is easy to use. Also, more than 50% of the participating students would recommend the widget to their colleagues. These results give to a certain extend evidence that such widget implemented in a LMS presenting learning goals is helpful for university students. From the log data analysis, we could deduce that the widget and all implemented features were used. Most of the clicks were made to access the "Mein Lernfortschritt"-view and for saving the own learning progress. This shows some evidence that the students seem to be interested in being able to track their own learning progress. The least used feature was the click on the learning goals in the "Lernziele"-view to directly access the learning content. The reason for this was twofold: While in L1 every learning goal was linked to respective content, in L2 and L3 this was only done for some of the learning goals. Additionally, one lecturer added the links to the relevant learning content only just before the exam.

RQ1c: Self-regulated Learning: Tracking own Learning Progress Along Learning Goals. By tracking their own learning progress, students approach their academic tasks in a strategic way as suggested by [20,23] and are on their way to become self-regulated learners. The usefulness of tracking the own learning progress along the learning goals presented in the widget could be shown objectively with the log data analysis. One-third of the log data activities could be related to the self-tracking feature of the widget. From the widget specific questionnaire of L3, we also received input that the students appreciated the tracking possibility. A common wish for improvement was that the selection of the progress should not be limited to the three options available, namely 0%, 50% and 100%, but should be more generic. This shows evidence that the students liked the feature and really thought about how to improve the widget. Additionally, they stated that estimating the own learning progress is not as easy as it seems. This proves that the widget initiates students to reflect about their learning progress [8,9].

10 Limitations of the Study

CoVid-19 Pandemic. The summer semester, in which our evaluation took place, lasted from March 2020 to June 2020. In Austria, this semester was strongly characterised by the CoVid-19 pandemic including the first declared lock-down affecting the whole country. Consequently, the face-to-face teaching at our university was transformed to virtual teaching on very short notice. As a result, students were unsettled and insecure, including if and how they could continue with their studies during the pandemic. Thus, introducing a new tool like the widget during the CoVid-19 pandemic was problematic and resulted in low engagement of students in the evaluation. This could be shown with a general questionnaire, which we sent to students of the lectures L1 and L2. We received only 8 complete responses, thus, we left out the description and corresponding results as they were not meaningful. And although the overall evaluation results were rather good, we had the impression that only motivated students who coped well with the CoVid-19 situation participated in the evaluation.

GDPR. The second limitation is related to the log data analysis. Due to very strict GDPR rules, we did not receive the log data per (anonmyized) user from the department hosting the LMS. Therefore, we were not able to conduct any user-related analysis of the interaction data, and thus we do not know, how many different users used the widget how often per lecture, instead, we could only provide some overall numbers.

11 Conclusion

In this work, we presented a learning goal systemic and a Learning Goal Widget that presents learning goals to students in the learning management system of our university. Our results confirm that learning goals can have an impact on teaching and learning. From the lecturers' perspective, the formulation of learning goals improves the structure of a lecture and to concentrate on the core topics. From the students' perspective, the learning goals and the widget can provide an easy-to-grasp lecture overview and an easy way to track the own learning progress in a self-regulated way. The contribution of our work lies in presenting how theory-based best practice in teaching can be transferred into a digital learning environment and that systematically defined learning goals positively impacts teaching and learning.

Acknowledgement. The 'TEL Marketplace' innovation program and 'Learning Goal Widget' pilot is funded within the project 'Digitale TU Graz' of the vice rectorate for 'Digitisation and Change Management' and 'Teaching' of Graz University of Technology. The iDev40 project has received funding from the ECSEL Joint Undertaking (JU) under grant agreement No. 783163. The Know-Center is funded within the Austrian COMET Program – Competence Centers for Excellent Technologies – under the auspices of the Austrian Federal Ministry of Transport, Innovation and Technology, the Austrian Federal Ministry of Economy, Family and Youth and by the State of Styria. COMET is managed by the Austrian Research Promotion Agency FFG.

References

1. Bloom, B.S., et al.: Taxonomy of educational objectives. vol. 1: cognitive domain. New York: McKay **20**, 24 (1956)

2. Brusilovsky, P., Hsiao, I.-H., Folajimi, Y.: QuizMap: open social student modeling and adaptive navigation support with TreeMaps. In: Kloos, C.D., Gillet, D., Crespo García, R.M., Wild, F., Wolpers, M. (eds.) EC-TEL 2011. LNCS, vol. 6964, pp. 71–82. Springer, Heidelberg (2011). https://doi.org/10.1007/978-3-642-23985-4_7
3. Brusilovsky, P., Sosnovsky, S., Shcherbinina, O.: QuizGuide: increasing the educational value of individualized self-assessment quizzes with adaptive navigation support. In: E-Learn: World Conference on E-Learning in Corporate, Government, Healthcare, and Higher Education. pp. 1806–1813. Association for the Advancement of Computing in Education (AACE) (2004)
4. Casey, R.J., Gentile, P., Bigger, S.W.: Teaching appraisal in higher education: an Australian perspective. High. Educ. **34**(4), 459–482 (1997)
5. Cushion, C.J., Townsend, R.C.: Technology-enhanced learning in coaching: a review of literature. Educ. Rev. **71**(5), 631–649 (2019)
6. DeLong, M., Winter, D., Yackel, C.A.: Mental maps and learning objectives: the fast-slo algorithm for creating student learning objectives. Probl. Resour. Issues Math. Undergr. Stud. **15**(4), 307–338 (2005)
7. DeLong, M., Winter, D., Yackel, C.A.: Student learning objectives and mathematics teaching. Probl. Resour. Issues Math. Undergr. Stud. **15**(3), 226–258 (2005)
8. Fessl, A., Blunk, O., Prilla, M., Pammer, V.: The known universe of reflection guidance: a literature review. Int. J. TEL **9**(2–3), 103–125 (2017)
9. Fessl, A., Bratic, M., Pammer, V.: Continuous learning with a quiz for stroke nurses. Int. J. TEL **6**(3), 265–275 (2014)
10. Fulkerth, R.: A case study from golden gate university: using course objectives to facilitate blended learning in shortened courses. J. Asynchronous Learn. Netw. **13**(1), 43–54 (2009)
11. Gagne, R.M., Leslie, J.: Briggs, Wagner, W.W.: principles of instructional design (1992)
12. Gagne, R.M., Wager, W.W., Golas, K.C., Keller, J.M., Russell, J.D.: Principles of instructional design (2005)
13. Guerra, J., Hosseini, R., Somyurek, S., Brusilovsky, P.: An intelligent interface for learning content: combining an open learner model and social comparison to support self-regulated learning and engagement. In: Proceedings of the 21st International Conference on Intelligent User Interfaces, pp. 152–163 (2016)
14. Hadwin, A.F., Webster, E.A.: Calibration in goal setting: examining the nature of judgments of confidence. Learn. Instr. **24**, 37–47 (2013)
15. Henderson, M., Selwyn, N., Aston, R.: What works and why? Student perceptions of 'useful' digital technology in university teaching and learning. Stud. High. Educ. **42**(8), 1567–1579 (2017)
16. Ivanović, M., Xinogalos, S., Pitner, T., Savić, M.: Technology enhanced learning in programming courses-international perspective. Educ. Inf. Technol. **22**(6), 2981–3003 (2017)
17. Kirkwood, A., Price, L.: Technology-enhanced learning and teaching in higher education: what is 'enhanced' and how do we know? A critical literature review. Learn. Media Technol. **39**(1), 6–36 (2014)
18. Krathwohl, D.R., Anderson, L.W.: Merlin C. Wittrock and the revision of bloom's taxonomy. Educ. Psychol. **45**(1), 64–65 (2010)
19. Mager, R.F.: Preparing instructional objectives (1962)
20. Marzano, R.J.: Designing & Teaching Learning Goals & Objectives. Solution Tree Press (2010)

21. McCardle, L., Webster, E.A., Haffey, A., Hadwin, A.F.: Examining students' self-set goals for self-regulated learning: goal properties and patterns. Stud. High. Educ. **42**(11), 2153–2169 (2017)
22. Pechenkina, E., Aeschliman, C.: What do students want? Making sense of student preferences in technology-enhanced learning. Contemp. Educ. Technol. **8**(1), 26–39 (2017)
23. Stronge, J.H.: Qualities of effective teachers. ASCD (2018)
24. Towns, M.H.: Developing learning objectives and assessment plans at a variety of institutions: examples and case studies. J. Chem. Educ. **87**(1), 91–96 (2010)
25. Winne, P., Hadwin, A.: Metacognition in Educational Theory and Practice. Studying As Self-regulated Learning, pp. 277–304 (1998)
26. Winne, P.H., Jamieson-Noel, D.: Exploring students' calibration of self reports about study tactics and achievement. Contemp. Educ. Psychol. **27**(4), 551–572 (2002)
27. Zhou, M., Winne, P.H.: Modeling academic achievement by self-reported versus traced goal orientation. Learn. Instr. **22**(6), 413–419 (2012)

Catching Group Criteria Semantic Information When Forming Collaborative Learning Groups

Yongchao Wu(✉), Jalal Nouri, Xiu Li, Rebecka Weegar, Muhammad Afzaal, and Aayesha Zia

Stockholm University, Stockholm, Sweden
{yongchao.wu,jalal,xiu.li,rebeckaw,muhammad.afzaal,aayesha}@dsv.su.se

Abstract. Collaborative learning has grown more popular as a form of instruction in recent decades, with a significant number of studies demonstrating its benefits from many perspectives of theory and methodology. However, it has also been demonstrated that effective collaborative learning does not occur spontaneously without orchestrating collaborative learning groups according to the provision of favourable group criteria. Researchers have investigated different foundations and strategies to form such groups. However, the group criteria *semantic information*, which is essential for classifying groups, has not been explored. To capture the group criteria semantic information, we propose a novel Natural Language Processing (NLP) approach, namely using pre-trained word embedding. Through our approach, we could automatically form homogeneous and heterogeneous collaborative learning groups based on student's knowledge levels expressed in assessments. Experiments utilising a dataset from a university programming course are used to assess the performance of the proposed approach.

Keywords: Collaborative learning group formation · Word embeddings · Natural Language Processing · Semantic information · Artificial Intelligence

1 Introduction

In recent decades, from diverse perspectives of theory and methodology, a great number of research works have shown that collaboration could help with students' learning processes. Over 1,000 research studies have consolidated and enhanced collaborative learning theories [1]. Against this background, there is broad agreement that collaborative learning has a significant impact on the individual cognitive growth compared to individualistic learning and standard teaching approaches [1–3]. Collaborative learning has also received considerable traction in educational systems, in addition to past and current research [1]. In [4], it is pointed out that knowledge levels and interests in the group could trigger better interactions. Pedagogical activities based on group interest generated by instructors, according to the work of [5], can also stimulate communications and cooperations among students. The topic of how to arrange students depending on their interests and knowledge levels, therefore, becomes interesting.

One of the most crucial procedures in collaborative learning is orchestrating groups. Traditional manual approaches consist of student formed groups [7], teacher formed groups [7] and randomly created groups [6]. However, these approaches face the problem of forming optimal groups [10]. Many researchers have looked at using computer-assisted methods to improve group optimisation in collaborative learning. Researchers in [8] tried to classify students by their knowledge interests and levels into different groups deploying Particle swarm-based optimisation. In [9,10], genetic algorithms (GA) were utilised to create collaborative learning groups considering several student attributes such as academic, cognitive, biographical, and personality characteristics. The effectiveness of particle swarm and GA-based approaches lies in the fact that experts design robust mathematical fitness functions. In another track, machine learning-based approaches have also been investigated. In the work of [11], SKmeans and Expectation maximisation were used to group learners in e-learning based on their collaboration competence. Work in [13] involved experimenting with vector-based modelling of student profiles in order to categorise students based on estimated vector similarity. These approaches face problems when creating heterogeneous groups, and additional procedures need to be designed. In [11], the authors first created homogeneous groups and then sampled students from each group to create heterogeneous groups. Genetic algorithms were deployed in [12] as a post step to assign students with different interests. Manually designed similarity thresholds in [13] were used to tell the level of difference between students.

We found that the majority of the group criteria come with semantic information. For instance, *Adventurous, Imaginative* could be used to describe a student's personality traits; we could also find topics like *function, array, class* in a computer science-related course. However, existing one-hot based machine learning algorithms ignore semantic information and treat group criteria as one or zero numerics. In the world of natural language processing, various pre-trained embeddings like word2vec [14], GloVe [15], and BERT [16] have significantly improved performance in various tasks of NLP. In [14], word embeddings have been proved with effectiveness at catching semantic information among words; the following equation exemplifies the ability to capture semantic information of word embeddings: $vec(Rome) - vec(Italy) + vec(Sweden) \approx vec(Stockholm)$. We argue that word embeddings could be helpful to catch semantic information from group criteria. Thus, we propose and describe an NLP based approach that creates collaborative learning groups in terms of students' knowledge levels without heavy post-procedures, which could:

- capture semantic relationships among group criteria.
- provide useful pedagogical information for teachers.

To the best of our knowledge, this is the first studies investigating how to use semantic information in group criteria when forming collaborative learning groups. The experiment results show that our approach outperforms the traditional one-hot based machine learning approach and can generate groups with good quality.

2 Method Formulation

2.1 Problem Description

We aim to automatically create distinct collaborative learning groups depending on student knowledge levels. The knowledge levels of students are established by the topics learned or not learned by the students.

Assume n students $s_1, s_2, \ldots, s_n$ enroll in a course with the goal of teaching k topics. A quiz of k questions is created for the course, with each question mapping to a topic. When taking the quiz, the student will be given a score of 1 or 0 for each question based on whether or not the correct answer is provided. The quiz results will show whether or not a student has mastered specific topics. The teacher might form two types of collaborative learning groups according to the quiz results: homogeneous learning groups G_{homo} and heterogeneous learning groups G_{hete}. Members of the homogeneous collaborative learning group should have similar levels of knowledge and a desire to learn similar topics. The teacher might provide unique tasks that correspond to the group's knowledge levels, allowing the students to work together to tackle comparable challenges. On the contrary, members of the heterogeneous collaborative learning group should have mastered a variety of topics. The teacher might plan learning activities in which students may assist one another by sharing their knowledge for such groups.

2.2 Proposed Approach

Students $\{s_1, s_2, \ldots\}$ make up a group G_i. Each student in the group has a mastery list M and an unmastered list L of topics. Topics in L and M are presented as single or multiple-word text. For example, a student could have a mastered topic list {*parallelism, design, operators, computer thinking, event*} and an unmastered topic list {*data, sequence, loop, reuse and remix, condition*}. The homogeneity and heterogeneity of a group are determined by the mastered topic lists M and unmastered topic lists L among the students. Motivated by the proven effectiveness of word embeddings at catching rich linguistic information, we proposed a word embedding based approach to formulate collaborative learning groups through modelling topics in L and M. The word embeddings we used is fastText[1] from the work of [17] which will map a word to a 300-dimensional vector.

In a topic list M or L, a certain topic could be mapped to a vector $t_i \in \mathbb{R}^{1 \times 300}$ by using fasttext word embeddings. If a topic contains multiple words, the topic will be the average embedding of these multiple words after removing stop words. We presume that the average embedding of all topics in the list will capture a student's knowledge level because the order of the topic list has no effect on the

---
[1] https://fasttext.cc/.

list's broad information. As a result, a student could be represented with vector $s_i \in \mathbb{R}^{1 \times 300}$ that can catch the knowledge level of the student with rich linguistic information.

$$s_i = \frac{\sum_{i=1}^{N_l} t_i}{N_l} \tag{1}$$

The topic list length is noted as N_l.

The distance between s_i and s_j is measured to determine how different or similar between knowledge levels of the two corresponding students. Here we choose cosine similarity as the similarity metric.

$$Sim(s_i, s_j) = \frac{s_i \cdot s_j}{\|s_i\| \times \|s_j\|} \tag{2}$$

$$Dif(s_i, s_j) = 1 - Sim(s_i, s_j) \tag{3}$$

We represent knowledge level difference between any two student pairs in $s_1, s_2, \ldots, s_n$ as cosine distance matrices M_{sim} and M_{dif}.

$$M_{sim} = \begin{bmatrix} 1 & Sim(s_1, s_2) & \cdots & Sim(s_1, s_n) \\ Sim(s_2, s_1) & 1 & \cdots & Sim(s_2, s_n) \\ \vdots & \vdots & \ddots & \vdots \\ Sim(s_n, s_1) & Sim(s_n, s_2) & \cdots & 1 \end{bmatrix}$$

and

$$M_{dif} = \begin{bmatrix} 1 & Dif(s_1, s_2) & \cdots & Dif(s_1, s_n) \\ Dif(s_2, s_1) & 1 & \cdots & Dif(s_2, s_n) \\ \vdots & \vdots & \ddots & \vdots \\ Dif(s_n, s_1) & Dif(s_n, s_2) & \cdots & 1 \end{bmatrix}$$

Then we run an unsupervised spectral clustering algorithm [18] with M_{sim} or M_{dif} to acquire candidate groups G_{init} for the homogeneous or heterogeneous collaborative learning groups G_{homo}, G_{hete}. The main reason not to use other clustering algorithms like K-means is that K-means is unsuitable for clustering different objects together. In contrast, through the use of distance matrices, spectral clustering may group both similar and dissimilar objects together. For n students, we set G_{init} cluster size as $\sqrt{\frac{n}{2}}$ suggested by the authors in [19]. It's worth noting that the recommended maximum group size in a collaborative learning group is eight [20]. As a result, we break down the bigger group with size exceeding eight in candidates in G_{init} into smaller groups. Homogeneous or heterogeneous groups can be obtained after the optimisation stage, with group sizes ranging from two to eight. In our approach, the following steps are required to construct G_{homo} or G_{hete}:

- Using fasttext $t_i \in \mathbb{R}^{1 \times 300}$ to represent each topic.
- Calculating average embeddings of the topic list to represent each student by a vector s_i.

- Creating M_{sim} similarity matrix or M_{dif} dissimilarity matrix.
- Formulating initial candidate groups G_{init} by feeding M_{sim} or M_{dif} to the spectral clustering algorithm.
- Composing G_{homo} or G_{hete} by breaking big groups in G_{init} into smaller groups.

3 Experiment

3.1 Dataset

We utilised a digital exam from a computer science course at Stockholm University carried in 2020 as the dataset for the experiment. The quiz consists of 16 questions, each of which is labelled with a programming-related topic by the course teacher., such as *class, abstraction, parallelism, operators, increment and iteration*. Each question gives a score in a binary fashion. Overall, the dataset contains 121 students' quiz performances. Students' private information like personal IDs and names are removed to completely anonymise the data. Consent for doing this research was received from all students participating through an online survey in the beginning of the course.

3.2 Group Quality Metrics

Considering that a group G_k in G_{homo} or G_{hete} consists of n_{S_k} students, and each student can be modelled with an unmastered topic list, thus G_k can also be represented as a list of unmastered topics $L_k = \{t_1, t_2, \ldots, t_l\}$, where l is the overall number of unmastered topics in this group and L_k covers n_{L_k} ($n_{L_k} \leq 16$) different topics.

To measure the homogeneity and heterogeneity of G_k, we assess intra-group similarities and topic coverage. For homogeneous groups, the intra-group similarity should be higher because students have comparable levels of expertise. While for heterogeneous groups, members of the group should lack expertise in a variety of topics, resulting in a higher number of unmastered topics per individual. We define the homogeneity and heterogeneity of group G_k as D_{ho_k}, D_{he_k}:

$$D_{ho_k} = \frac{2\sum_{i=1}^{l-1}\sum_{j=i+1}^{l-1} Sim(t_i, t_j)}{l \times (l-1)} \quad (4)$$

$$D_{he_k} = \frac{n_{L_k}}{n_{S_k}} \quad (5)$$

We calculate the mean homogeneity D_{ho} and heterogeneity D_{he} as:

$$D_{ho} = \frac{\sum_{k=1}^{N} D_{ho_k}}{N} \quad (6)$$

$$D_{he} = \frac{\sum_{k=1}^{N} D_{he_k}}{N} \quad (7)$$

where N is the size of the final cluster for collaborative learning groups. Since Chi-Square χ^2 and Log-likelihood G^2 could be used to measure the inter-document distance [21], in this study, inter-group distance is also measured as triangulate metrics to evaluate group homogeneity and heterogeneity. Assume we consider the group's unmastered topics to be features, higher χ^2 and G^2 scores indicate a larger inter-group distance and more prominent topic feature patterns for the group. Lower χ^2 and G^2 scores, on the other hand, indicate that inter-group distance is reduced and topic features are distributed equally across groups.

We add a random grouping based approach to create G_{rd} as a comparison set. G_{homo}, G_{hete}, and G_{rd} are formulated based on 10, 20, 30, ..., 90, 100 student sizes. We calculate the mean metrics D_{ho}, D_{he}, χ^2 and G^2 for G_{homo}, G_{hete}, and G_{rd} based on each random sampled student size out of the overall 121 students. We also compare our approach with the traditional one-hot based approach using the same experiment set.

3.3 Experiment Results and Discussion

The results of the experiment for group quality measurement in terms of Chi-Square χ^2, heterogeneity D_{he}, Log-likelihood G^2 and homogeneity D_{ho} for each experiment set can be found in Fig. 1 and Fig. 2

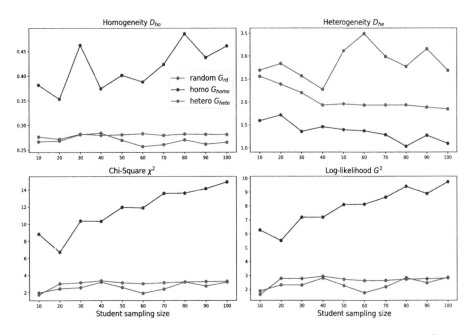

Fig. 1. Average metrics Chi-Square χ^2, heterogeneity D_{he}, Log-likelihood G^2 and homogeneity D_{ho} comparing with random approach

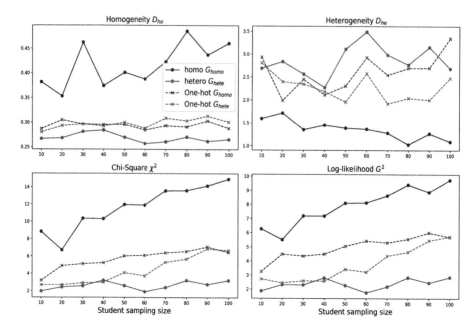

Fig. 2. Average metrics Chi-Square χ^2, heterogeneity D_{he}, Log-likelihood G^2 and homogeneity D_{ho} comparing with one-hot based approach

G_{homo} has the greatest chi-square and log-likelihood scores across all experiment sets with varying student numbers, indicating a significant inter-group distance and patterns in the homogenous collaborative learning groups formulated by our approach. Students in G_{homo} share similar knowledge levels, given that the groups hold the most outstanding homogeneity score. A homogenous group that share similar knowledge levels will also have fewer different unmastered topics, which is in accordance with the experiment result that G_{homo} obtains the lowest heterogeneity score. Students in a heterogeneous collaborative learning group have varying degrees of understanding on different topics, which will reflect a small inter-group distance. On homogeneity, Chi-Square, and log-likelihood, G_{hete} receives the lowest score. The greatest heterogeneity score goes to G_{hete}, indicating that students in a heterogeneous collaborative learning group generated by our approach might learn more topics from one other. The result in Fig. 2 shows that our approach achieves more competitive performance than the one-hot based approach. Specifically, our strategy scored higher on Chi-Square, homogeneity, and log-likelihood and lower on heterogeneity when generating G_{homo}. When constructing G_{hete}, our method scored lower on Chi-Square, homogeneity, and log-likelihood, and higher on heterogeneity.

3.4 Pedagogical Information Provided by Our Approach

To investigate what statistical insights could be provided by our approach, we grouped 30 students to generate G_{homo} and G_{hete}. For G_{homo}, five groups were generated. We calculated the percentage of students for each unmastered topic for all groups, illustrated in Fig. 3.

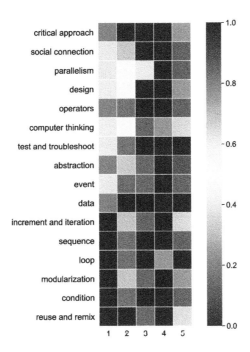

Fig. 3. Percentages of students on unmastered topics in G_{homo} based on 30 students (Color figure online)

The x-axis shows the group IDs, and the y-axis indicates each topic labelled by the course instructor. Warm colours reflect outstanding unmastered topics in each group. In contrast, cold colours indicate topics that have less impact on the group patterns. We extracted the top 2 topics that most students lacked in each group referred to in Fig. 4 which could provide useful pedagogical information. For example, there are six students in group 2. Five (83%) have not grasped the concept of *event*, and four (66%) need to increase their understanding of *abstraction*. As a result, the teacher might provide group comments or create tasks centred on *abstraction* and *event*. Similarly, seven (100%) of students in group 3 lacked knowledge of *data*, while four (100%) of students in group 4 lacked knowledge of *modularization*. *Data* and *modularization*-focused teaching and learning activities might be planned, respectively.

Five groups were created for G_{hete}, with the group information presented in Fig. 5. We start with group 5, which consists of two students, with id 149

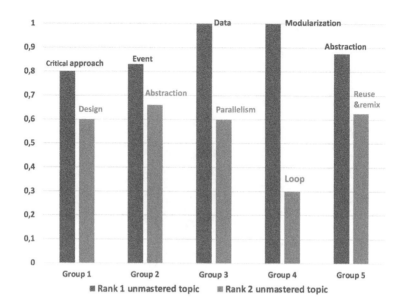

Fig. 4. Top 2 ranking unmastered topics for G_{homo} based on 30 students

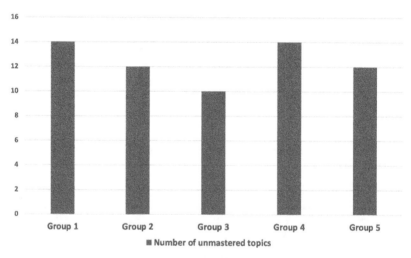

Fig. 5. Unmastered topics numbers for G_{hete} based on 30 students

and 116, whose knowledge levels can be found in Fig. 6. The result from Fig. 6 suggests that they have entirely different knowledge levels in the course and might bridge each other's knowledge gap through cooperation.

We created a knowledge-sharing map among students in group 1 (see Fig. 7) to see how they may fill certain knowledge gaps. The knowledge-sharing map indicates that unmastered topics encompass 14 of the 16 topics in group 1. The red-coloured ID represents a student who needs assistance with a certain topic,

Catching Group Criteria Semantic Information 25

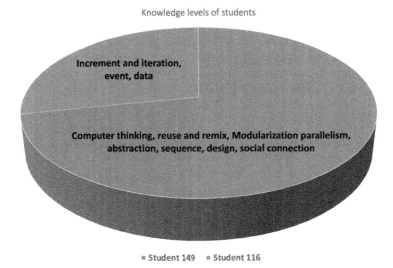

Fig. 6. Knowledge levels for student 149 and 116

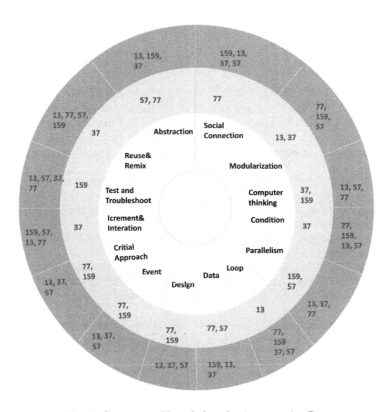

Fig. 7. Group one Knowledge-sharing map in G_{hete}

while the blue-coloured ID represents a student who can assist with a certain topic. For example, students 57 and 77 might gain support from students 13, 159, and 37 on the topic *abstraction*, while students 57 and 77 might aid students 159, 37 on the topic *computer thinking*. This knowledge-sharing map demonstrates that students in G_{hete} may receive and provide assistance on a wide range of topics. This information might be used by the teacher to plan knowledge-sharing sessions.

4 Conclusions, Limitations and Future Work

By deploying word embeddings, we have captured group criteria semantic information when forming collaborative learning groups based on students' knowledge levels. The development of homogeneous and heterogeneous collaborative learning groups might help teachers provide group feedback while also promoting successful collaborative learning. We also realize that our approach only addresses the student knowledge level in a binary manner, neglecting that a single topic can have multiple levels of complexity. We intend to address this limitation in the future. The application of word embeddings to other group criteria, such as student cognitive level and personality traits, would be another intriguing path for future research. We also plan to evaluate this approach in a formal learning setting.

References

1. Johnson, D., Johnson, R.: An educational psychology success story: social interdependence theory and cooperative learning. Educ. Res. **38**, 365–379 (2009)
2. Johnson, D., Johnson, R., Buckman, L., Richards, P.S.: The effect of prolonged implementation of cooperative learning on social support within the classroom. J. Psychol.: Interdisc. Appl. **119**, 405–411 (1985)
3. Slavin, R.E.: Research on cooperative learning and achievement: what we know, what we need to know. Contemp. Educ. Psychol. **21**(1), 43–69 (1996)
4. Yang, S.: Context aware ubiquitous learning environments for peer-to-peer collaborative learning. Educ. Technol. Soc. **9**, 188–201 (2006)
5. Michaelsen, L., Knight, A., Fink, L.: Team-Based Learning: A Transformative Use of Small Groups. Praeger Publishers, Westport (2002)
6. Huxham, M., Land, R.: Assigning students in group work projects. Can we do better than random? Innov. Educ. Train. Int. **37**(1), 17–22 (2000)
7. Hilton, S., Phillips, F.: Instructor-assigned and student-selected groups: a view from inside. Issues Account. Educ. **25** (2008)
8. Lin, Y.-T., Huang, Y.-M., Cheng, S.-C.: An automatic group composition system for composing collaborative learning groups using enhanced particle swarm optimization. Comput. Educ. **55**(4), 1483–1493 (2010)
9. Moreno, J., Demetrio, A.O., Vicari, R.M.: A genetic algorithm approach for group formation in collaborative learning considering multiple student characteristics. Comput. Educ. **58**(1), 560–569 (2012)
10. Chen, C.-M., Kuo, C.-H.: An optimized group formation scheme to promote collaborative problem-based learning. Comput. Educ. **133**, 94–115 (2019)

11. Nairobi, K., Elizaphan, M.M., Robert, O.O., Peter, W.W.: Using machine learning techniques to support group formation in an online collaborative learning environment. Int. J. Intell. Syst. Appl. **9**(3), 26–33 (2017)
12. Chen, L., Yang, Q.: A group division method based on collaborative learning elements. In: The 26th Chinese Control and Decision Conference (2014 CCDC), pp. 1701–1705 (2014)
13. Bourkoukou, O., Bachari, E.E., Boustani, A.E.: Building effective collaborative groups in E-learning environment. In: Ezziyyani, M. (ed.) AI2SD 2019. AISC, vol. 1102, pp. 107–117. Springer, Cham (2020). https://doi.org/10.1007/978-3-030-36653-7_11
14. Mikolov, T., Sutskever, I., Chen, K., Corrado, G., Dean, J.: Distributed representations of words and phrases and their compositionality. In: Proceedings of the 26th International Conference on Neural Information Processing Systems - Volume 2. NIPS 2013, pp. 3111–3119. Curran Associates Inc., Red Hook (2013)
15. Pennington, J., Socher, R., Manning, C.: GloVe: global vectors for word representation. In: Proceedings of the 2014 Conference on Empirical Methods in Natural Language Processing (EMNLP), pp. 1532–1543. Association for Computational Linguistics, Doha (2014)
16. Devlin, J., Chang, M.-W., Lee, K., Toutanova, K.: BERT: pre-training of deep bidirectional transformers for language understanding. In: Proceedings of the 2019 Conference of the North American Chapter of the Association for Computational Linguistics: Human Language Technologies, Volume 1 (Long and Short Papers), pp. 4171–4186. Association for Computational Linguistics, Minneapolis (2019)
17. Bojanowski, P., Grave, E., Joulin, A., Mikolov, T.: Enriching word vectors with subword information. Trans. Assoc. Comput. Linguist. **5**, 135–146 (2017)
18. Ng, A., Jordan, M.I., Weiss, Y.: On spectral clustering: analysis and an algorithm. In: NIPS (2001)
19. Han, J., Kamber, M., Pei, J.: 10 - Cluster analysis: basic concepts and methods. In: Han, J., Kamber, M., Pei, J. (eds.) Data Mining. The Morgan Kaufmann Series in Data Management Systems, 3rd edn., pp. 443–495. Morgan Kaufmann, Boston (2012)
20. Hooper, S., Hannafin, M.J.: Cooperative CBI: the effects of heterogeneous versus homogeneous grouping on the learning of progressively complex concepts. J. Educ. Comput. Res. **4**(4), 413–424 (1988)
21. Cavaglià, G.: Measuring corpus homogeneity using a range of measures for inter-document distance. In: Proceedings of the Third International Conference on Language Resources and Evaluation (LREC 2002). European Language Resources Association (ELRA), Las Palmas (2002)

The Role of Social Practices of Knowledge Appropriation for Sustaining TEL Innovations in the Classroom

Janika Leoste(✉) ⓘ, Tobias Ley ⓘ, Mati Heidmets, and Jelena Stepanova

Tallinn University, 10120 Tallinn, Estonia
janika.leoste@tlu.ee

Abstract. Schools strive to integrate emerging technologies via innovative TEL practices to ensure educational change. We examined social practices of knowledge appropriation (Social Practices) as indicators of TEL innovation process status, drawing data from interviews with 22 teachers who had adopted an innovative teaching method, the use of educational robots in Math, in their regular teaching practices. Results imply that teachers rely on different Social Practices in different innovation process stages. TEL innovation has become a part of teachers' practices after they have intensively adapted the innovation to their needs and they have started to actively create awareness about the method and formalize their knowledge.

Keywords: TEL innovation · Innovation process in education · Innovation process stages · Knowledge Appropriation Model

1 Introduction

Frontier technologies hold the promise to advance civilization while protecting nature [1]. Schools are encouraged to provide their students with relevant skills, needed to exploit frontier technologies. These skills are related to social networking, cloud computing, artificial intelligence, big data, machine learning, neural networks, robotics, and others [1]. In order to address this challenge, schools need to accept novel teaching strategies (how to teach with a certain technology), technological understanding (how this technology works), and subject matter knowledge (concepts that could and should be taught with this technology), i.e. they need to enhance their existing curricula with Technology Enhanced Learning (TEL) innovations.

Literature suggests that TEL innovations often do not lead to desired meaningful educational changes, being abandoned after the initial effort ends [2, 3]. According to some authors, planning educational TEL innovations as multistage processes while addressing certain sustainability factors in different innovation process stages can improve innovation's chances to become sustained in teaching and learning practices [4, 5]. In addition, there seems to be an adoption gap, causing otherwise promising TEL innovations to lose their momentum on the level of individual teachers and to become abandoned [6, 7]. The gap refers to the difference between teachers' existing practical knowledge and more theoretical knowledge that is related to proposed innovations. Mediation and knowledge transfer are needed for bridging this gap and for guiding teachers to adopt proposed innovations. These goals can be achieved by encouraging teachers to become involved in innovation-related Social Practices of Knowledge Appropriation (Social Practices) [8, 9].

In this article, we add to our previous work [10] by examining the importance of different Social Practices that manifest during different innovation process stages (Awareness, Acceptance and Adoption). For these purposes, we will examine Social Practices through the lenses of Knowledge Appropriation Model and study the experience of teachers who have adopted a certain TEL innovation, called Robomath. By looking at the whole innovation adoption process retrospectively over the course of three years, this research lets us to describe the dynamics of the knowledge appropriation practices over time.

1.1 Social Practices of Knowledge Appropriation

Introduction of an innovation has to consider already existing end-user work practices, while often significantly changing these and causing new ones to emerge, with the goal of making better use of the innovation. In education, teachers are commonly considered as the end users of TEL innovations. Relatively short TEL innovation cycles require teachers to become quick learners. Workplace located informal learning is an important way to develop and acquire innovation-related skills and competencies, relying on existing workplace practices and social context, and being driven by learner's work-related interests [11]. Through teachers' collaborative Social Practices, an innovation could become sustained in their everyday teaching practices. For example, teachers create, use, share and appropriate collaboratively new innovation-related knowledge. Ultimately, these processes lead to knowledge transformation between different levels of organization and beyond. These and similar social processes are explained by various social learning and knowledge creation theories [12, 13]. In the context of this article, the process of individuals relying on and participating in collective knowledge creation that takes place in teams, communities, and organizations, is called knowledge appropriation [8].

During knowledge appropriation, several manifesting Social Practices make the process observable. Many of these practices are prerequisite for successful adoption and adaption of innovations. Social Practices in the context of innovation adoption are described by Knowledge Appropriation Model (KAM) (Fig. 1) [8]. Previous studies have observed associations between KAM Social Practices and increased rates of classroom adoption of TEL innovations [9]. KAM model presents three types of practices that characterize learning during innovation adoption [8]: (a) **Knowledge Maturation** practices transform individual experience into shared community knowledge, potentially leading to widely available formalized knowledge; (b) **Knowledge Scaffolding** practices form a supporting structure, guiding those individuals who request help; (c) **Knowledge Appropriation** practices explain how knowledge is arranged into general patterns that can be later adapted to local needs.

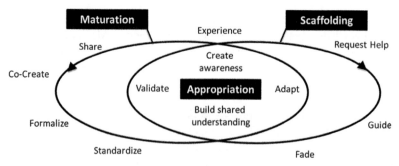

Fig. 1. Knowledge Appropriation Model to connect knowledge maturation and scaffolding [8].

KAM model supports viewing an innovation as a process with sustained use as its goal. In this paper, we view how Social Practices, described in KAM, could indicate the innovation process stage where the teachers currently are.

1.2 Research Question

The aim of this paper is to study the Social Practices, revealed in different TEL innovation process stages (Awareness, Acceptance, and Adoption), and determine their importance. For these purposes, the following **research question** guides this paper:

What Social Practices were, in teachers' opinion, important during the three innovation process stages?

In order to answer the research question we will interview the teachers who have permanently integrated Robomath method to their everyday teaching practices, and analyze their feedback with KAM model.

2 Method

The population of the study was 189 teachers who had used Robomath method in their lessons for more than a year. Via a direct email, we asked them to share their retrospective evaluation on how Robomath method became a sustained part in their teaching practices. Teachers were asked to take part in the study only in case they continued to use the method. Of these teachers, 20 female teachers and 2 male teachers (sample size n = 22, average duration of experience 5 years) agreed to give interviews.

Semi-structured interviews were used for data collections. The structure of questions was loose, and interviewees were encouraged to express themselves freely. The interviews were conducted by two researchers during evening hours (18:00–21:00), using the Zoom videoconferencing software. The exact time and interviewee location was decided by the participants. The average length of interviews was half an hour.

The course of a typical interview was the following. First, the duration of the interviewee's experience with educational robots was recorded. Next, the interviewing researcher introduced the interviewee to TEL innovation process stages and factors that influence this process. The list of KAM Social Practices with examples (Table 1) was shown and explained to the interviewee. Subsequently, the interviewee was asked to point out the practices that were evident in different innovation process stages.

The interviews were recorded with interviewees' consent, anonymized, transcribed and analyzed by two researchers. For the qualitative analysis, the retrospective phenomenological approach [14] and KAM framework were used. For quantitative analysis, the content analysis method [15] was used. The transcribed interviews were coded, using eight KAM categories. Each incidence of a certain KAM category was counted once per teacher.

Table 1. The list of knowledge appropriation practices with examples, presented to the participants during the interviews.

Please give specific examples of the practices you used in your school to support the application of Robomath method	
Social practice	Description
Seeking help	For example, contacting an investigator, colleague, using FB Messenger, etc., to ask questions from your colleagues, etc.
Guiding each other in applying the method	Guiding and counseling your peers, etc.
Sharing ideas	Shared your ideas or knowledge with colleagues who also tried Robomath
Validating the method in practice	Tried the method in your class, created learning designs, etc.
Adapting teaching materials to your class	I used materials created by someone else
Co-creating lesson designs	For example, with your colleagues, designed a Math task, created robotics tasks
Formalizing materials	For example, documented innovation-related materials in a way that these could be shared with other teachers in your school, wrote an article in the school newspaper, made changes to the procedures for using learning technology, etc.
Creating awareness	For example, conducted a demonstration lesson, talked to management or colleagues, etc.

2.1 Robomath Method

Robomath is a method used in Estonian basic education schools that employs educational robots in Math lessons. The aim of this method is to connect Math content via robotics exercises with real-life problems, making Math more meaningful to students, improving student learning engagement and learning outcomes [10]. Robomath method is designed to increase student autonomy and self-regulated learning, peer tutoring, and collaborative learning (i.e. 21th century skills), with the goal of transforming the learning and teaching dynamics in Math lessons [10]. Students work in small 2-member teams, using one educational robot per team, solving robotics exercises that are based on the lesson's Math topic. The focus of the robotics exercises is on using the robot as an agent for visualizing Math concepts like shapes, time, distance, speed, etc. Programming and robot building have only secondary importance, although most students become skilled in these areas also.

3 Results

Our research question was "What Social Practices were, in teachers' opinion, important during the three innovation process stages?" We used KAM model (Fig. 1) for systemizing and describing Social Practices that were present in teachers' behavior during the different stages of Robomath innovation process.

The quantitative data (Table 2, n = number of teachers) indicated that teachers acted remarkably differently in Acceptance and Adoption Stages compared to Awareness Stage. In **Awareness** Stage, the knowledge *appropriation* practices were in practical terms not represented (only two teachers had adapted materials, one had created awareness about the method in their school and one had tried material in their lessons). However, their method-related knowledge had started to *mature* by sharing their ideas (n = 12) and co-creating (n = 5) method-related artefacts (e.g. lesson designs or classroom practices). A teacher expressed *"I went home alone and was a few days busy with these exercises. Then I contacted another teacher and asked whether she'd like to join – as this is such an interesting project."* The practices with the highest presence were the knowledge *adoption* practices, namely seeking help (n = 14) and already guiding others (n = 5).

In **Acceptance** Stage, the most revealed KAM category was knowledge *appropriation* practices. Almost all teachers (n = 21) had adapted method's materials and tried it in their lessons (n = 17). More than half of them (n = 14) had disseminated the method in their schools. In knowledge *adoption* practices, there frequency of teachers guiding their peers increased greatly (n = 13), almost to the level of seeking help by themselves (n = 14). In addition, teachers' knowledge had started to *mature*: more than half of them shared their ideas (n = 14) and co-created (n = 13) method-related artefacts. By now, more than a third of teachers (n = 8) were offering their materials in a formalized format to other teachers (in open lesson design repositories, etc.). A teacher said: *"There was a lot of helping each other when using the method. Each time we discussed how to arrange the lesson better. Direct help we did not need anymore. The number of interested teacher had risen from one to five and I shared my materials with them."*

In **Adoption** Stage we saw rapid decline of material adaption (n = 10, instead of 21), whereas in the same knowledge *appropriation* practices category, validation continued strong (n = 17) and create awareness had also high presence (n = 17). Knowledge adoption practices started to lose their importance, especially seeking help (n = 11), but also guiding others (n = 12). The knowledge maturation practices retained their presence (compared to Acceptance Stage), with the exception of offering formalized materials to other teachers (n = 12). A teacher said: *"I had prepared good lesson designs, ready to be used whenever needed."*

Table 2. Presence of different Social Practices during innovation process stages (number of teachers).

KAM category	Innovation process stage	Awareness	Acceptance	Adoption
Knowledge appropriation practices	Adapt	2	21	10
	Create awareness	1	14	17
	Validate in practice	1	17	17
Knowledge maturation practices	Share	12	14	14
	Co-create	3	13	13
	Formalize	0	8	12
Knowledge adoption practices	Guide	5	13	12
	Seek help	14	14	11

The information from teachers indicates that in the first innovation process stage (Awareness) only a few KAM-described Social Practices (sharing and seeking help) are meaningfully present. In the later stages, all KAM Social Practices become observable (Table 2). Some practices that stand strongly out:

- **Adapting** TEL innovation related artefacts to their needs is practiced by almost all teachers (95%) in Acceptance Stage, and its importance fades remarkably later;
- Need for **validating** the innovation in practice becomes manifest as soon, as teachers start trying the innovation out in their classroom. In addition, its importance does not fade in time.
- The desire to **create awareness** about the method among their peers strengthens as teachers become more adept at using the innovation, reaching its maximum in Adoption stage.
- **Seeking help** is more practiced by teachers who are just starting to acquire the innovation related skills (i.e. in Awareness and Acceptance stages). The importance of this practice starts fading only in adoption stage.

The results suggest existence of three general patters for Social practices. First, **essential practices** (Adapt, Create Awareness, and Validate in Practice) seem to manifest with almost all teachers in either Acceptance or Adoption stage. These practices need to be present in teacher's daily practices if the innovation is to succeed. With the exception of Seek Help and Share, all other practices have little presence in Awareness stage but become rapidly more important in Acceptance and, with another exception of Formalize, remain at the same level. With Share and Seek Help, the difference between stages is negligible, with Seek Help fading and Share increasing in time.

These observations suggest that it is relatively easy to deduct whether a teacher is in Awareness or Acceptance stage: all Social Practices with an exception of "Seeking help" are little pronounced. It is much more difficult to determine the current stage when the teacher is in Acceptance or Adoption stage as Social Practices are exhibited very similarly in these stages. However, as stated above, four indicators could indicate if teacher has reached Adoption stage with the innovation in her classroom:

1. **Adaption** is not intensive anymore, meaning that the teacher has already prepared the lesson designs and other materials for her own needs.
2. The teacher is actively **creating awareness** about the innovation, meaning that she feels confident about her skills and knowledge about the innovation. This is the same reason why seeking help starts fading in Adoption.
3. The teacher is **formalizing** her knowledge in order to facilitate others to use it, meaning, again, that she has constructed a usable inner framework about the innovation and skills related to it.
4. The teacher **seeks** less **help** from others.

These four indicators as a set can demonstrate whether a teacher has acquired the innovation and started using it in their daily teaching practices, giving a positive sign about method's viability.

4 Conclusions and Discussion

Addressing certain Social Practices during different TEL innovation process stages may contribute to TEL innovations sustainability, as these help bridging the adoption gap between teachers' existing knowledge and innovation-related knowledge. Using KAM, we examined the importance of specific Social Practice in different TEL innovation process stages.

We discovered that teachers rely on different Social Practices in different innovation process stages. In Awareness Stage, teachers construct the foundations of their knowledge about the innovation – they are discussing innovation-related ideas and reach out to various sources for help. During this period, all other innovation-related Social Practices have rudimental presence. All Social Practices become manifest in the later innovation process stages, when teachers have begun trying out the innovation in their classrooms. In particular, the increase of co-creation (present from Acceptance stage) and formalize (having significant presence from Adoption stage) practices corresponds to the notions made by [16] and [9], implying that the odds of TEL innovation adoption increase when higher-level knowledge maturation and appropriation practices become prominent. It seems that TEL innovation has become a part of teachers' practices after they have intensively adapted the innovation to their needs, and they have started to actively create awareness about the method and formalize their knowledge.

Addressing Social Practices could prove valuable for designing targeted support mechanisms for teachers in the innovation adoption process. Information about the stage where teachers are at any certain moment makes it possible to scaffold teachers more efficiently. For example, if the teachers of a certain population are adapting or co-creating innovation-related artefacts, but are not formalizing these artefacts and are also seeking help from others, then most likely they are in Acceptance Stage (i.e. they are in the process of developing their opinion about the innovation). Alternatively, if these teachers are not adapting the artefacts anymore, are not seeking help, but are guiding their peers and sharing their own artefacts in a formalized manner, then most probably they are in Adoption Stage – the innovation has become a sustained in their practices. In addition, these observations suggest that if some Social Practices have only minimal presence in teacher's practices then this teacher should be supported by providing them with a relevant teacher professional development program. Such programs are discussed, for example, in [8].

5 Limitations and Future Work

TEL innovations are based on technologies that may require fundamentally different approaches. In this paper, we have more thoroughly studied the importance of Social Practices. For better understanding of the dynamics of TEL innovation sustainability, it is necessary to conduct further studies that examine the synergy of all innovation sustainability factors. We used robot-supported Math teaching as an example TEL method. Other TEL innovations could yield different results. The study sample consisted of a relatively small group of teachers who had successfully integrated the novel method to their teaching practices. Obtaining results that are more thorough could require additional examining of the experience of those teachers who had abandoned the method in some innovation process stage. In addition, the experience of other stakeholders, such as researchers and school management should be taken into consideration. This paper is a part of a wider three-year study that took place in Estonia – longitudinal studies in different national contexts could lead to results that are more reliable.

Based on these notes we suggest that broader international longitudinal studies that examine sustainability of TEL innovations that are based on different technologies. In addition, these studies should analyze the experience of different stakeholders in order to obtain in-depth knowledge about the subject.

Acknowledgments. This project has received funding from the European Union's Horizon 2020 research and innovation programme under grant agreement No. 669074.

Project "TU TEE – Tallinn University as a promoter of intelligent lifestyle" (No. 2014-2020.4.01.16-0033) under activity A5 in the Tallinn University Centre of Excellence in Educational Innovation.

References

1. United Nations: World Economic and Social Survey 2018. New York (2018)
2. Trentin, G., Alvino, S.: Faculty training as a key factor for Web Enhanced Learning sustainability. In: Repetto, M., Trentin, G. (eds.) Faculty Training for Web-Enhanced Learning. Nova Science Publishers Inc., Hauppauge (2011)
3. Niederhauser, D.S., Lindstrom, D.L.: Instructional technology integration models and frameworks: diffusion, competencies, attitudes, and dispositions. In: Voogt, J., Knezek, G., Christensen, R., Lai, K.-W. (eds.) Second Handbook of Information Technology in Primary and Secondary Education. SIHE, pp. 335–355. Springer, Cham (2018). https://doi.org/10.1007/978-3-319-71054-9_23

4. Owston, R.D.: School context, sustainability, and transferability of innovation. In: Kozma, R.B. (ed.) Technology, Innovation, and Educational Change: A Global Perspective. A Report of the Second Information Technology in Education Study, Module 2. IEA, Amsterdam (2003)
5. Cai, Y.: From an analytical framework for understanding the innovation process in higher education to an emerging research field of innovations in higher education. Rev. High. Educ. **40**(4), 585–616 (2017). https://doi.org/10.1353/rhe.2017.0023
6. Daniela, L., Visvizi, A., Gutiérrez-Braojos, C., Lytras, M.: Sustainable higher education and technology-enhanced learning (TEL). Sustainability **10**(11), 3883 (2018)
7. Sharples, M., et al.: New modes of technology-enhanced learning: opportunities and challenges. Becta (2009)
8. Leoste, J., Tammets, K., Ley, T.: Co-creating learning designs in professional teacher education: knowledge appropriation in the teacher's innovation laboratory. IxD&A Interact. Des. Archit. **42**, 131–163 (2019)
9. Rodríguez-Triana, M.J., Prieto, L.P., Ley, T., de Jong, T., Gillet, D.: Social practices in teacher knowledge creation and innovation adoption: a large-scale study in an online instructional design community for inquiry learning. Int. J. Comput.-Support. Collab. Learn. **15**(4), 445–467 (2020). https://doi.org/10.1007/s11412-020-09331-5
10. Leoste, J., Heidmets, M. Ley, T.: Classroom innovation becoming sustainable: a study of technological innovation adoption by estonian primary school teachers. IxD&A Interact. Des. Archit. (2021)
11. Arinaitwe, D.: Practices and strategies for enhancing learning through collaboration between vocational teacher training institutions and workplaces. Empir. Res. Vocat. Educ. Train. **13**(1), 1–22 (2021). https://doi.org/10.1186/s40461-021-00117-z
12. Kimmerle, J., Cress, U., Held, C.: The interplay between individual and collective knowledge: technologies for organisational learning and knowledge building. Knowl. Manag. Res. Pract. **8**(1), 33–44 (2010). https://doi.org/10.1057/kmrp.2009.36
13. Maier, R., Schmidt, A.: Explaining organizational knowledge creation with a knowledge maturing model. Knowl. Manag. Res. Pract. **13**(4), 361–381 (2015). https://doi.org/10.1057/kmrp.2013.56
14. Sloan, A., Bowe, B.: Phenomenology and hermeneutic phenomenology: the philosophy, the methodologies, and using hermeneutic phenomenology to investigate lecturers' experiences of curriculum design. Qual. Quant. **48**(3), 1291–1303 (2013). https://doi.org/10.1007/s11135-013-9835-3
15. Duriau, V.J., Reger, R.K., Pfarrer, M.D.: A content analysis of the content analysis literature in organization studies: research themes, data sources, and methodological refinements. Organ. Res. Methods **10**, 5–34 (2007)
16. Asensio-Pérez, J.I., et al.: Towards teaching as design: exploring the interplay between full-lifecycle learning design tooling and Teacher Professional Development. Comput. Educ. **114**, 92–116 (2017)

Visual Aids for Teaching Piano to Students with Autism: Designing a Web App Through Practice

Caterina Senette(✉), Maria Claudia Buzzi, Marina Buzzi, and Amaury Trujillo

IIT-CNR, Via Moruzzi 1, Pisa, Italy
{caterina.senette,claudia.buzzi,marina.buzzi, amaury.trujillo}@iit.cnr.it

Abstract. This paper describes an accessible web app for mobile devices that serves as a support tool to teach students with autism the basics of music using a virtual piano keyboard. Within the app, learning material is presented in a gradual and structured way, in which each educational unit can be customized according to students' needs and preferences; for instance, visual and auditory aids aimed at special-needs learners can be deactivated over time to make the learning outcomes independent from them. In order to study and improve both the user and use contexts for the interface design and interaction mechanisms, we recruited seventeen adolescents with autism at two different stages of the app development cycle. By collecting a variety of interaction data, we refined design choices and iteratively evaluated accessibility, usability, and acceptability aspects of the app. Results of this process appear to confirm the feasibility of our approach while providing valuable observational data for other researchers working on similar solutions. In addition, this work further corroborates the positive role of technology in motivating adolescents with low- and medium-functioning autism in their learning, and highlights the potential of music as a learning object per se, and not only as a medium for mastering other skills.

Keywords: Visual learning · Web application · Music · Autism · Graphic design

1 Introduction

Students with autism spectrum disorder may experience difficulty in classic learning environments; this is especially true for low-functioning individuals, since their attention and auditory channel may be impaired compared to neuro-typical students, making it difficult to concentrate without assistive visual elements and cues [3]. Structured learning offers students with autism a repeatable, predictable and consistent training environment, which can be tuned to the individual's needs, reducing anxiety and facilitating mastery of skills. Data monitoring and analysis enable caregivers to effectively verify progress as well as any difficulties experienced in the learning environment, and thus to better focus the intervention. To this aim, new approaches with Artificial Intelligence could also be used for automatic scheduling of practice trials in individualized learning paths to achieve better performance [22]. Intensive and early educational and behavioral intervention leads to better results, due to the great plasticity of a child's brain, which can be shaped more effectively [3]. Clear, predictable and accessible learning objectives reduce anxiety and prevent self-stimulation; thus, reinforcement is crucial for increasing motivation and attention when teaching students with autism.

Literature indicates that music is important for individuals with autism. For example, music is useful in the treatment of specific symptoms of autism (passive use of music) [14, 16, 27] and some individuals with autism show greater musical ability than the average person [15]. Unfortunately, very few studies have analyzed opportunities for individuals with autism (especially low- and medium-functioning) to learn music in an inclusive music class environment. Since the language of music is complex and playing an instrument well requires long training involving many skills, individuals with autism (especially low- and medium-functioning) often have problems decoding symbols and tempo, coordinating hands, and so on [3]. Therefore, to empower them it is necessary to exploit their strengths and mitigate their weaknesses. The use of mobile and web apps is a promising approach to achieving such empowerment. Indeed, several native and web apps are already available to teach music to children or novice learners, although none of them are fully accessible or usable by students with autism, mainly because they are too rich in stimuli and poorly adapted to their special needs.

Therefore, we have developed a structured, accessible and personalized web app, *Suoniamo*, designed for teaching music to students with autism. The main goal of the app is to deliver structured teaching in small elementary units, avoiding errors and modulating stimuli. The app's simple interface and its customization features enable a better match of the student's personal learning rhythm and preferences. This is the added value of the proposed app compared to other solutions currently available, either on the market or as research products. Moreover, the system will be free (after a longitudinal test with four schools across Italy) to encourage its adoption by music teachers, parents, and therapists who want to use music training programs for people with autism.

In the following sections we describe the app's theoretical background, the related research aspects and our proposed solutions to these. Then, we focus on the design and testing phases for assessing the effectiveness of visual elements intended to aid visual learners. Next, we discuss the main results gathered from the iterative design and testing process in terms of accessibility, usability, and user experience. Conclusions and future work end the paper.

2 Background

Autism is a disorder in which each patient is a whole world. The DSM-V [2] identified five diagnostic criteria and three levels of severity helpful for detecting both common and different traits among subjects with autism. Low-functioning children, categorized as Level 3, show severe deficits in verbal skills, and high impairment when interacting with others in social situations. Additionally, they may express disruptive behavior, especially in unknown contexts or routine transitions. Differently, children at Level 1 (high-functioning) express normal to high intellectual abilities and have verbal skills but may feel stressed when interacting with others or in routine transitions. At all levels, they may have sensory sensitivity (under or over), mainly auditory, that affects daily life experiences [2].

Literature reports the positive effects of music in treating specific symptoms in autism spectrum disorder at all levels [6, 27]. As reported in a recent review concerning music interventions for children with autism [27], most studies have focused their attention on music's influence on communication, socialization and behavior. Typical approaches included listening to music and music combined with social stories [7]. Other literature attempts to verify the expression of particular abilities in music perception, and sometimes the presence of higher than average skills, in people with autism [15]. Very few studies have focused on opportunities for people with low- and medium-functioning autism to learn music or to be included in music classes, instead mainly focusing on how to set up the didactic environment and schedule activities [1, 9, 16].

Our contribution is an attempt to fill this gap via a multidisciplinary study on effective strategies for including students with autism with higher severity levels (low- and medium-functioning) in a music class that provides accessible music programs via a web app. Some of these strategies come from literature. Our main point of reference is a doctoral thesis [17] that investigated how people with autism can have optimal learning experiences with music. The author used a qualitative approach [12] based on interviews with four music teachers who had many years of experience teaching music to students with autism. Among the several theses' contributions, the most valuable one concerns identifying strategies that can serve as guidelines for music teachers: (i) Concrete strategies (tools used to accommodate needs); (ii) Stylistic strategies (non-traditional and flexible teaching approaches); (iii) Attitudinal strategies (greater understanding of students).

Regarding software for learning music, several native apps are available in online stores (Google Play, Apple Store) to teach music to neuro-typical children or novice learners. Two of the most complete, Sinthesia[1] and Simply Piano[2], rely on colors and provide visual cues also suitable for teaching individuals with autism to play music. Unfortunately, both are very rich in stimuli and they lack structured and customized teaching, which is very important for students with autism.

3 Objectives and Methods

The main objective of this multidisciplinary study is to design an accessible and usable tool to support music learning in low- and medium-functioning students with autism by exploiting the potential of web technologies and gathering valuable data to facilitate designing user interfaces for people with autism in this domain, directly from the users. Moreover, the tool needs to be attractive enough to be accepted and continuously used by the target population. In this regard, to identify effective strategies for teaching music to people with autism using mobile devices, we focus on user-centered design and participatory design. The participatory design involved four ICT researchers, a music

---

[1] https://www.synthesiagame.com/.
[2] https://www.joytunes.com/simply-piano.

teacher and a psychologist, as well as two middle-school students with autism. They were helpful for collecting impressions and feedback at an early stage, in an ecological model of autism [20], but since both teacher and students already shared music class experiences, the context was highly predictable. To overcome this bias, we carried out the entire design and implementation phases with multiple tests involving other students with autism, as described in the following sections.

4 Research Approach

4.1 Thinking of a Framework

The first aspect of interest regards *a potential framework (theoretical or operational) for teaching music to students with low- and medium-functioning autism via an app.*

As previously described, literature offers suggestions for teaching music to students with autism, but interventions are often diverse and performed with few users, and to the best of the authors' knowledge, reproducible and generalizable guidelines are not available. Nonetheless, effectiveness of any guidelines for teaching music to people with autism varies from individual to individual, as it depends on the specific user skills and needs.

Music is part of the Italian school curriculum. In primary school, it is introduced gradually, with singing and playing a three-octave piano keyboard. Music theory and notation are introduced in middle school, which is the target age of our study (i.e., age 10–14 years). When students with low- and medium-functioning autism attend music classes in middle school, they are often assigned to perform small scores on the bass line to accompany the other instruments (classmates), playing a simple and repetitive pattern of notes that are easy to reproduce. The videos recorded by the teacher, part of the research team, show that their students with low- or medium-functioning autism always play guided by the teacher's finger, following a stimulus-response approach.

In order to go beyond a stimulus-response pattern, we identified the following four basic learning units as a framework to help the student familiarize him/herself with music notation and play simple scores autonomously: (i) Note discrimination module to learn the position of notes on the keyboard. (ii) Note value module to familiarize student with time duration (4/4, 2/4, 1/4); (iii) Harmonic progression module to familiarize student with the concept of harmony; (iv) Execution support module, to guide the student in playing the score. In this target population fine-motor coordination is challenging, so students usually play using only one finger at a time. For this reason, learning finger position has not been considered as a learning unit.

4.2 Requirements

The second aspect of interest is *the conveyance of such a framework in terms of functional and non-functional requirements that meet the user's needs and preferences.*

The aim is to create an app to support inclusion, improving current practices in music classes and offering better opportunities to students with autism. Functional requirements strictly related to the learning environment include: (i) Using alternative augmentative communication (AAC) that offers different ways to communicate (mainly visual aids) when children or adults have severe speech and language problems [29]; (ii) Offering an errorless environment, meaning that the student's actions are prompted in order to reduce occurrence of errors. According to ABA (Applied Behavior Analysis) principles, an error affects the learning process, breaking down the correct chain and requiring a big effort to reset the learning path [28]. (iii) Delivering structured and facilitated teaching, prompting the user when difficulty arises and using reinforcement in the case of positive behaviors, thus increasing the children's confidence in solving tasks as well as their self-esteem.

Besides the app's functional requirements, we took into consideration non-functional criteria to define the app's features -- for instance, how it implements errorless principles or provides a reward (reinforcement) to model the user's behavior. These criteria drove the design of the graphical user interfaces and the user interaction mechanisms within the identified learning framework, as described in the next section.

4.3 Design and Test GUIs

The third aspect of interest covers *the design of the graphical user interface components and the interaction mechanisms of the student's working area (WA).*

There are a plethora of works addressing computer-assisted learning (CAL) for students with autism, but only a few take into consideration specific design concerns (especially graphics) that are crucial to guaranteeing accessible and usable tools for this target population. Pavlov's work [23], focuses on the creation of an open book and indicates several user interface (UI) design recommendations covering different aspects. Kamaruzaman's work [18] applies the five principles of Lewis [19] (*Clustering principle, Visibility Reflects Usefulness Principles, Intelligent Consistency Principle, Colour as a Supplement Principle, and Reduced Clutter Principle*) in designing the UIs of a numeracy app for children with autism. Regarding web interfaces, Eraslan et al. (2019) [11] suggests that a minimalist design, reducing the number of elements on the screen, simplifies the interaction by decreasing the cognitive load for people with autism since they tend to look at details. All these studies offered guidelines for a general design that must be adapted to the current domain by adequately addressing specific autistic traits (low- and medium-functioning), besides guaranteeing high interactivity and good user experience to avoid frustration and preserve music as an engaging learning topic.

Involving Users in the Test Design

Participatory design sessions were performed every 2 weeks (for 6 months) with the design team members. Given the difficulties in involving users with low-functioning autism directly in the user interface design, preliminary schemas of UI components had been defined using a top-down approach starting from existing literature and exploiting experts' experience with learners with autism (the music teacher and the psychologist). Next, we organized cyclic tests (as part of the design phase) involving end users through an iterative and incremental design approach. It is worth noting that user tests are not easy to carry out on this target population due to lack of cooperation, low attention span, possible self-stimulation and problem behaviors. To avoid frustration, it is necessary to propose only a few tasks in each test session and allow participants to stop whenever they want. Therefore, we carried out two sessions of tests at different times, focusing our attention on one limited set of components at a time and involving different groups of users: (i) **First Level Tests (L1Ts)** were performed by a group of seven adolescents with autism with the aim of gaining feedback and evaluating possible in-between components of the UI's; (ii) **Second Level Tests (L2Ts)** to validate updated changes, involved ten participants (not previously recruited), some with musical knowledge, to investigate use patterns of both novice and more expert users. In the following, we describe participants, materials, methods, and results of both the L1Ts and L2Ts.

Participants – Data collection – Materials

Seventeen adolescents with diagnosed autism (age 11–19 years) participated; seven of them had some musical knowledge, only two played one or more musical instruments, and all were sufficiently familiar with the use of mobile touch screen devices. Additional details of the user sample are provided in Table 1.

Table 1. Characterization of participants in L1T and L2T tests

L1Ts					L2Ts				
User	Age	Gender	Severity Level[a]	Music Knowledge	User	Age	Gender	Severity Level[a]	Music Knowledge
P1	13	F	2	Y	P8	12	M	2	Y
P2	13	M	3	N	P9	11	M	2	Y
P3	14	M	2	N	P10	15	M	2	Y
P4	18	F	3	N	P11	16	F	3	Y
P5	15	M	2	N	P12	15	M	3	Y
P6	15	M	3	N	P13	15	M	3	Y
P7	17	M	3	N	P14	14	F	3	N
					P15	16	M	3	N
					P16	19	M	3	N
					P17	11	M	3	N

[a]Level 1: "Requiring support", Level 2: "Requiring substantial support", Level 3: "Requiring very substantial support" [2].

All participants performed the test in a natural setting (ten at school, five at home, and two in a lab where they carry out afternoon study sessions) and he/she could relax by doing something else for a while. Data collected during tests were mainly observational, focusing on user behavior while performing the proposed tasks (relevant to the specific module) and interacting with the UI elements. We also collected automatic data recorded through the app such as trial errors, successful tasks, task execution time and interactions with the UI components outside the virtual keyboard. Moreover, the participants were asked to evaluate their degree of acceptance and ease of use of each learning module using Likert visual scales. As suggested in literature, a Smiley-meter Likert scale (awful, not very good, neutral, good, very good) is an appropriate tool for collecting opinions from children and young users [13, 26]. Literature reports the feasibility of also applying this rating scale to users with autism [5, 21]. Questions were presented in a positive way: *Did you enjoy doing this type of exercise? How easy was it to do?*

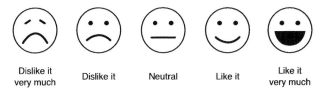

Fig. 1. Smiley Meter – Pleasantness

Materials and procedures were the same for both L1Ts and L2Ts (in L2Ts, the set of proposed tasks partially overlapped the set evaluated on L1Ts). Each test was performed using an Android Tablet with Wi-Fi connection, screen size 10.1". A Smiley-meter rating scale of five items (Fig. 1) was provided to each participant to collect subjective data on preferences from the users.

In the following, we will describe the main issues that arose when we proposed specific tasks to the participants and how they have driven the design process. We focused on two learning units (propaedeutic to the other ones): Note discrimination and Note value, containing all the UIs elements and the interaction mechanisms to be used in all the learning units.

Note Discrimination Module

The objective is learning the position of notes on the keyboard. First, notes are proposed in sequence to help memorize the scale; then the student can move to program generalization through random notes.

We designed the student's working area (WA) as a dynamic entity that exploits the user's visual channel to convey information, as people with autism are often visual learners [24, 25]. This WA consists of two sections (as illustrated in Fig. 2) the virtual piano keyboard at the bottom, and the informative area (IA) at the top, which is dynamic but not interactive except for the metronome. Depending on the objectives of each learning unit, the system adds or removes specific interface elements while respecting the basic scheme of the student WA. Tests with users helped us to verify overall interface components' intuitiveness as a medium to accomplish the proposed tasks.

Number of Octaves - Usability

L1Ts: A virtual keyboard with up to three octaves is a trade-off between the need to preserve the keyboard's usability on the target device (10" Tablet) and the typical tonal range of songs assigned at school to students with autism. Proposing three different versions of the keyboard did not show usability problems (evaluated observing users' finger positions on the keyboard). However, one participant with severity level 3 preferred the one-octave format.

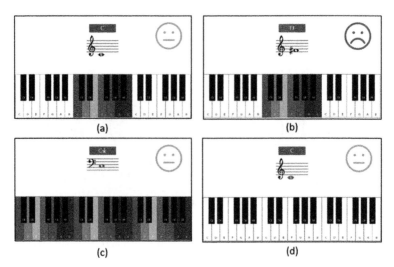

Fig. 2. Note discrimination module UIs

L2Ts: One participant (P8) played by placing his whole hand on the virtual keyboard, as he usually did on a real piano. Since keys on a virtual keyboard are different from those of a real piano, this leads to clumsy pattern interaction. Another participant (P13) rested their entire right hand on the keyboard, covering the interface elements; this suggests that it should be possible to customize elements' position on the screen. Moreover, some of these problems might be solved by the use of a physical keyboard that can be connected to the app via USB port, also allowing to generalize the learned concepts.

Note-Color Mapping: To simplify note identification and positioning on the keyboard we implemented the note-color mapping that is frequently and successfully used with neuro-typical children. Moreover, some people with autism have synesthesia, an ability to associate musical notes with colors, shapes, etc. [4]. Default note/color association proposes rainbow colors. During tests (both L1Ts and L2Ts), the visual color-based relation between notes and piano keys seemed intuitive for all participants, who were able to successfully accomplish the task without prompts. Moreover, when applying two different prompts (color and note label), which is the dominant one? We verified that when applying only one prompt at a time, the color prompt is dominant: using a white and labeled keyboard, 70% of the participants made several errors (on average 7 of 10 trials were unsuccessful). Instead, using the unlabeled and colored keyboard, on average for all the students only 2 of 10 attempts were unsuccessful.

Workflow – Error
L1Ts: The student's work environment should guarantee a logical workflow of tasks, and each task needs to be consistent. How should the system behave in case of error? How does it convey feedback to the user? The ABA errorless principle suggests avoiding errors, especially in the initial learning phase [28]. In our context, the error occurs if the

student presses the wrong key. The L1Ts showed that using additional sound effects to highlight errors could be annoying and disturbing.

L2Ts: considering the L1T results, the updated WA does not provide auditory error feedback. During the L2Ts, three out of ten users started touching the keyboard randomly, making many errors, noticing the absence of sonorous feedback from the UI. However, in the next interactions, the stimulus-action to produce a sound (playing the correct key on the keyboard) worked as a motivator for all participants.

Feedback

LT1s: Feedback from the system is conveyed via a visual reinforcement (animated smiley). The smiley icon appears neutral at the beginning (Fig. 2a) and becomes positive for each successful task completion (Fig. 3a). We did not propose the negative smiley icon for a failed task in order to prevent user frustration. L1Ts showed a crucial role of the dynamic smiley icon as instant feedback; participants demanded strong temporal synchronization between key pressing, sound released and emoticon status change. Desynchronization (mainly due to connection latency with the server) in fact caused user confusion and frustration.

L2Ts: Due to the issues observed in L1Ts, we changed the underlying architecture to a single application page that minimizes communication with the server for better performance and to allow the users to concentrate on the smiley's semantic role within the task. Moreover, during L2Ts, in order to highlight that semantic role, we propose the negative smiley (highlighted red, Fig. 2b) as negative feedback for a failed task. All L2Ts participants expected a change in the icon status because of their action on the screen, confirming to us that previous neutral status could be misunderstood. Seven participants were highly interested in its dynamic status, two participants seemed uninterested in the feedback icon (but they correctly performed the task and used the sound itself as a feedback) while one had some fine-motor-skills troubles, putting their hand on the icon and thus making it not visible.

Sharp Notes #: How to map sharp notes? Tagging the black piano keys with further colors could require additional mental effort of the user. Using the two colors of the closest notes on the keyboard's black keys made them unperceivable. Therefore, we chose to use these two colors only in the stimulus (note label) (Fig. 2b). During L2Ts: Two participants performed the task correctly without external prompts. Five out of ten participants experienced initial disorientation, but a little physical prompt helped them localizing the sharp note between the two keys colored as in the stimulus. Three participants found the task difficult to perform even when prompted.

Note Value Module

This second module is for learning the concept of note value, in terms of relative duration. An example task request is to press a specific note for a certain time. Moreover, the learning unit teaches the concept of rests. This module is more challenging since it requires good inhibitory control; it means thinking before acting. Like other *executive functions*, these skills are critical for success in all life's aspects and often need to be trained through specific strategies [10]. Users with low-functioning autism frequently show a lack of this skill, which affects day-to-day living [8]. Design proposal and tests of the WA elements are described below.

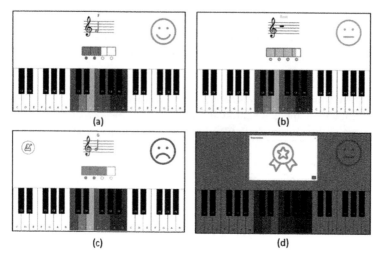

Fig. 3. Note value and dialogs UIs: Tolerance (a); Rest (b); Metronome (c); Reward Dialog (d)

Time Bar Progression: L1Ts: What is the best widget to convey the idea of time progression? At the early design stage, some hypotheses were discarded, and we oriented the choice towards a progress bar calibrated on the time signature (the default is 4/4). L1Ts guided us toward the idea of filling because when utilizing emptying dynamics, users show anxiety (a sort of countdown effect). Unfortunately, respecting the task request precisely in terms of key pressure duration is not easy and can induce user frustration. In L1Ts, all users were disoriented when they received negative feedback for not having performed the task request exactly.

Tolerance: To attempt to resolve the latter issue, we introduced tolerance value in the time progression bar (Fig. 3a). L2Ts show a good understanding of the task; two users out of ten performed the task easily, six users did so after verbal prompt, and the remaining two participants did not understand the task correctly (overall, 80% of users carried out the task). L2Ts confirmed that participants' behavior vs tolerance depends on personal attitudes; for some of them, the tolerance is initially perceived as an incongruity of the system behavior, but as they realize the difficulty of perfect timing, they accept this tolerance. For those who tend to do everything quickly (two participants showed this attitude in their overall interaction with the app), the tolerance helps minimize unsuccessful trials and correlated anxiety.

Rest: L1Ts: Is the standard rest symbol well-interpreted? We tried to add a specific AAC icon as a task stimulus, but during L1Ts we observed that it was a source of confusion for all participants. L2Ts guided us to introduce an extra stimulus to indicate stopping user interaction with the keyboard. The current implementation exploits the rest symbol using a soft gray color typically used for non-active elements in graphical interfaces. Proposing the tasks asking to play random notes including rests (Fig. 3b), LT2s tests showed that 80% of participants interpreted the concept of a rest very well, immediately stopping their interaction with the keyboard.

Metronome: How does the user count the time flow during the task? Can we add a metronome as an additional augmentative component to the WA? In order to better evaluate positive or negative effects of the metronome, during L2Ts we proposed two tasks without it (diatonic scale at 4/4 and at 2/4) and two tasks with it (diatonic scale at 4/4 and at 2/4) (Fig. 3c). L2Ts: Four out of ten participants showed they preferred tasks with the metronome, and its presence seemed to help them perform the task. Two of them explicitly requested to control the metronome, by starting or stopping it as needed. Two of ten participants were disturbed by the metronome and its sound and preferred to stop it. The behavior of the last four participants was indifferent to the metronome's presence.

App User Evaluation

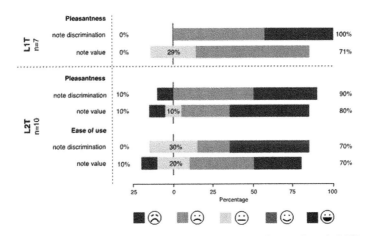

Fig. 4. User rating: pleasantness in L1Ts (top); pleasantness and ease of use in L2Ts (bottom)

Overall evaluation from participants regarding both modules, in terms of degree of acceptance (pleasantness) and ease of use (only for L2Ts) of the WA, was collected proposing the smiley-meter rating scale of five items as previously described. Results are summarized in Fig. 4. Most participants gave a positive evaluation; only one user (P13, who experienced usability problems, covering the interface elements with their hand) reported poor pleasantness and those tasks were not easy to perform. We plan to prevent this issue by allowing changing the elements' position on the screen. Nearly all participants easily gave their feedback through the smiley-meter; the mediator supported some users (younger, non-receptive) with additional vocal cues.

5 Discussion

Since each person with autism "is a whole world", each user contributed to collected data with a specific pattern of behavior in response to the proposed tasks. The behavior patterns observed were a valuable source of information towards refining design choices, but their nature is not objective. Considering the goals of the study (Sect. 3), an overall analysis of results in terms of observed behavior, especially coming from the L2Ts (test of the improved GUIs), should focus on four main questions:

1. **Is the app accessible?** As shown in the different app screenshots, we used a minimalist design, avoiding background and distractors, using soft or mild colors and appropriate fonts (clear, sans-serif fonts with contrast between font and background), as well as a workflow with clear task requests from the system. These design choices increase the app's accessibility for the target users, who are typically visual learners. All participants showed a good understanding of the proposed UIs: 50% of them had a clear understanding of the tasks, though in some cases (30%), prompting was necessary. Most of the selected WA components and the interaction mechanisms were not sources of disturbance or frustration, and when it occurred (as with the metronome), they could easily be controlled by the user him/herself, demonstrating the app's accessibility.

2. **Is the app usable?** The app simulates a three-octave piano, so the first usability request is physical. We tested it with participants of different ages and therefore different physical sizes, observing that generally playing with a single finger did not cause usability problems (80%). Physical usability was not satisfied when trying to reproduce some typical movements playing a real piano (1 user out of 10) or in the case of specific postural impairment (1 user out of 10). Other elements such as customizable task difficulty, visual aids, prompts, feedback, and rewards contribute to a good user experience avoiding frustration. As learned during tests, the latter is also influenced by instant feedback with no delays which is very important, especially in time-based tasks such as note-duration and rest training. Therefore, we use modern Web APIs to minimize latency within the interface and in the communication between client and server.

3. **Is the app well-accepted by students with autism?** Apart from positive feedback provided by participants through smiley-meter rating, we observed a very high acceptance and involvement from all of them. Although 70% of the sample normally exhibit repetitive behaviors and 40% also exhibit problem behaviors, neither occurred during any of the test sessions described herein (each lasting from 20 to 30 min). This suggests the potential role of the app as a tool to train inhibitory control [8, 10] – allowing the student to stay focused during learning through inhibition of mind wandering or external distractions. The app includes a 'Free play' module, a keyboard piano with different types of sound which was offered as a reinforcement after the execution of each task and was highly appreciated and requested by all the participants.

4. **Among the target users, who could benefit most from this tool?** Of the sample, 64% had a high severity level of autism (low-functioning autism). Typically, low-functioning users have great difficulty during activities requiring concentration;

however, as observed during tests, the attractiveness of the mobile device and the pleasantness conveyed by music could make the application suitable for them as well. Concerning the didactic content offered, the app seems to be well-accepted and appropriate even for medium-functioning users who still do not know music, while high-functioning students and/or students who already play piano may use it just for fun, due to the elementary learning modules offered.

6 Conclusion

Literature supports the positive effects of both music and digital technology in the treatment of autism. *Suoniamo*, described herein, is a mobile web app to help adolescents with low- and medium- functioning autism (severe autism) learn music, beyond its therapeutic use. The app's objective is to offer an accessible and customizable tool to improve users' autonomy while learning music, with the ultimate goal of easing integration with peers during music class. This paper describes early iterative design and test sessions of this app, conducted with two groups of adolescents with autism (in total 17 users). These tests helped us collect valuable data to improve the user experience, with attention to different profiles including severity levels, previous knowledge of music, etc. Results were positive in most aspects considered at this stage and confirmed the feasibility of this approach for teaching music to adolescents with autism, overcoming the stimulus-response paradigm. Furthermore, this study might offer valuable suggestions about research and software design principles to shape educational tools addressing the needs of users with severe autism in other domains.

For future work, the app will offer an execution support module completely adaptable to the students' preferences through which they can accompany their classmates in the performance of simple pieces. It is at this stage, playing with others, that the most relevant pedagogical objectives, mastered during training and affecting day-to-day living, could potentially be exploited: positive impact on concentration times, better inhibitory control, and reduction of problem behaviors. As a next step, we will investigate the app's effectiveness via a six-month test involving students with autism in four secondary schools geographically distributed around Italy.

References

1. Adamek, M., Darrow, A.A.: Music in special education. The American Music Therapy Association, Silver Springs (2007)
2. American Psychiatric Association: Diagnostic and Statistical Manual of Mental Disorders. 5th edn. American Psychiatric Publishing, Arlington (2013)
3. Baron-Cohen, S.: Autism: The Empathizing-Systemizing (E-S) Theory. Ann. New York Acad. Sci. **1156**(1), 68–80 (2009)
4. Baron-Cohen, S., et al.: Is synaesthesia more common in autism? Mol. Autism **4**(1), 40 (2013). https://doi.org/10.1186/2040-2392-4-40
5. Benton, L., Johnson, H., Ashwin, E., Brosnam, M., Grawemeyer, B.: Developing IDEAS: supporting children with autism within a participatory design team. In: Proceedings of the ACM SIGCHI Conference on Human Factors in Computing Systems, pp. 2599–2608 (2012)

6. LaGasse, B.A.: Effects of a music therapy group intervention on enhancing social skills in children with autism. J. Music Ther. **51**(3), 250–275 (2014)
7. Brownell, M.D.: Musically adapted social stories to modify behaviors in students with autism: four case studies. J. Music Ther. **39**, 117–144 (2002)
8. Christ, S., Holt, D., White, D., Green, L.: Inhibitory control in children with autism spectrum disorder. J. Autism Dev. Disord. **37**(6), 1155–1165 (2007). https://doi.org/10.1007/s10803-006-0259-y
9. Clements-Cortes, A.: Designing an inclusive music classroom for students with autism and autism spectrum disorders. In: Canadian Music Educator, pp. 35–37 (2012)
10. Diamond, D., Ling, D.S.: Conclusions about interventions, programs, and approaches for improving executive functions that appear justified and those that, despite much hype, do not. Dev. Cogn. Neurosci. **18**, 34–48 (2016)
11. Eraslan, S., Yaneva, V., Yesilava, Y., Harper, S.: Web users with autism: eye-tracking evidence for differences. Behav. Inf. Technol. **38**(7), 678–700 (2019)
12. Glaser, B.G., Strauss, A.L.: The Discovery of Grounded Theory: Strategies for Qualitative Research. Adline de Gruyter, New York (1967)
13. Hall, L., Hume, C., Tazzyman, S.: Five degrees of happiness: effective smiley face likert scales for evaluating with children. In: Proceedings of IDC 2016, pp. 311–321. ACM (2016)
14. Hallam, S.: The power of music: a research synthesis of the impact of actively making music on the intellectual, social and personal development of children and young people. International Music Education Research Centre (iMerc) (2015)
15. Heaton, P.: Assessing musical skills in autistic children who are not savants. Philos. Tran. R. Soc. Lond. B: BS **364**(1522), 1443–1447 (2009)
16. Hetland, L.: Learning to make music enhances spatial reasoning. J. Aesthetic Educ. **34**(3/4), 179–238 (2000)
17. Jimenez, S.D.: An exploration of teaching music to individuals with autism spectrum disorder (2014)
18. Kamaruzaman, M.F., Rani, N.M., Nor, H.M., Azaharia, M.H.: Developing user interface design application for children with autism. Procedia Soc. Behav. Sci. **217**, 887–889 (2016)
19. Lewis, C., Rieman, J.: Task-centered user interface design. A practical introduction (1993)
20. Loveland, K.A.: Toward an ecological theory of autism. In: The Development of Autism: Perspectives from Theory and Research, pp. 17–37 (2001)
21. Malinverni, L., Mora-Guiard, J., Padillo, V., Valero, L., Hervás, A., Pares, N.: An inclusive design approach for developing video games for children with Autism Spectrum Disorder. Comput. Human Behav. **71**, 535–549 (2017)
22. Pavlik, P., Anderson, J.: Using a model to compute the optimal schedule of practice. J. Exp. Psychol.: Appl. **14**(2), 101–117 (2008)
23. Pavlov, N.: User interface for people with autism spectrum disorders. J. Softw. Eng. Appl. **7**(02), 128 (2014)
24. Quill, K.A.: Visually cued instruction for children with autism and pervasive developmental disorders. Focus Autistic Behav. **10**(3), 10–20 (1995)
25. Rao, S.M., Gagie, B.: Learning through seeing and doing: visual supports for children with autism. Teach. Except. Child. **38**(6), 26–33 (2006)
26. Read, J.C., MacFarlane, S.: Using the fun toolkit and other survey methods to gather opinions in child computer interaction. In: Proceedings of IDC 06, pp. 81–88. ACM Press (2006)

27. Simpson, K., Keen, D.: Music interventions for children with autism: narrative review of the literature. J. Autism Dev. Disord. **41**(11), 1507–1514 (2011). https://doi.org/10.1007/s10803-010-1172-y
28. Terrace, H.S.: Discrimination learning with and without "error." J. Exp. Anal. Behav. **6**, 1–27 (1963). https://doi.org/10.1901/jeab.1963.6-1
29. Zangari, C., Lloyd, L., Vicker, B.: Augmentative and alternative communication: an historic perspective. Augment. Alter. Commun. **10**(1), 27–59 (1994). https://doi.org/10.1080/07434619412331276740

Interactive and Explainable Advising Dashboard Opens the Black Box of Student Success Prediction

Hanne Scheers and Tinne De Laet[(✉)]

Leuven Engineering and Science Education Center (LESEC), KU Leuven, Leuven, Belgium
`tinne.delaet@kuleuven.be`

Abstract. This paper presents exploratory research regarding the design and evaluation of a dashboard supporting the advising of aspiring university students incorporating a black-box predictive model for student success. While black-box predictive models can provide accurate predictions, incorporating them in dashboards is challenging as the black-box nature can threaten the interpretability and negatively impact trust of end-users. Explainable Learning Analytics aims to provide insights to black-box predictions by for instance explaining how the input features impact the prediction made. Two dashboards were designed to visualize the prediction and the outcome of the explainer. The dashboards supplemented the explainer with an interactive visualisation allowing to simulate how changes in the student's features impact the prediction. Both dashboards were evaluated in user tests with 13 participants. The results show the potential of explainable AI techniques to bring predictive models to advising practice. We found that the combination of the explainer with the simulation helped users to compare the predictive model with their mental models of student success, challenging understanding of users and influencing trust in the predictive model.

Keywords: Learning dashboards · Information visualization · Student advising

1 Introduction

Predicting success of aspiring students in higher education is challenging as success in a program of choice depends on a wide variety of aspects such as students' prior education, motivation, learning and study skills, intellectual capacity, socio-economic background, and effort level. On the one hand, many higher education institutes use professionally trained student advisors to coach and advice aspiring students. On the other hand, thanks to advances in Machine Learning (ML), Educational Data Mining, and Learning Analytics (LA) algorithms are built that can accurately predict students success [16]. To bring algorithmic outcomes to end users, Learning Analytics Dashboards (LADs) can be used as they provide a visual display of relevant learning data to provide insights, trigger reflection, and eventually and hopefully impact the educational process. The goal of this research is to bring predictive models for students success to advising practice by incorporating them in an advising LAD. The incorporation of predictive models in advising LADs has the potential to strengthen the data-based support for advisors and students during the advising process. While predictive models are powerful, their incorporation and adoption in higher education practice is still challenging due to legal, financial, and ethical considerations. Exemplary for the increased awareness around ethical use and privacy is the European GDPR regulation (Regulation 2016/679) and the "right to explanation" in particular. ML models underlying predictive models are often "black box" models who suffer from so-called algorithm opacity [1], which contradicts the "right to explanation". The opacity can alienate its users, create mistrust and suspicion, and hinders their actual adoption and deployment in real-world scenarios. XAI (eXplainable AI) aims to make the complex internal mechanisms of ML models transparent for humans and thereby increase understanding or event trust [20]. The XAI field by itself is fastly maturing as shown in the XAI survey of Adadi and Berrada [1]. Doshi stresses that explainability is not only a legal matter [9]. When users, such as advisors and students, cannot match algorithmic predictions and recommendations with their mental models they will not trust, and as a consequence not use, the algorithmic outputs. Adding explanations to predictions can enhance the understanding of the reality, and therefore give handles to reflect on potential ways to improve. This is particularly important in students advising where advisors not only have to provide insights in strengths and weaknesses of the aspiring student in relation to what is needed in the program to be successful, but also provide recommendations on top of predictors [3]. Finally, explanations can support the safety of automatic systems by providing explanations of algorithmic outputs in a wide variety of scenarios to create an understanding of where a system works and does not work. A natural way to obtain human interpretable explanations is through visualizations [20]. More recent work in Visual Analytics systems focuses on using interactivity for bridging the gap between user knowledge and the insights XAI can provide [20]. Finally, we want to highlight that explanations can serve very different purposes: justification (e.g. connected to GDPR), control (e.g. understanding where the prediction works or not), improvement (e.g. improve black-box based on user feedback), and discovery (e.g. discover features that are important for the prediction) [1]. A large set of research focuses on using explanations to increase trust in black-box predictions, while this is highly debatable [7]: users should not over-trust models and underestimate the uncertainty attached to the prediction, especially when the models are not accurate [23]. A shift to "appropriate trust" is needed.

This paper presents exploratory research with a user study of two advising LADs combining explanations and interactive visualizations of a black-box prediction of students success, building on students' prior education and learning and studying skills.

2 Background

The use of **predictive models** in the context of first-year student success has been intensively investigated. We highlight the studies of Pinxten et al. [16] and Mothilal [14] that focused on the same higher education context and build on the same as this paper. They show that nested regression models [16] and binary decision tree ensembles [14] can be use to predict students success based on self-reported prior-academic achievements (math background and high school grades) and Soft skills (motivation, concentration, time management, and study effort). **Dashboards** or visualisation tools concerning academic success, take many forms. Both student-facing dashboards [5,13] and dashboards supporting live advising sessions [6,8,12] have been studied. The Learning Analytics Dashboard for Advisors (LADA) of Gutiérrez et al. [12] includes a predictive component to classify study plans of students into one of the five categories ranging from "very easy" to "very hard", depending on students' characteristics and the study trajectories of past students. **Explainable student success prediction models** have been the subject of a very recent systematic review by Alamri and Alharbi [3]. Based on nine dimensions distributed over two domains of student performance models (educational level, performance level, problem type, predictors, predictors' type) and explainable models (method, stage, scope, and output type) they analysed 15 research papers published between 2015 and 2020, revealing the need for studies properly quantifying and evaluating accuracy and explainability. Interestingly, they found that less than 15% of the papers focused on predicting student success at the program level, and that the around 2/3th of the studies used ante-hoc explanations, i.e. they relied on non-black box (and often less powerful) ML models such as rule-based models that are explainable in their original format. As a particular example of explainable student success prediction models, we want to highlight the Student Success System, or S3, by Essa et al. [10], which builds on explanations of the success prediction using Win-Loss Charts. Each indicator showed if the student is above (green), within (orange), or below (red) average for a certain feature. They found that the explanations allowed faster and more efficient detection of problem causes, and provide points of focus for actions or interventions.

3 Context, Data, Predictive Model and Explainer

This section elaborates on the context, the data, and the prediction and explanation methods of this study. The classification according to the nine dimensions for explainable student performance prediction models [3] is indicated in *italic*.

3.1 Context

This research focuses on aspiring students of the first year of the Bachelor of Engineering Science at KU Leuven, at the *higher education level (education level)*. The open-admission policy for most university degrees in Flanders, allows for every student with a high school diploma to enroll in any bachelor program. This can cause students to choose a study program for which they do not have the appropriate knowledge or skill set, resulting in typical drop-out rates of 40%. Another effect is the higher heterogeneity in student background within a single program [16], challenging teaching and student support. KU Leuven provides professional student advisors who combine their advising role of aspiring students with tutoring and coaching of first-year students.

3.2 Data

The input features for the predictive model resulted from self-reported[1] data on prior-academic achievement collected using surveys (Math Hours in high school, High school grades in math, physics & chemistry, Effort level, and Pressure Preference) and a validated questionnaire for learning and studying skills (the Learning And Studying Skills Inventory [22] resulting in Motivation, Time management, Concentration, Anxiety, and use of Test Strategies). These features have been shown, despite being self-reported, to be predictive for student success [16]. The *predictors were therefore: pre-course data and other student data, and the predictor's types are categorical.*

The outcome variable is the academic achievement of a student after one semester, operationalized here by the Study Efficiency (SE, percentage of the booked ECTS credits that a student actually passed) after the first semester of the first academic year, which means we predicted achievement at the *program level (performance level)*. This data was collected from the universities data warehouse. Based on prior research [21] on the relation between SE and the years needed to obtain the bachelor diploma, the SE was discretized into three target classes: "no risk" for students with a SE of 75% or higher (622 data samples), "moderate risk" for students with a SE between 40 and 75% (464 samples), and "at risk" for students with a SE lower than 40% and dropouts (738 samples).

Data of four academic years, 2015–2016 up to 2018–2019, was collected resulting in 2016 student samples. After deleting incomplete entries, 1824 samples remain. More information on the data collection and the data structure can be found in prior work [14,16]. As high correlations were found between the three high school course grades (math, chemistry, and physics), the three high school grade variables were combined into a two-dimensional variables using a Principal Component Analysis (PCA), before using them in the predictive model.

3.3 Predictive Model and Explainer

Predictive models were trained to predict the academic achievement of aspiring students. A *Feed Forward Neural Network (method)*, shown to have potential for prediction of student success [2], was used to predict if a student belongs to the

---

[1] Due to Flemish regulations, no data on prior academic career is transferred from secondary to higher education.

three target classes ("no risk", "moderate risk", or "at risk"). We therefore handled the prediction as a *classification task (problem type)*. Students who belong to the "moderate risk" class can have very diverging study efficiencies. These are the students for whom no clear prediction can be made yet, since it can still go either way. Therefore, and based on the recommendation of student advisors, the emphasis while training the model was on correctly predicting the two outer classes ("no risk" and "at risk"), where the link between the early academic achievement and late academic achievement (obtaining the bachelor degree in nominal time) is strong. Another justification is the higher "damage" when misclassifying a student from the outer classes. For example, unfairly reassuring "at risk" students by erroneously predicting them as "moderate risk" or even "no risk", can have large consequences. At the same time, unnecessarily worrying "no risk" students by erroneously predicting them as "moderate risk" or "at risk" is also undesired. The data set was divided in a training (1459 samples) and a validation set (365 samples). Best classification performance was obtained when using a crossentropy loss with double weights for the outer classes. An accuracy of 78% and an f1-metric of 68% were achieved on the outer classes.

The Local Interpretable Model Agnostic Explainer (LIME) [17] was used as an explanation approach. LIME is a model-agnostic approach, which can be *post-hoc (stage)* combined with any predictive model. A LIME generates a *local (scope)* linear model that approximates the black-box predictive model in the neighbourhood of the student under investigation. From the approximate linear model, the contribution of each input feature to the probabilistic classification of the student can be readily derived. As output, LIME provides for a student and for each feature and output class, a numerical value indicating the strength of the feature's contribution to the predicted output class, which can be visualized, resulting in a *numeric and visual explainable output type*.

4 Interactive and Explainable Advising Dashboard

The goal of the dashboards (LADs) developed was to interactively visualize the aspiring student's features (prior education and learning and studying skills), the outcome of the predictive model, and the explanation of the prediction. Advisors can use the dashboard to gain information about the situation of the student, trigger discussions, and focus on specific points of interest. The advising LADs are only meant to be used by advisors in the preparation of an advising session or during such as session. The LAD is therefore not designed to be used by students independently. The goal of the explanations in the LADs are justification, control, and discovery [1].

Two LADs building on two different visualisations were created: the slider LAD and the rose LAD (Fig. 1). A prototype of each LAD was created in online design tool Figma and are available online at https://tinyurl.com/yynvqchq. The advising LADs included interactive visualisations to be able to simulate the impact of changes in the student's features on the prediction. This can provide support when assessing the strengths and weaknesses of a student and finding the most important features to act upon in order to optimize student success.

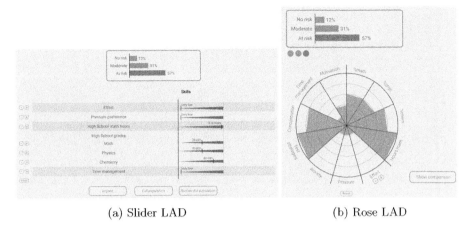

(a) Slider LAD (b) Rose LAD

Fig. 1. Two LA dashboards (LADs) visualizing the outcome of the prediction model for student success based on an aspiring student's features. In both LADS, the blue box contains the bar chart visualizing the outcome of the probabilistic model using a bar chart with color coding (green for 'no risk', orange for 'moderate risk', and red for 'at risk'). Below, the eight features/skills of the aspiring student are visualized on a linear scale with a slider indicating the skill level (slider LAD) or in a rose plot (rose LAD). The advisor can simulate changes of the features by clicking the − or + to the left of each feature (slider and rose LAD) or moving the slider (slider LAD). (Color figure online)

The slider and rose LADs share the same visualization for the outcome of the "black box" prediction model for student success (blue box) using a bar chart with color coding: the green bar represents the probability that the student is in the "no risk" class, the orange bar represents the probability that the student is in the "moderate risk" class, and the red bar represents the probability that the student is in the "at risk" class. The slider and rose LADs use a different approach to visualize the feature/skill level of the student, the impact of each feature on the prediction (explainer), and a comparison to the population.

The **slider LAD** uses a slider to visualize the **feature/skill** label and level (Fig. 1a). The mathematics, physics, and chemistry grade in secondary education, which were combined into one component in the PCA (see Sect. 3), are grouped together in a superclass "High school grades". All features/skills, also the three features within the "High school grades", have their own skill level slider, allowing to simulate changes in the student's skills and evaluating the impact on the prediction of academic success. Figure 2a shows the view of the slider LAD obtained by clicking the "Impact" button (Fig. 1a), revealing the visualization of the **explainer** output. The color of each impact circle corresponds to the risk class to which the specific feature/skills makes a positive contribution. The larger the circle, the larger this contribution. A big red circle for instance shows a large contribution to the prediction of the student to the "at risk" class (as the High School math hours in the example in Fig. 2a).

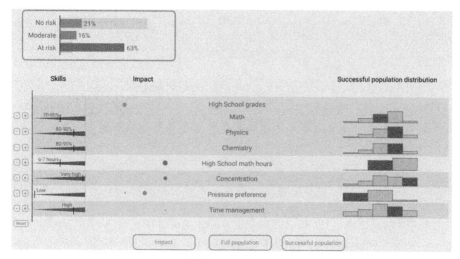

(a) Slider LAD

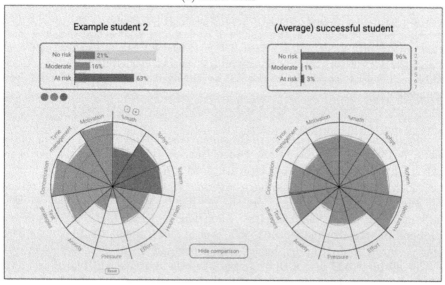

(b) Rose LAD

Fig. 2. Visualisation of the explainer output (left) by showing the impact of features on the prediction (i.e. outcome of the explainer) and comparison to a reference group (right) for both slider (top) and rose LAD (bottom).

The "Successful population distribution" (right in Fig. 2a) allows to **compare** the features of the student to the population of past successful students. The user can toggle between the full population (all enrolled students) and the successful population (all students in "moderate risk", or "no risk") as a reference.

The LAD allows to interactively **simulate** changes of a student's features. A change can be simulated by clicking on the corresponding + and - buttons. When adapting a feature, the prediction of academic success and the impact of the (simulated) features are also updated. In the prediction box, the original success levels are maintained in a lighter color (Fig. 2a). This allows to assess see the changes, caused by the simulation.

The start view of the **rose LAD** is shown in Fig. 1b. Each **feature/skill** has its own "pie slice" in which the size represents the skill level. Feature labels only become visible when hoovering over the rose with a cursor. The information of the **explainer**, i.e. the impact of a certain feature on the prediction of a specific risk class, is shown by colouring the slice that belongs to this skill into the color of the class it contributes to. A high color intensity is connected to a large impact. Pale coloured slices only have a small impact on the corresponding class. The most influencing feature for each class, is assigned the maximal intensity of 100%, and the least. As a feature can contribute to multiple output classes, a different rose is available per risk class, which the user can toggle by pressing the circle in the corresponding color (see the green, orange, and red circle beneath the blue box with the predication). Figure 2b shows the impact of the features on the "No risk" class. The rose LAD offers the possibility of **comparing** the current student with an averaged profile of the successful population. This profile is computed by taking all successful profiles ("Moderate risk" and "No risk") and rounding up the averaged value per feature. The option is left open to add six other specific profiles to compare with (numbers 1–7 next to the prediction box), which the user can toggle by clicking one of the numbers right of the blue box with the prediction. Changes in a feature/skill level can also be **simulated** by clicking the + or − that appear when hovering over a particular feature/skill pie slice (see effort in Fig. 2b).

5 Evaluation: Methods and Results

5.1 Methods

The LAD prototypes were evaluated using user studies. Gilpin et al. [11] indicated that humans can evaluate explanations for reasonableness (how well an explanation matches human expectations), completeness or substitute-task completeness (explanation enables a person to anticipate the behavior of the predictive model), and for helpfulness in revealing model biases. Supported by the recommendation of Davis et al. [7] we focused on the use and utility of the ML explanation in actual advising practice, rather than on attempting to measure trust. They argue that the explanations themselves have no intrinsic value, and that the goal of an explanation is, as for visualizations, to communicate useful information to a human and that methods to measure utility of visualization could therefore also be used to measure utility of explanations. We focused on model selection (which LAD is preferred), and the fit or clash of the explanations and mental models during advising and its impact on advisors [7].

A total of thirteen people participated: nine with experience in advising (advisors) and four with a background of designing and researching LADs (researchers). All participants were employees at KU Leuven. The user test consisted of an online interview where participants could see and interact with the LAD prototypes. Beforehand, participants received a document with information about the research and the two LADs. During the user test, the slider and rose LADs were compared. To avoid order effects, the order in which the LADs were shown to the users was alternated between participants. Participants expressed their train of thoughts out loud (Think-Aloud protocol) and were guided by directed questions from the interview conductor (e.g. "which information do you obtain from the visualization", "does the prediction match with your expectations", "what would you advice to students and why?"). After the interview, participants were asked to complete a survey, containing a version of the Evaluation Framework for Learning Analytics (EFLA) [18] and the System Usability Scale (SUS) [4] for their preferred LAD (slider or rose). They were also asked to elaborate on how the LAD would impact students if it was used in an advising conversation. Interviews and surveys were conducted in Dutch.

5.2 Results

Below, results of both interviews and questionnaires are discussed per topic. Quotes of users are in italic and were translated from Dutch.

Use and Usefulness in Actual Advising Sessions. The visualisation of the student features can help to provide a quick overview of the skills, confirming findings of earlier advising dashboards [6,12]. Especially for the rose plot, users indicated that it provided a clear, compact, and intuitive overview of the skills usable in practice: *"The large rose is an advantage when talking to a student since it give a clear overview that can be seen from a distance."* The advisors appreciate that the visualizations do not only focus on the top-impact features, but also show the importance of other features: *"The rose plot is useful to show that not only high school grades and hours of math are important. These skills occupy less than half of the rose, which puts their importance in perspective".*

Advisors acknowledge, consistently with [6], that the visualization provides them additional convincing power: *"The dashboard gives me a tool to actually show this [student can still improve time management, ...] to a student".* On the downside, adding explanations also increased the information load: *"I would not use the difference in color intensity to identify strengths or weaknesses of the student. Showing and explaining the meaning of the intensities would take up too much time in the conversation. The student can also be confused by the amount of information and leave the conversation with the wrong impression".*

The overall score of 76/100 of both the slider and rose LAD on the EFLA questionnaires, which take into account "Reflection & Awareness", "Impact", and "Data", indicate promising usefulness of the dashboards. The EFLA scores indicate that advisors believed the LADs will create similar reflection and awareness with advisors and users during advising conversations (around 67 for slider,

74 for rose) but will have more impact on advisors than on students (sliders 64 vs 58, rose 78 vs 64).

Usability. For the rose LAD, average **SUS scores** of 88.75 (advisors) and 85.83 (researchers) were obtained. For the slider LAD the average SUS scores were 78.5 (advisors) and 90 (researchers). A score above 80.3 points at a qualitative system but even the 78.5 of the advisors' slider LAD lies still far above the average SUS score of 68. Figure 3 details the SUS scores for the different questions. Looking at the results of the advisors, a minimum is seen for both LADs in question nine, targeting the confidence of the participant when using the system. Advisors believed more than researchers that most people would learn to use the system very quickly and that the system is not cumbersome to use (Q7 and Q8). In the interviews users provided many suggestions for usability improvements.

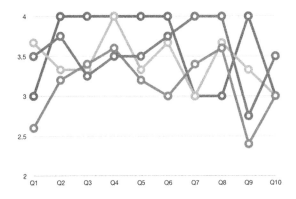

Fig. 3. Average scores on the 10 SUS-questions [4] by advisor (blue, preferring the rose LAD; green preferring the slider LAD) and researcher participants (yellow, preferring the rose LAD; red preferring the slider LAD). (Color figure online)

Use of Explanations. The users use the explanations to assess the current situation of the student and the impact on future student success: *"Probably, this student went through high school smoothly without significant problems. This prediction gives the possibility to show that the situation is not completely favourable."*, or *"During high school, the student obtained good grades without having to work really hard. This behavior got him/her through high school easily but won't work at university."*, or *"The student obtained good high school scores. And even though he didn't have 8h of math, I still believe him to be a model student. (...) I would tell the student he has a rather high success chance"*.

Advisors acknowledge that the visualization helps them to assess the impact of a student's features on student success. *"When visualising the impact, the rose plots give an overview per output class (e.g. at-risk) with the slider LAD is easier to see the impact of a specific feature"*. Particular features of the visualization helped to further focus on important features: *"Shades of impact colors are really useful. They make it possible to focus on the important features without wasting time on the ones that have less impact"*. Users also warn for possible wrong interpretations: *"Color intensity is not an intuitive way of representing a level. A large triangle with a bland red color has more visual impact than a small bright one. This might confuse students"*. Similar to [10], users found that the explanations helped to identify ways for the student to improve: *"The student can still improve Time management, Effort, and Motivation."*, or *"Maybe I would talk about Pressure preference and the Hours of math. I could show options of trajectories that can help"*. The explanations helped advisors focus on important features: *"By looking at the impact circles of all features (slider LAD), it is easy to focus on the features with a large influence on the prediction. No time needs to be spent on less relevant skills"* Users did not have a clear preference for the slider or rose LAD for visualizing explanations: five advisors and one researcher preferred the slider LAD, four advisors and three researchers preferred the rose LAD. Moreover, the feedback on the visualisation of the impact of the features on the prediction (explainer) was different between users and still shows room for improvement for intuitive, compact, yet complete visualizations of explanations of predictive models.

Trigger for Conversation. Consistent with [6], users indicate that explanations provide a trigger for further conversation: *"The students' effort can still improve. I would start a conversation with the student to find out why this is low and how it can be improved"*. They also see a conversation as a way to better understand, disproof, or dig deeper into the explanation of the prediction: *"A high motivation can possibly point to perfectionism but I would ask the student more questions in order to bring clarity"*. Advisors stress the importance of students' background stories when looking at a profile: *"The background story of the student is very important. There can be clear reasons why a certain skill is, for example "Very low"."*, hereby seeming to warn for the blind use of predictive models [7].

Interactive Visualization. The interactive visualization was appreciated by all users and was used in two ways: first, to test to what extent the predictive model fits with their mental model, and second, to discover features that help the student to improve their success. For the latter, users express and show a clear preference for simulating actionable or malleable skills (like Effort, Time management, and Concentration), and believe that simulating an actionable skill can motivate students to take action: *"The + and − buttons are very powerful to show to a student and persuade him that improvements can have a large payoff."*. The focus on actionable and malleable skills complies with the recommendation to improve the ability to act on LA information [19]. For the features High school grades and Hours of math, users had different opinions. Some users indicated it was strange one could still change these features, as the student could not change their grades or prior education any more: *"I would be less inclined to simulate high school grades. (...) I'd rather use this as a warning for certain courses, like chemistry"*. Other advisors believed that simulating changes in the features of High school grades and Hours of math could encourage students to enroll in for instance summer remediation courses. Users indicated that the grouping of features through PCA complicated the interpretation of the impact of feature while simulating: *"Combining high school grades is logical but still a disadvantage. Even though the use of a combined variable can be explained to a student, a high math grade can still have a red impact while this is actually caused by, for example, a low physics grade. This is confusing for a student."*, and *"The use of PCA might be confusing when grades are not lying close to each other"*.

Match or Conflict Between Predictive and Mental Model. Users reflected on the predictive model and their mental models of student success: *"[...] It makes me wonder more about why exactly a student is classified in a certain risk class"*. Especially when there was a conflict between the predictive and mental model, users started elaborating: *"The student has good grades for math and had 8 h of math per week. Even given the low score on effort, the chance of belonging to the at-risk class is too large"*. Almost all users reported somehow that it was "weird" and "counterintuitive" that a feature on which a student scored high (e.g. high secondary school grade) can contribute to the "at risk" class according to the explainer, and even reported that it diminished their trust in the predictive model: *"A very high skill having a negative influence on the prediction, is weird. It makes me question the reliability of the model"*. Advisors spontaneously starting providing possible intuitive explanations for the prediction: *"High motivation can possibly point to perfectionism, which can hinder the student"*. The fact that features could have a contribution to different output classes (e.g. both at-risk and medium-at-risk) was considered challenging to interpret: *"At first, it is difficult to give meaning to one skill contributing to two classes. (...) On the other hand, it can show a student that some skills are in between of classes and do not have a final impact yet. The future behaviour of the student can make the difference"*. As the interactive visualization was used to check to what extent the predictive model matched with their mental models, the interaction triggered additional conflicts: *"The decrease in prediction when decreasing the math score, is too large, compared to my experience. [...] I would still expect high success levels for this student"*.

6 Conclusions and Future Work

This research explored the use of interactive explanations of predictive black-box models for student success of first-year students in the Engineering Sciences degree at KU Leuven in a user study with thirteen users. With its evaluation of both the prediction and the explanation, this study addressed the need put forward by Alamri and Alharbi [3]. The results obtained through the interviews and questionnaires show that the interactive explainers can already be considered to be usable in advising practice and are expected to contribute to the awareness and reflection of both advisor and student users. Results indicate that the explanations helped to better understand how the aspiring student's features contributed outcome of the black-box prediction model, and to match or contrast the user's mental model to the prediction model. The simulations with the interactive visualizations, where users could change the students features, helped users to understand the behaviour of the prediction model and to find the essential features the student could be advised to acted upon and. The explanations and simulations in particular uncovered behaviour of the prediction model they believed was counter-intuitive and not consistent with their mental models, challenging their mental models, making them look for plausible explanations, and influencing their trust in the predictive models. Some users warn for overloading the LAD in case that explanations are added, connecting to the balance between overview of overload typically occurring in LAD design [15].

The proposed LAD can be introduced in advising practice to investigate impact on actual advising sessions. While our paper follows the recommendation of Davis et al. [7] to focus on the utility of ML explanations rather than trust, future work should use a systematic approach to evaluate if interactive explainers have a measurable impact on the utility and understanding and trust of the users in the predictive model. Relating trust of users to the prediction model's accuracy is of interest. Finally, more research is needed on how to visualize predictions relying on features preprocessed with PCA: while PCA is a key in preprocessing when features are correlated, it leads to less-interpretable features and predictions, hereby challenging understanding of end users.

References

1. Adadi, A., Berrada, M.: Peeking inside the black-box: a survey on eXplainable Artificial Intelligence (XAI). IEEE Access **6**, 52138–52160 (2018). https://doi.org/10.1177/0149206321997910
2. Al-Sudani, S., Palaniappan, R.: Predicting students' final degree classification using an extended profile. Educ. Inf. Technol. **24**(4), 2357–2369 (2019). https://doi.org/10.1007/s10639-019-09873-8
3. Alamri, R., Alharbi, B.: Explainable student performance prediction models: a systematic review. IEEE Access **9**, 33132–33143 (2021). https://doi.org/10.1109/ACCESS.2021.3061368
4. Brooke, J.: SUS - a quick and dirty usability scale (1996)
5. Broos, T., Pinxten, M., Margaux, D., Verbert, K., De Laet, T.: Learning dashboards at scale: early warning and overall first year experience. Assess. Eval. High. Educ. **45**(6), 855–874 (2020). https://doi.org/10.1080/02602938.2019.1689546
6. Charleer, S., Moere, A.V., Klerkx, J., Verbert, K., De Laet, T.: Learning analytics dashboards to support adviser-student dialogue. IEEE Trans. Learn. Technol. **11**(3), 389–399 (2018). https://doi.org/10.1109/TLT.2017.2720670
7. Davis, B., Glenski, M., Sealy, W., Arendt, D.: Measure utility, gain trust: practical advice for XAI researchers. In: 2020 IEEE Workshop on TRust and EXpertise in Visual Analytics (TREX), pp. 1–8 (2020). https://doi.org/10.1109/TREX51495.2020.00005
8. De Laet, T., Millecamp, M., Ortiz-Rojas, M., Jimenez, A., Maya, R., Verbert, K.: Adoption and impact of a learning analytics dashboard supporting the advisor-student dialogue in a higher education institute in Latin America. BJET **51**(4), 1002–1018 (2020). https://doi.org/10.1111/bjet.12962

9. Doshi-Velez, F., Kim, B.: Towards a rigorous science of interpretable machine learning. arXiv e-prints arXiv:1702.08608 (2017)
10. Essa, A., Ayad, H.: Student success system: risk analytics and data visualization using ensembles of predictive models. In: Proceedings of 2nd International Conference on Learning Analytics and Knowledge, LAK 2012, pp. 158–161. Association for Computing Machinery, New York (2012). https://doi.org/10.1145/2330601.2330641
11. Gilpin, L.H., Bau, D., Yuan, B.Z., Bajwa, A., Specter, M., Kagal, L.: Explaining explanations: an overview of interpretability of machine learning. In: 2018 IEEE 5th International Conference on Data Science and Advanced Analytics, pp. 80–89 (2018). https://doi.org/10.1109/DSAA.2018.00018
12. Gutiérrez, F., Seipp, K., Ochoa, X., Chiluiza, K., De Laet, T., Verbert, K.: LADA: a learning analytics dashboard for academic advising. Comput. Hum. Behav. **107**, 105826 (2020). https://doi.org/10.1016/j.chb.2018.12.004
13. Hilliger, I., et al.: For learners, with learners: identifying indicators for an academic advising dashboard for students. In: Alario-Hoyos, C., Rodríguez-Triana, M.J., Scheffel, M., Arnedillo-Sánchez, I., Dennerlein, S.M. (eds) EC-TEL 2020. LNCS, vol. 12315, pp. 117–130. Springer, Cham (2020). https://doi.org/10.1007/978-3-030-57717-9_9
14. Kommiya Mothilal, R.: Statistical modeling of students' performance in an open-admission bachelor program in Flanders (2018)
15. van Leeuwen, A.: Learning analytics to support teachers during synchronous CSCL: balancing between overview and overload. J. Learn. Anal. **2**(2), 138–162 (2015). https://doi.org/10.18608/jla.2015.22.11
16. Pinxten, M., Van Soom, C., Peeters, C., De Laet, T., Langie, G.: At-risk at the gate: prediction of study success of first-year science and engineering students in an open-admission university in Flanders—any incremental validity of study strategies? Eur. J. Psychol. Educ. **34**(1), 45–66 (2017). https://doi.org/10.1007/s10212-017-0361-x
17. Ribeiro, M., Singh, S., Guestrin, C.: "Why should i trust you?": explaining the predictions of any classifier. In: Proceedings of 2016 Conference of the North American Chapter of the Association for Computational Linguistics: Demonstrations. Association for Computational Linguistics (2016). https://doi.org/10.18653/v1/n16-3020
18. Scheffel, M.: Evaluation framework for LA (2017). http://www.laceproject.eu/evaluation-framework-for-la/. Accessed 06 May 2020
19. Schmitz, M., van Limbeek, E., Greller, W., Sloep, P., Drachsler, H.: Opportunities and challenges in using learning analytics in learning design. In: Lavoué, É., Drachsler, H., Verbert, K., Broisin, J., Pérez-Sanagustín, M. (eds) EC-TEL 2017. LNCS, vol 10474, pp. 209–223. Springer, Cham (2017) https://doi.org/10.1007/978-3-319-66610-5_16
20. Spinner, T., Schlegel, U., Schafer, H., El-Assady, M.: explAIner: a visual analytics framework for interactive and explainable machine learning. IEEE Trans. Vis. Comput. Graph. 1 (2019). https://doi.org/10.1109/tvcg.2019.2934629
21. Vanderoost, J., et al.: Engineering and science positioning tests in Flanders: powerful predictors for study success? In: Proceedings of 43rd SEFI Conference 2015, pp. 1–8. SEFI, Brussels (2015)

22. Weinstein, C.E., Palmer, D.R.: LASSI - Learning and Study Strategies Inventory. 2nd edn. (2002). www.collegelassi.com/lassi/. Accessed 22 May 2020
23. Yin, M., Wortman Vaughan, J., Wallach, H.: Understanding the effect of accuracy on trust in machine learning models. In: Proceedings of 2019 CHI Conference, pp. 1–12. Association for Computing Machinery, New York (2019). https://doi.org/10.1145/3290605.3300509

Investigating the Role of Educational Robotics in Formal Mathematics Education: The Case of Geometry for 15-Year-Old Students

Jérôme Brender[1,2], Laila El-Hamamsy[1,2(✉)], Barbara Bruno[2,3],
Frédérique Chessel-Lazzarotto[1], Jessica Dehler Zufferey[1],
and Francesco Mondada[1,2]

[1] Center LEARN, Ecole Polytechnique Fédérale de Lausanne (EPFL),
Écublens, Switzerland
{jerome.brender,laila.el-hamamsy,frederique.chessel-lazzarotto,
jessica.zufferey,francesco.mondada}@epfl.ch
[2] Mobots Group, Ecole Polytechnique Fédérale de Lausanne (EPFL),
Écublens, Switzerland
barbara.bruno@epfl.ch
[3] CHILI Lab, Ecole Polytechnique Fédérale de Lausanne (EPFL),
Écublens, Switzerland

Abstract. Research has shown that Educational Robotics (ER) enhances student performance, interest, engagement and collaboration. However, until now, the adoption of robotics in formal education has remained relatively scarce. Among other causes, this is due to the difficulty of determining the alignment of educational robotic learning activities with the learning outcomes envisioned by the curriculum, as well as their integration with traditional, non-robotics learning activities that are well established in teachers' practices. This work investigates the integration of ER into formal mathematics education, through a quasi-experimental study employing the Thymio robot and Scratch programming to teach geometry to two classes of 15-year-old students, for a total of 26 participants. Three research questions were addressed: (1) Should an ER-based theoretical lecture precede, succeed or replace a traditional theoretical lecture? (2) What is the students' perception of and engagement in the ER-based lecture and exercises? (3) Do the findings differ according to students' prior appreciation of mathematics? The results suggest that ER activities are as valid as traditional ones in helping students grasp the relevant theoretical concepts. Robotics activities seem particularly beneficial during exercise sessions: students freely chose to do exercises that included the robot, rated them as significantly more interesting and useful than their traditional counterparts, and expressed their interest in introducing ER in other mathematics lectures. Finally, results were generally consistent between the students that like and did not like mathematics, suggesting the use of robotics as a means to broaden the number of students engaged in the discipline.

Supported by the NCCR Robotics, Switzerland.
J. Brender, L. El-Hamamsy—Both authors contributed equally to this work

Keywords: Educational Robotics · Mathematics · Formal education · Secondary school curriculum · Visual programming language

1 Introduction

Research has shown that Educational Robotics (ER) can be used as a tool to enhance teaching [1] and learning [22], from early childhood [4] to tertiary education [3]. ER provides "an experimental platform for practice" [18] and improves students' motivation, engagement and learning [26]. While ER can be viewed as a tool fitting many and varied disciplines [17], it is most commonly associated with Computer Science [10] and STEM related disciplines [3,18] such as mathematics [30]. Papert, who instigated the learning theories on constructionism[1] [24], was one of the first to employ ER for mathematics, in the 80's. He used the LOGO programming language to teach geometry and found that ER improves children's motivation, learning and interaction in the classroom [24]. Given such premises, it is thus surprising to find that only a limited number of studies explore the benefits of introducing robotics into formal mathematics education [11,29]. In 2019, Leoste and Heidmets [21] conducted a longitudinal study with students from 20 classes, confirming that the use of ER in mathematics lessons improved students' learning outcomes on a national standardised assessment. Their results are coherent with recent studies on the use of the "Concreteness Fading" method in mathematics: Kim [19] found that starting with physical activities that include manipulatives (such as ER) and "gradually fading concreteness to access abstract concepts" effectively supports "students [access to] conceptual understanding in mathematics classrooms". These findings suggest that ER could play a pivotal role in a "Concreteness Fading Strategy" to improve learning outcomes in the formal mathematics curriculum.

Despite its numerous benefits, the use of robots in formal education settings, as opposed to extra-curricular activities, is still relatively sparse [3], both in terms of research and practice. A recent review by Zhong and Xia [30] on the use of educational robots in mathematics education concluded that more research was required "to further explore the integration of robotics and mathematics education". Progressing in such research requires facilitating the introduction of ER into regular classrooms. Unfortunately, teachers, who play a determining role in the classroom, are often preoccupied by time [6,10] and need to be assured that the use of Educational Robots will help reach the learning outcomes without incurring in a loss of time. Furthermore, the research is well aware of the importance of providing teachers with adequate guidelines for activity design [14] and intervention [5], to support the alignment of ER learning activities with the learning outcomes of the curriculum. However the reality is often far from these principles, leaving teachers to face the difficulties of integrating ER activities in their practices alone [8].

---

[1] The constructionist theory of learning stipulates that knowledge is built more effectively when people are actively engaged in building tangible and shareable artefacts.

In an effort to contribute to the study of effects and modalities of the integration of ER in mathematics formal education, in this article we specifically address the following research questions: *1) Should an ER-based theoretical lecture precede, succeed, or replace a traditional theoretical lecture? 2) What is the students' perception of, and engagement in, the ER-based lecture and exercises? 3) Do the findings differ according to students' prior appreciation for mathematics? I.e., can ER help broaden the number of students successfully engaged in the discipline?* The methodology devised to investigate the afore-listed questions (see Sect. 2), and the results herein reported (see Sect. 3), constitute the main contributions of this article. Additionally we provide in open-source all the ER-based pedagogical resources devised[2] and used in this study[3].

2 Methodology

A key requirement for the assessment of ER learning activities in the context of formal mathematics education is the presence of adequate ER content. Section 2.1 outlines the learning unit considered for this study and describes the proposed ER-based theoretical and exercise activities for a geometry lecture. Details about the study participants and experimental design are provided in Sect. 2.2.

2.1 Design of the ER Content

In our study, we consider the case of the formal mathematics curriculum at the level of secondary school in Switzerland. A common practice for Swiss mathematics teachers is to start with the theoretical introduction of a concept and then proceed to paper-based exercises. Students are often free to choose the order in which to do the exercises. Based on this pedagogical approach, and existing material, we thus designed an ER-based theoretical introduction lecture for the curriculum topic of "planar geometric figures" and a set of related ER-based exercises.

Choice of the ER Platform. All the learning activities we designed rely on the Thymio II robot [23] (henceforth referred to as Thymio), which was chosen because (1) its structure and shape is well suited for attaching a pencil and making it draw geometric figures; and (2) it is presently being introduced into classrooms in the region [10] and thus already familiar for a number of teachers. Moreover, Thymio has been successfully employed as an educational tool in a variety of settings, ranging from primary school [10] to university[4]. This

---

[2] For the open-source ER-based pedagogical resources devised see here 10.5281/zenodo.4649842.
[3] The proposed ER learning activities follow the structure outlined for 11th grade (15 y.o. students) mathematics in the mandatory curriculum of the Canton Vaud, Switzerland.
[4] https://edu.epfl.ch/coursebook/en/basics-of-mobile-robotics-MICRO-452.

versatility is rendered possible by the spectrum of programming languages that can be used with it (including three block-based visual programming languages: Blockly [23], VPL [23], Scratch [25]; and a text based programming language, ASEBA [23]). Scratch was selected for the present context as it is particularly adapted for our target group (15-year-old students) [12] and has already been used in various studies to teach mathematics [12,16].

ER-Based Theoretical Lecture. The ER lecture was designed starting from the guidelines for the theoretical introduction of planar geometric figures provided in the official regional study plan[5], and adhering as closely as possible to the way the teachers in the study introduce new mathematics topics. In the designed ER lecture, the teacher programs Thymio to illustrate the various concepts students are expected to acquire. Specifically, as the students are expected to understand what a regular polygon is, know its properties and how to construct it, the teacher illustrates the construction of complex polygons (e.g. hexagons, octagons...) by programming Thymio and making it draw polygons on a sheet of paper. Additionally, as the students are also expected to recognise and name the various angles in parallel lines[6], two Thymios are concurrently used to demonstrate the relationships between these angles. The material prepared for the lecture is available at 10.5281/zenodo.4649842. The lecture was designed to last 90 min, which equals the duration of the corresponding traditional theoretical lecture.

ER-Based Exercises. Starting from the 31 exercises present in the curriculum, we designed 6 robot-based activities which, while functionally equivalent to their pen-and-paper counterparts, are centred on the programming of, and/or interaction with, the Thymio robot for their resolution. As commonly done for robotics activities, our ER exercises envision that students work in pairs, a setup known to foster collaboration and often preferred to individual settings [15]. To detach the proposed ER exercises from programming, students were provided with pre-filled code snippets, and thus required only the basic programming skills that were covered during the ER introduction. Once a code snippet is loaded for execution on the robot (i.e., assumed by students to be the right answer), its correctness is immediately and directly assessed by observing the figure drawn by the robot. This is an interesting feature of ER activities, as the benefits of feedback mechanisms allowing learners to verify the correctness of their solutions have been shown in previous studies [2] and are typically lacking in traditional pen-and-paper exercises.

---

[5] The study plan and learning outcomes outlined for students throughout compulsory education in the french speaking region of Switzerland is publicly accessible at https://www.plandetudes.ch.
[6] Facing angles - or vertically opposite angles, corresponding angles, complementary angles and alternate exterior/interior angles.

Validation of the ER Content. The designed ER lecture and exercises were submitted to 5 teachers with diverse background and experience to ensure their alignment with learning objectives and methods. Specifically, our experts included one pre-service teacher, three experienced in-service mathematics teachers and a teacher who transitioned to research on digital education.

2.2 Participants and Study Design

The study was conducted in a public school in Switzerland, with two classes of grade 11 students (15 y.o.) taught by two different mathematics teachers. A total of 26 students participated in the study (16 boys and 10 girls), most of which had no prior experience in robotics, CS or Scratch-based programming. The overall outline of the study is reported in Fig. 1, with each class being split in two to avoid a confound between the teacher and the order effect. As anticipated, both the traditional and the ER-based theoretical lecture lasted 90 min, while the exercise session (in which students are presented with traditional and ER-based exercises) lasted approximately 225 min (5 teaching periods), corresponding to the time allocated to exercises in the official study plan. Details on the assessment tools used during the study are reported in Table 1. The surveys administered focused mainly on interest [27] and perceived utility [20] to gain insight into the students' intrinsic motivation [27] to introduce ER into mathematics formal education. Each question is administered on a 7-point Likert scale (score between –3 and 3, 0 being neutral).

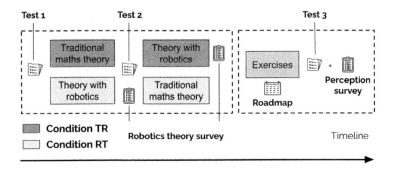

Fig. 1. Study design with each class being split in two to have half the students of each class in Condition TR and the other half in RT.

RQ1 - Should an ER-based Theoretical Lecture Precede, Succeed or Replace a Traditional Theoretical Lecture? Our hypothesis is that starting with a concrete experience (i.e. with the ER-based lecture) and moving to a theoretical lecture helps the students have a better "conceptual understanding" of geometry. To verify this hypothesis, we designed a between-subjects experiment comparing the condition *Traditional-Robotic (TR)* (i.e., starting with the traditional lecture and moving on to the ER-based lecture, shown in purple

Table 1. Summary of the data collected during the study (tests, surveys and roadmap)

Data	Objective	Content	Answer format
Test 1	Reference performance	3 exercises on prior geometry knowledge	Paper-based
Test 2	Performance after the first lecture	2 exercises of prior geometry knowledge, 2 on the first theme (polygons), 2 on the second (angles)	Paper-based
Test 3	End of unit performance	Similar to Test 2	Paper-based
Robotics theory survey	ER-based theory motivation	I found the theory with robotics 1) interesting; 2) useful	7-point Likert
Roadmap	ER-based exercises engagement	Order of exercise completion	Integer
		Activity type (ER-based done with the robot, ER-based done without the robot, Traditional)	Checkbox
		The exercises were 1) interesting; 2) useful	7-point Likert
Perception survey	Perception of ER-based content	1) Interest (I enjoyed doing them, was interested), 2) Collaboration (I discussed with my classmate, collaborated with my classmate to find the answers), 3) Ease (I found the activities easy, am sure of my answers, did well), 4) Effort (I was concentrated, did the activities as well as possible), 5) Future interest (I would like to do similar activities in maths, in other disciplines, would recommend such exercises to others for maths).	7-point Likert
	Maths appreciation	I generally like mathematics	7-point Likert

in Fig. 1) with the condition *Robotic-Traditional (RT)* (i.e., starting with the ER-based lecture and moving on to the traditional lecture, shown in orange in Fig. 1). Differences between the two conditions in terms of academic performance are assessed at three points in time (see Fig. 1). Test 1, administered prior to the start of the experiment, assesses students' knowledge in the geometry concepts identified as pre-requisite for the considered unit. Test 2, administered at the end of the first theoretical lecture, assesses students' understanding of the presented content, and is similar to test 3, administered at the end of the exercise sessions. All tests are based on the assessments in the official curriculum. RQ1 was therefore evaluated by checking the learning gains computed for Test 2 and Test 3 with respect to the baseline provided by Test 1, between the two experimental arms. To mitigate a possible teacher effect, half of each class was placed in condition RT and the other half in TR, with the responsible teacher giving the traditional lecture and a researcher (the same for both classes) giving the

ER-based one. Students were assigned to conditions to ensure they had similar distributions of competency in the discipline based on their performance in the course, as assessed by their teachers.

RQ2 - What Is the Students' Perception Of, and Engagement In, the ER-based Lecture and Exercises? Our hypothesis is that students would find the ER-based lecture and exercises interesting and useful, manifesting in high engagement in these activities and interest to integrate robotics into other mathematics lessons in the long term [21]. Students' appreciation for the proposed ER-based activities was assessed with a within-subjects experiment and via two complementary approaches: an objective assessment of their behaviour during the exercise session and a subjective assessment of their perception of the ER-based theoretical lecture and exercises. Throughout the exercise sessions students are free to decide which (among the 31 traditional and 6 ER-based) exercises to address, in which order and in which manner. Students could in fact pick a traditional exercise and solve it without using the robot (referred to as "traditional"); an ER-based exercise and solve it using the robot to validate their solutions (referred to as "robotics with robot"); or, lastly, the same ER-based exercises that the students decided to solve without using the robot (referred to as "robotics without robot"). In the *Roadmap*, students were thus asked to report the order in which they did the exercises and, for ER-based ones, whether they used the robot or not. Students' appreciation for the ER-based theoretical lecture and exercises was measured in terms of perceived interest and usefulness, respectively with the *Robotics theory survey* and the *Roadmap*, which also allows for the analysis of students' behaviour. At the end of the experiment, students were administered a final *Perception* survey, to evaluate their perception of the proposed ER-based content from the perspectives of interest, collaboration, facility (with respect to solving the exercises), effort and future interest (with respect to including robotics in future mathematics lessons, as well as lessons of other disciplines). Each of these items corresponded to a minimum of 2 questions, to acquire a more reliable estimate of the construct from the students [13]. Internal consistency is calculated using Cronbach's alpha [7].

RQ3 - Do the Findings Differ According to Students' Prior Appreciation for Mathematics? Our hypothesis is that ER would interest students and help engage those that are generally less invested in the mathematics curriculum, and thus compensate for differences in terms of prior mathematics appreciation. To investigate this question, we rely on the data collected for RQ1 and RQ2, categorising students based on their reported liking of mathematics on a 7-point Likert scale (13 do, 7 don't). More specifically, we consider differences in performance (learning gain), the level of engagement in the exercise sessions and the overall perception of the robotics-enhanced geometry lecture.

3 Results

3.1 RQ1 - Lecture Type and Students' Learning

Test 1 was administered prior to the start of the interventions and was used to ensure that the students in both conditions had similar levels of prior knowledge (Kruskal Wallis test fails to reject H_0, $p > 0.05$). The students' performance in Test 2 and Test 3 exceeded 80% for both experimental arms (Test 2: $84 \pm 11\%$ for condition RT, and $84 \pm 15\%$ for condition TR; Test 3: $86 \pm 8\%$ for condition RT and $87 \pm 11\%$ for condition TR). No significant difference was found between the two conditions (Kruskal Wallis test fails to reject H_0, $p > 0.05$). The finding thus seems to suggest that the ER-based lecture is equivalent to the traditional one in terms of students' learning, with both groups being sufficiently prepared to move on to the exercises after their first theory lecture. The lack of significant progress from test 2 to test 3 might be due to a ceiling effect in the test as to its focus on fundamentals.

3.2 RQ2 - Students' Perception and Engagement

Figure 2 reports the students' perception of the ER-based theoretical lecture, in terms of interest and utility, measured via the *Robotics theory* survey. Students in the RT condition, who started with the ER-based lecture, perceived it as significantly more interesting (Kruskal Wallis $p = 0.0073$, $H = 7.3$, $D = 1.43$), and, although not significantly, also more useful than those in the TR condition, who did it after the traditional lecture. This finding supports the results of RQ1 in suggesting that the two types of lectures are equally valid in transmitting relevant knowledge to the students, with those in condition TR thus finding the ER-based lecture of little interest and utility. Conversely, one of the teachers expressed a preference towards the TR condition, described as closer to the current practice and both manifested interest towards ER-based mathematics.

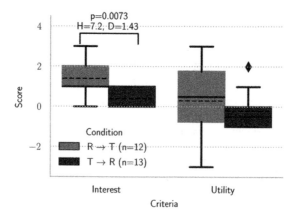

Fig. 2. Students' interest and utility assessment of the ER-based lecture. Significant Kruskal Wallis tests are indicated with p-value, H statistic and Cohen's effect size (D).

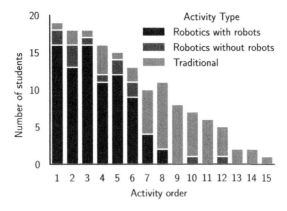

Fig. 3. Order in which the exercises were conducted.

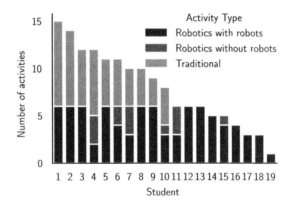

Fig. 4. Number of exercises conducted by each student.

To investigate students' engagement with the ER-based exercises proposed during the exercise sessions, we extracted from their *Roadmap* documents the order in which the activities were done by students (shown in Fig. 3) and the number of activities each student did individually (see Fig. 4). In both analyses, we distinguish between traditional exercises, ER-based exercises solved without using the robot ("robotics without robot") and ER-based exercises solved using the robot ("robotics with robot"). Figure 3 shows that most students started with "robotics with robot" exercises and finished with the traditional exercises, with few "robotics without robot" exercises being conducted overall. Since only 6 ER-based exercises were designed, the figure suggests that most students not only did many of them, but also did them in block, before transitioning to traditional ones. Indeed, Fig. 4 shows that all the students conducted at least one ER-based exercise with the robot ("robotics with robots", $\mu = 4.15 \pm 1.53$), with only 6 students engaging in "robotics without robot" exercises. Moreover, since the students who did the largest number of exercises also did all of the

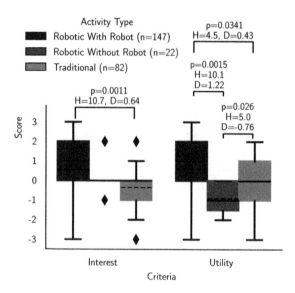

Fig. 5. Students' interest and utility assessment of the ER-based exercises. Significant Kruskal Wallis tests are reported with p-value, H statistic and Cohen's effect size (D).

"robotics with robot" exercises, it would seem that the time spent on ER-based exercises was not detrimental for their overall engagement with the exercises. It is important to note that 5 sessions were allocated to exercises (as per curriculum), and several students missed one or more of them[7], leading to lower-than-average number of exercises conducted within the allotted time.

Figure 5 reports the students' perception of the ER-based exercises, in terms of interest and utility, comparing the ratings of "robotics with robot", "robotics without robot" and "traditional" exercises. "Robotics with robot" exercises were perceived as interesting ($\mu = 0.5 \pm 1.5$)), while "robotics without robot" and traditional ones were rated more negatively ($\mu = 0.0 \pm 0.7$, $\mu = -0.33 \pm 1.2$ respectively). This contributes to a significant difference in interest between the ER-based exercises done with the robot and the traditional ones (Kruskal Wallis test $p = 0.0011$, $H = 10.7$, $D = 0.64$). Similarly, "robotics with robot" exercises are perceived as useful ($\mu = 0.6 \pm 1.6$) and significantly more so than the traditional ones (mediocre utility, $\mu = -0.9 \pm 0.8$) and "robotics without robot" ones ($\mu = -0.02 \pm 1.4$). "Robotics without robot" exercises are not only judged less favourably that their "with robot" counterparts, but also perceived as less useful than traditional activities, which suggests that the role of the robot in the ER-based exercises was meaningful, allowing for the creation of novel exercises relying on different modalities to convey and verify a same content.

In the *perception survey*, students evaluated the ER-based content from the perspectives of interest, collaboration, facility, effort put in, and future interest (see Fig. 6). Students had a globally positive opinion of the ER-based content and reported high interest, facility and effort with respect to integrating robotics

---

[7] also due to COVID-19 regulations concerning in-presence and distance learning.

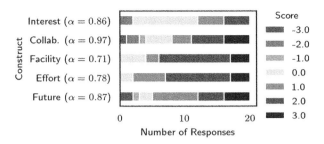

Fig. 6. Students' perception of the ER-based content. Cronbach's α internal consistency of the scale is calculated for each construct and shown in parenthesis.

in the geometry lecture. Although collaboration and future interest obtained slightly lower scores than the others constructs, the results remained globally positive ($\mu = 0.9 \pm 1.9$ and $\mu = 1.0 \pm 1.6$ respectively). However, some students observed that the robot "lacked a bit of precision for the constructions". Indeed, the robot's motion accuracy was not-always meeting the requirements of the application, which, together with some connectivity issues (causing the robot to skip certain instructions), caused some frustration for the students.

3.3 RQ3 - Effect of Prior Appreciation for Maths

The level of engagement in the exercise sessions (extracted from the *Roadmap*) was compared between the students who liked and those who did not like mathematics, to verify the effect of this variable on our observed ones. No significant differences were found between the students in terms of number of "robotics with robot", "robotics without robot", nor traditional exercises they engaged in (Kruskal Wallis test fails to reject H_0, $p > 0.05$). Similarly, no significant differences were found between the students in terms of knowledge acquired, both at the end of the theoretical lectures and at the end of the unit (Test 2 and Test 3, see Sect. 2.2), although it is possible that they were affected by a ceiling effect. Figure 7 compares the responses given to the final *Perception* survey by the students who liked and those who did not like mathematics. No significant differences were found between these groups (Kruskal Wallis test fails to reject H_0, $p > 0.05$) for collaboration, facility, effort and future interest. Conversely, students who don't like math perceive the ER-based content as less interesting than their classmates who appreciate the discipline, a finding that can be read as the proof that students were not fooled by the novelty introduced by the robot and perceived the ER-based content as geometry content. These findings (albeit limited in validity by the low number of students not liking mathematics) would seem to suggest that a hybrid between traditional and ER-based content has the potential to engage students who generally don't like mathematics as much as those who do. As a consequence, these students might possibly improve their competence in and appreciation of mathematics. Indeed, it would be interesting to verify this hypothesis in a longitudinal study, concurrently tracking students' perception of mathematics and of Robotics.

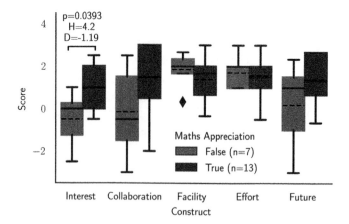

Fig. 7. Students' perception of the ER-based content depending on prior maths appreciation. Significant Kruskal Wallis tests are reported with p-value, H statistic and Cohen's effect size (D).

4 Discussion and Conclusion

This article investigates modes and benefits of the introduction of Educational Robotics in the formal curriculum of secondary school mathematics, specifically focusing on the 7-hours long learning unit about planar geometric figures, that students in Swiss schools address at grade 11 (15 y.o.). The study, involving 26 students from two classes, started with the preparation of a 90-minute long ER-based theoretical lecture and 6 ER-based exercises, validated by 5 experts to ensure their alignment with the learning objectives of the unit and state-of-art teaching practices. Rather than designing a fully robotics-based geometry course, our objective was to include a limited set of activities where the robot had an added value. Indeed, robotics should be considered as a tool, an extension to traditional paper-based methods, but not a total replacement. We specifically investigated (RQ1) the role of ER-based theoretical lectures, with respect to traditional ones; (RQ2) students' perception of and engagement in the proposed ER-based lecture and exercises; (RQ3) whether the findings of RQ1 and RQ2 differ according to students' prior appreciation for mathematics.

To investigate RQ1, half of the students started with the ER-based theoretical lecture and the other half with the traditional lecture, and then switched. Results showed that both groups of students, after their first lecture, reached a similar (and similarly high) level of competence, suggesting that ER, more often associated with exercises than theoretical lectures, can be as effective as traditional means to introduce abstract concepts. While the order in which students received the two types of theoretical lecture had no impact on their learning, likely due to the double exposure, the students evaluated the ER-based lecture more positively when done first. As different hypotheses can be made as to what caused these differences in perception, future studies should be envisioned to further and specifically investigate this topic. Students showed a generally positive perception of the ER-based content (RQ2), both through their assessment in terms of interest, utility, collaboration, facility, effort and interest for future integration and their behaviour during the exercise sessions. Indeed, most students started with, and engaged in all of, the ER-based exercises, despite the limitations of the platform sometimes frustrating their efforts. We hypothesise that a key reason for this success, to be verified in future studies, is that ER allows the student to be actively engaged in the exercise and provides immediate visual feedback that helps avoid the fear of errors and judgement. Lastly, results were generally similar between students who had declared liking mathematics, and those who had declared not to (RQ3), encouraging us to investigate in a future long-term study whether ER could possibly have a positive impact on students' competence in, and perception of, mathematics.

In more general terms, the findings highlight the importance of considering, and doing so as early as possible, the alignment between the learning outcomes and the robotics artefacts [14], the requirements posed by the classroom context [28], as well as discipline-specific ones (e.g., the need for precise localisation required by geometry). While our preliminary findings should be verified in broader and longer studies, the most important result of this study may be its standing as proof not only that ER can be introduced in formal education, but also, thanks to the increasing efforts to train teachers [9,10], that this can be done in a way that allows research and teaching practices to coexist and mutually benefit from their interplay within a context of translational research.

Acknowledgments. We would like to thank our colleagues (E.B, M.S), the members of the school (D.S., A.L.), teachers (M.H., S.K., B.J-D., Y.G.) and students who helped set afoot the experiments.

References

1. Alimisis, D.: Educational robotics: open questions and new challenges. Themes Sci. Technol. Educ. **6**(1), 63–71 (2013)
2. Azevedo, R., Bernard, R.M.: A meta-analysis of the effects of feedback in computer-based instruction. J. Educ. Comput. Res. **13**(2), 111–127 (1995)
3. Benitti, F.B.V., Spolaôr, N.: How have robots supported STEM teaching? In: Khine, M.S. (ed.) Robotics in STEM Education, pp. 103–129. Springer, Cham (2017). https://doi.org/10.1007/978-3-319-57786-9_5
4. Bers, M.U., Portsmore, M.: Teaching partnerships: early childhood and engineering students teaching math and science through robotics. J. Sci. Educ. Technol. **14**(1), 59–73 (2005)
5. Chevalier, M., Giang, C., Piatti, A., Mondada, F.: Fostering computational thinking through educational robotics: a model for creative computational problem solving. Int. J. STEM Educ. **7**(1), 1–18 (2020). https://doi.org/10.1186/s40594-020-00238-z
6. Chevalier, M., Riedo, F., Mondada, F.: Pedagogical uses of Thymio II: how do teachers perceive educational robots in formal education? IEEE Robot. Autom. Mag. (RAM) **23**(2), 16–23 (2016)

7. Cronbach, L.J., Shavelson, R.J.: My current thoughts on coefficient alpha and successor procedures. Educ. Psychol. Meas. **64**(3), 391–418 (2004)
8. Eguchi, A.: Educational robotics theories and practice: tips for how to do it right. In: Robots in K-12 Education: a new Technology for Learning, pp. 1–30. IGI Global (2012)
9. El-Hamamsy, L., et al.: The symbiotic relationship between educational robotics and computer science in formal education. Educ. Inf. Technol. (2021). https://doi.org/10.1007/s10639-021-10494-3
10. El-Hamamsy, L., et al.: A computer science and robotics integration model for primary school: evaluation of a large-scale in-service K-4 teacher-training program. Educ. Inf. Technol. **26**(3), 2445–2475 (2020). https://doi.org/10.1007/s10639-020-10355-5
11. Ferrarelli, P., Lapucci, T., Iocchi, L.: Methodology and results on teaching maths using mobile robots. In: Ollero, A., Sanfeliu, A., Montano, L., Lau, N., Cardeira, C. (eds.) ROBOT 2017. AISC, vol. 694, pp. 394–406. Springer, Cham (2018). https://doi.org/10.1007/978-3-319-70836-2_33
12. Foerster, K.T.: Integrating programming into the mathematics curriculum: combining scratch and geometry in grades 6 and 7. In: Proceedings of the 17th Annual Conference on Information Technology Education, pp. 91–96 (2016)
13. Fowler Jr., F.J., Fowler, F.J.: Improving Survey Questions: Design and Evaluation. Sage, Thousand Oaks (1995)
14. Giang, C.: Towards the alignment of educational robotics learning systems with classroom activities, p. 176 (2020)
15. Hanks, B., Fitzgerald, S., McCauley, R., Murphy, L., Zander, C.: Pair programming in education: a literature review. Comput. Sci. Educ. **21**(2), 135–173 (2011)
16. Iskrenovic-Momcilovic, O.: Improving geometry teaching with scratch. Int. Electron. J. Math. Educ. **15**(2), em0582 (2020)
17. Jung, S., Won, E.s.: Systematic review of research trends in robotics education for young children. Sustainability **10**(4), 905 (2018)
18. Karim, M.E., Lemaignan, S., Mondada, F.: A review: can robots reshape k-12 stem education? In: 2015 IEEE International Workshop on Advanced Robotics and its Social Impacts (ARSO), pp. 1–8. IEEE (2015)
19. Kim, H.J.: Concreteness fading strategy: a promising and sustainable instructional model in mathematics classrooms. Sustainability **12**, 2211 (2020)
20. King, W., He, J.: A meta-analysis of the technology acceptance model. Inf. Manag. **43**, 740–755 (2006)
21. Leoste, J., Heidmets, M.: The impact of educational robots as learning tools on mathematics learning outcomes in basic education. In: Väljataga, T., Laanpere, M. (eds.) Digital Turn in Schools—Research, Policy, Practice. LNET, pp. 203–217. Springer, Singapore (2019). https://doi.org/10.1007/978-981-13-7361-9_14
22. Miller, D.P., Nourbakhsh, I.: Robotics for education. In: Siciliano, B., Khatib, O. (eds.) Springer Handbook of Robotics, pp. 2115–2134. Springer, Cham (2016). https://doi.org/10.1007/978-3-319-32552-1_79
23. Mondada, F., et al.: Bringing robotics to formal education: the thymio open-source hardware robot. IEEE Robot. Autom. Mag. **24**(1), 77–85 (2017)
24. Papert, S.: Mindstorms: Children, Computers, and Powerful Ideas. Basic Books, New York (1980)
25. Resnick, M., et al.: Scratch: programming for all. Commun. ACM **52**(11), 60–67 (2009)
26. Rogers, C., Portsmore, M.D.: Bringing engineering to elementary school. J. STEM Educ. Innov. Res. **5**, 17–28 (2004)

27. Ryan, R.M., Deci, E.L.: Self-determination theory and the facilitation of intrinsic motivation, social development, and well-being. Am. Psychol. **55**(1), 68 (2000)
28. Shahmoradi, S., Kothiyal, A., Olsen, J.K., Bruno, B., Dillenbourg, P.: What teachers need for orchestrating robotic classrooms. In: Alario-Hoyos, C., Rodríguez-Triana, M.J., Scheffel, M., Arnedillo-Sánchez, I., Dennerlein, S.M. (eds.) EC-TEL 2020. LNCS, vol. 12315, pp. 87–101. Springer, Cham (2020). https://doi.org/10.1007/978-3-030-57717-9_7
29. Silk, E.M., Higashi, R., Shoop, R., Schunn, C.D.: Designing technology activities that teach mathematics. Technol. Teach. **69**(4), 21–27 (2010)
30. Zhong, B., Xia, L.: A systematic review on exploring the potential of educational robotics in mathematics education. Int. J. Sci. Math. Educ. **18**(1), 79–101 (2018). https://doi.org/10.1007/s10763-018-09939-y

Analysing Peer Assessment Interactions and Their Temporal Dynamics Using a Graphlet-Based Method

Fahima Djelil[1(✉)], Laurent Brisson[1(✉)], Raphaël Charbey[2], Cecile Bothorel[1], Jean-Marie Gilliot[1], and Philippe Ruffieux[3]

[1] IMT Atlantique, Lab-STICC, UMR CNRS 6285, 29238 Brest, France
{fahima.djelil,laurent.brisson,cecile.bothorel,
jm.gilliot}@imt-atlantique.fr
[2] Energiency, La Fabrique, 22 Avenue Jules Maniez, 35000 Rennes, France
[3] HEP Vaud, Avenue de Sévelin 46, 1014 Lausanne, Switzerland
philippe.ruffieux@hepl.ch

Abstract. Engaging students in peer assessment is an innovative assessment process which has a positive impact on students learning experience. However, the adoption of peer assessment can be slow and uncomfortably experienced by students. Moreover, peer assessment can be prone to several biases. In this paper, we argue that the analysis of peer assessment interactions and phenomena can benefit from the social network analysis domain. We applied a graphlet-based method to a dataset collected during in-class courses integrating a peer assessment platform. This allowed for the interpretation of networking structures shaping the peer assessment interactions, leading for the description of consequent peer assessment roles and their temporal dynamics. Results showed that students develop a positive tendency towards adopting the peer assessment process, and engage gradually with well-balanced roles, even though, initially they choose mostly to be assessed by teachers and more likely by peers they know. This study contributes to research insights into peer assessment learning analytics, and motivates future work to scaffold peer learning in similar contexts.

Keywords: Peer assessment · Temporal networks · Graphlets

1 Introduction

Peer assessment has emerged as a peer learning approach, which is an important research topic in education [15]. It has been presented as part of the concept of peer tutoring [27] or peer education [7], which is a specific form of student's engagement, having a powerful impact on active student participation [15].

A key way to bring learning and teaching together by engaging students in peer learning is through the assessment process [14]. Assessment used with students has been argued to have a significant impact on what, how and how much students study [13] and is therefore an essential element in the learning and teaching process. Bringing students into interactive learning and peer feedback around assessment activities is a good way for students to identify the strengthens and weaknesses of their work [30]. Allowing students to develop their own assessment activities is suggested as an innovative assessment practice enhancing tutor experience [2]. More importantly, engaging students in peer assessment has a positive impact on students learning experience, and helps improvement of performance [2]. Despite prior work in this field, the intrinsic mechanisms and temporal dynamics of peer interactions that drive peer assessment in hybrid classes remain understudied. A few online tools exist for supporting peer assessment [35], and support for transparent and meaningful peer assessment learning analytics is lacking [9]. For instance, such learning analytics may allow for reliability check of assessment [9].

This paper aims to provide insights on how students engage in peer assessment and address the following main questions: 1) How peer assessment interactions occur? 2) What are the consequent student roles regarding the peer assessment process? 3) How the student assessment roles evolve temporally? To this end, we applied a graphlet-based method, a meaningful and expressive network analysis approach, to a dataset collected across seven in-class courses integrating an online peer assessment platform called Sqily. This method allowed for the description of peer assessment roles students engage with, as well as their temporal dynamics, leading to a more understanding on how students involve in peer assessment.

In the following sections, we first present a state of research and practical issues in peer assessment. We describe the peer learning platform we used and how it implements peer assessment (Sqily). We also introduce the graphlet concept in the domain of Social Network Analysis. We then describe the graphlet-based method we adopt to analyse peer assessment interactions, and detect student roles and their temporal dynamics. We report our observations, and finally we discuss our contributions and pedagogical implications of this work.

2 Background

2.1 Peer Assessment Findings

Peer assessment is seen as a powerful tool to achieve evaluation of complex students' assignments at a large scale, as in the context of Massive Open Online Courses (MOOCs) [6,20]. Scalability in the evaluation is achieved since peer feedback is available in greater volume and with greater immediacy than teacher feedback [34]. It is also assumed that peer assessment is most generally formative, with the intent to make students help each other plan their learning, identify their strengths and weaknesses, target areas for remedial actions, and develop metacognitive, personal and professional skills [34].

This may seem to be an enriching system, but peer assessment evaluations can be prone to many biases. As it is reported in [35], biases for students can include inexperience in grading, but also friendship between peers [8], which implies rating friends favourably and making pacts with others [21]. A recent study [11] revealed that friendship-based favouritism in peer judgements was one of the most frequently cited by students, as posing a barrier for improvement, and so, a negative aspect of peer assessment. This is closely related to the problem of reliability and validity of students' peer assessment, which is one of the major concerns for both educators and researchers, that is rising in the literature, and which is mostly dealing with peer grading. For example, [5] found that when students are given guidance on peer assessment, they take the grading tasks seriously and their results are highly reliable and as valid as instructors' assessments. Other studies [17,33,35] indicated that peer assessment is of adequate reliability and validity compared to instructor or teacher assessments, when the process is carefully prepared and conducted.

It has also been expressed that peer assessment is a time-intensive process, as it requires students to engage in intellectually challenging tasks, and that students can feel socially uncomfortable [24]. The process of peer assessment may also take time before being adopted by students. It was reported that students, especially in the initial stages of peer assessment, are often critical of their peers' ability in assessing their work [1]. However, it was observed that although students have doubts and initially tend to resist being involved in peer assessment, such resistance subsides over time [1].

2.2 Peer Assessment Using the Platform Sqily

One of the objectives of Sqily [26] is to draw benefit from the peer assessment approach, by providing peer feedback (comments, documentation, ...) and certifying learning skills. Sqily also facilitates interactions between peers, by providing tools for sharing learning contents and engaging discussions. The platform enables to define a set of skills that can be certified by completing related assessment activities. An assessment activity can be an open question or an exercise created by a teacher or a peer. The creator of the activity, based on his or her own expertise and his own scoring, decides whether or not to validate the associated skill for another peer. A skill refers to a knowledge, a know-how or an ability. Each skill is added to the platform by a teacher or a peer who masters the related competency. Each learner refers to the platform, to acquire a new skill by interacting directly with the teacher or the tutor who acts as a teacher for that skill. Once a learner gets an activity certified, he can himself tutor other peers.

In the context of a classroom, this enables organising topics, or skills, to be learned as a tree of learning objectives' sequences. A learner progression is explicit, and interactions between peers are organised around skills through an assessment process. The learner is invited to progress in a learning path which is not imposed, since students can choose their own sequencing to certify skills (Fig. 1). Initially, the learning path is set by a teacher, but can be extended by the learners, i.e. learners are assessed either by teachers or peers, according to the activities they choose.

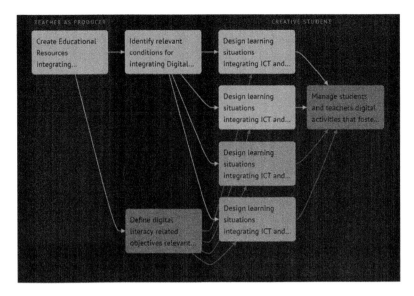

Fig. 1. A learning path in the Sqily platform: the skills coloured in yellow, blue and grey are respectively skills that have been certified, skills that are being certified, and skills that are not yet certified. (Color figure online)

The objective of peer assessment using the platform Sqily is to encourage the learner to adopt a peer tutoring approach: he must mobilise his newly acquired skills in order to explain them and help other students acquiring them. Thus, the learner puts himself into the role traditionally assigned to the teacher and deepens his skills [29]. In summary, students are encouraged to design their own assessment activities, ask for assessments to acquire new skills or give assessments and feedback on skills they master. Around assessment activities, students will alternatively assume both tutor (assessor) and tutee (assessed) roles.

2.3 Graphlet in the Social Network Domain and Potential for Peer Assessment Analysis

Since peer assessment involves social interactions and provides networking data, it is very worthy to look for the opportunities the domain of Social Network Analysis (SNA) may provide to analyse peer learning interactions. In fact, SNA is already known to be powerful at describing and analysing interaction behaviours in the field of learning analytics. SNA has mostly been applied to analyse student discussions in forums, a systematic review of literature covers more than 30 studies that analyse patterns of student discussions [3]. For example, the study [31] exhibits popular students who provide comments to others, who are reflectors and good communicators in the learning process. Graphlets have also potential to provide an automatic way to detect relevant, sometimes, non-obvious configurations of interaction inside complex networks [23]. By counting the positions in which the nodes appear (position enumeration), the graphlets offer a way to compare their topological role inside a social network. A previous study on the Sqily platform data [4] showed the relevance of the graphlet-based approach to detect roles. However, the limited number of graphlets used did not allow to differentiate the behaviors of students and teachers and thus to highlight statistically significant changes in behavior.

A social network, represented as an undirected or directed graph, consists, minimally, of a set of nodes (also referred to as vertices) representing social actors and a set of arcs (edges or ties) between pairs of nodes, representing social relations between actors [12]. Recently in the network analysis domain, methods that explicitly look at the connections between nodes inside subgraphs, called graphlets or motifs, have emerged [23]. Graphlets have been used in many tasks such as network comparison, link prediction, and network clustering, mainly in the computational biology domain (biological networks) [25,32]. On a more global perspective, graphlets have shown to be able to classify superfamilies of networks [22,37]. Graphlets are a collection of subgraphs representing all possible configurations of interconnection between a small number of k nodes, usually k is set to three in the case of a directed graph. Triadic configurations (directed graphlets with 3 nodes) represent a fundamental tool for social network theories and methodologies [12,16,36].

Figure 2 illustrates the process by which positions are enumerated in a directed graph. In this example, position enumeration is completed by visiting an initial complex graph (social network), to determine all the constitutive subgraphs of 3 nodes, classify the isomorphic ones and determine and count the nodes having equivalent positions. Each class defines a new graphlet, which is distinguished by the way the nodes are connected each other. We can also know for each graphlet, the number of its occurrences which is given by the count of isomorphic subgraphs defining the graphlet. An isomorphism between two subgraphs means that the subgraphs have the same number of nodes and are connected in the same way. In other words, if the two subgraphs were drawn, then we would only have to highlight their nodes, and keep the direction of connection between the nodes to get the exact copies (Fig. 2, (c)). Depicting the nodes inside each graphlet allows highlighting equivalent positions of nodes within a graphlet (Fig. 2, (d), (e)).

3 Method

Our work aims to examine interactions between students, that occur during peer assessment on the Sqily platform. We first consider the student interactions within the same time baseline, then we vectorise the student peer interactions, on the basis of their topological positions within graphlets (Question 1). To obtain student distinct roles, we applied a clustering over the aggregated vectors (Question 2), and finally we applied a likelihood metric to investigate relationships between two consecutive temporally unfolding roles (Question 3).

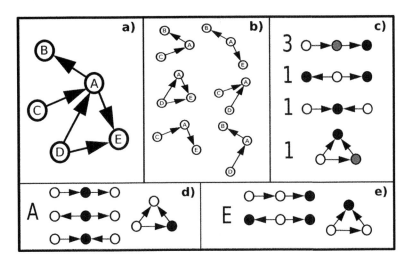

Fig. 2. Example illustrating the position enumeration process: a) initial directed graph; b) constitutive subgraphs of 3 nodes; c) classes of isomorphic subgraphs expressing the resulting graphlets, positions of nodes are depicted in shades of grey; d) node "A" in four positions; e) node "E" in 3 positions. Note that node "E" appears once in the same position as another node, hence the depicting of 4 nodes.

3.1 Context

The study was situated in seven courses that took place in a classroom using the Sqily platform in HEP Vaud (Lausanne, Switzerland), a higher education school that offers a university-level training to future teachers and educators. The courses were about the fields of mathematics, integration of ICT in teaching, web exploration and documentation, as well as images and media in teaching. Each of the courses involved different amounts of students rising from 11 to 171 students per course, and up to 7 teachers per course (this distribution is specific to the training program and the courses). Each course contains different assessment activities designed either by teachers or peers. To get involved in a peer assessment process, students are invited to certify exiting skills or to create their own assessment activities in the platform. Teachers are creators of skills and assessment activities, assessors and facilitators. Table 1 shows for each course, the proportions of assessment activities that have been created by peers in the platform.

3.2 Data Analysis

A Unique Time Baseline for Interaction Observation. In order to facilitate analysis of peer assessment interactions within the different courses and allow comprehensive comparisons, we first set an observation period to one week, to get observations with the same time baseline (time discretisation). Then, over each time period, we aggregate all the interactions between peers, as well as

Table 1. Number of teachers and students enrolled in each course, and the proportion of assessment activities created by peers.

Course	Nb. teachers	Nb. students	Nb. assessments	Peer assessments (%)
Maths 1	1	16	45	27
Maths 2	1	12	35	97
ICT 1	5	48	243	47
ICT 2	7	151	865	68
ICT 3	6	171	831	79
WebExplo	1	11	24	92
Image&Media	1	13	99	67

between teachers and students, to create a directed graph, where nodes are representing teachers or peers, and arcs the assessment interactions, i.e., a teacher assesses a student or a peer assesses another peer to certify at least one student skill. The obtained graphs are not weighted, i.e. there is no numerical values (weights) on the arcs, associated to the count of assessment interactions between the same individuals, and within the same time period.

Graphlets Shaping Student Interactions. Graphlets provide a meaningful way to express the student peer assessment roles. In each graphlet, peers are represented by nodes, the positions of nodes are visually depicted, and the arcs are directed from the peers taking the assessor role to the peers taking the assessed role. For instance, the graphlet ⌐, expresses a student who assesses other peers (depicted as a black node), ⌐ expresses a student who is assessed by other peers, and ⌐ expresses a student who assesses a peer after being assessed by another peer.

In order to be computed, the graph data obtained from the previous step of time discretisation, is structured using vectors. Each vector stores for each student, during a period of time, the ratio of the number of appearances of the student in a given position, with the total number of his appearances in other positions. More specifically, we defined all possible configurations of graphlets of size 3, which distinguish teachers (shown as a ☆) from students (shown as a ○). We obtained 20 graphlets allowing highlighting 48 distinct positions for the nodes, depicted with shades of grey (Fig. 3). Therefore, each student is characterised regarding these 48 distinct positions.

Student Roles. In order to determine peer assessment roles, we applied the kMeans clustering algorithm over the vectors obtained from the previous step. Each vector stores for each student information about its enumerated positions within a period of time. By applying the kMeans algorithm [18,19] to these vectors, we obtain clusters of similar distributions of positions. The clustering produced by this algorithm is dependent on its initialisation step and the number

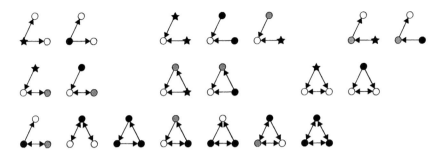

Fig. 3. The 48 possible positions expressed by 20 directed graphlets of size three, depicted by shades of grey. In each graphlet, the nodes with the same colour are in the same position. Students are represented by circles and teachers by stars.

of clusters c that is given as a parameter. Therefore, we ran the algorithm a hundred times for each value of c between 1 and 20 and kept the best result according to the silhouette score [28].

Peer Assessments Temporal Dynamics. In order to characterise student behaviours over time and analyse peer assessment dynamics, we analyse, for each student, transitions between two different roles at two consecutive time periods.

We applied a likelihood metric named a measure of transition likelihood, as proposed in [10]. In our context, the likelihood metric is expressed as $L(R_t \to R_{t+1})$ (Eq. 1). It measures to what extent the student roles R_t and R_{t+1} are associated, where R_t represents a student role at a current time t, and R_{t+1} a student role at the next time, t+1.

$$L(R_t \to R_{t+1}) = \frac{Pr(R_{t+1}|R_t) - Pr(R_{t+1})}{1 - Pr(R_t)} \quad (1)$$

The Likelihood metric, looks for association between two states R_t and R_{t+1}, using a conditional probability measure $Pr(R_{t+1}|R_t)$. The expected degree of association is $Pr(R_{t+1})$, because if R_{t+1} and R_t are independent, then $Pr(R_{t+1}|R_t) = Pr(R_{t+1})$. Therefore, the numerator of Eq. 1 is null, and so $L(R_t \to R_{t+1}) = 0$, i.e. no relationship between immediate role and next role [10].

The numerator of the likelihood may be interpreted as the degree of the association between the two consecutive roles minus the degree of the expected association between these roles at independence. If $Pr(R_{t+1}|R_t)$ is lesser than $Pr(R_{t+1})$ then $L(R_t \to R_{t+1}) < 0$, i.e. the association is less frequent than what would be expected under the hypothesis of independence (null hypothesis). On the contrary, if $Pr(R_{t+1}|R_t)$ is greater than $Pr(R_{t+1})$ then $L(R_t \to R_{t+1}) > 0$, i.e. the association is more frequent than what would be expected under the hypothesis of independence.

Likelihood is then averaged for each transition over the student population. In order to determine whether the average of our sample is statistically different from a null likelihood hypothesis, we perform a one-sample t-test (see Eq. 2) where $\bar{x}$ is the average of the likelihood for our population, S the standard deviation of the likelihood for the population, n the size of the population and $\mu = 0$ our hypothesis statement.

$$t = \frac{\bar{x} - \mu}{\frac{S}{\sqrt{n}}} \qquad (2)$$

4 Results and Discussion

4.1 Student Peer Assessment Roles

The clustering of the aggregated peer interaction data based on graphlets and positions enumeration led to four different categories of student positions, defining four distinct student roles (Table 2). Instead of focusing on all 48 possible positions (see Fig. 3), and in order to describe in a meaningful way each role category, we only keep the most frequent positions representing at least 75% of the positions within a cluster. We keep eight positions expressed with eight distinct graphlets to characterise the student peer assessment roles. Table 2 gives for each role, the statistical frequency of each of the eight positions, as well as the size of each role category.

Table 2. Resulting peer assessment roles described with the most frequent positions. Black depicted nodes represent distinct positions. Teachers are distinguished from students by star-shaped nodes.

Role	Size	Assessed positions				Assessor positions			Both
teacher-assessed	270	**0.92**	0.02	0	0	0	0.01	0	0
peer-assessed	412	0.04	**0.70**	0.07	0.07	0.01	0	0	0.01
assessor	260	0	0	0	0	**0.80**	0.07	0.05	0.02
assessed-and-assessor	459	0.05	0.09	0.08	0.06	0.10	**0.23**	0.09	0.08

We interpreted the four distinct roles on the basis of graphlet and position enumeration, as follows:

– **teacher-assessed:** This role is defined by a category that includes students who have been mostly assessed by the teacher (in 92% of cases). This shows that teachers are significantly present across courses, and that students choose to be assessed by teachers rather than peers at certain time periods.
– **peer-assessed:** This role is defined by a category that includes students who are mostly assessed by other peers (at least in 84% of cases). We note that it is common for the peers being assessed to have the same assessor (70%), but

that it is quite rare to be assessed by several peers ⋯ (7%), or to be assessed by a peer that has been himself assessed by another peer (a sequence of two assessments) ⋯ (7%). This can be explained by the fact that, over one week of observation, peers remain focused on one learning objective and do not move to other peer assessment activities.

- **assessor:** This role is defined by a category that includes peers who are assessors in 93% of the positions they hold, over a period of time. The majority of these students assess the same peers ⋯ (80%), more rarely different peers ⋯ (7%), and it is also uncommon that when a student assesses a peer, this peer assesses in turn another peer ⋯ (5%). This can be explained by the fact that students may know each other and favour their friends first in the assessments.
- **assessed-and-assessor:** This role is defined by a category that includes students who have the most balanced peer assessment interactions. This role is related to peers characterised by, at least, 42% of assessor positions and 28% of assessed positions. In contrast to what we observed for the category of assessor roles, students with this role are more likely to assess different peers ⋯ (23%), instead of assessing peers who are being assessed by other students ⋯ (10%).

Furthermore, in this role students are more likely to appear as first assessors of peers that are in turn assessors of other peers ⋯ (9%). They are less likely to be assessed by teachers ⋯ (5%), but they are rather assessed by other peers. They are assessed by the same peers ⋯ (9%), or different peers ⋯ (8%). They are also assessed by peers that have been assessed before by other peers ⋯ (6%). Finally, this role is characterised by the most frequent positions expressing both assessor and assessed peer interactions ⋯ (8% of the cases). These students, therefore, present a role that could be described as being strongly committed to peer assessment, both by creating assessments activities, and also mainly interacting with their peers as assessors or to be assessed and get skills certified.

4.2 Student Peer Assessment Dynamics

Equation 1 was used to compute the likelihood of all possible role transitions excluding repetitions between roles, leading to 3×4 or 12 possible transitions. Descriptive statistics on the transition likelihood and the results of the t-tests are presented in Table 3. We performed one-sample t-tests to test whether likelihood measures were significantly greater than or equivalent to zero, i.e. no relationship between immediate and next role.

Significance testing led to five transitions that occur above chance ($p < 0.05$, $\bar{x}¿0$), namely (teacher-assessed → peer-assessed/assessed-and-assessor; peer-assessed → assessed-and-assessor; assessor → peer-assessed/teacher-assessed), and three transitions whose occurrence was expected at chance levels ($p < 0.05$, $\bar{x} < 0$), namely (peer-assessed → assessor; assessed-and-assessor → assessor/teacher-assessed).

The first five transitions expressed an association between specific roles. This showed that peers assumed different roles as assessed and assessors after being assessed from the teacher or another peer. They also engage with their peers with assessed roles after being assessors. On the other hand, the three other transitions showed that peers engage as assessors more frequently regardless of their previous peer assessment roles. Moreover, students who are assessed by teachers are not most likely those who are engaging in peer assessment beforehand.

From these results, we can observe that peers have a positive tendency towards a more balancing role and engage in the peer assessment process progressively. We observe that teachers are significantly present in the courses, and students may need to be assessed by teachers before engaging themselves in reciprocal activities with peers. Another interesting result, is that students who are assessing first their friends (assessing frequently the same peers), are not likely those who have experienced peer assessment in a more balanced way. This shows that students may need time before feeling comfortable to interact with new peers, and so the process of peer assessment may take time before being adopted by students.

Table 3. Descriptive statistics of transition likelihood between two roles and results of the t-tests. **$p < 0.05$

Transitions	n	$\bar{x}$	S	One-sample t-test	
				t	p
From teacher-assessed role					
teacher-assessed → assessor	267	−0.000	0.409	−0.02	0.988
teacher-assessed → peer-assessed**	267	0.110	0.590	3.05	0.002
teacher-assessed → assessed-and-assessor**	267	0.061	0.401	2.48	0.014
From peer-assessed role					
peer-assessed → assessor**	250	−0.129	0.357	−5.70	0.000
peer-assessed → teacher-assessed	250	0.038	0.624	0.97	0.332
peer-assessed → assessed-and-assessor**	250	0.229	0.475	7.64	0.000
From assessor role					
assessor → peer-assessed**	168	0.251	0.578	5.62	0.000
assessor → teacher-assessed**	168	0.105	0.534	2.55	0.012
assessor → assessed-and-assessor	168	0.020	0.425	0.62	0.539
From assessed and assessor role					
assessed-and-assessor → assessor**	149	−0.200	0.293	−8.31	0.000
assessed-and-assessor → peer-assessed	149	−0.022	0.616	−0.44	0.659
assessed-and-assessor → teacher-assessed**	149	−0.218	0.411	−6.47	0.000

5 Conclusion and Implications

In this work, we have presented a graphlet-based method to analyse peer assessment interactions and their temporal dynamics, in the context of hybrid courses using a peer learning platform called Sqily. The graphlets allowed to shape peer interactions and provide a meaningful way to detect peer assessment roles, over the same time baseline. This approach makes it possible to meaningfully observe how students engage in peer assessment activities. And finally, examining dynamics brings insights on how peers adopt different roles over time. We observed that peers have a positive tendency to adopt the peer assessment process and engage progressively in reciprocal activities towards peers. Teacher presence was observed significantly across courses, and this may lead to enhance initial assessment activities between peers.

This study contributes fresh insights into better understanding how peer assessment occurs for informing future research. One of the main interesting empirical findings of this work is that students need some support to engage in a peer-assessment process, and that a direct guidance from a teacher can help them to initiate interactions with peers. Another main contribution of this paper consists in the effectiveness and expressiveness of the graphlet-based method used for analysing and interpreting assessment interactions between peers. This method has a great potential to address meany state of the art issues regarding peer assessment, such as friendship based favouritism between peers and resistance to being involved in peer assessment. This method would also be transferable to analyse other learning issues in similar contexts, as it allows shaping interactions between peers. One could focus, for example, on cooperation between students, such as co-development of learning content or analysing team work [14].

The work presented in this paper is of scholarly and practical implications. This work brings interesting insights on the design of learning analytics tools that allow for a meaningful reporting of peer learning dynamics. This may strengthen formative evaluation and provide learners with quick feedback during their learning. Future work is motivated to scaffold peer learning. Moreover, further information is required to improve peer interaction analysis and better understand peer learning phenomena. For example, it would be relevant to adapt the size of the observation time window to the intensity of interactions during a course, to get more rich information and improve the analysis of peer learning. It would be also interesting to analyse the quantity and the quality of feedback made to peers. This can extent the relative research on peer learning and peer assessment.

Acknowledgement. This work was financed by Carnot TSN/IMT Atlantique (2019–2020).

References

1. Ashenafi, M.M.: Peer-assessment in higher education-twenty-first century practices, challenges and the way forward. Assess. Eval. High. Educ. **42**(2), 226–251 (2017)

2. Bevitt, S.: Innovative assessment practice - evaluating and managing the impact on student experience. Working Paper, Higher Education Academy (HEA), May 2012. https://derby.openrepository.com/handle/10545/237191
3. Cela, K.L., Sicilia, M.Á., Sánchez, S.: Social network analysis in e-learning environments: a preliminary systematic review. Educ. Psychol. Rev. **27**(1), 219–246 (2015)
4. Charbey, R., et al.: Roles in social interactions: graphlets in temporal networks applied to learning analytics. In: Cherifi, H., Gaito, S., Mendes, J.F., Moro, E., Rocha, L.M. (eds.) COMPLEX NETWORKS 2019. SCI, vol. 882, pp. 507–518. Springer, Cham (2020). https://doi.org/10.1007/978-3-030-36683-4_41
5. Cho, K., Schunn, C.D., Wilson, R.W.: Validity and reliability of scaffolded peer assessment of writing from instructor and student perspectives. J. Educ. Psychol. **98**(4), 891 (2006)
6. Cooper, S., Sahami, M.: Reflections on Stanford's MOOCs. Commun. ACM **56**(2), 28–30 (2013)
7. Damon, W.: Peer education: the untapped potential. J. Appl. Dev. Psychol. **5**(4), 331–343 (1984)
8. Dancer, W.T., Dancer, J.: Peer rating in higher education. J. Educ. Bus. **67**(5), 306–309 (1992)
9. Divjak, B., Maretić, M.: Learning analytics for peer-assessment:(dis) advantages, reliability and implementation. J. Inf. Organ. Sci. **41**(1), 21–34 (2017)
10. D'Mello, S., Graesser, A.: Dynamics of affective states during complex learning. Learn. Instr. **22**(2), 145–157 (2012)
11. Ersöz, Y., Sad, S.N.: Facebook as a peer-assessment platform: a case study in art teacher education context. Int. J. Assess. Tools Educ. **5**(4), 740–753 (2018)
12. Faust, K.: 7. very local structure in social networks. Sociol. Methodol. **37**(1), 209–256 (2007)
13. Gibbs, G., Simpson, C.: Does your assessment support your students' learning. J. Teach. Learn. High. Educ. **1**(1), 1–30 (2004)
14. Healey, M.: Students as partners in learning and teaching in higher education. In: Workshop Presented at University College Cork, vol. 12, p. 15 (2014)
15. Healey, M., Flint, A., Harrington, K.: Students as partners: reflections on a conceptual model. Teach. Learn. Inquiry **4**(2), 1–13 (2016)
16. Holland, P.W., Leinhardt, S.: Local structure in social networks. Sociol. Methodol. **7**, 1–45 (1976)
17. Li, H., et al.: Peer assessment in the digital age: a meta-analysis comparing peer and teacher ratings. Assess. Eval. High. Educ. **41**(2), 245–264 (2016)
18. Lloyd, S.: Least squares quantization in PCM. IEEE Trans. Inf. Theory **28**(2), 129–137 (1982)
19. MacQueen, J., et al.: Some methods for classification and analysis of multivariate observations. In: Proceedings of the Fifth Berkeley Symposium on Mathematical Statistics and Probability, Oakland, CA, USA, vol. 1, pp. 281–297 (1967)
20. del Mar Sánchez-Vera, M., Prendes-Espinosa, M.P.: Beyond objective testing and peer assessment: alternative ways of assessment in MOOCs. Int. J. Educ. Technol. High. Educ. **12**(1), 119–130 (2015)
21. Mathews, B.P.: Assessing individual contributions: experience of peer evaluation in major group projects. Br. J. Edu. Technol. **25**(1), 19–28 (1994)
22. Milo, R., et al.: Superfamilies of evolved and designed networks. Science **303**(5663), 1538–1542 (2004)

23. Milo, R., Shen-Orr, S., Itzkovitz, S., Kashtan, N., Chklovskii, D., Alon, U.: Network motifs: simple building blocks of complex networks. Science **298**(5594), 824–827 (2002)
24. Praver, M., Rouault, G., Eidswick, J.: Attitudes and affect toward peer evaluation in EFL reading circles. Reading **11**(2), 89–101 (2011)
25. Pržulj, N., Corneil, D.G., Jurisica, I.: Modeling interactome: scale-free or geometric? Bioinformatics **20**(18), 3508–3515 (2004)
26. Haute École Pédagogique Vaud, S.: Plateforme de communication scolaire et de validation mutuelle de compétences. https://www.sqily.com/
27. Roscoe, R.D., Chi, M.T.: Understanding tutor learning: knowledge-building and knowledge-telling in peer tutors' explanations and questions. Rev. Educ. Res. **77**(4), 534–574 (2007)
28. Rousseeuw, P.J.: Silhouettes: a graphical aid to the interpretation and validation of cluster analysis. J. Comput. Appl. Math. **20**, 53–65 (1987)
29. Ruffieux, P.: Validation mutuelle des compétences dans une institution de formation d'enseignants. Distances et médiations des savoirs. Distance and Mediation of Knowledge **2017**(20) (2017). http://journals.openedition.org/dms/2044
30. Sambell, K.: Engaging Students Through Assessment. The Student Engagement Handbook: Practice in Higher Education, pp. 379–396. Emerald Group Publishing Limited, Bradford (2013)
31. Suh, H., Kang, M., Moon, K., Jang, H.: Identifying peer interaction patterns and related variables in community-based learning. In: Proceedings of the 2005 Conference on Computer Support for Collaborative Learning: Learning 2005: The Next 10 Years! CSCL 2005, pp. 657–661. International Society of the Learning Sciences (2005). http://dl.acm.org/citation.cfm?id=1149293.1149379
32. Sun, Y., Crawford, J., Tang, J., Milenković, T.: Simultaneous optimization of both node and edge conservation in network alignment via WAVE. In: Pop, M., Touzet, H. (eds.) WABI 2015. LNCS, vol. 9289, pp. 16–39. Springer, Heidelberg (2015). https://doi.org/10.1007/978-3-662-48221-6_2
33. Topping, K.: Peer assessment between students in colleges and universities. Rev. Educ. Res. **68**, 249–276 (1998)
34. Topping, K.J.: Peer assessment. Theory Pract. **48**(1), 20–27 (2009)
35. Vozniuk, A., Holzer, A., Gillet, D.: Peer assessment based on ratings in a social media course. In: Proceedings of the Fourth International Conference on Learning Analytics And Knowledge, pp. 133–137 (2014)
36. Wasserman, S., Faust, K., et al.: Social Network Analysis: Methods and Applications, vol. 8. Cambridge University Press (1994)
37. Yaveroğlu, Ö.N., et al.: Revealing the hidden language of complex networks. Sci. Rep. **4**, 4547 (2014)

VLE Limits and Perspectives for Digital Integration in Teaching Practices
Lessons Learned from the French Basic Education Teachers' Experience During the COVID-19 Pandemic

Christine Michel[1], Laëtitia Pierrot[1(✉)], and Melina Solari-Landa[1,2]

[1] TECHNE EA 6316, University of Poitiers, 86073 Poitiers, France
`{christine.michel,laetitia.pierrot,`
`melina.solari-landa}@univ-poitiers.fr`
[2] DRDUNE- Réseau Canopé, 86360 Chasseneuil du Poitou, France

Abstract. With the recent COVID-19 pandemic and general school closure, teachers had to teach remotely in an emergency. This study explores how this particular context enacts French Primary and Secondary Teachers' technology integration, with a specific focus on the virtual learning environment (VLE), by exploiting 441 teachers' answers to a survey and 13 in-depth interviews. The findings confirm previous studies: teachers intensified the practices they were already familiar with. But the need to keep a pedagogical link with students led them to more active, collaborative, and engaging learning forms. Our multidimensional analysis shows that teachers integrated technologies into their practices, according to two different logics: diversifying interaction with students and improving self-efficiency. VLE seems easier to use than other digital tools, yet it lacks the resources to fully support teachers' professional development. Finally, this article presents three strategies to redesign the UX and open up the VLE to resource creation, to promote the integration of digital tools within teachers' practices.

Keywords: Virtual learning environment · User experience · Teachers' digital practices · VLE practices redesign · COVID-19

1 Introduction

For the large majority of OECD countries, the Covid-19 pandemic led to the closure of schools in March 2020 and several governments chose to use digital tools to carry out teaching and learning activities, originally planned to be face-to-face, remotely [1]. To implement this strategy, the French government has relied on a policy of providing digital workspaces called "Environnement Numérique de Travail" deployed in primary and secondary schools since 2003 [2]. These digital workspaces follow nationally defined guidelines [2–4]. Thus, all teachers in France have a comparable solution that was initially dedicated to the administrative management of students (for example, attendance and grades) [5]. Over time, this solution has evolved to include communication and collaboration features, like any virtual learning environment (VLE), such as Moodle.

The massive use of digital tools provides great versatility and the opportunity for interaction and to transform learning activities [1, 6]. During the crisis, the main advantage of VLEs, according to teachers, was the ability to gather and foster activities involving different actors likely to accompany children's learning (teachers and other educational staff on the one hand, and children and parents on the other hand [7]). For teachers, distance learning activities can contribute to redefining their role (from instructor to mentor or facilitator) and, above all, to diversifying instructional and technical means [8]. This finding lines up with the "heroic handiwork" that Félix et al. [9] observed during this "quaranteaching" [10] period.

But various studies showed that VLEs were, in France and elsewhere, mainly used by primary and secondary school teachers for basic uses: information and content sharing, communication (mail, forums) and immediate assessment (quizzes) [11–13].

It is critical to understand how digital tools, and in particular VLEs, have been used during lockdown in order to adapt their deployment strategies or make design recommendations towards more useful and usable tools. For TEL researchers, this is essential since the deployment and use of the VLE is highly developed outside of France. For instance, in 2013 VLE had been deployed in 87% of Norwegian schools [14], and its use has been spreading in Lithuania since 2018 [13]). Other countries such as Spain [12] and Malaysia [11] have been experimenting with VLE use in secondary education and have observed some traditional class format transformations.

In this study, our first research question asks which tasks did teachers implement during this period and by what means: the VLE, other digital tools, or non-digital tools (Q1). Beyond contributing to longitudinal studies on the integration of digital technology in and for education, our goal is to identify how the injunction to provide distance learning has affected integration dynamics and how these observations can help formalise support strategies adapted to teachers' needs. The second research question is how to describe and explain the level of digital integration in schools (Q2). Globally, we are seeking to determine what lessons can be learned from this experience to foster the development of digital technology in schools (Q3).

We conducted a study from March to June 2020 to describe the teachers', students', and parents' experiences on the pedagogical continuity regarding digital technology. In association with Open Digital Education, the company that deploys two VLE solutions (Neo for primary school, One for secondary schools), a survey was disseminated through both VLEs. We conducted in-depth interviews to round off the results. Out of the 5000 answers collected from all actors' categories, in this article, we propose an analysis of 441 teachers' survey answers and 13 interviews.

2 Digital Technology in Teachers' Pedagogical Practices

The Deployment of Digital Technology in Education. Whereas the use of digital technology is widespread among teachers outside the classroom, especially for class preparation, its use remains limited within the classroom [15, 16]. There are many reasons for this.

One of the European Survey of Schools ICT in Education's [17] main findings is the consistently demonstrated link between teachers' experience and technology use. Most teachers who integrate digital tools into their classes have at least six years of teaching experience. When asked about their skills, they declared feeling more confident (score of at least 3 out of 4) with communication, information/literacy, collaboration, and safety tasks. They answered feeling less confident with content creation and problem solving.

Other causes are a lack of equipment or material dysfunctions [16], lack of technical and techno-pedagogical training [17], inequalities of access, or social inequalities [18]. Besides those external variables, beliefs, opinions, and the diversity of technology, integration policies [7] have a strong impact on determining the use or non-use of technologies. In the French context, 5 teacher's profiles have been identified by considering the frequency of use and the perceived benefit of technologies [15]. However, depending on the pedagogical approach adopted, studies have shown positive effects in using digital technology for learning. For instance, teacher-centred approaches work effectively with younger students for distance purposes [19]. Virtual environments help to break down spatio-temporal barriers and to promote synchronous/asynchronous communication [20].

VLE Introduction in French Schools. In 2006, the French Ministry of Education proposed a framework to deploy a solution designed to bring together all the educational actors in the same environment. Based on this framework, private publishers have deployed VLE solutions in primary and secondary schools.

Although the solution includes various services and resources, its uses are limited to certain activities or tasks: mail and planner services remain the most widely used tasks [4]. These services allow the reproduction of existing traditional practices with other means [4], which explains its popularity. The feeling of additional workload, the lack of usability of some services such as the forum [21], or the negative perception that teachers have of VLEs can explain the low level of use [5]. This solution also competes with "cobbled together" solutions, preferred by the most enthusiastic teachers [5], because they existed before the arrival of VLEs [3]. Moreover, the VLE deployment strategies follow the institutional will to homogenise services, to the detriment of matching the needs of users with a tool's functionalities [2].

However, new practices are emerging [20], and VLEs have built up new forms of enhancing teachers' work [22]. The VLE seems to contribute to the implementation of activities inside and outside the classroom [15].

Observation of Digital Uses and Teaching Practices. The observation of teachers' digital uses of VLEs sets different objectives: producing descriptive studies of uses, identifying and explaining the factors that condition uses/non-uses, the effects linked to uses, or modelling and formalising the appropriation dynamics.

When addressing a large scale, surveys through questionnaires are usually representative of a population's general trends. They are useful for producing descriptive studies or appropriation models. They generally question teachers on their sociodemographic characteristics, professional background, work environment (including computer equipment), and on their opinions and practices about a given type of technological service. The usefulness, usability, and acceptability [23] is often analysed, with standardised tests [24], to identify all the "practical" aspects of use [25]. Several studies cited in the previous section [3, 7, 11] use these factors to explain teachers' uses/non-uses. These methods are also useful for modelling technology integration in order to describe and understand the innovation diffusion [25, 26].

These methods remain questionable in many aspects. Certain criteria on teachers' skill levels are poorly formalised. The Technological Pedagogical Content Knowledge (TPACK) model [27] could be considered because of its differentiating aim. It describes the three main fields of knowledge that teachers have to mobilise when integrating a technology (knowledge related to the content, knowledge on pedagogy, and knowledge on technology). Furthermore, this quantifying use approach tends to ignore the use purpose that contributes to understanding teachers' objectives and justifying one service's choice over another [21]. Open-ended questions of the "why" type are precious help in understanding these motivations (lack of usefulness, lack of technical or techno-pedagogical skills, too much effort) [17, 28]. Nevertheless, a more systematic analysis of the benefits [24] or the value constructed by use [29] can be carried out. One last methodological element is questionable. The linear character of these models does not allow us to understand the use progression that is not unified for all the services or applications considered [5], and multidimensional classification processes are potentially more suitable [4, 30].

Despite its limitations, the questionnaire, remains the most used form, especially to situate our study results in a long-term extension of other studies' results. We propose to complement classic questionnaires by introducing other information gathered, regarding the tasks and objectives that motivate teachers' use, their more precise opinions about the services and the VLE design, as well as their own evolution in terms of motivation, self-efficacy feeling and competence at the beginning and the end of the lockdown. We also propose to use multidimensional classification methods.

3 Open Digital Education-Nunc Study

Context of the Study. The survey[1] was proposed to users of the VLE solution provided by the publisher Open Digital Education between May and June 2020. The invitation to answer the questionnaire was proposed directly on the VLE. The questionnaire consists of 3 parts (Fig. 1). The first part addresses the respondent's profile. The second part tackles digital technology and VLE experience: uses of digital technology/VLE for school tasks, the experience of VLE (UMUX usability scale [24], and preferred services). The third part concerns the overall experience of the pedagogical continuity period in terms of motivation, sense of efficacy, competence (characterised according to the TPACK dimensions [27]), social ties, and autonomy. We considered the feelings expressed at the beginning and end of this period to calculate the benefits/damages individually. In addition to the questionnaire, in-depth interviews and a collection of experience stories were carried out remotely between June and July 2020.

Participants. The corpus of analysis was composed of 441 responses to the teacher questionnaire (279 in primary school, 162 in secondary school) and 13 in-depth interviews. The respondents were mostly women (79%), between 25 and 55 years old (89%),

---

[1] The survey is part of the larger Nunc project, started in March 2020 to understand how families and teachers adjusted teaching and learning activities to lockdown with TEL.

Section	Description
1 – Profile	Sociodemographic characteristics (gender, age, seniority, level and discipline of teaching)
	Characteristics of the institution (size, private/public, department, primary school/secondary school/high school)
	Working conditions at home (number of children in remote learning at home, help available to manage them)
2 – Digital technologies and VLE	Method of carrying out school tasks (4 methods of carrying out, 24 tasks)
	UMUX VLE score (4 items, 6-point scale)
	Preferred VLE services (ranking of 25 services)
3 – Feelings about remote learning activity	Overall feelings about the confinement at the beginning and the end (12 items, 7-point scale).

Fig. 1. Structure of the questionnaire

with a permanent position (94%), more than 11 years of service in the national education system (90%) and working in public institutions (97%). Nearly a quarter (24%) of the teachers reported that less than 5% of their students did not complete the proposed activities, while 14% reported that half or more of their students were in this situation. Teachers' responses come from different parts of France with a predominance for two departments (Somme, 24% of teachers, and Martinique, 10%).

Data Analysis. We identified teachers' adaptation strategies (Q1) by adding up the answers regarding how they performed (with a VLE, other digital tools or non-digital tools) or not in 24 school tasks (Sect. 2 of the questionnaire). We regrouped these 24 tasks according to the pursued higher-level objectives (design, transmission, facilitation, verification, communication, and self-training). Then, we used a K-means classification method on the tasks answers grouped by objectives in order to identify groups of teachers that use VLEs, and/or other digital tools for equivalent purposes and to model technology integration (Q2). We determined 5 levels for each means in order to respect the TIM scale of technology integration [30]. For description purposes, we calculated the average of the objective performed and the number of teachers in each level. Next, to explain the teachers' motivation, we conducted a co-variance analysis (significance level at 0.05) of the integration level with the variables: profile, UMUX VLE, overall experience of pedagogical continuity (motivation, self-efficacy, competence, social ties, and autonomy). All statistical analyses (bivariate or multivariate analysis) were performed using Excel, XLStat, and Jmp. In this paper, interviews are used to illustrate the results.

4 Results

4.1 Teachers' Adaptation Strategies During the Lockdown

Figure 2 presents the answers from primary and secondary school teachers about the means used to perform 24 school tasks, reorganised according to the pursued higher-level objectives. The behaviours of primary and secondary school teachers are overall quite similar. The most performed tasks are transmission, communication, design, and information retrieval.

Objectives	Tasks	Secondary school - VLE	Primary school - VLE	Secondary school - Digital	Primary school - Digital	Secondary school - Not digital	Primary school - Not digital	Secondary school - None	Primary school - None
Design	1-Adapting activities for specific students	41%	38%	40%	42%	7%	13%	11%	6%
	2-Creating activities	14%	27%	74%	63%	8%	7%	4%	3%
Transmission	3-Making available courses, resources	73%	79%	24%	18%	1%	1%	2%	2%
	4-Making available the activities of the day	71%	78%	22%	16%	1%	2%	6%	4%
	5-Making available exercises	72%	75%	23%	21%	2%	3%	2%	2%
	6-Making available activity sequences	61%	62%	23%	21%	4%	4%	12%	13%
	7-Making available pedagogical activities to develop interaction and collaboration between students	42%	51%	18%	19%	2%	4%	38%	26%
Facilitation	8-Working with video (YouTube, tutorials, etc.)	39%	57%	43%	33%	0%	1%	18%	10%
	9-Publishing or writing with students (journal, blog, pad, etc.)	33%	67%	15%	7%	2%	1%	49%	25%
	10-Working with audio (audio files, webradio, podcast, etc.)	24%	36%	36%	32%	1%	2%	40%	30%
	11-Teaching with specific dedicated applications (Excel, Edumedia, Sesamath, Quidoo…)	7%	5%	22%	20%	1%	0%	70%	75%
	12-Organizing virtual classes with video	6%	3%	43%	61%	1%	1%	51%	33%
	13-Organizing virtual classes with forums	6%	4%	26%	25%	1%	0%	67%	71%
Verification	14-Receiving student productions	80%	55%	10%	32%	6%	6%	4%	8%
	15-Checking that the work has been done	61%	42%	20%	39%	10%	8%	9%	12%
	16-Assessing students	49%	12%	29%	34%	10%	18%	12%	36%
Communication	17-Managing individual requests	77%	59%	14%	33%	6%	5%	4%	3%
	18-Maintaining the link between students despite the distance	67%	58%	22%	36%	4%	2%	7%	4%
	19-Organizing regular checkpoints with families	44%	29%	24%	46%	14%	19%	18%	6%
	20-Making everyone's questions visible	31%	30%	9%	14%	5%	6%	54%	50%
Self-training	21-Cooperating with teachers from my school	49%	17%	38%	61%	7%	15%	6%	7%
	22-Training me on the technologies to use	11%	13%	67%	69%	4%	2%	18%	16%
	23-Cooperating with teachers from other institutions	15%	5%	39%	38%	3%	5%	43%	52%
	24-Searching for information on activities to be done by students	6%	4%	77%	85%	10%	8%	6%	3%

Fig. 2. Task completion modalities by primary and secondary school teachers

The transmission of activities concerns courses, resources, and exercises (T3, T6) that are mostly carried out with the VLE and on a one-off basis (often daily) (T4). "This year I am using the blog that allows me to deliver content and for the students to interact. This is the added advantage over the multimedia notebook, they can ask questions through the comments and also share with each other," (Primary school teacher, n°8). "Each day was fully detailed with all the topics. So for each topic, [I wrote] which activity to do with the reference of the document to be found in the document area," (Primary school teacher, n°13). The teachers less often proposed activity sequences (T6) or activities in groups (T7), sometimes to avoid losing students.

Communication through the VLE is mostly to keep contact with students (T18) or to manage individual requests (T17), mainly inter-personally. In primary school, teachers also used other communication means. "There was the textbook which acted as a messaging system, and the parents' email addresses which also acted as a double messaging system, and also the multimedia workbook" (Primary school teacher, n°7). The teachers do not share questions with other students (T20).

Self-training is mainly performed by searching on the Internet (T24) and exchanging practices between teachers of the same school via the VLE or other digital tools (emails, telephone) (T21). Teachers designed activities (T2) using tools available online. "I go and look for videos on YouTube, I go to the BBC website and then I make a lot of things myself from images that I look for on the internet. (…) After the videos, I often rework them, I split them up, I re-adapt them, I do it to measure for them" (Secondary school teacher, n°1). For self-training purposes, teachers mostly favour the Internet to the VLE, except for some primary teachers. "I have many different textbooks, and I create my sequences from documents that I find in them. I don't use a particular textbook, and I create all the sequences, and then I go and look on sites, Spanish sites for articles, videos that can enrich the sequence, (…) then I look, I create everything by myself" (Secondary school teacher, n°5).

Verifying the students' work (T14, 15, 16) is achieved mainly using the VLE in secondary school and with other digital tools in primary school.

"They would leave in the digital locker the work they had to hand in to me" (Secondary school teacher, n°2). "I asked students to send me their notebook's pictures with what they had done every day, so I can be able to correct them live. So they would send me all the pictures either on Messenger or on WhatsApp" (Primary school teacher n°9). Assessing the student work was not generalised.

The least performed tasks are facilitation ones. The teachers mainly used video resources transmitted directly on or with VLE services to facilitate the lessons. "And when there was a new concept, for example, 'What is a verb?', I put them in a separate notebook where there are only videos to learn. The video of 'What is a verb?' explains how to look up for a verb and then I put the lesson in. So, every time they had exercises, they could refer to the video to better understand" (Primary school teacher, n°9). The other forms of facilitation (collaborative writing, oral work, virtual classes, use of specific tools) remain less developed. However, the VLE allows writing activities (T9) and the other digital tools organising virtual classes (T12, 13).

4.2 Levels of Digital Technology Integration in Teachers' Practices

Figures 3 and 4 present the VLE and others digital tools levels of integration produced with the K-means analysis of the objectives performed. Figure 3 describes the level of integration according to the objectives completed. The higher the level, the more objectives the teachers achieve. Figure 3 describe the number of teachers in each level.

Digital Integration Strategies. Integration strategies for VLE (Fig. 3) involve varying and intensifying the interaction methods with the students, starting with the transmission of courses (level 2), and adding verification and communication (level 3) or design, communication and facilitation (level 4). Level 5 corresponds to an intensification of these five types of objectives. At all levels, the self-training objectives are weak. Conversely, the integration of digital technologies mainly serves first productivity objectives (levels 1–2–3) (self-training, design) and then increases for interactions purposes with students (levels 4–5). Most of the teachers are counted at level 5 (139).

Comparing the joint integration of the two means (Fig. 4), we observe 5 types of behaviours. In green, 3 groups with advanced uses: G1 includes 57 and 80 teachers using exclusively VLEs at level 5 and other digital tools for design and self-training (level 1 and 2); G2 includes 63 teachers using only other technologies at level 5 and G3 includes 51 and 30 teachers having integrated the two ways concomitantly at level 3 or 4. Example for G1: "The blog allowed me to send them the work by inserting PDF

	TIM Level	Self-training	Design	Transmission	Verification	Communication	Facilitation	Nb teachers
VLE	1	0.08	0.07	0.12	0.13	0.21	0.11	91
	2	0.07	0.00	0.77	0.10	0.31	0.27	68
	3	0.15	0.00	0.76	0.70	0.58	0.22	79
	4	0.13	0.63	0.83	0.17	0.48	0.34	64
	5	0.20	0.64	0.85	0.85	0.69	0.32	139
Digital tools (except VLE)	1	0.32	0.07	0.04	0.06	0.09	0.13	103
	2	0.72	0.45	0.09	0.09	0.16	0.28	127
	3	0.60	1.00	0.14	0.16	0.22	0.33	73
	4	0.74	0.62	0.09	0.78	0.47	0.36	70
	5	0.68	0.85	0.84	0.67	0.57	0.50	68

Fig. 3. Description of technology integration levels (TIM) by objectives completed (normalised values between 0 and 1)

	TIM Level	VLE 1	VLE 2	VLE 3	VLE 4	VLE 5	Nb teachers
Diigotal Tools	1	10	7	13	16	57	103
	2	10	9	11	17	80	127
	3	6	16	51	0	0	73
	4	2	34	3	30	1	70
	5	63	2	1	1	1	68
	Total	91	68	79	64	139	441

Fig. 4. Description of technology integration levels (TIM) by number of teachers in the level

attachments, or videos. I used the pad for two things, for registration when I did the videoconf, because I wanted small groups (…) and I used it for collaborative writing too. I absolutely wanted to find a way of doing written expression without having 28 copies of 15 pages to correct, so they did stories together (…), and then I published them in the multimedia book so that everyone could see them." (Primary school teacher, n°4). Example for G2: "We used Discord (…) on request (…) of my students. We were able to chat every day, I was able to motivate those who were dropping out. In short, it was extremely valuable" (Secondary school teacher, n°1).

Example for G3: "Some students told me, after two months 'We're no longer motivated, we don't feel like it anymore', so I said to myself, 'Come on, I'm going to do something on video to talk to them and motivate them,' a colleague told me to register on Zoom" (Primary school teacher, n°9).

In yellow a group (G4) of 93 teachers with limited use of other technologies but progressing in the integration of VLE in their practices. Only 3 teachers (G5 in red) have advanced uses with all the tools.

Factors Explaining VLE Integration. The following paragraphs present the variables that have a significant co-variance (with a threshold of 0.05) with the integration levels. The linear correlation coefficient r is specified.

The profile variables (age, gender, seniority, characteristics of the institution) of teachers do not significantly explain the level of VLE integration. The variables that contributed significantly to the VLE integration were a positive opinion on the VLE design (UX) (r = 0.27), knowing that they could count on a community (0.15), realising that they could discover new practices (r = 0.09), evolve professionally (r = 0.02) and work autonomously (r = 0.07). Other variables that contributed are realising that using VLE does not require much effort specially for content design (r = 0.05), that they are able to produce activities (r = 0.05) that activities are useful to pupils (r = 0.02). "I am satisfied with the use of the VLE. It had to be set up to handle the large number of notifications generated because of the lockdown, and I like that I can attach large files easily" (Secondary school teacher, n°5). "Yes, I think my work has improved in quality. For me, it's a very good experience because it forced me to push certain things further that I wouldn't have done. It's going to improve my preparation work essentially" (Secondary school teacher, n°1).

The variables that contributed significantly to the non-integration of VLE were a high level of integration of other digital tools (r = −0.62), feeling difficulties with digital technology use (r = −0.39), feeling that the effort to produce was too great, in particular to create content (r = −0.05), and also the fear of losing the relationship with colleagues (r = −0.01) or parents and pupils (r = −0.01). The correlation coefficient r = −0.62 shows that when the integration is completed (level 5) teachers keep only one way of working. These results are consistent with those in Fig. 4 (groups 1 and 2). During the interviews, teachers explained their difficulties in integrating the VLE due to design flaws. "Without all these problems of multiple locations, if it was more rational, I think it would be a good tool" (Secondary school teacher, n°1). Others explained their practices according to the students' and families' digital technology troubles or previous habits. Primary school teacher n°7 explained how "For those who didn't pass the login challenge, I had taken my phone and created a small WhatsApp group so I would sometimes have two screens, and then I would flip the phone over and show the reading." These teachers belong to groups 3 and 4 and choose the technology according to the context of uses.

To refine the analysis of difficulties in the uses of VLE, we looked at the services that were preferred by users with the highest level of integration [31]. The results are globally coherent with previous surveys concerning the massive use of email, textbook, multimedia notebook, and blog [4]. We can observe a strong progression in the notification manager's use, mobile version of the VLE, and news feed, which confirms the VLE's interest in organising collective activities. Some services are starting to be reused for activity design: the blog, multimedia workbook, exercise and evaluation, competencies, collaborative wall. Nonetheless, even when the user experience is good and the community is present, barriers persist for facilitation and self-training purposes. Teachers do not use the communication and collaboration features of the platform to help each other and few of them adapt their facilitation practices with the forum, mind map or collaborative pad proposed in the VLE.

Factors Explaining Other Digital Tools' Integration. As with VLE, contextual and sociodemographic variables do not significantly explain the level of digital integration. The variables that contributed significantly to the integration of digital tools (other than VLE) were the feeling of having difficulties in creating content or with digital tools in general (r = 0.12), the feeling that it would be useful to students (r = 0.05), in particular for creating or maintaining links with them (r = 0.05). These observations are consistent with previous findings such as looking for information on the internet to create content and using the tools that pupils use, to keep in touch with them and improve their motivation. "So I asked the parents to go to the One VLE, but there were a lot of them who couldn't send me back the exercises, I don't know why, to post the pictures… so as a result, they were sending me all the pictures either on Messenger or on WhatsApp" (Primary school teacher n°9). Very few teachers (only 3) have integrated all the tools in the highest levels.

A positive experience with VLE combined with the fact of knowing that a community could help them in the school also significantly improved the integration of digital tools ($r = 0.04$). The fact that a positive experience with the VLE reinforces the use of other digital tools shows its potential as a tool that promotes digital tools in schools more generally. These teachers combined tools: they designed activities and search for information via the Internet and used the VLE for transmission, verification and communication. They represent the group 3 identified in Fig. 4.

The variables that contribute significantly to the non-integration of digital technology are the fact of already regularly working with VLE ($r = -0.62$), the feeling of having to work alone ($r = -0.52$), the impression of having difficulties with digital tools ($r = -0.13$) or that the effort to be made would be too great ($r = -0.04$).

5 Lessons Learned to Promote the Development of Digital Technology in Schools

Lessons Learned. To answer the first research question, this study showed that overall, teachers' behaviours were quite consistent in terms of practice with what previous studies have shown: they used the VLE mainly for communication tasks and transmission of activities [4, 17], and the other digital tools (resources on the internet and applications on their computer) for self-training and design [16]. The French teachers mainly used the technologies they were already familiar with, but some teachers develop new practices to address the imperative need to keep in touch with students, as identified by Pace et al. [10]. Using the Internet and personal applications fostered a discovery on new practices and new learning resources (video, text documents, exercises) which were often directly reused or adapted to create new activities. Students' and families' difficulties in using the VLE also led teachers to make more use of their personal email and instant messaging. Moreover, the VLE has encouraged the emergence of collaborative writing practices with students or the design of activity sequences that integrate more multimedia resources, or verification. In this sense, the crisis led the teachers who were more reluctant to technologies to more active, collaborative and engaging teaching practices. This experience made teachers more confident about their personal effectiveness and the quality of their professional practice. Like Tække [19], we believe that this crisis has triggered a significant evolution in teachers' practices, which can be fully achieved with better training of teachers in the use of TEL [1, 32]. As with all methods, data collection by questionnaire sent via the VLE might have induced some bias; the teachers who responded might also have been those most involved in school activities and in the use of digital technology in general. The consistency of our observations with other international studies leads us to believe that this is probably not the case.

To answer the second question, the integration of digital technology and the VLE are done jointly. The integration of digital technology was more effective for the VLE than for other tools. Many teachers quickly developed practices covering several objectives related to their activity, whereas fewer teachers were able to do so with other tools. However, this integration could not have been achieved without the use of the Internet or applications external to the VLE. Both resources stimulate teachers' creativity and ability to design new activities or to find resources adapted to students' and families' needs. The Internet pushes the VLE use towards pedagogical innovation (design, facilitation), and the VLE pushes the collective and collaborative organisation's activity (transmission, communication).

These observations on the integration of digital technology into teachers' practices must be placed in perspective with the results of the 2016 Profetic annual survey results [15]. Teachers who have a daily practice with VLE or other digital tools (in this study, groups 1 and 2) find it easy to access to online resources which may explain their ability for self-training. Teachers in group 3 share same integration level on VLE and other digital tools mostly because they try to adapt and diversify resources to students' and families' needs. Finally, group 4 is similar to those Profetic teachers who use digital technology the least and are less convinced of its relevance. For these profiles, institutional resources, such as the VLE, must be favoured because they are already available and do not require additional equipment. This might explain the increase in the use of VLEs and not other digital tools in this group.

Promoting Digital Technology in Schools. Two axes are critical to develop digital technology in schools: creating new resources (activities, applications, documents...) accessible on the internet, and improving the VLE UX. The VLE design, as a global platform, is a strength for stimulating the development of digital schooling because it integrates a variety of useful services, and the design is rather good. But it is also a weakness because many services are unnecessary or redundant, and others are still missing.

As recommended by Pace et al. [10], it would be interesting to offer teachers the means to personalise the services of their personal or class work-space: by (un)selecting the services (following a store model) and by proposing a "default" model integrating only the most relevant services. Teachers should also configure the implementation of services, for example concerning notifications or storage synchronisation. The VLE would offer more flexible uses.

Additional studies on pedagogical continuity show that teachers, students, and parents are often lost between the different possible ways of identifying, carrying out, transmitting, or getting feedback on pedagogical activities [32, 33]. To overcome the complexity of certain operations, a redesign of the VLE information architecture could be carried out based on the user path design method to identify ways to better articulate services (e.g., document management, notification, communication, activity production, and control/verification), to streamline their access in workspaces by functionality and also to optimise certain processing (synchronisation of resources in document spaces, type of notification/alert oriented according to activity).

The third strategy for redesign is to better identify and develop self-training means, especially in facilitation forms of training. Looking at teachers' overall strategies (Fig. 2

and 3), self-training occurs through the search for documentation resources, then through collaboration within the institution and, to a lesser extent, outside the institution. The VLE's only means of self-training are communication with peers (messaging) and the exchanging of activity models (the library service opened in early March 2020). This service seems extremely promising but needs to be redesigned to also include other resources such as training resources or links to external resources. Furthermore, it would be relevant to open the VLE to academic actors in charge of teacher's training, such as referent teachers or inspectors in charge of the digital education mission, in order to disseminate information related to the training, facilitation and innovation activities of this community.

6 Conclusion and Prospects for Fostering VLE Use

The pedagogical continuity episode experienced during Spring 2020 was an opportunity to address digital technology integration into French teachers' pedagogical practices. A study conducted among VLE One and Neo users revealed that teachers who intensified their practices were already familiar with the following tasks: transmission and communication with the VLE, design and self-training with others tools. Facilitation practices are less developed, but the imperative need to keep in touch with the students led teachers to incorporate more active, collaborative, and engaging learning forms. By exploring how teachers integrate technologies in their practices, we have identified two different logics: (1) diversifying communication channels and working ways with students, and (2) improving self-efficiency in resources and activities design through self-training. VLE seems easier to integrate into teachers' practices than other digital tools. It holds a privileged place due to its status as a shared work environment with students and parents, but it lacks resources to support teachers' professional development using digital technology. We propose ways for VLE redesign and evolution: personalising, rationalisation of the user path, and self-training services. These changes will allow better technology integration in teachers' practices, where parents' and students' contexts are favourable.

Acknowledgments. This research was supported by the French "FUI AAP21".

References

1. Gouëdard, P., Pont, B., Viennet, R.: Education responses to COVID-19: implementing a way forward. OECD Education Working Papers (2020)
2. Bruillard, E.: Le déploiement des ENT dans l'enseignement secondaire: entre acteurs multiples, dénis et illusions. Rev. Fr. Pédagogie **177**, 101–130 (2011)
3. Voulgre, E.: Espace numérique de travail en collège. Distances Savoirs **8**, 585–600 (2010)
4. Poyet, F., Genevois, S.: Vers un modèle compréhensif de la généralisation des usages des ENT dans l'enseignement secondaire. Rev. Fr. Pédagogie **181**, 83–98 (2012). https://doi.org/10.4000/rfp.3927
5. Schneewele, M.: Représentation sociale d'un ENT dans l'enseignement secondaire: une étude pour comprendre et analyser les usages. Carrefours Educ **37**, 211–226 (2014)

6. Trestini, M.: Modeling of Next Generation Digital Learning Environments: Complex Systems Theory. Wiley, New Jersey (2018)
7. Rashid, A.H.A., Shukor, N.A., Tasir, Z., Na, K.S.: Teachers' perceptions and readiness toward the implementation of virtual learning environment. Int. J. Eval. Res. Educ. **10**, 209–214 (2021)
8. Hamnett, C., Butler, T.: Distance, education and inequality. Comp. Educ. **49**, 317–330 (2013)
9. Félix, C., Filippi, P.-A., Martin, P., Gebeil, S.: École et famille en temps de confinement. Et après? (2020). https://www.cahiers-pedagogiques.com/ecole-et-famille-en-temps-de-confinement-et-apres/
10. Pace, C., Pettit, S., Barker, K.: Best practices in middle level quaranteaching: strategies, tips and resources amidst COVID-19. Becoming **31** (2020)
11. Ramli, N., Saleh, S.: FrogVLE application in science teaching in secondary schools in North Malaysia: teachers' perspective. Educ. Sci. **9**, 262 (2019)
12. Serrano, I., Sahagún, H.: Una experiencia con Entornos Virtuales de Aprendizaje en Enseñanza Secundaria Obligatoria. Model. Sci. Educ. Learn. **10**, 19–35 (2017)
13. Kliziene, I., Taujanskiene, G., Augustiniene, A., Simonaitienė, B., Cibulskas, G.: The impact of the virtual learning platform EDUKA on the academic performance of primary school children. Sustainability **13**, 2268 (2021)
14. Johannesen, M.: The role of virtual learning environments in a primary school context: an analysis of inscription of assessment practices. Br. J. Educ. Technol. **44**, 302–313 (2013)
15. MENSR: Synthèse de l'Enquête PROFETIC 2016 auprès de 5 000 enseignants du 2nd degré (2016)
16. Jalal, G., Lachand, V., Tabard, A., Michel, C.: How teachers prepare for the unexpected bright spots and breakdowns in enacting pedagogical plans in class. In: Pammer-Schindler, V., Pérez-Sanagustín, M., Drachsler, H., Elferink, R., Scheffel, M. (eds.) EC-TEL 2018. LNCS, vol. 11082, pp. 59–73. Springer, Cham (2018). https://doi.org/10.1007/978-3-319-98572-5_5
17. European Commission. Directorate General for Communications Networks, Content and Technology, Deloitte, Ipsos MORI: 2nd survey of schools: ICT in education: objective 1: benchmark progress in ICT in schools, final report. Publications Office, LU (2019)
18. MENJS: EVALuENT Synthèse globale. Ministère de l'Éducation nationale, de l'Enseignement supérieur et de la Recherche (2018)
19. Tække, J., Laursen, P.F., Cuban, L.: The Corona crisis has been a revelation for schools – but not a revolution (2020). https://arts.au.dk/aktuelt/nyheder/nyhed/artikel/the-corona-crisis-has-been-a-revelation-for-schools-but-not-a-revolution-1/
20. Awang, H., Aji, Z.M., Yaakob, M.F.M., Osman, W.R.S., Mukminin, A., Habibi, A.: Teachers' intention to continue using virtual learning environment (VLE): Malaysian context. J. Sci. Educ. Technol. **8**, 439–452 (2018)
21. Pacurar, E., Abbas, N.: Analysis of French secondary school teachers' intention to integrate digital work environments into their teaching practices. Educ. Inf. Technol. **20**(3), 537–557 (2015). https://doi.org/10.1007/s10639-013-9301-9
22. Codreanu, E., Michel, C., Bobillier-Chaumon, M.E., Vigneau, O.: Assessing the adoption of virtual learning environments in primary schools: an activity oriented study of teacher's acceptance. In: Costagliola, G., Uhomoibhi, J., Zvacek, S., McLaren, B. (eds.) Computers Supported Education. CSEDU 2016. CCIS, vol. 739, pp. 513–531. Springer, Cham (2017). https://doi.org/10.1007/978-3-319-63184-4_27
23. McCulloch, A.W., Hollebrands, K., Lee, H., Harrison, T., Mutlu, A.: Factors that influence secondary mathematics teachers' integration of technology in mathematics lessons. Comput. Educ. **123**, 26–40 (2018)
24. Finstad, K.: The usability metric for user experience. Interact. Comput. **22**, 323–327 (2010)
25. Nelson, M.J., Voithofer, R., Cheng, S.-L.: Mediating factors that influence the technology integration practices of teacher educators. Comput. Educ. **128**, 330–344 (2019)

26. Dogan, S., Dogan, N.A., Celik, I.: Teachers' skills to integrate technology in education: two path models explaining instructional and application software use. Educ. Inf. Technol. **26**, 1311–1332 (2021). https://doi.org/10.1007/s10639-020-10310-4
27. Mishra, P., Koehler, M.J.: Technological pedagogical content knowledge: a framework for teacher knowledge. Teach. Coll. Rec. **108**, 1017–1054 (2006)
28. Gamage, S.N., Tanwar, T.: Factors affecting teachers' use of ICTs in the classroom: a systematic review of the literature. Inf. Technol. **14**, 11 (2018)
29. DeLone, W., McLean, E.: The DeLone and McLean Model of information system success: a ten-year update. J. Manag. Inf. Syst. **19**, 9–30 (2003)
30. Kozdras, D., Welsh, J.: Enter the matrix: a pedagogy for infusing technology. In: Society for Information Technology & Teacher Education International Conference, pp. 536–541. AACE, Waynesville (2018)
31. Michel, C., Pierrot, L.: Stratégies pour de nouvelles formes d'appropriation des ENT. Impact de l'école à la maison dans le développement des usages et pratiques numériques des enseignants. In: Actes de la 10e Conférence EIAH'21, Fribourg, pp. 128–139 (2021)
32. Blume, C.: German teachers' digital habitus and their pandemic pedagogy. Postdigit. Sci. Educ. **2**, 879–905 (2020)
33. Genevois, S., Lefer-Sauvage, G., Wallian, N.: Questionnaire d'enquête auprès des enseignants - Confinement et continuité pédagogique. Research report, ICARE (2020)

First-Year University Students in Distance Learning: Motivations and Early Experiences

Maria Aristeidou(✉)

Institute of Educational Technology, The Open University, Milton Keynes MK7 6AA, UK
Maria.Aristeidou@open.ac.uk

Abstract. Acquiring new learning and assessment styles, maintaining old and creating new relationships, and learning how to function as independent adults are some of the stressors that first-year university students face. Yet, we know little about the transition of students from school/college to distance learning higher education. This study drew from survey responses of 377 first-year students, aged 18–19, at The Open University, UK. This study aimed to explore the motivations of students who join distance learning universities and to examine their early experiences. Findings showed that the main motivations for joining distance learning higher education include flexible study alongside other commitments, earning money alongside their studies, and demonstrating self-motivation. Motivations for joining were significantly different among various student groups. Further, the decision of 22% of the respondents to study via distance learning was impacted by the Covid-19 pandemic. 'Course structure' was identified as the factor that supported them the most with their transition from school/college to a distance learning university, while 'interactions with students' was identified as the main area of suggested improvement. This study has gone some way towards enhancing our understanding of the expectations and needs of first-year distance learning students. The present findings have important implications for designing suitable transition and support networks in the distance and online learning environments.

Keywords: Distance learning · Online learning · Higher education · Transition · First-year students · Motivations · Student support · Student retention

1 Introduction

The transition from school/college to the university can cause concerns for many students. Acquiring new learning and assessment styles, maintaining old and creating new relationships, and learning how to function as independent adults are some of the stressors that first-year university students face [1]. Beyond causing significant stress, the reality of university life can also lead to poor academic performance and increased dropout rates, if these issues are not successfully addressed [2]. To tackle the unpreparedness and unrealistic perceptions of first-year students, a number of studies have been conducted on students' motivations (and expectations) for joining higher education, and on their transition experiences.

Kahu, Nelson and Picton [3] highlight the importance of understanding the students' interests and goals to trigger situational interest and student engagement, and to further prevent students from dropping out of university. To that end, a number of studies investigated the motivations of students for joining higher education. For instance, Lowe and Cook [4] in their research with 691 first-year students found that most students attended university because they wanted to enhance their academic and vocational prospects, and only a few because of reactive decisions (parental pressure and social norms); female, social and health science students were less likely to make reactive decisions. Similarly, a more recent study with 77 participants, conducted by Hassel and Ridout [2], reports that the majority of first-year students attended university with the expectation to receive help in making decisions about their careers and starting those careers.

Regarding anticipated transition struggles, Lowe and Cook [4] note that students find themselves unprepared for the more 'relaxed' form of teaching at university, while Hassel and Ridout [2] explain that about half of the students battle with workload and the fast pace of teaching and learning. These difficulties are suggested to appear due to the transition from a relatively small-scale and supportive environment of school/college to a much larger and faceless university environment [5]. However, supporting students in their transition can be challenging, since it relates to many factors, such as the learners' profile, their context of prior learning, and the higher education provision in terms of programmes, disciplines and flexibility [6]. Further to identifying factors that affect students' transition, Whittaker [6] suggests that student retention and progression could be achieved by involving a coordinated institutional strategic approach, providing university pre-entry support and longitudinal approach to induction, promoting social integration and progressive skills development, embedding support in learning, developing a sense of belonging, and allowing student control and choice.

In light of the Covid-19 disruption around the globe, distance learning has recently become a critical issue in higher education. However, the transition of students from school/college into distance learning higher education has not yet been widely researched. Previous work emphasised the extra difficulties that remote students experience because of their social transition [4], and suggested guidelines for designing spaces to provide support to first-year distance learning students. For instance, Winnard and Eilliot [7] stress the importance of induction in minimising the feelings of isolation, navigating the online learning environment, familiarising themselves with university regulations and concepts, meeting tutors and support staff, and initiating a working relationship with their tutors. Further to the induction, Foley and Marr [8] propose the creation of extracurricular, collaborative, online spaces that allow distance learning students to learn from each other, guided by an academic leader. Likewise, Forrester and Parkinson [9] suggest developing social cohesion with the group and facilitating a sense of belonging, as well as running a pre-course diagnosis of students' IT skills.

The aim of this study is to extend and shed new light on current knowledge of first-year student transition from school/college to distance learning higher education in online settings. For this purpose, we explored the motivations and early experiences of first-year students at The Open University (OU), an institution with a long tradition of distance learning in the UK. The OU supports an open entry system, and its learning model includes the delivery of courses via virtual learning environments, online tutorials and small tutor group forums. Student performance is evaluated via tutor or computer-marked summative or formative assessments. Since students at the OU are typically older than those of campus-based universities, in this study we only focused on the portion of first-year students that have recently finished school (aged 18–19). The reason for this is that age has been shown to have a bearing on the nature of issues experienced during the transition, with younger students found to be less academically oriented [10] and less focused [11] than older students. To understand the motivations and early experiences of younger students at the OU we explored the following research questions (RQs):

1. What motivates students, aged 18–19, to join distance learning higher education?
2. Are there any significant differences among student groups (gender, race, disability, faculty, previous qualifications) in their motivations for joining distance learning?
3. What are the areas that support and facilitate the transition of first-year distance learning students?
4. What are the areas that need improvement in order to better support the transition of first-year distance learning students?

Findings from our study contribute to improving the learning design of activities in technology-enhanced learning (TEL), especially for newcomers in higher education institutions. Current research on learning design highlights its importance as a driver for learning and focuses on conceptualising learning design principles (e.g. [12]) and the outcomes of the design process via student logs and experiences of a particular course (e.g., [13]). However, there is little work around the early and overall student experience and transition from the face-to-face school/college environment to a TEL environment. The learning experiences of university students, who have recently transitioned from school/college to distance learning higher education, can be used to guide deliberate choices in relation to the pedagogy and technology used for the delivery of a course. These choices may include the structure and sequence of learning activities, content, pedagogy, assessment type and frequency, and mainly the learning technologies used to better support the overall learning experience.

2 Methods

For the current study, we recruited students, aged 18–19 years old, who joined the university in October 2020, to take part in an online survey. Ethical approval was obtained from the author's university ethics committee, and participation in the survey was voluntary. Prior to completing the survey, the respondents were provided with an online information sheet and a consent form. The survey was initially piloted with four students, aged 19, who were members of the OU student association, and minor changes took place. The survey was then administered to a random university-wide sample of students. The survey ran between 2–28 February 2021 and received 377 responses. The dataset was anonymised on the 1st of March 2021, prior to initiating the process of data analysis.

2.1 Data Collection

Collected data included student responses in a 5-item Likert scale, ranging from 1 (strongly disagree) to 5 (strongly agree), with an extra 'not applicable' (N/A) option, exploring motivations for joining a distance learning university (RQ1). The set of statements were developed based on student open-ended responses to previous internal studies on their motivations. The selection of statements drew from the Self-Determination Theory (STD) [14], by which people choose to engage in activities because they are inherently interesting or enjoyable (intrinsic motivation) or because they will lead to separable outcomes (extrinsic motivation). For example, potential motivations for joining distance learning higher education at the OU included enjoying studying via online learning (intrinsic motivation), but also saving money on living expenses (extrinsic motivation). The final list of motivation statements was reviewed and agreed upon with the university's strategy office. Moreover, a closed-ended question gathered information as to whether the Covid-19 pandemic has impacted their decision for joining.

In order to identify any differences in motivations for joining distance learning among student groups (RQ2), student demographics and study information were retrieved from the university's database. Table 1 presents the demographics and study information for all the 377 survey respondents.

Table 1. Demographics and study information of survey respondents.

Demographics	Frequency	Study information	Frequency
Gender		Faculty	
Female	304 (80.6%)	STEM	92 (24.4%)
Male	73 (19.4%)	WELS	74 (19.6%)
		FASS	145 (38.5%)
BAME		FBL	54 (14.3%)
Yes	44 (11.7%)	Entry level	12 (3.2%)
No	324 (85.9%)		
No records	9 (2.4%)	PEQ	
		No formal qualification	2 (0.5%)
Declared disability		Less than A-levels	100 (26.5%)
Yes	73 (19.4%)	A-levels or equivalent	261 (69.2%)
No	304 (80.6%)	HE Qualification	14 (3.7%)

These included gender; race summarised in Black, Asian and minority ethnic (BAME) and non-BAME students; declared disability; faculty; and previous qualifications (PEQ), such as A-levels (the traditional subject-based qualifications that are offered by schools and colleges in the UK and can lead to university or further studies). Faculty included Social Sciences and Humanities (FASS); Science, Technology, Engineering and Maths (STEM); education, languages, health and sport studies (WELS); business and law (FBL). Two further open-ended questions invited students to report their positive transition and support experiences (RQ3), and to suggest areas of improvement (RQ4).

2.2 Data Analysis

In the first phase of analysis, a visualisation of the motivation Likert scale was used to answer what motivated students to join distance learning education (RQ1). Then, to determine how gender, race, disability, faculty and PEQ relate to particular motivations (RQ2), chi-square tests were performed. For the tests, dichotomous variables were used for each motivation statement, in which option 1 included all the 'agree' and 'strongly agree' responses to the statement and 0 all the 'disagree' and 'strongly disagree'. N/A and 'neither agree nor disagree' were excluded from the chi-square test analysis. An alpha level of .05 was used for all the analysis. Groups with chi-square expected frequencies less than five were excluded from the analysis (i.e., PEQ = No formal qualification, PEQ = HE Qualification, Faculty = Entry level, BAME = No records).

In the second phase and to answer RQ3 and RQ4, content analysis was used for making valid inferences from participants' open-ended responses focusing on the meaning in context [15]. The author went through the comments ascribing descriptive codes to each student comment. The codes represented areas of positive experience (RQ3) and areas of suggested improvement (RQ4). By coding the data in this way, early frequencies and patterns were identified, leading to the construction of exclusive categories (themes). The codes and themes were reviewed and agreed upon with the university's strategy office. Once all the data had been coded and categorised into themes, the frequency of each code and each theme was calculated, and the latter is presented in this study.

3 Results

3.1 Motivations to Join Distance Learning Higher Education (RQ1)

The following graph (Fig. 1) presents the set of motivations for joining the OU that we shared with the survey respondents. The motivations are visualised in ascending order of agreement and highlighted findings are also described in mean (M) and standard deviation (SD), with scores ranging from 1 (strongly disagree) to 5 (strongly agree).

The most popular motivation for joining the OU, selected by 94% of the survey respondents, was 'I can study flexibly alongside other commitments' ($M = 4.55$, $SD = 0.68$). Other motivations selected by at least 4 out of 5 students were 'I can earn money by having a job alongside study' (83% of students, $M = 4.57$, $SD = 0.87$) and 'I can demonstrate my self-motivation by studying via online/distance learning' (81% of students, $M = 4.20$, $SD = 0.91$). The least popular motivation was 'I don't want to/can't move away from my part-time job' selected by 23% of the students, and including a 25% N/A response ($M = 3.55$, $SD = 1.82$). Only around 1 in 3 agreed that they had chosen the OU because they did not have the entry requirements for a selective university ($M = 2.73$, $SD = 1.76$). The latter was also the motivation that scored the lowest.

Further, of the study population, 22% reported that the Covid-19 pandemic impacted their decision on enrolling with a distance learning university.

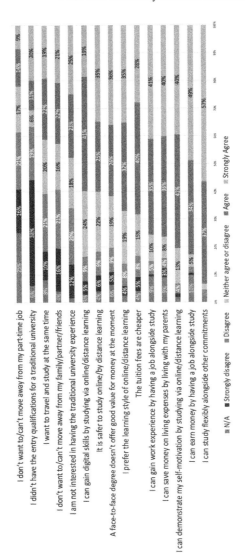

Fig. 1. Motivations for joining distance learning higher education, presented in ascending order of agreement with each statement.

3.2 Motivations and Student Groups (RQ2)

Our analyses showed that there were significant associations between motivation and:

- Gender: Female were more likely than males to select that 'it is safer to study online/by distance learning' ($X^2[1, N = 377] = 5.87, p = 0.015$) and 'I can gain digital skills by studying via online/distance learning' ($X^2[1, N = 377] = 6.36, p = 0.012$).
- Race: BAME students were more likely than non-BAME students to select 'I can earn money by having a job alongside study' ($X^2[1, N = 368] = 4.12, p = 0.04$) and 'I

can gain work experience by having a job alongside study' ($X^2[1, N = 368] = 4.61$, $p = 0.03$).
- Disability: Students without a declared disability were more likely than those with a declared disability to select that 'I prefer the style of online/distance learning' ($X^2[1, N = 377] = 8.49, p < 0.01$), 'I can demonstrate my self-motivation by studying via online/distance learning' ($X^2[1, N = 377] = 5.67, p = 0.02$), 'I don't want to/can't move away from my part-time job' ($X^2[1, N = 377] = 7.90, p < 0.01$).
- Faculty: Students in WELS were more likely than students in other faculties to select that 'it is safer to study online/by distance learning' ($X^2[4, N = 377] = 10.52, p = 0.03$), 'I prefer the style of online/distance learning' ($X^2[4, N = 377] = 10.01, p = 0.04$), 'I can gain digital skills by studying via online/distance learning' ($X^2[4, N = 377] = 17.03, p < 0.01$) and 'I can demonstrate my self-motivation by studying via online/distance learning' ($X^2[4, N = 377] = 9.71, p = 0.046$).
- Previous qualifications: Students with A-levels or equivalent were more likely than students with less than A-levels to select 'I don't want to/can't move away from part-time job' ($X^2[1, N = 361] = 4.69, p = 0.03$); and students with less than A-levels were more likely than those with A-levels or equivalent to select 'I can save on living expenses by living with my parents' ($X^2[1, N = 361] = 4.22, p = 0.04$).

3.3 Positive Experiences (RQ3)

The area with the largest proportion of positive mentions (32%) was 'course structure', followed by 'support' (21%), 'course content' (19%), 'induction' (13%), 'assessment' (8%), and 'interactions' (7%).

Course Structure. This theme included comments reporting the liking of students in the material being presented in weeks/blocks, the ability to self-regulate and study flexibly in terms of time (including getting ahead) the clear expectations with checkboxes and deadlines, the gradation of difficulty, and the easy-to-use website.

"I like the fact it is all online and structured into weeks (week 1, 2, 3) so this allows me to schedule one week's worth of work around my work schedule and days off" (female, mixed, no disability, HE qualification, FASS).

Support. Support included mentions of students' supportive tutors, the availability of plentiful and accessible resources, the overall support by the university (including mental health support and student buddies) and the frequent communication from the university services.

"Tutor support has been really good, and the support given to independently study as best you can, has been brilliant" (female, white, disability declared, less than A-levels, FASS).

Course Content. Students reported positive areas with regards to the course content, such as a paced start to the course, optional and recorded tutorials with many time options, easy to understand and interesting content in multiple formats, a balanced course workload, access to study skills sections, and overlapping content with A-levels.

"My course had only a few activities in the first weeks, so it wasn't overwhelming" (male, white, no disability, less than A-levels, WELS).

Induction. Induction activities that students found very useful for their transition from school/college to the university included induction tutorials, freshers' events, list with contacts, study planning advice, introduction forums, and an OpenLearn (https://www.open.edu/openlearn/) course explaining what it's like to study at a distance.

"The introductory week was very helpful as there were introductory videos on how to navigate the course websites and how to use Adobe Connect (for tutorials)" (female, white, no disability, A-levels or equivalent, FBL).

Assessment. The assessment theme included students' positive comments on good instructions to assignments and exams, detailed feedback on results, access to assessment templates and booklets so that they have an idea of how the exam will be like or what they are expected to write in an assignment, deadline extensions, self-assessment quizzes, assignments to be a good fit to the course content, regular assessment via assignments, the lack of stressful competition, and the 'pilot' assignments at the beginning of the course.

"The guidance for the assignments is very helpful in outlining exactly what is expected" (female, white, no disability, A-levels or equivalent, FASS).

Interactions. In regard to opportunities to interact with others, students found beneficial the access to discussion forums and university-organised events, frequent communication with their tutor, being a part of a small tutor group, joining the Student Hub Live series of events, and communicating via the OU community (the university's central hub for services and events).

"The forums help you talk to a range of people who are going through the same thing" (female, white, no disability, A-levels or equivalent, STEM).

3.4 Areas of Suggested Improvement (RQ4)

The largest proportion of the student comments (33%) mentioned 'interactions with other students' as the area that needs the most improvements. This area was followed by suggestions to improve aspects in relation to 'tutor support and communication' (18%), 'assessment' (16%), 'induction and support' (13%), 'tutorials' (10%), 'course content and structure' (5%), and 'younger student-focused issues' (5%).

Interactions with Other Students. This theme included students' comments in relation to improving interactions with other students. Students suggested that the university could provide more organised meetups and face-to-face meetings, and to make the events more visible to students. Moreover, they proposed that meetings could be organised to invite students of the same age, interest or location. Further to the meetups, students recommended some improvements to the forum's structure, and the addition of features that will allow more course interaction, as well as the use of WhatsApp groups for more direct communication.

"I find it difficult to put myself out there to meet fellow students, I'd like it if resources were available to help us meet other students and make friendships" (female, black, no disability, A-levels or equivalent, WELS).

Tutor Support and Communication. Students expressed their need for more personalised support and more frequent communication with their tutors. Further, they suggested that tutors should set up more check-ins with their students.

"More individual support from tutors instead of asking the students to always reach out to them, I think as a younger student it's intimidating to do that, especially if I have a problem because there's not already a pre-existing relationship there" (female, white, no disability, A-levels or equivalent, FASS).

Assessment. Students' suggestions in relation to improving assessment included the following: supplementing them with more practice questions and assignment examples, providing them with more explicit instructions and detailed feedback, allowing more time between assignments, and allowing them access to more detailed marking criteria.

"Examples of how the university would like assignments to look would be helpful" (male, white, no disability, A-levels or equivalent, FASS).

Induction and Support. This theme comprised induction and support during the first year of their studies, with mentions of personalised inductions by their tutors and organised student introductions, more information about how tutorials work, and more course introduction materials. Furthermore, they suggested being provided with more opportunities for training for academic writing and time management, and to have better signposting for resources and expectations. Finally, students suggested some more financially and administrative oriented improvements, such as having access to funding aid, career advice and support for organising full-time studies.

"Explaining some of the more basic skills when it comes to things like essay writing - we're told what they don't want or what we have done wrong but not how to improve" (female, white, no disability, less than A-levels, FASS).

Tutorials. Tutorials was one of the suggested areas of improvements with students proposing the provision of more tutorials, including compulsory and questions and answer (Q&A) tutorials, longer or with more time options tutorials. Further to the existing tutorials, students suggested having assisted hours with tutors, and access to tutorials of other courses that they are not currently enrolled in.

"Maybe some more online lectures with question-and-answer sections" (female, white, no disability, A-levels or equivalent, STEM).

Course Content and Structure. Mentions in relation to the course content and structure involved having more visual content and variety, and smaller blocks of learning.

"More range of learning methods e.g. presentations, videos" (female, Asian, no disability, A-levels or equivalent, WELS).

Younger Students Focused. Several student comments were focusing on aspects related to the age group of our study population (i.e., 18–19-year-olds). Our participants suggested the creation of social media groups, forum groups, skill courses and resources that are particular to students of this age. In addition, they suggested that the course material could be more relevant to younger students.

"The university could include a more younger student-friendly social media platform or chat room. The forums and tutorials could be tailored more towards younger people (every time I go on, it's adults talking about their children etc.). It's also obvious that the courses and 'skills' (such as how to Google, open a new tab, read Wikipedia entries etc.) are targeted towards the older generation and people with more life experience" (female, white, disability declared, A-levels or equivalent, FASS).

4 Discussion

While students have a mix of motivations for choosing the OU, the survey suggests that many in the study cohort are making a relatively 'active' choice to study by distance learning, rather than only choosing it due to open entry, which may have been the case for a high proportion of younger students in the past. Hence, more than two-thirds of the survey respondents joined distance learning higher education because of the flexibility it allows, financial reasons, and the chance to gain work experience in parallel to their studies. Interestingly, the Covid-19 pandemic was an important factor for 22% of the survey respondents in their decision to join distance learning, with more than half of the survey population reporting that studying by distance learning is safer and that a face-to-face degree doesn't offer good value for money at the moment. The value of understanding why students joined distance education lies in the evidence-based creation of activities and policies that, as Kahu, Nelson and Picton [3] suggest, aim to trigger students' interest and engagement. Such actions may involve a longer-term strategy to significantly and actively increase younger students in distance learning universities, as well as to form the basis for recruiting students in distance learning programmes located at campus-based universities during or post-pandemic.

Yet, similarly to Lowe and Cook's [4] research in campus-based universities, motivations for joining distance learning were slightly different for some student groups. Female students were more interested in the safety and digital skills that distance learning offers; BAME students selected motivations related to finances and work; Disabled students were less interested in the learning style, demonstrating self-motivation and moving away from their jobs; Students in WELS selected motivations in relation to the learning style, safety and self-development. Finally, both students with A-levels or equivalent and with less than A-levels were motivated by not changing their location, the former because of their job's location and the latter because of living expenses. Insights into the expectations and drivers of each group could possibly support decision-makers in the recruitment and onboarding of students coming from specific backgrounds.

The areas that supported students with their transition from school/college into university were mainly related to the course structure, university support, course content, induction, assessment and interactions. In particular, students greatly appreciated the weeks/blocks format that material was presented, which help them to self-regulate their studies. Other important aspects involved having frequent communication with their tutors and university; a slow start to the course and many tutorial options; many induction activities and resources; detailed instruction, examples and feedback for their assignments; and opportunities to communicate with their tutor and others. These findings could form practical solutions to students' battles with the workload, fast pace, and issues with self-regulation reported in previous research on anticipated transition struggles of first-year campus-based students (e.g., [2, 4]). More importantly, these findings could eventually serve as a stepping stone for the development or alteration of online and distance learning programmes.

The areas that students thought need improvement to better support their transition tended to be a mirror image of the areas commented on positively. These areas mainly related to interactions with other students, and to a smaller extent, to tutor support and communication, assessment, induction and support, tutorials, course content and structure, and issues related to younger students. Specifically, students expressed their need for more opportunities for interaction with other students for learning and socialising, supporting previous findings in the literature stressing the importance of collaborative spaces for interaction among students in distance learning [8]. Other popular suggestions included more personalised communication with their tutors, more assignment examples, more tutorial options, more visual content, and the creation of social media groups and skills courses that are particular to younger students. The latter can be attributed to the reduced domestic commitments, and therefore the more available time that younger students have, compared to older students [11], as well as the different skill set that they may have. Overall, students' suggestions of areas that need improvement have several implications for research into embedding these aspects into distance learning in order to support student retention and success.

Insights from our study corroborate previous research [16] that highlights the need for learning design in TEL to emphasise not only on cognition activities but also focus on the social elements of learning. Our findings have also revealed the need of first-year students to organised and structured socialising with their tutors and fellow students for study and other purposes. Finally, our study provides some recommendations for good practice for academic and practitioners involved in the learning design of first-year courses. This guidance includes the importance of structuring the material in blocks/weeks to reinforce self-regulation and independent learning, and the positive effects of securing a slow start to the course and providing many tutorial options.

This exploratory study has examined the motivations and early experiences of students studying in one distance learning university. Although the OU welcomes a diverse group of students from different locations, backgrounds and disciplines, the outcomes should be discussed within the context of this study and the OU's learning and support models, and to be interpreted with caution. Future work should concentrate on how these early experiences of students in distance learning higher education associate with academic retention, and whether changes to the learning design of first-year courses could improve their transition experience.

5 Conclusions

This study explored the motivations of 377 first-year students in joining distance learning higher education, and their early experiences. The evidence from this study suggests that flexibility and finances are the main drivers for students to join distance learning education, with the Covid-19 disruption playing an important role in their decision. However, motivations for joining distance learning were significantly different among various student groups. Furthermore, considerable insight has been gained with regard to factors that supported students the most with their transition, such as the course structure, and areas that need improvement, such as student interactions.

Our findings add to a growing body of literature on the transition of first-year students from school/college into university. Further, this study provides an agenda for universities and policymakers to develop or improve ways that students or particular groups of students are recruited to distance learning universities and distance learning programmes in campus-based universities. Findings in this study also highlight areas that programme leaders, learning designers, and tutors in distance learning could incorporate into or improve in their programme's design and teaching.

Acknowledgements. I would like to thank the 377 first-year OU students who took part in the 'younger students' survey, and the OU strategy and student offices who contributed their insights and experiences to the instrument development and data analysis.

References

1. Parker, J.D.A., Summerfeldt, L.J., Hogan, M.J., Majeski, S.A.: Emotional intelligence and academic success: examining the transition from high school to university. Personality Individ. Differ. **36**, 163–172 (2004). https://doi.org/10.1016/S0191-8869(03)00076-X
2. Hassel, S., Ridout, N.: An investigation of first-year students' and lecturers' expectations of university education. Front. Psychol. **8**, 2218 (2018). https://doi.org/10.3389/fpsyg.2017.02218
3. Kahu, E., Nelson, K., Picton, C.: Student interest as a key driver of engagement for first year students. Stud. Success **8**, 55–66 (2017). https://doi.org/10.5204/ssj.v8i2.379
4. Lowe, H., Cook, A.: Mind the Gap: Are students prepared for higher education? J. Furth. High. Educ. **27**, 53–76 (2003). https://doi.org/10.1080/03098770305629
5. Ingram, R., Gallacher, J.: Making the Transition from College to University, Glasgow (2013)
6. Whittaker, R.: The first year experience: transition to and during the first year. QAA Scotland, Glasgow (2008)
7. Winnard, Y., Elliott, V.: The freshers' week experience in a VLE: can it be achieved? - ARRO - Anglia Ruskin Research Online. Eur. J. Open, Distance E-Learn. **2**, 8 p. (2012). Article No. 2
8. Foley, K., Marr, L.: Scaffolding extracurricular online events to support distance learning university students. J. Interact. Media Educ. **1**, 17 (2019). https://doi.org/10.5334/jime.525
9. Forrester, G., Parkinson, G.: "Mind the gap": students; expectations and perceptions of induction to distance learning in higher education. In: British Educational Research Association Annual Conference, 16–18 September. University of Manchester (2004)
10. Power, C., Robertson, F., Baker, M.: Success in higher education (1987)
11. Ozga, J., Sukhnandan, L.: Undergraduate non-completion: developing an explanatory model. High. Educ. Q. **52**, 316–333 (1998). https://doi.org/10.1111/1468-2273.00100
12. Hernández-Leo, D., Moreno, P., Chacón, J., Blat, J.: LdShake support for team based learning design. Comput. Hum. Behav. **37**, 402–412 (2014). https://doi.org/10.1016/j.chb.2012.05.029
13. Rienties, B., Toetenel, L.: The impact of learning design on student behaviour, satisfaction and performance: a cross-institutional comparison across 151 modules. Comput. Hum. Behav. **60**, 333–341 (2016). https://doi.org/10.1016/j.chb.2016.02.074
14. Ryan, R.M., Deci, E.L.: Self-determination theory and the facilitation of intrinsic motivation, social development, and well-being. Am. Psychol. **55**, 68–78 (2000)
15. Krippendorff, K.: Content Analysis: An Introduction to Its Methodology. SAGE Publications Inc., Thousand Oaks (2018)
16. Ferguson, R., Shum, S.B.: Social learning analytics: five approaches. In: ACM International Conference Proceeding Series, pp. 23–33 (2012). https://doi.org/10.1145/2330601.2330616

The Dire Cost of Early Disengagement: A Four-Year Learning Analytics Study over a Full Program

Mohammed Saqr[1,2](✉) and Sonsoles López-Pernas[3,2]

[1] KTH Royal Institute of Technology, Stockholm, Sweden
mmas3@kth.se
[2] University of Eastern Finland, Joensuu, Finland
[3] Universidad Politécnica de Madrid, Madrid, Spain

Abstract. Research on online engagement is abundant. However, most of the available studies have focused on a single course. Therefore, little is known about how students' online engagement evolves over time. Previous research in face-to-face settings has shown that early disengagement has negative consequences on students' academic achievement and graduation rates. This study examines the longitudinal trajectory of students' online engagement throughout a complete college degree. The study followed 99 students over 4 years of college education including all their course data (15 courses and 1383 course enrollments). Students' engagement states for each course enrollment were identified through Latent Class Analysis (LCA). Students who were not engaged at least one course in the first term was labeled as "Early Disengagement", whereas the remaining students were labeled as "Early Engagement". The two groups of students were analyzed using sequence pattern mining methods. The stability (persistence of the engagement state), transition (ascending to a higher engagement state or descending to a lower state), and typology of each group trajectory of engagement are described in this study. Our results show that early disengagement is linked to higher rates of dropout, lower scores, and lower graduation rates whereas early engagement is relatively stable. Our findings indicate that it is critical to proactively address early disengagement during a program, watch the alarming signs such as presence of disengagement during the first courses, declining engagement along the program, or history of frequent disengagement states.

Keywords: Learning analytics · Early disengagement · Trajectories of engagement

1 Introduction

Engagement is concerned with students' participation, efforts and time investment to learn, develop and optimize their learning outcomes [1, 2]. The society aspirations for better education as well as the increasing interests in graduating students have prompted an increasing interest in engagement as a malleable quality that holds the hope for better education [3]. Research has consistently confirmed a positive link between engagement and academic achievement and disengagement has been linked to worse outcomes, dropout and behavioral problems [4].

Engagement has several temporal dimensions, e.g., engagement with a learning task, engagement within a course, or engagement through a full program [5]. Longitudinal engagement –the subject of this study– seems to be the least studied, as collecting data for the same students over the years during a complete undergraduate study is not a trivial task and requires exhaustive work over several years [6]. The timeline of longitudinal engagement is often referred to as engagement trajectory, while a trajectory is a sequence of engagement states that unfold over time [6]. Research on engagement trajectories of face-to-face education has shown that engagement has a cross-time correlation pattern, i.e., engagement states are sequentially alike. Therefore, students who are engaged in a course, are more likely to be engaged in the next [6]. Research has also shown that the cross-time correlation varies among subgroups of students (e.g., consistent in engaged students while turbulent in disengaged students) [7].

While research on online engagement is abundant [8], most of the studies have investigated engagement within a course or two [9, 10]. Studies in the higher education context that have studied the longitudinal trajectory of online engagement are almost non-existent. As online learning has become increasingly common and witnessed an exponential growth during the COVID-19 pandemic [11], it has become increasingly important to focus on longitudinal engagement or the lack thereof. Our study addresses this gap, i.e., investigates the longitudinal engagement trajectory throughout a complete university program over four years. Our interest is in how early disengagement or engagement unfolds, and how accurately it predicts the completion of the program.

We split students into two groups: *Early engagement* and *Early disengagement*. We then follow the students along their whole program and study their trajectory of engagement or disengagement, the stability or the lack thereof (transitions between trajectories), and how these trajectories of student engagement predict persistence in the program. Our research questions are:

- **RQ1:** What are the engagement states that students have over a full program and what are the characteristics of such engagement states?
- **RQ2:** What are the differences between the early engaged students and early disengaged students regarding their longitudinal engagement trajectory, transitions between engagement states and stability?
- **RQ3:** What is the relationship between early engagement and students' outcome in terms of graduation (or dropping out) and final grades?

2 Background

The concept of student engagement started to gain mainstream acceptance around the eighties as a means for supporting students' involvement, achievement as well as preventing alienation and dropout [1, 2]. Back then, engagement was defined as "the student's psychological investment in and effort directed toward learning, understanding, or mastering the knowledge, skills, or crafts that academic work is intended to promote" [1].

While agreement on a unified definition of engagement may be far from realizable, there is wide agreement that engagement is a multi-dimensional concept that includes a behavioral dimension (behavior related to learning activities and learning process), an emotional dimension (feelings about school, studies, and peers), and a cognitive dimension (investment in learning and going beyond the required). Such dimensions are dynamically closely interrelated, e.g., positive feelings about school motivate behavioral engagement in school activities, and cognitive engagement [2, 3, 5]. Researchers have demonstrated that all domains of engagement (behavioral, emotional and cognitive) are significant catalysts of academic achievement. Such relationship has been repeatedly confirmed in all levels of education [4, 12, 13].

Engagement has obvious qualities that can be observed, tracked and easily understood by teachers [8, 14, 15]. More importantly, engagement is malleable and therefore, disengaged students are amenable to intervention. Underachievement, and consequently dropout, could be traced back to events which showed obvious "distress signals" of disengagement [15, 16]. Students may show signs of low effort, truancy, declining grades that may lead to failing a course or more. Several other distress signals can be observed, e.g., missing assignments, procrastination or lack of participation, disinterest in school or social activities [2, 3, 5, 17]. Since persistence in the program or school, and consequently graduation, are the ultimate goals of educational institutions, strategies at keeping learners engaged or at prevention of disengagement have gained increasing attention across the years [3, 18].

2.1 Trajectories of Engagement

Research on the trajectories of engagement is inconclusive. Some studies have shown a cross-time correlation between engagement states, in which students who are engaged in a course or an academic year are more likely to remain engaged in the next. However, these cross-time correlations should not be interpreted as an indication that engagement is a fixed trait. In fact, research on the dynamics of engagement offers evidence on the contrary, i.e., that engagement is both malleable and dynamic. Some researchers have reported that engagement declines with time [19], while others claimed that engagement can grow with time under optimal conditions [20]. Such variability has been recently explained by the heterogeneity of students' subgroups, where subgroups of students have a stable trajectory, while others have a declining or troubled trajectories [7, 21]. The previous studies on the trajectories of engagement have all been conducted in face-to-face settings.

Most of the studies on online engagement have looked into a course or two while the longitudinal online engagement remains an uncharted territory especially in higher education settings [22]. Very few exceptions can be mentioned here. Lust et al. investigated students' engagement with an online learning tool in two consecutive offerings of a course [10]. They found that students used different strategies in each iteration of the course. However, the students were different in each iteration. In another recent example, which studied a full MOOC program, the authors grouped students into distinct engagement profiles and followed the changes in such profiles across the program. The three clusters they identified were 1) *consistent*: who are engaged are more likely to remain engaged, 2) *get-it-done*: assessment-oriented but still able to follow up with the program, 3) *disorganized*: who are mostly disengaged. Similar results were reported by [23], who identified three trajectories along a professional development course.

2.2 Learning Analytics and Modeling the Engagement

As online learning environments became increasingly common, along with all types of technology-enhanced learning [24], a wealth of online data has driven interest in learning Analytics (LA) for understanding and supporting learning and teaching. Research in LA has produced valuable insights regarding, e.g., engagement patterns, students' profiles and the relationship between engagement and achievement [9, 25–27]. Within LA, Sequence Pattern Mining (SPM) is among the methods that was established to model the sequential patterns of students learning [17, 28]. SPM accounts for the chronological, time ordered relationships between events [29]. Therefore, the method has been embraced widely by social scientists in modeling life course studies, e.g., the trajectories of careers, marital status or health trajectories [30]. Our study takes advantage of the developments of LA, life course studies, and data-mining methods to model the longitudinal trajectories of engagement.

3 Methods

3.1 Context

The study included a full blended Problem-Based Learning (PBL) higher education program. The learning management system (LMS) is the platform for online collaboration (weekly PBL forum discussions), distribution of lectures, announcements, and interaction with the teachers and peers. The online weekly PBL discussions are mandatory, in which students in small groups discuss a problem scenario that follows the objectives of the course [31, 32]. The courses are similar in educational underpinning (PBL), arranged sequentially (therefore, referred to as blocks). Some practical courses are longitudinal (over the full year) and therefore were excluded as they did not share the same educational underpinning or evaluation method.

3.2 Data Collection

Every student who joined the program in the academic year 2014–2015 was included in the study (n = 99). The logs of the students in the 15 sequential courses (1,383 enrollments) over four years of education (2014–2015, 2015–2016, 2016–2017, 2017–2018) were retrieved from the Moodle LMS. Only learning-related events were collected. We included only students who completed the first term of the college to avoid including students who were dis-interested in the type of program or had early problems moving to the city or any other problems. Seven students were excluded as they early withdrew during the first course and left the program. *Early disengagement* (n = 43) group comprised students who had at least one course with a disengagement state in the first term (first two courses). This definition was adopted since the first course is introduction about the teaching and learning methods of the program, whereas the second course is the first subject matter course. As such, disengagement in either of these courses could be cortical. The remainder (n = 56) of students belong to the group of *Early engagement*.

Online engagement in learning was operationalized following the approach proposed in [8], through collecting logs of "frequency of logins to website; number and frequency of postings, responses, and views ... or other website resources accessed; time spent creating a post; and time spent online." To capture the full breadth of students' activities in the program, three types of indicators were collected: I) indicators representing the **frequencies of engagement** with the course learning resources: a) frequency of access to lectures, links to lectures, or course materials (e.g., videos), b) frequency of forum discussion contribution (posting, updating, or rating), c) frequency of forum reading, and d) frequency of course browsing and thus getting course updates, announcements, and links to resources; II) indicators of **activity level and regularity** of activities: a) number of active days where the student had at least made one click on learning related activities, and b) regularity of course access calculated according to [33]; III) general indicators representing the total **time and effort** of online activities: a) number of unique sessions—a session was considered as a an uninterrupted sequence of online actions (see [33] for details of the computation method)—, and b) the total time spent online accessing learning related activities. Since the data were collected from several courses, the indicators were discretized into equal width bins, so all indicators have a similar measurement scale, are easy to compare, and the outliers are neutralized [34].

3.3 Analysis

To classify students according to their engagement states at the course-level (**RQ1**), Latent Cluster Analysis (LCA) was performed using the LMS indicators (frequencies, activities and time indicators) [35]. LCA offers a robust method for clustering of educational data (see [9] for a review and advantages). To select the optimum number of clusters we relied on best Akaike information criterion (AIC), Bayes information criterion (BIC), as well as the separation of clusters with best effect size [9, 35, 36]. Students were clustered according to their engagement level in each course offering (we refer to clusters as *engagement states*). The resulting clusters were compared with Kruskal–Wallis non-parametric one-way analysis of variance (ANOVA) [37]. To test the magnitude of the obtained results and the quality of separation of clusters, we calculated the epsilon-squared effect size [36]. Post-hoc pairwise comparisons were also performed through Dunn's test using Holm's correction for multiple testing [38].

To answer **RQ2**, SPM was performed to study and visualize the longitudinal trajectory of engagement states throughout the whole program, patterns of transitions, stability of engagement states and the characteristics thereof. The TramineR R package [39] was used to construct a state sequence object from the chronologically ordered course engagement states. Sequence distribution plots were used to demonstrate the ratio of each course engagement state at each time point. Sequence index plots were used to visualize the longitudinal timeline of engagement states for each single student. Mean time plots were used to demonstrate the number of courses each student spent in each engagement state on average. To test how homogenous the sub-groups of engagement are, intra-students stability was measured using entropy [40]. Chi-squared test with Bonferroni correction was computed to compare the patterns of transitions of engagement states in each subgroup.

To find if there are subgroups or pattern within the groups, we implemented clustering, which a standard sequence mining technique. Each group (the early engaged and early disengaged) was clustered using agglomerative hierarchical clustering based on Ward's method using distances based on optimal matching (see [41] for details of the method).

To answer **RQ3**, a Kaplan-Meier (KM) survival curve was performed to estimate the probability of students persisting in the program (survival). For each group, we report the number of events (of dropouts) and the survival probability at each time point. To compare the difference between trajectories, we performed the recommended tests: Log-rank, Gehan, Tarone-Ware and Peto-Peto [42]. Lastly, a non-parametric Wilcoxon-Mann-Whitney (WMW) was used to compare students Grade Point Average (GPA) at the end of the program which is the total grades of all courses [43].

4 Results

The extracted data included 1,052,807 recorded logs, which became 790,956 log records after removal of non-learning events (e.g., clicks on profile pages). The median number of students per course was 92 and ranged from 85 to 99. The median number of events per course offering (in the final data set after removal of non-learning events) was 15,345 and ranged from 3,925 to 36,417. The median number of forum consumption events was 48.5 per student per course offering; the median of forum contribution per student per course offering was 50; the median of sessions per student per course offering was 48, and the median duration of online time was 4.99 h per student per course offering.

To answer **RQ1**, an LCA model was fitted using students' learning activities. We tested models with two to ten clusters (similar to [9]). The model with three clusters had the lowest AIC = 43,748.7 and BIC = 44,891 as well as had clearly separable clusters and high epsilon-squared effect size (ranging from 0.3 to 0.8). Table 1 shows the three identified clusters. Throughout this manuscript we will refer to each cluster as an engagement state as it describes the students' state of engagement in each course. They can be described as follows:

- *Actively engaged cluster:* Students in this cluster had the highest values of activity indicators (between the 7th and 9th decile), frequent access to course resources, frequent forum posting and reading. They had the highest frequency of active days, longer sessions, and the highest regularity. These indicators ranged between the 7th and 9th decile.
- *Averagely engaged cluster:* Students in this cluster had moderate (mostly around the 5th decile) values of activity indicators: average frequency of access to course resources, forum posting, forum reading, active days and regularity.
- *Disengaged cluster:* Students in this cluster had the lowest levels of activities that lied between the 1st decile and the 3rd decile.

Table 1. Comparison (ANOVA) of the three clusters according to their mean activity indicators

Indicator	State	Mean	SD	p	ε^2
Frequency of course browsing	Actively engaged	8.47	1.487	<.001	0.686
	Averagely engaged	4.91	1.820		
	Disengaged	1.95	1.211		
Frequency of lecture access	Actively engaged	7.31	2.413	<.001	0.304
	Averagely engaged	5.17	2.506		
	Disengaged	2.94	2.057		
Frequency of forum reading	Actively engaged	7.95	2.074	<.001	0.456
	Averagely engaged	4.89	2.218		
	Disengaged	2.67	1.901		
Frequency of forum contribution	Actively engaged	7.25	2.421	<.001	0.277
	Averagely engaged	5.13	2.509		
	Disengaged	3.09	2.298		
Active days	Actively engaged	8.51	1.432	<.001	0.726
	Averagely engaged	4.95	1.738		
	Disengaged	1.79	0.938		
Session count	Actively engaged	8.71	1.095	<.001	0.796
	Averagely engaged	4.87	1.553		
	Disengaged	1.70	0.851		
Total online time	Actively engaged	8.02	1.995	<.001	0.500
	Averagely engaged	4.94	2.187		
	Disengaged	2.45	1.663		
Regularity	Actively engaged	8.15	1.832	<.001	0.609
	Averagely engaged	5.10	2.034		
	Disengaged	1.96	1.032		

To answer **RQ2**, the engagement states were used to construct a sequence object in each of the two study groups (*Early engagement* and *Early disengagement*) which was mined used SPM. We then compared the two groups and the characteristics of each of their trajectories.

Early Disengagement Group: The sequence index plot (Fig. 1A) shows each trajectory of a student as a sequence of horizontally colored stacked bars: the colors reflect their engagement states. The hierarchical clustering (Fig. 1A) shows two distinct groups of students: *G1*, a mostly disengaged group (n = 9) who eventually drop out, *G2* with fluctuating engagement trajectories which can be further divided into two subgroups: *G2a* with fluctuating engagement trajectory dominated with disengagement states, and *G2b*, a relatively stable group dominated with active engagement states. Overall, among the group of *Early disengagement*, the total number of students who dropped-out was two students at the 3rd course, six at the 6th course, nine students at the 9th course, and 13 students by the 15th course. A noticeable observation that students who were able to catch up and engage again in the second course were more likely to maintain such an engaged state (11/13), while students who were disengaged for two successive courses had more dropouts (11/28). The distribution plot (Fig. 1B) shows the distribution of engagement states at each time point, highlighting that dropout occurred immediately after the first term. The mean time plot (Fig. 1C) shows that these students spent an average of 7.7 courses as disengaged or dropout and 7.3 as averagely or actively engaged.

Early Engaged Group: The index plot (Fig. 2A) shows that the students in this group had more stable trajectories that were dominated with average and active engagement states with very infrequent disengagement states (an average of 13.6 courses were active or average engagement per student, Fig. 2C). Two distinct subgroups can be revealed with hierarchical clustering: *G1*, a subgroup with mostly average engagement with frequent transition to engagement states, and *G2*, a subgroup with mostly engaged states with infrequent transition to other engagement states. The distribution plot (Fig. 2B) confirms that students in this group were mostly highly engaged or averagely engaged. Only a single student dropped at the course 12.

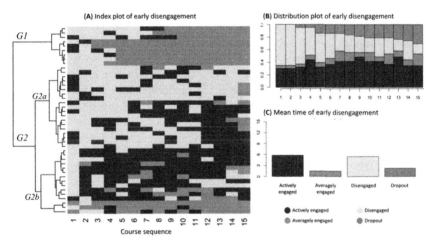

Fig. 1. The sequence plots of the *Early disengagement* group: A) index plot, B) distribution plot, and C) mean time plot.

The Dynamics of Engagement Trajectories

Comparing both trajectories helps understand the dynamics of events (transitions, sequences of transitions, stability and persistence. Firstly, we compare the transition probabilities between engagement states to investigate how each group changes across time. Secondly, we compare the frequent transition subsequences that are characteristic of each group. Thirdly, we compare the stability of trajectories in each group using transversal-entropy curves.

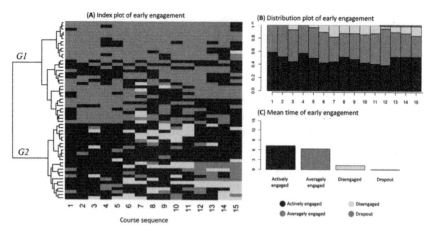

Fig. 2. The sequence plots of the *Early engagement* group: A) index plot, B) distribution plot, and C) mean time plot.

Students in the *Early disengagement* group were more likely to descend from the "actively engaged" state to the "disengaged" state (transition probability 28%) compared to the *Early engagement* group (transition probability 11%), which highlights the vulnerability of the former group of students to transition to disengagement states in the future (Table 2). Similarly, students in the *Early disengagement* group were also more likely to stay in a "disengaged" state with a probability of 59% compared to 39% in the *Early engagement* group. The top statistically significant discriminating subsequences in the *Early disengagement* group were characterized by persisting in a "disengaged" state, descending from an engagement state (averagely or actively engaged) to a "disengaged state", or ascending to an engagement state.

Table 2. Transition probability matrix among engagement states for each engagement group.

Early disengagement	Actively engaged	Averagely engaged	Disengaged	Dropout
Actively engaged >	0.6	0.09	0.28	0.03
Averagely engaged >	0.30	0.55	0.11	0.04
Disengaged >	0.35	0.04	0.59	0.02
Dropout >	0.00	0.00	0.00	1.00
Early engagement	Actively engaged	Averagely engaged	Disengaged	Dropout
Actively engaged >	0.65	0.24	0.11	0.00
Averagely engaged >	0.30	0.69	0.02	0.00
Disengaged >	0.45	0.16	0.39	0.00
Dropout >	0.00	0.00	0.00	1.00

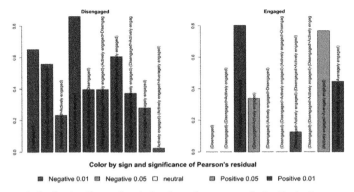

Fig. 3. Top statistically significant discriminating subsequences in the *Early disengagement* group

Figure 3, shows the Chi-squared test for discriminating subsequences. The *Early disengagement* group had more frequent and statistically significant (Disengaged) and (Disengaged)-(Disengaged > Actively engaged) subsequences, while less likely to have (Averagely engaged > Actively engaged) subsequences. In summary, the *Early disengagement* group were more likely to persist in a "disengaged" state, descend from an engagement state to a disengagement state as well as showed an unstable trajectory. These findings add to the previous findings, that not only being in a disengagement state is an alarming distress signal, but also the persistence or transition to a disengaged state is similarly alarming.

To investigate the likelihood to persist in the program, we estimate the survival probability (probability of completing the program) using KM curves, comparing *Early engagement* and *Early disengagement* groups (Fig. 4A). The survival probability of the *Early disengagement* group at the end of the 1st year was 0.86 CI (0.76:0.97), at the end of 2nd year the survival probability dropped to 0.81 CI (0.7:0.94), while it was 1.00 in the *Early engagement* group. By the end of the program, the survival probability in the *Early disengagement* group was 0.7 CI (0.57:0.85), while it was 0.98 CI (0.95:1.0) in the *Early engagement* group. The Log-rank, Gehan, Tarone-Ware and Peto-Peto tests were all statistically significant at the level of $p < 0.001$ emphasizing the difference between the groups. In summary, the *Early disengagement* group had a higher and statistically significant probability of dropping out of the program.

Lastly, the results of the WMW test revealed that performance (measured as GPA) in the *Early engagement* group (85.15/100) was significantly higher than that of the *Early disengaged* group (79.73/100) with a medium effect size (rank-biserial correlation coefficient of -0.38). The findings indicate that not only does early engagement predict persisting in the program, but it is also a catalyst of higher performance.

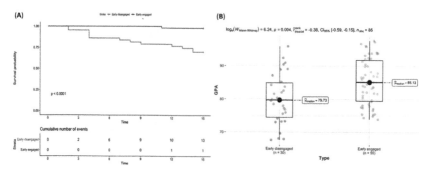

Fig. 4. A) KM survival curves comparing both groups. B) WMW test comparing the GPA of both groups

5 Discussion

There are several studies that have addressed students' online engagement. The majority of such studies have focused on engagement with a learning task or within a course [8, 9, 25]. Notwithstanding the wealth of insights that we have learned over the years, the longitudinal engagement remained a much-needed area of research. Our study has sought to address such a gap and, in particular, we investigated the longitudinal trajectories of early engaged versus early disengaged students.

Our **RQ1** sought to identify the course-level engagement states of the students over a full program using LCA clustering method. While few studies have looked into a full program, the three engagement states at the course level identified in our study were in line with the existing literature [9, 23, 44]. Our three identified engagement clusters were: 1) an *actively engaged* cluster similar to the intense, highly active groups reported by others [9, 23, 44]. The *actively engaged* cluster invests a significant amount of energy and effort in learning which has been linked to *deep* learning [5, 15]. 2) An *average engagement cluster*, constituted by selective learners investing a moderate amount of effort. Such cluster is similar to *get-it-done cluster* reported in other studies [9, 23]. 3) A *disengaged cluster*, who invest the least amount of effort, focus on assessed resources, or use a *surface* approach to learning [15]. Our clusters may have been more uniform than which can be explained by the fact that our context has a uniform course design, homogeneous course structure and similar underpinnings.

Our **RQ2** investigated the longitudinal trajectories of early disengaged students in comparison to their early engaged counterparts. The results have shown that students in the *Early disengagement* group are not a uniform group but rather a heterogenous group with two main identifiable subgroups: a group with rapid declining engagement that eventually ended by dropping out early in the program, and another group that maintained a turbulent course with occasional dropping-out. In addition to frequent disengagement states, this group has shown frequent alarming transitions too, that is, transitions from an engagement state to a disengagement state (declined). These findings highlight the importance of course to course transitions as another alarming sign that should alert educators of the imminent risk that these students may have (dropping out). The fact that *Early disengagement* group had a high number of dropouts is an indication of the high risk that early disengagement incurs on students' outcomes. The presence of alarming signs is a sign of tractability that should be taken seriously. Similarly, the *Early engagement* group was not a uniform group of learners, but rather presented two subgroups with two engagement patterns.

The findings of this study align with face-to-face studies [7, 21] that reported the presence of engagement heterogeneity among students, as well as the presence of subgroups of students with different trajectories. A stable subgroup who remain engaged most of the program has been reported by [7, 21], those students were referred to as "Stable High Trajectory" or "Persistent engagement group" and were around 70% of all enrolled students [7, 21]. A declining trajectory has also been reported by studies in face-to-face settings, referred to as "Descending engagement group" and were around 17% in [7] and around 8% in [21]. Similar results have been obtained in the scarce research on longitudunal engagement in online settings [9], where the "consistent" and "get-it-done" groups to be around 67% of students if combined and a *disorganized* group (33%) who are mostly disengagement.

RQ3 investigated the relationship between early disengagement and graduation using survival analysis. The results showed that early disengagement projects a substantial risk on students' graduation and is linked to frequent and statistically significant dropout. Since troubled, unstable or early disengagement have been strongly linked to dropping out of school, the early identification and support of such students is thus of paramount importance to educators [2, 3, 5].

This study contributes to the body of the literature regarding longitudinal engagement, an area that is rarely studied. We show that early online engagement—regardless of the grades—is a significant predictor of persistence in the program. More importantly, we describe the trajectories of early disengaged students and show that in addition to the state of disengagement, the transitions and their stability can also be alarming. Another contribution of this study is a methodological one: we used SPM methods in modeling longitudinal engagement, a use that is novel in LA and education.

6 Conclusions

This study followed 99 students over four years of college education including all their course data (15 courses and 1383 course enrollments). The results have shown that early disengagement is associated with significant higher rates of dropouts, lower scores, and lower graduation rates. Our findings indicate that it is critical to proactively watch the alarming signs of disengagement during the first program courses, such as low engagement with the course materials, declining engagement along the program or history of frequent disengagements. Most of existing approaches to disengagement focus on a single course; such approaches are far from optimal as they miss an important aspect of engagement i.e., program-level engagement. This study points to the dire consequences of ignoring program-level disengagement and the loss it incurs in terms or attrition and loss of resources. Therefore, we call for institutions to have program-level monitoring mechanisms that early identify at-risk students and offer a timely relevant support. It must be noted that the generalizability of this study is subject to investigation and replication within different contexts. The quality of data captured from the LMS are far from perfect and students' usage may differ. Therefore, further confirmation with different samples is required.

References

1. Newmann, F.M.: Student Engagement and Achievement in American Secondary Schools. ERIC (1992)
2. Fredricks, J.A., Blumenfeld, P.C., Paris, A.H.: School engagement: potential of the concept, state of the evidence. Rev. Educ. Res. **74**, 59–109 (2004). https://doi.org/10.3102/00346543074001059
3. Finn, J.D., Zimmer, K.S.: Student engagement: what is it? Why does it matter? In: Christenson, S., Reschly, A., Wylie, C. (eds.) Handbook of Research on Student Engagement, pp. 97–131. Springer, Boston (2012). https://doi.org/10.1007/978-1-4614-2018-7_5
4. Lei, H., Cui, Y., Zhou, W.: Relationships between student engagement and academic achievement: a meta-analysis. Soc. Behav. Pers. **46**, 517–528 (2018). https://doi.org/10.2224/sbp.7054
5. Azevedo, R.: Defining and measuring engagement and learning in science: conceptual, theoretical, methodological, and analytical issues. Educ. Psychol. **50**, 84–94 (2015). https://doi.org/10.1080/00461520.2015.1004069
6. Skinner, E.A., Pitzer, J.R.: Developmental dynamics of student engagement, coping, and everyday resilience. In: Christenson, S.L., Reschly, A.L., Wylie, C. (eds.) Handbook of Research on Student Engagement, pp. 21–44. Springer, Boston (2012). https://doi.org/10.1007/978-1-4614-2018-7_2
7. Zhen, R., et al.: Trajectory patterns of academic engagement among elementary school students: the implicit theory of intelligence and academic self-efficacy matters. Br. J. Educ. Psychol. **90**, 618–634 (2020). https://doi.org/10.1111/bjep.12320
8. Henrie, C.R., Halverson, L.R., Graham, C.R.: Measuring student engagement in technology-mediated learning: a review. Comput. Educ. **90**, 36–53 (2015). https://doi.org/10.1016/j.compedu.2015.09.005
9. Barthakur, A., Kovanovic, V., Joksimovic, S., Siemens, G., Richey, M., Dawson, S.: Assessing program-level learning strategies in MOOCs. Comput. Hum. Behav. **117**, 106674 (2021). https://doi.org/10.1016/j.chb.2020.106674
10. Lust, G., Elen, J., Clarebout, G.: Regulation of tool-use within a blended course: student differences and performance effects. Comput. Educ. **60**, 385–395 (2013). https://doi.org/10.1016/j.compedu.2012.09.001
11. Saqr, M., Wasson, B.: COVID-19: Lost opportunities and lessons for the future. Int. J. Health Sci. **14**, 4–6 (2020)
12. Wang, M.T., Degol, J.: Staying engaged: knowledge and research needs in student engagement. Child Dev. Perspect. **8**, 137–143 (2014). https://doi.org/10.1111/cdep.12073
13. King, R.B.: Sense of relatedness boosts engagement, achievement, and well-being: a latent growth model study. Contemp. Educ. Psychol. **42**, 26–38 (2015)
14. Fredricks, J.A., McColskey, W.: The measurement of student engagement: a comparative analysis of various methods and student self-report instruments. In: Christenson, S.L., Reschly, A.L., Wylie, C. (eds.) Handbook of Research on Student Engagement, pp. 763–782. Springer, Boston (2012). https://doi.org/10.1007/978-1-4614-2018-7_37
15. Redmond, P., Abawi, L.A., Brown, A., Henderson, R., Heffernan, A.: An online engagement framework for higher education. Online Learn. J. **22**, 183–204 (2018). https://doi.org/10.24059/olj.v22i1.1175

16. Balfanz, R., Herzog, L., Mac Iver, D.J.: Preventing student disengagement and keeping students on the graduation path in urban middle-grades schools: early identification and effective interventions. Educ. Psychol. **42**, 223–235 (2007). https://doi.org/10.1080/00461520701621079
17. López-Pernas, S., Saqr, M., Viberg, O.: Putting it all together: combining learning analytics methods and data sources to understand students' approaches to learning programming. Sustainability. **13** (2021). https://doi.org/10.3390/su13094825
18. Saqr, M., Fors, U., Tedre, M.: How learning analytics can early predict under-achieving students in a blended medical education course. Med. Teach. **39**, 757–767 (2017). https://doi.org/10.1080/0142159X.2017.1309376
19. Wigfield, A., Eccles, J.S., Schiefele, U., Roeser, R.W., Davis-Kean, P.: Development of achievement motivation and engagement. Handb. Child Psychol. **3**, 657–700 (2007)
20. You, S., Sharkey, J.: Testing a developmental-ecological model of student engagement: a multilevel latent growth curve analysis. Educ. Psychol. **29**, 659–684 (2009). https://doi.org/10.1080/01443410903206815
21. Archambault, I., Dupéré, V.: Joint trajectories of behavioral, affective, and cognitive engagement in elementary school. J. Educ. Res. **110**, 188–198 (2017). https://doi.org/10.1080/00220671.2015.1060931
22. López-Pernas, S., Saqr, M.: Idiographic learning analytics: a within-person ethical perspective. In: Companion Proceedings 11th International Conference on Learning Analytics & Knowledge (LAK21), pp. 310–315 (2021)
23. Mirriahi, N., Jovanovic, J., Dawson, S., Gašević, D., Pardo, A.: Identifying engagement patterns with video annotation activities: a case study in professional development (2018)
24. Palvia, S., et al.: Online education: worldwide status, challenges, trends, and implications. J. Glob. Inf. Technol. Manag. **21**, 233–241 (2018). https://doi.org/10.1080/1097198X.2018.1542262
25. Joksimović, S., et al.: How do we model learning at scale? A systematic review of research on MOOCs (2018). https://doi.org/10.3102/0034654317740335
26. Vytasek, J.M., Patzak, A., Winne, P.H.: Analytics for student engagement (2020)
27. Saqr, M.: Learning analytics and medical education. Int. J. Health Sci. **9** (2015)
28. Uzir, N.A.A.A., et al.: Analytics of time management and learning strategies for effective online learning in blended environments. In: ACM International Conference Proceeding Series, pp. 392–401. Association for Computing Machinery, New York (2020). https://doi.org/10.1145/3375462.3375493
29. Agrawal, R., Srikant, R.: Mining sequential patterns. In: Proceedings of the Eleventh International Conference on Data Engineering, pp. 3–14. IEEE (1995)
30. Ritschard, G., Studer, M.: Sequence analysis: where are we, where are we going? In: Ritschard, G., Studer, M. (eds.) Sequence Analysis and Related Approaches. LCRSP, vol. 10, pp. 1–11. Springer, Cham (2018). https://doi.org/10.1007/978-3-319-95420-2_1
31. Saqr, M., Viberg, O., Vartiainen, H.: Capturing the participation and social dimensions of computer-supported collaborative learning through social network analysis: which method and measures matter? Int. J. Comput.-Support. Collab. Learn. **15**(2), 227–248 (2020). https://doi.org/10.1007/s11412-020-09322-6
32. Saqr, M., Nouri, J., Jormanainen, I.: A learning analytics study of the effect of group size on social dynamics and performance in online collaborative learning. In: Scheffel, M., Broisin, J., Pammer-Schindler, V., Ioannou, A., Schneider, J. (eds.) EC-TEL 2019. LNCS, vol. 11722, pp. 466–479. Springer, Cham (2019). https://doi.org/10.1007/978-3-030-29736-7_35
33. Jovanović, J., Mirriahi, N., Gašević, D., Dawson, S., Pardo, A.: Predictive power of regularity of pre-class activities in a flipped classroom. Comput. Educ. (2019). https://doi.org/10.1016/j.compedu.2019.02.011

34. Hung, J.-L., Shelton, B.E., Yang, J., Du, X.: Improving predictive modeling for at-risk student identification: a multistage approach (2019)
35. Goodman, L.A.: Exploratory latent structure analysis using both identifiable and unidentifiable models. Biometrika **61**, 215–231 (1974)
36. Tomczak, M., Tomczak, E.: The need to report effect size estimates revisited. An overview of some recommended measures of effect size. Trends Sport Sci. **21**, 19–25 (2014)
37. Ostertagova, E., Ostertag, O., Kováč, J.: Methodology and application of the Kruskal-Wallis test. In: Applied Mechanics and Materials, pp. 115–120. Trans Tech Publ (2014)
38. Holm, S.: A simple sequentially rejective multiple test procedure. Scand. J. Stat. **6**, 65–70 (1979)
39. Gabadinho, A., Ritschard, G., Müller, N.S., Studer, M.: Analyzing and visualizing state sequences in R with TraMineR. J. Stat. Softw. **40** (2011). https://doi.org/10.18637/jss.v040.i04
40. Gabadinho, A., Ritschard, G., Studer, M., Nicolas, S.M.: Mining sequence data in R with the TraMineR package: a users guide for version 1.2, p. 1. University of Geneva, Geneva (2009)
41. Fincham, E., Gašević, D., Jovanović, J., Pardo, A.: From study tactics to learning strategies: an analytical method for extracting interpretable representations. IEEE Trans. Learn. Technol. **12**, 59–72 (2019). https://doi.org/10.1109/TLT.2018.2823317
42. Blossfeld, H.P., Golsch, K., Rohwer, G.: Event History Analysis with Stata. Routledge (2007). https://doi.org/10.4324/9780203936559
43. McKnight, P.E., Najab, J.: Mann-Whitney U test. The Corsini encyclopedia of psychology, p. 1 (2010)
44. Kovanović, V., et al.: Examining communities of inquiry in massive open online courses: the role of study strategies. Internet High. Educ. **40**, 20–43 (2019). https://doi.org/10.1016/j.iheduc.2018.09.001

Analysis of the "D'oh!" Moments. Physiological Markers of Performance in Cognitive Switching Tasks

Tetiana Buraha[1], Jan Schneider[2(✉)], Daniele Di Mitri[2], and Daniel Schiffner[2]

[1] Goethe University, Frankfurt am Main, Germany
[2] DIPF, Frankfurt am Main, Germany
{schneider.jan,dimitri,schiffner}@dipf.de

Abstract. The link between the body and mind has fascinated philosophers and scientists for ages. The increasing availability of sensor technologies has enabled the possibility to explore this link even deeper, providing some evidence that certain physiological measurements such as galvanic skin response can have in the performance of different learning activities. In this paper, we explore the link between learners' performance of cognitive tasks and their physiological state with the use of Multimodal Learning Analytics (MMLA). We used MMLA tools and techniques to collect, annotate, and analyse physiological data from 16 participants wearing an Empatica E4 wristband while engaging in task-switching cognitive exercises. The collected data include temperature, blood volume pulse, heart rate variability, galvanic skin response, and screen recording from each participant while performing the exercises. To examine the link between cognitive performance we applied a preliminary qualitative analysis to galvanic skin response and tested different Artificial Intelligence techniques to differentiate between productive and unproductive performance.

Keywords: Multimodal learning analytics · Psychophysiology · Game analytics · Sensors

1 Introduction

Aristotle says: "Soul and body, I suggest react sympathetically upon each other. A change in the state of the soul produces a change in the shape of the body and conversely, a change in the shape of the body produces a change in the state of the soul." Similarly, in the 17th century, René Descartes proposed that mind and matter exert causal effects on one another. It was until the 19th century when William James started to systematically study this proposition examining the causal links among behaviour, physiology, and psychology providing the foundations of modern psychology [1]. These causal links have shown to be bi-directional meaning that internal psychological states have an influence on observable attributes of behaviour such as posture and movements, and also posture and movements influence internal states [2]. For example, engaging the muscles of a smile or a frown has a strong influence on the perception and interpretation of different scenarios, as well happy or sad states of mind lead to naturally smile or frown [2, 3].

These links are not restricted to basic emotional states. Embodied cognition theorizes that the cognition of humans and other biological creatures is strongly influenced by physiological aspects that go beyond the brain itself [4]. Executive cognitive functions such as reasoning, attention control, task flexibility and performance can be undermined by states of powerlessness that have also a clear influence on behaviour and the physiology of an individual [5]. The levels of stress, which can be inferred by the secretion of glucocorticoids, have shown to influence different types of cognitive tasks in different ways. For example, moderate levels of stress before implicit memory tasks tend to have a positive influence on performance. In terms of explicit memory tasks, stress has shown to improve the retention of words with a negative connotation but also leads to the creation of false memories [6]. Embodied cognition is a very broad area of research that usually produces mixed results like the aforementioned stress example. While there is much evidence supporting the embodiment of cognition, the interpretation of results and their significance is an unsettled topic in the scientific discourse [7].

Traditional interactive e-learning environments such as learning management systems (LMS) or intelligent tutoring systems (ITS) automatically log the interactions from learners. These systems offer opportunities to evaluate learning theories, learning technologies, and the development of future learning applications giving rise to the field of Learning Analytics (LA) [8]. However, these types of data sources represent only a small portion of the learning activities and not the whole learning process [9], e.g. the physiological state of learners is not captured.

To gain a more thorough view of the learning process, inspired by recent technological developments such as wearable sensors and Internet of Things (IoT) devices, the field of Multimodal Learning Analytics (MMLA) emerged [10]. Several studies on MMLA have explored the link between physiological data and learning performance for multiple learning tasks such as video game skill acquisition [11], collaborative learning scenarios [12, 13], inquiry tasks [14], arithmetic tasks [15], physics exams [16], problem solving [17], etc. MMLA uses the idea that behavioural cues can be considered as "markers of expertise" in learning context [18].

The data collected, analysis methods, and reported results in MMLA studies attempting to describe the link between physiological data and learning/cognitive performance remain heterogeneous. While recent studies like the one in Sharma et al. [19] shows that it is possible to extract features out of physiological data including Heart Rate Variability (HRV), Galvanic Skin Response (GSR), Blood Volume Pulse (BVP), facial expressions, etc., and use them in combination with different machine learning techniques to make predictions about cognitive workload for a diverse set of cognitive tasks that require problem-solving, decision-making, and learning processes. There are some other studies that even the same physiological data and analysis methods produced different results for different learning tasks. For example, the study in Ryu & Myung [20] showed that HRV is an indicator for cognitive workload in flying simulation tasks, but not for arithmetic tasks. Similarly, the example in Larmuseau et al. [17] shows that GSR and skin temperature (TMP) are indicators of mental effort, but these indicators are not shown when the complexity of the task changes.

Regardless of recent advances in MMLA, identifying the link between physiology and performance is not trivial. These data modalities are produced at high and different frequencies, they are noisy, their synchronization is challenging, and several important methodological decisions require high competence and contextual knowledge, which goes from the treatment of low-level signals to the interpretation of high-level abstractions, such as features and measurements [21].

To contribute to the state-of-the-art exploration of the connection between physiology and cognition, in this paper we introduce a methodology based on qualitative analysis and machine learning to establish a connection between physiological markers of performance in task switching. Task switching is an executive function that belongs to the concept of cognitive flexibility. It involves the ability to rapidly and efficiently adapt to different situations [22], and has been associated with academic achievement [23]. Our methodology makes use of the MMLA pipeline [24], which consists of a set of methods and Open Source applications. Instead of looking at the overall game performance, in our analysis, we focus on each answer in the task switching game, which we refer to as one "attempt". The purpose of analysing the attempts is to identify physiological markers which can represent some precise learning states. In particular, we are interested in isolating the moments when the learner realises having committed a mistake. We call these the "D'oh!" moments, referencing the famous expression of the cartoon character Homer J. Simpson.

2 Method

Task switching is an ability that varies during the lifespan of an individual [25], thus suggesting that it is influenced by changing factors and leading us to our first research question:

RQ1: Do measurable physiological factors influence executive functions such as task switching?

To answer RQ1 we first need to select appropriate methods and techniques to collect and make sense of physiological data during the performance of task switching, leading us to our second research question:

RQ2: To what extent can we use the MMLA Pipeline to identify physiological markers of performance in individual attempts of a task switching game?

To answer RQ2, we applied the MMLA Pipeline including the *LearningHub* [26] for collecting data and the *Visual Inspection Tool* [27] for manual annotation and visual understanding of the patterns.

First, we conducted a qualitative analysis of the collected sessions inspecting visually and manually the GSR of the participants in presence of mistakes. Later, we used the collected annotations to train various supervised-machine learning models to classify both the presence of mistakes and the optimal game performance by considering also the duration of each attempt.

2.1 Data Collection and Annotation

Our data sample consists of 48 multimodal recordings of 16 participants (8 females and 8 males) aged 19 to 22 years playing the Brain Shift game. Each participant played the game three times, this means three sessions per participant and each session lasted 60 s. The Brain Shift game requires the user to switch rapidly between two different tasks. Two cards are presented on the screen. On each attempt, a number and a letter appear on one of the cards. If the stimulus appears on the top card, then the user should indicate "yes" if the number is even and "no" if the number is odd. On the other hand, if the stimulus appears on the bottom card, the user should indicate "yes" if the letter is a vowel and "no" if the letter is a consonant.

We used the *LearningHub* [26] to create the multimodal recordings. Each multimodal recording includes a screen recording of the played game, and the TMP, BVP, GSR, HRV, interbeat interval (IBI), and 3d acceleration (ACC) that was collected from an Empatica E4 wristband[1].

We used the *Visual Inspection Tool* [27] to visually inspect and annotate the multimodal recordings. The process of annotation consisted of first identifying the time interval for each attempt to select "yes" or "no" based on the shown card. Then annotating each attempt with a 0 for correct responses and a 1 for mistakes.

3 Analysis and Results

3.1 Qualitative Analysis

To get a first impression of the physiological data collected we first plotted them. Values from BVP showed a wave function behaviour making it difficult to perceive any details just by pure visual inspection. Values from HRV, IBI, TMP and ACC, presented no clear patterns that could be identified through a visual inspection. On the other hand, GSR values presented patterns that could be visually identified.

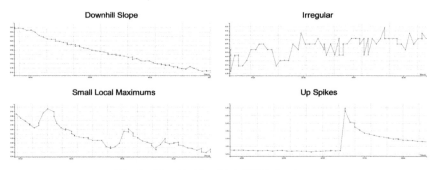

Fig. 1. Visually identified GSR behaviours.

We were able to identify four main different types of sessions by examining the GSR plot: (1) Downhill Slope, (2) Irregular, (3) Small Local Maximums (SLM), and (4) Up

---
[1] https://www.empatica.com/research/e4/.

Spikes (see Fig. 1). Table 1 provides a summary of the descriptive values found for the different types of sessions.

Table 1. Descriptive statistics grouped by the visually identified session type based on the GSR plot.

Type of session	No. of sessions	GSR Avg	Proportion GSR change	Mistakes	Avg Attempt duration (seconds)	Game Score	Corr. GSR vs score
Downhill slope	18	m = 0.817 sd = 0.65	m = −0.0777 sd = 0.12	m = 2.4 sd = 2.12	m = 1.506 sd = 0.77	m = 14292 sd = 8051	R = −0.35 p = 0.148
Irregular	9	m = 2.088 sd = 2.41	m = 0.2483 sd = 0.27	m = 3 sd = 2.55	m = 1.287 sd = 0.22	m = 14055 sd = 3961	**R = −0.68 p = 0.04**
SLM	5	m = 1.307 sd = 1.11	m = −0.0004 sd = 0.0003	m = 2.4 sd = 3.05	m = 1.373 sd = 0.31	m = 13860 sd = 2742	R = −0.75 p = 0.13
Up spikes	4	m = 0.611 sd = 0.61	m = 0.0008 sd = 0.0007	m = 4.25 sd = 2.75	m = 1.050 sd = 0.06	m = 18750 sd = 2817	R = −0.73 p = 0.26
All	36	m = 1.179 sd = 1.42	m = −0.0386 sd = 0.146	m = 2.61 sd = 2.29	m = 1.389 sd = 0.58	m = 14604 sd = 6231	**R = −0.35 p = 0.03**

As seen in Table 1, on average for all the GSR diminished throughout the sessions (m = −0.0386). The collected data shows a moderate negative Pearson correlation between the GSR and the Game Score. Results were statistically significant for the aggregate of all sessions and for sessions that presented Irregular GSR behaviour.

For the SLM, and Up Spikes sessions, we conducted a qualitative analysis with the purpose to identify explanations for the observed SLM and Up Spikes. Table 2 shows the summary of the observations before and after the occurrence of an SLM. For all cases, there was at least one long attempt before an SLM appeared/happened.

Table 3 summarizes the observations of GSR Up Spikes before and after their occurrence. We found that before the spike in four of the five cases there was a distinctive event. Moreover, in three out of the five cases, the spike led to a mistake or a slow attempt.

3.2 Machine Learning Classifiers

To deepen the exploration of physiological markers of performance in the individual attempts, we explored the use of different machine learning models. First, we applied these models for the identification of mistakes (Sect. 3.2.1). The optimal performance of the Brain Shift has two components, correctness of the attempts and response time. Therefore, we also conducted a second classification considering the variable of attempt duration (Sect. 3.2.2).

Table 2. Observations for Small Local Maximum (SLM).

Session	Before GSR SLM	After GSR SLM	Avg duration attempt (seconds)	Mistakes
g4_2	Slow attempts 3.1 s, 2.35 s	Slow Attempt 3.4 s	m = 1.6 sd = 0.63	0
g4_3	Slow attempt 2.1 s	Nothing distinctive	m = 1.4 sd = 0.37	0
g4_3	Slow attempts 2.4 s, 2.1 s, 2.1	Nothing distinctive	m = 1.4 sd = 0.37	0
k4_2	1 slow attempt (3.99 s)	Nothing distinctive	m = 1.1 sd = 0.33	7
k4_2	Erratic GSR readings	Erratic GSR Readings	m = 1.1 sd = 0.33	7
k4_2	2 mistakes then slow attempt 2.8 s	Mistake, rapid guess 0.2 s, Mistake	m = 1.1 sd = 0.33	7
k4_2	Slow attempt 2.4 s	Nothing distinctive	m = 1.1 sd = 0.33	7
m4_1	Slow attempt 3.7 s	1 mistake	m = 1.8 sd = 1.02	1
p4_1	Slow attempts 1.9 s, 1.2 s, 1.9 s	Nothing distinctive	m = 1.0 sd = 0.44	4

Table 3. Observations for up spikes

Session	Before GSR spike	After GSR spike	Avg duration attempt (seconds)	Mistakes
h4_1	3 mistakes in 6 attempts	Slow attempt 2.8s	m = 0.9 sd = 0.17	6
k4_1	Rapid guess 0.2 s	1 Mistake	m = 1.1 sd = 0.65	2
k4_1	Mistake, Slow attempt 3.3 s	Nothing distinctive	m = 1.1 sd = 0.65	2
n4_3	Nothing distinctive	Nothing distinctive	m = 1.1 sd = 0.45	3
p4_3	Slow attempt 2.2 s	1 Mistake	m = 1 sd = 0.25	1

3.2.1 Mistake Classification

The first analysis for our machine learning classifiers consisted of classifying the presence or the absence of a mistake using the physiological data as input data. Among all the annotated sessions, we selected 14 sessions and discarded the ones having one or more sensor attributes missing. We considered five sensor attributes, TMP, BVP, GSR, HRV, and IBI. The Empatica E4 samples these attributes at different frequencies. To overcome the problem of unevenly spaced time series, each attempt was resampled into a fixed number of time-bins that correspond to the median length of each sample. We obtained a 3D tensor of shape: 1927, 35, 5 *(no. samples × no. bins × no. attributes)*.

From the five input signals, we extracted more than 1920 features using the Tsfresh time-series library[2]. To reduce the dimensionality of the extracted features and select the best ones, we used Recursive Feature Elimination using the estimator Decision Tree. We also set the number of desired best features at different thresholds: 1% (19 features) and 2.5% (48 features). The 3D tensor was therefore aggregated in a matrix of size 1927, 19 (no. samples × no. attributes).

The target class values and other metadata including the id of the session and the attempt duration (in seconds) were kept in a separate data frame. Consequently, a cluster of machine learning classifiers was selected including (1) Decision Trees (DT), Gradient Boosting (GB), k-Nearest Neighbours (KNN), Naïve Bayes (NB), Random Forests (RF), Support Vector Machines (SVM). The hyperparameters of the classifiers were tuned using Grid Search on a subset of the dataset to optimise the convergence time.

Since the target class (presence or absence of a mistake) exhibited a highly unbalanced distribution (9% mistake - 91% not-mistake) we applied oversampling using the Synthetic Minority Oversampling Technique using 10-fold-cross validation. We made sure to oversample only the nine training folds and not the validation fold. The dataset was between training and testing using leave-one-session-out: we trained the models on 13 sessions and tested on the remaining one, iteratively. We then averaged the results obtained. Additionally, we applied feature scaling using min-max normalisation with a range of −1 and 1. The scaler was fitted on the training set and applied on both validation and test sets.

Table 4. Classification results of the target class "mistake".

Model	No. best features: 19 (1%)				No. best features: 48 (2.5%)			
	Accuracy	Precision	Recall	F1-score	Accuracy	Precision	Recall	F1-score
DT	0.793	0.933	0.836	0.880	0.804	**0.933**	0.847	0.886
GB	0.765	0.930	0.794	0.853	0.796	0.933	0.839	0.881
KNN	0.699	0.926	0.733	0.816	0.688	0.925	0.722	0.808
NB	0.277	0.928	0.234	0.333	0.263	0.922	0.231	0.344
RF	0.839	**0.934**	0.883	0.903	0.824	0.930	0.868	0.896
SVM	0.653	0.929	0.664	0.764	0.830	0.930	0.885	0.905
HMM	**0.931**	0.931	**1.000**	**0.963**	**0.931**	0.931	**1.000**	**0.963**

All the classifiers mentioned treating the variables as independent *and identically distributed*. Although there are no constraints about the independence of the observations, for example, required by the logistic regression, all these models do not capture the sequential nature of the physiological signals. For this reason, we considered two sequential models, Recurrent Neural Networks (RNN) and Hidden Markov Models (HMM). As the RNNs require high amounts of data, we focused on HMM, adding it to the stack of our models. In particular, we used the multivariate Hidden Markov Models

---
[2] https://tsfresh.com/.

[28], tuned for supervised machine learning using a multivariate Gaussian distribution. The transition probability matrix calculated of the HMM is directly inferred by the data using the Maximum Likelihood Estimation.

3.2.2 Performance Classification

In the Brain Shift game, the presence or absence of a mistake alone is not sufficient to describe the optimal solution of the game. The duration of the attempt also matters. The game requires the user to react fast, therefore attempts of long duration are sub-optimal for the game objective. Similarly, players sometimes lose focus and start selecting their answer randomly and very quickly. This behaviour is called "random guessing" and is also sub-optimal for the game objectives. To better separate the optimal from the ineffective strategies, we introduced a "score" that divides the presence (class 0) or absence (class 1) of a mistake for the duration of the attempt. In these terms, the mistaken attempts will always be 0. The correct attempts will be inversely proportional to its duration e.g. 1/0.5 s = 2 score, 1/2 s = 0.5 score. A histogram of the scores is shown in the left plot in Fig. 2.

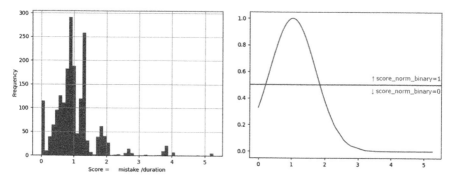

Fig. 2. Left: score histogram; Right: Gaussian function fitting the distribution.

The histogram in Fig. 2 presents a normal distribution: the peak in the middle reflects the best and most common scores according to the population. Hence, we fitted a Gaussian curve on the distribution (right-end plot of Fig. 2). The Gaussian curve maps the scores (x-values) into y-values between 0 and 1. The y-values (right-end plot of Fig. 2) close to 0 are mistakes or slow correct answers or fast correct answers (probably due to "random guessing"). These y-values close to 1 are the most optimal answers. We transformed this range into 2 binary classes, by labelling the values in the range 0–0.5 with 0 and the values in the range 0.5–1 with 1. This gave a new target class "score_norm_binary", distributed 82% positive and 18% negative. We repeated the same analysis performed with the target class "mistake" in Sect. 3.2.1 and reported the results in Table 5.

Table 5. Classification results of the target class "score norm binary".

Model	No. best features: 19 (1%)				No. best features: 48 (2.5%)			
	Accuracy	Precision	Recall	F1-score	Accuracy	Precision	Recall	F1-score
DT	0.638	**0.819**	0.695	0.746	0.648	**0.818**	0.729	0.763
GB	0.624	0.808	0.695	0.739	0.663	0.799	0.775	0.779
KNN	0.530	0.797	0.566	0.654	0.502	0.805	0.518	0.622
NB	0.384	0.815	0.269	0.361	0.352	0.805	0.242	0.337
RF	0.648	0.810	0.729	0.756	0.649	0.798	0.760	0.767
SVM	0.473	0.761	0.471	0.568	0.656	0.806	0.758	0.775
HMM	**0.802**	0.804	**0.996**	**0.884**	**0.757**	0.805	**0.928**	**0.841**

4 Discussion

In this study, we used MMLA tools such as the *LearningHub* and the *Visual Inspection Tool* together with their corresponding approaches to collect, annotate and support the analysis of multimodal physiological data to gain deeper insights into the influence of physiological factors in executive functions such as task switching (RQ1). Results from our manual qualitative analysis revealed distinctive types of behaviour for GSR during task switching. It also showed a moderate negative correlation between GSR and performance. These results suggest a possible alignment with the findings in Larmuseau et al. [17] that show a positive correlation between GSR and mental effort. Thus, suggesting that people that find the switching task easier perform better. Nonetheless, this observation contrasts the findings from Pijeira et al. [16] where moments of GSR activation were positively correlated with good grades in physics exams. Therefore, showing that these findings are task-specific and additional research is needed.

The visual inspection of GSR data conducted in our qualitative analysis, allowed us to identify several points of interest in the sessions, which on closer inspection displayed interesting facts that affected the performance of different task switching attempts (RQ2). While the occurrences of these points of interest are too small to obtain statistically significant results, our analysis suggests studying these types of incidents with a larger data sample. This would allow deeper insights into the physiology of the "D'oh!" moments where the learner recognises having committed a mistake.

The applied machine learning classifiers provided further insights into our research questions. As shown in Table 4, the multivariate HMM outperforms by a big margin all other classifiers in terms of accuracy, precision, recall and F1-score, both for the 1% and 2.5% best features thresholds. In our understanding, this proves the idea that Bayesian probabilistic models are better suited for the proposed supervised classification tasks as they better consider the temporality of the physiological signals. Among the remaining and more traditional classifiers, the best performing ones are RF and DT. When compared to HMM, they score higher in Precision but lower in Recall, resulting in lower F1 scores. Both DT and RF are more flexible in accommodating high dimensional datasets and more transparent in terms of feature importance. Concerning what is the best number of features for the classification task, the results suggest that it depends on the model. For instance, the DT and RF have a higher F1-score with a 2.5% threshold while the HMM has a better F1-score with a 1% threshold. In sum, we can assert it was possible to classify correctly the mistakes analysing the physiological responses (RQ1).

When it comes to performance classification, as presented in Table 5, the performances follow a similar tendency to the mistake classification. HMM is confirmed to be the best performing classifier followed by RF and DT. However, the scores are generally worse when compared to the mistake classification. We think this is because when participants make mistakes they are presented with visual feedback, green ticks or red crosses. This feedback is likely to influence their physiological markers and trigger the so-called "D'oh!" moments. In contrast, adopting the sub-optimal strategies such as "correct guessing" or taking too much time to answer, do not have an immediate negative reward and are less likely to alter the player's emotional and physiological state. Nevertheless, the HMM can be used to classify the ideal performance with the ideal amount of accuracy (80.2%) and F1-score (88.4%). The results of this other analysis suggest that, in principle, an evidence-based approach based on the analysis of the physiological signals can be used also to classify successful from unsuccessful question-answering strategies.

5 Conclusion

In this study, we performed first a qualitative analysis to discover emerging patterns in the physiological markers examining their influence on performance. Then we continued our analysis by training various machine learning classifiers to distinguish the correct from incorrect attempts and optimal from sub-optimal performances. From different perspectives, both analyses allowed us to establish a connection between physiological factors and their influence on executive functions providing answers to RQ1.

The main limitation of our study relies on the limited number of participants and sessions played by them. Some interesting points of observation like Up Spikes appeared only six times, too few to draw any statistically significant conclusion. More data is needed to be able to distinguish between random effects and true links between physiology and task switching performance.

While the qualitative analysis shows a correlation between one of the physiological markers (GSR) and overall performance, the results seem to be specific for the task switching case. For this reason, we can neither generalise across different cognitive tasks nor make claims concerning the causal relationships of physiological states and task performance. However, from the results of our study, we can derive that we can use physiological markers to distinguish optimal from sub-optimal task switching performance. This approach could provide feedback in (near) real-time or can trigger modifications to the environment or the learning tasks to nudge the learner towards the zone of optimal performance.

References

1. James, W.: The Principles of Psychology, vol. 1. Cosimo, Inc. (2007)

2. Marmolejo-Ramos, F., et al.: Your face and moves seem happier when i smile. Exp. Psychol. (2020)
3. Duncan, J.W., Laird, J.D.: Positive and reverse placebo effects as a function of differences in cues used in self-perception. J. Pers. Soc. Psychol. **39**(6), 1024 (1980)
4. Foglia, L., Wilson, R.A.: Embodied cognition. Wiley Interdisc. Rev. Cogn. Sci. **4**(3), 319–325 (2013)
5. Derakshan, N., Eysenck, M.W.: Anxiety, processing efficiency, and cognitive performance (2009)
6. Sandi, C.: Stress and cognition. Wiley Interdisc. Rev. Cogn. Sci. **4**(3), 245–261 (2013)
7. Raab, M., Araújo, D.: Embodied cognition with and without mental representations: the case of embodied choices in sports. Front. Psychol. **10**, 1825 (2019)
8. Greller, W., Drachsler, H.: Translating learning into numbers: a generic framework for learning analytics. J. Educ. Technol. Soc. **15**(3), 42–57 (2012)
9. Pardo, A., Kloos, C. D.: Stepping out of the box: towards analytics outside the learning management system. In: Proceedings of the 1st International Conference on Learning Analytics and Knowledge, pp. 163–167 (2011)
10. Di Mitri, D., Schneider, J., Specht, M., Drachsler, H.: From signals to knowledge: a conceptual model for multimodal learning analytics. J. Comput. Assist. Learn. **34**(4), 338–349. Ew developments from attentional control theory. Eur. Psychol. **14**(2), 168 (2018)
11. Giannakos, M.N., Sharma, K., Pappas, I.O., Kostakos, V., Velloso, E.: Multimodal data as a means to understand the learning experience. Int. J. Inf. Manage. **48**, 108–119 (2019)
12. Sharma, K., Pappas, I., Papavlasopoulou, S., Giannakos, M.: Towards automatic and pervasive physiological sensing of collaborative learning. In: Lund, K., Niccolai, G.P., Lavoué, E., Gweo, C.H., Baker, M. (eds.) Thirteenth International Conference on Computer Supported Collaborative Learning (CSCL), pp. 684–687 (2019)
13. Chanel, G., Bétrancourt, M., Pun, T., Cereghetti, D., Molinari, G.: Assessment of computer-supported collaborative processes using interpersonal physiological and eye-movement coupling. In Proceedings of Humaine Association Conference on Affective Computing and Intelligent Interaction, pp. 116–122 (2013)
14. Spann, C.A., Schaeffer, J., Siemens, G.: Expanding the scope of learning analytics data: preliminary findings on attention and self-regulation using wearable technology. In: LAK17, pp. 203–207 (2017)
15. Bleck, M., Le, N.T., Pinkwart, N.: Physiology-aware learning analytics using pedagogical agents (2020)
16. Pijeira-Díaz, H.J., Drachsler, H., Kirschner, P.A., Järvelä, S.: Profiling sympathetic arousal in a physics course: How active is students? J. Comput. Assist. Learn. **34**(4), 397–408 (2018)
17. Larmuseau, C., Vanneste, P., Cornelis, J., Desmet, P., Depaepe, F.: Combining physiological data and subjective measurements to investigate cognitive load during complex learning. Frontline Learn. Res. **7**(2), 57–74 (2019)
18. Worsley, M., Blikstein, P.: What's an expert? Using learning analytics to identify emergent markers of expertise through automated speech, sentiment and sketch analysis. In: EDM 2011, pp. 235–240 (2011)
19. Sharma, K., Niforatos, E., Giannakos, M., Kostakos, E.: Assessing cognitive performance using physiological and facial features: generalizing across contexts. Proc. ACM Interact. Mob. Wearable Ubiquit. Technol. **4**(3), 1–41 (2020)
20. Ryu, K., Myung, R.: Evaluation of mental workload with a combined measure based on physiological indices during a dual task of tracking and mental arithmetic. Int. J. Ind. Ergon. **35**(11), 991–1009 (2005)
21. Sharma, K., Giannakos, M.: Multimodal data capabilities for learning: what can multimodal data tell us about learning? Br. J. Edu. Technol. **51**(5), 1450–1484 (2020)

22. Scott, W.A.: Cognitive complexity and cognitive flexibility. Sociometry 405–414 (1962)
23. Jacob, R., Parkinson, J.: The potential for school-based interventions that target executive function to improve academic achievement: a review. Rev. Educ. Res. **85**(4), 512–552 (2015)
24. Di Mitri, D., Schneider, J., Specht, M.M., Drachsler, H. J.: Multimodal pipeline: a generic approach for handling multimodal data for supporting learning. In: First workshop on AI-based Multimodal Analytics for Understanding Human Learning in Real-world Educational Contexts (2019)
25. Chelune, G.J., Baer, R.A.: Developmental norms for the Wisconsin card sorting test. J. Clin. Exp. Neuropsychol. **8**(3), 219–228 (1986)
26. Schneider, J., Di Mitri, D., Limbu, B., Drachsler, H.: Multimodal learning hub: a tool for capturing customizable multimodal learning experiences. In: Pammer-Schindler, V., Pérez-Sanagustín, M., Drachsler, H., Elferink, R., Scheffel, M. (eds.) EC-TEL 2018. LNCS, vol. 11082, pp. 45–58. Springer, Cham (2018). https://doi.org/10.1007/978-3-319-98572-5_4
27. Di Mitri, D., Schneider, J., Klemke, R., Specht, M., Drachsler, H. : Read between the lines: an annotation tool for multimodal data for learning. In: LAK19, pp. 51–60 (2019)
28. Blasiak, S., Rangwala, H.: A hidden Markov model variant for sequence classification. In: Twenty-Second International Joint Conference on Artificial Intelligence (2011)

Examining the Effect of Self-explanations in Distributed Self-assessment

Cheng-Yu Chung(✉) and I-Han Hsiao

Arizona State University, Tempe, AZ, USA
{Cheng.Yu.Chung,Sharon.Hsiao}@asu.edu

Abstract. Self-assessment is a twofold activity consisting of self-evaluation and self-explanation, which are considered imperative metacognitive strategies in learning science. Although the self-explanation effect has been scaffolded in numerous learning systems, it remains unclear whether the effect can still occur to students in a voluntary setting of learning such as remote learning that requires self-regulation to persist in making progress. Furthermore, it is inconclusive what students' behavioral patterns can be when they exercise self-evaluation and self-explanation overtime. In this study, we investigate the effectiveness of self-assessment and the embedded self-explanation by dissecting semantic elements in the explanations in a multilevel analysis. The result showed that the low-performing students were challenged by the complexity of topics, which resulted in an increased error rate when they ventured into more learning opportunities. However, the self-explanation effect might occur to them and improved their performances, especially when they reflected on the content of questions that were relevant to the concepts. In summary, this study provides an insight into effective self-assessment. Specifically, it shows that students can potentially improve performances by writing compact and relevant explanations over time.

Keywords: Self-explanation · Self-regulated learning · Distributed practice · Learning analytics

1 Introduction

Recently, in the community of learning analytics, many researchers have focused on the theory of self-regulated learning (SRL) and developed various computational models to trace SRL in students' learning processes [1]. With the help of learning management systems, there have been numerous approaches to scaffold students' metacognitive skills and engage them in their learning processes consciously over time [2]. One instructional design based on SRL theories is *self-assessment*. Self-assessment aims to improve to develop the students' metacognitive skills and self-efficacy by a twofold process: evaluation with a standard rubric and reflection to fill the gap between his/her prior knowledge by explanations. Although explanation-based learning [3] has shown beneficial for students to learn in problem-solving activities, it remains unclear whether the progression of self-explanation in self-assessment improves students' performances over time.

Self-explanation is considered an effective strategy that invokes students to learn from active comprehensions of concepts, actions, and goals in solving problems [4, 5] Many studies have shown that a good problem solver can follow a sophisticated procedure to self-explain by examining the relationship between actions and goals, connecting to principles, and making domain-relevant comments. Essentially, *the self-explanation effect* hypothesizes that students can learn better when they explain learning content to themselves while solving problems [3]. The effect has been found across various fields of study, e.g., mathematics, physics, geometry, and computer programming [3, 6, 7]. However, a student's learning is dynamic. For example, s/he may change the schedule, style, or strategies throughout a course of study due to internal cognitive factors like interests, self-efficacy, and motivations, or external factors like pressure from other academic activities. These factors are also correlated to the development of knowledge and understanding, which could further complicate the effectiveness of self-explanation.

Researchers have developed many reliable research instruments to control and measure the self-explanation effect in both laboratory and classroom settings. Computational models in the literature have also provided empirical evidence about how good and poor solvers construct declarative knowledge [3] and integrate supportive tools into the learning in self-explanation [4]. These research works indeed advance the use of scaffolded learning in classrooms by technologies; nevertheless, the relationship between self-explanation and a student's long-term development remains somewhat ambiguous and presumptuous. For example, [5] documented a year-to-year comparison of students who used the material with self-explanation questions and those who did not. The results, however, did not reveal explicitly how the self-explanation effect occurred over time together with students' learning activities. Students might lose interest and disengage from the learning activity, which suggests that they might not learn from the self-explanations in the way researchers expect.

This work aims to dissect the correlation of the self-explanation effect and students' learning processes in self-assessment (i.e., a natural and voluntary self-regulated setting). To develop significant and replicable learning analytics, the research design is grounded on the Knowledge-Learning-Instruction (KLI) framework and empirical evidence of the self-explanation effect from learning science. Specifically, the development of this study is guided by the following research questions:

1. What is the pattern of students' progression of learning in different programming topics on the self-assessment platform? What is the relationship between the number of opportunities taken and students' performance?
2. Does the self-explanation effect transfer from self-assessment to students' performance in formal exams? What is the difference between high- and low-performing students in their self-explanation behavior?
3. What are effective and ineffective elements in explanations that affect students' performance in self-assessment over time?

2 Related Work

2.1 The Self-explanation Effect in Problem-Solving

The self-explanation effect hypothesizes that students who self-explain examples in problem-solving activities learn better than those who do not [3]. This effect has been examined and shown effective in different fields of study like geometry, physics, mathematics, etc. Researchers have also found several key differences between novice and expert students in the ways they self-explain. An early study from Chi et al. [6] showed that in a self-explanation process, the good solvers were able to fill in the gaps in their knowledge by making domain-relevant comments that aimed to support the relationship between actions and goals. On the contrary, the "poor" solvers were more likely to make superficial and less-accurate explanations. These findings were further examined by a computational model in the following study [3]. It revealed that the good solvers learned from self-explanation through a sophisticated search control to localize a defect and derive a piece of knowledge to patch it. In the context of computer science and engineering, [5] examined in-code commenting activities in computer programs by cluster analysis and identified five patterns of students' explanations: goal-based, limited, principle-based, mechanistic, and original solution. The study pointed out that despite in different contexts the students wrote different kinds of explanations, the principle-based approach was linked to high-quality explanations that connected background knowledge and outcomes.

The results from these studies to some extent cross-validate the self-explanation effect and show there are discrepancies between good and poor problem solvers in their ways of self-explanation. They shed light on how to leverage self-explanation and its embedded elements to support students to learn efficiently and effectively by learning analytics and systems. For example, [8] elaborated a quantitative coding system identifying explanation artifacts for algorithms and data structures. The system constituted an overarching concept of explanation-oriented programming. In a broader context, the self-explanation effect can also be scaffolded as reflective activities after assignments (or exams) to improve the students' metacognition and self-regulation skills [1]. All of these studies unanimously suggest that it is feasible to design instructions for promoting and encouraging students to write explanations while they are solving problems. The underlying assumption is that the self-explanation effect will occur to students when they are being prompted or instructed to do so. In our work, we inspect when and how the self-explanation effect occurs in a voluntary setting. The results are expected to contribute towards and complement literature of self-explanation in the perspective of scalable, dynamic, and close-to-reality instructional designs.

2.2 Tracing the Relationship Between Metacognitive Skills and Learning Outcomes

Numerous studies have tried to leverage students' activities in log data and learning analytics to trace the relationship between students' metacognitive skills and learning outcomes. For example, Cicchinelli et al. explored activity streams from a learning management system and correlated the students' self-regulation behaviors including planning, monitoring, and regulating, to their performances [9]. Asano et al. investigated the effectiveness of optional self-explanation scaffolded by two kinds of prompts, which were shown after online programming homework, in terms of the frequency of writing explanations, the correctness of problem-solving, and proficiency in the language of instruction [10]. By long-term tracking on reflection activities, one study also pointed out that the students' self-regulation behaviors were highly variable and, therefore, required adaptive strategies to support [11].

The self-explanation effect, however, has been traditionally analyzed in laboratory settings that are well-controlled [7]. Although the self-explanation effect and different modes where students react to self-explanation prompts can be well explained in a laboratory setting, the correlation between the effect and the development of learning status is less explored and remains unclear in practice. One related work from Loksa et al. who conducted a 10-week study to analyze students' self-regulation processes by in-situ observations showed that the students' reflection was highly variable [11]. But their work focused on a broader self-regulation process instead of the embedded self-explanation effect. The study from Asano et al. [10] described above was also closely related to our research goals, but their analysis mainly focused on summary statistics of contextual variables rather than capturing the continuous learning progress and semantics elements in written explanations.

Our study aims to fill the gap by using learning analytics to examine how students write their self-explanations when they solve problems on a self-assessment platform, which allows us to observe the students' learning progress and how they react to self-explanation activities at the same time. We believe this observation is of interest for both researchers and educational practitioners since the understanding could not only improve the ecological validity of the self-explanation effect in practice but also suggest potential factors to improve the design of scaffolded self-explanation in a learning system.

3 Methodology

3.1 Guiding the Research by the KLI Framework

The KLI framework consists of three kinds of events related to student learning: assessment events (AEs), instructional events (IEs), and learning events (LEs) [12]. LEs entails knowledge components (KCs) which are an abstract representation of cognitive knowledge to learn. The interaction, dependency, and iteration of these events and KCs, either observable or unobservable, capture students' learning processes. The KLI framework can be used to help different groups of researchers elaborate their research agendas and formulate hypotheses on the same set of constructs. This process ensures that the yielded results contribute to the potential generality of learning theories analytics. In this study, we choose to use the KLI framework as the underlying guidance when asking research questions due to its simplicity and closeness to computational models and learning analytics [13].

In this study, the subject course (which is an introductory programming course as described in Sect. 3) focuses on the basics and intermediate topics in the object-oriented programming of Java. Those topics are a kind of KCs under the KLI framework. A practice of self-assessment consists of two parts: assessment and evaluation. The assessment part, as a kind of AE, tests a student's prior knowledge about the concept to learn. The evaluation part, as a kind of LE, provides an opportunity for the student to reflect and learn from his/her success/failure in the assessment. The self-assessment per se is a kind of IE that is, different from a typical instructional design, scheduled and controlled dynamically throughout a semester by the student but not the instructor.

3.2 Modeling Self-assessment by the Learning Curve Analysis

The derived instance of the KLI framework pinpoints the unit of analysis in this study as individual self-assessment activities (i.e., attempts to answer questions and make self-evaluations). There are many mature statistical tools in the community of learning analytics to analyze observable events. In this study, we choose to use the learning curve analysis that embodies the essence of the KLI framework and involves the time dimension in the analysis [12]. This method not only is close to our research design but also meets our need to trace the dynamics of students' learning processes in self-assessment over time.

To apply this method, the KCs were refined and grouped into five categories of topics: Basics (e.g., syntax, variables), Arithmetic, Flow Control, Data Structure (e.g., arrays), and OOP (e.g., class and object in Java). The IEs were modeled as students' first attempts to answer questions and treated as opportunities to practice and learn. AEs were simply represented by the error flag of those attempts, i.e., 1 is incorrect and 0 is correct. The LEs, or students' learning processes in self-assessment, were modeled as learning curves, or more specifically, non-linear curves of error rates over the number of questions that have been answered by students.

We followed the implementation based on a specialized mixed linear model that is referred to as Additive Factors Model (AFM) [13]. We evaluated the model performance by Akaike information criterion (AIC) and Bayesian information criterion (BIC) as suggested in [14]. Additionally, the self-explanation effect was explained by semantic features in the written explanations. The features were included as a separate factor in the AFM model (see the following section for more details).

3.3 Semantics and Elements in Self-explanation

The difference in explanations between good solvers and poor solvers has been discovered extensively in the literature. An early study from Chi et al. is one of the pioneers in this area exploring the two-way process where a student constructs explanations and learns from them [6]. The study found that the good solvers involved their prior-knowledge in self-explanation (relevance), accurately identified their successes and failures (accuracy), and infrequently but succinctly made references to examples (frequency and precision of references). Although these findings were based on protocols and observations made by the researchers, a follow-up study showed that a computational model could accurately simulate and verify those results with further details of processes that triggered the self-explanation effect [3].

These findings effectively pave the way for researchers to leverage self-explanation to support students and analyze the self-explanation effect by computationally scalable schema together with other learning analytics. Our study follows this track of research to understand how students' self-explanation affects their learning in an introductory programming class. It is worth noting that explanations have also been found beneficial in programming learning [5]. The coding schema developed by researchers [7] in the context of programming and engineering provides a domain-specific tool for us to explore self-explanation activities conducted by our subjects. We adapted their schema for our research data and used aggregated semantic elements as shown in Table 1.

Table 1. Coding schema and extracted semantic features of explanation content.

Level & element [15]	Semantic features	Examples (keywords are quoted by brackets)
None/Outcome	(DR) Domain-relevant keywords extracted from topics in a Java textbook, e.g., *syntax, data, variable, Boolean, integer, type, comment, statement, control, if-else, switch, loop, for, break, continue, object, method*, etc.	• "[Syntax] errors occur before one can compile" • "The '//' makes the [statement] a [comment]" • "I got confused and thought there was no semicolon after x was [initialized]" • "The code means numbers cannot be outside of those [parameters]"
Shallow/Description	(B1) Action verbs in Bloom's Remember and Understanding [16] including *recognize, recall, remember, interpret, exemplify, classify, summarize, infer, explain, understand*	• "I [remembered] there are two for [integers]..." • "I know that there are 8 [types] of [primitive data types]" • "I [remember] the [main method] by hear"
Shallow/Description	(QR) Relevance to question content [a]	• "That's not actually a line so no semicolon anymore" • "I didn't know it was object-oriented"

[a] Measured by latent semantic analysis instead of keyword mapping so no keywords are marked in examples.

3.4 Experiment Platform and Data Collection

QuizIT [20] was an online self-assessment platform developed by the researchers in this study. The platform provided opportunities for novice students to self-monitor their learning status in the study course. The platform released one programming-related, multiple-choice question a day for the students to practice and review the learning content. There were two kinds of questions supplied on the platform: concept questions and code comprehension (i.e., code tracing) questions. The topics of questions included a range from the basics, like data types and flow controls, to the advanced data structures and object-oriented programming in Java. When the students attempted to answer a question, they had an opportunity to self-explain how they reached the answer. This process was served as a way to reflect on the concept asked by the question. All activities on the platform were logged as transactions including question content, self-explanation content, timestamps, and correctness.

The dataset in this study was collected from an introductory programming course offered in Spring 2018 at a four-year public university in the United States. There were 249 undergraduate students enrolled in the course. The platform was introduced to students as an optional learning tool for them to practice and monitor their learning progress. The students were told that their activities on the platform would not be graded, which primed them to take questions for their benefit but not the requirements of the course. Throughout the semester we collected in total 2228 transactions from 112 students in the course.

The analysis focused on the comparison between and within the high-performing (HP) and low-performing (LP) students. To categorize HP and LP students, we normalized the grades from the three midterm exams in the course and calculated the average exam grades. The students who achieved 60% or higher normalized grades were grouped into HP; the others were grouped into LP. In total, there were 51 HP students and 61 LP students. On average, the HP students answered 22.27 distinct questions and the standard deviation (SD) was 31.64; the LP students answered 17.90 and the SD was 26.62. No significant difference was found in the number of questions answered by the HP and LP students. This indicated that both HP and LP students probably shared a similar self-assessment pattern on a macro level since they attempted a similar number of questions on average.

4 Results

4.1 Mixed Regression Outcomes Between the Error Rate and Learning Opportunities

Each self-assessment question in this study is considered an opportunity for students to learn and improve their knowledge in the course. It is intuitive to assume that the more questions students practice, the more chances they can learn and acquire knowledge, and as a result achieve better performance in self-assessment (i.e., a lower error rate). We analyzed this factor by looking at the regression plot between the total number of questions taken by the students and the error rate as shown in Fig. 1. We found that the HP and LP students had mixed outcomes. The error rate of the HP students was not sensitive to the total number of questions they took (a relatively flat regression line in Fig. 1). On the contrary, the error rate of LP students had a stronger positive correlation, which was further verified by a significant main effect from the total number of opportunities on the error rate ($F(1, 59) = 7.98, p = 0.01$). While the result seemed that the self-assessment platform favored HP students over LP students (since the more LP students worked, the higher the error rate they received); nonetheless, it could also be a signal of the LP students' vulnerability and incapability.

To look deeper into the root cause, we factored in the topic complexity levels and found out that the error rates were more sensitive in some topics than the others. The ANOVA analysis with question topics controlled verified that there was no significant effect from the total number of opportunities on the error rate. Since the topics of questions on the self-assessment platform were aligned with the progress of the class syllabus, it was likely that questions released at a later time were coupled with multiple complex topics that the students were struggling with (or early topics were challenging enough since they were novices in computer programming), which therefore resulted in higher error rates in some topics.

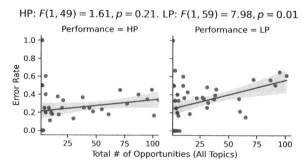

Fig. 1. The relationship between the total number of questions and the error rate. We can see that LP students have the trend where more attempts resulted in higher error; and the trend from HP is relatively flat, which reveals some LP students might suffer from ineffective practices.

Overall, this analysis illustrated that the HP and LP students had different levels of problem-solving abilities. The complexity of questions had an impact on the performance as the class progressed forwards. However, what the students did in self-assessment that was correlated to their performance remained unclear. Therefore, we further investigated their self-explanation activities to find out whether the written explanations made any difference to the performances.

4.2 Comparing the Number of Self-explanations Between HP and LP

Because the self-explanation part on the self-assessment platform was optional in this study, we needed to find out whether there was a difference between HP and LP students in the willingness of writing optional explanations. We calculated the ratio of attempts with prior explanations (AwE) to those without ones (AnE) for each student and compared the values from HP and LP.

The result showed that both groups of students made many attempts without prior explanations, which was not surprising because the self-assessment platform did not force students to write explanations. Instead, students were self-regulated by themselves and decided whether to self-explain for their benefit. It was expected that only a part of students who were aware of the benefits of self-explanation would do so. However, it was surprising to see that there was no significant difference found between HP and LP students in the amount of self-explanation. Both groups had very similar ratios (around 35%). This result indicates that both HP and LP students probably had a similar level of metacognitive strategies regarding self-explanation.

4.3 Correlating the Error Rate to Self-explanation

After confirming that there was no difference in the number of explanations, we further compared the error rate between AwE and AnE. When a student attempted on the self-assessment platform, s/he would get a chance to self-explain how or why he/she chose the answer no matter it was correct or not. We assumed that a student's attempt to answer a question would be considered *influenced by the potential self-explanation effect* if the student wrote explanations in the prior attempt to another question. We also controlled the level of questions (i.e., the difficulty) in this analysis because we assumed that the level of questions might indirectly affect students' willingness to make explanations. For example, a student might answer an easy question correctly without the need to further self-explain how to solve the question.

We found out that the HP and LP students had a very similar pattern of error rate, and the self-explanation effect was mixed. In most cases, AwE did not have a significantly lower error rate than AnE. However, in the case where the LP students working on questions of moderate difficulty, AwE had a significantly lower error ($M = 0.24, SD = 0.21$) than the others ($M = 0.47, SD = 0.32$) ($t(34) = -2.20, p = 0.03$).

To control the level of questions, we conducted an ANOVA with 3 (level of questions) by 2 (having previous explanations) factorial design. The result showed that for HP students, only the main effect of the level of questions on the error rate was significant such that attempts of easy and moderate questions had lower error rates than those of difficult questions. ($F(2, 1132) = 14.99, p = 0.00$). For LP students, the analysis further showed that the main effect of having prior explanation on the error rate was significant such that attempts with prior explanations had a lower error rate ($F(1, 1088) = 23.27, p = 0.00$); the effect of the level of questions was also significant with a pattern similar to one of HP students ($F(2, 1088) = 14.77, p = 0.00$).

Also, there was a significant interaction found between the two variables ($F(2, 1086) = 4.21, p = 0.01$) such that for easy and moderate questions, having prior explanations led to lower error rates. But, for difficult questions, prior explanations did not affect the error rate. These outcomes indicated that the level of questions was, unsurprisingly, correlated to the error rate, and the self-explanation effect could occur to LP students when they practiced questions of certain difficulty.

4.4 Multilevel Semantics: Relevance to Question and Learning Content is the Key to the Self-explanation Effect

To find out the correlation between the content of explanations and the error rate, we extracted several semantic features (Table 1) and analyzed them by the learning curve analysis (Table 2) for their effects on students' learning progress, and multilevel ANOVA analyses for main effects from different levels of semantics.

In the following discussion, we will first explain the detail of extracted semantic features and report the result from the learning curve analysis. Afterward, we will focus on analyzing the main effects of different semantic features by multilevel analysis.

Learning Curves from HP and LP Students were Sensitive to the Level of Questions and the Number of Explanations Respectively. As shown in Sect. 4.3, the difficulty of questions and the existence of explanations had different correlations to the error rate for HP and LP students. To figure out the effect of these two factors, we looked at the fitness of models that incorporated these two factors. For HP students, the number of explanations did not improve the model from the baseline and random models. Instead, the level of questions improved the model and decreased AIC and BIC from the baseline by around

Table 2. Comparing the performance of different learning curve models.

Factors in the model	AIC in HP	BIC in HP	AIC in LP	BIC in LP
(Random) Error ~ (1 | Student) - 1	1374.502	1384.573	1434.384	1444.375
(Baseline) Error ~ (1 | Student) + (Opportunity | Topic) - 1	1347.982	1373.158	1355.501	1380.480
Baseline + Num of Explanations	1355.946	1381.123	1352.717	1377.696
Baseline + Question Level	1337.188	1372.435	1357.296	1392.266
Baseline + Question-Explanation Relevance	1318.004	1342.951	1302.280	1326.972
Baseline + Number of Domain-relevant Keywords	1318.080	1343.026	1304.008	1328.700
Baseline + Action verbs in Bloom's Remember and Understand	1317.808	1342.755	1300.207	1324.898

10 and 1 respectively. For LP students, the number of explanations improved the model but not the level of questions. The improvement from the baseline was around −3 in AIC and −3 in BIC. Overall, these findings provided another piece of evidence showing that students' learning progress was not only related to the number of opportunities taken but intertwined with the complexity of topics, the level of questions, students' learning status (modeled by the student intercept), and the self-explanation process.

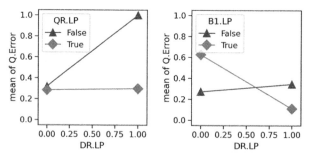

Fig. 2. Interaction plots of two multilevel self-explanation processes for LP students. The left plot shows the process DR + QR. The right plot shows DR + B1. The plots and accompanied ANOVA analyses indicated that there were significant main effects on the error rate from the interaction between DR and QR, and the one between DR and LP. In other words, domain-relevant explanations without question relevance led to a higher error rate; those involving the Remember and Understand processes led to lower error rates.

Domain- and Question-Relevant Explanations Mattered Especially for LP Students. Next, we analyzed the semantics in the students' self-explanations. In the fitted models, we found that all semantic features of explanations improved the baseline by decreasing around 30 and 50 in AIC/BIC for both HP and LP students, respectively. This result indicated that the semantic elements in the explanations were somewhat correlated to the students' performances in self-assessment. When examining the marginal distribution of error rates and the semantics, we did not find a significant main effect from individual semantic features on the error rate.

When we further examined the interaction of processes, we found that for LP students, with the variance from levels of questions controlled, there was a significant main effect on the error rate from the interaction between DR and QR ($F(1, 309) = 6.10, p = 0.01$), and another one from DR and B1 ($F(1, 309) = 8.19, p = 0.00$)). Interpreted together with the interaction plot (Fig. 2), this result indicated that for the domain-relevant explanations (DR = 1), no question relevance led to higher error rates; for domain-irrelevant explanations (DR = 0), whether they had question relevance did not affect the error rate. Besides, the domain-relevant explanations involving the Remember and Understand processes led to lower error rates; the domain-irrelevant explanations involving the same sets of processes, on the contrary, led to higher error rates. To summarize, these outcomes suggested that the LP students' written explanations in self-explanation could be effective when they involved the retrieval of domain-relevant content instead of merely mentioning that s/he remembered or understood the answer (e.g., "I remembered learning this in the class"). Also, the explanations irrelevant from the questions would not be effective even though they were somehow domain-relevant.

In terms of HP students, we did not find any significant pattern in the semantics of explanations but found their explanations contained more domain-relevant keywords marginally than LP students ($F(1, 472) = 17.55, p = 0.00$). This result suggested that HP students tended to include domain-relevant content in their explanations.

5 Conclusions and Discussion

This study aimed to examine the correlation of the self-explanation effect and students' learning processes in a natural and voluntary setting (i.e., self-assessment). We dissected the self-explanation effect over a semester by analyzing semantic features in the written explanations. The result showed that the receptive low-performing students could benefit more from writing explanations. The questions that were attempted by the student after explanations had a significantly lower error rate. Besides, the effectiveness of practices was positively correlated to the domain- and question-relevance from self-explanation, especially for the low-performing students.

We found that the more questions a student took, the higher the error rate was due to the complexity of topics and ineffective practices. This outcome answered our RQ1. At the first glance, the result seemed to contradict the intuition behind "the power law of practice" [17] and the distributed practice [18]. However, such a result could be the case that when a student practiced more and more questions, they would eventually exhaust easy and moderate questions and failed to solve difficult ones. It could also be the case that the self-assessment was not easy for the novice students to achieve effectiveness because effective self-assessment might require not only a sufficient amount of practice but also the students' engagement [19], persistence [Author 2020], and other metacognitive strategies (like the self-explanation effect found in this study).

When the instructions are less restrictive and schedules are relatively flexible (e.g. massive open online courses (MOOCs)), students may tend to procrastinate and participate less over time, and result in the use of scaffolded SRL becomes imperative. Our study revealed that it may be helpful for students to learn in such a voluntary setting by enabling self-explanation opportunities. We found that the high-performing students had lower error rates than the low-performing students on the self-assessment platform. Also, the explanations were associated with lower error rates, especially for the low-performing students. These findings effectively addressed our RQ2 and adhered to the self-explanation effect which suggests explanations are helpful for students to learn in solving problems [3].

The literature shows that students who benefit the most from the self-explanation effect are those who provide high coherence in their written reflection texts [6]. Our results are aligned with the literature. The students benefited from the self-explanation effect when they wrote explanations involving high domain- and question-relevance. We found that as long as the students made explanations including domain-relevant keywords and question-relevant content, plus their own "actions" like understanding or remembering, they were able to achieve better performance. This finding answered our RQ3 and provided an encouraging implication for supporting more and more distributed learning environments nowadays, e.g., during the COVID-19 pandemic high self-regulation is demanded for students to keep progress when they study online. Although an extensive and complex scaffolding may be useful to support students, a rather compact but consistent design of scaffolding could be as effective.

5.1 Limitations

There are a few limitations in this study. First, our self-assessment platform supplied only MCQs, even though they included both conceptual and code comprehension questions. Programming learning requires diverse problem-solving skills that the current system and the problem set do not offer. For example, actual code writing is not included. This might limit the scope of topics students could learn on the self-assessment platform and deterred students who planned to focus on code-writing problems when they practiced on their own. Second, our analyses did not consider time intervals between attempts of questions. Some students could practice a lot of questions in a short time (i.e., cramming), some could space their practices evenly over time. The current study follows the assumption that students would never forget content they had learned through their attempts to solve questions in self-assessment. This assumption inherently limits our understanding of the spacing effect in self-assessment and the students' strategies in self-regulated learning. Finally, it was noted that there were potential overlaps in the semantic features. For example, Java's "class" overlaps the "class" in school. In our implementation we shortened the keyword lists by removing overlapping words; however, there could still be multifaceted words across different aspects of the semantics that we were not fully aware of. This limitation requires future studies to use more sophisticated natural language models to overcome.

References

1. Prather, J., Becker, B.A., Craig, M., Denny, P., Loksa, D., Margulieux, L.: What do we think we think we are doing? Metacognition and self-regulation in programming. In: Proceedings of the 2020 ACM Conference on International Computing Education Research, pp. 2–13. ACM, New York (2020). https://doi.org/10.1145/3372782.3406263
2. Becker, B.A., Quille, K.: 50 years of CS1 at SIGCSE: a review of the evolution of introductory programming education research. In: Proceedings of the 50th ACM Technical Symposium on Computer Science Education - SIGCSE 2019, pp. 338–344. ACM Press, New York (2019). https://doi.org/10.1145/3287324.3287432
3. VanLehn, K., Jones, R.M., Chi, M.T.H.: A model of the self-explanation effect. J. Learn. Sci. **2**, 1–59 (1992). https://doi.org/10.1207/s15327809jls0201_1
4. Aleven, V.A.W.M.M., Koedinger, K.R.: An effective metacognitive strategy: learning by doing and explaining with a computer-based cognitive tutor. Cogn. Sci. **26**, 147–179 (2002). https://doi.org/10.1207/s15516709cog2602_1
5. Vihavainen, A., Miller, C.S., Settle, A.: Benefits of self-explanation in introductory programming. In: Proceedings of the 46th ACM Technical Symposium on Computer Science Education - SIGCSE 2015, pp. 284–289. ACM Press, New York (2015). https://doi.org/10.1145/2676723.2677260
6. Chi, M.T.H., Bassok, M., Lewis, M.W., Reimann, P., Glaser, R.: Self-explanations: how students study and use examples in learning to solve problems. Cogn. Sci. **13**, 145–182 (1989). https://doi.org/10.1207/s15516709cog1302_1
7. Vieira, C., Magana, A.J., Roy, A., Falk, M.L.: Student explanations in the context of computational science and engineering education. Cogn. Instr. **37**, 201–231 (2019). https://doi.org/10.1080/07370008.2018.1539738
8. Young, J., Walkingshaw, E.: A Domain analysis of data structure and algorithm explanations in the wild. In: Proceedings of the 49th ACM Technical Symposium on Computer Science Education, pp. 870–875. ACM, New York (2018). https://doi.org/10.1145/3159450.3159477
9. Cicchinelli, A., et al.: Finding traces of self-regulated learning in activity streams. In: Proceedings of the 8th International Conference on Learning Analytics and Knowledge. pp. 191–200. ACM, New York (2018). https://doi.org/10.1145/3170358.3170381
10. Asano, Y., Solyst, J., Williams, J.J.: Characterizing and influencing students' tendency to write self-explanations in online homework. In: Proceedings of the Tenth International Conference on Learning Analytics & Knowledge, pp. 448–453. ACM, New York (2020). https://doi.org/10.1145/3375462.3375511
11. Loksa, D., Xie, B., Kwik, H., Ko, A.J.: Investigating novices' in situ reflections on their programming process. In: Proceedings of the 51st ACM Technical Symposium on Computer Science Education, pp. 149–155. ACM, New York (2020). https://doi.org/10.1145/3328778.3366846
12. Koedinger, K.R., Corbett, A.T., Perfetti, C.: The Knowledge learning instruction framework: bridging the science-practice chasm to enhance robust student learning. Cogn. Sci. **36**, 757–798 (2012). https://doi.org/10.1111/j.1551-6709.2012.01245.x
13. Cen, H., Koedinger, K., Junker, B.: Learning factors analysis – a general method for cognitive model evaluation and improvement. In: Ikeda, M., Ashley, K.D., Chan, T.-W. (eds.) ITS 2006. LNCS, vol. 4053, pp. 164–175. Springer, Heidelberg (2006). https://doi.org/10.1007/11774303_17
14. Liu, R., Koedinger, K.R.: Variations in learning rate: student classification based on systematic residual error patterns across practice opportunities. In: Proceedings of the 8th International Conference on Educational Data Mining, pp. 420–423. Educational Data Mining, Madrid (2015)

15. Jung, Y., Wise, A.F.: How and how well do students reflect? Milti-dimensional automated reflection assessment in health professions education. In: Proceedings of the Tenth International Conference on Learning Analytics & Knowledge, pp. 595–604. ACM, New York (2020). https://doi.org/10.1145/3375462.3375528
16. Adams, N.E.: Bloom's taxonomy of cognitive learning objectives. J. Med. Libr. Assoc. **103**, 152–153 (2015). https://doi.org/10.3163/1536-5050.103.3.010
17. Newell, A., Rosenbloom, P.S.: Mechanisms of skill acquisition and the law of practice. Cogn. Ski. their Acquis. **1**, 1–55 (1981)
18. Benjamin, A.S., Tullis, J.: What makes distributed practice effective? Cogn. Psychol. **61**, 228–247 (2010). https://doi.org/10.1016/j.cogpsych.2010.05.004
19. Chi, M.T.H., Wylie, R.: The ICAP framework: linking cognitive engagement to active learning outcomes. Educ. Psychol. **49**, 219–243 (2014). https://doi.org/10.1080/00461520.2014.965823
20. Alzaid, M., Hsiao, I.-H.: Behavioral analytics for distributed practices in programming problem-solving. In: 2019 IEEE Frontiers in Education Conference (FIE). IEEE (2019). https://doi.org/10.1109/FIE43999.2019.9028583

Examining the Relationship Between Reflective Writing Behaviour and Self-regulated Learning Competence: A Time-Series Analysis

Wannapon Suraworachet[1](✉) , Cristina Villa-Torrano[2] , Qi Zhou[1] ,
Juan I. Asensio-Pérez[2] , Yannis Dimitriadis[2] , and Mutlu Cukurova[1]

[1] UCL Knowledge Lab, University College London, London, UK
{wannapon.suraworachet.20,qtnvqz3,m.Cukurova}@ucl.co.uk
[2] GSIC-EMIC Research Group, Universidad de Valladolid, Valladolid, Spain
cristina@gsic.uva.es, {juaase,yannis}@tel.uva.es

Abstract. Self-Regulated Learning (SRL) competence is imperative to academic achievement. For reflective academic writing tasks, which are common for university assessments, this is especially the case since students are often required to plan the task independently to be successful. The purpose of the current study was to examine different reflection behaviours of postgraduate students that were required to reflect on individual tasks over a fifteen-week-long higher education course. Forty students participated in a standardised questionnaire at the beginning of the course to assess their SRL competence and then participated in weekly individual reflection tasks on Google Docs. We examined students' reflective writing behaviours based on time-series and correlation analysis of fine-grained data retrieved from Google Docs. More specifically, reflection behaviours between students with high SRL and low SRL competence were investigated. The results show that students with high SRL competence tend to reflect more frequently and more systematically than students with low SRL competence. Even though no statistically significant difference in academic performance between the two groups was found, there were statistical correlations between academic performance and individual reflective writing behaviours. We conclude the paper with a discussion on the insights into the temporal reflection patterns of different SRL competence student clusters, the impact of these behaviours on students' academic performance, and potential suggestions for appropriate support for students with different levels of SRL.

Keywords: Self-regulated learning · Time series analysis · Writing analytics · Seasonal decomposition · Writing behaviours

1 Introduction and Background

In contrast to many face-to-face learning scenarios, in online learning students are not as restricted in managing their schedules and learning process such as what to study, when to study and for how long [1]. In this aspect, students who are successful in their learning appear to be those who can control their learning process and take an active role in achieving their academic goals [2]. These students are generally referred to as self-regulated learners. The theory of Self-Regulated Learning (SRL) views learning as a self-monitoring and planning process where students monitor the effectiveness of their learning methods and adjust them to their needs [3]. There are different theoretical models of SRL that describe regulation phases during learning situations, such as the one proposed by Zimmerman [4] and Winne and Hadwin [5]. Despite the difference in their theoretical backgrounds, there are common phases within them: preparation (forethought), performance and appraisal (self-reflection) [6]. Throughout these phases, students may adopt different strategies for tackling the challenges posed by the learning task. The strategies could be grouped into time management, metacognition, effort regulation, critical thinking, rehearsal, elaboration, organization, peer-to-peer learning and help-seeking [1]. Literature shows that planning (i.e., organization, goal setting, effort regulation, etc.) during the forethought phase and following a good time management strategy during the performance phase are important aspects of SRL that can lead to an improvement in learning [7]. Many studies in the literature analyse how the level of student regulation is related to their performance. For instance, in the study by Broadbent [8] the authors highlighted the importance of time management and elaboration during a MOOC course and a positive relationship between the SRL strategies used by the students and their grades. In another study by Tempeelar, Rienties, and Nguyen [9], it was found that students who use help-seeking strategies by using examples with worked-out solutions achieve higher scores.

A significant approach to studying Self-Regulated Learning is through writing reflections. Reflection is an essential learning process by consciously pondering upon past experience to evaluate and gain new insights which could shape better future actions [10]. As noted by Schunk and Zimmerman [11], self-reflective practices allow students to i) assess their learning progress and the effectiveness of their strategies modify such practices when needed and ii) adjust environmental and social factors to improve their learning settings. For instance, Baggetun and Wasson's study [12] analyses students' use of weblogs for open-ended writing. Specifically, it looks at how SRL manifested in these writings based on four categories: reflection, motivation, ownership, and customization and categorization. The study suggested that weblogging can contribute to SRL in several ways: allowing students to publicly reflect on a topic and initiate conversations about it; building personal knowledge bases by providing relevant links on certain topics; and, providing solutions to challenges that they have encountered. In addition, during the study carried out by Nückles, Hübner and Renkl [13], the authors supported the writing process using prompts to encourage SRL while drafting learning protocols. Learning protocols are artefacts created by students where they are instructed to write down their reflections on previously presented learning contents. Moreover, students should ask themselves what they did not understand and what they could do to improve it. Students received different types of prompts: cognitive prompts, metacognitive prompts and mixed prompts with and without planning of remedial strategies. The results show that prompts are very effective in stimulating cognitive and metacognitive strategies. Providing students with prompts on organisation, elaboration, monitoring and planning increases the use of strategies related to these phases of regulation and improves students' learning protocols.

As mentioned above, engaging in writing reflection practices about the learning process may provide benefits for learners, and supporting students during this process by enhancing their SRL strategies can improve their results. Unfortunately, it is very difficult for teachers to gain insight into their students' writing process, which could be one of the reasons why they only provide feedback on the final product [14]. Therefore, it is necessary to use tools that can provide meaningful information about the students' writing process to i) understand students' reflective writing behaviours, and ii) provide timely support to the students [14]. There are many tools developed to support writing instruction and assessment including automated essay scoring systems to assess writing quality [15], automated writing evaluation systems to provide feedback and correction suggestions [16] and intelligent tutoring systems that can provide automated feedback and provoke students' reflection through questions [17]. Even so, most of the tools are research-based and therefore, not pervasively available. Moreover, educators and students might lack experience using educational technology tools that are not familiar to them or might find it challenges to setting up and implementing these tools in real-world settings.

In this study, we applied time-series analysis to examine the temporal reflective writing behaviour of students with varying SRL competence levels (according to their self-reported data) to better understand their reflection processes. Contrary to most previous research, we explored students' reflective writing behaviours using trace data from a commonly used, user-friendly and easily accessible cloud platform (Google Docs). The supportive insights from reflection behaviours could generate a model to predict students' performance and therefore pave the way towards educational technology solutions that can provide personalised support and trigger timely interventions aimed at students with different levels of SRL competence. As noted by Zimmerman [18], there are different profiles of regulation among students (i.e., experts and novices) and it is possible to support them according to their regulation level. More specifically, this study aims to answer the following main research questions:

RQ1) How do students with different levels of SRL competence approach their reflective writing tasks?
RQ2) To what extent do students with high SRL competence approach the individual reflective writing tasks more systematically?
RQ3) What is the relationship between students' individual reflective writing behaviours and their performance?

2 Context of Study

2.1 Educational Context

The study was conducted within an online selective MA module called 'Design and Use of Technology for Education' (DUTE). Over the 15-week course, students were introduced to topics related to educational technology design and had to collaboratively work on their chosen educational challenges and propose a technological solution to overcome them. To illustrate, they might select a challenge of an assessment at scale and propose artificial intelligence (AI) as a solution. Within each week, students had to 1) read the weekly materials on the weekends, 2) participate in the class debate expectedly by Monday, 3) study lectures released on Tuesday, 4) organize an online weekly group meeting preferable between Wednesday and Friday to discuss their design case, and 5) individually reflect on what they have learnt, what went well and what needed to be improved via a single Google Docs every week, preferably before the next week started. This study focused on the 5th weekly task (Individual reflective writing task). The module started on 28 Sep (week 1) to 7 Dec 2020 (week 10) with a pause in the middle from 9–15 Nov 2020 (after week 6) known as the reading week. The final submission was on 11 Jan 2021 (5 weeks later). There were nine weeks in total for students to reflect upon since the first week was an orientation week. This reflection part accounted for 40% of the students' overall grade. The feedback was provided twice: formative feedback on the use of evidence, tone, misconceptions, suggestion for improvement and a balance between personal experience and academic practice at mid-term (week 6) and summative feedback of the final grade at the end. Both types of feedbacks were provided and marked by three reviewers. For the final grade, thirty-five percent of the students were double marked, achieving high inter-rater reliability (96%).

Participants. There were 54 students enrolled in the course but only 42 students completed it. They were mixed gender (65% female vs. 35% male), varied backgrounds from pedagogy (60%), multidisciplinary (20%), technology (5%) to others (14%), and based in different time zones. On average, students reported moderate familiarity with the collaborative writing tool used in this study (Google Docs). At the beginning of the study, ethical approval was received through the institutional processes.

2.2 Data Collection Tools

As mentioned above, we decided to collect student's individual reflective writing behaviours using Google Docs (http://docs.google.com). It is an online collaborative web-based platform for word processing. There are various platforms for reflective writing tasks such as Input Log. However, installation and activation are required and this might not be practical for real-time teaching and learning contexts where reflective writing happens at students' personal computers. Google Docs, on the other hand, can keep track of every change by chronologically storing versions of the file (called 'revisions') in the cloud database. Each revision has a unique and auto-incremental identification number. However, Google Docs occasionally merges revisions for space optimization purposes[1] which results in minor changes or some revisions lost. Moreover, Google Docs stores revision history as a file that requires pre-processing to extract changes but in combination with Draftback (http://draftback.com), an open-sourced Chrome extension, it can offer extracted data and save processing time. As a result, given the popularity, the accessible analytics and student and educators' familiarity with it, students were invited to reflect weekly on Google Docs which were processed with Draftback for generating analytics on students' writing behaviours.

---
[1] https://developers.google.com/drive/api/v3/change-overview.

Draftback provides a statistical summary of the writing sessions and visualizations, namely a timeline of the activity and change locations in the document (see Fig. 1). Since this plugin is open-sourced, we modified the extension to be able to export the extracted data in the csv format for further analysis. Draftback data contained information about: (1) type—of change made whether the contents were inserted or deleted, (2) starting index—of the document in which the contents were inserted/deleted, (3) ending index—of the document in which the contents were inserted/deleted, (4) string—the actual contents that were inserted but this field is blank when the contents were deleted, (5) revision number—an incremental number recorded by Google Docs to refer to a particular change, (6) user ID—Google account ID of the person who made the change, and (7) timestamp—recorded time of when the change was made.

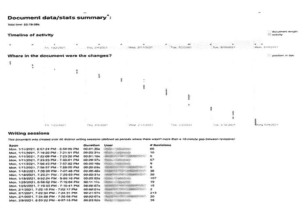

Fig. 1. Statistical summary and visualization provided by Draftback. The top part shows the timeline of the activity (red dots represent editing actions and the blue shade refers to the document length) whereas the second part shows the edited location within the document. The bottom part contains a summary of the writing sessions. (Color figure online)

2.3 SRL Questionnaire and Clustering Students According to Their SRL Competence

At the beginning of the module, students were asked to fill in a standardised self-report questionnaire about their SRL levels. Four aspects of SRL namely goal-setting (GS), effort (E), self-efficacy (SE) and persistence (P) were shown to be together accounted for the highest variance of learning performance in a well-validated meta-analysis of SRL and academic performance [19]. Questionnaire items were then selectively gathered from GS [20], E and P [21] and SE [22] to maintain optimum length and coverage of SRL dimensions and were adapted accordingly to the context. The inter-item reliability was tested per dimension (Cronbach' Alpha: $GS = 0.796$, $E = 0.879$, $P = 0.891$, $SE = 0.902$). Students' scores on these dimensions were clustered with the K-means clustering approach [23] to categorise students with different levels of SRL competence. To maximize the average centroid distance with high interpretability of the clusters, three clusters (average centroid distance $= -0.674$) were selected: (1) high SRL cluster (25 students), (2) medium persistence & effort, low goal setting & self-efficacy group (5 students), and (3) medium goal setting & self-efficacy, low persistence & effort group (10 students). Similar to previous SRL competence comparison studies in the field [24], we merged clusters 2 and 3 into the low competence SRL group and created one high competence SRL cluster (25 students) and one low SRL competence students (15 students).

3 Methodology

3.1 Pre-processing

Out of 42 students, 2 students were excluded because they did not submit the reflections via Google Docs. As a result, 40 students remained for processing. Another three students submitted the weekly reflections through multiple Google Docs, thus merging was performed. Additionally, the changes that did not belong to the students (e.g., the reviewer accidentally edited the document) or the changes that were made after the submission date, were filtered out. In the end, the resulting dataset described approximately 600000 editing actions (revisions) in total.

3.2 Derived Features

Two datasets were created to be investigated: the 'Activity' dataset composed of the actual changes that students have made and timestamps, 'Student' dataset contained information related to students, their SRL level and their grade. For each editing action described in the 'Activity' dataset, two features were added. By integrating timestamp and students' timezones, we inferred (1) DayOfWeek_local—day of the week in which the change happened at the student's local timezone. By considering the type of changes, starting index and ending index, (2) strCount—number of letters added or deleted was counted regardless of the change types. For individual students, seven features were derived: (1) TotalRev—number of total revisions, (2) FinalStringCount—number of strings in the final document, (3) AvgRevPerDay—the average number of revisions made per day, (4) AvgStrCountPerDay—the average number of strings added/deleted per day, (5) TotalActiveDay—number of days that students have made changes (possible 99 days), (6) AvgStrCountPerWeek—the average number of strings added/deleted per week, and (7) TotalActiveWeek—number of weeks that students have made changes (possible 15 weeks). Apart from the two datasets, a time-series 'Date' was created. It has dates as indexes (from the first day of the course to the submission date) and clusters as columns: all students, students with high SRL competence (cluster 1) and students with low SRL competence (cluster 2). This time-series data contained an average number of strings added or deleted per day (AvgStringCountPerDay) for comparison across clusters.

3.3 Time Series Analysis of Students' Reflective Writing Behaviours

To answer the research questions posed, we needed an analysis approach to explore the commonalities and differences between different clusters of students' writing behaviours, and potentially build models that would help us predict their future outcomes. Such explorations are particularly difficult for time-dependent data. In this study's context as students were free to reflect at any particular point in time, these voluntary and time-dependent behaviours can most appropriately be explored using time series analysis [25]. Time series analysis is very common for economic forecasting yet rarely implemented in learning sciences and education despite the time-dependent characteristics of the collected data [26]. Compared to other common techniques in social sciences such as regression analysis, time series analysis provides an opportunity to explore time-dependent behaviours such as long-term trends or short-term fluctuation as seasonality which could further help to identify the causes of the temporal patterns. Two major characteristics of time series data are trend and seasonality. Trend refers to a long-term changing direction of the data. While an upward trend refers to an increasing mean over time, a downward trend conversely refers to a decreasing mean over time. On the other hand, Seasonality is a recurrent short-term pattern found over a fixed period of time. Concerning the research questions: RQ1) How do students with different levels of SRL competence approach their reflective writing tasks?, trends of the reflection behaviours at multiple frequencies (e.g., day of the week and over the period of observation) will be explored. For the second research question: RQ2) To what extent do students with high SRL competence approach the individual reflective writing tasks more systematically?, seasonality will be extracted and investigated. For the final research question, RQ3) What is the relationship between students' individual reflective writing behaviours and their performance?, a correlation analysis will be used.

4 Results

4.1 Overall Individual Reflective Writing Behaviours

To observe the overall reflection behaviours more clearly, the trend was extracted from the time series data across clusters using 7-day and 30-day rolling means as shown in Fig. 2. Visual inspection of the average string count per day showed a steady trend across 14 weeks and increased exponentially towards the final week. Whereas the trend plot of cluster 1 was steady, cluster 2's trend showed higher variance and a distinct trend especially a seasonal increase during week 9.

To investigate further, the average string count per day across 15 weeks and the two clusters are compared in Fig. 3. This analysis confirmed that the trend of cluster 1 tends to be steadier. On the contrary, cluster 2 revealed a different trend with lower number of reflections (denoted by the sparser number of asterisks) and a lower number of edited contents (denoted by the lower magnitude) in general. More specifically, cluster 1 showed more editing frequency (93 times) with a larger amount of edited contents (M = 7927.07) as compared to cluster 2 (70 times, M = 6945.93). During the 10-week studying period, cluster 1 reached its local peak on week 7 (the week after the midterm feedback) whereas cluster 2 followingly reached this peak on week 9. Considering the break period before the final submission, the global maxima was located at the end of the course (Week 14) in any group.

Apart from daily trends throughout the course, reflecting behaviours were explored as weekly interactions to see the overlap between the actual behaviours and the anticipated

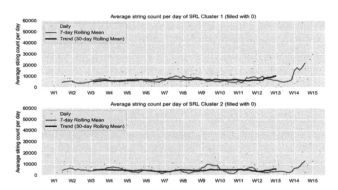

Fig. 2. Plot of average string count per day, 7-day and 30-day rolling mean of cluster 1 and 2

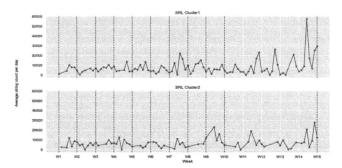

Fig. 3. Average string count per day across different clusters in which the multiple dotted red lines represent Monday of the week, the final dotted red line refers to the final submission date and the asterisks (*) show the number of edited contents on a particular day

weekly tasks of the module. Figure 4 demonstrated the average string count on each day of the week across clusters. In general, both clusters reflected the most on Monday. While this number dropped significantly to the lowest on Tuesday (lecture day of the week in the course), it progressively increased towards the end of the week. Among these days, cluster 1 had a higher amount of average string count than cluster 2 except on Wednesday where cluster 2's average string count slightly surpassed cluster 1's.

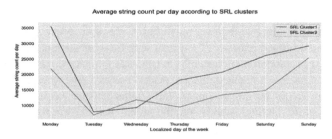

Fig. 4. Average string count for each day of the week across clusters (localized time zones)

4.2 Systematic Reflection Patterns

Apart from the overall trends above, seasonal decomposition as a part of time series analysis was applied to investigate recurrent short-term patterns of students' writing behaviours. The seasonal decomposition of cluster 1 and 2 are illustrated in Fig. 5 (upper) and Fig. 5 (lower), respectively. Aligned with the above results, both clusters adopted similar trends, yet higher variance was observed in cluster 2's seasonal model. When considering the extracted seasonalities in Fig. 5 (upper), cluster 1's seasonality had a similar cycle as found in the aforementioned 'day of the week' graph (Fig. 4). In other words, the interaction in terms of the average number of string counts was lowest at the beginning of the week (Tuesday) and raised towards the end of the week (Saturday). Compared to cluster 2, the extracted seasonality was more fluctuating which can be seen as multiple peaks (Fig. 5 (lower)). The seasonality detection should be considered in accordance with the residuals to ensure its validity. The normally-distributed and zero mean residuals suggest randomness and hence supports the validity of the seasonality model extracted.

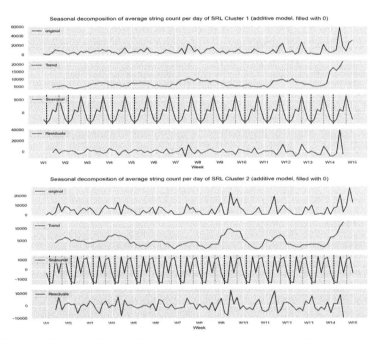

Fig. 5. Seasonal decomposition of the average string count per day of cluster 1 (upper) and cluster 2 (lower) which displayed the original, trend, seasonal and residuals components from top to bottom, respectively. In the seasonal component, red and green dotted lines refer to Tuesday and Saturday of the week, respectively. (Color figure online)

4.3 Academic Performance

At last, to investigate the differences between the reflection scores between two clusters, an independent sample t-test was used. There was no significant difference ($t(38) = -0.047, p = 0.936$) in academic performance between cluster 1 ($M = 2.04, SD = 0.49$) and cluster 2 ($M = 2.05, SD = 0.54$). To get a better sense of the relationship between the individual reflective writing behaviours and academic performance Pearson's r correlations were calculated. Table 1 shows the correlation coefficients between the reflection score calculated from two parts of the rubric criteria for reflective writing, and the computed features from reflection behaviours: total number of revisions, final string count, average revisions per day, average string count per day, total active day, average string count per week, and total active week. There were moderate and significant correlations between the reflection scores and the total number of revisions ($r_s = 0.484, p < .01$), the average revisions per day ($r_s = 0.423, p < .01$) and the total active weeks ($r_s = 0.417, p < .01$). On the other hand, the reflection scores and the final string count ($r_s = 0.374, p < .05$) and the total active day ($r_s = 0.387, p < .05$), were found to be statistically significant yet weakly correlated.

Table 1. Correlation matrix between student performance and reflection behaviours

	Reflection score	TotalRevisions	Final string count	AvgRev PerDay	AvgStr Count PerDay	TotalActiveDay	AvgStr CountPerWeek	TotalActiveWeek
Reflection score	1.00	.484**	.374*	.423**	.037	.387*	.215	.417**

**Correlation is significant at the 0.01 level (2-tailed)
*Correlation is significant at the 0.05 level (2-tailed)

5 Discussion

RQ1: How do students with different levels of SRL competence approach their reflective writing tasks?: According to the overall trends, students tended to reflect more after the reading week in which the mid-term feedback was provided and increased their efforts towards the end of the course as the submission date approaches. Comparing between the high and low SRL competence groups, the high SRL group tended to have a higher frequency of reflective writing behaviours and a higher quantity of contents written while reflecting. One potential interpretation of these results is that students with high SRL competence were also able to regulate their reflective writing behaviours better. A higher amount of interaction after the reading week, when there were no lectures and students were sent their mid-term feedback on their writing tasks, may be associated with students' reactions to their feedback. One interesting observation is that, whilst these trends can easily be spotted right after the feedback for the high SRL group, such higher interaction was delayed by two weeks for the low SRL group. Timely reaction to feedback was a representative behaviour of the high SRL group. According to the observation from the reflection data, out of twelve interactions from low SRL students within week 9, three students reflected on the contents before the reading week, another three students reflected on the contents of the week before and the last six reflected timely on the current week.

Looking at the weekly interactions, both clusters of students had the lowest reflection behaviours on Tuesdays (when the course lectures took place) and gradually increased their reflective writings towards the end of the week. This aligned with the anticipated learning activities of the module in which students were expected to study the lectures on Tuesdays and reflect during the week. Despite the higher reflection contents of students with high SRL throughout the week, an interesting reflection pattern was observed on Wednesdays. Wednesdays were the only day of the week that students with low SRL outperformed students with high SRL in terms of the amount of reflective writing content produced. Based on a further investigation of the actual reflection contents, we found out that 5 out of 6 students with low to medium SRL competence showed catching up behaviours after Tuesday's lectures in which they reflected on the contents of the week before rather than the current week. These results are aligned with the SRL theory, which suggests that students with high SRL competence tend to approach their learning tasks more timely and strategically to achieve their goals [8].

RQ2: To what extent do students with higher SRL competence approach the individual reflective writing tasks more systematically?: Based on the seasonal decomposition analysis, students with high SRL competence exhibited more periodic patterns weekly: reflecting the lowest on Tuesdays and the highest on Saturdays. However, students with lower SRL competence showed more random behaviours. In other words, students with high SRL approached their reflective writing task more systematically. One potential explanation for this observation is that students with high SRL competence are better at planning and enacting their tasks by deploying time management strategies. Therefore, they tend to plan when they will do the task to better ensure task completion rather than do the task when it was necessary (e.g., right before submission deadlines) [27]. Although the type of data analysis we have undertaken in this study doesn't help us answer such "why?" questions, they lead to hypotheses that should be explored with further qualitative investigations in future research studies. Perhaps, more importantly, these results highlight the value of structuring individual reflective writing tasks in ways that would allow students to approach them more systematically. To achieve this, there are multiple forms of metacognitive scaffolding that can be incorporated into the task itself such as static predefined questions or dynamic support within the learning environment [28]. At the learning design level, since the results highlight the value of regularity in individual reflective writing behaviours, once reflective writing tasks are set, students can be regularly reminded about the expected contributions as well as being supported on how to do so (i.e., prompt-embedded templates sent to students every week on certain times).

RQ3: What is the relationship between students' reflective writing reflecting behaviours and their academic performance?: Even though there was no statistically significant difference between academic performance and students' SRL competence as measured through self-declared data, there were significant correlations found between academic performance and certain reflective writing behaviours such as the total number of revisions, final string count, average revisions per day, total active day, and total active week. Surprisingly, average string count per day and average string count per week had no correlation with students' performance. One potential interpretation of this result is that the reflective writing behaviours that relate to organisational behaviours are more fundamental to academic performance than the amount of reflective writing itself. In other words, high performing students appeared to make more regular visits to their reflective writing tasks and they spread their writing across days and weeks. However, they didn't necessarily write significantly more than low performing students. Recognising the limitations of such correlational interpretations, we suggest that further research in more controlled designs and with potential content analysis of individual reflective writing pieces should be conducted to draw more conclusive results.

5.1 Limitations and Future Research

Before we conclude, it is important to note that even though permissions were given, it is undeniable that collecting log data from Google Docs might introduce privacy concerns for students due to its invasiveness and high granularity of collected data [29]. As a result, multiple methods to ensure transparency have been applied in our study such as available information on data collection and objectives, choices to opt-in/out and recognition of tracker (ibid). Moreover, our recent study [30] suggested that participants reported concerns over being monitored by the system only at the beginning of the course and the perceived effects were reduced as the module progresses. More importantly, as the reflecting engagement was not a part of the summative assessment, monitoring such behaviours might be neglectable for them. Apart from the ethical issues, this study involved a relatively small number of students from a single course. Therefore, the results might not be generalized into other contexts due to the context-specific nature of the SRL processes. Besides, previous research highlights the potential content-specific [31] and context-specific [32] nature of students' SRL behaviours. More studies are required to explore consistency in the reflection patterns across domains and learning design. Moreover, the log data captured from Google Docs is limited and might overlook other significant aspects of the writing process such as duration of pause, document formatting and mouse movement. Another limitation concerns the selected proxy to represent students' reflection behaviours. In this study, the number of strings added/deleted was used to represent the number of reflection interactions. However, this proxy might not be a good presenter in situations where students frequently cut-and-paste the contents. Thus, other proxies such as the number of the writing sessions or time consumed on the tasks could further be explored. Regarding the current analysis, we currently only focus on the low-level quantity measures of students' reflecting behaviours whereas most SRL research infers SRL processes from the contents of reflection which could provide more information about students' thinking processes. Their reflective writing behaviours in combination with reflective contents could reveal more insights into how students plan and enact the task. This aligned with the recent participatory research in the design of the writing analytics tools that the experts expected higher level and content-related feedback to support writing processes and assessment [14]. Future work should also focus on analytics from the individual reflective writing contents of students.

6 Conclusion

This exploratory study investigated the reflection behaviours of postgraduate students with different levels of SRL competence over the fifteen-week module in an ecologically valid educational setting. Data on fine-grained reflection writing were retrieved from Google Docs and analyzed using time series decomposition. The results showed that students with different levels of SRL competence present different reflective writing behaviours. Students of high SRL competence carried out the task more frequently, and produced greater quantities of writing, and did so in line with the expectations of the modules. Regarding students with lower SRL, they appear to be catching up and presenting more random reflection behaviours. Moreover, time-series analysis shows that both low SRL and high SRL competence students' reflective writing behaviours fit well in certain seasonal trends with low residuals. This exploration opens up future opportunities for early prediction of less productive reflective writing behaviours and timely interventions from educators, learners themselves and/or educational technology.

Acknowledgement. We would like to thank DUTE 2020/2021 students for granting permissions to collect data for this study. The Universidad de Valladolid co-authors would like to acknowledge funding of the European Regional Development Fund and the National Research Agency of the Spanish Ministry of Science, Innovation and Universities, under project grants TIN2017-85179-C3-2-R and PID2020-112584RB-C32, and the European Regional Development Fund and the Regional Government of Castile and Leon, under project grant VA257P18.

References

1. Araka, E., Maina, E., Gitonga, R., Oboko, R.: Research trends in measurement and intervention tools for self-regulated learning for e-learning environments—systematic review (2008–2018). Res. Pract. Technol. Enhanc. Learn. **15**(1), 1–21 (2020). https://doi.org/10.1186/s41039-020-00129-5
2. Zimmerman, B.J.: Self-regulated learning and academic achievement: an overview. Educ. Psychol. **25**(1), 3–17 (1990)
3. Milikić, N., Gašević, D., Jovanović, J.: Measuring effects of technology-enabled mirroring scaffolds on self-regulated learning. IEEE Trans. Learn. Technol. **13**(1), 150–163 (2018)
4. Zimmerman, B.J.: Attaining self-regulation: a social cognitive perspective. In: Handbook of Self-regulation, pp. 13–39. Academic Press (2000).
5. Winne, P.H., Hadwin, A.F.: Studying as self-regulated learning. In: Hacker, D.J., Dunlosky, J., Graesser, A.C. (eds.) The Educational Psychology Series. Metacognition in Educational Theory and Practice, pp. 277–304. Lawrence Erlbaum Associates Publishers (1998)
6. Puustinen, M., Pulkkinen, L.: Models of self-regulated learning: a review. Scand. J. Educ. Res. **45**(3), 269–286 (2001)
7. Eilam, B., Aharon, I.: Students' planning in the process of self-regulated learning. Contemp. Educ. Psychol. **28**(3), 304–334 (2003)
8. Broadbent, J.: Comparing online and blended learner's self-regulated learning strategies and academic performance. Internet High. Educ. **33**, 24–32 (2017)
9. Tempelaar, D., Rienties, B., Nguyen, Q.: Investigating learning strategies in a dispositional learning analytics context: the case of worked examples. In: Proceedings of the 8th International Conference on Learning Analytics and Knowledge, pp. 201–205. Association for Computing Machinery, New York (2018)

10. Boud, D., Keogh, R., Walker, D.: Promoting reflection in learning: a model. In: Boud, D., Keogh, R., Walker, D. (eds.) Reflection: Turning Experience into Learning, pp. 18–40. Routledge Falmer (1987)
11. Schunk, D. H., Zimmerman, B. J.: Self-regulated Learning: From Teaching to Self-reflective Practice. Guilford Press (1998)
12. Baggetun, R., Wasson, B.: Self-regulated learning and open writing. Eur. J. Educ. **41**(3–4), 453–472 (2006)
13. Nückles, M., Hübner, S., Renkl, A.: Enhancing self-regulated learning by writing learning protocols. Learn. Instr. **19**(3), 259–271 (2009)
14. Conijn, R., Martinez-Maldonado, R., Knight, S., Buckingham Shum, S., Van Waes, L., Van Zaanen, M.: How to provide automated feedback on the writing process? A participatory approach to design writing analytics tools. Comput. Assist. Lang. Learn. **35**, 1–31 (2020). https://doi.org/10.1080/09588221.2020.1839503
15. Dikli, S.: An overview of automated scoring of essays. J. Technol. Learn. Assess. **5**(1), 1–36 (2006)
16. Cotos, E.: Automated writing analysis for writing pedagogy: from healthy tension to tangible prospects. Writ. Pedag. **6**, 1 (2015)
17. Ma, W., Adesope, O.O., Nesbit, J.C., Liu, Q.: Intelligent tutoring systems and learning outcomes: a meta-analysis. J. Educ. Psychol. **106**(4), 901 (2014)
18. Zimmerman, B.J.: Becoming a self-regulated learner: an overview. Theory Pract. **41**(2), 64–70 (2002)
19. Sitzmann, T., Ely, K.: A meta-analysis of self-regulated learning in work-related training and educational attainment: what we know and where we need to go. Psychol. Bull. **137**(3), 421 (2011)
20. Barnard, L., Lan, W.Y., To, Y.M., Paton, V.O., Lai, S.-L.: Measuring self-regulation in online and blended learning environments. Internet High. Educ. **12**(1), 1–6 (2009)
21. Elliot, A.J., McGregor, H.A., Gable, S.: Achievement goals, study strategies, and exam performance: a mediational analysis. J. Educ. Psychol. **91**(3), 549 (1999)
22. Pintrich, P. R.: A manual for the use of the Motivated Strategies for Learning Questionnaire (MSLQ). National Center for Research to Improve Postsecondary Teaching and Learning (1991)
23. MacQueen, J.: Some methods for classification and analysis of multivariate observations. In: Proceedings of the Fifth Berkeley Symposium on Mathematical Statistics and Probability, vol. 1, no. 14, pp. 281–197 (1967)
24. Littlejohn, A., Hood, N., Milligan, C., Mustain, P.: Learning in MOOCs: motivations and self-regulated learning in MOOCs. Internet High. Educ. **29**, 40–48 (2016)
25. Box, G.E., Jenkins, G.M., Reinsel, G.C., Ljung, G.M.: Time Series Analysis: Forecasting and Control, 4th edn. Wiley, Hoboken (2008)
26. Shin, Y.: Time Series Analysis in the Social Sciences: The Fundamentals, 1st edn. University of California Press, Oakland (2017)
27. Wolters, C.A., Won, S., Hussain, M.: Examining the relations of time management and procrastination within a model of self-regulated learning. Metacogn. Learn. **12**(3), 381–399 (2017). https://doi.org/10.1007/s11409-017-9174-1
28. Azevedo, R., Hadwin, A.F.: Scaffolding self-regulated learning and metacognition–implications for the design of computer-based scaffolds. Instr. Sci. **33**, 367–379 (2005)
29. Alwahaby, H., Cukurova, M., Papamitsiou, Z., Giannakos, M.: The evidence of impact and ethical considerations of multimodal learning analytics: a systematic literature review. In: Giannakos, M., et al. (eds.) The Handbook of Multimodal Learning Analytics. Springer, Cham (2021). https://edarxiv.org/sd23y/

30. Zhou, Q., et al.: Investigating students' experiences with collaboration analytics for remote group meetings. In: Roll, I., McNamara, D., Sosnovsky, S., Luckin, R., Dimitrova, V. (eds.) AIED 2021. LNCS, vol. 12748, pp. 472–485. Springer, Cham (2021)https://doi.org/10.1007/978-3-030-78292-4_38
31. Winne, P.H., Hadwin, A.F.: nStudy: tracing and supporting self-regulated learning in the Internet. In: Azevedo, R., Aleven, V. (eds.) International Handbook of Metacognition and Learning Technologies, vol. 28, pp. 293–308. Springer, New York (2013). https://doi.org/10.1007/978-1-4419-5546-3_20
32. Zhou, Q., Suraworachet, W., Cukurova, M.: Different modality, different design, different results: exploring self-regulated learner clusters' engagement behaviours at individual, group and cohort activities (2021). https://doi.org/10.35542/osf.io/u3g4n

From Paper to Online: Digitizing Card Based Co-creation of Games for Privacy Education

Patrick Jost[✉] [iD] and Monica Divitini

Department of Computer Science, Norwegian University of Science and Technology,
Trondheim, Norway
{patrick.jost,divitini}@ntnu.no

Abstract. Education is rapidly evolving from co-located settings to remote and online learning. However, many proven educational tools are designed for collaborative, co-located classroom work. Effective sketching and ideating tools, such as card-based workshop tools, cannot be applied in remote teaching.

This paper explores how the paper-based card and playboard metaphor can be digitized for remote student co-creation via video call sessions. Therefore, a card-based toolkit for co-creating educational games is transformed into a digital representation for remote application. In a between-subject trial with two university student groups ($n = 61$), it is investigated how users perceive ideation/balancing support and applicability of the technology-enhanced card toolset compared to the paper-based variant. Both groups thereby created an analytic game concept for privacy education.

The results remarkably revealed that remote co-creation using the technology-enhanced card and playboard in video call sessions was perceived as significantly more supportive for ideation and game concept balancing. Students also felt more confident to apply the digitized card toolset independently while being more satisfied with their created game concepts. The designed educational game concepts showed comparable patterns between the groups and disclosed the students' preferences on how games for privacy education should be designed and when and where they would like to play them. Conclusively, design implications for digital card ideation toolsets were synthesized from the findings.

Keywords: Serious games · Game design · Education games · Co-design · Remote co-creation · Design card set · Privacy

1 Introduction

With the transformation of our surroundings in a technology-enhanced environment, driven by ambient data-processing and data-sharing, humans face continuous privacy decision-making. One strategy to reach teenagers/young adults who are more likely to share fake information [1] and make less reflected privacy choices [2], is creating awareness by video games. Learning by playing games as well as learning through creating games are well explored and are often applying co-creational activities involving the card and board metaphor [3]. Research has shown that co-located workshops utilizing paper cards facilitate discussion, support generating new ideas/knowledge [4] and help optimizing concepts [5]. They have also proven to be valuable in co-design scenarios for eliciting tacit knowledge and integrating the perspectives of multiple disciplines/perspectives [6]. These qualities are of particular interest for the design of Serious Games for educational purposes.

As pointed out by Dörner et al. [7], Serious Games are games with the intention to entertain and to achieve at least one or more additional goals. In the case of privacy awareness, for example, factors such as risk-taking behavior [8] or peer pressure [9] may be assessed in the game to improve both the game experience and the efficacy of the learning game. Thus, complementing the educational goal with a researching goal. At the same time, disruption through in-game assessment or extraneous cognitive influences from interaction design should be avoided in such *analytic educational games* to preserve an engaging game flow [10]. While card-based tools have proven helpful in co-located/classroom education and co-creational design activities, their benefits in the increasingly important distance learning scenarios are under-explored. This study thematizes the application and benefits of the card and board metaphor in the case of co-creating games for privacy education via videoconferencing.

1.1 Card-Based Co-creation of Educational Game Concepts

Considering the educational, analytical, and interactional aspects in a Serious Game (SG) from an early stage of game design can help maintain an engaging game experience. Prior work has shown that participatory approaches to the co-creation of SG concepts can support ideation of game challenges and help to balance SG concepts.

Tokens and cards with game design suggestions for the player, teacher, researcher and designer roles

Playboard with slots for each role/game part to co-create a balanced concept

Fig. 1. Paper-based co-creation toolset for ideation of analytic educational games

A card-based toolset – the *Challenge Game Frame* (CGF) – that integrated the perspectives of teachers/researchers with the roles of the player and interaction designer through affordance analysis has been demonstrating the applicability and balance/ideation support in a previous study [5]. The paper-based co-creation toolset (Fig. 1) consists of game design suggestion cards for the *player, teacher, researcher* and *interaction designer* roles and an associated board to lay out a balanced Serious Game concept.

It can be applied in classroom settings with students and teachers for co-creation of analytic learning games.

The collaborative design approach empowers all involved roles to discuss conflicts and adapt the game challenge to generate a harmonious game concept. The current educational game design toolset provides card decks for each role – 12 decks in total. The role-oriented decks (affordance cards) for the player consist of *achieving, acting, progressing, engaging, and adapting* while the teacher decks comprise *reflecting and examining*, the researcher card decks cover *researching, reporting, and monitoring* and the interaction designer decks include *interacting and presenting* suggestions.

To set the frame for optimizing the game concept, the toolset additionally features 4 role-independent card decks with design suggestions to define the game's context, target group, and educational domain. The design proposals in these decks outline *who* will play the game, *where and when* the game is planned to be played and what *challenging* privacy issue is addressed as the domain goal. Privacy challenges described in detail include, for example, unnoticed third-party data sharing, the risk of aggregation/profiling, and large-scale tracking of health or private behavior. Each of the toolset's 150 cards describes a suggestion on how to actualize/design a part in the educational game concept. With the provided design suggestion cards, playing board and stepwise playbook/instructions, non-game experts such as student groups are supported in collaboratively ideating and balancing the game concept for engaging privacy education [5].

However, a non-digital toolset is constrained to offline/co-located use cases while educational institutions are increasingly faced with technology-enhanced remote collaboration scenarios. This paper addresses the digitalization of the card-based offline activity to learn more about remote co-creation with the card and board metaphor. Applicability and ideation/balancing support are studied by comparative co-located and remote co-creation sessions with student groups co-creating educational privacy game concepts.

1.2 Related Work and Research Gap

Non-digital card toolsets for collaborative idea generation have been studied intensively over the last decades, as summarized by Wölfel and Merritt [11] and more recently by Roy and Warren [12] as well as Aarts et al. [13] and Peters et al. [14]. Several card toolsets address gamification [15] or general game design [16]. Similar to other tools, the paper-based CGF supports students in on-site classroom settings in the co-creation process but additionally includes the learning and assessment perspectives. As with other ideation sets [4, 17], using the card metaphor and a scaffolding board structure supported discussing, ideating and balancing the concept [5]. However, rapidly evolving online learning situations and current social interaction restrictions originating from the covid-19 pandemic prevent much of the utility of physical, co-located ideation. While many educational institutions shift to online learning and remote seminars, physical collaboration toolsets cannot be applied. Yet, there is a paucity of research that addresses remote co-creation with student groups. Only few researchers addressed remote ideation or synchronous online co-creation scenarios. One study looked at paper sketching via Skype [18] and found that face-to-face communication remains important in remote collaboration. Stockleben et al. [19] point out in this regard that traditional emotional cues are diminished in remote collaboration and suggest implementing substitutes in the online tool. Ho and Tomitsch [20] recently investigated brainstorming tools for collaborative game ideation and found most strategies at game jams rely on paper or whiteboard. They concluded that there is a need for idea sharing and arrangement platforms with strategies to overcome issues of unguided idea creation sessions. In their integrative model created from a recent review of electronic brainstorming, Maaravi et al. [21] emphasize the benefits of clear goal descriptions for ideation. Their suggestions include assigning quantity and quality goals and setting success criteria. Further, they recommend combining asynchronous and synchronous ideation phases, encouraging working individually, having explicit discussion guidance as well as rank-order procedures and mechanisms to maintain motivation. However, the focus of their work was on settings not using face-to-face communication and idea generation via text messages/typing.

Despite the substantial research on traditional collaborative card ideation, no studies were found to investigate the transfer of a paper-based card-toolset to a digital representation for remote co-creation and the corresponding effects on user support and applicability.

1.3 Research Objectives

This present study addresses the outlined research gap and investigates the effects of remote co-creation with digitized cards and playboard. By comparing the co-located paper-based card toolset and the digitized remote co-creation variant, implications concerning support for ideation, balancing and applicability are researched. Additionally, the co-created concepts are analyzed for frequency patterns to learn more about the potential impact of the distinct toolsets and students' preferred approaches to privacy games. The research questions guiding the investigation were accordingly:

1. How does remote co-creation with digital cards and playboard support ideation, concept balancing, and toolset applicability compared to a paper-based co-located variant?
2. What are the preferred privacy education game patterns co-created by students using the remote and co-located toolsets?

2 Research Approach

In our work, we followed the cyclic design science research model [22]. The described paper-based card and board toolset (Sect. 1.1) is thereby transformed in this design cycle into a digital representation/artefact. The card decks, the role tokens and the playboard instructions are digitized to an online tool that supports remote co-creation (Sect. 2.1) of educational game concepts. The digital card-toolset is planned to be applicable in combination with video chat tools used in distant education settings. In the subsequent evaluation/relevance cycle, the technology-enhanced version and the non-digital toolset are evaluated in a between-subject trial. Both variants are applied by student groups for co-creating engaging privacy education games (Sect. 2.2). The user trials were evaluated by pre/post questionnaires assessing perceived support for *ideation, balancing* and *application* of the two toolsets. According to the *first research objective*, the null hypothesis established for the empirical investigation was:

H_0: 'There are no significant differences in perceived support for game concept ideation, balancing or applicability between co-located and remote card-based co-creation.'

To address the *second research objective*, the outcomes of the classroom and remote co-creation sessions were comparatively analyzed to determine design choice frequency patterns for each card deck.

2.1 Digitizing the Paper-Based Card Toolset

The following paragraphs describe the transformation of the paper-based toolset to the technology-enhanced digital tool. The digital cards, board, and instruction process were designed with the aim to closely retain the card and board metaphor for the online context.

Technical Background. As the digital toolset is planned to be used together with video call software and run on all platforms without restrictions, it was chosen to be a web browser application. However, it should also be possible for future mobile adaption to build it as an app for all popular mobile platforms. Moreover, flexibility regarding the visual representations of cards, boards, and roles was an aim since improvements must be easy to implement during the iterative design science cycles. Therefore, the technical base was chosen to be the Unity Engine (unity.com). Data storage was realized by secure communication via https to a MySQL database under the researchers' authority.

Cards. The card and card deck metaphors were kept in the transformation process in a general approach of skeuominimalistic aesthetics [23]. Thereby, the proportional shape, fonts and colored frame of the cards were kept. On the other hand, there was no attempt to simulate paper card depth with shadows (Fig. 2).

Fig. 2. Selecting paper-based cards and digital card selection

While in the paper-based toolset, blank cards were provided for writing own suggestions, the digital version featured a "+" button to add own ideas to a deck. The technology-enhanced ideation tool is thought to be used in distant learning and with video conferences on the desktop/notebook. As not every device in this context possesses a touch screen enabling swipe gestures, the card browsing featured previous/next buttons.

Board. Similarly, the digital playboard was closely oriented on the design of the paper board. The game concept was presented as one stream from left to right with slots for each role-oriented card suggestion (Fig. 3). For each card deck, one slot was reserved in this main game challenge stream (stream A).

Fig. 3. Placing cards on the paper-based playboard and on the digital playboard slots

To encourage card matching and discussion, slots for an alternative stream B were presented below stream A. Placement of cards in the slots was translated to the digital board as drag-and-drop action. To ensure that all co-creators could follow the events, card movements were synchronized over the network.

Roles and Playbook. The role tokens of the paper-based toolset were digitized as displayed in Fig. 4. As emotional cues between participants are diminished in remote settings [19], a mechanism for expressing content/happiness with the current concept was integrated. Each group member/role was provided with the possibility to state their happiness with the current concept using a rating slider (0 to 100%). The picture of the digital role avatar changes accordingly from a neutral to a happier expression. The combined group satisfaction (mean) for both alternative game concepts (A/B) was also displayed synchronously for all co-creators. As Maaravi et al. [21] proposed, this may serve the remotely collaborating group as a quality success criterion.

Fig. 4. Role token in the physical toolset and digitized role token including feedback sliders for the co-created concept

Clear goal description and stepwise instructions are recommended by several researchers for non-digital [4, 17] and digital collaborative idea finding [21]. The paper-based toolset features instructions and time for each step on the bottom of the A0 playboard (Fig. 5, left).

Utilizing the benefits of a digital representation, time for the step was implemented as a countdown (Fig. 5, right). To synchronize guidance for a group working remotely, the instructions were announced by a digital instructor character before each step (Fig. 5, center).

Fig. 5. Stepwise instructions in the paper-based toolset and stepwise digital instructions

2.2 Co-located and Remote Co-creation of Privacy Education Game Concepts

Both toolsets were applied in trials with student groups. Two classes of Computer Science students ($n = 61$) at a Norwegian university participated in the co-creation sessions. In one class ($n = 29$) the paper-based toolset was applied by eight co-located groups in the classroom. The seven groups in the other class ($n = 32$) were holding physically distanced remote sessions via video conference and using the digital co-creation toolset (Fig. 6).

Participants. Before the activity, participants (aged 20 to 29) provided informed consent and indicated their game design and software development skills via questionnaire on a seven-point Likert scale (1, none; 7, professional). Both classes showed a comparable skill average in game design (remote $M = 2.7$, co-located $M = 2.2$) and software development (remote $M = 4.3$, co-located $M = 4.1$).

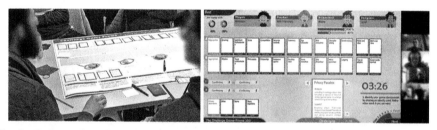

Fig. 6. *Co-located* session with the paper-based toolset (left) and *remote* co-creation using the digital card toolset (right)

Procedure and Data Collection. The task for the student groups was to co-create an engaging game that educates about privacy issues with players working collaboratively together in the game. The co-creation sessions were organized for two hours in total. Participants were first introduced to Serious Game Design theory and the balancing process between game goal/domain goal and engagement/assessment. Secondly, the basic principles of the toolset were explained. After this 30-min introduction, participants filled out the pre-questionnaire to report their skills and proceeded to the one-hour co-creation activity. Each step of the co-creation process was to be completed in a certain number of minutes. For the paper-based toolset, these minutes were written on the playboard, and the lecturer announced when to proceed to the next step. The remote ideation tool stopped being interactive when the step time expired, and a defined group manager could initiate the next step for all participants by clicking a button on the playboard. Each step time and step instruction were inscribed on the bottom of the paper-based playboard. For the online toolset, the step instructions were displayed at the beginning of a step and read out by a voiceover before the group manager clicked the start button. The steps in both, remote and co-located co-creation were as follows:

1. Pick a role of either player, teacher, researcher or designer
2. Define the context of the game: domain, target group, location/time of play
3. Individually read through role-assigned cards and pick favorites
4. Co-create/balance a game challenge: starting from left to right, discuss ideas from cards or create custom cards
5. Identify conflicting pairs in the game concept and balance out the potential flow breaks by discussing alternative picks or another group agreement
6. Agree on the final picks, define a working title and write a game plot summary

Finally, after the co-creation session, all participants filled out the post-questionnaire individually on their experience regarding tools, activity, and outcome. A seven-point Likert scale (1, strongly disagree; 7, strongly agree) was used to assess the participants' judgement. The questionnaire items asked about perceived ideation/balancing support and perceived applicability of the combined toolset, cards, roles and playboard. While the ideation and application dimensions consisted of four items each, balancing support was assessed with eight items. Exemplary items/statements included: *'Using the cards helped to focus on ideas' (ideation); 'The roles helped identifying conflicts between the game parts.' (balancing); 'I can imagine using the game design tool on my own for group co-creation' (application).*

3 Results

Data analysis showed that collected data was not consistently normally distributed but displayed comparable distribution and homogeneity of variance. As suggested by Field [24], non-parametric Mann-Whitney U analysis ($\alpha = 0.05$) was performed and showed significant differences between the two variants. The subsequently reported results concerning H_0 were corrected to control false discovery by Benjamini-Hochberg procedure [25] as multiple pairwise tests were conducted. Nonetheless, following McDonald [26], the raw p-values of the remaining significant results are stated to indicate authentic probabilities. In none of the assessed items was the paper-based ideation valued as more supportive than the digital representation.

Ideation. When first analyzing the ideation support results, the groups co-creating with the remote tool perceived the digitized cards as more helpful for finetuning ideas than the groups using the paper-based version (Fig. 7). A majority of 75% of the students using the remote tool agreed on support through the digital cards, $U = 634.5, z = 2.83, p = .005, r = .36$. Contrarily, only 39% of the students in the co-located group were experiencing help for improving existing ideas from the paper cards.

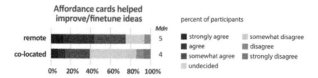

Fig. 7. The digital cards were perceived as more helpful in finetuning existing ideas

Balance. Looking next at the support for balancing the game concept, the technology-enhanced CGF co-creation activity was perceived in total as significantly more supportive (Fig. 8). While 46% of the participants considered the paper-based toolset in general as helpful for balancing the game concept parts (playing, teaching, researching, and designing), 80% felt supported by the remote co-creation tool, $U = 612.5, z = 2.52, p = .012, r = .32$. In detail, participants expressed more perceived balancing support from every component of the digitized toolset. The remote co-creation groups felt more support from the digital cards for balancing the concept between the parts than the groups using paper cards, $U = 653, z = 2.81, p = .005, r = .36$.

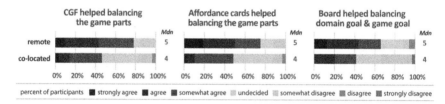

Fig. 8. The digitized tool was found significantly more helpful for balancing the game concept

Similarly, the paper board was experienced as significantly less helpful than the digital playboard for balancing the privacy education goal to the game goal, $U = 623.5, z = 2.36, p = .018, r = .30$. The groups felt particularly differently about help for balancing originating from the roles (Fig. 9).

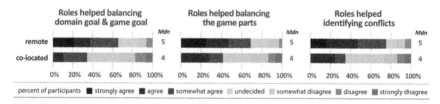

Fig. 9. Digital implementation of the role tokens was perceived as significantly more supportive

The remotely collaborating groups perceived significantly more support from the digital role representation for balancing the game parts, $U = 634, z = 2.5, p = .012, r = .32$, balancing the educational goal to the game goal, $U = 659.5, z = 2.88, p = .004, r = .37$, and for identifying conflicts in the educational game concept, $U = 649, z = 2.73, p = .006, r = .35$.

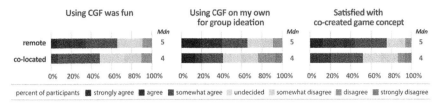

Fig. 10. The digital co-creation was perceived as significantly more applicable and enjoyable

Application. When analyzing the two toolset variants' applicability, three significant differences between the toolsets were identified (Fig. 10). First, remote co-creation with the digital CGF was perceived as more fun than the paper-based idea finding sessions, $U = 610.5, z = 2.19, p = .029, r = .28$. Second, students were expressing more confidence to use the digital remote co-creation tool on their own than the co-located paper toolset, $U = 599.5, z = 1.99, p = .047, r = .25$. Third, the remotely collaborating groups also felt more satisfied with their co-created privacy education game concepts than their colleagues using the paper-based toolset, $U = 626, z = 2.41, p = .016, r = .31$.

The median (*Mdn*) value for all the above-reported results was 5 on the Likert scale regarding the remote co-creation and 4 for the co-located variant. The effect sizes were hovering around $r = 0.3$ and thus indicating medium effect sizes for all findings [27]. Statistical analysis consequently suggests rejecting H_0 as support from remote and co-located toolsets was perceived significantly different by the student groups.

Co-created Game Concepts. Finally, the co-created outcome was analyzed regarding the most frequent game design choices. Table 1 lists the design suggestions per card deck that were selected more than once.

Table 1. Student groups' preferred design choices for analytic privacy education games

Card deck (*context* or role affordance)	Groups' preferred design choices (no. of co-located groups/remote groups) combined frequency in percent
Who	Yourself (4/2) 40%, School Class (1/1) 13%, Group of Kids (0/2) 13%
Where	Home (3/3) 40%, University (3/0) 20%, School (0/2) 13%, Outside (0/2) 13%
When	Voluntary Repetition (4/4) 53%, Once/Timeless (4/1) 33%, Repetition (0/2) 13%
Challenging	Movement Tracking (1/2) 20%, Aggregation (1/1) 13%, Knowledge Gap (2/0) 13%
Achieving	Mission (2/2) 27%, Outwit a Team (2/1) 20%, Maximize Score (0/2) 13%

(*continued*)

Table 1. (*continued*)

Card deck (*context* or role affordance)	Groups' preferred design choices (no. of co-located groups/remote groups) combined frequency in percent
Acting	Single Collaboration (3/3) 40%, Team Collab. (4/1) 33%, Team Rivalry (1/2) 20%
Progressing	Score (2/4) 40%, Turn Based (2/1) 20%, Mini Quests (2/0) 13%
Engaging	Competition (2/4) 40%, Gaining Awards (1/1) 13%, Fellowship (2/0) 13%
Adapting	Increase Rewards (2/2) 27%, Introduce Elements (1/3) 27%, Difficulty (3/1) 27%
Reflecting	Decision Tree (1/4) 33%, Summary (1/2) 20%, In-Game Questions (1/1) 13%
Examining	Move Patterns (1/2) 20%, Spy Character (1/2) 20%, Interact./Time Log (2/0) 13%
Researching	Risk Behavior (4/3) 47%, Decision Making (4/1) 33%, Presentation (0/2) 13%
Reporting	Micro Questions (2/3) 33%, Experience Sampling (2/3) 33%, Character Asking (3/1) 27%
Monitoring	Event Tracing (1/4) 33%, Team Decisions (3/1) 27%, Interaction Patterns (2/2) 27%
Interacting	Point and Click (3/2) 33%, Tap on Display (2/1) 20%, Location Change (0/2) 13%
Presenting	Bird's Eye View (2/1) 20%, Augmented Reality (1/2) 20%, Dynamic 2D World (2/0) 13%, Real World Scenarios (1/1) 13%

Note. Card-decks researching/acting were constrained to privacy research and collaborative acting

4 Discussion

4.1 Supporting Remote Co-creation with the Digitized Card/Board Metaphor

When looking at the results with respect to the *first research question*, the study disclosed that the technology-enhanced card/playboard metaphor considerably supports groups with idea finetuning and concept balancing. In fact, remote co-creation with the digitized toolset was perceived as more supportive, applicable and enjoyable than the paper-based co-located ideation card activity. The feeling for more support thereby originated from all investigated parts of the digitized toolset.

First, concerning *ideation support*, the digital cards were found more helpful in finetuning existing ideas. However, it was the only significant difference between the groups regarding ideation. From the study findings, the digitized card metaphor as designed in this toolset comparison can be seen as equivalent for idea finding to paper-based cards but more supportive for idea improvement. The benefits for idea finetuning with the digital cards could result from an improved speed to try out combinations in the game concept. Compared under Fitts' law [28], placing cards in the slots on the screen with drag-and-drop support is more efficient than laying out cards on a big A0 paper. This is further supported by the fact that the digital cards were found more supportive for balancing between the game concept parts.

Second, balancing support was found to be significantly better with the digital than with the paper tool. While the digital cards were found as helpful to balance between the game parts, the board supported matching of educational goal to game goal. As the playboard was featuring very similar areas and layout in both versions, the digital playboard's advantage likely originates from the more guided approach. The synchronizing effects of time countdown and introductory voice instructions before each step are guiding structures that could support the balancing process as suggested by previous research [20, 21]. However, the most improvement for balancing was found with the digital representation of the roles. The inclusion of emotional feedback for each role in the remote co-creation scenario can be one factor contributing to this (Fig. 4). It represents a quality goal [21] that is both an emotional cue and a measure of each role's current satisfaction with the overall concept that can help maintain discussion between the co-creators. Consequently, discussing discrepancies in the satisfaction rating may support finding conflicts in the concept.

Finally, regarding *application* of the toolsets, it is remarkable that the digital co-creation in the remote setting was found as the more enjoyable activity that creates a more satisfying game concept outcome. Even more remarkably, about 70% of students would use the digital toolset independently, compared to only 40% for the paper-based option. The reasons for this might be found in the same digital design factors that are behind the improved ideation/balance support. The more guided approach can be a factor that contributes to this higher applicability. In the same way, the emotional feedback for the roles can add to a more engaging discussion and, as a result, to a more satisfying co-creation outcome.

Conclusive synthesis of the results provides *design implications for technology-enhanced co-creation card toolsets:*

- The digital card/board metaphor with drag-and-drop interaction supports ideation in remote settings comparable to co-located paper-based tools and helps improving ideas.
- Feedback options that allow to emotionally rate the overall concept at any time support balancing between role-oriented concept parts.
- Guiding mechanisms such as a stepwise introduction before each phase and step countdowns support applicability and concept balancing during remote co-creation.

4.2 Co-created Outcome of Preferred Privacy Education Game Designs

Concerning the *second research question*, several patterns emerged through frequency analysis of the co-created game concepts (Table 1). In general, the outcomes of both card-based co-design activities display similar design choice patterns. The results suggest that co-located and remote card-based co-creation can be employed complementary or interchangeably for designing educational game concepts. However, further research with co-creation sessions including students with more diverse backgrounds is required to confirm this implication. When looking at the combined frequency patterns, students revealed a preference of choosing themselves as the games target group and building a game for continual voluntary/free play at home. A clear alternative pattern, however, was the university/school context. Selected privacy challenges showed no apparent preferences but addressed movement tracking, data aggregation, data security knowledge and privacy trade-off behavior.

Design choices for the *player* role showed preferences for competitive, mission-oriented games that progress by scoring and adapting by increasing rewards/difficulty or introducing new elements. In terms of the *teacher* parts, most groups suggested encouraging reflection about privacy choices by displaying retrospective decision trees/summaries and examining progress by tracking time/movement patterns or asking subtle questions by characters. Looking at the *researcher* role, most of the students chose to research risk-taking or decision-making. The groups most frequently suggested investigating these objectives with monitoring of events, team decisions or interaction patterns while asking story integrated questions by characters or including micro questions/experience sampling. No strong preferences could be identified for the *designer* perspective. Game presentation choices ranged from Augmented Reality to map/bird perspectives or other 2D presentations. However, most groups chose to design games for classical point-and-click or tap interaction.

5 Conclusion

The performed study outlined the digitalization of a paper-based card ideation tool and applied it in a remote co-creation scenario to investigate applicability and user support compared to using the paper tools in the classroom. The between-subjects trial displayed that co-creation with the digital card/playboard metaphor in a video conference session is equally supportive for idea generation than using co-located paper tools and significantly more helpful to improve ideas and balance concepts. In addition, the results showed that integrating guiding/feedback mechanisms that become available for a digitized toolset improves balancing support and applicability. Providing options to rate the concept freely and narrated stepwise instructions showed to increase students' satisfaction with the outcome, enjoyment of co-creation and confidence to independently use the digitized tool.

The design patterns in the co-created privacy education game concepts indicate that the remote and co-created co-design resulted in comparable game concepts. Students showed a preference for competitive, mission-oriented games that progress through scoring, taking turns, or solving mini-quests and adapting to player skill by introducing new rewards and increasing difficulty. Students also showed a preference to integrate decision summaries about privacy choices for reflection and examine progress by logging and subtle in-game questions. Regarding privacy research factors, the student groups preferred to investigate risk-taking or decision-making by equally unobtrusive strategies. Future research should extend on these favored game design strategies when creating privacy education games. As the digitized card toolset has demonstrated applicability and user support in this study, upcoming research endeavors are encouraged to research and improve this utility further by dedicated co-creation sessions, including educators and researchers.

Acknowledgements. This research was funded by the NFR IKTPLUSS project ALerT, #270969 and Excited, The Norwegian Center for Excellent IT Education. We thank the students who participated in the game co-creation sessions.

References

1. Jost, P.: The quest game-frame: balancing serious games for investigating privacy decisions. In: Ahlin, K., Mozelius, P., Sundberg, L. (eds.) Proceedings of the 11th Scandinavian Conference on Information Systems (SCIS2020), pp. 1–17. AIS, Atlanta (2020)
2. Jost, P.: Because it is fun: investigating motives of fake news sharing with exploratory game quests. In: Sampson, D.G., Ifenthaler, D., Isaías, P. (eds.) Proceedings of the 17th International Conference on Cognition and Exploratory Learning in the Digital Age (CELDA 2020), pp. 35–42. IADIS Press, Lisbon (2020)
3. Marquez, J.: Designing card games for learning the pragmatics of a second language. In: Proceedings of the 2018 Annual Symposium on Computer-Human Interaction in Play Companion Extended Abstracts, pp. 45–49. ACM, New York (2018)
4. Mora, S., Gianni, F., Divitini, M.: Tiles: a card-based ideation toolkit for the internet of things. In: Proceedings of the 2017 Conference on Designing Interactive Systems - DIS 2017, pp. 587–598. ACM, New York (2017)
5. Jost, P., Divitini, M.: The challenge game frame: affordance oriented co-creation of privacy decision games. In: Fotaris, P. (ed.) Proceedings of the 14th International Conference on Game Based Learning (ECGBL 2020), pp. 277–286. Academic Conferences International (ACI), Reading (2020)
6. Chung, D.W., Liang, R.-H.: Interaction tarot: a card-based design of knowledge construction for brainstorming in HCI. In: Proceedings of the 6th IASDR Conference on Design Research (IASDR 2015), pp. 1–19. Queensland University, Brisbane (2015)
7. Dörner, R., Göbel, S., Effelsberg, W., Wiemeyer, J. (eds.): Serious Games: Foundations, Concepts and Practice. Springer, Cham (2016). https://doi.org/10.1007/978-3-319-40612-1
8. Jia, H., Wisniewski, P.J., Xu, H., Rosson, M.B., Carroll, J.M.: Risk-taking as a learning process for shaping teen's online information privacy behaviors. In: Proceedings of the 18th ACM Conference on Computer Supported Cooperative Work & Social Computing, pp. 583–599. ACM, New York (2015)
9. Stuart, A., Bandara, A.K., Levine, M.: The psychology of privacy in the digital age. Soc. Personal. Psychol. Compass **13**, e12507 (2019)
10. Nakamura, J., Csíkszentmihályi, M.: Flow theory and research. In: Snyder, C.R., Lopez, S.J. (eds.) Handbook of Positive Psychology, pp. 195–206. Oxford University Press, Oxford (2009)
11. Wölfel, C., Merritt, T.: Method card design dimensions: a survey of card-based design tools. In: Kotzé, P., Marsden, G., Lindgaard, G., Wesson, J., Winckler, M. (eds.) INTERACT 2013. LNCS, vol. 8117, pp. 479–486. Springer, Heidelberg (2013). https://doi.org/10.1007/978-3-642-40483-2_34
12. Roy, R., Warren, J.P.: Card-based design tools: a review and analysis of 155 card decks for designers and designing. Des. Stud. **63**, 125–154 (2019)
13. Aarts, T., et al.: Design card sets: systematic literature survey and card sorting study. In: Proceedings of the 2020 ACM Designing Interactive Systems Conference, pp. 419–428. ACM, New York (2020)

14. Peters, D., et al.: Toolkits, cards and games – a review of analogue tools for collaborative ideation. CoDesign, 1–25 (2020). https://doi.org/10.1080/15710882.2020.1715444
15. Lucero, A., Arrasvuori, J.: The PLEX cards and its techniques as sources of inspiration when designing for playfulness. Int. J. Arts Technol. **6**, 22–43 (2013)
16. Wetzel, R., Rodden, T., Benford, S.: Developing ideation cards for mixed reality game design. Trans. Digit. Games Res. Assoc. **3**, 175–211 (2017)
17. Bergen, E., Solberg, D.F., Sæthre, T.H., Divitini, M.: Supporting the co-design of games for privacy awareness. In: Auer, M.E., Tsiatsos, T. (eds.) ICL 2018. AISC, vol. 916, pp. 888–899. Springer, Cham (2020). https://doi.org/10.1007/978-3-030-11932-4_82
18. Weibel, N., Signer, B., Norrie, M.C., Hofstetter, H., Jetter, H.-C., Reiterer, H.: PaperSketch: a paper-digital collaborative remote sketching tool. In: Proceedings of the 16th International Conference on Intelligent User Interfaces, pp. 155–164. ACM, New York (2011)
19. Stockleben, B., et al.: Towards a framework for creative online collaboration: a research on challenges and context. Educ. Inf. Technol. **22**, 575–597 (2017). https://doi.org/10.1007/s10639-016-9483-z
20. Ho, X., Tomitsch, M.: Affordances of brainstorming toolkits and their use in game jams. In: Proceedings of the 14th International Conference on the Foundations of Digital Games, pp. 1–10. ACM, New York (2019)
21. Maaravi, Y., Heller, B., Shoham, Y., Mohar, S., Deutsch, B.: Ideation in the digital age: literature review and integrative model for electronic brainstorming. Rev. Manag. Sci. **15**, 1431–1464 (2021). https://doi.org/10.1007/s11846-020-00400-5
22. Hevner, A.R.: A three cycle view of design science research. Scand. J. Inf. Syst. **19**, 4 (2007)
23. Urbano, I.C.V.P., et al.: From skeuomorphism to flat design: age-related differences in performance and aesthetic perceptions. Behav. Inf. Technol. 1–16 (2020). https://doi.org/10.1080/0144929X.2020.1814867
24. Field, A.: Discovering Statistics using IBM SPSS Statistics. SAGE, Thousand Oaks (2017)
25. Benjamini, Y., Hochberg, Y.: Controlling the false discovery rate: a practical and powerful approach to multiple testing. J. Roy. Stat. Soc. Ser. B Methodol. **57**, 289–300 (1995)
26. McDonald, J.H.: Handbook of Biological Statistics. Sparky House Publishing, Baltimore (2009)
27. Cohen, J.: A power primer. Psychol. Bull. **112**, 155–159 (1992)
28. Fitts, P.M.: The information capacity of the human motor system in controlling the amplitude of movement. J. Exp. Psychol. **47**, 381–391 (1954)

Open Access This chapter is licensed under the terms of the Creative Commons Attribution 4.0 International License (http://creativecommons.org/licenses/by/4.0/), which permits use, sharing, adaptation, distribution and reproduction in any medium or format, as long as you give appropriate credit to the original author(s) and the source, provide a link to the Creative Commons license and indicate if changes were made.

The images or other third party material in this chapter are included in the chapter's Creative Commons license, unless indicated otherwise in a credit line to the material. If material is not included in the chapter's Creative Commons license and your intended use is not permitted by statutory regulation or exceeds the permitted use, you will need to obtain permission directly from the copyright holder.

An In-Depth Methodology to Predict At-Risk Learners

Amal Ben Soussia[(✉)], Azim Roussanaly, and Anne Boyer

LORIA, Lorraine University, Nancy, France
{amal.ben-soussia,azim.roussanaly,anne.boyer}@loria.fr

Abstract. Nowadays, the concept of education for all is gaining momentum thanks to the widespread use of e-learning systems around the world. The use of e-learning systems consists in providing learning content via the Internet to physically dispersed learners. The main challenge in this regard is the high fail rate particularly among k-12 learners who are our case study. Therefore, we established an in-depth methodology based on machine learning models whose objectives are the early prediction of at-risk learners and the diagnosis of learning problems. Going through this methodology was of a great importance thus it starts by identifying the most relevant learning indicators among performance, engagement, regularity and reactivity. Then, based on these indicators, we extract and select the adequate learning features. For the modeling part of this methodology, we apply machine learning models among k-nearest neighbors (K-nn), Support Vector Machine (SVM), Random Forest and Decision tree on a real data sample of 1361 k-12 learners. The evaluation step consists in comparing the ability of each model to correctly identify the class of learners at-risk of failure using both accuracy and False Positive Rate (FPR) measures.

Keywords: At-risk learners · Early prediction · Methodology · Learning indicators · Machine learning · Evaluation

1 General Introduction

Many educational institutions are now opting for e-learning by offering their courses through their own private online Learning Management Systems (LMS). While adopting a technology-driven approach allows these institutions to maintain their competitiveness, it comes with many challenges. Indeed, the main issues detected in e-learning environments are the high number of no-shows, early dropouts and low completion rates which lead to a total failure of the learner [12]. In this paper, we are interested in systems designed for teachers to help them detecting the potential learning difficulties.

In the context of a fully distance learning institution, data is generally multi-source as we have more than one application, which may provide us with informative, heterogeneous and different types of data. The heterogeneity of data is explained by having administrative data describing the demographics of learners profiles, traces of use and interaction between learners and the learning environment as well as data about the academic performance and assessments. These learning applications provide a time-independent data that is stable over time or a time-dependent data type that is evolutive over time. Given the volume and diversity of data, teachers are no longer able to assist all their learners at the same time with a pedagogical follow-up adapted to the situation of each of them. Therefore, teachers need a summary of how each learner's experience unfolds through four learning indicators: performance, engagement, regularity and reactivity. Each indicator is represented by features extracted and computed from learning data sources. The identification of these learning indicators has more than one intention. They are useful for the prediction of at-risk learners as well as for the diagnosis of learning gaps of each learner.

In this paper, we propose an in-depth methodology that exploits the numeric traces generated by learning applications. This methodology is based on machine learning (ML) models whose objective is the early and accurate prediction of learners at-risk of failure. The depth of this methodology comes from the fact that we first start with the identification of the most relevant learning indicators among performance, engagement, regularity and reactivity. Second, and based on these indicators, we extract and select the adequate features representing the activity of an online learner. The last parts of this methodology are for modeling and evaluation. Using the False Positive Rate (FPR) measure, we conclude on the best ML model that correctly predicts the class of at-risk learners. For this end, we build a real data sample of 1361 k-12 learners following the same module. We identify the learning indicators and extract features from two available applications. Then, we follow a weekly prediction approach and formalize the problem into a 3-class classification problem: success, medium risk of failure and high risk of failure. The trained and tested ML models in this paper are: k-nearest neighbours (k-nn), Support Vector Machine (SVM), Random forest and Decision tree. These models are the most used in literature and show a good predictive performance. Several techniques of filtering, wrapper and embedded methods for feature selection are applied. The techniques of filtering and wrapper methods give a very promising result. Also, the FPR evolution confirm that the Decision tree model has a good ability to predict at-risk learners on the first prediction weeks.

The paper is organized as follows. Section 2 presents the state of art projects related to our work. Section 3 explains the proposed methodology. Section 4 introduces the application of the methodology in our case study. Section 5 explains the experiments and the results. Section 6 concludes on the study.

2 Related Work

The high dropout and failure rates registered in k-12 are rarely discussed in the literature especially when it comes to online education and when learners are in total autonomy. One of the main solutions to reduce failure is to predict correctly and at the earliest at-risk learners. Therefore, studies that are interested in solving this problem start generally by proposing working methodologies and frameworks. The major common point between all strategies and methodologies proposed is the importance of work done on the collection, extraction, engineering and selection of features to aliment the machine learning models. [9] proposes an integrated framework to predict the dropout in MOOCs. This framework includes three main steps: feature generation, feature selection and dropout prediction. They used an ensemble feature selection method as it does not depend on a specific learning algorithm for feature scoring. [5] proposes an analytics framework for Moodle that abstracts out the most relevant elements of prediction models. This framework goes through the steps of analysing raw data and dividing it into features and target variable, modelisation and insights given by some predictions about the learners potential difficulties. These later projects propose solutions for one specific online learning context which are Moodle and MOOCs respectively. In addition, they extract data from one application. The methodology we propose shows the importance of going through almost the same processes and phases but it is more general and emphasizes the use of heterogeneous and multi-source data. Other studies of the field focus more on the relevant and effectiveness of data for the prediction of at-risk learners in the context of online education. [7] reviews on the most used data types to discover at-risk students. The learning behaviour data including number of logs into the course, number of views, clicks and downloads, the time spent on teaching materials... is in the top list of the most used data. Learning network data such as the number of forums discussions posts, replies and comments is a very used data type in the state of the art. The third data type is related to the learning level. It includes data about tests and grades. One other used type is the learning emotional data which includes non-cognitive assessment, self-efficacy and self assessed level. Other common used data is related to learners demographics and characteristics. The Open University (OU) records also a high dropout rate. In order to solve this problem, the OU project interests in detecting as early as possible the students who are likely to dropout by identifying the less engaged ones at an early stage of a course [1]. In addition to demographic data, the models used features expressing the engagement of a learner and his interaction with the VLE [11]. Student Success System (S3) is an analytical system based on ensemble models to identify and treat at-risk students [3]. S3 is based on the calculation of a generic measure called the success index composed of five indicators: attendance, participation, preparation, completion and social learning [2]. A first step in the approach is developing basic models to predict each indicator. Thus, simple logistic regression was used for the prediction of presence while social network analysis (SNA) is more appropriate for the index of social learning. The methodology we propose and apply shows also the importance of the performance and engagement learning indicators, gives a new definition of the regularity indicator and defines the reactivity indicator. These later indicators are important to follow the learning rhythm of in total autonomy learner.

3 Methodology

Data is the fuel of ML projects and is the start point of the methodology we propose. As shown in Fig. 1, the first step in a learning analytics project is the collection of the different learning traces from the available data sources and cleaning it. This first phase allows us having the raw data ready to be used and analyzed in the next phase, which is feature extraction. The overall goal of the feature extraction is to prepare a new dataset composed of a set of computed features representing learning indicators. The third step is modeling using ML algorithms. Each model takes as input the set of features previously computed and gives as output the predicted class of each learner. The prediction results are then evaluated according to one general measure, which is the accuracy. Based on these results, we select for next experiments only algorithms with the highest prediction accuracy. Then, we go through the feature selection process to identify the most relevant features as well as learning indicators to predict the learner class with no accuracy degradation. The selected features are the input for the second modeling phase. To finally evaluate the ability of models to predict learners at-risk of failure, we use the FPR measure.

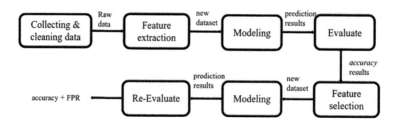

Fig. 1. The in-depth methodology phases

3.1 Feature Extraction

A feature is a representation of raw data [4]. Input features are the most important factor for ML models. Therefore, feature extraction is a central task in every ML project workflow as illustrated in Fig. 1. The idea is to define a learner activity through learning indicators. First of all, we identify these indicators which are the basis when extracting features from raw data. An indicator is an observable that is pedagogically significant, computed or established with the help of observations, and testifying to the quality of interaction, activity and learning. It is defined according to an observation objective and motivated by an educational objective. According to this definition, each learning indicator is defined by a subset of features. The identification of the above learning indicators was established based on a deep study of the behavioural profile of an at-risk learner given by the education sciences as well as on the pertinent results of multiple state-of-the-art projects which are interested in solving this issue. In addition, we have taken into consideration the specificity of distance learning available tools and data and the particular characteristics of an in total autonomy learner:

- performance: it is a very used learning indicator. It represents all features related to marks and exams that are highly correlated with a learner final result [1,3,8].
- engagement: it reflects the involvement of a learner toward his work. Features related to learners participation in the online platforms are frequently used in literature [11].
- regularity: in the state of the art, the learning regularity was proven to be highly correlated with the prediction of learners final results. Regularity can be defined in two domains: actions and time, or a combination of both. Regularity in actions is repeating patterns in user's actions sequence. Regularity in time corresponds to repeating patterns in timing of study sessions. Regularity in the combined domains is reflected by the dependencies between action types and their occurrence time [10]. As it is important to follow the regular progress made by an in total autonomy learner, we introduce the regularity of progress.
- reactivity: as far as we know, reactivity has not been used in the literature as a learning indicator. In fact, unlike face to face education, each online learner has its own learning rhythm. Reactivity in the context of an online learning corresponds to the time required to become active in the LMS and to respecting deadlines for exams submissions. This indicator serves to analyze the learner behaviour and to compare it to those of his peers.

For each indicator, we extract features from raw data. To obtain such features, we go through multiple computations of raw data such as composition and combinations.

3.2 Feature Selection

ML models need relevant features to give accurate results. However, a high dimension set of input features could contain noisy, redundant and irrelevant data. Such a data weakens the predictive performance of the model, causes overfitting and increases the error rate. To handle this issue, the feature selection process aims at selecting a subset of relevant features from the initial set based on redundancy and relevance [13]. To this end, several techniques are used in classification problems that fall into three categories:

- Filtering: based on statistical tests, the model selects from the initial set a k-dimension subset of the most correlated features with the target variable [13].
- Wrapper methods: features subset is selected based on inductive algorithms.
- Embedded methods: they aim at selecting the best features during the training phase [13]. The embedded feature selection could use two methods: Regularization and tree-based methods.

3.3 Approach

For the early prediction of at-risk learners, the problem is generally formalized into a n-class classification problem. The classes of learners are usually identified based on the required results fixed by the grading system of each teaching institution. Depending on the needs of each project as well as on the frequency of learners activity follow-up required by teachers, we choose a period of time after which we make a regular prediction. To represent the activity of a learner during this learning period p_i, all features of learning indicators are grouped in the same vector X. Thus, on each prediction time p_i, a learner is represented by a vector X composed of features going from f_1 to f_n and the class y to which he belongs to. Each learner belongs to one and only class over the year.

$$X = <f_1, f_2, ..., f_n, y>$$

Each feature f_1 to f_n represents one learning activity till the prediction time p_i. For each prediction time p_i, the value of one feature is added to that of prediction time p_{i-1}: we proceed to an accumulation of values.

4 Case Study: CNED

4.1 CNED Presentation

The CNED[1] is the french largest national center for distance education. It offers multiple and fully distance courses to a very large number of physically dispersed learners. These learners are from different demographic profiles and cannot go to traditional schools for multiple reasons. Each learner is unique, in total autonomy and follows his own learning rhythm and schedule. The only information we have about him are the exams he submits and the traces of his activity within the LMS. Learning is also quite specific and provided through more than one application. It is multi-modal as the courses contents are available online and in printed papers. Moreover, by relying on traditional teaching methods, teachers monitor the progress of a large number of heterogeneous learners (up to thousands of learners) at the same time. These methods are no longer effective and teachers need help as well as new techniques and tools, which allow them a better tracking of learners performance and an early detection of their potential learning difficulties. In fact, CNED records among its k-12 learners a high failure rate every year. K-12 learners are the main focus of this study.

4.2 Data Description

In this project, learning traces are collected from two data sources. The first one is the LMS, which generates the interaction traces between learners and learning environment. This data is related to learners actions within the platform and

---

[1] Centre National d'Enseignement á Distance created in 1939.

their use of its different components. The second one is the students administrative management application GAEL[2]. This application provides two types of data. The first data type is demographic such as gender, age, native country, place of birth, city of residence, having or not a scholarship, repeating or not the year. The second type of data is related to modules, exams and their submission dates, marks, and correctors. The k-12 learners enrolled in the physical-chemistry module during the school years 2017–2018 and 2018–2019 are the case study of this paper. The school year starts on September 1 and ends on July 7. It is composed of 44 weeks. As the registration in CNED is open during the year, the start activity date t_0 of each learner is defined as the maximum date between the start school year date and the registration date. Depending on t_0, learners don't have the same number of activity weeks. In addition, study programs for learners who register after October 31 of each year go through adjustments. In this project, we focus on learners who subscribed before October 31. According this information, we collect the learning traces of 663 and 698 learners respectively from 2017–2018 and 2018–2019. All learners of 2017–2018 and 2018–2019 have respectively 37 and 35 activity weeks. From these two dates, we have a decrease in the number of learners per activity week.

4.3 Feature Extraction

In the context of CNED, in addition to the demographic data provided by GAEL, the activity of a learner is represented by the four learning indicators introduced in the Sect. 3.1. Based on the available and extracted features from both data sources, these indicators are defined as follows:

- performance: grades and exams are the current criteria for CNED tutors to evaluate their learners. The performance of a learner is represented by 3 features. These features are about the academic assessments and grades. They are evolutive over time.
- engagement: as CNED learners are in total autonomy, the only way to track their engagement is the online presence. In addition, CNED teachers push especially the k-12 learners to be more active on the LMS. The engagement is represented by 36 features. These features are time-dependent and are about the learner's use of the LMS and his interaction with its components.
- regularity: it is defined by the progress made by a learner in terms of number of actions within the LMS and number of submitted exams. The regularity is represented by 2 features. These features are also evolutive over time.
- reactivity: it is represented by features about the reactivity of a learner to submit an exam or to connect to the online course. The reactivity is represented by 7 features. These features are time-dependent, evolve over time and are computed based on the exams schedule calendar.

Thus, each learner is defined by 10 demographic features (which are constant) and learning indicators represented by the extracted features. In total, each learner is defined by 58 features.

---

[2] Gestion Administrative des ÉLèves.

4.4 Application of the Approach

CNED teachers need to have a regular and frequent tracking of their learners' activity. Therefore, the temporal granularity chosen here is the activity week as the period of time to apply the approach. This makes it possible to predict, for the context of CNED, learners in learning difficulties on a weekly basis and to compare their reliability over time. The prediction weeks, for each learner, depend on his start activity day t_0. More explicitly, the first prediction week of one learner is $w_1 = t_0 + 7 days$, the second prediction week is $w_2 = w_1 + 7 days$ and so on until w_n corresponds to the school year end date. With the exception of demographic data, which is of course time-independent, the rest of extracted learning features are therefore weekly updated. Demographic and features of learning indicators are grouped together in the same vector X to represent the weekly activity of a learner. The French system allows teachers to give marks between 0 and 20. The average of 10 in a module generally determines the success or failure of a learner. However, it is of great importance to have more focus on learners in the uncertainty zone with an average between 8 and 12. Therefore, for each module, learners are classified into three classes based on the obtained marks average by the end of the school year:

- success: when the marks average is superior to 12
- medium risk of failure: when the marks average is between 8 and 12
- high risk of failure learner: when the marks average is inferior to 8.

The Table 1 gives the number of learners belonging to each of the three classes during each of the school years. As the majority of state of art projects, most of learners are classified as successful.

The experimental part will focus on comparing the prediction performance of the following supervised machine learning models: Random Forest, Decision tree, K-nn and SVM. These models are frequently used showing good prediction results in the majority of the state of art projects [7,11].

Table 1. Number of learners per class.

School year	Learner class		
	Success	Medium risk	High risk
2017–2018	488	111	64
2018–2019	538	101	59

5 Methodology Implementation and Results

5.1 Experimental Protocol

The models are tested with 5-fold cross validation and have as input features those of the vector X. To evaluate the performance of the ML models to give an output y_{pred} similar to the y_{test}, we followed a two-step method allowing the identification of the models with the best accuracy. First, we randomly select 80% of learners vectors from the 2017–2018 school year to train the models and use the remaining 20% for the test phase. Then, to be sure of the first obtained results, we train the models with the school year $n - 1$ (2017–2018) learners vectors and test them with those of the school year n (2018–2019).

5.2 Accuracy Results

Comparing the accuracy curves of Fig. 2, SVM, Random Forest and Decision tree are the most performing models and keep an increasing accuracy evolution. K-nn has not stable results throughout the school year. On the first prediction week, the accuracies of SVM, Random forest and Decision tree were respectively 0.729, 0.706 and 0.639. The highest accuracies obtained by SVM, Random forest and Decision tree were respectively on week 32, 36 and 35. The results of the second step of the experimental protocol presented in Sect. 5.1 are shown in Fig. 3. Indeed, SVM, Random forest and Decision tree keep a high and increasing accuracy during the prediction dates. The selected models are pertinent.

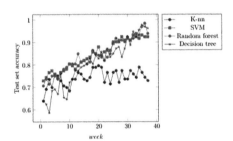 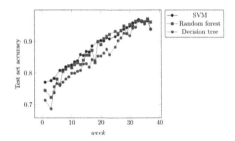

Fig. 2. First step of the accuracy evaluation

Fig. 3. Second step of the accuracy evaluation

Table 2. Models accuracy when using only demographic features.

Evaluation step	Model		
	Random Forest	Decision tree	SVM
First step results	0.608	0.655	0.756
Second step results	0.713	0.614	0.770

The Table 2 presents the models prediction accuracy when only using as input features the demographic ones. The first and second rows of the table are respectively the results of applying the two-step method of Sect. 5.1. These results show that the prediction performance of the algorithms during the early dates given in Fig. 2 and Fig. 3 is due to demographic features. This makes sense since during the first weeks we do not have enough data about learner's activity. We want to gain in dimension, computing time and why not in accuracy. For these reasons, we proceed to the feature selection process.

5.3 Feature Selection Process

For this study, we follow the accuracy curves of Fig. 2. Then, we apply, for each model, the feature selection techniques with learners vectors that give the maximum accuracy. For the next experiments, we train and test models with the 2017–2018 learners vectors.

Filtering Methods. Two statistical tests are applied as filtering methods: Chi-square and ANOVA [13]. We set the number of features to be selected to $k = 20$ which is the optimum value for k. We applied these two tests, on the same data, with other values for k that did not give better accuracy results. Therefore, on every prediction week, each learner is now represented by a vector X of 20 features and his success/risk class y. Most of the selected features by both tests belong to the engagement indicator. These features are about the learner activity within the LMS. Features related to the performance indicator such as number of exams and marks obtained up to the prediction week w_i are selected by both tests. ANOVA test selects features of regularity such as the progress in number of actions and submitted exams made by a learner comparing to the previous prediction date. The demographic features selected by Chi-square test are country of residence and city and those selected by ANOVA are having or not a scholarship and repeating or not the year. Applying the Chi-square and ANOVA tests, there is no degradation in the models accuracy. The curves shapes of Fig. 4 and Fig. 5 keep the same properties of those of Fig. 2 but with a faster accuracy evolution especially during the first prediction weeks. On some prediction weeks, the input features selected with the ANOVA test seems to give a higher prediction accuracy of y_{test} than with the Chi-square test. The selected learning features by the ANOVA test are relevant and independent of algorithms.

Wrapper Methods. The Recursive Feature Elimination with Cross Validation (RFECV) [6] is used here as a technique of wrapper methods. The number of features selected by RFECV technique with SVM, Random forest and Decision tree are respectively 13, 10 and 29. With the three models (SVM, Random forest and Decision tree), RFECV selects features indicating the engagement of a learner such as the amount of logs. Features of the learner performance given by the number of submitted exams and marks are always selected. With the three models, features expressing the reactivity of a learner such as the number of days between the start of the activity date and the first connection to the LMS date are selected to confirm their high correlation with the prediction of y_{test}. Features of regularity of the progress are selected with SVM and Decision tree. As for demographic features, place of birth and city are selected by the

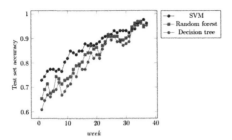
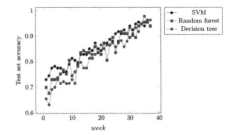

Fig. 4. Accuracy evolution-chi-square-

Fig. 5. Accuracy evolution- Anova-

three models. The feature concerning having or not a scholarship is selected by Random forest and Decision tree. Age and gender are selected by SVM and Decision tree. The curves shapes of Fig. 6 have the same properties of those of Fig. 2. In fact, there is no degradation in accuracy and the input features selected by the RFECV method seems to have a better impact on the prediction accuracy of the three models. The curves of the Fig. 6 have a faster accuracy evolution on the first prediction weeks. The RFECV technique gives good results with the three models. The selected features by the RFECV technique are relevant but are dependent to the models.

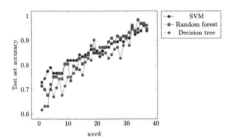
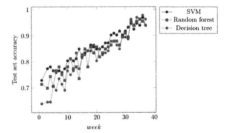

Fig. 6. The accuracy evolution-RFECV-

Fig. 7. The accuracy evolution-embedded method-

Embedded Methods. Due to their powerful structure, tree-based algorithms, have the feature importance hyperparameter that serves to select the most important features to make an accurate prediction. In this experiment, the Random Forest is the tree-based algorithm used for feature selection. To train SVM, Random forest and Decision tree and test their prediction accuracy, the tree-based algorithm selects 8 relevant features. The main selected features in this case are about the learner performance given by marks and average. Features of the reactivity of a learner to connect to the LMS are selected too. The demographic features selected are city, place of birth and age. The curves of Fig. 7 still have the same properties as those of Fig. 2. In fact, there is no degradation in accuracy results. The selected features here are also dependent of the tree-based model and have generally better accuracy with models of the same category.

Features of the performance indicator are selected by all the feature selection techniques. Features about the engagement of a learner are selected by the ANOVA, Chi-square and RFECV techniques. Features expressing the regularity of progress are selected by the ANOVA and RFECV techniques. Features of the reactivity indicator are selected by the wrapper and embedded methods.

5.4 FPR Results

Classification performance without focussing on a class is the most general way of comparing algorithms. Thus, the accuracy measure does not distinguish between the number of correct labels of different classes. Therefore, opting for a more specific performance metric is necessary to identify the model which correctly predicts learners at medium and high risk of failure (at-risk learners). It is with these learners that the educational interventions will take place. The aim is to minimize at-risk learners classified as successful. To this end, we propose to track the evolution of FPR measure during the learning period given by:

$$FPR = \frac{FP}{FP + TN}$$

The lower FPR is, the more the model is qualified to have a significant ability to predict at risk learners. The Fig. 8, Fig. 9, Fig. 10 and Fig. 11 show that SVM is the algorithm with the highest FPR during the first prediction dates. Despite having the highest overall accuracy, SVM doesn't correctly predict at-risk learners on the first prediction dates. Decision tree is the algorithm with the lowest FPR during the first weeks. Decison tree shows a better ability to correctly predict at-risk learners.

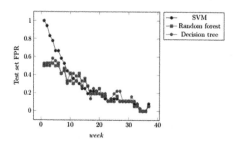

Fig. 8. The FPR evolution-Chi-square-

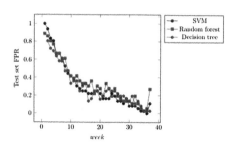

Fig. 9. The FPR evolution-ANOVA-

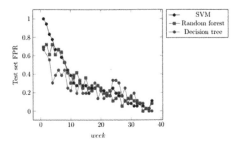 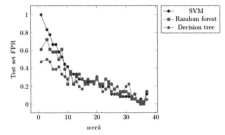

Fig. 10. The FPR evolution-RFECV-

Fig. 11. The FPR evolution-embeded method-

5.5 Results Analysis

Going through the feature selection process allows gaining in dimension and keeping a high prediction accuracy of models. In addition, it shows the pertinence of the identified learning indicators particularly the performance and engagement ones. These indicators serve for the diagnosis of learning problems. Some techniques are related to algorithms and others are independent of algorithms. The ANOVA test selects features which are correlated with the target variable independently from the models. SVM is the model with the highest accuracy and the highest FPR during the first weeks. These results come from the fact that this model predicts very well successful learners. On the other hand, Decision tree is the algorithm with the lowest accuracy and lowest FPR during the first weeks. Decision tree is the best to predict at-risk learners during the first weeks. Random forest performs slightly worse than decision tree in predicting at risk learners but is still much better than SVM. From week 10, all algorithms show almost the same accuracy and FPR values. From week 20, we predict with the minimum of error the at-risk learners.

6 Conclusion

The early prediction of students with learning difficulties is one of the most popular studies in the literature. However, this issue is less discussed when it comes to k-12 online and in total autonomy learners. The CNED is not an exception and records a high failure rate every year. Thus, it aims at providing its instructors with a tool to identify correctly and at the earliest k-12 at-risk learners. In addition to the challenges of dealing with multi-source, heterogeneous and of different types data, we proposed an in-depth methodology which gives ML based solutions to early predict at-risk learners. This methodology starts with the identification of learning indicators among: performance, engagement, regularity and reactivity. Then, we extract features from raw data to define each indicator. The identification of learning indicators is of a great importance as it serves on one hand for the prediction of at-risk learners and on the other hand for the diagnosis of each learner situation and learning gap. Then, we formalized the problem into a 3-class classification problem and followed a weekly prediction approach. For the evaluation phase of the methodology, we used the FPR measure to compare the ability of the used algorithms to well identify the classes of at-risk learners. The findings show that decision tree is the best model that correctly predicts at-risk learners especially on the first weeks. Through these experiments, we also affirmed that the prediction of at medium and high risk of failure learners is given with the minimum error starting from week 20. The perspectives of this study are numerous. We have to extend the application of the methodology on other learning levels and modules. We have also the intention to evaluate these findings with teachers and in a real learning situation. To make the methodology more generic and complete, we aim at adding a phase for the suggestion of academic actions for learners from their teachers.

Acknowledgement. This project is funded by the CNED which provides us with data for this work.

References

1. Akub, K., Martin, H., Drahomira, H., Zdenek, Z., Jonas, V., Wolff, A.: OU analyse: analysing at-risk students at the open university. LAK (2015)
2. Alfred, E., Hanan, A.: Improving student success using predictive models and data visualisations. Research in Learning Technology (2012)
3. Alfred, E., Hanan, A.: Student success system: risk analytics and data visualization using ensembles of predictive models. LAK (2012)
4. Alice, Z., Amanda, C.: Feature Engineering for Machine Learning. O'REILLY (2018)
5. David, M.O., Du, Q.H., Mark, R., Martin, D., Damyon, W.: A supervised learning framework: using assessment to identify students at risk of dropping out of a MOOC. J. Comput. High. Educ. (2020)
6. Jiliang, T., Salem, A., Huan, L.: Feature selection for classification: a review. In: Data Classification, pp. 37–64. CRC Press (2014). https://doi.org/10.1201/b17320
7. Kew, S.N., Zaidatun, T.: Identifying at-risk students in online learning by analysing learning behaviour: a systematic review. In: IEEE Conference on Big Data and Analytics (ICBDA) (2017)
8. Kimberly, E.A., Matthew, D.P.: Case study: a traffic lights and interventions: signals at Purdue University. LAK 2012, April 2012
9. Lin, Q., Yanshen, L., Yi, L.: An integrated framework with feature selection for dropout prediction in massive open online courses. IEEE Access **6** (2018)
10. Boroujeni, M.S., Sharma, K., Kidziński, Ł, Lucignano, L., Dillenbourg, P.: How to quantify student's regularity? In: Verbert, K., Sharples, M., Klobučar, T. (eds.) EC-TEL 2016. LNCS, vol. 9891, pp. 277–291. Springer, Cham (2016). https://doi.org/10.1007/978-3-319-45153-4_21
11. Mushtaq, H., Wenhao, Z., Wu, Z., Syed Muhammad Raza, A.: Student engagement predictions in an e-learning system and their impact on student course assessment scores. Comput. Intell. Neurosci. (2018)
12. Papia, B.: Retention in online courses: exploring issues and solutions - a literature review. Sage Open 1–11 (2016)
13. Venkatesh, B., Anuradha, J.: A review of feature selection and its methods. Cybern. Inf. Tech. **19**(1) (2019)

A Framework to Guide Educational Technology Studies in the Evolving Classroom Research Environment

Tomohiro Nagashima(✉), Gautam Yadav, and Vincent Aleven

Human-Computer Interaction Institute, Carnegie Mellon University, Pittsburgh, USA
{tnagashi,gyadav,va0e}@andrew.cmu.edu

Abstract. Despite the drastic change to school environments due to the COVID-19 pandemic, it is still important that educational technology researchers conduct school-based research to understand the impact of technology in an authentic learning context, even remotely. However, the transition to remote research has made it challenging for researchers to collect classroom data, observe teacher-student-technology interactions, and facilitate study sessions. To explore how researchers can effectively plan and conduct technology-based educational studies in the new, evolving classroom research environment, we interviewed seven US teachers, investigating their perceptions of participating in remote classroom studies. Based on the findings and the authors' experience of running classroom studies, we propose a framework that educational technology researchers can refer to when planning and conducting research in the evolving classroom research environment. Specifically, the framework informs researchers of several types of questions they can explore with teachers, students, and researchers themselves to be better prepared to address potential confusion, unexpected issues, and practical benefits in remote classroom research. Our work contributes by providing a practical guide for running technology-based research remotely, which may remain as a means of classroom research in the future. Some of the findings and the framework would also be applied to in-person classroom research setting.

Keywords: Classroom research · COVID-19 · Remote teaching and learning

1 Introduction

1.1 Classroom Studies in Educational Technology Research

For decades, researchers of educational technologies have studied the effectiveness and use of educational technologies in the context of school classrooms. For example, researchers conduct "in-vivo" experiments to examine the effectiveness of instructional approaches embedded in educational software in a classroom context [1]. An in-vivo experiment in education research is a study conducted in an actual classroom setting, as opposed to in a research lab setting, in an attempt to maximize both internal and external validity of the study [1]. Examples of an in-vivo study include efficacy studies using learning software and classroom evaluations of AI-based tutoring software where students are assigned to use learning software and researchers collect data generated from the software and other instruments such as online surveys and tests [1, 2]. Classroom studies are also employed in other types of educational research conducted with practitioners, such as in Design-Based Research and Researcher-Practitioner Partnerships [3, 4]. Classroom studies with educational technologies can take a variety of formats (e.g., observational studies, randomized control trials). Regardless of the study format, classroom studies consider regular classroom features, such as teacher-student interactions and resources available in the classroom, as part of the study context.

The current paper considers how classroom research with educational technology can be conducted effectively in the *evolving classroom research environment* in which different levels of remote involvement by researchers is possible, brought about mainly by the COVID-19 pandemic [5, 6]. We believe that remote involvement in classroom research may continue to exist in some form in the near future due to its advantages (e.g., remote classroom research allows researchers to conduct research with schools located in areas where study participation opportunities are not available) [7]. From among the various types of classroom studies, we focus on in-vivo educational studies.

1.2 Conducting Classroom Research Remotely

In the year 2020, due to the spread of the coronavirus disease (COVID-19), a vast number of schools across the globe were forced to make a transition to remote instruction [8]. In response to the shift, researchers were required to pivot to collecting data remotely using technologies such as video conferencing systems [7, 9]. Conducting classroom studies remotely, however, can be challenging and can affect study design and outcomes significantly. First, the mode of teaching at the school and that of researcher participation affect ways in which communications, data collection, and study facilitation happen. Figure 1 shows six different modes in which classroom research can be conducted, the traditional in-person classroom research mode and five remote classroom research modes. We developed this schematic based on our experience of running in-person and remote classroom studies at six schools with ten teachers before and during the pandemic [2]. Compared to the traditional classroom research mode (Fig. 1, A), where all stakeholders are physically located in the same classroom, remote classroom research can vary depending on whether the school/class adopts in-person or remote teaching, synchronous or asynchronous teaching, and whether and how the researcher helps run the study with the teacher synchronously or asynchronously, including any technical and logistical support the research team may provide. For instance, direct researcher-student interactions are more likely to happen when the researcher, teacher(s), and students are all synchronously connected in a video-conferencing system than in situations where students participate in classroom research asynchronously (i.e., completing assigned study tasks whenever students have time).

Secondly, data collection can be affected by the affordances and constraints of communication technologies used for remotely connecting researchers and participants (e.g., video conferencing systems) [5]. For example, in a fully-remote synchronous session (Fig. 1, D), it becomes difficult to observe teacher-student interactions if the study uses a platform that allows participants to privately message each other. Also, it is challenging to observe students' gestures and facial expressions since students might not have a web camera, or even when they have one, students might not turn it on [10].

Finally, it is important to consider teachers' and students' experiences (e.g., benefits and concerns) in participating in research conducted remotely. Classroom studies are a means for researchers to visit an *authentic* learning environment and understand the impact of the technology *in situ* [1]. Understanding what practical benefits educational technology research (remote or in-person) can offer to teachers and students, and what concerns may be mitigated, will help design classroom research as a mutual learning opportunity between researchers and teachers and students rather than as a mere means of data collection. It is particularly important to understand such practitioners' perspectives on participating in remote research, caused due to the COVID-19 pandemic. As the pandemic has already created and will continue creating many struggles for students (e.g., lack of emotional support and device access, increased family responsibilities) [11] and for teachers (e.g., increased workload, burnout) [12], educational technology research should not cause any additional burdens and stress to teachers and students. Therefore, it is critical that researchers understand practical benefits and challenges/concerns that teachers and students might have and appropriately address them when conducting research in the evolving classroom research environment.

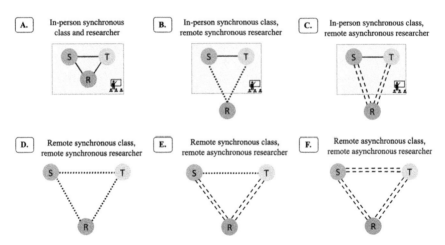

Fig. 1. Modes of remote and in-person classroom research. "S", "T", and "R" represent student, teacher, and researcher, respectively. Solid lines indicate in-person synchronous interaction, dotted lines show remote synchronous interaction, and double dashed lines indicate remote asynchronous interaction. Gray squares show that stakeholders in the square are in the physical classroom. Model A shows the in-person classroom research model. The authors experienced all six modes in their classroom research. Hybrid (mix of in-person and remote) teaching mode can be represented by combining Models B and D (synchronous hybrid class, remote synchronous researcher) or C and E (synchronous hybrid class, remote asynchronous researcher).

Given these considerations for classroom research conducted remotely, it is essential that researchers of educational technology understand potential factors that might affect data collection, communications, and teacher and student experience when conducting technology-based educational research. Understanding such pragmatic factors will help create a sustainable model for running research in the evolving classroom research environment. Prior related work provides some guidance for how to conduct remote data collection, such as when conducting co-design activities with children [5] and remote user studies in the field of Human-Computer Interaction [6, 13]. However, to the best of our knowledge, there is no prior work that guides remote research studies in (physical or virtual) school environments. Educational studies in classrooms are uniquely different from typical user studies or other types of studies that are conducted in a lab, or in a relatively *confined* setting. In a teaching and learning environment, interactions are complex since multiple stakeholders (e.g., teachers, students, and peers) interact with each other dynamically in unpredictable ways [14]. To inform researchers what aspects to be mindful of in running classroom studies, particularly in the remote setting, we conducted interviews with US teachers exploring their perceptions of participating in classroom studies. Based on the findings and our own experience of running in-person and remote studies, we propose a framework that researchers can use to help develop their remote study plans.

2 Method

2.1 Participants

To conduct interviews, we recruited middle-school ($n = 6$) and high-school ($n = 1$) mathematics teachers in the United States. We specifically targeted mathematics teachers because mathematics is the task domain of our on-going research. We targeted teachers who, in earlier interactions, had expressed an interest in participating in classroom studies with us during their remote instruction (March–June 2020). Three of the participating teachers had remotely participated in a study with us during May–June 2020, prior to the interview. In the study, their students used an Intelligent Tutoring System for algebra [2]. One other teacher had participated in classroom research with their students before the COVID-19 pandemic. The remaining three teachers had not participated in classroom research before. The teachers were recruited either via teacher groups on a social networking site or from previous contacts. Their level of experience in using educational technology varied. Lastly, all teachers' schools were affected significantly by the pandemic; they were required to make a transition to either fully-remote synchronous instruction ($n = 4$) or fully-remote asynchronous instruction ($n = 3$).

Interviews were conducted individually and remotely using a video conferencing system. Each interview lasted approximately an hour. The interviews were semi-structured; the researchers asked both pre-planned questions and un-planned questions as the conversation evolved. The interviews explored teachers' perceptions regarding participating in classroom research in general (e.g., "What kinds of benefits do you think participating in classroom research will bring to you and your students?" and "how would you describe the study participation opportunity to your students?") and those specific to remote study participation (e.g., "What kinds of emerging factors during remote teaching you think might affect data collection and student learning?"). Three of the teachers participated in one or two additional sessions to continue the interview. In total, we conducted 11 one-hour interview sessions.

2.2 Data Collection and Analysis

All interviews were video-recorded and transcribed for analysis. Two learning sciences graduate students analyzed the data following an Affinity Diagramming approach, a commonly-used method for analyzing qualitative data through grouping and organizing quotes and codes into a hierarchy of themes [15]. The graduate students communicated frequently to resolve any disagreements. We obtained a total of 179 codes, clustered into 70 mid-level themes. We grouped the mid-level themes into seven major themes.

3 Results

Our analysis revealed seven major themes regarding teachers' perceptions on participating in remote classroom studies, categorized into benefits and concerns/challenges (Table 1). In what follows, we describe these themes in the two categories in turn.

Table 1. Benefits and concerns/challenges teachers perceive for participating in remote classroom studies.

Perceived benefits	Perceived concerns/challenges
B1: Teachers appreciate the opportunity to make a real-world connection by remotely welcoming researchers to the classroom	**C1**: Teachers find it hard to calibrate their level of intervention/facilitation during studies
B2: Teachers consider that remote study participation can be a motivating activity for students	**C2**: Teachers prefer customizability and flexibility regarding research participation and content to-be-covered
B3: Teachers will have an opportunity to understand their students from a different perspective	**C3**: Teachers are concerned with the lack of synchronous, immediate support for students in remote studies
	C4: Teachers are concerned with students' learning environments during remote teaching

3.1 Perceived Benefits of Participating in Remote Classroom Research

B1: Teachers Appreciate the Opportunity to Make a Real-World Connection by Remotely Welcoming Researchers to the Classroom. All teachers strongly emphasized the importance of connecting their students with researchers, consistent with findings in prior literature [16]. Teachers view welcoming researchers in the classroom as an opportunity for students to learn about real-world jobs (e.g., knowing what researchers do). For instance, one teacher, who participated in a study in June 2020 when the teacher remotely and asynchronously taught students, stated that their students had had very limited exposure to the outside world even before the transition to remote teaching:

[We] are a very small community [...] so a lot of kids don't know what's out there [...]. They haven't been out in the real world. A lot of them haven't even traveled beyond our edge of our city. [...]. So I was looking for ways to connect what we're doing in math to either like a career field or something in their real life.

Importantly, the need for real-world connections in classrooms has become more critical during remote learning because students have fewer opportunities to interact with the world outside the classroom and their homes. As an overall trend, we found that teachers who teach in a suburban area, including the teacher whose quote is shown above, shared that remote classroom research gives a meaningful research participation experience to their students, who used to have limited access to such opportunities before the transition to remote instruction.

B2: Teachers Consider that Remote Study Participation Can Be a Motivating Activity for Students. Teachers mentioned that, as it became very challenging for students to keep up their motivation and engagement during remote teaching, participating in a study could be a huge motivator that would "bring students back to the classroom," which they hoped to do but found challenging. Indeed, several of the teachers we interviewed reported that their virtual class participation rate was only about 10–15%. They also said that they expect that an opportunity to contribute to the science of teaching and learning will be motivating for their students. They told us that they would emphasize that helping researchers would make the world better and that their students' effort would be key to the success of the research.

B3: Teachers will Have an Opportunity to Understand their Students from a Different Perspective. Teachers noted that participating in a study would allow them to view their students from a different perspective. Specifically, teachers said that they would appreciate an opportunity to observe how students perform the assigned tasks in the educational technology used. Teachers stated that watching how their students approach the task would give them a new point of view regarding individual students that they would not otherwise gain from their daily instruction. In this sense, teachers are curious about researchers' scientific inquiries and keen to learn from research results.

Teachers also consider research participation an opportunity to try new types of instruction or digital technologies and find out what kinds of educational technology or tools their students find engaging. Although the benefit of being able to understand students from a different perspective could well apply to an in-person setting, all interviewed teachers had a hard time coping with students' low motivation and engagement and they were therefore looking for ways to maintain or enhance participation and engagement more often during remote teaching than before.

3.2 Perceived Concerns and Challenges Regarding Participation in Remote Classroom Research

C1: Teachers Find it Hard to Calibrate their Level of Intervention/Facilitation during Studies. As the data collection became virtual, interactions among teachers, students, and researchers during the study, including during the study sessions themselves, became dependent on the affordances and constrains of the technology used for having interactions. For example, the use of a synchronous video conferencing system might facilitate researcher-student interactions; by contrast, if email is the only technology used for communications, there is no opportunity for synchronous interaction. Therefore, depending on the type of technology used for running remote studies, a situation could conceivably happen where, for example, students and researchers directly communicate with each other without including their teacher. Conversely, researchers might be able to interact with students only through the help of teachers (e.g., researchers are not allowed to send emails to students directly). This tension regarding how much researchers' and teachers' involvement are ideal came up frequently during the interviews. Although teachers said they would want the researchers to lead the study, they stressed that it was important that they could be a "facilitator" of the study. They noted that it is important that researchers describe the study because that would motivate students but they consider their own involvement essential, especially during remote teaching. This desire comes from concerns regarding the lack of cues and strategies that they used to have during in-person teaching as well as limited communication channels between students and teachers during remote teaching [17].

Another reason that teachers gave for wanting to be actively facilitating research studies is that they have better knowledge than researchers about which students are struggling and how to help them (e.g., they know which students regularly ask for help). Therefore, they would like to be informed or involved when researchers communicate with students. One teacher shared how much researcher involvement would be ideal:

> I do think it's important to have a teacher being the facilitator of that kind of the relationship then between [our] students and the actual study. The idea that the students have formed a relationship with me [...]. But on the other hand, it's not my project. So I think it's a good idea for [a researcher] to explain the research to them [...]. I do think it's good for [a researcher] to be involved [...] but also, I think they are more comfortable if they know that I'm explaining the procedure.

C2: Teachers Prefer Customizability and Flexibility regarding Research Participation and Content To-be-Covered. Teachers prefer having the ability to customize what content their students will work on during the study, or at least having a few options for the task assignment. They also prefer studies that are aligned with their teaching practices. Customization and flexibility in research design are perceived as a critical factor for teachers to decide whether or not to participate in the remote study.

C3: Teachers Are Concerned with the Lack of Synchronous, Immediate Support for Students in Remote Studies. All teachers expressed concern regarding what to do if a student would face technical trouble or struggle with the content in the technology used in the study during a remote study (e.g., students might have trouble when they log into the system). Supporting students remotely during such an event would be challenging, compared to doing so in the in-person regular classroom environment. In fact, teachers' concern that it would be challenging for their students to learn to use the technology was a major reason that some of them decided not to participate in our proposed study during remote teaching, despite having previously expressed interest in doing so.

C4: Teachers are Concerned with Students' Learning Environments During Remote Teaching. Teachers indicated that there are new, unique challenges that affect student learning during remote teaching. As reported in the literature [11, 12], teachers stated that their students were struggling due to lack of access to the internet, lack of parental and peer support, and lack of access to the physical books that they had used. As both students and teachers found it very challenging to connect with each other to keep the classroom instruction going [17], in spite of trying hard, teachers were hesitant to introduce anything new (technology or topic) to their students during remote teaching, lest it causes their students additional confusion and adds to their workload.

4 Discussion

4.1 A Framework for Conducting Remote Classroom Research

The interviews highlight benefits of participating in educational research in the evolving classroom research environment and concerns/challenges perceived by teachers. All the themes we found (except C3 and C4) could arguably be applied to in-person research setting, but we found that these themes have much greater importance in a remote setting (e.g., teachers' desire for students to get exposed to a real-world experience would still apply to in-person classroom research, but teachers stressed the importance of it in a remote setting). Despite the unpredictable future, we believe that conducting classroom studies virtually will remain important as schools may consider a virtual learning environment as one of the possible teaching modes or researchers may keep conducting research remotely due to a school's policy regarding visitors and/or due to advantages of remote research (e.g., researchers do not need to travel to the study site and their sample will not be constrained in specific locations).

Based on the interviews, we offer a framework that researchers can use to guide their research in the evolving classroom research environment (Table 2). The framework captures factors that researchers need to be aware of when preparing for and running classroom studies remotely. We think that providing such a framework, rather than concrete recommended strategies, would be more useful because of the unpredictable and uncontrollable nature of remote research [5]. The framework provides guiding questions that researchers can use to explore needs, preferences, and expectations among teachers, students, and researchers themselves. The questions help researchers better address dimensions that we consider are critical when planning and conducting remote classroom research. During our own remote classroom studies, we found these guiding questions helped understand the school's context, teachers' needs and preferences, and realize our (researchers') own expectations. We describe each of the dimensions below.

Study Facilitation. It is important that researchers clearly understand teachers' expectations and preferences regarding whether and how teachers want to take the lead in running study sessions. We found that teachers are concerned with how to help run the study and provide appropriate, immediate support for students. Although it is important to understand teachers' and students' needs and preferences in any classroom study, including those conducted in-person, it is especially important in remote research. Such

Table 2. A framework for addressing factors that might affect remote classroom research. Each question in a cell represents a guiding question that the researcher can ask the corresponding stakeholder (teacher, student, or researcher themselves). Code in parentheses (e.g., B1) represents the associated theme(s) that the dimension is drawn from.

Dimension and Objective	Question for:		
	Teacher	Student	Researcher
Study Facilitation (C1, C3) - To communicate expectations and preferences on what to do when unexpected events occur	- What are the teacher's expectations and preferences regarding who will lead study sessions, and how they will do so?	- How would students feel about communicating directly with researchers?	- How critical is it that the researcher takes the lead in facilitating study sessions? - How can researchers help teachers be prepared for their preferred role as a facilitator?
Resource Access (B2, B3) - To understand and address the needs and desires of participants regarding resource access	- What data, resources, and tools, would the teacher want to use for their own teaching or for understanding their students better?	- What data, resources, and tools would students find useful if they were given free access?	- How to make the data, resources, and tools *open* enough so that participants can use them outside the research context (e.g., platform choice, customization)?
Motivation (B1, B2) - To understand and address participants' motivations for participating in the research	- What would the teacher want to learn about students, the research, and the educational technology used? - What would the teacher want students to gain from participating in the study?	- What would help motivate students to participate and engage in the research? - What kinds of real-world connections would students be interested in making or hearing about?	- What would the researcher want the teacher and students to gain from participating in the research? - What kinds of real-world connections could the researcher provide to students?
Study Logistics and Context Alignment (C2, C3) - To make the study participation easy and straightforward - To ensure that the study is aligned with the classroom practice	- What tool does the teacher use that could be integrated into the research (or that the research could be integrated into)? - How closely is the study topic aligned with classroom teaching?	- What tools are students already familiar with? - Are there topics that students are interested in (e.g., out-of-school interests) that could be integrated into the research?	- What are some possible ways that the study activities can be streamlined and made as simple as possible so that participants can carry out these activities easily?

(*continued*)

Table 2. (*continued*)

Dimension and Objective	Question for:		
	Teacher	Student	Researcher
Equity in Participation (C4) - To understand individual differences in participants' learning environments	- What does the teacher know about their students' learning environments and about how to effectively support students during remote learning?	- What kinds of learning environments and support (e.g., from parents, and siblings) do students have access to?	- How can the research address/consider students' learning environments? - What are alternative ways for students to participate in the research if they do not have adequate learning environments?

understanding will help researchers develop a study plan that the teachers and students feel comfortable with and that can accommodate unique situations that might happen in remote setting. For instance, researchers need to ensure that teachers understand what to do when a sudden internet or electricity outage happens in a remote study because it can be challenging to make decisions dynamically in such a situation [5].

Resource Access. Teachers like to be informed about study results to better understand their students. As well, they are curious to learn about research-based instructional knowledge and possibly incorporate it into their practices. Understanding these needs of practitioners will help researchers share resources that are most useful for the practitioners. For example, teachers might not only want access to students' learning data that researchers typically provide but might also appreciate receiving other types of data, such as how frequently students access the system in an asynchronous setting, to get insights into their students' behaviors that the teachers would not otherwise know. Also, if teachers and students are interested in further customizing study resources, it is important that researchers provide access to their resources in a customizable way (e.g., use an editable file and an open license).

Motivation. To maximize practical benefits for teachers and students, we recommend that researchers understand teachers' and students' motivations for participating in classroom research. As the interview findings suggest, teachers find it hard to motivate and engage their students especially during remote teaching. Remote classroom research, if it adequately addresses participants' motivation, can be a powerful motivating experience for them. Exploring participants' motivation will help researchers find ways to address these motivations. For example, when students are curious about what it is like to be a researcher, researchers can consider setting aside time for students to ask questions about the researchers' background and future career goals.

Study Logistics and Context Alignment. Researchers need to ensure that the technology used can be navigated intuitively with no technical bugs. They also need to be prepared for unexpected events during remote studies [5] such as sudden internet outages and technical difficulties (e.g., students cannot log into the system in an asynchronous setting). Also, researchers are expected to make a study plan that allows for flexibility regarding multiple aspects of the study (e.g., the difficulty of the problems assigned to students) to accommodate any needs or preferences that the teacher or students have. Understanding such needs and preferences will help make study participation easier, more streamlined, and more aligned with classroom practices and curriculum requirements.

Equity in Participation. We suggest that researchers consider equity in student participation as a core component of the studies they design for remote classroom research. As the findings of the present study as well as other recent work [11, 12, 18] suggest, the shift to remote learning due to COVID-19 has exacerbated existing inequalities regarding the support and resources students have access to, including access to learning technologies, increased family responsibilities, and lack of support from parents and peers. These gaps among students might affect study participation, engagement, and learning in remote classroom research [17]. Exploring what kinds of inequalities researchers need to expect will help them make the study more accessible. For instance, by understanding individual differences in device access among students in advance, researchers can adjust their study design, develop an alternative study participation plan for students with limited access to internet and devices, and design ways for assessing variability in students' learning environment to appropriately consider any potential influence such differences may have on study results.

4.2 How Would the Teaching Mode Affect Remote Classroom Research?

The proposed framework offers guidance for how researchers could prepare for remote classroom data collection, but the teaching mode and that of researcher participation (Fig. 1) would also significantly influence the planning. We propose that all five dimensions in the framework need to be considered in accordance with the modes of teaching and researcher participation (Fig. 2). Based on our interviews and prior work [7, 13, 14, 19], we think that, as the mode of teaching and researcher participation become less *connected* (i.e., from physical to remote, from synchronous to asynchronous interaction), the importance of considering the dimensions will increase. When communication channels are limited, it becomes more challenging to intervene and support students (e.g., hard to observe what students are doing and offer help in a timely manner) [7, 10, 19]. Therefore, in a *less-connected* classroom research environment, it would be more important to carefully consider study facilitation strategies, develop ways to motivate participants, give sufficient access to resources for students' individual learning, streamline study procedure and consider the alignment between the study and classroom practices, and offer an opportunity to participate in the study for students who have limited internet or device access. On the other hand, when the study is conducted in a more *connected* setting (e.g., Fig. 2, B), it would be easier to have direct, synchronous communications and provide support, it would not be as hard to motivate participants, and there would be strong need for resource access for classroom use (by teachers, rather than access for students' individual learning). Researchers could also consider more complicated study designs and could expect narrower gaps among students regarding their learning environment since they are all joining from their classroom synchronously, instead of their own home environment [7].

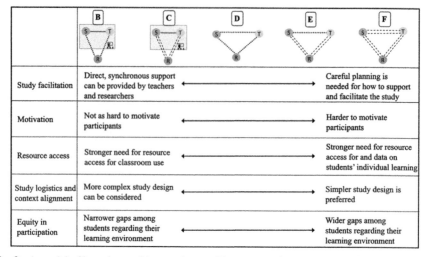

Fig. 2. A model of how the teaching mode can affect remote classroom research. As the teaching mode becomes less *connected* (from B to F), more careful planning and coordination are needed between researchers and the classroom teacher (and students) to ensure that students can participate in and complete the study and benefit from the study participation experience.

Finally, it is important to note that the framework and many of our findings could be generalized to in-person in-vivo classroom research where it is equally important to consider practitioners' viewpoints. In fact, practical considerations in classroom research, especially in the in-vivo research context, are underexplored [20]. Also, even after some challenges might be mitigated after the *chaotic* time in 2020–21, many of the proposed considerations would still be useful as remote classroom research may continue to exist as a means of classroom research. Therefore, although the proposed model is designed for remote classroom research based on teacher interviews during the COVID-19 pandemic, we think that there are elements that will be useful for remote and in-person classroom studies conducted when schools are *back to normal*.

5 Conclusion

The transition to a new learning environment has forced educational technology researchers to make a transition from in-person to remote data collection, which created new challenges. Our interviews with teachers illustrated that teachers perceive both benefits and challenges in participating in remote classroom studies. Our framework for conducting remote classroom research provides guidance for how educational technology researchers can plan and facilitate remote classroom research, which would continue to exist. We acknowledge, however, that our findings with seven mathematics teachers, who already had an interest in participating in research, may not cover a full range of potential benefits and challenges that teachers and students might experience, and their perceived benefits and challenges might not reflect the actual benefits and challenges they would receive. Also, the small sample is not likely to be representative of school teachers as a whole; it is, however, representative of teachers interested in using educational technology. Our work contributes to the educational technology research community by offering a practical guide that can be used widely by researchers.

Acknowledgements. This research was supported by NSF Award #1760922. We thank all the participating teachers.

References

1. Koedinger, K.R., Aleven, V., Roll, I., Baker, R.: In vivo experiments on whether supporting metacognition in intelligent tutoring systems yields robust learning. In: Handbook of Metacognition in Education, pp. 897–964 (2009)
2. Nagashima, T., et al.: Using anticipatory diagrammatic self-explanation to support learning and performance in early algebra. In: de Vries, E., Ahn, J., Hod, Y. (eds.) 15th International Conference of the Learning Sciences, pp. 474–481. International Society of the Learning Sciences (2021)
3. Amiel, T., Reeves, T.C.: Design-based research and educational technology: rethinking technology and the research agenda. J. Educ. Technol. Soc. **11**(4), 29–40 (2008)
4. Coburn, C.E., Penuel, W.R.: Research–practice partnerships in education: outcomes, dynamics, and open questions. Educ. Res. **45**(1), 48–54 (2016)
5. Lee, K.J., et al.: The show must go on. A conceptual model of conducting synchronous participatory design with children online. In: Proceedings of the 2021 CHI Conference on Human Factors in Computing Systems (CHI '21), pp. 1–16. Yokohama, Japan (2021)
6. Ratcliffe, J., Soave, F., Bryan-Kinns, N., Tokarchuk, L., Farkhatdinov, I.: Extended reality (XR) remote research: a survey of drawbacks and opportunities. In: Proceedings of the 2021 CHI Conference on Human Factors in Computing Systems (CHI '21), pp. 1–13. Yokohama, Japan (2021)
7. Rhodes, M., et al.: Advancing developmental science via unmoderated remote research with children. J. Cogn. Dev. **21**(4), 477–493 (2020)
8. Middleton, K.V.: The longer-term Impact of COVID-19 on K–12 student learning and assessment. Educ. Meas. Issues Pract. **39**(3), 41–44 (2020)
9. Nussenbaum, K., Scheuplein, M., Phaneuf, C.V., Evans, M.D., Hartley, C.A.: Moving developmental research online: comparing in-lab and web-based studies of model-based reinforcement learning. Collabra: Psychol. **6**(1) (2020)
10. Castelli, F.R., Sarvary, M.A.: Why students do not turn on their video cameras during online classes and an equitable and inclusive plan to encourage them to do so. Ecol. Evol. **11**, 3565–3576 (2021)
11. Patrick, S.W., et al.: Well-being of parents and children during the COVID-19 pandemic: a national survey. Pediatrics **146**(4) (2020)
12. Reich, J., Buttimer, C.J., Coleman, D., Colwell, R.D., Faruqi, F., Larke, LR.: What's lost, what's left, what's next: lessons learned from the lived experiences of teachers during the 2020 novel coronavirus pandemic. EdArXiv (2020)
13. Smith, C.J.: Getting the most out of remote research and testing. Interactions **24**(2), 82–84 (2017)

14. Doyle, W.: Ecological approaches to classroom management. In: Handbook of Classroom Management: Research, Practice, and Contemporary Issues, pp. 97–125 (2006)
15. Lucero, A.: Using affinity diagrams to evaluate interactive prototypes. In: Abascal, J., Barbosa, S., Fetter, M., Gross, T., Palanque, P., Winckler, M. (eds.) INTERACT 2015. LNCS, vol. 9297, pp. 231–248. Springer, Cham (2015). https://doi.org/10.1007/978-3-319-22668-2_19
16. Laursen, S., Liston, C., Thiry, H., Graf, J.: What good is a scientist in the classroom? Participant outcomes and program design features for a short-duration science outreach intervention in K–12 classrooms. CBE—Life Sci. Educ. **6**(1), 49–64 (2007)
17. Stelitano, L., Doan, S., Woo, A., Diliberti, M.K., Kaufman, J.H., Henry, D.: The digital divide and COVID-19: teachers' perceptions of inequalities in students' internet access and participation in remote learning. RAND Research Report (2020)
18. Panaoura, R.: Parental involvement in children's mathematics learning before and during the period of the COVID-19. Soc. Educ. Res. **2**, 65–74 (2021)
19. Gills, A., Krull, L.: COVID-19 remote learning transition in spring 2020: class structures, student perceptions, and inequality in college courses. Teach. Sociol. **48**(4), 283–299 (2020)
20. Farell, C.C., et al.: A descriptive study of the IES Researcher-Practitioner Partnerships in Education Research Program: Final report. National Center for Research in Policy and Practice (2018)

Using Prompts and Remediation to Improve Primary School Students Self-evaluation and Self-efficacy in a Literacy Web Application

Thomas Sergent[1,2](✉)[iD], François Bouchet[1][iD], Morgane Daniel[2], and Thibault Carron[1][iD]

[1] Sorbonne Université, CNRS, LIP6, 75005 Paris, France
{thomas.sergent,francois.bouchet,thibault.carron}@lip6.fr
[2] Lalilo, Paris, France
{thomas,morgane}@lalilo.com

Abstract. Self-regulation skills are critical for students of all ages in order to maximize their learning. A key aspect of self-regulation is being aware of one's performance and deficits in self-evaluation. Additionally, a clear consensus has not been reached regarding the age one can start learning these self-regulation processes. In order to investigate the possibility to raise awareness to some self-regulation deficits in 5 to 8 years old children, we have introduced two prompts triggered randomly after 1 out of 15 exercises into a literacy web-application for primary school students, to evaluate perceived difficulty [Too easy, Good, Too difficult] and desired difficulty [easier, same level, harder]. Comparing students' actual performance with their responses to self-regulatory prompts can provide information about their ability to self-regulate their learning, in particular in terms of self-evaluation and self-efficacy. We collected 2,600,142 responses from 467,116 students for our experiments. The goal of this paper is to assess the impact of two different remediation strategies to reduce the two types of deficits initially measured in students.

In a first study, we measured the impact of a gauge (resp. an audio recording) showing (resp. telling) the number of correct and incorrect answers to help students evaluate their actual performance during answers to the self-regulation prompts. In a second study, we measured the impact of giving self-evaluation and self-efficacy remediation to students who showed a deficit in self-regulated learning abilities from their answers to the self-regulation prompts.

The results show (a) a significant reduction of self-evaluation deficits when answers were supported by a visual gauge, (b) no significant impact on self-evaluation deficits when answers were supported by an audio recording, (c) a significant reduction of future self-evaluation deficits when giving students audio feedback advising them not to repeat a detected deficit.

This underlines the possibility of scaffolding self-regulated learning skills in a web based application from a young age while learning another skill.

Keywords: Self-regulated learning · Primary school · Web based application · Scaffolding · Remediation · Self-evaluation · Self-efficacy

1 Introduction

Children's self-regulated learning (SRL) skills are a key component of their academic performance, as self-regulated students generally know better "how to learn", which can have a positive impact in all disciplines [15]. The earlier children begin to develop these skills, the greater the impact on their overall schooling, and self-regulation training programs for elementary school students have already been developed for this purpose [4]. Nevertheless, it can be difficult for teachers to provide individualized help to each student, both in terms of the task at hand (e.g., learning to read) and in terms of their self-regulation skills.

The SRL scaffolding using computer tools has also been studied: a meta-analysis of SRL support implemented up to 2016 shows their significant positive effect on progression [14]. However, these tools have several limits: firstly, they only targeted older students (beyond 5th grade), secondly they focused on the performance phase (one of the three phases of the SRL cycle described, along with the anticipation and self-reflection phases [15]), and thirdly they measured whether the student's progression was improved by the SRL support, rather than whether the student was improving their SRL skills. Thus, SRL is mostly seen as supporting learning, not as a skill to be evaluated and trained in itself.

Previous work has shown that among young students, self-evaluation and self-efficacy deficits are two prevalent issues [12]. In this paper, our goal to investigate how to train self-evaluation and self-efficacy through scaffolding (helping the student to assess their level) and feedback (suggesting what to do in the future), and to measure the impact of these two strategies from a data analysis point of view. More particularly, we investigate the following research questions:

(RQ1) Can scaffolding help students in correcting their self-evaluation deficits?
(RQ2) Can a remediation feedback help students in answering to future self-evaluation and self-regulation prompts?

The remainder of this paper is organized as follows: in Sect. 2 we will present briefly some related work on self-regulation support in particular for younger children. In Sect. 3 we will introduce the experimental context, the designed prompts and the data collected. We will then describe the two experiments led to answer to RQ1 and RQ2 respectively in Sects. 4 and 5, before concluding with a discussion.

2 Related Work

SRL is a three-phase cycle that repeats itself with each new task the learner is confronted with [15]. First the learner prepares for the task (anticipation phase), then they perform the task and can monitor their progress (performance phase). Finally, they assess the effectiveness of their learning to draw conclusions for future learning (self-reflection phase).

As previously mentioned, some SRL training programs have been shown to have a significant positive effect in primary school children [4] but outside of a computer-based context. Some works have already tried to assess the effect of self-regulatory prompts to show their positive effects on self-efficacy [10]. For instance, Müller [7] showed that prompting university students had an immediate impact which did not transfer over time. Hoffman [5] also showed a positive impact of prompting for self-efficacy but before accomplishing the task and measured the impact on performance more than in self-efficacy itself. More generally, a meta-review [9] has shown that self-assessment has a positive impact on learners self-efficacy.

It is worth noting that although young children's abilities to use SRL strategies may be more limited than in teenagers, they seem to have comparable monitoring skills [11]. Indeed, recent work on a dashboard supporting SRL in a mathematics software program for 9–10 years old (only slightly older than our targeted students) showed a significant improvement in SRL skills for students in the dashboard group compared to those without the dashboard [6]. Finally, young students not detected as having a self-evaluation deficit seemed to rely mainly on their success rate when asked to self-evaluate [13].

3 Experimental Context and Data Collection

3.1 A Literacy Software

Lalilo is one of the many web applications used by teachers in the classroom to help them implement differentiated instruction strategies. At the beginning of 2021, it is used by 40,000 English and French speaking kindergarten and primary classes every week to strengthen literacy through series of exercises adapted to the students' level. It also provides the teacher with a dashboard to evaluate the students' activities and progress. It is therefore a relevant testing ground for attempting to correct students' SRL deficits and measuring the impact of different strategies. A typical session lasts 20 min (on average) with the student performing around 15 short exercises with 3 to 7 questions each, chosen by an adaptive learning algorithm, as pictured by Fig. 1. Student activities (e.g. logging in, time spent on a question/exercise, mistakes) are traced and we focus here only on students' answers to an exercise, thus calling **trace** only the answers to a set of questions of the same type.

3.2 Self-evaluation and Self-efficacy Prompts

To assess some aspects of students' SRL skills, we introduced two self-regulatory prompts [1] which are randomly shown successively once every fifteen exercises when a student finishes an exercise (i.e. a student answers them on average once per typical learning session). First, the **perceived difficulty** prompt asks the

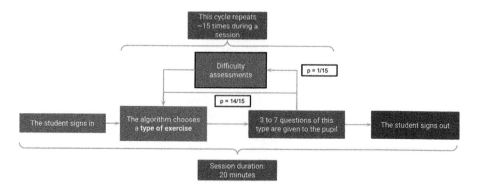

Fig. 1. Chronology of a typical student session

student *"How difficult was this exercise for you?"* with 3 possible answers: "Too hard", "Just-right", "Too easy"). Then, if we don't detect any self-evaluation deficit (which are described in the next subsection), the student is asked to reply to the **desired difficulty** prompt *"I would like exercises that are..."* with 3 possible answers: "easier", "the same level", "harder". The perceived difficulty prompt aims at measuring the **self-evaluation** ability of the students, i.e. their ability to correctly estimate the difficulty of the questions they just answered. The desired difficulty prompt aims at measuring their **self-efficacy**, i.e. how they would react to their representation of the difficulty. The visuals for these two prompts are displayed in Fig. 2. Before introducing the assessments, we checked qualitatively in a classroom using Lalilo that prompts were understood by 1st grade students (details not presented here).

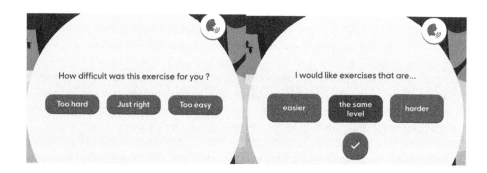

Fig. 2. Perceived (left) and desired (right) difficulty prompts

3.3 Data Collection

We collected traces from Kindergarten, 1st grade and 2nd grade classes based in France, Canada and USA learning in French (FR) or English (EN) between January 18 and April 8, 2021 on the Lalilo platform. We kept only the traces for which students had answered to self-regulation prompts (i.e. on average $1/15^{\text{th}}$ of all traces) and hereafter we call trace the answers to the exercise with the associated answers to SRL prompts.

3.4 Data Preprocessing

Deficit Tagging. As a trace registers answers to each exercise question as well as to the two SRL prompts, one can compute the success rate of a trace defined as the number of correct answers over the total number of questions of the trace. From the success rate, we can determine a **performance tag** of a trace with one of those three values: excellent (all answers are correct), poor (34% or less of the answers are correct), and medium (for the remaining cases). We have chosen a threshold of 34% for "poor" performance so that traces that have only one correct answer out of 3 are considered poor. Indeed, the expected probability of succeeding questions is always at least at 1/3 which means students having a success rate of 1/3 or less do not perform better than chance. It is also worth noting that the "excellent" tag is quite conservative, as one could argue that a student who answered correctly to 6 out of 7 questions could be considered as having a very good performance as well.

From the performance, the perceived difficulty and the desired difficulty, we generate the so-called **trace deficit tag** displayed in Table 1. The "Desired difficulty" column is empty for the first four listed trace deficits: these deficits are self-evaluation deficits and in these cases students were not asked the desired difficulty prompt. Indeed, we considered that if the student did not have a proper representation of the difficulty of the exercise, it was not relevant to ask them the desired difficulty prompt.

Table 1. Trace deficit tag determination

Actual performance	Perceived difficulty	Desired difficulty	Deficit
Excellent	Too hard		Underevaluation
Excellent	Just-right		Slight underevaluation
Poor	Too easy		Overevaluation
Poor	Just-right		Slight overeval
Excellent	Too easy	Easier/same	Avoiding difficulty
Poor	Too hard	Harder/same	Seeking difficulty

4 Impact of a Gauge or an Audio Recording During Answers to Self-evaluation and Self-efficacy Assessments

4.1 Method

To answer to our first research question on how scaffolding can help with self-evaluation deficits, we focused only on the deficits involving self-evaluation only, i.e. only the four first deficits in Table 1. In order to measure the impact of visual cues on the answers to the perceived difficulty prompt (=self-evaluation prompt), students were randomly given one of two visuals for the prompts: one similar to the initial prompts (Fig. 2) and one with an additional gauge displaying the number of correct and incorrect answers in the past exercise (Fig. 3). Additionally, in order to measure the impact of auditory cues, students were randomly given an audio recording stating their number of correct answers and total number of answers in their last exercise: e.g. "In the last exercise, you found three correct answers out of four questions". This sentence is read instead of shown to not bias answers simply because younger students may not be able to read it well. For the same reason, every text displayed on the screenshots is also read aloud to the student, and they can replay the instruction using the top right-hand button. The choice of alternative modalities is therefore only because of the particular audience (young students who are not necessarily fully literate yet), and not because of an hypothesis on learning styles which have been proven to be a neuromyth [8].

Overall, when a student got a self-evaluation prompt, they were assigned randomly in one of four options: (a) no gauge and no audio recording (control condition); (b) gauge and no audio recording; (c) no gauge but audio recording; (d) gauge and audio recording. Our hypothesis was that visual or audio cues could support self-evaluation for students.

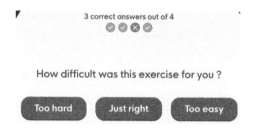

Fig. 3. The gauge shown for scaffolding, visible above both SRL prompts

4.2 Results

In this experiment, we only kept the first answer of students to the self-evaluation prompt so that our data would not be interfered by students answering repeatedly to the self-evaluation prompt and sometimes having visual or audio support or not. This also allows us to isolate the effect of the gauge and audio recording alone. We then selected traces with excellent performance (100% success rate as described above) and computed the answer deficit distribution using Table 1 depending on the presence of the gauge and audio recording. The results are summarized in Fig. 4. We can observe that there is a significant difference in the answer deficit distribution if there is a gauge or not: students with excellent performance having a gauge as a visual support are less likely to show an underevaluation ($d = 0.05$, $p < 0.001$, two tailed hypothesis). There is also a significant difference between the answers with an audio recording support or not: however the effect is that students with excellent performance having an audio recording are *more* likely to show an underevaluation.

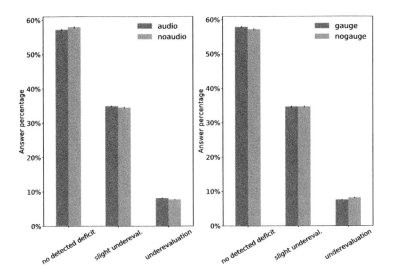

Fig. 4. Self-evaluation deficit distribution depending on gauge and audio recording presence for excellent performance answers with confidence interval at 95%. N("audio") = 136,210, N("no audio") = 137,156; N("gauge") = 136,716, N("no gauge") = 136,650. No "avoiding difficulty" as it is not a self-evaluation deficit.

Similarly, we selected traces with poor performance (less than 34% success rate as described above) and computed the answer deficit distribution using Table 1 depending on the presence of the gauge and audio recording. The results are summarized in Fig. 5. We can observe that there are significant differences in the answer deficit distribution both when there is a gauge ($d = 0.06$, $p < 0.001$, two tailed hypothesis) and auditory support ($d = 0.04$, $p < 0.001$, two tailed hypothesis), and both impact lead to less over-evaluation by students.

We can note that the baseline percentage of deficits is a lot higher for poor performance than excellent performance traces (51% against 34%). This is consistent with the fact that students who got an excellent performance are more likely to correctly self-evaluate. Moreover, the effect size - which measures the impact of the intervention - is larger for traces with poor performance than for traces with excellent performance, which indicates that students who had a poor performance seem to benefit more from visual or auditory support than those who had an excellent performance. As the impact of the gauge is positive and significant for both excellent and poor performance traces, we measured the impact of having the audio or not when there was a gauge to support a student's self-evaluation. The results are summarized in Fig. 6. They indicate that having

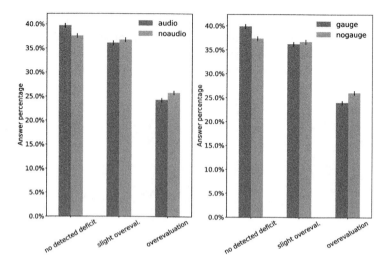

Fig. 5. Self-evaluation deficit distribution depending on gauge and audio recording presence for poor performance answers with confidence interval at 95%. N("audio") = 35,700, N("no audio") = 36,394; N("gauge") = 36,048; N("no gauge") = 36,046. No "seeking difficulty" as it is not a self-evaluation deficit.

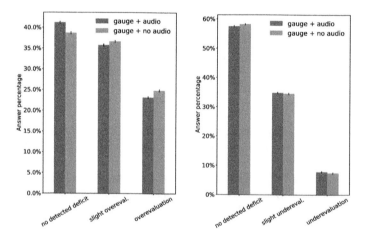

Fig. 6. Self-evaluation deficit distribution depending on audio recording when there is a gauge for poor (left) and excellent (right) performance answers with confidence interval at 95%. For the poor performance answers, N(gauge + audio) = 17,698, N(gauge + no audio) = 18,350. For the excellent performance answers, N(gauge + audio) = 68,068, N(gauge + no audio) = 68,648.

an audio recording stating the number of correct answers over the total number of questions (e.g. "In the last exercise, you found three correct answers out of four questions") had a significant impact on decreasing the number of student overevaluating when the students performance was poor on the last exercise

($d = 0.05$, $p < 0.001$). There was a significant impact on *increasing* the number of student underevaluating when their performance was excellent ($d = 0.03$, $p < 0.01$).

Overall we can therefore answer positively to RQ1 as the provided scaffoldings seem to have helped students in reducing their self-evaluation deficits.

5 Impact of Audio Remediation Feedback on Self-evaluation and Self-efficacy Deficits

5.1 Methods

To answer to our second research question, we designed four possible remediation feedback recording (cf. Table 2) to be played after the student displayed one of the four deficit tags from Table 1. Students who displayed a slight overevaluation or slight underevaluation did not receive any remediation feedback. We did the randomization so that half of the students would always get a remediation when they showed a self-evaluation or a self-efficacy deficit (remediation group) and half of the students would never get it (control group).

Table 2. Audio remediation recordings. See Table 1 to get the corresponding answers to the perceived and desired difficulty prompts.

Deficit tag	Audio recording
Underevaluation	You said it was too hard, but you did great! It seems like this exercise was actually pretty easy for you!
Overevaluation	You said it was too easy, but you made some mistakes. That's okay! Maybe this exercise was a bit too hard for you right now
Avoiding difficulty	You said it was too easy and that you wanted easier exercises. You can challenge yourself next time and ask for harder exercises. You're doing great!
Seeking difficulty	You said it was too hard, and you're right, this was a tricky exercise. That's okay. You can keep trying. Instead of doing something harder, you can ask for an easier exercise to help you practice

5.2 Results

Impact of Underevaluation Remediation. In order to measure the impact of the underevaluation remediation, we selected the traces with excellent performance for students in both the control group and the remediation group. In these traces, we selected students whose first trace with an excellent performance showed an underevaluation (see Table 1 for the definition of deficits). We then computed the answer deficit distribution on their next trace with an excellent performance where they got a self-evaluation assessment. The results for both groups are shown in Fig. 7 (left). We remind that all students had shown an underevaluation deficit on their first answer to the self-evaluation assessment. We notice that the number of students showing *again* an underevaluation is significantly smaller for students in the remediation group than for students in the control group ($d = 0.17$, $p < 0.001$, two-tailed hypothesis). Conversely, there are significantly more students for whom we detect no deficit. There are also significantly more students for whom we detected a slight underevaluation, which corresponds to students for whom the deficit was partially addressed only (indeed, students with slight underevaluation did not receive any feedback, so there is no reason to expect a change otherwise).

Impact of Overevaluation Remediation. We did the same analysis to measure the impact of the overevaluation remediation. In these traces, we selected students in both groups whose first trace with a poor performance showed an overevaluation. We then computed the answer deficit distribution on their next trace with a poor performance where they got a self-evaluation assessment. The results for both groups are shown in Fig. 7 (right). We remind that all students had shown an overevaluation deficit on their first answer to the self-evaluation assessment. We notice that the number of students showing *again* an overevaluation is significantly smaller for students in the remediation group than for students in the control group ($d = 0.18$, $p < 0.001$, two-tailed hypothesis). Conversely, there are significantly more students for whom we detect no deficit. Also there are significantly more students for whom we detect a "slight overevaluation" which means they had a poor performance but declared the difficulty of the exercise they got was "Just right". We can interpret these students as students that may feel close to succeeding at this exercise, even though their current performance is not good yet. For example, a student that had 3 questions in the last exercise and got two wrong answers and then a good answer may feel the difficulty is "Just right" as their last answer was correct, though their performance is considered "poor".

Impact of Avoiding Difficulty Remediation. We conducted a similar analysis to measure the impact of the avoiding difficulty remediation. We selected in both groups the traces with an excellent performance and in these traces, we selected students whose first trace with an excellent performance showed they wanted to avoid difficulty. We then computed the answer deficit distribution on their next trace with an excellent performance where they got the SRL assessments. The results are shown in Fig. 8 (left). We can notice that the number of students detected as wanting to avoid difficulty (see Table 1 for the definition) decreases drastically the next time students are asked the SRL assessments in the remediation group, when compared to students in the control group ($d = 0.30$, $p < 0.001$, two-tailed hypothesis). However, we also detect an increase in the number of students showing some underevaluation which will be addressed in the discussion section.

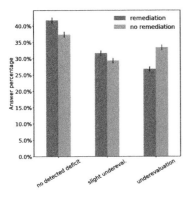 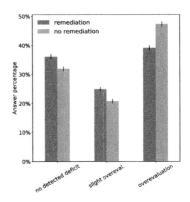

Fig. 7. Left: self-evaluation answer distribution of the 2nd trace with excellent performance of a student when the 1st one was a *underevaluation* depending on remediation. N(remediation) = 11,397, N(no remediation) = 11,196 **Right:** self-evaluation answer distribution of the 2nd trace with poor performance of a student when the 1st one was an *overevaluation*, depending on remediation. N(remediation) = 11,513, N(no remediation) = 11,476.

Impact of Seeking Difficulty Remediation. Finally, we conducted a similar analysis to measure the impact of the seeking difficulty remediation. We selected in both groups the traces with a poor performance and in these traces, we selected students whose first trace with a poor performance showed they wanted to seek difficulty (see Table 1). We then computed the answer deficit distribution on their next trace with a poor performance where they got the SRL assessments. The results are shown in Fig. 8 (right). We can observe that there is no significant difference between the answer distribution of the remediation group and the answer distribution of the control group ($p > 0.05$, two-tailed hypothesis), therefore we cannot conclude that the seeking difficulty remediation that we designed had any effect.

Overall, thanks to remediation there is a significant reduction in the number of students showing overevaluation or underevaluation. As we only do the analysis on the second trace with excellent (resp. poor) performance of a student and students were randomized into the two possible conditions, we can infer a causal relationship between the presence or not of the remediation and the difference in the answer distribution to the self-evaluation prompt. Moreover, as the self regulation prompts are only given with a probability $\frac{1}{15}$ after finishing an exercise, the impact of one remediation is seen not immediately after it was given but later, suggesting lasting effects of remediation. We can therefore answer partially positively to RQ2.

6 Discussion and Limits

In the first experiment, we noticed that the audio recording seemed to have a positive impact on students who had a poor performance and a negative impact

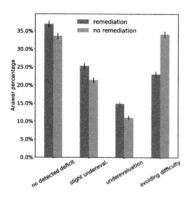 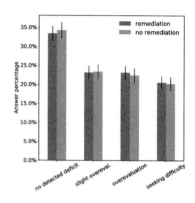

Fig. 8. Left: self-evaluation answer distribution of the 2nd trace with excellent performance of a student when the 1st one was "avoiding difficulty", depending on remediation. N(remediation) = 10,913, N(no remediation) = 10,908 **Right:** self-evaluation answer distribution of the 2nd trace with poor performance of a student when the 1st one was "seeking difficulty", depending on remediation. N(remediation) = 2,145, N(no remediation) = 1,939

on students who had an excellent performance. This indicates that the audio recording could allow a potentially distracted student to focus again after a poor performance. Conversely, it could distract a student who was focused after an excellent performance.

The most reliable way to assess SRL deficits is through direct questions to the students [2] and currently the frequency of the SRL statements is one out of fifteen. On the one hand, increasing the frequency of SRL remediation could improve SRL skills, however constant prompting can lead to an overall degraded perception of the learning environment [3]. Moreover SRL skills training should not come at the expense of literacy training which remains the main goal of the software. On the other hand, once we are able to detect that a student has good self-evaluation and self-efficacy skills, we could consider reducing the prompts, precisely so as not to waste time unnecessarily, paving the way for adaptive prompting.

The results of our second experiment showed that self-efficacy deficits (avoiding difficulty and seeking difficulty) are not ideally tackled with the audio remediation we designed. For the avoiding difficulty remediation, the number of students showing an underevaluation is higher in the remediation group than in the control group. Therefore, there should be a trade-off in the implementation of this remediation so that it does not impact students' self-evaluation negatively. In other words, it appears that some students who were self-evaluating well but avoiding difficulty seem to resolve this contradiction not by asking harder exercise, but by declaring they did not feel like they were doing so well after all. This behavior could indicate either that they were not so sure in their self-evaluation in the first place, and that challenging their assessment made them hesitate, or that they are somehow "gaming the system" by thinking that answering differently to the first question would prevent the system from raising the difficulty too much, which would be confirming the diagnosis of their difficulty avoidance behavior.

For the "seeking difficulty" deficit, we didn't detect any significant effect. We can notice however that the sample size is smaller here than in previous analysis, so it possible that with a similar number of samples, an effect would appear. Nonetheless there can also be explanations why this behavior is not as easy to impact as the other one, as "seeking difficulty" is a behavior consistent with a form of overconfidence, and discarding a system feedback is also consistent with overconfidence. For these students, a teacher intervention might be more appropriate. Alternative strategies could involve letting the student feel that they are incorrect by actually giving them a much harder exercise, or also asking them before an exercise how well they think they will succeed to confront their actual performance with their own self-evaluation a priori (and not only a posteriori).

Finally, we focused only on the first and second answers to students to the SRL prompts which are very local metrics. This allows us to measure precisely the impact of features on students' answers. However, we did not describe the global SRL state of each student and its evolution over time after the first two SRL answers.

7 Conclusion and Future Works

In this work, we studied the answers to ponctual self-evaluation and self-efficacy prompts of primary school (K-2) aged students on a literacy platform. We determined, using local metrics, the impact of visual and audio cues while answering self-evaluation prompts. The impact of visual cues (a gauge) is always significantly positive by decreasing the number of self-evaluation deficits. The impact of audio cues is mixed: it helps decrease the number of overevaluations but increases the number of underevaluations. Therefore it should be triggered only for poor performance students.

We also determined the effect of a remediation that was triggered when self-evaluation and self-efficacy deficits were detected. We manage to reduce significantly these deficits for some students with our actions locally (for self-evaluation more than for self-efficacy). Future works include the study of how remediation lasts in time or if it has to be reinforced regularly. We limited our scope to self-evaluation and self-efficacy in the SRL skills because we considered that these skills were measurable and could possibly be improved for students from Kindergarten to grade 2. Future works thus include the study of other SRL skills in primary school aged students.

This work underlines the possibility of scaffolding self-regulated learning skills in a web based application from a young age while learning another skill.

References

1. Bannert, M., Reimann, P.: Supporting self-regulated hypermedia learning through prompts. Instr. Sci. **40**(1), 193–211 (2012). https://doi.org/10.1007/s11251-011-9167-4
2. Barnard, L., Lan, W.Y., To, Y.M., Paton, V.O., Lai, S.L.: Measuring self-regulation in online and blended learning environments. Internet High. Educ. **12**(1), 1–6 (2009). https://doi.org/10.1016/j.iheduc.2008.10.005
3. Bouchet, F., Harley, J.M., Azevedo, R.: Evaluating adaptive pedagogical agents' prompting strategies effect on students' emotions. In: Nkambou, R., Azevedo, R., Vassileva, J. (eds.) ITS 2018. LNCS, vol. 10858, pp. 33–43. Springer, Cham (2018). https://doi.org/10.1007/978-3-319-91464-0_4
4. Dignath, C., Buettner, G., Langfeldt, H.P.: How can primary school students learn self-regulated learning strategies most effectively? Educ. Res. Rev. **3**(2), 101–129 (2008). https://doi.org/10.1016/j.edurev.2008.02.003
5. Hoffman, B., Spatariu, A.: The influence of self-efficacy and metacognitive prompting on math problem-solving efficiency. Contemp. Educ. Psychol. **33**(4), 875–893 (2008). https://doi.org/10.1016/j.cedpsych.2007.07.002
6. Molenaar, I., Horvers, A., Dijkstra, R., Baker, R.S.: Personalized visualizations to promote young learners' SRL: the learning path app. In: Proceedings of the Tenth International Conference on Learning Analytics & Knowledge, pp. 330–339 (2020)
7. Müller, N.M., Seufert, T.: Effects of self-regulation prompts in hypermedia learning on learning performance and self-efficacy. Learn. Instr. **58**, 1–11 (2018). https://doi.org/10.1016/j.learninstruc.2018.04.011
8. Newton, P.M.: The learning styles myth is thriving in higher education. Front. Psychol. **6** (2015). https://doi.org/10.3389/fpsyg.2015.01908
9. Panadero, E., Jonsson, A., Botella, J.: Effects of self-assessment on self-regulated learning and self-efficacy: Four meta-analyses. Educ. Res. Rev. **22**, 74–98 (2017). https://doi.org/10.1016/j.edurev.2017.08.004
10. Schmitz, B., Wiese, B.S.: New perspectives for the evaluation of training sessions in self-regulated learning: time-series analyses of diary data. Contemp. Educ. Psychol. **31**(1), 64–96 (2006). https://doi.org/10.1016/j.cedpsych.2005.02.002
11. Schneider, W.: The development of metacognitive knowledge in children and adolescents: major trends and implications for education. Mind Brain Educ. **2**(3), 114–121 (2008). https://doi.org/10.1111/j.1751-228X.2008.00041.x
12. Sergent, T., Daniel, M., Bouchet, F., Carron, T.: Assessing children's self-regulation deficits and their teachers' perception: towards a co-designed remediation through a literacy web application. In: Proceedings of ICALT 2021 (2021)
13. Sergent, T., Daniel, M., Bouchet, F., Carron, T.: Predicting young students' self-evaluation deficits through their activity traces. In: International Conference on Educational Data Mining (EDM 21) (2021)
14. Zheng, L.: The effectiveness of self-regulated learning scaffolds on academic performance in computer-based learning environments: a meta-analysis. Asia Pac. Educ. Rev. **17**(2), 187–202 (2016). https://doi.org/10.1007/s12564-016-9426-9
15. Zimmerman, B.J.: Investigating self-regulation and motivation: historical background, methodological developments, and future prospects. Am. Educ. Res. J. **45**(1), 166–183 (2008). https://doi.org/10.3102/0002831207312909

Harnessing Student Creativity to Design Fake News Literacy Training: An Overview of Twelve Graduate Student Projects

Christian Scheibenzuber[1(✉)], Marvin Fendt[1], and Nicolae Nistor[1,2]

[1] Faculty of Psychology and Educational Sciences, Ludwig-Maximilians-Universität, Leopoldstr. 13, 80802 München, Germany
`c.scheibenzuber@psy.lmu.de, ma.fendt@campus.lmu.de,
nic.nistor@uni-muenchen.de`
[2] Richard W. Riley College of Education and Leadership, Walden University, 100 Washington Avenue South, Suite 900, Minneapolis, MN 55401, USA

Abstract. Fake news is an increasing problem for many areas of the social life, prominently for politics and democracy. Falling for fake news is largely due to deficient cognitive processing of online news, which we address as fake news illiteracy. One of the many ways of combating fake news consists of training media literacy with a focus on online news. Currently, there are few examples of fake news literacy training approaches. Against the background of a brief research overview on the cognitive processing of online news, we aim to generate and propose ideas for approaches to online fake news literacy training. To achieve this, we exploit the expertise and creativity of graduate students of educational sciences who were asked to design and carry out such pilot programs. This study provides an analysis and overview of 12 successfully conducted training programs, focusing on the cognitive processing aspects they address, intervention types, instructional designs, and the use of technologies. We conclude by pointing out productive directions of this development and suggesting corresponding educational technology development.

Keywords: Fake news literacy · Online training · Instructional design · Educational technology

1 Introduction

Fake news poses an increasing problem as social life can be compromised by a misinformed public [1]. People's susceptibility towards fake news is regarded as a synthesis of various deficits in the cognitive processing of fake news—the so-called fake news illiteracy [2]. So far, educational interventions against fake news illiteracy remain limited, hence the necessity to develop further interventions and specific training approaches. Online environments are essential for fake news literacy training, because this is where most fake news is found and many fake news consumers can be reached. To approach fake news literacy training, we aimed at harnessing student expertise and creativity generating ideas for pilot training programs in the context of the Covid-19 lockdown and consequential online learning.

The remainder of this paper gives an overview over current psychological and educational fake news research with a focus on the cognitive processing of fake news and current intervention approaches. Identifying a research gap, we address it with our research questions, describe the employed methodology, present and discuss the findings. We draw conclusions on development directions for fake news literacy training and suggest subsequent development of educational technology.

2 Theoretical Background

Fake news is defined as verifiably false statements that are intentionally misleading [1] and politically polarizing [3]. Furthermore, it "mimic[s] news media content in form but not in organizational process or intent" [4]. Whereas media literacy [5] should provide a safety net against fake news, we believe that news consumers need a more specialized fake news literacy to overcome their own oftentimes flawed cognitive processes when dealing with online media content.

The **cognitive processing** of (fake) news can be broken down into four different levels: reception, information acceptance, cognitive integration and sharing [2]. At *reception level*, fake news needs access to recipients' cognition, therefore to captivate news consumers' attention. This may happen out of interest towards a certain topic, and can also be enhanced by negativity bias that makes humans focus more on negative information, which a vast amount of fake news is comprised of. This can be further exploited by emotional framing, i.e. the intentional activation of certain, usually negative, emotions (e.g., fear) through specific language [6].

At *acceptance level* truth evaluation becomes the main focus. New information can be evaluated in various ways: not at all [7], intuitively through "gut instinct" [8], or analytically by applying truth evaluation techniques such as fact checking. Intuitive truth evaluation is prone to bias in several ways. The illusory truth effect [9] makes repeated claims more likely to be believed than completely new ones. Relatedly, the mere exposure effect [10] implies a positive evaluation of information that has already been encountered before. Analytic truth evaluation can be subjected to confirmation bias [11]. In line with Festingers' [12] cognitive dissonance theory, humans tend to actively search and accept information that is consonant with their pre-existing beliefs, and dismiss dissonant information. In addition, emotional content such as fake news is remembered better and therefore reinforces confirmation bias [13]. Technologically, filter bubbles reinforce both confirmation bias and naïve realism. They emerge from algorithms recommending new content based on internet users' history, i.e., in line with their pre-existing interests, knowledge and current beliefs [14].

Once accepted, fake news is *cognitively integrated* resulting in hard to correct misconceptions [15]. Should news recipients, still influenced by the confirmation bias, aim to uphold their misconceptions, they may end up in a state known as naïve realism [16], where humans believe their view of the world to be objectively true, with opposing opinions being assessed as irrational, ill-informed, or—ironically—biased [17].

Finally, at *sharing level*, filter bubbles and their social equivalents, the echo chambers, promote an environment where alternative facts and fake news stories are shared among like-minded individuals [18] and perpetuate a naïve worldview highly resistant towards counteracting interventions.

Interventions aimed at combating fake news follow two main directions: the preemptive inoculation approach and the more reactive fact-checking methods. According to the *inoculation* theory [19], people can be inoculated against the effects of certain messages by being exposed to a weaker version. Inoculation may be promising at the reception, acceptance, and integration levels by making news consumers aware of commonly used fake news design elements, its framing, and its effects [20]. *Fact-checking*, which falls under the relatively broad umbrella of information literacy, mainly addresses the acceptance level where analytic truth evaluation can increase the likelihood of recognizing fake news as such [21]. A more elaborated form of fact-checking, lateral reading, was proven to enhance students' ability to choose reliable news sites when looking for new information [22]. This may also come in handy at the sharing level, where such techniques can stop the spread of fake news.

Specific **instructional design** can sustain fake news literacy interventions that involve news consumers in complex learning activities with higher cognitive requirements. In first line, *learning motivation* needs to be stimulated. This requirement is met in problem-based learning [23], either in its basic form, or in more elaborated versions such as experiential learning [24], goal-based scenarios [25], game-based learning [26], or cognitive apprenticeship [27]. The development of *complex cognitive skills* is prominently fostered by instructional designs such as cognitive apprenticeship [27] or 4C/ID [28]. Finally, the transfer of knowledge and skills to real world situations is promoted by authenticity [29] as provided in constructivist problem-based learning environments [23].

The Role of Educational Technology. In the last three decades, an important line of educational research was dedicated to the implementation of instructional designs as those mentioned above based on information and communication technology. This forwarded the development of educational technology from lab prototypes to standard tools included in content management systems. For instance, moodle integrates an increasing number of ubiquitous educational tools. Some technologies are, however, closer to fake news and still hard to find in technology-enhanced learning contexts. Automatically assessing and attaching warning labels to dubious news articles [30] are first steps towards automatic fact-checking [31]. As fake news predominantly spreads through social media and social bots [32] or user profiling [33], such technologies could also be borrowed and further developed for fake news literacy training.

Generating Technology-Based Fake News Literacy Training Approaches. While generic approaches for fake news literacy interventions might appear obvious, concrete educational applications remain scarce [2]. As one of the many methods to generate ideas and develop concrete intervention approaches, we analyze in this study pilot online training sessions developed by graduate students. Methodologically, this was inspired by projects harnessing student creativity [34] and by the expert interviews method [35]. We believe that graduate students are familiar with the online medium and its specific technologies and tools, and familiar with a first target group, undergraduate students, that is widely involved in educational studies. Furthermore, we perceive our graduate students as holding in-depth knowledge of educational sciences and related domains, engaged with current political themes, and highly creative. Therefore, we chose them as actors for generating ideas of fake news literacy training. This has been already done in diverse contexts. As Bairaktarova [36] observes, "attempts to harness the power of creativity in the engineering classroom are more widespread than formal literature indicates. Creative faculty find ways to let our students take risks, collaborate, and create."

3 Research Questions

As explained above, the purpose of this study was to investigate how graduate students of educational sciences conceive, design, and carry out online fake news illiteracy training programs. This resulted into four specific research questions, as follows:

RQ1: Which fake news illiteracy aspects do the graduate students find appropriate as a starting point for literacy training?
RQ2: Which interventions do they find appropriate?
RQ3: Which instructional designs do they find appropriate?
RQ4: Which technologies do they find appropriate?

4 Methodology

Research Design. We conducted an explorative study utilizing basic qualitative methodology inspired by techniques such as expert interviews [37], Delphi interviews [38], paired with content analysis of text-based products in the form of the course papers.

Setting. This study was conducted as part of the "Training Methods" course for graduate students of the educational sciences. The course was offered during the winter term 2020/2021 and aimed at giving students an insight into training conception, design, and implementation with the topic being the ever-relevant fake news problem.

Participants. A total of $N = 55$ graduate students (51 female, 4 male, aged 24 on average) took part in the course in the first semester of their masters' program. The participants built 12 small groups each with their own training project.

Treatment. The graduate students were tasked with developing and conducting a pilot fake news literacy training program. Their trainees were first-year undergraduate students of educational sciences. There were 5–10 freshmen in each pilot training. Due to the Covid-19 pandemic and social distancing measures, both the Training Methods course and all pilot training had to be conducted entirely online. At term end, the graduate students were asked to synthesize their work in a course paper.

Instrumentation. We applied content analysis to students' course papers and coded the collected material based on the RQs (see Table 1): fake news illiteracy aspects addressed in the training (e.g., confirmation bias), type of intervention (inoculation or fact checking), instructional design (e.g., cognitive apprenticeship), technology support (moodle, zoom, and specialized tools).

Procedure. The course opened in week 1 with a short introduction to the fake news topic, an overview of the course goals, and the small group building. During weeks 2–4, students searched for, and synthesized research literature on the three main topics: fake news cognitive processing, intervention approaches, and instructional design. In weeks 5–6 the graduate students developed their training concepts, and subsequently submitted them for feedback in week 7. The undergraduate students used week 8 and the winter break to revise their training concepts according to the instructor feedback. After the winter break, each group presented their revised training concepts in week 9 before implementing them in weeks 10–12, during which they worked with the freshmen. In weeks 13 and 14, each student group presented their training results and experiences, then submitted their course papers in week 15. The papers featured a conceptual framework, a description of the online training design, and a summary of the training results. Shortly after the course papers were submitted, the content analysis began with two instructors coding the text.

5 Findings

All 12 groups could design and develop fake news literacy training pilots as assigned. Moreover, the training sessions could be completely conducted as planned. In terms of fake news illiteracy aspects, the graduate students mostly chose to focus on filter bubbles (4 of 12 groups), confirmation bias (3 groups), combinations of these, and single, further effects. In terms of interventions results, 6 groups chose fact-checking, 5 groups inoculation, and one group combined the two approaches. The array of instructional designs was more diverse, however the majority (4 groups) chose to utilize cognitive apprenticeship [39] and 3 groups chose goal-based scenarios [25]. Regarding the technology support, students were somewhat constrained to the standard platforms provided by the university, i.e., moodle as content management system and zoom as video conference tool. While all groups used the generic moodle and zoom for their pilot training programs, 3 groups combined the moodle tools in a more advanced way: two groups developed an online computer game inspired by "Bad News" [20] and one group developed a role playing game. A more specific overview of the pilot training design in all groups is provided in Table 1.

To provide a more in-depth insight into graduate students' work, we describe in the following two of the pilot training approaches, one based on inoculation, and the other on fact checking. Each intervention was used by several student groups; from these, we chose two examples we deemed most representative.

Group 1 explained the fake news effects by *confirmation bias*. They chose *inoculation* as an intervention. Exposing their training participants to a weaker fake news version was achieved by asking them to play a game in which they had to create fake news posts. First, the trainers (graduate students) demonstrated the participants' (freshmen's) confirmation bias by presenting fake news and asking for the freshmen's opinions on the fake news themes. Then the trainers inoculated their participants with a game in which the participants had to create their own fake news post for a social media platform utilizing journalistic techniques such as polarizing or emotionalizing, which had to be learned first. As learning such journalistic techniques can be very demanding, both explicit information and instructional support had to be provided and the *cognitive apprenticeship* design [39] was applied. The training was hosted in one synchronous session via the video conference software zoom. First, they were shown how to create fake news (modeling) always being encouraged to discuss every step (articulation). After that, the participants had to create their own fake news post for a social media platform utilizing fake news techniques such as polarizing or emotionalizing language to learn these mechanisms while receiving support by the trainers (coaching and scaffolding). After presentation and feedback on their results they created fake news posts again, receiving less support by the trainers (fading). This training made use of several technologies as moodle and zoom were a key part of the intervention as well as the game that was created by the trainers.

Group 5 explained the impact of fake news as *illusory truth* effect. To cope with this effect, the source was checked without reading it thoroughly, but using lateral reading. As this approach relies heavily on third-party sources about the news website, it is not always applicable on lesser-known sources. Therefore, it sometimes had to be combined with fact-checking the text. The resulting goal of this training was to enable the participants to correctly apply fact-checking as well as lateral reading. Group 5 applied the *4C/ID* design, because the tasks required for fact-checking and lateral reading consist of both routine and non-routine aspects. First, the tasks were demonstrated by one of the trainers. Then, supporting information was provided to deal with the non-routine aspects. After that, procedural information consisting of a checklist was given to solve the routine tasks during fact-checking. Following the input phases, the training participants practiced identifying fake news by following the beforementioned strategies. This training was provided in a live and in an asynchronous version. Technology usage included the software platforms Zoom and Moodle to create a training that fit the participants' needs.

6 Discussion

This study aimed at harnessing graduate students' expertise and creativity to generate approaches for fake news literacy training. In a graduate course of educational sciences, the students designed and developed 12 pilot training programs, all of which could be entirely caried out with freshmen as trainees. The training design was based on diverse cognitive theories explaining the effects of fake news, mainly filter bubbles [14] and confirmation bias [13]. The intervention approaches were quasi equally divided between inoculation [19, 20] and fact checking [21, 22]. Inoculation was mainly positioned at information acceptance level, mainly addressing confirmation bias and related phenomena such as filter bubbles. Fact checking was often positioned at cognitive integration level, addressing naïve realism and illusory truth. While several combinations of these were possible and occurred in some of the 12 projects, not all combinations were conceptually possible, for instance fact checking was not considered to be compatible with

Table 1. Overview of student projects

Group	Fake news cognitive processing approach	Intervention approach	Instructional design	Supporting technology
1	Confirmation bias	Inoculation	Cognitive apprenticeship	Moodle & Zoom, computer game
2	Naive realism	Fact checking	Goal-based scenarios	Moodle & Zoom, role play
3	Mere exposure	Fact checking	Goal-based scenarios	Moodle & Zoom
4	Confirmation bias	Inoculation	Goal-based scenarios	Moodle & Zoom
5	Illusory truth	Fact checking (lateral reading)	4C/ID	Moodle & Zoom
6	Confirmation bias	Inoculation	Experiential learning	Moodle & Zoom
7	Filter bubbles, echo chambers	Fact checking	Basic problem-based learning	Moodle & Zoom
8	Filter bubbles, echo chambers	Inoculation	Game-based learning	Moodle & Zoom, computer game
9	Filter bubbles, illusory truth	Fact checking	Cognitive apprenticeship	Moodle & Zoom
10	Filter bubbles	Inoculation, Fact-checking	Basic problem-based learning	Moodle & Zoom
11	Emotional framing	Inoculation	Cognitive apprenticeship	Moodle & Zoom
12	Filter bubbles	Fact-checking	Cognitive apprenticeship	Moodle & Zoom

confirmation bias, because the fake news consumers will probably avoid the cognitive dissonance resulting from information aimed to correct their misconceptions [12].

In terms of instructional design, inoculation was done in most cases using problem-based approaches such as goal-based scenarios [25], probably because these build upon authenticity [29] and stimulate learning motivation [23]. Fact checking required analytic truth evaluation [8], thus more complex cognitive activities and corresponding skills, which were trained in many projects by cognitive apprenticeship [27]. All training programs utilized the available moodle platform and the video conferencing tool zoom, thus confirming the versatile applicability of these technologies. However, in special cases additional technologies were needed. Complex, problem-based training activities such as games and role plays [25, 26] called for more advanced technology that was not integrated in the standard moodle. Both instructional designs aimed at training complex cognitive skills, cognitive apprenticeship [27] and 4C/ID [28] required diverse forms of instructional support at levels adapted to the momentary performance level reached by the trainees—adequate technologies were for the graduate students of educational sciences not accessible or not available. Technologies that were more directly related to fake news, such as automated fact checking [31], social bots [32] or user profiling [33] were missed, as well.

7 Conclusion

While this exploratory study demonstrated that fake news illiteracy can be combated using various cognitive approaches and available technologies, the training design and development was limited by technological factors. This clearly suggests that specific technology needs to be developed in order to support the educational efforts aimed at fostering fake news literacy. Standard content management systems would profit from integrating more flexible tools (e.g., based on learning analytics) that assess student performance, paired with more flexible instructional support (coaching and scaffolding [27]). Thus, adaptive training environments could be more easily deployed which, in turn, would enable the implementation of complex instructional designs like cognitive apprenticeship [27]. Content management systems for higher education may also profit from gamification and simulation tools that may better support experiential and game-based learning [24, 26]. In the same vein, automated content and sentiment analysis may be used for identifying and labeling emotional framing, thus inoculating news consumers against falling for fake news [2]. Furthermore, for future course iterations a broader set of tools could be made available to the students, such as the InVID Plug-in, a web-video verification tool for browser [40].

Indeed, such technologies may be available, though not standard. Beyond standards, a challenge for educational technology may be to develop tools that are closer to the current fake news technology. For instance, how can an average user track and visualize cookies, and thus grasp filter bubbles?

References

1. Allcott, H., Gentzkow, M.: Social media and fake news in the 2016 election. J. Econ. Perspect. **32**(2), 211–236 (2017)
2. Scheibenzuber, C., Hofer, S., Nistor, N.: Designing for fake news literacy training: a problem-based undergraduate online-course. Comput. Hum. Behav. (2021). https://doi.org/10.1016/j.chb.2021.106796
3. Van der Linden, S., Roozenbeek, J.: Psychological inoculation against fake news. In: Greifender, R., Jaffe, M., Newman, E., Schwarz, N. (Hrsg.) The Psychology of Fake News, pp. 147–169. Routledge (2020)
4. Lazer, D.M.J., et al.: The science of fake news. Science **359**(6380), 1094–1096 (2018). https://doi.org/10.1126/science.aao2998
5. Potter, W.J.: Media Literacy. Sage (2018)
6. Jaffé, M.E., Greifeneder, R.: Can that be true or is it just fake news? New perspectives on the negativity bias in judgements of truth. In: Greifender, R., Jaffé, M.E., Newman, E.J., Schwarz, N. (eds.) The Psychology of Fake News: Accepting, Sharing, and Correcting Misinformation, pp. 111–126. Routledge (2020)

7. Pennycook, G., Rand, D.G.: Lazy, not biased: Susceptibility to partisan fake news is better explained by lack of reasoning than by motivated reasoning. Cognition **188**, 39–50 (2019). https://doi.org/10.1016/j.cognition.2018.06.011
8. Schwarz, N., Jalbert, M.: When fake news feels true. In: Greifeneder, R., Jaffé, M.E., Newman, E.J., Schwarz, N. (eds.) The Psychology of Fake News: Accepting, Sharing, and Correcting Misinformation, pp. 71–86. Routledge (2020)
9. Fazio, L.K., Brashier, N.M., Payne, B.K., Marsh, E.J.: Knowledge does not protect against illusory truth. J. Exp. Psychol. Gen. **144**(5), 993–1002 (2015)
10. Bornstein, R.F.: Exposure and affect: overview and meta-analysis of research, 1968–1987. Psychol. Bull. **106**(2), 265–289 (1989)
11. Nickerson, R.S.: Confirmation bias: a ubiquitous phenomenon in many guises. Rev. Gen. Psychol. **2**(2), 175–220 (1998). https://doi.org/10.1037/1089-2680.2.2.175
12. Festinger, L.: A Theory of Cognitive Dissonance. Stanford University Press (1957)
13. Haddock, G., Maio, G.: Einstellungen. In: Jonas, K., Stroebe, W., Hewstone, M. (eds.) Sozialpsychologie, 6th edn. Springer (2014)
14. Pariser, E.: The filter bubble: how the new personalized web is changing what we read and how we think. Penguin (2016)
15. di Sessa, A.A.: Knowledge in pieces: an evolving framework for understanding knowing and learning. In: Amin, T.G., Levrini, O. (eds.) Converging Perspectives on Conceptual Change: Mapping an Emerging Paradigm in the Learning Sciences, pp. 9–16. Routledge (2018)
16. Cheek, N.N., Blackman, S.F., Pronin, E.: Seeing the subjective as objective: people perceive the taste of those they disagree with as biased and wrong. J. Behav. Decis. Mak. **34**(2), 167–182 (2021). https://doi.org/10.1002/bdm.2201
17. Ross, L., Ward, A.: Naive realism in everyday life: implications for social conflict and misunderstanding. In: Reed, E.S., Turiel, E., Brown, T. (eds.) Values and Knowledge, The Jean Piaget Symposium Series, pp. 103–135. Lawrence Erlbaum Associates (1996)
18. Nguyen, C.T.: Echo chambers and epistemic bubbles. Episteme **17**(2), 141–161 (2020). https://doi.org/10.1017/epi.2018.32
19. McGuire, W.J., Papageorgis, D.: The relative efficacy of various types of prior belief-defense in producing immunity against persuasion. J. Abnorm. Soc. Psychol. **62**(2), 327–337 (1961). https://doi.org/10.1037/h0042026
20. Roozenbeek, J., van der Linden, S.: Fake news game confers psychological resistance against online misinformation. Palgrave Commun. **5**(1) (2019). https://doi.org/10.1057/s41599-019-0279-9
21. Jones-Jang, S.M., Mortensen, T., Liu, J.: Does media literacy help identification of fake news? Information literacy helps, but other literacies don't. Am. Behav. Sci. **65**(2), 371–388 (2021). https://doi.org/10.1177/0002764219869406
22. McGrew, S.: Learning to evaluate: an intervention in civic online reasoning. Comput. Educ. **145** (2020). https://doi.org/10.1016/j.compedu.2019.103711
23. Sinatra, G.M., Pintrich, P.R.: Intentional Conceptual Change. Lawrence Erlbaum (2003)
24. Kolb, D.: Experiential Learning: Experience as the Source of Learning and Development. Prentice-Hall (1984)
25. Schank, R.C., Fano, A., Bell, B., Menachem, J.: The design of goal-based scenarios. J. Learn. Sci. **3**(4), 305–345 (1984)
26. Plass, J.L., Homer, B.D., Kinzer, C.K.: Foundations of game-based learning. Educ. Psychol. **50**(4), 258–283 (2015)
27. Collins, A., Brown, J., Newman, S.: Cognitive apprenticeship: teaching the craft of reading, writing, and mathematics. In: Resnick, L. (ed.) Knowing, Learning, and Instruction: Essays in Honor of Robert Glaser, pp. 453–493. Erlbaum (1989)

28. van Merriënboer, J.J., Kirschner, P.A.: 4C/ID in the context of instructional design and the learning sciences. In: Fischer, F., Hmelo-Silver, C.E., Goldman, S.R., Reimann, P. (eds.) International Handbook of the Learning Sciences, pp. 169–179. Routledge (2018)
29. Gulikers, J.T., Bastiaens, T.J., Martens, R.L.: The surplus value of an authentic learning environment. Comput. Hum. Behav. **21**(3), 509–521 (2005)
30. Yaqub, W., Kakhidze, O., Brockman, M.L., Memon, N., Patil, S.: Effects of credibility indicators on social media news sharing intent. In: Proceedings of the 2020 CHI Conference on Human Factors in Computing Systems, CHI 2020, pp. 1–14, April 2020. https://doi.org/10.1145/3313831.3376213
31. Ciampaglia, G.L., Shiralkar, P., Rocha, L.M., Bollen, J., Menczer, F., et al.: Correction: computational fact checking from knowledge networks. PLOS ONE **10**(10) (2015). https://doi.org/10.1371/journal.pone.0141938
32. Shao, C., Ciampaglia, G.L., Varol, O., Flammini, A., Menczer, F.: The spread of fake news by social bots. arXiv preprint arXiv:1707.07592, 96, 104 (2017)
33. Heawood, J.: Pseudo-public political speech: democratic implications of the Cambridge Analytica scandal. Inf. Polity **23**, 429–434 (2018)
34. Snowball, J.D., McKenna, S.: Student-generated content: an approach to harnessing the power of diversity in higher education. Teach. High. Educ. **22**(5), 604–618 (2017). https://doi.org/10.1080/13562517.2016.1273205
35. Dorussen, H., Lenz, H., Blavoukos, S.: Assessing the reliability and validity of expert interviews. Eur. Union Polit. **6**(3), 315–337 (2005). https://doi.org/10.1177/1465116505054835
36. Bairaktarova, D.: The new renaissance artificers: harnessing the power of creativity in the engineering classroom. In: Bairaktarova, D., Eodice, M. (eds.) Creative Ways of Knowing in Engineering, pp. 1–22. Springer, Cham (2017). https://doi.org/10.1007/978-3-319-49352-7_1
37. Bogner, A., Littig, B., Menz, W.: Introduction: expert interviews—an introduction to a new methodological debate. In: Interviewing Experts, pp. 1–13. Palgrave Macmillan (2009)
38. van Dijk, J.A.: Delphi questionnaires versus individual and group interviews: a comparison case. Technol. Forecast. Soc. Chang. **37**(3), 293–304 (1990)
39. Collins, A., Brown, J.S., Holum, A.: Cognitive apprenticeship: making thinking visible. Am. Educ. **15**(3), 6–11, 38–46 (1991)
40. Teyssou, D., et al.: The InVID plug-in: web video verification on the browser. In: Mezaris, V., Nixon, L., Papadopoulos, S., Spangenberg, J. (eds.) Proceedings of the First International Workshop on Multimedia Verification, pp. 23–30. Association for Computing Machinery (2017). https://doi.org/10.1145/3132384.3132387

Recommendations for Orchestration of Formative Assessment Sequences: A Data-Driven Approach

Rialy Andriamiseza[1](✉), Franck Silvestre[1], Jean-François Parmentier[2], and Julien Broisin[1]

[1] IRIT, Université de Toulouse, 118 Route de Narbonne, 31062 Toulouse Cedex 9, France
[2] Toulouse INP, R4 Allée Emile Monso, 31030 Toulouse, France

Abstract. Formative assessment aims to improve teaching and learning by providing teachers and students with feedback designed to help them to adapt their behavior. To face the increasing number of students in higher education and support this kind of activity, technology-enhanced formative assessment tools emerged. These tools generate data that can serve as a basis for improving the processes and services they provide. Based on literature and using a dataset gathered from the use of a formative assessment tool in higher education whose process, inspired by Mazur's Peer Instruction, consists in asking learners to answer a question before and after a confrontation with peers, we use learning analytics to provide evidence-based knowledge about formative assessment practices. Our results suggest that: (1) Benefits of formative assessment sequences increase when the proportion of correct answers is close to 50% during the first vote; (2) Benefits of formative assessment sequences increase when correct learners' rationales are better rated than incorrect learners' ones; (3) Peer ratings are consistent when correct learners are more confident than incorrect ones; (4) Self-rating is inconsistent in peer rating context; (5) The amount of peer ratings makes no significant difference in terms of sequences benefits. Based on these results, recommendations in formative assessment are discussed and a data-informed formative assessment process is inferred.

Keywords: Technology-enhanced formative assessment · Learning analytics · Peer instruction · Decision-making

1 Introduction

Formative assessment aims to improve learning by providing teachers and students with feedback designed to help them to adapt their behavior. However, according to Andersson, formative assessment is often used in an informal and approximate way [1]. Ellis also emphasized the difficulty of capturing all learning interactions in a face-to-face context [14]. Providing practitioners and students with meaningful and effective feedback is thus a complex task, especially in large scale settings where the amount of learning interactions to capture increases with the number of learners.

To address this challenge and to support the growing number of students in higher education, Technology-Enhanced Formative Assessment (TEFA) and its interactive voting systems emerged. Such systems implement different processes offering teachers the opportunity to conduct formative assessment sequences. Among them, a group of processes, namely the "two-votes-based processes", requires learners to vote twice during the sequence. Peer Instruction, as described by Mazur [9], is one of the earliest forms of two-votes-based formative assessment processes. Basically, a two-votes-based sequence includes the following phases: (1) Teachers ask a question; (2) Students give their first answer; (3) Students reflect on peers answers and think about their own knowledge; (4) Students give their second answer to the same question; (5) Teachers discuss with students about the results. With two-votes-based processes, the number of students providing the correct answer at the fourth phase is expected to be higher than at the second phase. When this is the case, we qualify such sequence as *beneficial* because it means that students understanding of the topic has been enhanced [34].

These five phases comprise a wide variety of learning interactions. However, due to the lack of data related to two-votes-based processes [3], little work has explored how to use these interactions to bring new knowledge about formative assessment. Hence, in this paper, we address the following research questions: Which meaningful information can be inferred from the analysis of data gathered from a tool implementing a two-votes-based process and used in authentic contexts? How can such information contribute to facilitate two-votes-based process orchestration?

The three main contributions are the followings:

- findings about formative assessment, based on a dataset gathered from the use of a formative assessment tool in authentic learning contexts in higher education;
- recommendations to assist designers of formative assessment systems;
- recommendations to assist teachers when orchestrating two-votes-based sequences.

The paper is structured as follows. Section 2 introduces formative assessment and emphasizes limits of prior TEFA initiatives. Section 3 describes the formative assessment system used as the data provider of our study, as well as the dataset. Section 4 details the analysis we conducted and gives the main results. Starting from these results, Sect. 5 proposes an orchestration model of formative assessment sequences implementing the two-votes-based process. Section 6 discusses the limitations of our study. Section 7 concludes and discusses future work.

2 Related Works

2.1 Formative Assessment

Although assessment is often used as assessment *of* learning, it can also be used as assessment *for* learning [22]. On one hand, summative assessment is used to evaluate student's level of achievement at the end of an instructional unit. On the other hand, formative assessment is crucial to make teachers able to evaluate students' understandings and adapt their lessons [11]. Hattie highlighted formative assessment as one of the most efficient methods to improve student achievement [17]. In 1998, Black and

William suggested the following definition: "Formative assessment is to be interpreted as encompassing all those activities undertaken by teachers, and/or by their students, which provide information to be used as feedback to modify the teaching and learning activities in which they are engaged" [4]. This definition emphasizes the importance of collecting data to provide feedback designed to improve learning and teaching.

For instance, in face-to-face settings, Meltzer and Mannivan reported on the usage of visual artefacts (such as pieces of papers or cardboards) to allow students to answer questions asked by teachers [25]. Thanks to this feedback, teachers can collect learners' answers at a glance and adapt their teaching. However, this method hardly fits large scale educational settings since collecting and processing several answers is time consuming. Technology is then needed to collect and process interaction data efficiently, making Learning Analytics relevant for improving formative assessment.

2.2 Technology-Enhanced Formative Assessment

TEFA is one of the emerging solutions for delivering formative assessment with immediate feedback [33]. Since questioning an audience enters in the frame of formative assessment [4], Classroom Response Systems (CRS) are one of the most commonly used systems supporting TEFA in face-to-face context [2].

A generic formative assessment process of CRS is implemented by web-based platforms such as Poll Everywhere [8]. It allows teachers to ask a question, and learners to vote for the correct answer. Histograms or pie charts are then immediately displayed as feedback in order to show the distribution of votes and help teachers and learners engage in a debriefing phase. Several platforms such as Kahoot [18] support the same process. However, beyond the overview of learners' vote for the question, they propose a feedback providing teachers with the answers of each learner regarding all the formative assessment sequences she has been involved in.

Activating learners as instructional resources is an efficient way to implement formative assessment [5]. Student performance over a course of an academic programme can be significantly affected and positively influenced through a series of feedback processes handled by peers [26]. Hence, a richer formative assessment process implemented by ComPAIR [31] lets teachers ask open-ended question, while learners provide textual answers. Afterwards, learners engage in a peer review loop. They are asked to give a textual feedback about two peers answers, but also to justify why one answer is more relevant than the other. During and after this phase, teachers are provided with a feedback about each learner interaction such as her chosen answer, the textual feedback she provided, and the comparisons she submitted for the presented pair of answers.

Elaastic [13, 30] and myDalite [6] offer even richer processes with even more interactions. Both systems implement the two-votes-based process illustrated in Fig. 1. The processes proposed by Elaastic and myDalite consist in asking learners to vote a first time and to provide a written explanation (also called "rationale") to justify their choices. Then the process allows learners to vote a second time. At this point, both platforms differ. On one hand, myDalite allows learners to select one rationale as their second vote. Then, it provides teachers with a feedback detailing how many learners went from being wrong to right, right to wrong, wrong to wrong and right to right. On the other hand, Elaastic engages learners in a peer rating phase before they submit their second answer, as they are asked to rate several peers rationales. At anytime of the sequence, Elaastic can display first and second votes of learners and provide teachers with each learner written explanation and the mean rate attributed by peers (see Sect. 3.1).

This section showed that advanced technology-enhanced formative assessment processes such as two-votes-based processes offer a wide variety of interactions. Previous quantitative studies emphasized the benefits of such interactivity-rich processes [23,29,34]. Furthermore, qualitative works about the usage of a two-votes-based process emphasized learners' growing sense of self-regulation and awareness of their own explanation [6]. According to Crouch and Mazur [9] and to the ICAP framework [7], this process cognitively engages students at different levels. Finally, based on Black and William's theory of formative assessment [5], we argue that two-votes-based processes have a very satisfying coverage of formative assessment requirements [32]. Consequently, we tackle our research questions by (i) identifying hypotheses based on a review of literature, and (ii) applying various data mining techniques to evaluate these hypotheses and infer relevant information about formative assessment.

3 Design of the Dataset

We present here the formative assessment platform used for our study, together with the dataset gathered from its usage in authentic learning contexts in higher education.

3.1 Elaastic, a Technology-Enhanced Formative Assessment Tool

Elaastic is a web platform [30] used since 2015 in different higher education contexts across various disciplines such as computer science, physics or project management.

During phase 1, teachers ask learners to answer a question. If the question is closed-ended, it can be either a multiple- or exclusive-choice question. Phase 2 requires learners to answer the question and provide a written rationale to justify their choice(s). They are also asked to provide their confidence degree about their answer on a four-items Likert scale (see Fig. 2). This scale has 4 items because a neutral value would be difficult to interpret [27] regarding confidence degree. Phase 3 engages learners in a peer rating activity. As shown in Fig. 3, they are provided with peers' rationales or their own and are asked to evaluate each of them by reporting their level of agreement using a five-items Likert scale (1 = "Strongly disagree", 2 = "Disagree", 3 = "Not agree and not disagree", 4 = "Agree", 5 = "Strongly agree"). To avoid middle response bias [19], learners can also select a null response option ("I'm not giving my opinion"). Teachers can configure the number of rationales (up to 5) evaluated by each learner. Then, phase 4 begins and learners have the opportunity to vote a second time for the correct answer(s). Finally, teachers can start the phase 5. The distribution of learners scores, the rationales and their mean rate are displayed for a debriefing.

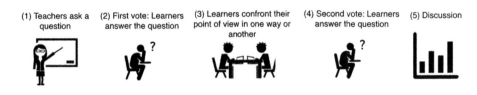

Fig. 1. The 5 phases of the two-votes-based process.

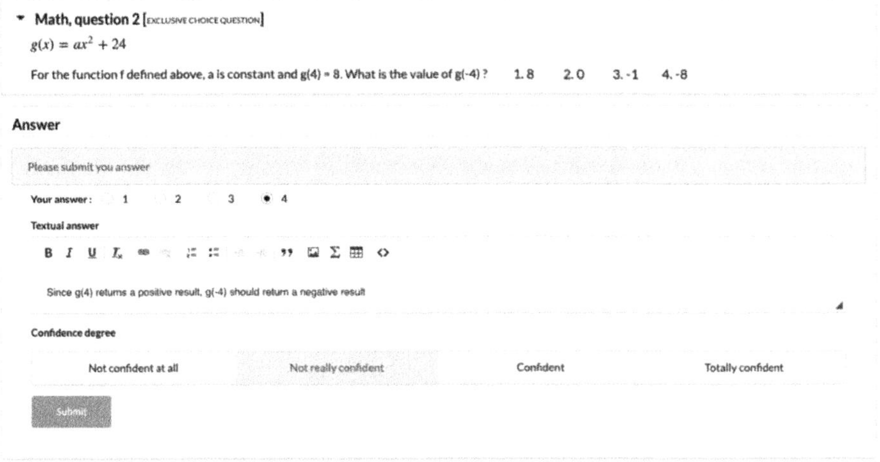

▼ **Math, question 2** [EXCLUSIVE CHOICE QUESTION]

$g(x) = ax^2 + 24$

For the function f defined above, a is constant and g(4) = 8. What is the value of g(-4) ?   1. 8   2. 0   3. -1   4. -8

Answer

Please submit you answer

Your answer :   1   2   3   ● 4

Textual answer

B I U I₂ ∞   ≔ ≔   ,, 🖼 Σ ⊞ <>

Since g(4) returns a positive result, g(-4) should return a negative result

Confidence degree

Not confident at all   Not really confident   Confident   Totally confident

Submit

Fig. 2. Elaastic: submission form of first vote.

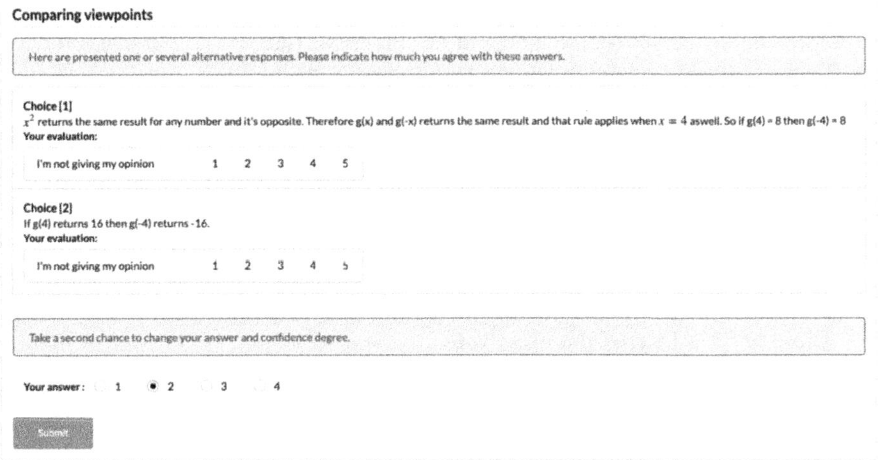

Comparing viewpoints

Here are presented one or several alternative responses. Please indicate how much you agree with these answers.

Choice [1]
x^2 returns the same result for any number and it's opposite. Therefore g(x) and g(-x) returns the same result and that rule applies when $x = 4$ aswell. So if g(4) = 8 then g(-4) = 8
Your evaluation:

I'm not giving my opinion   1   2   3   4   5

Choice [2]
If g(4) returns 16 then g(-4) returns -16.
Your evaluation:

I'm not giving my opinion   1   2   3   4   5

Take a second chance to change your answer and confidence degree.

Your answer :   1   ● 2   3   4

Submit

Fig. 3. Elaastic: submission form of second vote.

3.2 The Dataset

We conducted our analysis on data gathered from the use of Elaastic in higher education from 2015 to 2019. Until now, we collected 623 sequences conducted by 53 teachers where 1769 learners provided 8757 answers and performed 9256 peer ratings.

A sequence is characterised by a learning context (i.e. face-to-face, distant or hybrid), the answers of the first and second votes, as well as the number of participants. For each answer, the following data are collected: the learner identifier, the content of the rationale, the score and the selected choice(s) when applicable. If the answer is a first vote, it is characterised by additional data such as the mean grade assigned by peers to the rationale associated with the answer, and the confidence degree of the learner who provided the answer. Questions are described by their statement, their type (e.g. open ended, multiple- or exclusive-choice) and, in case of choice questions, by the number of different choices proposed to learners. Finally, for each evaluation resulting from the peer rating activity, the following data are collected: the rated rationale, the identifier of the rater, and the rate she assigned.

4 Data Analysis

The whole dataset has been filtered in order to reduce influential external factors and outliers. First, we only considered choice questions so as to be able to evaluate correctness of answers. In our analysis, in order to classify an answer as right or wrong, we considered answers as incorrect if the score is lower than the maximum score that can be obtained (i.e. 100). Also, since the asynchronous nature of distant and hybrid execution contexts in Elaastic doesn't require full orchestration from teachers [30], we kept face-to-face sequences only. Then we removed sequences where there were less than 10 participants because we wanted to focus on large scale settings. Finally, we considered the variables $p1$ and $p2$ which are the proportion of learners who answered correctly at the first and second vote respectively. Sequences where $p1 = 0$ were removed, since the confrontation can not operate under these conditions (there is no rationales for correct answers to convince incorrect peers). Sequences where $p2 = 1$ or $p1 = 1$ were removed as well, as they point out questions that were too easy to measure an effect size. After cleaning our data, we obtained 104 sequences conducted by 21 teachers where 616 learners provided 1981 answers and performed 4072 peer ratings. For our analysis, even though our sample does not follow a normal distribution of the variables, we consider it as large enough to conduct analysis with parametric tests [16].

4.1 Benefits of Sequences Increase When the Proportion of Correct Answers Is Close to 50% During the First Vote

In 2001, Crouch and Mazur defined [35%–70%] as the desired interval of $p1$ for optimal benefits of formative assessment sequences [9]. Later works suggested [30%–80%] as the threshold values [20]. Finally, in 2010, Watkins and Mazur [23] noticed that their implementation of Peer Instruction is of high benefits for students when between 30–70% of their first answers are correct. Based on these statements, we make the hypothesis that benefits of a sequence are linked to the distance between $p1$ and 50%.

In order to verify this hypothesis, we measured the effect size between the first and second votes. To this end, we used the estimation of Cohen's effect size d proposed by Parmentier [29]: $d = 0.6 ln\left(\frac{p2}{1-p2} \frac{1-p1}{p1}\right)$. Based on this estimation, we define sequences as *beneficial* when $d > 0$ (since it implies that $p1 < p2$). Figure 4a shows the mean effect size depending on the distance between $p1$ and 50%. As an example, the first bar represents 37 sequences where the distance of $p1$ to 50% is between 0% and 10%. In other words, when $p1$ is comprised between 40% (50% − 10%) and 60% (50% + 10%), the mean effect size is close to 0.4. The chart suggests that the effect size of a sequence decreases when the distance between $p1$ and 50% increases.

The Pearson correlation between $|p1 - 0.5|$ and d is -0.31 with p-value = .001 and a 95% confidence interval equal to [−0.48:−0.13], which supports our hypothesis.

The distance between $p1$ and 50% is a useful indicator to predict benefits of a two-votes-based sequence. In other words, benefits of peer interactions are maximized when correct and incorrect answers are equally represented. We argue that too few correct answers may indicate that learners lack understanding or knowledge to engage in productive discussions, whereas too many correct answers may indicate that the question is too easy and does not require discussions.

> **Recommendations for system designers:** Formative assessment systems implementing a two-votes-based process should provide teachers with the proportion of correct answers at the first vote. They should also feature flexibility regarding the way to conduct the sequence, especially according to the proportion of correct answers at the first vote and its distance to 50%.

As Lasry stated [21], the threshold values of the ideal percentages of correct answers are indicative. In our context, the interval that best suits our result is [20%–80%]. Indeed, Fig. 4a suggests that when $p1$'s distance from 50% is greater than 30%, the effect size is significantly lower.

> **Recommendations for orchestration:** If there are too few correct answers at the first phase ($p1 < 20\%$), teachers should either provide detailed explanations and restart the sequence, or provide learners with hints before engaging learners in a confrontation phase. If there are a lot of correct answers ($p1 > 80\%$), teachers can interrupt the sequence and provide learners with a brief explanation. ❶

4.2 Benefits of Sequences Increase When Peer Ratings Are Consistent

Double et al. argue that reflecting on peers answers is expected to lead to a higher percentage of correct answers [12]. Since correct learners are expected to convince incorrect learners, we make the hypothesis that the consistency of the peer rating phase is linked to the sequence benefits.

In order to measure the consistency of peer ratings in a sequence, we used ρ_{peer} which is the correlation between the level of agreement given by peers to a rationale, and the correctness of the matching answers (self-rating included). Since these two variables are latent [15], the polychoric correlation is the adequate tool [28]. More precisely, ρ_{peer} will tend to be close to 1 if the rationales matching with correct answers are positively evaluated by peers, whereas those matching with incorrect answers are negatively evaluated. Conversely, ρ_{peer} will tend to be close to −1 if the rationales matching with incorrect answers are better evaluated than those matching with correct answers. Figure 4b shows a plot diagram of the effect size d depending on ρ_{peer}.

The Pearson correlation between ρ_{peer} and d is 0.34 with a p-value < .002 and a 95% confidence interval equal to [0.14:0.52], which supports our hypothesis. Let us note that ρ_{peer} is not significantly correlated to the distance between $p1$ and 50% (p-value = 0.25). Consequently, this subsection and Subsect. 4.1 identified two independent predictors of the benefits of a sequence, namely ρ_{peer} and $|p1 - 50\%|$.

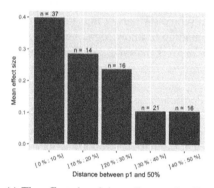
(a) The effect size d depending on the distance between $p1$ and 50%.

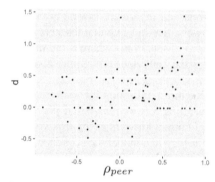
(b) The effect size d depending on the consistency of peer ratings ρ_{peer}.

Fig. 4. d given $|p1 - 50\%|$ and ρ_{peer}.

When $\rho_{peer} < 0$, it means that incorrect answers are more popular than correct answers which should be addressed by teachers.

Recommendations for system designers: Formative assessment systems implementing a peer rating process should provide teachers with the consistency of peer rating and feature flexibility regarding the selection of the rationales in the focus of the discussion (phase 5), especially according to the consistency of peer rating.

Recommendations for orchestration: If peer rating is inconsistent ($\rho_{peer} < 0$), teachers should focus on incorrect rationales during the discussion. Else ($\rho_{peer} \geq 0$), teachers should focus on correct rationales during the discussion. ❷

4.3 Peer Ratings Are Consistent When Learners Confidence Degrees Are Consistent

Back to the first vote, Curtis used the confidence of learners about their answers as a way to identify misinformed learners [10]. More precisely, he defined misinformed learners as confident but incorrect learners. Starting from this research, we propose an indicator to measure the consistency of learners confidence degree given the correctness of their answers. Since correct learners are expected to be more confident than incorrect learners, we believe that misinformed learners are not able to consistently rate peers rationales. As a consequence, we make the hypothesis that consistency of peer ratings is linked to the consistency of learners confidence degree.

Similarly to ρ_{peer}, confidence consistency ρ_{conf} can be computed by using the polychoric correlation between learners confidence degree and correctness of their first answers. If correct learners are confident whereas incorrect ones aren't, ρ_{conf} will tend to be close to 1. Conversely, if incorrect learners are confident whereas correct ones aren't, ρ_{conf} will tend to be close to -1. Figure 5a is a plot diagram of ρ_{peer} according to ρ_{conf}. The Pearson correlation between ρ_{conf} and ρ_{peer} is 0.38 with a p-value $< 4e - 4$, and a 95% confidence interval equal to [0.18:0.55], which supports our hypothesis.

> **Recommendations for system designers:** Formative assessment systems implementing a two-votes-based process should provide teachers with the consistency of learners confidence degree. They should also feature flexibility regarding the way to conduct the sequence, but also regarding the selection of the rationales in the focus of the discussion (phase 5) according to this consistency.

ρ_{conf} is an adequate measure of learners understanding of the concept targeted by the question. Beyond learners correctness, their confidence degree allows teachers to obtain more precise feedback, including the proportion of misinformed learners (incorrect but confident) and lucky learners (correct but not confident). Similarly to ρ_{peer}, when $\rho_{conf} < 0$, it means that incorrect answers are more popular than correct answers. This may indicate that some misconceptions need to be addressed by teachers.

> **Recommendations for orchestration:** When there are too many correct answers in the first vote, teachers should focus the discussion on incorrect rationales if learners are inconsistently confident ($p1 > 80\%$ and $\rho_{conf} < 0$), and on correct rationales if learners are consistently confident ($p1 > 80\%$ and $\rho_{conf} < 0$). When there are too few correct answers, teachers should provide detailed explanations and restart the sequence if learners are inconsistently confident ($p1 < 20\%$ and $\rho_{conf} < 0$). If learners are consistently confident ($p1 < 20\%$ and $\rho_{conf} > 0$), teachers should provide learners with hints before starting the confrontation phase. ③

4.4 Self-rating Is Inconsistent in Peer Rating Contexts

Regarding peer interactions-related factors, some studies about self-rating [12, 24] provide support for its use as a formative practice to improve academic performances.

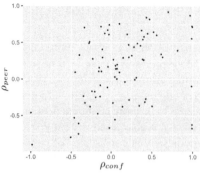
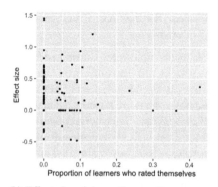

(a) Peer rating consistency ρ_{peer} depending on the confidence consistency ρ_{conf}.

(b) Effect size d depending on the percentage of learners who rated themselves.

Fig. 5. ρ_{peer} given ρ_{conf} and d given the proportion of self-grades

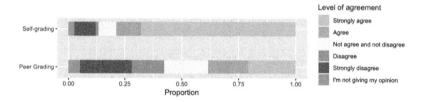

Fig. 6. Stacked bar chart of the grade attributed depending on the type of rating.

Consequently, we make the hypothesis that there is a relationship between the number of self-rated students and the benefits of a sequence.

Our results suggest that self-rating tends to nullify the effect size (see Fig. 5b). We explored the data and found out that learners who rated themselves during the confrontation of viewpoints tend to give their rationale the highest grade whether they where correct or not. We compared grades given when learners rated themselves with grades given when learners rated peers (see Fig. 6). The difference in means was significant (95% CI = [−1.68:−1.014] and p-value < 10e − 11). Furthermore, self-rating was less consistent ($\rho_{self_r} = 0.139$) than peer rating ($\rho_{peer_r} = 0.219$).

This result rejects our hypothesis and suggests that self-rating does not benefit learners within peer rating contexts. An informal discussion with 9 learners has been conducted and allowed us to make three hypotheses. First, learners stated that they logically agree with themselves. This implies that they do not revise their own answer based on peers rationales as expected. Second, learners know that rationales with the highest grades are more likely to be noticed. Therefore, learners game the system in order to receive oral feedback from teachers during phase 5. Third, learners perceive this activity as competitive and, therefore, want to obtain the highest mean grade.

> **Recommendation for system designers:** Peer rating activities in formative assessment systems should not include self-rating.

4.5 The Amount of Peer Ratings Makes No Significant Difference in Terms of Sequences Benefits

Group discussion in formative assessment is a challenging task. Depending on the context (e.g. the physical location of learners or the nature of the course), different ways to confront learners' viewpoints can be found in literature. Some implementation paired learners with their neighbour in classes [34], whereas others involved teachers in the collective discussion [35]. Therefore, we want to explore the impact of the number of learners involved in group discussions. With Elaastic, the number of learners involved in group discussion is represented by the number of peers rationales rated by each learner. We believe that the effect size depends on such a number.

Since there were not enough sequences with 1 and 4 rates given, we ran a t-test with various grouping methods (see Table 1). According to our result, the number of learners involved in peer interactions has no significant impact, which rejects our hypothesis.

Table 1. Results of the two sample t-test with various grouping methods.

Group 1			Group 2			Two sample t-test	
nb rates given	mean	sd	nb rates given	mean	sd	95% CI	p-value
1, 2	0.18	0.39	3	0.26	0.42	[−0.3:0.13]	0.42
1, 2	0.18	0.39	4, 5	0.29	0.34	[−0.31:0.08]	0.25
3	0.26	0.42	4, 5	0.29	0.34	[−0.2:0.14]	0.73
1, 2	0.18	0.39	3, 4, 5	0.28	0.38	[−0.09:0.29]	0.29
1, 2, 4, 5	0.25	0.36	3	0.26	0.42	[−0.17:0.15]	0.88
1, 2, 3	0.23	0.41	4, 5	0.29	0.34	[−0.2:0.09]	0.44

> **Recommendation for system designers:** Formative assessment systems should feature flexibility regarding the number of peers involved in group confrontation.

> **Recommendation for orchestration:** Teachers can decide the number of peers involved in group confrontation.

5 Resulting Orchestration Model

Figure 7 summarises our recommendations for orchestration of formative assessment sequences. The presented model is derived from Vickrey's model designed to support orchestration of Peer Instruction [36]. When sequences are not beneficial, deep and detailed explanations are needed from teachers during the oral feedback. Consequently, we added the following recommendation to our model:

> **Recommendation for orchestration:** After the second vote, teachers explanation should be more detailed if the proportion of correct answers did not increase ($d \leq 0$). ④

6 Limitations

Our main limitations come from the dataset itself. The 104 sequences that we analysed addressed mainly STEM topics from higher education classes. A more refined study of sequences from various topics and educational levels could lead to broader findings.

In the context of multiple choice answers, if a learner obtains a score of 33/100 during the first vote and 66/100 during the second vote, both her answers are considered as wrong, and the information stating that she improved is lost. Even though multiple choice questions are only a small portion of our sample (~10%), a deeper study addressing this distinction would be a more adequate way to refine our results.

Moreover, as stated earlier, Elaastic does not capture all learning interactions in a face-to-face context, thus making us unable to identify every decisive aspects of a formative assessment sequence such as its context (i.e. the subjects and themes of the questions) as well as oral and informal interactions between learners and teachers.

Finally, we consider rationales associated to correct answers as correct rationales. However, learners can answer correctly and provide incorrect rationales. As an example,

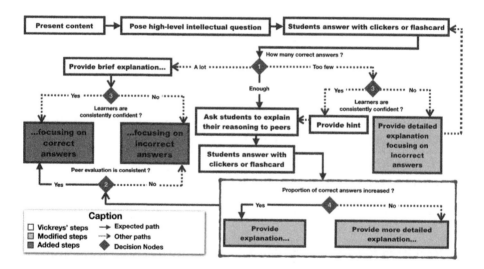

Fig. 7. Orchestration model of two-votes-based processes based on [36]. Each white number represents the matching recommendation for orchestration.

if learners give a low rate to an incorrect rationale corresponding to a correct answer, ρ_{peer} will decrease even though this rationale was rightfully given a low rate. Such a possibility is not addressed by our works regarding the quality of peer interactions.

7 Conclusion and Future Works

This paper focused on formative assessment and emphasized the challenge of its application in face-to-face contexts. We introduced TEFA as the solution that emerged to perform face-to-face formative assessment and also introduced rich formative assessment processes generating a lot of meaningful interactions. Based on literature and on a dataset gathered from the usage of a two-votes-based process in an authentic learning context, we proposed to study these interactions to (i) highlight new understandings of formative assessment; (ii) provide system designers with evidences intended to help them to design a formative assessment system; (iii) identify meaningful indicators to assist teachers when orchestrating a face-to-face formative assessment sequence.

Future works will implement our orchestration model within Elaastic while taking in account the explainability issues regarding our indicators. After the first vote, teachers will receive textual description to help them make decisions regarding the next phase to engage. After the second vote, teachers will be provided with recommended learners' rationale to address during the discussion phase. Then, we will measure this evolution's impact on teaching and learning thanks to a qualitative and quantitative analysis.

References

1. Andersson, C., Palm, T.: The impact of formative assessment on student achievement: a study of the effects of changes to classroom practice after a comprehensive professional development programme. Learn. Instr. **49**, 92–102 (2017)
2. Beatty, I.D., Gerace, W.J.: Technology-enhanced formative assessment: a research-based pedagogy for teaching science with classroom response technology. J. Sci. Educ. Technol. **18**(2), 146–162 (2009)
3. Bhatanagar, S., Zouaq, A., Desmarais, M.C., Charles, E.: A dataset of learner sourced explanations from an online peer instruction environment. Int. Educ. Data Min. Soc. **13**, 350–355 (2020)
4. Black, P., Wiliam, D.: Assessment and classroom learning. Assess. Educ. Princ. Policy Practice **5**(1), 7–74 (1998)
5. Black, P., Wiliam, D.: Developing the theory of formative assessment. Educ. Assess. Eval. Account. (Formerly: J. Pers. Eval. Educ.) **21**(1), 5 (2009)
6. Charles, E.S., et al.: Harnessing peer instruction in-and out-of class with myDALITE. In: Education and Training in Optics and Photonics, p. 11143_89. Optical Society of America, SPIE, Quebec City (2019)
7. Chi, M.T.H., Wylie, R.: The ICAP framework: linking cognitive engagement to active learning outcomes. Educ. Psychol. **49**(4), 219–243 (2014)
8. Clark, S.: Enhancing active learning: assessment of poll everywhere in the classroom. University of Manitoba, Technical report (2017)
9. Crouch, C.H., Mazur, E.: Peer instruction: ten years of experience and results. Am. J. Phys. **69**(9), 970–977 (2001)

10. Curtis, D.A., Lind, S.L., Boscardin, C.K., Dellinges, M.: Does student confidence on multiple-choice question assessments provide useful information? Med. Educ. **47**(6), 578–584 (2013)
11. Davis, M.: Technology fed growth in formative assessment. Education Week, p. 11 (2015)
12. Double, K.S., McGrane, J.A., Hopfenbeck, T.N.: The impact of peer assessment on academic performance: a meta-analysis of control group studies. Educ. Psychol. Rev. **32**, 481–509 (2020)
13. Elaastic. https://elaastic.irit.fr. Accessed 25 June 2021
14. Ellis, C.: Broadening the scope and increasing the usefulness of learning analytics: the case for assessment analytics. Br. J. Edu. Technol. **44**(4), 662–664 (2013)
15. Everett, B.: An Introduction to Latent Variable Models. Springer Science & Business Media, Dordrecht (2013). https://doi.org/10.1007/978-94-009-5564-6
16. Ghasemi, A., Zahediasl, S.: Normality tests for statistical analysis: a guide for non-statisticians. Int. J. Endocrinol. Metab. **10**(2), 486 (2012)
17. Hattie, J.: Visible Learning for Teachers: Maximizing Impact on Learning. Routledge, New York (2012)
18. Ismail, M.A.A., Mohammad, J.A.M.: Kahoot: a promising tool for formative assessment in medical education. Educ. Med. J. **9**(2), 19–26 (2017)
19. Kulas, J.T., Stachowski, A.A., Haynes, B.A.: Middle response functioning in Likert-responses to personality items. J. Bus. Psychol. **22**(3), 251–259 (2008)
20. Lasry, N.: Clickers or flashcards: is there really a difference? Phys. Teach. **46**(4), 242–244 (2008)
21. Lasry, N., Mazur, E., Watkins, J.: Peer instruction: from Harvard to the two-year college. Am. J. Phys. **76**(11), 1066–1069 (2008)
22. Martinez, M.E., Lipson, J.I.: Assessment for learning. Educ. Leadersh. **46**(7), 73–75 (1989)
23. Mazur, E., Watkins, J.: Just-in-time teaching and peer instruction. In: Just-in-time Teaching: Across the Disciplines, Across the Academy, pp. 39–62. Stylus Publishing, LLC, Sterling (2010)
24. McMillan, J.H., Hearn, J.: Student self-assessment: the key to stronger student motivation and higher achievement. Educ. Horizons **87**(1), 40–49 (2008)
25. Meltzer, D.E., Manivannan, K.: Transforming the lecture-hall environment: the fully interactive physics lecture. Am. J. Phys. **70**(6), 639–654 (2002)
26. Montebello, M., et al.: The impact of the peer review process evolution on learner performance in e-learning environments. In: Proceedings of the Fifth Annual ACM Conference on Learning at Scale, London, UK, pp. 1–3. ACM (2018)
27. Muijs, D.: Doing Quantitative Research in Education with SPSS. Sage Publications, London (2004)
28. Olsson, U.: Maximum likelihood estimation of the polychoric correlation coefficient. Psychometrika **44**(4), 443–460 (1979)
29. Parmentier, J.F.: How to quantify the efficiency of a pedagogical intervention with a single question. Phys. Rev. Phys. Educ. Res. **14**(2), 020116 (2018)
30. Parmentier, J.F., Silvestre, F.: La (dé-)synchronisation des transitions dans un processus d'évaluation formative exécuté à distance: impact sur l'engagement des étudiants. In: 9ème Conférence sur les Environnements Informatiques pour l'Apprentissage Humain (EIAH 2019), pp. 97–108. ATIEF, Sorbonne Universite, LIP6, Paris, France (2019)
31. Potter, T., Englund, L., Charbonneau, J., MacLean, M.T., Newell, J., Roll, I., et al.: ComPAIR: a new online tool using adaptive comparative judgement to support learning with peer feedback. Teach. Learn. Inquiry **5**(2), 89–113 (2017)
32. Silvestre, F.: Conception et mise en oeuvre d'un système d'évaluation formative pour les cours en face à face dans l'enseignement supérieur. Ph.D. thesis, Université de Toulouse, Université Toulouse III-Paul Sabatier (2015)

33. Spector, J.M., et al.: Technology enhanced formative assessment for 21st century learning. Int. Forum Educ. Technol. Soc. **19**(3), 58–71 (2016)
34. Tullis, J.G., Goldstone, R.L.: Why does peer instruction benefit student learning? Cogn. Res. Princ. Implic. **5**(1), 1–12 (2020). https://doi.org/10.1186/s41235-020-00218-5
35. Turpen, C., Finkelstein, N.D.: Not all interactive engagement is the same: variations in physics professors' implementation of peer instruction. Phys. Rev. Spec. Topics Phys. Educ. Res. **5**(2), 020101 (2009)
36. Vickrey, T., Rosploch, K., Rahmanian, R., Pilarz, M., Stains, M.: Research-based implementation of peer instruction: a literature review. CBE-Life Sci. Educ. **14**(1), es3 (2015)

Surveying Teachers' Preferences and Boundaries Regarding Human-AI Control in Dynamic Pairing of Students for Collaborative Learning

Kexin Bella Yang[1](✉), LuEttaMae Lawrence[1], Vanessa Echeverria[2], Boyuan Guo[1], Nikol Rummel[3], and Vincent Aleven[1]

[1] Carnegie Mellon University, 5000 Forbes Avenue, Pittsburgh, USA
{kexiny,llawrenc,boyuang,va0e}@andrew.cmu.edu
[2] Escuela Superior Politécnica del Litoral (ESPOL), Guayaquil, Ecuador
vanechev@espol.edu.ec
[3] Ruhr-Universität Bochum, Universitätsstraße 150, 44801 Bochum, Germany
nikol.rummel@rub.de

Abstract. Orchestration tools may support K-12 teachers in facilitating student learning, especially when designed to address classroom stakeholders' needs. Our previous work revealed a need for human-AI shared control when dynamically pairing students for collaborative learning in the classroom, but offered limited guidance on the role each agent should take. In this study, we designed storyboards for scenarios where teachers, students and AI *co-orchestrate dynamic pairing* when using AI-based adaptive math software for individual and collaborative learning. We surveyed 54 math teachers on their co-orchestration preferences. We found that teachers would like to share control with the AI to lessen their orchestration load. As well, they would like to have the AI propose student pairs with explanations, and identify risky proposed pairings. However, teachers are hesitant to let the AI auto-pair students even if they are busy, and are less inclined to let AI override teacher-proposed pairing. Our study contributes to teachers' needs, preference, and boundaries for how they want to share the task and control of student pairing with the AI and students, and design implications in human-AI co-orchestration tools.

Keywords: Classroom · Human-AI collaboration · CSCL · HCI · Design orchestration tools

1 Introduction

While teachers need to facilitate students' collaborative activities and monitor their progress, these activities can be cognitively demanding for teachers [1–4]. Orchestration

---

Electronic supplementary material The online version of this chapter (https://doi.org/10.1007/978-3-030-86436-1_20) contains supplementary material, which is available to authorized users.

broadly refers to the planning and real-time management of learning activities in the classroom [5]. Various orchestration tools and prototypes have been designed to help lessen teachers' load of class management or allow them to focus on teaching and helping students [3, 4, 6–8]. Recently, much work focuses on *"co-orchestration,"* referring to technology that is explicitly designed so that the orchestration responsibilities are shared across multiple agents (e.g., teachers, students, and AI systems) [4, 5, 7].

Much research has focused on designing tools to support teachers orchestrating either individual (e.g. [9]) or collaborative learning scenarios [2, 10]. These tools have typically been designed with the assumption that students progress through activities in a pre-planned, relatively synchronized manner. By contrast, little work has focused on supporting *fluid social transitions* (with recent exceptions [3, 6, 11]). *Fluid social transitions,* as defined by Olsen et al. [3], refer to transitions between classroom activities that "occur asynchronously between students - not all at the same time for everyone in the class." Different from the static, planned transitions, fluid social transitions may be needed in technology-enhanced classrooms, to support students to flexibly move between activities at a pace that suits their specific circumstances and knowledge level. It is a hypothesis that technologies that support fluid transitions can better support students' learning [3]. To be able to test this hypothesis, the high-level goal for the current study is to design a co-orchestration tool to help teachers easily and effectively manage fluid social transitions in class. Specifically, we focused on dynamic pairing, which means teaming up students opportunistically based on unfolding learning situations [3, 11].

To design effective tools that can help K-12 teachers co-orchestrate their students' learning activities in classrooms, it is critical that the tools "support the needs and respect the boundaries of both teachers and students" [12]. Researchers have begun exploring questions such as: How should orchestration responsibilities be divided among different classroom stakeholders? Who should be accountable for particular instructional decisions? How should such hybrid control adapt to context and learning scenarios [5, 11, 12]? Our previous work reveals that classroom stakeholders have nuanced preferences regarding the co-orchestration of classroom activities. From design research with K-12 teachers, researchers found "a delicate balance between automation and respecting teachers' autonomy", and that "over-automation risks threatening teachers' authority in class and flexibility to set their own goals, yet under-automation may burden teachers with tasks they'd rather not perform" [12]. Similarly, Olsen et al. found from design research with primary school teachers that instructors prefer to "maintain an elevated position above AI systems and need to have some degree of accountability and control" [3]. Echeverria et al. found from a Wizard-of-Oz technology probe in K-12 classrooms a need for hybrid control between students, teachers, and AI systems over dynamic transitions from individual to collaborative learning. They also found a need for such hybrid control to be adaptable to classroom contexts, such as class size and students' prior knowledge.

This study investigates the following questions: *In co-orchestrating dynamic student pairing, how do teachers want to share control with AI systems and students, regarding proposing, evaluating, and deciding pairings?* (RQ1) *What criteria do teachers prefer when dynamically pairing students?* (RQ2) In the current study, we designed storyboards of possible scenarios of human-AI co-orchestration of dynamic pairing. We surveyed

54 math teachers' preferences on them, in the context of using adaptive AI-tutoring software for individual and collaborative K-12 math learning.

2 Methods

2.1 Study Design

The overall goal of the research project, that the current study is part of, is to design a co-orchestration tool that helps teachers manage fluid transitions back-and-forth between individual and collaborative learning in the classroom. This study concerns finding teachers' needs and preferences on one key aspect in managing fluid transitions: dynamically teaming up students (i.e., dynamic pairing). Dynamic pairing may not happen at the same time for every student, and managing the process in real-time may be overwhelming for teachers.

Many design-based research activities, such as user interviews, can require significant time input from researchers, often resulting in a relatively smaller participant pool. Surveys, while being easily scalable, are often hard to adequately convey the nuanced designs to the participants. To concisely communicate potential designs to a larger user population, we incorporated storyboards into a survey. We created storyboards that illustrate different co-orchestration tool features in the context of different dynamic scenarios. We surveyed teachers' opinions on these scenarios, to make sure the tool we design can be aligned with teachers' needs and preferences. These scenarios take context in two intelligent tutoring systems (ITSs) that support learning of middle school math algebra, specifically, equation solving. The individual ITS, Lynnette, has been proven to improve students' equation solving skills in several classroom studies (e.g., [13]). The collaborative ITS, APTA, extends Lynnette's functionality to support reciprocal peer tutoring.

Using storyboards is a standard method in human-centered design. Storyboards show how users interact with different versions of a proposed system in specific contexts [14]. According to Davidoff et al., in the need validation process, storyboards may "help designers prioritize user needs, more clearly map spaces for innovation, and use that focus to narrow the design space for potential applications" [14].

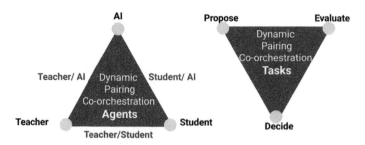

Fig. 1. Agents (left) and Tasks (right) in Human-AI Orchestration of Dynamic Student Pairing

Co-orchestration Scenarios and Survey Design. To inform the design space, we reviewed literature at the intersection of orchestration tools, dynamic pairing, fluid social transitions, and computer-supported collaborative learning (CSCL) [3, 11, 15–17]. As shown in Fig. 1, for co-orchestrating dynamic pairing, there are three main *agents* and three main *tasks*. The three main agents are teacher, AI, and student (Fig. 1, left), and the three main tasks are how the student pairings are proposed, evaluated, and decided (Fig. 1, right). The design space for dynamic pairing co-orchestration is about which *agent(s)* have control over each *task*. Two authors collaboratively brainstormed 22 design concepts for potential co-orchestration scenarios. We used our past research on teachers' needs in pairing co-orchestration [3, 11] to prioritize scenarios that teachers may find more useful. We also included scenarios that push social boundaries or maybe controversial among teachers, as it may help to uncover where these boundaries lie [14]. We went through four rounds of clustering and refining the 22 design concepts, and finalized five co-orchestration scenarios, described in Table 1 (first column).

Based on these five scenarios, we designed a survey that had three sections: 1) teachers' demographics and teaching experience, 2) five co-orchestration scenarios and related questions, and 3) teachers' general preferences on pairing co-orchestration. The five scenarios were presented in a random sequence for every participant, to reduce bias and carry-over effects. Each scenario has 1) a three-panel storyboard with a short title with a simple visual and description (e.g., Fig. 2), 2) a seven-point Likert scale question asking how likely it is that the teacher would use the technology shown in the storyboard in their classroom, 3) a follow up open-ended question asking why or why not, 4) an open-ended question asking what improvements or changes teachers would want to make to the scenario, 5) 1–2 focused seven-point Likert question specific to the main design element in the scenario. In addition, some scenarios had 6) 1–2 multiple choice probing questions. The complete survey questions can be found in <u>supplementary materials</u>.

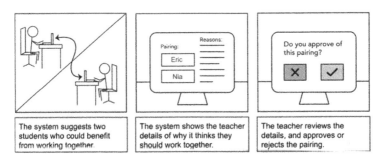

Fig. 2. Storyboard Example (Co-orchestration Scenario 3)

Procedure. The survey was hosted online using Qualtrics and available for seven days. Teachers were introduced to the context and asked to consent to the research. Before large-scale deployment, researchers conducted 8 pilot sessions including 2 think-aloud studies, with math teachers and researchers with 5+ years experience in classroom orchestration. Based on results from the pilot, researchers iteratively refined the survey and storyboards to ensure clarity.

Participants. 54 math teachers (36 females, 18 males) were recruited from math teacher groups on social media. They were asked to complete the 20 to 30-min survey and paid $10 USD Amazon Gift Card. Most teachers (75%) taught in middle school and had taught math for 4 or more years (88%). Participants were mostly white (80%) and mainly taught in the United States of America (96%). At the time, 52% were teaching fully online or remote settings, 41% were in a hybrid mode of online and in-person teaching, and only 2 teachers (4%) were teaching fully in-person. Most teachers (85%) used collaborative learning activities in their classrooms for 50% of the time or more. Other demographics can be found in the supplementary materials.

Table 1. Co-orchestration Scenario Descriptions and Teachers' Stated Likeliness of Use

Scenario titles and descriptions	Co-orchestration roles	Stated likeliness of use	
		M (SD)[a]	Median
S1. Teacher Informs Automated Pairing: Teacher entered information for the AI to use when making student pairings	*Proposes*: Teacher and System *Evaluate*: N/A *Decides*: AI	4.96 (1.58)	5
S2. AI Auto-Pairs When Teachers are Busy: AI paired students up on its own because the teacher was busy and in "Do not disturb" mode	*Proposes*: AI *Evaluate*: N/A *Decides*: AI	4.70 (1.59)	5
S3. AI Explains Pairing Suggestions: AI paired students up, explained to the teacher why it paired them up and asked the teacher to approve or reject the pairing	*Proposes*: AI *Evaluate*: Teacher *Decides*: Teacher	5.89 (1.13)	6
S4. AI Identifies Risky Pairs: Students proposed a partner, the AI reviewed the pairing and notified teachers of potentially risky pairings for teachers to approve or reject	*Proposes*: Student *Evaluate*: AI+ Teacher *Decides*: Teacher	5.33 (1.41)	6
S5. AI Reviews and Decides: Teachers paired students up, the AI evaluated the pairings, and changed risky ones without notifying teachers	*Proposes*: Teacher *Evaluate*: AI alone *Decides*: AI	4.00 (1.76)	4

[a]Likert Scale Labels: 1 - Definitely No, 2 - Very Unlikely, 3 - Probably not, 4 - Neither likely nor unlikely, 5 - Probably yes, 6 - Very likely, 7 - Definitely yes

2.2 Data Analysis Approach

To ensure response quality, we manually reviewed survey responses, and filtered out duplicate or invalid ones (e.g., coming from the same IP address).

For the *quantitative analysis,* we computed the mean and SD for each seven-point Likert scale questions (e.g., how likely teachers thought it was that they would use the technology depicted in the storyboard), and analyzed teachers' responses to each of the multiple-choice probing questions (e.g., what student information the system should consider in dynamic pairing). For the *qualitative analysis,* we analyzed a total of 540 open-ended teacher responses to the two open-ended questions: 1) why they would or would not use the technology in their classroom, and 2) what they wish to see changed or improved. We conducted iterative affinity diagramming [18], where two members of the research team grouped and regrouped individual pieces of data (i.e., raw teachers' response to the two questions above) to find common themes representing teachers' opinions. These teachers' comments were iteratively clustered into 117 first level themes and 63 second-level themes.

To synthesize findings, we laid out all the analysis results *within each scenario,* which allowed us to see, from quantitative data, how teachers' *preferences* on design elements in the co-orchestration tool were distributed, and *why they felt this way* from qualitative data. We then organized the quantitative results and qualitative themes *across different scenarios* according to research questions. Based on this organization, we then formulated insights regarding teachers' co-orchestration preferences, attending both quantitative distribution and qualitative sentiments.

3 Results

In Sect. 3.1, we report quantitative and qualitative results, organized by *scenario,* regarding teachers' needs and preferences for co-orchestration of dynamic pairing. In Sect. 3.2, we report teachers' opinions on hybrid control in proposing and deciding who to pair. The supplementary materials contain complete survey questions and detailed statistics for all Likert scale questions responses.

3.1 Quantitative and Qualitative Results for Each Scenario

Scenario 1 Results. In the first scenario (S1), teachers can enter information about each individual student, which the AI uses to make student pairings later that week. S1 was third-highest regarding teachers' stated likeliness of use ($M = 4.96$, $SD = 1.58$). The survey then asked whether teachers wanted to *spend the time to enter student information that the AI could use to pair up students*. In answer to this question, 37% of teachers chose "very likely" or "definitely yes" in the seven-point Likert scale ($M = 4.65$, $SD = 1.85$). In response to the question asking whether different students should be paired using the *same or different criteria,* the majority of teachers (70%) wanted *different* (personalized) pairing criteria for each student, 26% wanted to have the *same* pairing criteria for all students, and 4% chose "other". When asked what *factors* the system should consider when pairing students, and given a list from which they could select multiple factors, almost all teachers thought the system should consider *students' level of knowledge mastery* (98%). Other factors included students' error rate (76%), students' pairing history (76%), students' personality (66%), number of collaborative sessions students already did (64%), students' friendship/ relationship (52%) and gender (34%).

Qualitative analysis from scenario 1 showed that teachers generally like that the technology could pair students in a data-driven way and that it may increase their work efficiency and reduce orchestration load ($N = 7$)[1]. They also liked the fact that such a system may allow them more work flexibility because they could front-load the preparation work for students pairing prior to class sessions ($N = 6$). However, some teachers were hesitant to use such technology in their classroom, mainly because they were concerned that manually entering students' information would be time-consuming ($N = 12$). Such concerns were amplified for teachers with larger classes: *"I would not spend even 5 min entering a bunch of data about individual students to be used in pairing later. I have 130 students - I can't imagine how time-consuming that would be"* (T3). Some teachers mentioned privacy concerns ($N = 2$), e.g., *"I am also concerned about the type of data the system will ask for in regards to students. Personality? Friendships? I do not think this is appropriate information to enter into an educational software system."* (T3) Accordingly, teachers wished for a more efficient, less burdensome way to achieve the same effect as manually entering the information ($N = 7$). For example, some teachers prefer *"the system to collect the data rather than enter it myself."* (T7) or *"students taking a self-assessment"* (T19).

Scenario 2 Results. In the second scenario (S2), the AI system auto-pairs students when the teacher turns on a "Do not disturb" mode in the orchestration tool, to signal they are busy helping a student. In other words, in this scenario, the AI sometimes has full autonomy over pairing decisions. S2 has the *second-lowest* stated likeliness of use among teachers ($M = 4.7$, $SD = 1.59$). There was substantial variability in teachers' answers to the question of whether teachers think the system should pair students without asking teachers' approval when they are busy. Only 37% of teachers chose "agree" or "strongly agree" ($M = 4.35$, $SD = 1.78$). The survey also asked *when* teachers preferred the AI to pair students up without asking for their approval. Most (57%) teachers chose *when helping other students*, 22% chose when they are *off work*, and 9 teachers (17%) chose *never*.

From the qualitative analysis, we found teachers generally think that auto-pairing by the co-orchestration tool when the teacher is busy could help *reduce interference and distraction* in teachers' work (e.g., *"It can effectively reduce the disturbing information for teachers"* [T46]). They also opined that it could improve their work efficiency ($N = 19$). They also liked the fact that such a system may help students to get help sooner, (e.g., *"I like the fact it can partner students without teacher action"* [T41]), engage better in class, and learn collaboratively ($N = 8$). However, many teachers had reservations about a possible auto-pair feature ($N = 32$). Specifically, some teachers did not want the system to have such a high degree of control over the pairing process and wished to be able to review the pairing, and change or override the system's pairing decisions when needed ($N = 26$). As one teacher described *"If a computer can pair students at random, then what is the point of a teacher being present? This seems to undermine the authority of a teacher in the classroom"* (T54). Some other teachers ($N = 7$) thought this feature *"seems needlessly complicated"* and preferred that the system *"just give[s]*

---

[1] N refers to the number of teachers' comments.

a notification to the side that's unobtrusive" (T10) or *"quickly ask[s] me for approval, even if I'm doing something else"* (T14).

Teachers wanted to be able to review and change the tool's proposed pairings because they wanted to ensure the pairing choices were good ($N = 9$). They thought *"there may be recent social changes that [affect] the effectiveness of the pair the software may not be able to decipher or be aware of yet"* (T11). If the system auto-paired students, teachers still wanted to be able to distinguish auto-paired students from those already approved by teachers ($N = 4$). Teachers suggested that the tool might *"put the pairing in yellow to show that [they] would not have gotten paired if the teacher was not busy"* (T26). Along with the teachers' preference for being able to front-load preparation tasks, teachers said they wanted to be able to set up *restricted pairing* (i.e., *"pairs that should not happen no matter what."* [T8]) and *pre-approved* pairings ($N = 5$). Teachers also wanted to monitor students' pairing status and collaboration progress ($N = 4$), *"It would help to not only see who students are working with but also what they are working on"* [T5].

Scenario 3 Results. In the third Scenario (S3), the system proposes a student pairing, shows the teacher details of why these students might work together, and asks the teacher to approve or reject the pairing (Fig. 2). S3 was the *most* favorable scenario among teachers ($M = 5.89, SD = 1.13$). The survey asked in a seven-point Likert scale question whether the system should *explain* its reasoning behind the suggested pairing. 77% of teachers agreed or strongly agreed, and only one (2%) teacher disagreed to some extent ($M = 6.07, SD = 0.93$). The survey probed further into what information teachers wanted to see *when approving or rejecting a pairing*. Most teachers responded they wanted to see students' math skill mastery (94%), the problem each student is working on (92%), and students' recent errors (88%). They were much less interested in seeing factors such as students' personality (40%), friendship (32%), and gender (27%) when approving proposed pairings.

Qualitative analysis showed that teachers' overall attitudes towards the scenario were overwhelmingly positive. The majority of teachers ($N = 38$) liked the idea that the system would suggest pairs and give reasoning and justification for the suggested pairs. One teacher expressed, *"THIS IS AMAZING!!! If the system shows me reasonings based on evidence on why [I should] pair some students I would consider it. I love this idea!"* (T43). Teachers found explanations (the scenario did not specify the particular type of explanations) to be valuable as it *"might be something the teacher doesn't realize"* (T1) and could *"provide another pair of eyes"* (T12). Teachers liked that the technology might ensure pairing quality and thought it could increase their work efficiency ($N = 10$). They also liked the idea that in this scenario, even though the system would suggest a pairing, teachers would *have full control* to make final decisions, and the ability to approve or deny the pairing ($N = 11$).

Some teachers ($N = 13$) expressed ideas to further improve this scenario, such as the ability to change pairings occasionally. They also wanted the tool to provide an easy way to find an alternative partner for a student ($N = 2$), such as providing *"a list of other students who would be good pairs"* (T3), or *"a button where I can ask the program to suggest another pair in case I don't like the pair that it suggested"* (T9). Teachers also wanted the system to be accessible (e.g., providing both English and Spanish translation), and compatible with their current contexts and practices (e.g., *"...be able to run on tablets, phones and computers* [T43]" ($N = 4$).

Scenario 4 Results. In the fourth scenario (S4), students suggest their preferred partner, the AI reviews the pairing and notifies teachers of potentially risky pairings (i.e., pairings that may not lead to fruitful collaboration). The teacher then approves or rejects risky pairings and the system pairs all students based on the teacher's decisions. This scenario has the second-highest likeliness of use among teachers ($M = 5.33, SD = 1.41$). One of the survey questions asked teachers whether they thought the AI should *notify* them when student pairings are potentially risky and ask them to decide. Most teachers (70%) agreed or strongly agreed ($M = 5.72, SD = 1.19$). The survey further asked how teachers wanted students to be notified when they (teachers) rejected student-proposed risky pairings. Some teachers (28%) wanted students to simply be paired with a different partner without further explanation. A similar number of teachers wanted students to be told that *teachers and AI* together rejected the pairing (30%), or the *teachers* rejected their pairings (20%). Some teachers (15%) want students to be told the *AI* rejected their pairing, even though it was, in fact, the teachers who would do so, showing some of them may prefer students to "blame" the AI instead of teachers for not being paired with their preferred partner.

Qualitative analysis showed that teachers' generally viewed the technology used in this scenario in a positive light ($N = 37$). They especially liked that this technology valued students' voice in proposing peer tutors ($N = 16$) and that the systems could act as a safety net and detect if the student-proposed pairings are risky ($N = 13$). Similar to S3, teachers liked the fact that they can make final decisions to approve and reject pairings ($N = 8$). Although teachers thought students' voices were essential ($N = 16$), some were concerned that students' pairing decisions may not be ideal for their learning ($N = 13$). Moreover, many teachers were concerned that rejecting student-proposed pairs may *"affect the relationship between teachers and students and cause unnecessary trouble"* (T53). For example, one teacher thought that *"students should not be able to request in the program. This can lead to many problems in a middle school classroom. Misuse, hurt feelings, etc."* (T1). Teachers also wanted to see the pairing history and results from analysis ($N = 9$; e.g., *"It is hoped that the history of student matchmaking can be added"* [T46]).

Scenario 5 Results. In the fifth scenario (S5), the teachers pair students to work collaboratively, and the AI system reviews teacher-proposed pairings. The AI changes the teachers' proposed pairing when it detects a risky pairing without notifying teachers. S5 was the *least* favorable and most controversial scenario, having both the lowest mean likeliness of use and the highest SD ($M = 4.00, SD = 1.76$). To separate design elements teachers like and dislike, the survey then asked teachers on a 7-point Likert scale if the AI should *review* their proposed student pairings. To this, 47% teachers agreed or strongly agreed ($M = 4.87, SD = 1.64$). However, when asked whether the system should *override* teachers' proposed pairing if it determined a pair was potentially risky, only 15% agreed or strongly agreed, and 44% of teachers disagreed or strongly disagreed ($M = 3.39, SD = 1.86$).

Qualitative analysis showed that teachers' preferences regarding the technology used in the scenario were very divergent. Some teachers liked the fact that the technology could serve as an extra pair of eyes and help them make reasonable pairings ($N = 7$). About one-fifth of teachers expressed that a system that changes risky pairs for teachers can increase teachers' efficiency ($N = 10$). However, the majority of teachers indicated they would decline to use this technology design in their classroom because it would give them too little control ($N = 53$). Specifically, teachers want to have the final say and ultimate control over student pairing; they think they know their students the best and trust their judgment more than the system's ($N = 10$). One teacher explained, *"As a teacher, I will decide what to do and not to do. System modifying without notifying is not the service I am seeking for"* (T5). Instead, teachers wanted the system to *notify* them when it would change their proposed pairings, and allow them to override the system's decisions ($N = 21$).

3.2 Other Results on Teachers' Preferences on Hybrid Control in Pairing

We report how teachers want to share the control of *proposing* and *deciding* with AI and students (RQ1), as stated in the *general preferences* section of the survey.

Regarding **who should propose pairings**, most teachers (90%) think *teachers* should be involved. Interestingly, more teachers thought the *system* (76%) should be involved than *students* should be involved (53%). In addition, 80% of teachers thought suggesting or proposing student pairing should be *shared*. Among them, the two most popular co-orchestration choices were sharing control *between teacher, student, and system* (41%), or *between teacher and system* (30%). Regarding **who should make the final decisions** about pairings, 95% of the teachers thought *teachers* should be the ones to do so. Only two teachers (4%) thought students should make the final decision about student pairing, and only one thought the system should.

4 Discussion

4.1 Insights Related to the Research Questions

We discuss the roles teachers think each agent (i.e., teacher, AI system, students) should or should not take when co-orchestrating dynamic pairing (RQ1), and their preferences regarding dynamic pairing criteria (RQ2).

Teachers' Role. Across all scenarios, teachers prefer to *prepare for student pairing before class, make final pairing decisions,* and *customize the orchestration tool*. Firstly, teachers want to contribute knowledge to help pair up students and to front-load such preparation work prior to class. They want to set pairing restrictions (i.e., identify students who should not be teamed up) and pre-approve pairings. However, many teachers, especially those who teach large classes, do not want to enter information into the system to help the AI pair students, as it may have privacy concerns, or maybe too time-consuming. Given the survey question did not specify either the type or the amount of student information teachers would need to enter, it seems possible that many teachers might be willing to enter a small amount of information, in line with Olsen's finding from co-design studies with teachers [19]. Thus a simple and time-efficient design that allows teachers to set restricted and pre-approved pairings may be needed. Secondly, teachers want to be able to review and modify student pairings proposed by other agents; they strongly want to have the final say. Thirdly, teachers want to be able to customize and configure the co-orchestration tool (e.g., pairing criteria, frequency of changing pairs), to fit their classroom context.

AI Systems' Role. Teachers like the AI to propose personalized pairings, explain the reasoning behind proposed pairings, help evaluate proposed pairings, and lessen teachers' orchestration load. They do not want the AI to make final pairing decisions. Teachers like for the system to propose pairings that are personalized to each student's characteristics. The top three factors that teachers think the system should consider in dynamic pairing are students' knowledge mastery, overall error rate, and past pairing partners. Teachers consider students' friendships, relationships, and gender to be less important in pairing. Most teachers want to use different criteria for different students, suggesting students' characteristics may be weighed in the pairing decision in a manner that varies by situation.

Additionally, teachers want to see reasoning and explanations for why the AI proposes to pair two students or considers a pair to be risky. Teachers want the AI system to act as an extra pair of eyes to review and evaluate proposed pairings, no matter if they are student-proposed or teacher-proposed. Furthermore, teachers want the AI system to lessen their orchestration load, increase work flexibility (e.g., by allowing them to front-load pairing preparation tasks), and minimize distractions while working with students. Interestingly, while teachers want to reduce students' time waiting for their help, they do not all agree that the AI should auto-pair students even when they are busy. Though teachers like being assisted by the AI, most teachers rejected the idea for the AI to pair students without teachers' review or approval.

Students' Role. Teachers see value in allowing students to have a say in the pairing process and provide feedback on pairing, as *"students are more likely to be productive if they are given the opportunity to have a sense of ownership in their partnership"* (T23). One teacher mentioned it may be helpful to notify teachers if *"one partner was unwilling to work [with another student]"* (T41). Compared to teachers' and AI's roles, teachers made fewer comments about the role that students should have, which may be explained by the fact that we have more scenarios describing teacher-AI co-orchestration than student-AI or teacher-student-AI.

4.2 Design Challenges and Directions

Design Challenges. Our findings uncover several *design challenges*. First, teachers' wish to reduce students' waiting time and avoid being the bottleneck blocking students' progress suggests that some degree of system autonomy may be needed. The design challenge is to do so without letting teachers feel their authority in class is threatened. Secondly, there may be a tension between teachers' desired awareness and control, and their desires to avoid interference and distraction when working with students. Relatedly, since teachers often need to make fast decisions when teaching and managing classroom activities, there may be limited time for them to "consume and digest" explanations systems give. It may be necessary to investigate what information will be most helpful to teachers in these explanations and create a design that provides interpretable explanations at a glance. These explanations should take teachers minimal time to read and interpret, *and* still give teachers enough evidence to support their decisions (e.g., approving or rejecting pairings). Finally, it may be hard for a co-orchestration tool to allow students to have a say in pairing decisions and ensure teachers have the final say while avoiding harming teacher-student relationships if students' proposals are rejected.

Design Directions. In connection with the three tasks in dynamic pairing - *propose, evaluate and decide* pairing (Fig. 1, right), our study three design directions, including having the AI system *be a teacher's helper that explains its reasoning (Propose), be an extra pair of eyes (Evaluate),* and *notify instead of deciding (Decide)*.

Firstly, it may be fruitful for the AI system to monitor the class and help teachers to prioritize their attention to those who need it the most. For example, if the AI can keep track of students' working progress and pairing needs, and display the class' status to the teacher in *"a queue with time of any students not already being paired"* (T8), it may help teachers to prioritize so students get help sooner than when no AI-monitor is involved. A promising direction is for the AI helper to explain its reasoning when proposing or suggesting certain educational decisions.

Secondly, while teachers want to have the final say in educational decisions (e.g., student pairing), they want the AI to provide an extra pair of eyes, capture things that may escape teachers' consideration, and augment teachers' memory as a form of "distributed cognition." For example, given an AI can keep track of student pairing history, it may suggest to teachers whether or not two students should be paired again. The AI can base its suggestions on the total number of times students have been paired and perhaps their past collaboration quality, information that teachers may not readily have.

Lastly, our study suggests that it may be fruitful to use the AI systems to *notify* teachers of worrying classroom activities that are worth their attention (e.g., risky pairings or unproductive students), and ask them to make final decisions. This may prove much more preferable for teachers than if the AI makes decisions, as it ensures teacher awareness and control. More iterative work is needed to design the orchestration tool, attending to both teachers' preferences and practical feasibility of different pairing policies [20] for pairing students in a given classroom.

4.3 Implications and Outlook

Firstly, this study confirmed, with larger sample size, findings from prior design research and classroom studies [3, 4, 11, 12] that teachers want to: 1) have the final say over pairing students, 2) enable students to get help from other sources when teachers are busy, 3) flexibly front-load preparation tasks for collaborative activities *before class*, and 4) minimize interruptions and orchestration load *during class*. Secondly, we uncover new insights into teachers' needs regarding how to share aspects of dynamic pairing with the AI and with students. The insights include 1) teachers want to see brief reasoning given by the system in at least two situations: when the AI system proposes a pairing, and when it detects a risky pairing. 2) Although teachers want to contribute to student pairings, they are concerned that entering student information into the system may be time-consuming. Thirdly, this study explored how teachers' preferences of orchestration control may depend on certain *dynamic contexts,* including when teachers are busy, when risky pairings occur, when the teacher (S5), system (S2,3), student (S4) proposed pairings.

Future Work. Future work may explore 1) how the dynamic pairing criteria can be personalized based on factors such as class context, students' characteristics, or teachers' demographics and expertise, 2) how co-orchestration tools may afford customizability and adaptability in areas *where teachers have varied opinions,* e.g., whether and how students should be "allowed" to propose pairings, and 3) whether teachers' opinions would change under the time pressure when using the tools in the classroom (e.g., whether and how teachers still wish to review explanations from AI).

5 Conclusion

As researchers start envisioning more sophisticated and personalized interactions in future smart classrooms, fluid social transition become an interesting issue to study [20]. We contribute to the literature of orchestration for fluid social transitions and dynamic pairing. Based on results of the user-centered, mixed-method research through surveying 54 math teachers, the current study extends and complements prior research in human-AI co-orchestration by validating teachers' preferences with a larger sample size, revealing new, nuanced, and context-dependent needs and preferences, and proposing design implications. As the community increasingly adopts a co-orchestration lens to leverage human and AI's complementary strength to achieve synergy, we are hopeful that teacher needs validated and uncovered in this study can help inform future design and research of tools.

Acknowledgement. This work was supported in part by Grant #1822861 from the National Science Foundation (NSF). Any opinions presented in this article are those of the authors and do not represent the views of the NSF. We thank all participating teachers and the anonymous reviewers.

References

1. Hämäläinen, R., Vähäsantanen, K.: Theoretical and pedagogical perspectives on orchestrating creativity and collaborative learning. Educ. Res. Rev. **6**, 169–184 (2011). https://doi.org/10.1016/j.edurev.2011.08.001
2. van Leeuwen, A., Rummel, N.: Orchestration tools to support the teacher during student collaboration: a review. Unterrichtswissenschaft **47**(2), 143–158 (2019). https://doi.org/10.1007/s42010-019-00052-9

3. Olsen, J.K., Rummel, N., Aleven, V.: Designing for the co-orchestration of social transitions between individual, small-group and whole-class learning in the classroom. Int. J. Artif. Intell. Educ. **31**(1), 24–56 (2020). https://doi.org/10.1007/s40593-020-00228-w
4. Santos, L.P.P.: Supporting orchestration of blended CSCL scenarios in distributed learning environments (2012)
5. Holstein, K., Olsen, J.K.: Human–AI co-orchestration: the role of artificial intelligence in orchestration. In: Handbook of Artificial Intelligence in Education. Edward Elgar Publishing (2021)
6. Tissenbaum, M., Slotta, J.: Supporting classroom orchestration with real-time feedback: a role for teacher dashboards and real-time agents. Int. J. Comput.-Support. Collab. Learn. **14**(3), 325–351 (2019). https://doi.org/10.1007/s11412-019-09306-1
7. Sharples, M.: Shared orchestration within and beyond the classroom. Comput. Educ. **69**, 504–506 (2013). https://doi.org/10.1016/j.compedu.2013.04.014
8. Holstein, K., McLaren, B.M., Aleven, V.: Intelligent tutors as teachers' aides: exploring teacher needs for real-time analytics in blended classrooms. In: Proceedings of the Seventh International Learning Analytics & Knowledge Conference, pp. 257–266. Association for Computing Machinery, New York (2017)
9. Alavi, H.S., Dillenbourg, P., Kaplan, F.: Distributed awareness for class orchestration. In: Cress, U., Dimitrova, V., Specht, M. (eds.) Learning in the Synergy of Multiple Disciplines, pp. 211–225. Springer, Heidelberg (2009). https://doi.org/10.1007/978-3-642-04636-0_21
10. Martinez-Maldonado, R., Clayphan, A., Yacef, K., Kay, J.: MTFeedback: providing notifications to enhance teacher awareness of small group work in the classroom. IEEE Trans. Learn. Technol. **8**, 187–200 (2015). https://doi.org/10.1109/TLT.2014.2365027
11. Echeverria, V., Holstein, K., Huang, J., Sewall, J., Rummel, N., Aleven, V.: Exploring human–AI control over dynamic transitions between individual and collaborative learning. In: Alario-Hoyos, C., Rodríguez-Triana, M.J., Scheffel, M., Arnedillo-Sánchez, I., Dennerlein, S.M. (eds.) EC-TEL 2020. LNCS, vol. 12315, pp. 230–243. Springer, Cham (2020). https://doi.org/10.1007/978-3-030-57717-9_17
12. Holstein, K., McLaren, B.M., Aleven, V.: Designing for complementarity: teacher and student needs for orchestration support in AI-enhanced classrooms. In: Isotani, S., Millán, E., Ogan, A., Hastings, P., McLaren, B., Luckin, R. (eds.) AIED 2019. LNCS (LNAI), vol. 11625, pp. 157–171. Springer, Cham (2019). https://doi.org/10.1007/978-3-030-23204-7_14
13. Holstein, K., McLaren, B., Aleven, V.: Student learning benefits of a mixed-reality teacher awareness tool in AI-enhanced classrooms. In: Rosé, C.P., et al. (eds.) AIED 2018. LNCS (LNAI), vol. 10947, pp. 154–168. Springer, Cham (2018). https://doi.org/10.1007/978-3-319-93843-1_12
14. Davidoff, S., Lee, M.K., Dey, A.K., Zimmerman, J.: Rapidly exploring application design through speed dating. In: Krumm, J., Abowd, G.D., Seneviratne, A., Strang, T. (eds.) UbiComp 2007. LNCS, vol. 4717, pp. 429–446. Springer, Heidelberg (2007). https://doi.org/10.1007/978-3-540-74853-3_25
15. Holstein, K., Aleven, V., Rummel, N.: A conceptual framework for human–AI hybrid adaptivity in education. In: Bittencourt, I.I., Cukurova, M., Muldner, K., Luckin, R., Millán, E. (eds.) AIED 2020. LNCS (LNAI), vol. 12163, pp. 240–254. Springer, Cham (2020). https://doi.org/10.1007/978-3-030-52237-7_20
16. van Leeuwen, A., et al.: Orchestration tools for teachers in the context of individual and collaborative learning: what information do teachers need and what do they do with it? In: Symposium at ICLS (2018)
17. Sankaranarayanan, S., et al.: Designing for learning during collaborative projects online: tools and takeaways. Inf. Learn. Sci. **121**, 569–577 (2020). https://doi.org/10.1108/ILS-04-2020-0095

18. Miles, M.B., Huberman, A.M., Saldana, J.: Qualitative Data Analysis: A Methods Sourcebook. Sage, Thousand Oaks (2013)
19. Olsen, J.: Orchestrating combined collaborative and individual learning in the classroom. https://kilthub.cmu.edu/ndownloader/files/12255413
20. Yang, K.B., et al.: Exploring policies for dynamically teaming up students through log data simulation. In: Educational Data Mining (2021)

What Do Learning Designs Show About Pedagogical Adoption? An Analysis Approach and a Case Study on Inquiry-Based Learning

María Jesús Rodríguez-Triana[(✉)], Luis P. Prieto, and Gerti Pishtari

Tallinn University, Tallinn, Estonia
{mjrt,lprisan,gpishtar}@tlu.ee

Abstract. The usage of educational technologies does not necessarily imply the adoption of the pedagogical approaches they are designed to support. Existing works analysing learning design practices often focus on the usage metrics of the authoring platform, the authoring process or structural aspects of the designs themselves. While such usage metrics are useful to understand technology adoption, to understand pedagogical adoption we need to take into account the content of the designs created by practitioners as well. For example, in the case of inquiry-based learning, such content-related aspects include whether the learning designs scaffold the inquiry, promote engagement and collaboration. This paper proposes a concrete content-oriented design analysis approach for inquiry-based learning, which can be applied to digitally-authored inquiry designs. To illustrate its application and usefulness, we have applied this framework to learning designs created within Go-Lab (an initiative to promote inquiry learning in primary and secondary school). More concretely, we manually analyzed 44 learning designs published by Estonian practitioners using content analysis. Despite the small scale of the illustrative case study, the results from the content analysis show the potential of our analytical approach to inform teacher training and the development of authoring tools.

Keywords: Learning design · Inquiry-based learning · Content analysis · Conceptual framework · Pedagogical adoption

1 Introduction

Critical thinking is an essential skill for citizens to face current global challenges like fake news and misinformation. To promote such critical thinking, we can guide learners to apply the scientific method, helping them to make informed decisions in a systematic way [23]. Inquiry-based learning (IBL) can be especially valuable in this regard, helping learners to develop their questioning skills, make hypotheses, design experiments, and extract conclusions from the data gathered, and to reflect on its implications and the learning process itself. Although this pedagogical approach has many benefits, it is notoriously demanding for teachers, who need to scaffold the inquiry process to be more effective [16], promote engagement [3], and often combine individual and collaborative work [13].

There have been attempts in the field of Learning Design to support teachers in implementing IBL, providing them not only with guidelines [10] but also with digital platforms that scaffold the design process (e.g., nQuire, weSPOT, WISE, Graasp, and TraceReaders). While we often measure the adoption of these platforms by looking at usage metrics or amounts of artifacts created, these numbers do not necessarily tell us whether and how practitioners are actually adopting the pedagogical approach itself. In fact, while technology may play a supportive role, what leads to better learning is *how* those platforms are used [1]. Existing work in the area of Learning Design has also analysed the authoring process, for example, to understand how social practices relate to IBL adoption in the classroom [19]. Other authors have investigated the structural components of teacher IBL designs, looking at, e.g., the kind of media and apps included in them [9]. Yet, in order to understand *pedagogical* adoption, it is also necessary to look at the specific *content* and activities proposed by teachers in the designs, analysing scaffolding [16], engagement [3] and collaborative aspects [13]. The results of such content-oriented analyses would help IBL tool providers to identify the most challenging aspects of the pedagogy, and to design technologies and training that can better support teachers in IBL implementation.

To reach that goal, this paper proposes an analysis approach to better understand the adoption of core IBL aspects, within teacher-generated (IBL) designs. To illustrate its usefulness, we have carried out a case study in the context of Go-Lab, a European initiative devoted to promote IBL in primary and secondary schools. In Go-Lab, thousands of teachers from around the world can create, implement and share their designs. More concretely, we have analysed the learning designs published in the context of one European country (Estonia), looking at whether they scaffold the inquiry, promote engagement and collaboration.

The paper is structured as follows: Sect. 2 provides an overview of existing research analysing learning designs and on core aspects of IBL designs to be included in our analytical approach (Sect. 3); Sect. 4 focuses on the illustrative case study of applying our analytical approach; and finally, Sect. 5 provides a wrap-up of the main implications and future work.

2 Related Work

2.1 Learning Design Analysis

There exist a plethora of tools developed to support the learning design process. Systematic literature reviews on the adoption of learning design tools concluded that tool evaluations have mainly focused on the effectiveness of the methods proposed to support the design process, as well as on technical aspects (e.g., usability) [4,17]. However, they also note that the underlying pedagogical approaches and practitioners' actual design practices remained under-explored. To better understand the pedagogical adoption of learning design tools, researchers have recently analyzed elements of the authoring process itself, as well as structural components of its end product (i.e., the learning design artifacts).

For instance, various authors have also analyzed learning designs elements to evaluate the impact that pedagogical decisions had on students' performance, such as Toetenel and Rienties [25]that analyzed the types of learning activities included in the designs, or Nguyen et al. [15] that analyzed the configuration of the designs over time. Based on the analysis of traces from the design process and the structure of digital design artifacts, de Jong et al. [9] found that designs that practitioners had shared or co-created with peers, tended to be richer in content (e.g., being more pedagogically mature, or including more resources). In a parallel example, Rodrguez-Triana et al. [19] analyzed digital traces of practitioners' social practices during the design, and how they related to the adoption of specific pedagogical approaches (such as IBL). They concluded that practices of scaffolding (i.e., when teachers require/receive guidance) and maturation (e.g. when teachers exchange ideas and collaborate during the design) were positively related to the usage of those learning designs in the classroom. Yet, they acknowledge that there is still a need for complementary research that qualitatively analyses the *content* of the design artifacts [19]. Such content-oriented analyses, when guided by relevant theoretical models and frameworks, may inform about practitioners' design practices and needs which may promote (or impede) adoption. In the following subsections, we discuss several such models and frameworks that are particularly relevant for IBL design analysis.

2.2 Pedagogical Guidelines for IBL

In traditional educational approaches, the responsibility for the learning process rested on the teacher and learners played a passive, receptive role. In contrast, constructivist approaches to learning, such as IBL, highlight the importance of transferring part of that responsibility to the learner, who should be actively involved in the learning process [27]. In this line, the ICAP framework categorizes engagement into one of four modes [3]: interactive[1], constructive, active[2], and passive (see definitions and examples in Table 1). These four modes are organized hierarchically, meaning that interactive behaviors subsume constructive behaviors, constructive behaviors subsume active ones, and active behaviors subsume passive ones. According to the studies carried out by Chi and Wylie [3], when learners become more engaged with the learning materials, from passive to active to constructive to interactive, their learning increases. But as the authors mention, the framework has instructional implications, being necessary to encourage and lead the learners to engage in making sense of the learning activity.

---

[1] Note that "interactive engagement" refers to dialogues (between humans or a human and a computer agent) where both partners' utterances are constructive, and there is a sufficient degree of turn taking [3].

[2] Note the difference between "active engagement" (motoric actions that require learners to manipulate the learning material [3]) and "active learning" (the constructivist approach where the learner is actively involved in the learning process [27]).

Hattie and Donoghue [6], based on a meta-analysis of existing educational literature, highlight less favourable effect sizes for forms of active learning (like IBL) when they are introduced in the curriculum when the necessary surface knowledge has not yet been acquired. Also, Schneider and Preckel [21] in their meta-synthesis of research studies, found that prior instruction is a moderator variable for the effectiveness of engaged forms of learning such as problem-based and inquiry learning. It seems, therefore, likely that IBL needs to be a guided process [8,11,22]. However, providing such guidance to IBL is not straightforward. It requires more advanced competence and knowledge from teachers. Providing practitioners with best learning design practices and adequate technical solutions is paramount to promote effective adoption [22].

In order to guide IBL, the learning process is often organized into inquiry phases similar to those in the scientific method. In their review, Pedaste et al. identified five typical inquiry phases: orientation, conceptualization, investigation, conclusion, and discussion (see their description in Table 1) [16]. All phases could interleave communication [1,16] or collaboration [1,13] with peers, teachers, etc. Among other purposes, these interactions allow learners to co-design an experiment, receive feedback about their learning process, share their domain-related outcomes and process-related ideas with others. In terms of the social nature of the learning, Lakkala et al. identified four categories: individual activities, individual products, collective activities, and collective products [13]. Also, looking at the kind of activity carried out, learners may be requested to talk, work, or share materials with others[3].

3 A Content Analytic Approach for IBL Designs

How to analyze a learning design to understand whether the learning experience will be an effective inquiry (and hence, whether the designing teachers have successfully adopted the IBL pedagogy into their practice)? Drawing from the strands of IBL guidelines mentioned in the previous section, we can define four main aspects to be analyzed in the designs:

1. Whether the designed learning activities actually *guide* learners through the phases of a scientific inquiry (orientation, conceptualization, investigation, conclusion and discussion) [16]. This requires not only to look at the labels of the design's structure (e.g., a design section called "investigation"), but also to corroborate that what is asked of students in that activity is of the appropriate nature (i.e., that it really asks students to investigate a phenomenon, including, e.g., data collection).
2. What level of *engagement* do the learning activities proposed by the teacher actually require from learners? Let us remember that IBL cannot be passive, it requires active engagement (and even more, constructive and interactive engagement) [3]. Again, an in-depth look at what activities are proposed by the teacher in the design, is needed to determine this issue.

---
[3] IPAC framework: http://www.mobilelearningtoolkit.com/app-rubric1.html.

3. Following the work of Lakkala et al. [13], we can delve into whether the teacher-designed learning experience is *social in nature*, by looking at whether the activities and/or the learner-generated products, are individual or collective.
4. Communication is a critical, cross-cutting activity in any inquiry [16]. Therefore, we can also look at the nature of the *collaborative activities* featured in the IBL design, analyzing whether learners are asked to talk with each other, share material, or rather go into more constructivist activities where they work together to create or modify content.

These four dimensions can be operationalized into, e.g., a coding scheme for content analysis by researchers or IBL platform providers. Table 1 provides an example codebook for such a content analysis, outlining the dimensions above, common codes, their definitions and typical examples of IBL design elements that would be categorized under those codes.

It is worth noting that, although such content analysis will be most likely performed manually by humans (as in the illustrative case study that follows). Yet, the real potential and usefulness of this approach for IBL platforms and initiatives is to be able to eventually perform platform-wide automated analyses of learning designs using similar schemes. Recent advances in automated content analysis, exploiting natural language processing (NLP) and machine learning, are starting to make such automated approaches a very tangible possibility (e.g., the automated analysis of mobile learning designs featured in [18]).

4 Case Study: An Analysis of Estonian Learning Designs

To illustrate the application of our analytical approach, this section presents how we used it in a case study to better understand the adoption of IBL among practitioners publishing their learning designs in Go-Lab, in the Estonian context. The section is structured as follows: first, we briefly present the context of the case study and the methodology used; later, we summarize the results obtained from the content analysis process. The section ends with a discussion of the main findings and implications of applying this approach, for the particular case study context.

4.1 Technological Context: Go-Lab

Go-Lab is a European initiative to promote IBL in primary and secondary schools. The Go-Lab ecosystem is made up of two platforms: Golabz[4], a repository where teachers can find apps, labs, learning designs ready to be used, and support materials; and Graasp[5], a platform for authoring and implementing learning designs in the classroom.

---

[4] Go-Lab repository: https://www.golabz.eu.
[5] Go-Lab authoring tool: https://graasp.eu.

Table 1. Codebook for the content-oriented analysis of IBL designs.

Category	Code name	Code description	Code examples in an IBL design
Engagement [3]	Passive	Learners receive information from instructional materials without overtly doing anything else related to learning.	Listening, observing, reading, watching an animation.
	Active	Learners do overt motoric action or physical manipulation. It does not necessarily entail the creation of a learning product.	Making notes, talking, answering a quiz, playing a video, using a lab/app, using instruments (e.g., an observation sheet) and devices (e.g., meters, scales, chronometers ...).
	Constructive	Learners generate externalized products beyond what was provided in the learning materials.	Creating a concept map/hypothesis, elaborating the answer to a question
	Interactive	Learners dialogue with another person or intelligent system. It does not necessarily entail the creation of a learning product.	Being in a dialogue, arguing, discussing, answering a quizz that provides automatic feedback.
Social nature [13]	Individual activities	Learners are asked to accomplish certain activities individually, not necessarily involving the creation of a learning product.	Reading a text, watching a video, measuring temperature/distance/...
	Individual product	Learners are asked to produce an individual product.	Collecting data, making observations, writing down answers, reporting results.
	Collective activities	Learners are asked to accomplish certain activities with other people (e.g., peers, teacher, parents, ...), not necessarily involving the creation of a learning product.	Brainstorming, discussing, doing coordinated activities, presenting ideas/results in group, providing feedback to each other.
	Collective product	Learners are asked to produce a collective product with other people (e.g., other peers, teacher, parents, ...).	Co-creating learning products such as reports, slides, concept maps, ...
Collaborative activity	Talking	Learners are asked to talk (but not necessarily share material or work together) to achieve a certain learning goal.	Brainstorming, discussing, providing feedback
	Sharing material	Learners are asked to share material with other peers (but not necessarily to talk or work with them) to achieve a certain learning goal.	Sharing learning products such as concept maps, observations, pictures, reports, presentations, ...
	Working together to create or modify content	Learners are asked to work together to achieve a certain learning goal.	Coordinated activities where each student has to do a different task (e.g., measuring, taking notes, ...), and joint creation of learning products (e.g., answer questions, concept maps, ...).
Inquiry phases [16]	Orientation	The process of stimulating curiosity about a topic and addressing a learning challenge through a problem statement.	This phase usually contains: textual descriptions, pictures or videos presenting the problem; the motivation/purpose/goal of the learning design; and/or an introduction to the activity.
	Conceptualization	The process of generating research questions and/or hypotheses regarding a stated problem.	This phase usually contains: apps to create hypotheses, research questions or concept maps.
	Investigation	The process of planning exploration or experimentation, collecting and analysing data based on the experimental design or exploration.	This phase usually contains: guidelines to conduct the experimentation or a request to design the experiment; online labs or descriptions about the physical materials for the inquiry; apps or descriptions of the instruments for data gathering.
	Conclusion	The process of drawing conclusions from the data, comparing inferences made based on data with hypotheses or research questions.	This phase usually contains apps to extract conclusions, establishing connections with the previously posed hypotheses/questions and the gathered evidence.
	Discussion	The process of presenting findings to others and/or engaging in reflective activities.	This phase usually contains apps to report and reflect on learning process.

In Go-Lab, learning designs are by default structured according to the different phases of an inquiry process (orientation, conceptualization, investigation, conclusion and discussion, see Pedaste et al. [16]). Teachers can later modify this structure depending on their particular goals. Also, teachers can enrich each of these phases with multimedia content, apps and labs, to scaffold the learners' work (e.g., proposing hypotheses, designing an experiment, interacting with a virtual lab, collecting observations of a phenomenon, and justifying their conclusions).

As of January 2021, there were 69,835 users from 175 countries registered in Graasp, out of which 25,438 had created at least one learning design, and 4,020 had implemented a learning design at least once. By that date, teachers and IBL experts had already published more than 1,300 learning designs in Golabz, in 31 languages[6].

4.2 Methodology

While thousands of learning designs have been created by teachers in Go-Lab, to test drive our analytic approach we have chosen a set of learning designs that are publicly available (due to pragmatic concerns). Given the depth of (qualitative) analysis involved, we decided to analyze all published learning designs done by Estonian teachers (where the authors' research team is based). Analyses at the country level are especially relevant in Go-Lab and similar platforms, since this is the level at which most of the training and other actions are planned and implemented (i.e., more direct practical implications).

While this dataset of published Estonian inquiry designs is probably not representative of the typical pedagogical adoption of IBL in the Go-Lab platform, it represents, in theory, an interesting high-end reference subset of the inquiries designed by teachers in Go-Lab. In terms of knowledge maturation theory [14], formalized designs (i.e., those designed and published to be reusable by other teachers outside the narrow group that created them [19]) are the most mature—hence should abide the most by the IBL guidelines suggested in Sect. 2. Furthermore, Estonia is one of the countries with highest PISA scores in the science subject (actually, it is the top European country in this particular ranking [20]). Thus, our hypothesis at the outset of the case study was that the inquiry learning designs under analysis would have high levels of pedagogical (IBL) adoption.

To guide the content analysis, a codebook was created to support the coding team (similar to Table 1). The coders (one senior researcher and four master students) analysed the content of each phase of a learning design according to the aforementioned analytical framework. The coding process was organized in four rounds, with inter-coder reliability checks after each round. Each coding round was followed by a joint meeting where coders discussed the disagreements, reached an agreed decision, and modifications were made accordingly to the codebook (e.g., when ambiguities or new criteria for inclusion into a code arose). While English-language learning designs were analysed by all coders (in rounds

---

[6] Complete list of published learning designs: https://www.golabz.eu/spaces.

1 and 2), Estonian- and Russian-language ones were coded by only two coders (based on the language skills of coders).

Once an acceptable level of inter-coder agreement was achieved in the fourth round, and in order to determine the "ground truth" of whether a particular designed inquiry phase adheres to a particular IBL guideline/dimension in the proposed approach, the final labeling of all coders has been taken into account. Rather than use a simple majority vote, we have used "fuzzy" or "non-binary" codes, to explicitly account for the inherent uncertainty of assessing pedagogical adoption of a guideline by a teacher, by just looking at a learning design artifact.

To understand the level of pedagogical adoption of IBL in this subset of (theoretically highly mature) Go-Lab designs, simple descriptive summaries have been performed of the resulting codes, at the phase and learning design levels. Furthermore, to account for the fact that different IBL phases are expected to display activities of very different nature (e.g., discussion phases are more, in theory, likely to involve communication, than orientation ones), similar summaries have been taken for IBL phases of each kind. Given the non-binary codes used as the ground truth mentioned above, such summaries can include fractional numbers, as shown in Tables 2 and 3 (signifying that phases in which coders disagree, are considered less likely to actually represent pedagogical adoption in that dimension, than those in which coders agree).

4.3 Results

In November 12th 2020, we identified a total of 44 learning designs published by Estonian practitioners (27 of them in Estonian language, 9 in Russian and 8 in English). All in all, these 44 designs contained a total of 259 phases, i.e., close to 6 phases per design, on average. In this section, we present the results of applying the analytic approach described in Sect. 3, at two granularity levels: at the individual phase level, and at the learning design level (i.e., for each inquiry).

In relation to Chi and Wylie's hierarchy of engagement and its relation to the learning outcomes [3], in Table 2 we can see that:

- Most phases (91%) include activities requiring *passive* engagement (e.g., in the form of texts or images to be read by the learners), whose learning outcomes are often associated with minimal understanding.
- 49% of the phases present activities promoting *active* engagement (such as videos to be played or labs to manipulate), which the ICAP framework relates to shallow understanding;
- 68% of the phases contained activities envisioned to trigger *constructive* engagement (e.g., asking learners to create a hypothesis, a concept map, make observations, extract conclusions, etc.), which is associated with deep understanding and potential for learning transfer;
- 24% of the phases also include activities requiring *interactive* engagement (e.g., collaborating or discussing ideas with other peers), thus aiming at a deepest understanding with potential for novel ideas.

– Higher levels of engagement are rarer than lower levels in our dataset. Yet, looking at the learning design level, we can see that all analyzed designs reached the constructive level at least in one of their phases. Interactive levels of engagement were only reached in a part of our dataset (66% of the designs).

Regarding Lakkala's classification of social nature of learning [13], the results presented in Table 2 show that:

– Most phases include either *individual activities* (e.g., reading, playing a video, measuring, or interacting with a lab) or the *individual* creation of *products* such as hypotheses or conclusions.
– Only 9% and 3% of the phases include *collective activities or products* (e.g., a discussion or joint concept map, respectively).
– At the phase level, practitioners are more prone to include activities than to request the creation of products.
– At the learning design level, it is interesting to see that all designs include individual work, but close to 40% also involve some kind of collaboration in at least one of their phases.
– Similarly, all designs contained *both* activity and product creation (either at the individual or collaborative level).

In terms of collaboration, Table 2 shows that:

– Most phases containing collaborative work focus on talking with other peers, while sharing and working together are less frequent.
– Looking at the learning design level, we can observe similar trends.

Looking at the phases from an inquiry perspective, i.e., based on the phases proposed by Pedaste et al. [16], we can observe that:

– As shown in Table 2, some types of inquiry phases were more prominent than others, e.g., all designs contained orientation and investigation phases, 98% contained conclusion phases, 90% contained conceptualization phases, and discussion phases were somewhat less frequent (75% of analyzed designs contained one).
– In several cases, we observed overlapping between IBL phases (e.g., orientation and conceptualizations are sometimes joined in a single phase).
– We also detected that 29% of the designs contained phases devoted to purposes beyond inquiry-related ones, such as: suggesting further work, providing support or reference material, evaluation, and teacher feedback.
– Looking at how each type of IBL phase was designed in terms of engagement, Table 3 shows that, while all types of engagement appear to some extent in all IBL phases, the ratios vary widely. For example, 97% of conceptualization phases include some kind of *interactive* engagement, while only 32% of investigation phases do (indeed, it is the rarest of engagement levels there). Also, *constructive* engagement is most frequent in investigation and conclusion phases. *Active* engagement, on the other hand, is especially high in conceptualization and investigation phases.

- Based on the social nature observed in each IBL phase, we can see in Table 3 that all types of IBL phases include *individual activities* very frequently. *Individual products* were mainly associated with the conceptualization, investigation and conclusion phases, where students are normally requested to formulate research questions or hypothesis, provide evidence, and extract conclusions. At the collective level, the most prominent was the appearance of *collective activities* in orientation, investigation, and discussion phases, prompting learners to brainstorm, collectively interact with labs, and discuss their conclusions.
- In terms of collaborative work, Table 3) shows that sharing material was the least frequent option, while talking with peers the most predominant type of collaborative work across all IBL phases.

Table 2. Overview of individual phase- and learning design-level analyses of engagement, collaboration and types of IBL phases.

Category	Code	Phases (N = 259)	Learning designs (N = 44)
Engagement	Passive	236.3 (91%)	44 (100%)
	Active	126.1 (49%)	44 (100%)
	Constructive	176.9 (68%)	44 (100%)
	Interactive	61.3 (24%)	28.9 (66%)
Social nature	Individual activities	242.1 (93%)	44 (100%)
	Individual product	188.6 (73%)	43 (98%)
	Collective activities	22.2 (9%)	17.2 (39%)
	Collective product	8.7 (3%)	7.7 (18%)
Collaboration	Talking	19 (7%)	15 (34%)
	Sharing material	7.2 (3%)	7.2 (16%)
	Working together	8.2 (3%)	7.7 (18%)
IBL phase	Orientation	79.7 (31%)	44 (100%)
	Conceptualization	65.7 (25%)	39.6 (90%)
	Investigation	79.4 (31%)	44 (100%)
	Conclusion	60.3 (23%)	42.9 (98%)
	Discussion	53.1 (21%)	32.9 (75%)
	Others	18.5 (7%)	12.7 (29%)

4.4 Discussion

While initially learning designs should aim at higher levels of engagement [3], exclusively using highly complex learning tasks would yield excessive cognitive load for the learners, having a negative impact on learning, performance, and motivation [24]. Thus, the results of our case studyanalysis seem to align with

Table 3. Analysis of engagement and collaboration per type of IBL phase.

	Orientation	Conceptualization	Investigation	Conclusion	Discussion	Others
Number of phases	79.7	65.7	79.4	60.3	53.1	18.5
Passive	78.7 (99%)	61.7 (94%)	74.7 (94%)	52.2 (87%)	49.7 (94%)	10.6 (58%)
Active	43.9 (55%)	61.7 (94%)	70.7 (89%)	24.2 (40%)	23.8 (45%)	4.7 (25%)
Constructive	40.3 (51%)	34.1 (52%)	63.3 (80%)	50 (83%)	35.6 (67%)	7.8 (42%)
Interactive	29.5 (37%)	63.6 (97%)	25.1 (32%)	17.4 (29%)	19.4 (37%)	1.3 (7%)
Individual activities	77.9 (98%)	65.5 (100%)	79.1 (100%)	54.3 (90%)	49.8 (94%)	11.5 (62%)
Individual product	42.1 (53%)	62.3 (95%)	70 (88%)	55.7 (92%)	41.6 (78%)	9.6 (52%)
Collective activities	12.9 (16%)	8 (12%)	13.4 (17%)	8.5 (14%)	11.8 (22%)	0 (0%)
Collective product	6 (7%)	4.3 (7%)	3 (4%)	1.3 (2%)	6.5 (12%)	0 (0%)
Talking	13 (16%)	9 (14%)	12 (15%)	13 (22%)	16 (30%)	0 (0%)
Sharing material	6.2 (8%)	3.2 (5%)	0 (0%)	1 (2%)	6.2 (12%)	0 (0%)
Working together	7.2 (9%)	4.2 (6%)	2.5 (3%)	1.5 (2%)	7.2 (14%)	0 (0%)

the common approach of moving progressively from relatively simple to more complex learning tasks [26], requesting in each IBL phase different levels of engagement so that activities are complex enough to provide learners with new information and, on the other, easy enough so that they can integrate such information [1]. Also, we can observe that the distribution of engagement modes varies across IBL phases in our dataset, fitting generally the kind of work expected in each type of IBL phase. The main unexpected result from our case study's analysis of engagement was the *small proportion of learning designs explicitly including interactive engagement*, especially in the discussion phase where communicating with others is highly recommended [16]. Nevertheless, it is also possible that, when the learning design is implemented in the classroom, oral discussion may be prompted face-to-face (e.g., depending on the time available at the end of the session) without explicit mentions to it in the design artifact.

Regarding the social nature of inquiry learning [13] and the collaboration types identified in the IPAC framework, collective activities took most often the form of talking with peers (and, slightly less often, with sharing materials). Likewise, collective products show similar proportions than working together to create/generate content. Worth noticing is the fact that the proportion of interactive engagement more than doubles the collective and collaborative phases. This means that the interactive engagement designed into the Estonian published designs is not only with humans (mainly peers), but also with intelligent systems (such as interactive quizzes that provide automatic formative feedback and recommendations about what to do next).

While all phases could interleave communication and collaboration with peers, teachers, and other stakeholders [13,16], our results show that orientation, investigation and discussion phases involve more social interaction. However, it is surprising the *rare appearance of phases requiring working together*. Also, while most designs contained orientation, conceptualization, investigation and conclusion phases, the presence of the discussion one was unexpectedly low, meaning that *learners received less guidance to discuss their results and reflect on the inquiry* [16].

Even if the sample of learning designs under analysis may differ from the learning designs created by the average Estonian practitioner for use in their own classrooms, these findings lead us to think that it may be necessary to reinforce (e.g., in teacher training events): 1) the added value of prompting interactive engagement; 2) the benefits of collaborative work; and 3) the importance of covering and guiding the discussion phases of an inquiry. To support teachers in this endeavour, the authoring platform could also integrate feedback and recommendations to take those aspects into account (e.g., recommending interactive activities, collaborative apps, or explicitly including a discussion phase in teachers' designs).

This illustrative case study does not come without limitations. First, the size of the dataset (3.06% of the 1,436 existing by March 2021) and the sample chosen (learning designs published in the Estonian context) does not enable us to generalize about all the designs publicly available in Go-Lab. Also, the fact that we are only looking at published designs, instead of implemented ones (more than 5,000), may not provide a representative sample. Another limitation is that our coding process focuses on the (observed) intended engagement, social nature, collaboration and inquiry. However, there may be a discrepancy between how the learning activity is designed by the teacher and enacted by the learners. Thus, in the future, a content analysis of learners' activities and responses would help to confirm the coding of the learning designs. Furthermore, the "fuzzy coding" approach followed to produce the final version of the content analysis by multiple coders, is a methodological innovation whose soundness in terms of qualitative methods rigour, may be debated. Thus, this study is just a small first step to illustrate the applicability of our analytical approach, and the real potential would be to eventually automate these analyses across the whole platform.

5 Conclusions and Future Work

This paper started with the critical reflection that adoption (i.e., usage) of a learning technology does not necessarily imply the adoption of the underlying pedagogical approach such technology is design to support. Learning designs developed by teachers provide us with a rich window into the extent to which the ideas of a certain pedagogical approach has been actually adopted. Yet, practically-relevant content-oriented design analysis approaches are scarce. Our paper contributes to start addressing this challenge, focusing on one of the most challenging pedagogical approaches to orchestrate: IBL. Our illustrative case study shows how digital platform and training providers can extract pedagogical adoption insights from the analysis of teacher-created digital artifacts, and apply them to the design of technologies and training events to support teachers in this complex endeavour.

Following the idea of "analytics for learning design" [7] our future work will focus on replacing human-driven manual coding (which is laborious and time-consuming) with artificial intelligence solutions that enable us to analyze *all* designs present in a massive digital learning design platform like Graasp. We could use such wide-scale analyses to extract "community analytics" to understand how different teacher communities design and adopt IBL pedagogy differently. We could also refine and extend existing authoring tools with (built-in) personalized solutions to support practitioners in the learning design process, in a way that further develops their pedagogical skills (i.e., encouraging guidelines such as the ones presented in Sect. 2).

The particular coding scheme proposed in this paper is not meant to be definitive or exhaustive. Other complementary coding schemes could be applied, e.g., according to Bloom's [12] (on instructional goals) or the SOLO taxonomy [2] (on student understanding), or based on the instructional design model for complex learning [26] (on student cognitive load required). From the collaborative point of view, we could also analyse the learning designs using orchestration graphs [5].

Acknowledgements. This research has been partially funded by the European Union in the context of CEITER (Horizon 2020 Research and Innovation Programme, grant agreements no. 669074). The authors would like to thank the rest of the coding team (Aleksandr Trofimov, Jaanika Lukk, Katariina Vainonen, and Mariell Miilvee) for their contribution to this study.

References

1. Bell, T., Urhahne, D., Schanze, S., Ploetzner, R.: Collaborative inquiry learning: models, tools, and challenges. Int. J. Sci. Educ. **32**(3), 349–377 (2010)
2. Biggs, J.B.: Teaching for Quality Learning at University: What the Student Does. McGraw-hill Education, England (2011)
3. Chi, M.T., Wylie, R.: The ICAP framework: linking cognitive engagement to active learning outcomes. Educ. Psychol. **49**(4), 219–243 (2014)
4. Dagnino, F.M., Dimitriadis, Y.A., Pozzi, F., Asensio-Pérez, J.I., Rubia-Avi, B.: Exploring teachers' needs and the existing barriers to the adoption of learning design methods and tools: a literature survey. Br. J. Edu. Technol. **49**(6), 998–1013 (2018)
5. Dillenbourg, P.: Orchestration Graphs. EPFL Press, Lausanne (2015)
6. Hattie, J.A., Donoghue, G.M.: Learning strategies: a synthesis and conceptual model. npj Sci. Learn. **1**(1), 1–13 (2016)
7. Hernández-Leo, D., Martinez-Maldonado, R., Pardo, A., Muñoz-Cristóbal, J.A., Rodríguez-Triana, M.J.: Analytics for learning design: a layered framework and tools: analytics layers for learning design. Br. J. Edu. Technol. **3**, 153 (2018)
8. Hmelo-Silver, C.E., Duncan, R.G., Chinn, C.A.: Scaffolding and achievement in problem-based and inquiry learning: a response to Kirschner, Sweller, and Clark (2006). Educ. Psychol. **42**(2), 99–107 (2007)
9. de Jong, T., et al.: Understanding teacher design practices for digital inquiry–based science learning: the case of Go-Lab. Educ. Technol. Res. Dev. **69**(2), 417–444 (2021)
10. Kali, Y., Linn, M.C.: Technology-enhanced support strategies for inquiry learning. In: Handbook of Research on Educational Communications and Technology, pp. 145–161 (2008)
11. Kirschner, P.A., Sweller, J., Clark, R.E.: Why minimal guidance during instruction does not work: an analysis of the failure of constructivist, discovery, problem-based, experiential, and inquiry-based teaching. Educ. Psychol. **41**(2), 75–86 (2006)

12. Krathwohl, D.R.: A revision of Bloom's taxonomy: an overview. Theory Pract. **41**(4), 212–218 (2002)
13. Lakkala, M., Lallimo, J., Hakkarainen, K.: Teachers' pedagogical designs for technology-supported collective inquiry: a national case study. Comput. Educ. **45**(3), 337–356 (2005)
14. Ley, T., Maier, R., Thalmann, S., Waizenegger, L., Pata, K., Ruiz-Calleja, A.: A knowledge appropriation model to connect scaffolded learning and knowledge maturation in workplace learning settings. Vocat. Learn. **13**(1), 91–112 (2019)
15. Nguyen, Q., Rienties, B., Toetenel, L.: Unravelling the dynamics of instructional practice: a longitudinal study on learning design and VLE activities. In: Proceedings of the Seventh International Learning Analytics & Knowledge Conference, pp. 168–177 (2017)
16. Pedaste, M., et al.: Phases of inquiry-based learning: definitions and the inquiry cycle. Educ. Res. Rev. **14**, 47–61 (2015)
17. Pishtari, G., et al.: Learning design and learning analytics in mobile and ubiquitous learning: a systematic review. Br. J. Educ. Technol. **51**(4), 1078–1100 (2020)
18. Pishtari, G., Rodríguez-Triana, M.J., Prieto, L.P., Ruiz-Calleja, A., Väljataga, T.: How practitioners design for learning in mobile learning environments: two in-the-wild case studies. J. Comput. Assist. Learn. (under review)
19. Rodríguez-Triana, M.J., Prieto, L.P., Ley, T., de Jong, T., Gillet, D.: Social practices in teacher knowledge creation and innovation adoption: a large-scale study in an online instructional design community for inquiry learning. Int. J. Comput.-Support. Collab. Learn. **15**(4), 445–467 (2020)
20. Schleicher, A.: Pisa 2018: Insights and interpretations. OECD Publishing (2019)
21. Schneider, M., Preckel, F.: Variables associated with achievement in higher education: a systematic review of meta-analyses. Psychol. Bull. **143**(6), 565 (2017)
22. Schuster, D., Cobern, W.W., Adams, B.A., Undreiu, A., Pleasants, B.: Learning of core disciplinary ideas: efficacy comparison of two contrasting modes of science instruction. Res. Sci. Educ. **48**(2), 389–435 (2018)
23. Seymour, E., Hunter, A.B., Laursen, S.L., DeAntoni, T.: Establishing the benefits of research experiences for undergraduates in the sciences: first findings from a three-year study. Sci. Educ. **88**(4), 493–534 (2004)
24. Sweller, J., Van Merrienboer, J.J., Paas, F.G.: Cognitive architecture and instructional design. Educ. Psychol. Rev. **10**(3), 251–296 (1998)
25. Toetenel, L., Rienties, B.: Analysing 157 learning designs using learning analytic approaches as a means to evaluate the impact of pedagogical decision making. Br. J. Edu. Technol. **47**(5), 981–992 (2016)
26. Van Merriënboer, J.J., Kirschner, P.A., Kester, L.: Taking the load off a learner's mind: instructional design for complex learning. Educ. Psychol. **38**(1), 5–13 (2003)
27. Von Glasersfeld, E.: Cognition, construction of knowledge, and teaching. In: Matthews, M.R. (ed.) Constructivism in Science Education, pp. 11–30. Springer, Dordrecht (1998). https://doi.org/10.1007/978-94-011-5032-3_2

On the Linguistic and Pedagogical Quality of Automatic Question Generation via Neural Machine Translation

Tim Steuer[✉][iD], Leonard Bongard, Jan Uhlig, and Gianluca Zimmer

Technical University of Darmstadt, Darmstadt, Hesse, Germany
tim.steuer@kom.tu-darmstadt.de

Abstract. Allowing learners to self-assess their knowledge through questions is a well-established method to improve learning. However, many educational texts lack a sufficient amount of questions for self-studying. Hence, learners read texts passively, and learning becomes inefficient. To alleviate the lack of questions, educational technologists investigate the use of automatic question generators. However, the vast majority of automatic question generation systems consider English input texts only. Therefore, we propose a simple yet effective multilingual automatic question generator based on machine-translation techniques. We investigate the linguistic and pedagogical quality of the generated questions in a human evaluation study.

Keywords: Automatic question generation · Self-assessment technologies · Educational technology

1 Introduction

Reading is a crucial way of learning. However, readers often do not learn efficiently with texts, due to possibly misread facts or missing conceptual connections. Thus, reading texts passively is not enough to fully understand the texts' content. To help learners understand even difficult texts, actively engaging them is a useful teaching method. Hence, adjunct questions may improve the learning outcome [1]. However, many texts lack an appropriate amount of questions needed for efficient learning. State-of-the-art natural language processing techniques allow the generation of factual questions on given texts with minimal manual intervention. They receive a sentence or short paragraph and a desired answer. Given the inputs, they transform them into an appropriate question asking about the desired answer. In education, such Automatic Question Generators (AQGs) could alleviate the lack of textbook questions by generating questions on-the-fly, increasing learning efficiency. However, state-of-the-art neural network-based methods mainly work in English. Hence, in this article, we would like to address how to transfer an English AQG into other languages via neural machine translation (NMT). We investigate the linguistic and pedagogical qualities of the generated questions and explore the following research question (RQ): To what extent can a combination of NMT and AQG be utilized to generate linguistically and pedagogically sound questions about texts?

2 Related Work

The research field around AQG has recently shifted from rule-based (e.g. [7]) and template-based approaches (e.g. [10]) towards neural network-based models [5]. The main reason is the superior language generation capabilities of neural models compared to rule-based models [5]. State-of-the-art systems apply large-scale language model pre-training before fine-tuning on SQuAD to improve the general English token prediction capabilities before predicting the task [4]. In education, the LearningQ [2] and RACE [8] datasets are two large-scale datasets comprising questions with explicit educational intent. Furthermore, there have been studies exploring the educational use of neural question generation approaches in empirical studies [6,15,16]. Besides the English language, there also exist AQGs in other languages. For Japanese, using sequence-to-sequence learning and classical statistical learning techniques as AQG have been explored on a small-scale dataset with promising results [12]. Another study uses the over-generate and rank approach in Chinese, combining a rule-based system with a statistical ranking in a factual AQG, outperforming the rule-based system [9]. Recently XNLG [3] has been proposed, a multilingual neural language model pre-trained in fifteen languages. For Chinese, it has been demonstrated that if XNLG is fine-tuned for AQG on SQuAD, it can generate plausible questions [3]. However, to achieve those results, XNLG was pre-trained using computational resources often not available to researchers on a large-scale multilingual corpus [3]. If the corpus does not contain the language target for generation, there is currently no way to import it into XNLG later. Hence, in such cases, pre-training needs to be repeated. Consequently, although the multilingual model may be a good option for some languages, it heavily relies on computational resources and cannot easily be extended with novel languages later.

3 Approach

The proposed approach combines two NMT models and an AQG model. The general idea is to start with a text in a source language, translate it to English, apply the AQG on the translated text, and finally back-translate the resulting question. The input consists of small paragraphs written in the source language, and the output contains the generated question also written in the source language. The AQG takes a paragraph and an answer-candidate as input. The answer-candidate is needed to specify which question we aim to generate. Hence, before generating with the AQG, an answer-candidate must be selected. While the answer-candidate selection is an active field of research and multiple methods exist to detect promising answer-candidates in a text (e.g. [16,17]), we opt for a relatively simple approach for our initial experiments. We extract the longest noun phrase in the paragraph, expecting that it carries the most information in the small paragraphs. Having the answer-candidate and input sentence, we translate them into English using the WMT19 NMT model by Ng et al. [11]. The NMT model consists of transformer-based neural architecture that is trained in large-scale on filtered parallel corpora. It is built on top of the open-source FAIRSEQ sequence modelling toolkit and is developed to be used in research and production [13]. The neural AQG employed in our work is UNILM by Dong et al. [4]. The UNILM model consists of a transformer-network that is pre-trained on a large corpus using multi-task learning with different sequence masks [4].

4 Empirical Evaluation

The evaluation study comprises two human annotators with a background in educational sciences, annotating 80 generated questions in random order. The questions are generated for 48 educational texts, written by teachers based on Wikipedia articles, as first used by Rüdian et al. [14]. We randomly select 26 texts with a total of 80 questions from the initial 48 articles. The dataset has question-worthy sentences in the texts already marked by educational experts. During data annotation, annotators apply the hierarchical scheme by Horbach et al. [6]. We achieve a average Krippendorff's $\alpha = 0.35$ over the nine categories.

An overview of the results in the levels of the annotations scheme is given in Fig. 1. We report the results relative to the remaining questions and to all questions, since some questions will not be annotated fully, due to the hierarchical nature of the evaluation scheme. Hence the reported metrics have the form in the form *Relative% (All%)*. The provided percentages are averaged over the two annotators and it is important to notice that the bars are relative to the remaining questions in an evaluation level and not to all questions. In total, 88% of the questions are rated as semantically meaningful and understandable. The remaining 12% are rated as not understandable. We found 93% (82%) of the questions to be related to the texts' domains, and 97% (85%) of the questions to be free of language-errors. The most problematic factor on the second level was the clarity of the generated questions with: *clear* 52% (46%), *more or less clear* 32% (28%) and *not clear* 16% (14%). The majority of questions is answerable 80% (59%) with only 20% (15%) being unanswerable. Furthermore 63% (46%) of questions are accepted without rephrasing whereas 37% (27%) should be rephrased. The questions usually ask for information directly given in one position of the text 62% (35%) or in multiple positions in the text 36% (21%). Using additional external knowledge is only rarely needed 2% (1%). The information inquired is central in 82% (48%) and not central in 18% (11%). Finally, 43% (25%) of the questions would be used, 32% (19%) would *maybe* be used and 26% (15%) would not be used in an educational setting according to our experts.

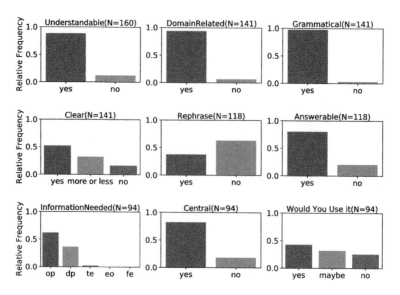

Fig. 1. The results obtained in the evaluation study. The N indicates how many questions where remaining for the bar plot of the given evaluation item.

5 Conclusion

In regard to our research question, the results highlight the important properties of the generated questions. First, the syntactic linguistic quality of the generated questions is high. The majority is understandable and free of language-errors. A look in the data suggests that the incomprehensible questions often stem from a faulty translation of domain terminology. Second, the semantic linguistic quality, the clarity of questions seems to be of concern. Although the questions were mainly answerable and domain-related, annotators found them often to be only more or less clear. In terms of the pedagogical quality, we are able to generate central factual questions aiming directly at the knowledge stated in the text in roughly 50% of all inputs. Our annotators report that they may use around 34% of all generated questions in an educational setting. Consequently, we conclude the approach generated too many pedagogically unimportant questions to give them directly to learners. Currently, we only applied basic answer selection and did not use any question re-ranking method. Related work has shown that answer selection [16] or question ranking [9] may influence the output quality significantly. In future work, we will thus explore these methods. Given sufficient question quality, the approach could then be used to recommend questions to a respective passage to a teacher. The teacher quickly evaluates which of them make sense and marks the good ones as additional self-assessment material with the click of a button.

Acknowledgements. This work is funded by the Hessian State Chancellery in the Department of Digital Strategy and Development in the Förderprogramm Distr@l (Förderprodukt: Digitale Innovations- und Technologieförderung, Förderlinie: 2A Digitale Innovationsprojekte).

References

1. Anderson, R.C., Biddle, W.B.: On asking people questions about what they are reading. In: Psychology of Learning and Motivation, vol. 9, pp. 89–132. Elsevier (1975)
2. Chen, G., Yang, J., Hauff, C., Houben, G.J.: LearningQ: a large-scale dataset for educational question generation. In: Proceedings of the International AAAI Conference on Web and Social Media, vol. 12 (2018)
3. Chi, Z., Dong, L., Wei, F., Wang, W., Mao, X.L., Huang, H.: Cross-lingual natural language generation via pre-training. In: Proceedings of the AAAI Conference on Artificial Intelligence, vol. 34, pp. 7570–7577 (2020)
4. Dong, L., et al.: Unified language model pre-training for natural language understanding and generation. arXiv preprint arXiv:1905.03197 (2019)
5. Du, X., Shao, J., Cardie, C.: Learning to ask: neural question generation for reading comprehension. arXiv preprint arXiv:1705.00106 (2017)
6. Horbach, A., Aldabe, I., Bexte, M., de Lacalle, O.L., Maritxalar, M.: Linguistic appropriateness and pedagogic usefulness of reading comprehension questions. In: Proceedings of The 12th Language Resources and Evaluation Conference, pp. 1753–1762 (2020)
7. Huang, Y., He, L.: Automatic generation of short answer questions for reading comprehension assessment. Nat. Lang. Eng. **22**(3), 457 (2016)
8. Lai, G., Xie, Q., Liu, H., Yang, Y., Hovy, E.: Race: large-scale reading comprehension dataset from examinations. arXiv preprint arXiv:1704.04683 (2017)
9. Liu, M., Rus, V., Liu, L.: Automatic Chinese factual question generation. IEEE Trans. Learn. Technol. **10**(2), 194–204 (2016)
10. Mazidi, K., Nielsen, R.D.: Pedagogical evaluation of automatically generated questions. In: Trausan-Matu, S., Boyer, K.E., Crosby, M., Panourgia, K. (eds.) ITS 2014. LNCS, vol. 8474, pp. 294–299. Springer, Cham (2014). https://doi.org/10.1007/978-3-319-07221-0_36
11. Ng, N., Yee, K., Baevski, A., Ott, M., Auli, M., Edunov, S.: Facebook fair's WMT19 news translation task submission. In: Proceedings of the Fourth Conference on Machine Translation (Volume 2: Shared Task Papers, Day 1), pp. 314–319 (2019)
12. Nio, L., Murakami, K.: Intelligence is asking the right question: a study on Japanese question generation. In: 2018 IEEE Spoken Language Technology Workshop (SLT), pp. 771–778. IEEE (2018)
13. Ott, M., et al.: fairseq: a fast, extensible toolkit for sequence modeling. arXiv preprint arXiv:1904.01038 (2019)
14. Rüdian, S., Heuts, A., Pinkwart, N.: Educational text summarizer: which sentences are worth asking for? DELFI 2020-Die 18. Fachtagung Bildungstechnologien der Gesellschaft für Informatik eV (2020)
15. Steuer, T., Filighera, A., Rensing, C.: Exploring artificial jabbering for automatic text comprehension question generation. In: Alario-Hoyos, C., Rodríguez-Triana, M.J., Scheffel, M., Arnedillo-Sánchez, I., Dennerlein, S.M. (eds.) EC-TEL 2020. LNCS, vol. 12315, pp. 1–14. Springer, Cham (2020). https://doi.org/10.1007/978-3-030-57717-9_1

16. Steuer, T., Filighera, A., Rensing, C.: Remember the facts? Investigating answer-aware neural question generation for text comprehension. In: Bittencourt, I.I., Cukurova, M., Muldner, K., Luckin, R., Millán, E. (eds.) AIED 2020. LNCS (LNAI), vol. 12163, pp. 512–523. Springer, Cham (2020). https://doi.org/10.1007/978-3-030-52237-7_41
17. Willis, A., Davis, G., Ruan, S., Manoharan, L., Landay, J., Brunskill, E.: Key phrase extraction for generating educational question-answer pairs. In: 2019 Proceedings of the Sixth ACM Conference on Learning@ Scale, pp. 1–10 (2019)

Developing a Prototype of an Open Educational Resource on Research Methods for PhD Candidates in Technology-Enhanced Learning

Lorena Sousa(✉) , Luís Pedro , and Carlos Santos

University of Aveiro, Aveiro, Portugal

Abstract. Open Educational Resources (OER) are teaching and learning materials that are licensed to provide everyone the access to engage with them in several manners, such as adapting and reusing it. This work aims at developing an OER to support PhD candidates' learning of research methods in Technology-enhanced Learning (TEL) as part of the Doctoral Education in Technology-enhanced Learning (DE-TEL) project. A survey was conducted by the DE-TEL project to collect information on the practices and challenges of doctoral education in TEL and to find out the topics that are relevant to the area but have few educational materials available. Preliminary results reveal that 103 PhD candidates from 25 different countries answered the survey. The main topic of their research in TEL is computing or information technology applied to learning, and the most relevant research method is design-based research. For this reason, a prototype of the OER module about design-based research is being designed and developed first. This paper presents the first outline of the prototype using the H5P tool, an open source and free to use tool that enables authors to create, share and reuse interactive HTML5 content, without the need for any technical skills. Then, this module is going to be piloted and evaluated by PhD candidates, so that the complete OER can be planned and created, encompassing the most relevant research methods to doctoral programs in TEL.

Keywords: Open Educational Resource · Research methods · Technology-enhanced learning

1 Theoretical Background

Technology-enhanced learning (TEL) is considered an interdisciplinary field of research since it intersects several disciplines related to teaching and learning, such as education and psychology, and technology, such as computer science and information science [1]. Kalz and Specht [2, pp. 416] recognize TEL "as an interdisciplinary research field rooted in several academic disciplines like educational science, psychology/cognitive science, and computer science." In short, TEL investigates how technology can be used in education. Because of this, the approach adopted in TEL investigations combines researchers with different experiences, knowledge, and practices, resulting in multidisciplinary studies [1].

Despite the advantages in conducting interdisciplinary investigations, especially in finding innovative solutions for ordinary problems, there are also some challenges. As academic institutions are structured along disciplinary groups, interdisciplinary projects usually consume more integration and planning time [3]. Pammer-Schindler et al. [4] have found that most doctoral programs are associated with a single discipline and they argue that doctoral training in TEL "needs to be situated at the intersection of disciplines in order to facilitate innovation" [4, pp. 1].

In order to integrate the programs for doctoral education in TEL in Europe, nine European universities and the European Technology Enhanced Learning Association (EA-TEL) created the Doctoral Education for Technology Enhanced Learning (DE-TEL) project. The DE-TEL project aims to identify the best teaching practices in doctoral programs in TEL and to develop a proposal for a new program. This new program will have modules encompassing research methods and key topics in TEL and will be supported by Open Educational Resources (OER). This study, in particular, will focus on developing a prototype of an OER on research methods.

According to the United Nations Educational, Scientific and Cultural Organization (UNESCO), "OER are teaching, learning and research materials that make use of appropriate tools, such as open licensing, to permit their free reuse, continuous improvement and repurposing by others for educational purposes" [5, pp. 9]. As stated in this definition, these educational materials must be under open licenses or reside in the public domain, free of copyright restrictions, to give users free permission to adapt and reuse them [6]. The types of materials can vary from videos, images and textbooks, to podcasts, games, and courses [5].

Wiley [7] claims that a content is open not only when it is freely available to be used in other contexts. It is open when it gives everyone permission to engage with the material through different activities, known as the 5R: retain (the right to make, own, and control copies of the content), reuse (the right to use the content in a wide range of ways), revise (the right to adapt, adjust, modify, or alter the content itself), remix (the right to combine the original or revised content with other material to create something new), and redistribute (the right to share copies of the original content, your revisions, or your remixes with others).

There are some motivations for educators, institutions and governments to be involved with the development and sharing of OER [8–10]. Educators, for example, are able to share content as well as reuse and adapt it according to their context, optimizing their time in creating materials from scratch [11]. Consequently, by reusing and sharing these resources, there might be an improvement in their quality, and the costs of content development can be reduced, which can be a benefit to the institutions. From the governmental perspective, OER projects make learning more accessible to society, particularly to nontraditional groups of learners, bridging the gap between non-formal, informal and formal learning [8–10].

2 Description of the Work

This work aims to develop an Open Educational Resource (OER) on research methods in Technology-enhanced Learning (TEL) to support PhD candidates' learning. Firstly, a survey was conducted by the DE-TEL project, between December 2020 and March 2021 through DE-TEL webpage [12], in order to collect information on the practices and challenges of doctoral education in TEL, and to find out the topics that are relevant to the area but have few educational materials available.

Preliminary results reveal that 103 PhD candidates from 25 different countries, most of them from Europe, answered the survey, being 50% female and 50% male, at the age of 30–39 (43,7%), 20–29 (21,4%), 40–49 (18,4%), and 50 and above (15,5%). The main topic of their research in TEL was 'Computing or Information Technology applied to learning' (41,7%), followed by 'Education using technologies' (21,4%) and 'approximately equal efforts in development of educational technologies and applying them for learning' (16,5%).

The most relevant research methods to PhD candidates in TEL were design-based research (46,6%) and qualitative methods (45,6%), followed by quantitative methods (36,9%) and experimental research (35%), respectively, as can be seen in Fig. 1.

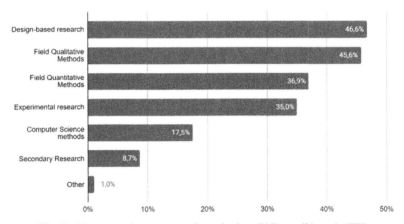

Fig. 1. The most relevant research methods to PhD candidates in TEL

As this work aims to develop an OER on research methods in TEL to support PhD candidates' learning, and the preliminary results showed that design-based research is the most relevant research method, the module on design-based research is going to be designed and developed first, until September 2021.

Then, it is going to be piloted and evaluated by PhD candidates, and improvements are going to be carried out. This cycle will be repeated until a final version of the prototype is concluded. When the prototype is finished, the modules about the other research methods are going to enter this iterative cycle of development, evaluation, and revision.

3 Preliminary Results

The tool that is being used to develop the prototype is H5P (an abbreviation for HTML5 Package) [13] because it is an open source and free to use tool that enables authors to create, share and reuse interactive HTML5 content, without the need for any technical skills. With H5P, authors can create several content types such as videos enriched with interactions, presentations with interactive slides, interactive books, drag and drop tasks with images and text, images with multiple information hotspots, and quizzes with various question types.

Figure 2 shows an example of the content type called *drag the words*. In this activity, users are asked to drag the characteristics of design-based research into the correct explanation. Then, they can check their answers and a score is generated. They can also choose between retrying or visualizing the solution. Figure 2, for example, presents the solution with the correct responses.

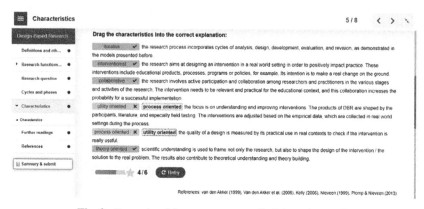

Fig. 2. Example of the content type called *drag the words*

The content type that is being adopted in the creation of the OER on research methods is interactive books because it allows authors to combine other interactive content types, like interactive videos, presentations, and quizzes, through multiple pages. Figure 2 shows a part of the page about the characteristics of design-based research. On the left side of the image, it is possible to visualize the contents of the book. Besides, at the end of the book, there is a summary displaying the total score obtained by the learner resulting from the interaction with the book (Fig. 3).

Fig. 3. Summary of an interactive book

As H5P content may be integrated into Learning Management Systems (LMS) like Canvas, Blackboard, and Moodle, the idea is to pilot this interactive book on Moodle.

On Moodle, it is possible to add gamification elements to the content, such as generating badges according to the score and interactions performed by the user with the interactive book. Furthermore, through Moodle, it is also possible to create discussion forums so that PhD candidates and other researchers can communicate with one another, and share references and other important resources to the area.

The future research plans of this work are to pilot and evaluate the module about design-based research with PhD candidates first, so that the whole course on research methods can be planned and built later, encompassing the most relevant research methods to doctoral programs in TEL.

References

1. Scanlon, E., Conole, G.: Interdisciplinarity in technology enhanced learning: an interview study. J. Interact. Media Educ. **12**(1), 1–8 (2018)
2. Kalz, M., Specht, M.: Assessing the cross-disciplinarity of technology-enhanced learning with science overlay maps and diversity measures. Br. J. Edu. Technol. **45**(3), 415–427 (2014)
3. Net4Society: Report on the Integration of Socio-economic Sciences and Humanities (SSH) in Horizon 2020 (2014)
4. Pammer-Schindler, V., et al.: Interdisciplinary doctoral training in technology-enhanced learning in Europe. Front. Educ. **5**, 1–12 (2020)
5. UNESCO: Guidelines on the development of open educational resources policies. UNESCO, France (2019)
6. Wiley, D., Bliss, T.J., McEwen, M.: Open educational resources: a review of the literature. In: Spector, J.M., Merrill, M.D., Elen, J., Bishop, M.J. (eds.) Handbook of Research on Educational Communications and Technology, pp. 781–789. Springer, New York (2014). https://doi.org/10.1007/978-1-4614-3185-5_63
7. Wiley, D.: Defining the "open" in open content and open educational resources. Open content (2014)
8. Hylén, J.: Open educational resources: opportunities and challenges. In: Open Education 2006: Community, Culture, and Content. OECD's Centre for Educational Research and Innovation, France (2006)
9. OECD: Giving Knowledge for Free: The Emergence of Open Educational Resources. Source OECD, France (2007)
10. D'Antoni, S.: Open educational resources: reviewing initiatives and issues. Open Learn. J. Open Distance Learn. **24**(1), 3–10 (2009)
11. Hodgkinson-Williams, C.: Benefits and challenges of OER for higher education institutions. In: Open Educational Resources Workshop for Head of Commonwealth Universities, South Africa (2010)
12. DE-TEL. https://ea-tel.eu/de-tel/survey. Accessed 29 June 2021
13. H5P. https://h5p.org/. Accessed 29 June 2021

Comparing Usage in and Between Primary and Secondary Schools for a Blended TEL Portal

Sohum Mandar Bhatt[1,2](✉), Lien De Bie[1,2], and Wim Van Den Noortgate[1,2]

[1] Faculty of Psychology and Educational Sciences, KU Leuven, Campus Kulak Kortrijk, E. Sabbelaan 51, 8500 Kortrijk, Belgium
sohummandar.bhatt@kuleuven.be
[2] Imec Research Group ITEC, KU Leuven, Kortrijk, Belgium

Abstract. Blended learning has risen in primary and secondary schools due the COVID-19 pandemic, and is expected to remain after the pandemic. Despite this, the large majority of research into blended learning has studied university student populations. Thus, this paper seeks to research differences in usage between and in primary and secondary schools. Data were collected from a prototype learning portal, resulting in a dataset of 803 students from 12 schools with 45 teachers. Teachers and students could perform diverse actions on the platform, coded as 19 student features and 6 teacher features. These features were used to perform cluster analysis with k-means clustering on the entire dataset, split between teachers and students. Differences in primary and secondary schools were also analyzed. Clustering on the entire student dataset resulted in two clusters that differed on amounts of learning activities and learning tracks. Primary and secondary school students differed on the amount of learning activities, amount of learning tracks, and ratings of fun. Clustering on teachers resulted in two clusters differing in exploration and personalization. These results might be due to differences implementations of blended learning, where young students begin with simple rotation and complexity in implementation increases with age. These results might also be due to differences in teacher competencies. These results belie the importance of research into blended learning in pre-university education, filling a gap in literature and providing guidelines for coaching and use of multiple learning applications.

Keywords: Blended learning · Technology enhanced learning · Clustering · Pre-university education · Learning analytics · Teacher analytics

1 Introduction

Blended learning integrates traditional, face to face education with online distance learning [14]. It has become more prominent in recent years, particularly in higher education [14]. The recent COVID-19 pandemic has also accelerated the rise of blended learning, forcing teachers to use online distance education or blended learning. Expectations are that the technology utilized for distance education will remain for blended learning after the pandemic. Blended learning has also grown pre-university education, but not to the same degree, and thus is rarely investigated [9, 10].

Despite the growing use of educational technology within the classroom and its potential benefits, little research on learning analytics has been done in pre-university education [7]. Various stakeholder reports note interest in learning analytics and potential benefits like the prediction and improvement of learner outcomes, or the ability to develop and focus interventions [2, 3].

Therefore, this paper seeks to fill in gaps in learning analytics and blended learning literature by analyzing the usage statistics of primary and secondary students and teachers who use an experimental portal with multiple learning applications. We specifically investigate the differences in use between clusters of students, and between primary and secondary students. We also investigate differences in teacher use.

2 Methods

Data were collected from i-Learn, a prototypical technology enhanced learning portal which offers learning tracks with learning activities (e.g. exercises, communication tools, engagement activities, etc.) from several educational applications. On i-Learn, teachers can support students, and assign them to groups and learning tracks.

Our dataset consists of 803 students (228 from 5 primary schools, and 575 from 7 secondary schools), and 45 teachers from 12 schools who used the portal from November 2020 to March 2021. In total, 13,184 student events were logged. All students could rate activities on how fun an activity was, from 1 (not very fun) to 5 (very fun). Secondary school students could also rate on difficulty, from 1 (very easy) to 5 (very hard). From these events and ratings, 19 aggregate student features were extracted for clustering, resulting in one value per feature. The same logging and extraction procedure was completed for teachers, resulting in 6 features. All features, code for analyses, tables of differences, and figures can be found in the supplemental material linked below[1].

Cluster analyses were performed to discover usage differences between students and teachers. These analyses used k-means clustering programmed in scikit-learn [5, 8]. To determine a suitable number of clusters, the average silhouette width was maximized between 2–15 clusters following the work of [6]. We also analyzed the differences in usage between primary and secondary school students and teachers.

To explore general group differences, multivariate ANOVAs were used, with follow-up ANOVAs and t-tests used to investigate group differences.

3 Results

3.1 Student Results

In summary, students started an average of 16.4 learning activities (SD = 16.8) and 2.1 learning tracks (SD = 1.8). Few unassigned learning activities were completed (M = .17, SD = .9). The average fun rating was 3.5 (SD = .8), while the average difficulty rating was 2.7 (SD = .6), indicating that students found activities slightly fun and slightly easy.

---
[1] https://github.com/SohumBhatt/ECTELClustering2021.

Two clusters led to the highest silhouette with of .67, indicating a reasonable cluster structure [6]. Across all features, differences were found between clusters ($F(13, 617) = 38.38, p < .001$), though fun was not significantly different between the two ($t(631) = 1.61, p = .11$). The high use cluster started more learning tracks ($t(801) = 18.08, p < .001$) and activities ($t(801) = 44.41, p < .001$), primarily related to languages.

The average primary school student started 32.1 learning activities ($SD = 19.6$) and 4.1 learning tracks ($SD = 2.2$). The average fun rating was 3.9 ($SD = .7$), with primary students finding activities fun. Secondary school students started 10.2 learning activities ($SD = 10.3$) and 1.3 learning tracks ($SD = .6$) on average. The average fun and difficulty ratings were 3.4 ($SD = .9$) and 2.4 ($SD = .1$) respectively.

Across all features, there are differences between primary and secondary schools ($F(13, 617) = 87.63, p < .001$). Importantly, primary schools had higher amounts of starting learning activities ($t(801) = 20.54, p < .001$), starting learning tracks ($t(801) = 27.80, p < .001$), and rating them as more fun ($t(631) = 6.22, p < .001$). Primary school students also had a higher proportion of high use students than secondary schools ($t(801) = 19.90, p > .001$).

3.2 Teacher Results

Teachers on average added 8.0 learning tracks ($SD = 8.0$) to their libraries, edited 0.8 tracks ($SD = 1.9$), created 3.6 groups ($SD = 3.5$), edited groups 5.7 times ($SD = 7.5$), assigned a total of 5.0 learning tracks ($SD = 6.0$) to students, for an average of 1.8 tracks per group ($SD = 2.8$).

Two clusters led to a maximized silhouette score of .56, suggesting a reasonable cluster structure [6]. With all features, difference between clusters was found ($F(6, 33) = 15.40, p < .001$). A cluster of 7 teachers had high learning track additions ($t(43) = 7.92$), group creations ($t(43) = 8.13$), group edits ($t(43) = 5.96$), and assigned many learning tracks per group ($t(43) = 6.14$), all with $p < .001$. Despite that, the ratio of assigned learning tracks per group created was not significantly different ($t(43) = 0.08, p = .94$). However, with all features, no significant difference was found between primary school teachers and secondary school teachers ($F(6, 33) = 1.6473, p = .1654$).

Interestingly, the learning tracks assigned by high use teachers were rated as more fun than other learning tracks ($t(257) = 4.12, p < .001$). This is despite not having significant differences between amount of learning activities ($t(964) = 1.27, p = .20$) or subject of learning track ($t(967) = 1.06, p = .29$). When comparing primary and secondary learning tracks, number of learning activities ($t(964) = 5.98, p < .001$), number of communication activities ($t(967) = 13.83, p < .001$), and average fun rating ($t(257) = 4.48, p < .001$) of the learning tracks were significantly different.

4 Discussion

This study is among the first to apply cluster analysis for primary and secondary schools utilizing blended learning. With the general high use of exercises and engagement activities, it is likely that teachers and students often used a rotation model of blended learning [10]. Given low video usage, students were likely taught face to face or via video conferencing tools, rotating to i-Learn for short supplementary exercises.

The two usage clusters found were likely due to differences in activity complexity in teacher chosen learning tracks. High use students completed more language learning tracks and were more likely to be primary school students. This suggests that high use students completed simpler exercises.

In contrast, differences found between primary and secondary schools might be due to differences in types and length of learning activity. As secondary school students started fewer learning activities and learning tracks, they likely moved to a project-based rotation model where students complete longer tasks at their own pace [10]. Teachers also assigned more communication activities, but secondary school students didn't use them. This might be due to increased disengagement due to 'Zoom Fatigue', fatigue caused by the increased use of teleworking tools, or simply a desire to work face to face [12].

Another significant difference between primary and secondary school students is in the amount of fun. The difference in fun might be due to age, as primary school students are more engaged in school than secondary school students, and might have been exacerbated by the COVID-19 pandemic, in which many students saw mental health decline due to social distancing and stay at home measures [1, 13].

Teachers differ on how much they personalize and explore content. One group of teachers add and trial more learning tracks, despite assigning average amounts of learning tracks. This usage pattern might indicate that (a) some teachers are more comfortable exploring and understanding which tracks might be best for their students, or (b) that some teachers find it easier to use the platform, allowing them integrate their knowledge into the platform more quickly. These explanations are supported by the higher perceived fun of the high-use teacher learning tracks with no difference to other tracks. In both cases, the underlying difference between groups might be a question of teacher competency.

Successfully integrating technology into education depends on teacher competencies [4]. For blended learning, teachers may lack technological knowledge or instructional design skills [9]. Teachers might also have a negative disposition towards blended learning and personalized learning [9]. This is evidenced in our results by the low amount of high use teachers, and that low use teachers explore few learning tracks and create few groups. Blended learning may be adopted more widely if the aforementioned competencies are increased through coaching, though this requires more research [11]. Reducing the need for some teacher competencies may also help increase the adoption of blended learning.

In conclusion, this paper has compared primary and secondary school usage to show a more complete picture of blended learning in a time of higher use. Some limitations of our work are that our portal may have been improperly used, that different features could show different results, and that few background data on schools and students could be collected. This research is just a first step into investigating blended learning with multiple applications. Our future work in this clustering will investigate the use of hierarchical clustering to understand if there are class differences within this dataset. Even further, based on the results of this clustering, our future work will create a recommender system to help reduce the need for teacher competencies. More generally, future research should elucidate gaps in the literature on blended learning in primary and secondary schools, along with comparisons between the two, given lack of such research. Further research should more generally explore the use of learning analytics in order to better understand and compare learning in pre-university education.

References

1. Corso, M.J., Bundick, M.J., Quaglia, R.J., Haywood, D.E.: Where student, teacher, and content meet: student engagement in the secondary school classroom. Am. Second. Educ. **41**, 50–61 (2013)
2. Freeman, A., Becker, S.A., Cummins, M.: NMC/CoSN Horizon Report: 2017 K-12 Edition. The New Media Consortium, Austin, Texas (2017)
3. Gonski, D., et al.: Through growth to achievement: review to achieve educational excellence in Australian schools. Department of Education and Training, Australia (2018)
4. Harris, J.B., Hofer, M.J.: Technological pedagogical content knowledge (TPACK) in action. J. Res. Technol. Educ. **43**, 211–229 (2011). https://doi.org/10.1080/15391523.2011.10782570
5. Hartigan, J.A., Wong, M.A.: A K-means clustering algorithm. J. Roy. Stat. Soc.: Ser. C (Appl. Stat.) **28**, 100–108 (1979)
6. Kaufman, L., Rousseeuw, P.J.: Finding Groups in Data: An Introduction to Cluster Analysis. Wiley, Hoboken (2005)
7. Li, K.C., Lam, H.K., Lam, S.S.Y.: A review of learning analytics in educational research. In: Lam, J., Ng, K.K., Cheung, S.K.S., Wong, T.L., Li, K.C., Wang, F.L. (eds.) ICTE 2015. CCIS, vol. 559, pp. 173–184. Springer, Heidelberg (2015). https://doi.org/10.1007/978-3-662-48978-9_17
8. Pedregosa, F., et al.: Scikit-learn: machine learning in Python. J. Mach. Learn. Res. **12**, 2825–2830 (2011)
9. Pulham, E., Graham, C.R.: Comparing K-12 online and blended teaching competencies: a literature review. Distance Educ. **39**, 411–432 (2018)
10. Staker, H., Horn, M.B.: Classifying K-12 blended learning. Innosight Institute (2012)
11. Stevens, G.H., Frazer, G.W.: Coaching: the missing ingredient in blended learning strategy. Perform. Improv. **44**, 8–13 (2005)
12. Wiederhold, B.K.: Connecting through technology during the coronavirus disease 2019 pandemic: avoiding "zoom fatigue." Cyberpsychol. Behav. Soc. Netw. **23**, 437–438 (2020). https://doi.org/10.1089/cyber.2020.29188.bkw
13. Zhai, Y., Du, X.: Addressing collegiate mental health amid COVID-19 pandemic. Psychiatry Res. **288**, 113003 (2020). https://doi.org/10.1016/j.psychres.2020.113003
14. Zhang, W., Zhu, C.: Review on blended learning: identifying the key themes and categories. Int. J. Inf. Educ. Technol. **7**, 673–678 (2017)

Investigating the Associations Between Emotion, Cognitive Load and Personal Learning Goals: The Case for MOOCs

Maartje Henderikx[✉], Karel Kreijns, and Kate M. Xu

Faculty of Educational Sciences, Open Universiteit, Heerlen, The Netherlands
{maartje.henderikx,karel.kreijns,kate.xu}@ou.nl

Abstract. The purpose of this study was 1) to validate the measures for achievement emotion as well as the measures for perceived cognitive load and 2) to explore the relationships between achievement emotions, perceived cognitive load and personal goal achievement in MOOCs. Participants were 1361 students who completed a survey at the end of the MOOCs. Rasch analyses confirmed the construct validation and dimensionality of all measures. Results of the SEM analyses revealed no statistically significant relationships between any of the variables with personal goal achievement except for enjoyment. Enjoyment positively affected cognitive load in the sense that enjoyment resulted in 1) the investment of more mental effort rather than less mental effort and 2) the perception of low mental load rather than high mental load. Boredom also positively affected cognitive load but in the sense that boredom resulted in 1) the investment of less mental effort rather than more mental effort and 2) the perception of high mental load.

Keywords: MOOCs · Achievement emotions · Cognitive load · Personal learning goals

1 Introduction

Research based on the Cognitive Load Theory [14] suggests that learner's affect plays a role in the learning processes: emotions, either positive or negative, can serve as facilitators or suppressors to cognitive attention thereby influencing the load experienced during learning. In particular, a positive emotion has shown to lower perceived cognitive load and facilitate learning [1]. In addition to the frequently studied general emotions and mood states of learners, learning related emotions - achievement emotions - have also been identified to affect learning [3]. For example, enjoyment is often found to positively affect learner engagement and achievement whereas boredom negatively does so [12]. Achievement emotions are essential to understand how learning occurs as they can affect a learner's effort, motivation to persist and achievement [13]. However, most studies, regarding achievement emotions and cognitive load and their interplay [15] are set in traditional face to face classroom-based learning contexts and have not been studied in the context of Massive Open Online Courses (MOOCs). MOOCs offer learners easily accessible online personal development opportunities, in which they can expand their knowledge on many topics at their own time and pace [7].

In MOOCs, learners can each determine personal learning goals they intent to achieve [5]. Chen, Woolcott & Sweller [4] theorized that perceived cognitive load is important for study success in MOOCs, thus also for personal goal achievement. Based on studies primarily staged in face-to-face contexts, we expected enjoyment to serve as a facilitator and boredom as a suppressor to cognitive load, thereby respectively negatively or positively influencing the load or effort experienced during learning in MOOCs and subsequently affecting personal goal achievement.

The current study provides two contributions to the field of learning in open online environments: 1) we examined and validated measures for the two dimensions of achievement emotions (enjoyment, boredom) and for the four dimension of cognitive load; that is, the two dimensions of mental load (high and low mental load) and the two dimensions of mental effort (more and less mental effort) in MOOC context because these measures were not yet or only partly [6] validated in online learning context, and 2) we explored the association between achievement emotions (enjoyment and boredom), perceived cognitive load (i.e., mental load and mental effort) and personal goal achievement in MOOCs. The findings will provide information for developing instructional design interventions that can support effective learning and subsequently support MOOC learners reaching their personal learning goals.

2 Method

2.1 Participants

The participants were students who took part in self-paced MOOCs about the concept of 'SAP model company' (89%; runtime 5 weeks, study load 3–4 h per week) or about building mobile applications (11%; runtime 6 weeks, study load 4–5 h per week). A total 1361 students completed the survey (81% male, 18% female, 1% other).

2.2 Materials, Procedure and Analysis

The achievement emotions were measured using the Achievement Emotions Questionnaire developed by Pekrun et al. [12]. In the current study we focused only on the learning related emotions enjoyment and boredom; measures for both dimensions used five-point Likert scales. Cognitive load was measured using the mental load and mental effort measures by Krell [8]. Mental load had two dimensions: high and low; mental effort had too two dimensions: more and less effort; measures for the four dimensions all use seven-point Likert scales. All items were slightly adjusted to fit the learning context of MOOCs. Because MOOCs provide students with the possibility of forming their own learning goals, personal goal achievement was determined by asking them to rate their success on a seven-point Likert scale.

The MOOC platform from Hasso Plattner Institute (HPI) was utilized for data collection. Data was collected by inviting students to participate in the survey in the last week of the MOOC.

The analyses were performed in two steps. In the first step, Rasch analysis were performed in Winsteps 4.8.0 [9] for construct validation and dimensionality determination. In the second step, SEM analyses in MPLUS 8.6 [11] were performed.

3 Results

The Rasch analyses in the first step confirmed that 1) enjoyment and boredom were two dimensions of achievement emotions; 2) high and low mental load were two dimensions of mental load; and 3) more and less mental effort were two dimensions of mental effort. Furthermore, the Rasch analyses revealed good construct validation of all measures. That is, all measures' person separation indices exceeded the value of 2.00 which means that each measured item could well separate persons into low, average and high endorsing persons. Alternatively said: all measures had a Cronbach's alpha exceeding .91 except the less mental effort dimension, which had a Cronbach's alpha of .82. Furthermore, the Rasch analyses showed that the seven-point Likert scales for all four measures for the dimensions of cognitive load needed to collapse into five-point Likert scales.

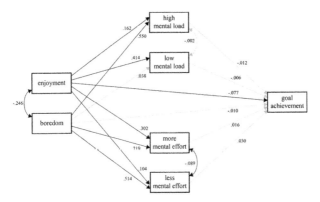

Fig. 1. SEM model with imputed Rasch person measures (i.e., scores).

The SEM model which resulted from the second analysis step is depicted in Fig. 1 and shows the results of the SEM analyses with the imputed Rasch person measures (dark lines indicate a statistically significant relationship). Therefore, the SEM model does not show the latent variables with their observed indicators because the imputed Rasch person measures function here as 'observed' variables Fit indices for the SEM model indicated perfect fit: RMSEA = 0.0; CFI = 1.0; and TLI = 1.0 [16]. The SEM analyses revealed that none of the variables could predict personal goal achievement except for enjoyment; however, the relationship between enjoyment and goal achievement was very weak. The analyses also revealed that enjoyment and boredom have strong to good relationships with all dimension of cognitive load except for the relationship between boredom and low mental load, which was not found to be statistically significant.

4 Discussion

The purpose of this study was 1) to validate the measures for achievement emotion as well as the measures for perceived cognitive load and 2) to explore the relationships between achievement emotions (i.e., enjoyment and boredom), perceived cognitive load (i.e., mental high and low load, and more and less mental effort), and personal goal achievement in MOOCs. Regarding the first purpose, the Rasch analyses revealed good psychometric properties of all measures for all dimensions: enjoyment, boredom, high mental load, low mental load, more mental effort, and less mental effort. All measures were unidimensional which means that they have no further underlying dimensions. Given these properties, the analyses demonstrated that these measures are suitable for use in the online learning context of MOOCs.

Regarding the second purpose of the study; it was expected that all variables would positively or negatively affect personal goal achievement. The results revealed that this was not the case. In fact, none of the variables was capable to predict personal goal achievement except enjoyment but as explained above, the relationship between enjoyment and goal achievement was weak.

It was further expected that enjoyment would have a positive relationship with more mental effort and low mental load, and negative relationships with less mental effort and high mental load. The analyses confirmed the first expectation but did not for the latter (the negative expected relationships). Though, the unexpected (positive) relationships were much weaker than those of the expected positive relationships. We, therefore, may conclude that enjoyment positively affected cognitive load in the sense that enjoyment resulted in 1) the investment of more mental effort rather than in less mental effort and 2) the perception of low mental load rather than high mental load.

It was also expected that boredom would have a positive relationship with less mental effort and high mental load, and negative relationships with more mental effort and low mental load. The analyses again confirmed the first expectation but did not confirm the latter (the negative expected relationships). However, the unexpected (positive) relationships were weaker than those of the expected positive relationships, and the relationship between boredom and low mental load was not significant. From this finding we may, therefore, conclude that boredom positively affected cognitive load in the sense that boredom resulted in 1) the investment of less mental effort rather than in more mental effort and 2) the perception of high mental load.

As every study, the current study has some limitations. First, personal goal achievement was assessed with a one-item scale whereas the other scales had more items. While a one item scales may not be a problem per se, it may have problems as outlined by the Rasch community; for example, a single item may not have the power to differentiate persons well enough. Also, the use of a single item may not assess the full breadth and depth of the construct [10]. Second, the current study only included activity-related achievement emotions enjoyment and boredom using respective items from the AEQ [12]. Future studies may shift the focus from achievement emotions to epistemic emotions, as these are defined as emotions that specifically relate to cognitive tasks and activities [2].

Given these limitations, we need to develop a reliable multi-item instrument for assessing personal goal achievement in order to replicate the current study so to better understand what effects personal goal achievement.

References

1. Brom, C., Stárková, T., D'Mello, S.K.: How effective is emotional design? A meta-analysis on facial anthropomorphisms and pleasant colors during multimedia learning. Educ. Res. Rev. **25**, 100–119 (2018)
2. Brun, G., Doğuoğlu, U., Kuenzle, D. (eds.): Epistemology and Emotions. Ashgate, Aldershot (2008)
3. Camacho-Morles, J., Slemp, G.R., Pekrun, R., Loderer, K., Hou, H., Oades, L.G.: Activity achievement emotions and academic performance: a meta-analysis. Educ. Psychol. Rev. (2021). https://doi.org/10.1007/s10648-020-09585-3
4. Chen, O., Woolcott, G., Sweller, J.: Using cognitive load theory to structure computer-based learning including MOOCs. J. Comput. Assist. Learn. **33**(4), 293–305 (2017)
5. Henderikx, M.A., Kreijns, K., Kalz, M.: Refining success and dropout in massive open online courses based on the intention–behavior gap. Distance Educ. **38**(3), 353–368 (2017)
6. Henderikx, M., Lohr, A., Kalz, M.: Enjoyed or bored? A study into achievement emotions and the association with barriers to learning in MOOCs. In: Scheffel, M., Broisin, J., Pammer-Schindler, V., Ioannou, A., Schneider, J. (eds.) EC-TEL 2019. LNCS, vol. 11722, pp. 15–27. Springer, Cham (2019). https://doi.org/10.1007/978-3-030-29736-7_2
7. Hew, K.F.: Promoting engagement in online courses: what strategies can we learn from three highly rated MOOCS. Br. J. Edu. Technol. **47**(2), 320–341 (2016)
8. Krell, M.: Evaluating an instrument to measure mental load and mental effort considering different sources of validity evidence. Cogent Educ. **4**(1), 1280256 (2017)
9. Linacre, J.M.: Winsteps® Rasch measurement computer program user's guide. Winsteps.com, Beaverton (2018)
10. Messick, S.: Validity and washback in language testing. Lang. Test. **13**(3), 241–256 (1996)
11. Muthén, L.K., Muthén, B.O.: Mplus user's guide, 8th edn. Muthén & Muthén, Los Angeles (1998–2017)
12. Pekrun, R., Goetz, T., Frenzel, A.C., Barchfeld, P., Perry, R.P.: Measuring emotions in students' learning and performance: the Achievement Emotions Questionnaire (AEQ). Contemp. Educ. Psychol. **36**(1), 36–48 (2011)
13. Pekrun, R., Linnenbrink-Garcia, L.: Academic emotions and student engagement. In: Christenson, S., Reschly, A., Wylie, C. (eds.) Handbook of Research on Student Engagement, pp. 259–282. Springer, Boston (2012). https://doi.org/10.1007/978-1-4614-2018-7_12
14. Plass, J.L., Moreno, R., Brünken, R.: Cognitive Load Theory. Cambridge University Press, Cambridge (2010)
15. Plass, J.L., Kalyuga, S.: Four ways of considering emotion in cognitive load theory. Educ. Psychol. Rev. **31**(2), 339–359 (2019). https://doi.org/10.1007/s10648-019-09473-5
16. Xia, Y., Yang, Y.: RMSEA, CFI, and TLI in structural equation modeling with ordered categorical data: the story they tell depends on the estimation methods. Behav. Res. Methods **51**, 409–428 (2019). https://doi.org/10.3758/s13428-018-1055-2

"I Need More Motivation": Engaging Students in the Gamification Design Process

Valeria Barzola[✉], Harlyn Pichardo, Julio Macías, Dick Zambrano, and Vanessa Echeverria

Escuela Superior Politécnica del Litoral, ESPOL, Guayaquil, Ecuador
{vbarzola,hpichard,jumacias,dzambra,vanechev}@espol.edu.ec

Abstract. Gamification in a technology-enhanced learning context has drawn much attention to increasing students' motivation, engagement, and learning performance; however, past research points to a bag of mixed results from these. These results could be partially due to the lack of involvement of end-users (i.e., students and teachers) in the design process. To this end, this work reports a pilot study to explore students' feelings, perceptions, and engagement with EasyNewton, a gamified application to practice physics-related problems. This pilot study gathered 1) students' interactions with EasyNewton and 2) design workshops and interviews with students. We report design recommendations based on students' engagement and perceptions to inform the next design iteration of EasyNewton. This work is a step towards engaging students early in the design process and using engagement metrics to understand students' behaviors.

Keywords: Gamification · Engagement analytics · Human-centred gamification

1 Introduction and Background

Gamification, known as the application of game playing elements (e.g., point scoring, competition with others, rules of play) to other domains, has recently become an important research topic in the development of Educational Technologies [1]. Correctly structured and designed, a gamified application brings a new approach to learning that can positively support motivation and engagement towards the learning process, thus be more effective than traditional class instruction. Despite the significant benefits studied in gamification for education, such as the impact of gamification elements on cognitive engagement and student learning [2], research shows certain cases where students' performance is not as expected [3]. These results could be partially due to the lack of involvement of end-users (i.e., students and teachers) in the design process, or the misalignment between the gamification intentions and teachers' and students' needs. Kleme et al. [4] introduced Gadep (The Gamification Design Process), which aims to design a practical application grounded in game theory. Prior investigations have reported the evaluation, usefulness, and acceptance of a gamified application with final users (e.g., [2]). However, there is a lack of empirical evidence reporting teachers' and students' involvement during the design process, with some exceptions (c.f., [5]). This work takes a user-centered design approach and aims to include students' perspectives in the design process of a gamified application called EasyNewton. Our pilot study aims to explore: 1) *How are students engaged when using EasyNewton?* And 2) *What are students' perceptions of usefulness EasyNewton for practicing physics-related problems?*

2 Context and Pilot Study Design

EasyNewton is a gamified application to help first-year bachelors' students practice physics-related problems [6]. This first version is a middle-fidelity prototype and includes *four levels*: easy, medium, hard, and expert (e.g., Fig. 1, home screen). Each of these levels has a set of problems. Students can *request hints*, or they can *ask for the solution*. EasyNewton uses a *point scoring system* to unlock the next level if they have reached a minimum score. Students can *collect badges* that they unlock depending on how they progress within the application (e.g., answering five questions without hints). It also captures students' actions (e.g., login time, time spent on the application, questions answered without hints, among others). Given that this is the first version of the application, we aim to inform the next design iteration by considering students' perspectives in an early stage of the application development.

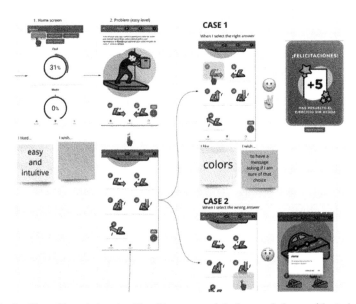

Fig. 1. Shared board showing EasyNewton used during workshops with students.

Participants and Task. Twenty-four first-year undergraduate students (19 males; 5 females, avg age: 19.6, min age: 18, max age: 28) enrolled in the Mechanics course from a local university participated in the study. Students were asked to use EasyNewton to practice Newton's Laws concepts. The task consisted of two parts. In *part 1*, they interacted with EasyNewton for two weeks by solving problems, progressing through four levels, and collecting badges. We logged all students' actions (e.g., login, right and wrong answers, unlocked a new level) with its timestamps. After two weeks, students took the usual test for the Newton's Laws unit. In *part 2*, eleven students participated in a follow-up workshop session. We ran four workshop sessions using a video-conferencing system (e.g., zoom) that lasted around 60 min each. We also prepared a shared board (e.g., see Fig. 1) aiming to understand students' perceptions and elicit their feelings when interacting with EasyNewton. Participants were asked to provide answers to questions such as *what did you like? what would you wish to improve?* All workshop sessions were video recorded and transcribed verbatim.

3 Analysis and Results

We analyzed quantitative data (i.e., users' logs) and qualitative data (i.e., video recordings from workshops). From users' logs, we analyzed students' interactions with EasyNewton during the two weeks. Similar to the engagement metrics presented in [7], we calculated how many students completed the different levels and how many students solved extra problems on each level. We also counted the number of interactions per day. A total of 664 interactions were captured from EasyNewton. From the video recordings, we transcribed and analyzed around five hours of videos. This analysis aims to 1) understand if students liked the game design features and 2) define improvements to inform the next design iteration of the application. Two researchers analyzed students' quotes following an affinity diagram technique and grouped quotes according to the game design principles (DP) presented in [8].

3.1 Students' Engagement

We observed that almost half (n = 10) of students did not complete any level (they only logged in and out into the application), According to [9], game elements not leading to intrinsic motivation could be due to two factors: elements not offering enough feedback to help participants judge their performance, and lack of challenges to allow participants experience competitive feelings. This may suggest that EasyNewton may need to upgrade its reward system. From the logs, we found out that only 8.3% completed the expert level. Results showed that 37.5% of students solved *extra problems* in the easy level, 20.8% of students in the medium level, and 8.3% of students in the hard level. We found that most of the interactions happened the day before (38.1%) and few hours (24.1%) before the test, these interactions corresponding to 25% of students. This behavior is in line with the comments expressed during interviews. Seven students mentioned they felt engaged and motivated to keep using the application. By contrast, four students stated that while the application was easy to use, they were expecting more gaming elements and features to keep them motivated (e.g., *"something is missing, I would need more challenges to keep playing"* – S3). A student that finished all levels (S1) mentioned that the application *"is a good resource to study and practice while playing on it."* On the contrary, a student who used the application before the test and only completed the easy and medium levels (S10) expressed that the application was *"not novel."*

3.2 Students' Feelings, Perceptions of Usefulness and Design Improvements

Most students (n = 10) had positive feelings (i.e., happy, motivated, proud) when *selecting a correct answer*, except for one student who mentioned that he felt confused because he guessed the correct answer. All students had negative feelings (i.e., confused, worried, disappointed) when *selecting a wrong answer*. Students mentioned that they would like to see an explanation about why the answer was wrong (S5) using additional resources (e.g., videos, external links). Students had mixed feelings when *asking for a hint*. Most students (n = 9) felt confused and disappointed as they were expecting to see detailed information about formulas and procedures. Few students (n = 2) felt happy and motivated when reading the hints. Next, we present five design principles (DP) to express students' perceptions of usefulness and to inform the design improvements.

DP 1: Creating Progressive Goals That Build on Each Other. Goals were an important feature for students because it was one of the factors that kept them motivated to keep using the application. One student expressed that *"the application was engaging due to its reward system"* (S1). However, seven students expressed that the application should have a better reward system to challenge them (i.e., based on the total of points they accumulate). This was expressed as follows: *"I would like the total points to have a purpose, to be more challenging"* (S2).

DP 2: Use a Profile/Avatar That the Player Can Own and Can Relate To. Three students expressed that they would like to have a *"nickname"*. We consider this as an improvement for EasyNewton to have a profile screen, where the student is represented by an avatar with a nickname, and it provides the user with all the information related to his/her progress.

DP3: Provide the Status of the Game Process and Next Available Actions. EasyNewton has a home screen showing the student progress of each level. Ten students positively responded to this feature. One student expressed that he liked how the progress bar and its percentage of completion represented his actual status (e.g., *"I liked that the percentage shows me my progress"* - S4). However, they also gave suggestions to show more information, such as the problem's history. (e.g., "*I would like to see a total of exercises resolved*" - S4, S6).

DP4: Favor Simple Interaction. The simplicity of EasyNewton encouraged students to start playing since their first interaction with the application. Most students agreed that the application was attractive due to its simplicity (e.g., *"The application was very intuitive and pleasant to use"* – S5, *"it's easy to use and useful resource"* - S8). For further designs, it must remain simple to use, meaning that more features should not increase students' cognitive load.

DP5: Provide Immediate, Positive, and Useful Feedback. Feedback is one of the most important motivators because students are interested in knowing when they do something right or wrong, so they can learn from their mistakes. Students liked the option to see the solution when they did not know the answer. However, they suggested also to include positive feedback (e.g., *"see the explanation of the solution even if I answer correctly"* - S10) and constructive (e.g., *"see explanations on why we are answering incorrectly"* - S9).

4 Discussion and Further Work

In this work, we presented a study to engage students in designing a gamified application to practice physics-related problems. We conducted a pilot study to understand students' perceptions, feelings, and engagements when using EasyNewton. We used log data and students' interviews to inform the next design iteration of this application. This study suggests that students' motivation and engagement are linked to the gamified elements, as we observed with data logs and through the workshop sessions. Most of the students showed a lesser motivation and disengagement towards the use of EasyNewton due to the lack of challenging features of the application and expressed that they would benefit from detailed feedback when they get wrong answers. Here, we showed how engaging with students could help designers and researchers understand and align design gaps and stakeholders' needs. We are aware that these results cannot be generalizable due to the small sample we report in this work. Instead, this work in progress opens up opportunities to design and develop adapted gamified applications, where students can also have a voice. Further work will extend this study by engaging with more students and also promoting co-design practices with teachers and students. We also plan to embed a tutor system for tracking skills mastery and give more intelligent and adapted problems and feedback to students.

References

1. Fitz-Walter, Z.: Achievement unlocked: investigating the design of effective gamification experiences for mobile applications and devices. Ph.D. thesis, Queensland University of Technology (2015)
2. Ibanez, M., Di-Serio, A., Delgado-Kloos, C.: Gamification for engaging computer science students in learning activities: a case study. IEEE Trans. Learn. Technol. **7**, 291–301 (2014)
3. Seaborn, K., Fels, D.I.: Gamification in theory and action: a survey. Int. J. Hum. Comput. Stud. **74**, 14–31 (2015)
4. Klemke, R., Antonaci, A., Limbu, B.: Designing and implementing gamification: GaDeP, Gamifire, and applied case studies. Int. J. Serious Games **7**, 97–129 (2020)
5. Tenório, K., Dermeval, D., Monteiro, M., Peixoto, A., Pedro, A.: Raising teachers empowerment in gamification design of adaptive learning systems: a qualitative research. In: Bittencourt, I.I., Cukurova, M., Muldner, K., Luckin, R., Millán, E. (eds.) AIED 2020. LNCS (LNAI), vol. 12163, pp. 524–536. Springer, Cham (2020). https://doi.org/10.1007/978-3-030-52237-7_42
6. Macias, J.: Implementación de una aplicación para estudiantes que aprenden Física en cursos de Ingeniería. Master's thesis, ESPOL - FCNM (2020)
7. Ruipérez-Valiente, J.A., Gaydos, M., Rosenheck, L., Kim, Y.J., Klopfer, E.: Patterns of engagement in an educational massively multiplayer online game: a multidimensional view. IEEE Trans. Learn. Technol. **13**, 648–661 (2020)
8. Laine, T.H., Lindberg, R.S.: Designing engaging games for education: a systematic literature review on game motivators and design principles. IEEE Trans. Learn. Technol. **13**, 804–821 (2020)
9. Mekler, E.D., Brühlmann, F., Tuch, A.N., Opwis, K.: Towards understanding the effects of individual gamification elements on intrinsic motivation and performance. Comput. Hum. Behav. **71**, 525–534 (2017)

Augmented Reality as Educational Tool: Perceptions, Challenges, and Requirements from Teachers

Matthias Heintz[✉], Effie Lai-Chong Law, and Pamela Andrade

The University of Leicester, University Road, Leicester L1 7RH, UK
{mmh21,lc19,pyas2}@leicester.ac.uk

Abstract. In the recent decade the number of augmented reality educational applications (AR-EAs) has increased, but their actual uptake in real-life contexts remains low. To identify reasons for the limited uptake and resolutions for this issue, we conducted a teacher survey. Based on the analysis of 65 valid responses, we derived teacher requirements that could improve the adoption of AR-EAs.

Keywords: Augmented Reality · Education · Teacher · Survey · UX · Requirement

1 Introduction and Background

Augmented Reality (AR) combines real and virtual content, is interactive in real-time, and registered in 3D [1]. These three characteristics render AR technologies particularly attractive and useful for educational uses. Consequently, the recent decade has seen a visible increase in the number of AR educational applications (AR-EAs).

However, according to a recent survey [2] the actual usage of AR-EAs in schools remains low, limiting the opportunity to unleash the potential benefits of these emergent educational tools. A critical obstacle is the unavailability of equipment and infrastructure [2]. The lack of requisite knowledge and skills and thus confidence makes teachers reluctant to introduce AR-EAs in their teaching [3–6]. As teachers can be key gatekeepers for the introduction of new technologies to their students, their related perceptions, experiences and opinions need to be identified, heeded, and valued. Hence, we were motivated to design and conduct a survey to analyse the usage of AR-EAs from the teacher perspective, as the related literature is rather thin.

While the AR technology first emerged in the 1960s, the research work on deploying AR in education has only been published since 2000 (cf. the Scopus database). Given that students are the bigger target group (based on the teacher to student ratio alone), only a small number of studies explore *exclusively* teachers' views on deploying AR-EAs (e.g. [3–6]). All four studies had two common shortcomings: the teacher participants involved had no or little experience in using AR applications and the scale of the individual study was limited to a certain region of a single country.

Meanwhile, several systematic literature reviews (SLRs) on AR-EAs have been conducted (e.g. [7–9]). However, most of these reviews address primarily the educational impacts. To gain deeper insights into the interaction quality of AR-EAs to inform their future research and development, we conducted a SLR on AR-EAs designed for K-12 education by following the related guidelines and principles [10, 11]. The process resulted in a batch of 49 papers (31 journal, 18 conference). While the complete results from the student perspective are documented [12], the results from the teacher perspective are yet to be reported. In fact, the related data on teachers are so meagre that there is little to present. There are two teacher-specific aspects to report on. First, concerning the perceived quality of AR-EAs, 36 out of the 49 papers did *not* take any measures with teachers. Second, concerning the effectiveness of the AR-EAs for teaching, 46 out of 49 did *not* specify it at all. The overall limited attention ascribed to teachers' perception of AR-EAs motivated us to conduct a teacher survey. Our main contribution is to identify teachers' experience-based needs and requirements for enhancing AR-EAs and thus their uptake, unleashing the potential of this emerging technology.

2 Method and Results

We created a homegrown survey with closed- and open-ended questions to address the shortcomings identified in the existing work. Its design was based on our AR/HCI expertise and inspired by related work and similar surveys [13, 14]. Originally developed in English, the survey was translated into Dutch, German, Greek, Italian, and Spanish.

Introduction and Section 1: Demographics. The introduction page outlines the prerequisite of having used AR for teaching and asks for the teacher's consent to participate. The six demographic questions are about the type of school they teach at, gender, age, country of residence, main teaching subject, and years of teaching experience.

Section 2: General AR Usage for Teaching. A description of AR is given to ensure that all participants have a similar understanding, followed by 10 questions on the teacher's reasons to use AR-EAs, frequency and duration of usage, conditions of usage (i.e. class size, hardware), confidence in using them, and how the usage can be increased.

Section 3: Most Recent AR Usage for Teaching. Participants are asked to provide the name of the AR app and (optionally) write a short description. The subsequent questions ask details about the app usage, the app itself, the perceived usefulness and user experience of students and teachers with the app, the domain and topic of the app covered, and the age group of the students using it.

The research work underpinning the survey was run under the auspices of an EU-funded project. The survey was implemented with the open-source survey tool *LimeSurvey* and was live from September 2020 to March 2021. To reach teacher participants, the survey was publicised in the news section of the project website, distributed by the project partners to their networks of teacher and school contacts, and promoted on the project's social media channels several times. Altogether there were 1746 visits to the survey website, only 65 responses were complete (i.e. all the questions of the survey were answered), resulting in a completion rate of only **3.7%**. Like most user-based studies, our survey was severely affected by the pandemic. However, the low percentage is also an indicator that the actual usage of AR-EAs in everyday teaching is still a nascent phenomenon, as having used AR in their teaching was a requirement for teachers to participate in the survey.

Due to the space constraints we can only report the demographics and usage data collected, showing the variety within the participants, as well as needs and improvement suggestions gathered, which have the highest relevance of all the information collected when it comes to deriving requirements.

The 65 complete responses came from 17 countries (Belgium, Bulgaria, Croatia, Czech Republic, Finland, Greece, Israel, Italy, North Macedonia, Portugal, Romania, Serbia, Slovakia, Spain, Turkey, United Arab Emirates, and Ukraine) and 2 unspecified ones. In the sample, 35 teachers were in secondary schools, 27 in primary schools, one in an infant school, and two in further education colleges. The gender distribution with 44 female and 21 male participants is higher than a typical ratio of 3:1 in the teaching profession. In terms of age-group, the distribution is as follows: 31–40 (n = 20), 41–50 (n = 26), 51–60 (n = 16), >60 (n = 3). With regard to teaching subjects, the majority of respondents reported to teach mostly STEM subjects. The average teaching experience in years was 17.2 (SD = 7.02, Range = 4–45).

The majority of respondents said to have used AR in their teaching for less than a year (n = 15), between 1–2 years (n = 20), or between 3–4 years (n = 14), whereas few teachers have used it for more than four years (n = 7); the rest did not specify (n = 9). As for the frequency of usage, several teachers, who used AR weekly or fortnightly (17%, n = 10), could be considered as active AR users whereas 45% (n = 26) were moderately active with the usage frequency between monthly and every-three-months. Nonetheless, 38% (n = 22) of the teachers were less active, using AR educational apps for teaching every six months or less frequently.

When asked about their needs to increase the usage of AR technologies in their teaching 44 participants selected the option *to have better access to AR hardware*, 38 *know which AR applications are suitable*, 27 *find the time*, and 19 *more help to use AR apps* (Note: they could choose more than one option). When asked to expand about these needs, most participants said to have significant **financial constraints** (n = 24) such as the lack of budget and equipment at their schools, followed by the need of **training** to be able to use AR apps (n = 21). Teachers also explained to be facing other types of **restrictions** (n = 15) such as the lack of time or national laws forbidding students to use electronic devices in the classroom. The limited availability of **quality materials** (n = 18) in AR apps was also mentioned several times by the respondents. At last, **technical improvements** (n = 4) on the software were said to be needed for teachers to increase their usage of AR for teaching.

In answering the question on how existing AR apps could be improved to better support their teaching, most participants considered that technical enhancements could benefit them the most. Specifically, they wanted the AR apps to be faster, to have more functionalities, and to work on different operating systems. Increasing the scope of the materials available was another common suggestion. There could be more resources that would help teachers to save time and different applications suitable for the student level, which should include not only a larger catalogue of apps, resources, and scenarios, but also their availability in different languages.

Based on the survey results, three types of user (teacher) requirements have been derived, namely, **functional requirements** (i.e. what the system should do, e.g. *'AR apps should support different styles of presentation (e.g. teacher to class, students in groups, or students individually).'*), **non-functional requirements** (i.e. quality in use that the system should satisfy, e.g. *'AR apps should be usable and learnable.'*), as well as **organisational and pedagogical requirements** (i.e. enabling teachers to deploy AR as educational tool, e.g. *'School management should care about providing the appropriate infrastructure and hardware/equipment, including the Internet and mobile devices to run AR apps (tablets, smartphones), and ease regulatory constraints.'*).

3 Discussion and Limitations

The survey responses show clearly that teacher needs are not only technical but also financial and organisational. Besides highly usable and useful software they need more access to hardware and training in order to use AR more often in their teaching. The availability of basic hardware like mobile phones, tablets, and computers with camera for running AR applications is generally low. Hence, the need for even more expensive equipment, like HMDs, to support cutting-edge AR apps as currently developed in the general AR research community, seems very difficult to meet.

Furthermore, the teachers pointed out that a repository of apps and lessons on topics from their countries' curricula would be ideal for them to best utilize these tools and their time. Nonetheless, ready-made materials, while convenient, may not be able to address particularities of specific learning contexts. Hence, it is recommendable to provide teachers with usable and useful *authoring tools*. Such tools can support teachers to customize the existing as well as create new contents to meet their specific needs.

There are some limitations of our study. First, the inherent drawbacks of using survey as a research method are applicable, including the lack of opportunity to ask follow-up questions or clarify responses as well as the constraint of given options, although the option "other" is included for participants to elaborate. Second, the sample size was low, which could partly be attributed to the pandemic and partly to the screening criterion (i.e. experience in using AR for teaching was a prerequisite).

4 Conclusion and Future Work

To capture user requirements for future development of AR we developed a survey to explore teachers' general as well as specific needs in respect to AR apps for educational purposes. Overall, the majority of the participants recognised the potential of AR as educational tool, given its interactivity and visualization effect. However, they pointed out the different challenges – technical, financial, pedagogical and organisational – that need to be overcome to enhance the uptake of AR in real life teaching. These findings support the results of previous work [2–6] while at the same time expanding on it.

The functional and non-functional requirements we derived, albeit not particularly fine-grained, can serve as relevant factors for designers and developers to consider when creating AR-EAs. To address the pedagogical and organisational requirements, it is necessary to mobilise professional bodies such as teacher associations and negotiate with policymakers to invest sufficient resources in requisite infrastructure and equipment.

Acknowledgement. The publication has been supported by European Union's Horizon 2020 research and innovation program under grant agreement No 856533, project ARETE.

References

1. Azuma, R.T.: A survey of augmented reality. Presence Teleoper. Virtual Environ. **6**(4), 355–385 (1997)
2. Research report: UK. The road to digital learning. https://www.birmingham.ac.uk/Documents/HEFI/FUJ-EducationReport-UK.pdf
3. Tzima, S., Styliaras, G., Bassounas, A.: Augmented reality applications in education: teachers point of view. Educ. Sci. **9**(2), 99 (2019)
4. Alkhattabi, M.: Augmented reality as e-learning tool in primary schools' education: barriers to teachers' adoption. Int. J. Emerg. Technol. Learn. **12**(02), 91–100 (2017)
5. Putiorn, P., Nobnop, R., Buathong, P., Soponronnarit, K.: Understanding teachers' perception toward the use of an augmented reality-based application for astronomy learning in secondary schools in Northern Thailand. In: Global Wireless Summit, pp. 77–81. IEEE (2018)
6. Alalwan, N., Cheng, L., Al-Samarraie, H., Yousef, R., Alzahrani, A.I., Sarsam, S.M.: Challenges and prospects of virtual reality and augmented reality utilization among primary school teachers: a developing country perspective. Stud. Educ. Eval. **66**, 100876 (2020)
7. Ibáñez, M.B., Delgado-Kloos, C.: Augmented reality for STEM learning: a systematic review. Comput. Educ. **123**, 109–123 (2018)
8. Garzón, J., Baldiris, S., Gutiérrez, J., Pavón, J.: How do pedagogical approaches affect the impact of augmented reality on education? A meta-analysis and research synthesis. Educ. Res. Rev. **31**, 100334 (2020)
9. Pellas, N., Fotaris, P., Kazanidis, I., Wells, D.: Augmenting the learning experience in primary and secondary school education: a systematic review of recent trends in augmented reality game-based learning. Virtual Reality **23**(4), 329–346 (2019)
10. Moher, D., Liberati, A., Tetzlaff, J., Altman, D.G., Prisma Group: Preferred reporting items for systematic reviews and meta-analyses: the PRISMA statement. PLoS Med. **6**(7), e1000097 (2009)
11. Siddaway, A.P., Wood, A.M., Hedges, L.V.: How to do a systematic review: a best practice guide for conducting and reporting narrative reviews, meta-analyses, and meta-syntheses. Annu. Rev. Psychol. **70**, 747–770 (2019)
12. Law, E.L.C., Heintz, M.: Augmented reality applications for K-12 education: a systematic review from the usability and user experience perspective. Int. J. Child-Comput. Interact. **30**, 100321 (2021)
13. Sáez-López, J.M., Cózar-Gutiérrez, R., González-Calero, J.A., Gómez Carrasco, C.J.: Augmented reality in higher education: an evaluation program in initial teacher training. Educ. Sci. **10**(2), 26 (2020)
14. Ghavifekr, S., Kunjappan, T., Ramasamy, L., Anthony, A.: Teaching and learning with ICT tools: issues and challenges from teachers' perceptions. Malays. Online J. Educ. Technol. **4**(2), 38–57 (2016)

Towards a Self-assessment Tool for Teachers to Improve LMS Mastery Based on Teaching Analytics

Ibtissem Bennacer[✉], Rémi Venant[✉], and Sébastien Iksal[✉]

University of Le Mans, Avenue Olivier Messiaen, 72085 Le Mans, France
{Ibtissem.Bennacer,Remi.Venant,Sebastien.Iksal}@univ-lemans.fr

Abstract. While learning management systems have spread for the last decades, many teachers still struggle to fully operate an LMS within their teaching, beyond its role of a simple resources repository. To elicit these learning situations, we suggest a web environment based on teaching analytics to provide teachers with self and social awareness of their own practices on the LMS. This article focuses on the behavioral model we designed on the strength of (i) a qualitative analysis from interviews we had with several pedagogical engineers and (ii) a quantitative analysis we carried out on three years of teachers' activities on an LMS at the scale of the University. This model describes teachers' practices through six major explainable axes: evaluation, reflection, communication, resources, collaboration as well as interactivity and gamification. It can be used by the institution to detect particular teachers who may be in need of specific individual support or conversely, experts of a particular usage of the LMS who could bring constructive criticism for its improvement. While instrumented in our environment, this model enables supplying teachers with self-assessment, automatic feedback and peer recommendations in order to encourage them to improve their skills with the LMS.

Keywords: Teaching analytics · Learning management system · Self-assessment · Peer recommendation · Clustering analysis · Principal component analysis

1 Introduction

The trend of using Learning Management Systems (LMS) is now spreading quickly across all areas of education. Most universities offer LMSs as a "one size fits all" technology solution for all teachers of any discipline. However, many teachers face several difficulties to integrate these platforms into their practices. The main problems of teachers appear to be technical or organizational, due to the lack of support and the lack of time devoted to its learning [2]. Furthermore, most universities are hiring pedagogical engineers (PE), especially to support and train teachers in order to ensure a proper use of their LMS and ensure their pedagogical fit. With few PE compared to teachers, the formers struggle to support every teacher. For instance, in France, these problems were one of the reasons that led the Ministry of Higher Education to launch the HyPE-13 project(Hybridizing and Sharing Teachings). It aims to accompany teachers and students towards success by promoting the hybridization of training.

On the other hand, the use of LMS allows the capture of large amounts of quantitative data concerning the behavior of users and designers, and thus paves the way for Learning and Teaching Analytics (LA, TA). In our University, the LMS has been in place for more than 10 years. However, the University is facing the same issues we identified previously (LMS use expectations are not met and only 5 PE have to deal with more than 600 teachers). Our main objective is then to provide teachers with personal and social awareness [3], in order for them to engage in learning situations that aim at improving their LMS skills.

To reach this objective, we propose the design and the instrumentalisation of a teachers' behavior model to support their self-assessment and leverage peer-learning through automatic recommendations. We address here two first research questions: (i) How to model the exploitation of an LMS a teacher does and could do in an intelligible way? (ii) What TA indicators can be instrument from this model to support self-assessment and enable feedback and recommendations?

2 Related Work

Some researchers have focused on TA to understand how teachers deliver their lessons. For instance, to support the teacher inquiry process, [7] identified TA as a necessary component, exploited in synergy with Learning Analytics (LA). For this purpose, [5] used TA to automatically extract teachers' actions. To get out of the dependence on the technological context, [1] proposed a theoretical referential of good e-learning practices (DISC), while [4] empirically built a model to describe hybrid learning systems. On the other hand, some studies have been conducted to analyze teachers' behavior for different purposes as [8] aimed to uncover course design archetypes across multiple institutions and identified 5 groups consider courses with: mainly content and low interactions, one-way communication, strong peer interactions, more evaluation activities and those with a balance between content, communication and evaluation. Or, [6] that proposed a method to automatically certify teachers' skills from LMS data and they were able to identify 6 types of courses based on teachers' practices (non-active, submission, deposit, communicative, evaluative, balance). Overall, these different studies show the importance of using analytical tools on the actions of teachers themselves, but it appears that the use of these behaviors for self-assessment has not yet been explored. In addition, they depict current platform usage, with the rejection of unused variables and cannot adapt to expected future uses.

3 Methodology

In order to qualify the current and expected teachers' uses of the LMS, we applied a quantitatively driven mixed method. We started with a quantitative analysis to deduce statistically different profiles of LMS use, in order to find groups of teachers or profiles of interest, based on the LMS log data. We performed a Principal Component Analysis (PCA) and a clustering analysis. PCA analysis allows to highlight diversity of the dataset in a reduced set of variables (components) while the clustering one aims to regroup the different instances of the dataset regarding their similarity. Afterwards, we conducted semi-structured interviews (i.e.: qualitative interview) with 3 female engineers on the same day (each lasted 40 to 50 min). In a series of open-ended questions prepared in advance to guide our interview, we collected information to improve the quantitative study which was analyzed by 2 researchers. This qualitative method was chosen because we needed the interviewee to answer freely, express a specific point of view, and bring out potential new working hypotheses.

We then performed a second quantitative analysis using the same previous method to address the engineer's comments by adding or modifying some variables. In order to design a behavior model that can handle both present and future expected usages of the LMS, we merge both results we obtained from this latest analysis and those we obtained from the interviews. Particularly, some of the discussed LMS features are still not used enough to appear in the results of the quantitative analysis. Moreover, the choice of the model axes (i.e.: the structure and how variables are grouped by axis) is also based on the results of the last PCA analysis and those of the qualitative interviews.

Finally, this model allowed to design several TA metrics. We applied clustering methods (K-Means, Dbscan, Agglomerative clustering and Gaussian Mixture) to be able to provide a social awareness based and defined interpretable scores to offer a more detailed personal awareness. Based on these metrics, we eventually designed a tool mainly dedicated to teachers, that supports self-assessment and awareness, but also can provide automatic peer recommendations using our model and metrics.

4 Teachers' Behavior Model

4.1 Model Definition

Through the intersection of the qualitative and quantitative studies, we designed a teacher behavioral model. It describes along six axes the behavior of teachers in a comprehensive way, and includes features that can be used to represent the current or potential use of the platform. The first axis (a.1 - Evaluation) represents the different tools used by the teacher to assess his students (quiz, assignment, attendance, calendar, grade). The second axis (a.2 - Reflection) concerns the LMS features that can provide teachers with a way to get feedback from students on their teaching and the digital resources they use (survey and choice). The third axis (a.3 - Communication) is devoted to the different means of communication used by the teacher to facilitate the transfer of information to the students and to improve the sharing between them (forum and chat). The fourth axis (a.4 - Resources) refers to the diversity of resources the teacher provides to students, and include then the file, book, folder, page, glossary and url features. Whereas the fifth one (a.5 - Collaboration) concerns the promotion of collaboration between students with different LMS features (workshop, wiki, via, choice and data), the last axis (a.6 - Interactivity and Gamification) gathers the interactive or playful activities used by teachers to animate their courses and make them more attractive (lesson, course format, img, gallery, game and lti).

4.2 Teaching Analytics Indicators

Based on the teachers' behavior model derived from the quantitative and qualitative analysis, we designed two TA metrics for awareness and self-assessment. The first metric is the LMS usage trends, it provides teachers with a current view by axis of their position relative to their colleagues. It was calculated by testing several clustering algorithms, and the results allowed teachers to identify the axes on which they are active and those on which they are not. The second metric propose two complementary scores for self-awareness to measure how the teacher profits from the LMS, based on the complete model we designed: (a) The score of curiosity that indicates the teacher's degree of curiosity according to each axis, takes into account the number of non null variables over all the teacher's courses. It aims to encourage to discover other LMS features within the axis.(b) The score of regularity that considers how often teachers exploit the features related to an axis with respect to their courses. In other terms, it helps validating a skill based on the repetition of practice.

4.3 Model and Metrics Exploitation

We started the development of a tool to engage teachers into learning situations regarding the different axes of our model. The main dashboard is represented in Fig. 1. Once logged, the teacher can have an overview of his situation. Each axis is detailed within a card, with a different background color and subtitle whether the teacher was clusterized as active or inactive, and including the two different

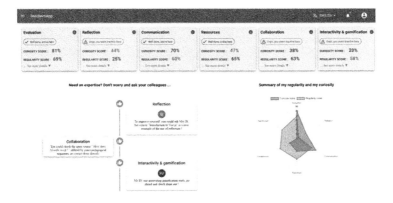

Fig. 1. Teacher dashboard for self-assessment and recommendations

scores of curiosity and regularity. In the bottom right corner of the figure, we provide a radar visualisation that sums up the two scores for the teacher to have a quick comparative view of the different axes. Moreover, according to the different metrics our system can provide several automatic recommendations to improve the teacher's skill by recommending an active teacher if there is one, otherwise the system uses a fallback and recommends the PE.

5 Conclusion and Perspectives

In this paper, we designed a behavioral model of teachers based on a qualitative analysis from interviews we had with three PE and a quantitative analysis we performed on teachers' activities on the University's LMS. This model describes teachers' practices through six major axes of mastery: evaluation, reflection, communication, resource, collaboration as well as interactivity and gamification. From this model, we designed several TA indicators. We proposed clustering models to make out non active and active teachers in a particular axis, as a metric for social awareness. For self-awareness, we took into account the complete model, including variables that relate unused features so far, into two different scores also proposed by axis (score of curiosity and score of regularity). However, our study presents several limitations. We have integrated all teacher traces on the University's LMS to analyze their behavior, knowing that many teachers use other technologies to manage their teaching, whom we do not have access to. Moreover, our study does not take into account what happens in a class, outside the technological environment and considers all teachers in the same way regardless of context. We will continue in the short term to refine our model with the inclusion and analysis of new features that would consolidate our axes and also our TA indicators. Indeed, once the first version of the tool will be operational, we will experiment it at the scale of our University to evaluate its usability, the interest teachers will show in it, and then test whether it allows inducing learning situations and if recommendations are followed and relevant.

References

1. Coomey, M., Stephenson, J.: Online learning: it is all about dialogue, involvement, support and control-according to the research, pp. 37–52 (2001)
2. Fung, H., Yuen, A.: Factors affecting students' and teachers' use of LMS – towards a holistic framework. In: Cheung, S.K.S., Fong, J., Kwok, L.-F., Li, K., Kwan, R. (eds.) ICHL 2012. LNCS, vol. 7411, pp. 306–316. Springer, Heidelberg (2012). https://doi.org/10.1007/978-3-642-32018-7_29
3. Gutwin, C., Stark, G., Greenberg, S.: Support for workspace awareness in educational groupware (1995)
4. Peraya, D., Charlier, B., Deschryver, N.: Apprendre en présence et à distance: une définition des dispositifs hybrides. Dist. Savoirs **4**, 469–496 (2006)
5. Prieto, L.P., Sharma, K., Dillenbourg, P., Jesús, M.: Teaching analytics: towards automatic extraction of orchestration graphs using wearable sensors (2016)

6. Regueras, L.M., Verdú, M.J., De Castro, J.P., Verdú, E.: Clustering analysis for automatic certification of LMS strategies in a university virtual campus (2019)
7. Sampson, D.: Teaching and learning analytics to support teacher inquiry. In: 2017 IEEE Global Engineering Education Conference (EDUCON). IEEE (2017)
8. Whitmer, J., Nuñez, N., Harfield, T., Forteza, D.: Patterns in blackboard learn tool use: five course design archetypes (2016)

Uncovering Latent Profiles Based on How Students Review Paper-Based Assessments

Yancy Vance Paredes[✉] and I-Han Hsiao

Arizona State University, Tempe, AZ 85281, USA
{yvmparedes,Sharon.Hsiao}@asu.edu

Abstract. Blended learning environments offer a rich amount of data that encompasses various learning interactions. Despite advancements in technology, there have been several learning activities that remain offline, thus preventing us from fully understanding certain aspects of student learning. An example of this is how students review their paper-based assessments. Using a homegrown educational technology that addresses this gap, we analyzed students' clickstream data to uncover latent profiles based on how they review these graded assessments. Such behavior could provide insight into their self-regulated learning strategies as they attempt to correct their misconceptions. We leveraged latent profile analysis and presented our preliminary findings and interpretations of the five student profiles we uncovered to understand the effects of their varying efforts to learn the course material.

Keywords: Clickstream data · Reviewing behavior · Latent profile analysis

1 Introduction

Students use various readily available resources as they prepare for exams. In one survey, they responded that they review their past quizzes or exams, in addition to reading the lecture materials or notes [6]. They look back at old questions with the hopes of encountering a similar question. This exposes them to the possibility of seeing past mistakes, which would present a problem if not addressed soon. In fact, it was found that difficulty of material affects the total time it takes for students to read and study it [9]. Reviewing assessments enables students to demonstrate metacognitive skills such as monitoring mistakes or evaluating any learning strategy's success and adjusting. Knowing how they performed in a graded assessment allows them to formulate a plan to address their misconceptions. This highlights the importance of guidance on approaching learning materials to ensure that the learning activity is beneficial. For guidance to be effective, it has to be personalized [2]. However, to be able to do so, the system needs to know something about the students.

This paper aims to uncover various profiles of students based on how they review their paper-based assessments. *What are the characteristics of students who performed well? Can we use such discovery to provide appropriate guidance to make them more accountable in addressing their misconceptions?* These questions can be answered by looking at how students interact with an educational technology that captures their reviewing behaviors. These strategies are captured in the form of clickstream data. Many approaches can be employed to model and interpret such behaviors. In this paper, we attempt to discover such latent profiles through Latent Profile Analysis [1].

In earlier works, the distribution of the students' review actions and how this affects their succeeding exam performance was investigated [4,5]. However, in those studies, the questions' context, such as the difficulty, was not factored into the analysis. Furthermore, these studies only used arbitrary thresholds to group events into sessions instead of using a more accurate approach (i.e., determined by the server). Lastly, students in these works have always been classified based on their class performance (e.g., high- and low-performing students; A-B-C students). Their behaviors were not looked into to come up with these groupings or profiles. Therefore, this paper aims to address such limitations.

2 Methods

2.1 Data Collection and Pre-processing

The clickstream data were collected from a classroom study from an Object-Oriented Programming and Data Structure class in a higher education institution. The course had a total of 17 paper-based assessments. Three of which were exams, while the other 14 were quizzes. Among the quizzes, two were for credit, while the rest were not. Students still had to answer these quizzes and were awarded full points regardless of whether their answers were correct or not (i.e., extra questions). These were only used for attendance. A total of 317 students were enrolled, mostly in their second year. *WebPGA* [5] was used to capture students' reviewing behavior (a total of 88,111 unique events).

This preliminary analysis focuses on three specific actions representing the three levels of how students can review an assessment. The first level is the *dashboard overview*, where students can see a list of all their assessments and their scores at a glance. Students choose an assessment from the list, which redirects them to the second level, *assessment overview*. Students can see a listing of all the questions from the selected assessment. This includes individual scores for each question. Color codings were used to help students identify which questions they had more mistakes. Students can freely choose a question to review, redirecting them to the *question overview*, the third level. In this view, students can see fine-grained detail about their performance, such as the rubrics and written annotations from the grader. From here, students can use the navigation buttons (left and right) to go to other questions; or close the current window to go back to the assessment overview and choose another question from the list.

Students' perception of a question's difficulty varies. We provided context to the different questions based on the student's performance. For every graded question, we obtained the class performance for this question and used this as a cutoff point to determine whether, for a given student, this question requires urgent attention. For example, if the cutoff point for Q1 is 0.75 and students A and B obtained scores of 0.65 and 0.92, respectively, Q1 will be tagged as urgent for student A and non-urgent for student B. The rationale behind this approach is to let students focus on questions that were relatively difficult for them. Lastly, the student's overall performance was obtained from the average of his or her three exam scores. The class average is 0.83 (s = 0.12).

Students accessed the platform throughout the semester at their convenience. Announcements were posted on Blackboard as an assessment becomes available for review. Each student is represented by a string of symbols that describes the student's different actions in the system. Actions performed in a single session as determined by the system were grouped. Two different session groups are separated with a session marker symbol. Finally, we computed the relative frequency distribution of the six different symbols (D, A, N, U, X, S) of every student.

2.2 Latent Profile Analysis

The goal of this study is to identify subgroups based on their behavioral data to be able to provide appropriate guidance or intervention. The student's relative frequency distribution was used to represent his or her reviewing behavior. To uncover these various profiles, we performed latent profile analysis by leveraging Gaussian mixture models (GMMs) [3]. GMM was used over k-means clustering as the former performs soft classification providing us with probabilities. In this exploratory analysis, the number of components (i.e., latent profiles) is unknown. We used Bayesian Information Criterion (BIC) [8] as the metric in determining the number of components from the range of 1 to 10, inclusive. A GMM with five components yielded the best BIC and was used to group the students. Figure 1 provides an overview of the relative frequency of the five student profiles.

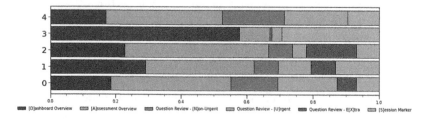

Fig. 1. Relative frequency distribution of symbols of the five student profiles.

3 Preliminary Results

Table 1 provides an overview of the characteristics of the five student profiles. We wanted to investigate whether there is a significant difference between students' overall performance across the different profiles. We performed a Kruskal-Wallis test and found a statistically significant difference ($H = 36.14, p < .01$). To further investigate the differences between the groups, we performed Dunn's post hoc test. We repeated the same set of analyses for the sequence lengths ($H = 116.35, p < .01$) and the number of unique sessions ($H = 56.87, p < .01$). In terms of overall performance, the following groups had no significant differences 0-3, 1-4. This potentially suggests that there are three groupings for the users. Only the 0-2 pair had no significant differences in terms of sequence lengths, suggesting four different sequence lengths. In terms of the number of unique sessions, two groupings can be formed, namely 0-1-2 and 3-4.

Table 1. Overview of the five student profiles

Profile	Student count	Overall performance	Sequence length	Unique sessions	Urgent ratio
0	67	0.79	171	11	0.56
1	87	0.82	102	13	0.58
2	94	0.88	174	11	0.37
3	21	0.77	021	5	0.86
4	48	0.82	67	5	0.51
Overall	**317**	**0.83**	**128**	**10**	**0.52**

We further looked at the relationship of the relative frequency distribution values to provide some explanations or characterize the various profiles. When comparing distributions of dashboard and assessment actions, only profile 3 had more dashboard actions than assessments. This provides evidence of their shallow reviewing behavior, which is made evident by their relatively low number of unique sessions. Interestingly, this profile had the lowest overall performance. When looking at the distribution of assessment and question review actions, we found that only profiles 0 and 4 had fewer assessment actions than question reviews. This could indicate that these students simply did not explicitly choose which questions to review based on their performance (i.e., simply followed what was being presented by the system). More assessment actions could indicate an intentional part of the student choosing and planning which question to review next since the system was designed to handle such a situation. It should be noted that profiles 0 and 4 are entirely different in terms of their sequence lengths and number of unique sessions.

Not all the questions that can be reviewed are for credit. Among the five, only profiles 0, 1, and 2 made an effort to review extra questions. Students from profiles 3 and 4 may have missed this opportunity to learn more about the topic. A closer look at profile 2 shows that more review on extra questions was higher than graded questions (urgent and non-urgent). This shows their willingness and determination to learn more and take advantage of any available resources. Finally, we computed the urgent ratio (Table 1), which is the ratio of the urgent and non-urgent review question actions. Only profile 2 had a value less than 0.50. Notably, despite the high urgent ratio for profile 3, it seems that such behavior is not enough. The length of their sequences could potentially explain this.

4 Conclusion and Future Work

This exploratory analysis has demonstrated the potential of uncovering student profiles based on their reviewing behavior. A follow-up study to ask students why they behaved the way they did in the system could validate such interpretation of the student profiles. Furthermore, it is worth investigating data from other educational systems used in the class. In terms of adaptive personalization, using the identified profiles, various models could be trained to provide the right nudge or recommendation to make the student more engaged in addressing their misconceptions. Finally, other methodologies can be explored (e.g., hidden Markov models). Many works have leveraged this technique to understand behavioral patterns. An advantage of this approach is that it incorporates the temporal information of the data as opposed to simple clustering [7]. Another is to apply sequential pattern mining techniques to understand what constitutes effective and ineffective reviewing strategies.

References

1. Gibson, W.A.: Three multivariate models: factor analysis, latent structure analysis, and latent profile analysis. Psychometrika **24**(3), 229–252 (1959)
2. Hsiao, I.H., Sosnovsky, S., Brusilovsky, P.: Guiding students to the right questions: adaptive navigation support in an e-learning system for Java programming. J. Comput. Assist. Learn. **26**(4), 270–283 (2010)
3. Oberski, D.: Mixture models: latent profile and latent class analysis. In: Robertson, J., Kaptein, M. (eds.) Modern Statistical Methods for HCI. HIS, pp. 275–287. Springer, Cham (2016). https://doi.org/10.1007/978-3-319-26633-6_12
4. Paredes, Y.V., Azcona, D., Hsiao, I.-H., Smeaton, A.: Learning by reviewing paper-based programming assessments. In: Pammer-Schindler, V., Pérez-Sanagustín, M., Drachsler, H., Elferink, R., Scheffel, M. (eds.) EC-TEL 2018. LNCS, vol. 11082, pp. 510–523. Springer, Cham (2018). https://doi.org/10.1007/978-3-319-98572-5_39
5. Paredes, Y.V., Huang, P.K., Hsiao, I.H.: Utilising behavioural analytics in a blended programming learning environment. New Rev. Hypermedia Multimed. **25**, 89–111 (2019)
6. Paredes, Y.V., Huang, P.K., Murphy, H., Hsiao, I.H.: A subjective evaluation of web-based programming grading assistant: harnessing digital footprints from paper-based assessments. In: MMLA-CrossLAK@LAK, pp. 23–30 (2017)

7. Perera, D., Kay, J., Koprinska, I., Yacef, K., Zaane, O.R.: Clustering and sequential pattern mining of online collaborative learning data. IEEE Trans. Knowl. Data Eng. **21**, 759–772 (2009)
8. Schwarz, G., et al.: Estimating the dimension of a model. Ann. Stat. **6**(2), 461–464 (1978)
9. Van Etten, S., Freebern, G., Pressley, M.: College students' beliefs about exam preparation. Contemp. Educ. Psychol. **22**(2), 192–212 (1997)

Orchestrating an Ubiquitous Learning Situation About Cultural Heritage with Casual Learn

Adolfo Ruiz-Calleja[✉], Sara Lorena Villagrá Sobrino, Miguel L. Bote-Lorenzo, Sergio Serrano-Iglesias, Pablo García-Zarza, Víctor Alonso-Prieto, and Juan I. Asensio-Pérez

GSIC/EMIC Research Group, Universidad de Valladolid, Valladolid, Spain
{adolfo,sergio,pablogz,victor}@gsic.uva.es, sarena@pdg.uva.es,
{migbot,juaase}@tel.uva.es

Abstract. This paper presents a case study that analyzes the orchestration of a ubiquitous learning situation involving a teacher and 89 secondary-school students using Casual Learn. This case study allows us to illustrate how teachers can use Casual Learn to orchestrate ubiquitous learning situations to learn Cultural Heritage. During the case study, Casual Learn played a key role as it enabled to bridge in- and out-classroom activities across physical and virtual learning spaces.

Keywords: Ubiquitous learning · Cultural heritage learning · Case study

1 Introduction

Cultural Heritage learners highly benefit from active on-site learning: learners get a better understanding of a monument and its context when visiting it, than when studying it from a book or online site [3]. For this reason, ubiquitous learning -typically defined as "using mobile technologies to facilitate learning" [4]- is a promising approach to teach and learn Cultural Heritage. UL promotes autonomous and active learning across different spaces and contexts. In many cases, UL situations bridge formal and informal learning spaces, where learning tasks of different formality may occur. Thus, an UL situation can combine the advantages of different learning spaces [1].

All these UL benefits come to a price: using mobile technology to bridge learning across spaces may require a significant effort for the teacher. UL typically implies using new technological tools and platforms. Moreover, there are important pedagogical issues in the orchestration [6] of UL situations, including their learning design (e.g., how to define the sequence of activities that will be carried out, including how the tools will support them) and enactment (e.g., scaffolding the students or solving their doubts). In the last few years, the research community is making a significant effort to overcome these issues, but few researchers explored them in the context of UL situations that bridge in-classroom and out-classroom learning [1].

Overcoming the aforementioned limitations of UL could be highly beneficial for Cultural Heritage learning situations: since school trips are scarce [3], it is convenient to help the teacher to orchestrate learning situations that connect in-classroom activities with on-site activities that students may carry out in informal contexts. However, the potential of UL for the Cultural Heritage domain has not been explored in depth [1,4]. Some researchers reported UL situations either inside museums [8] or around the city [2]. But these are purely informal learning experiences, not related to formal learning or contexts. Furthermore, they do not promote active learning as the supporting technology limits its functionality to offering [2] or recommending [8] information about places to visit.

An example of a mobile application that may support UL for Cultural Heritage is Casual Learn [7]. Casual Learn, designed and developed by the authors, makes use of semantic technologies and linked open data to define 10 000 active learning tasks related to Cultural Heritage sites from the Spanish region of Castile and Leon (see Fig. 1). Casual Learn enables the learners to do these tasks and share their answers in Instagram, Twitter, or Microsoft Teams. Casual Learn is already available in Google Play Store for downloading and installation[1], and it has already been tested by a set of individual users. This paper goes a step forward and presents the results of a study focused on the difficulties faced by a secondary-education teacher when designing and enacting an UL situation supported by Casual Learn, under the umbrella of the so-called orchestration metaphor [6]. The rest of the paper summarizes the research method (Sect. 2) and the main results (Sect. 3) of this case study.

2 Methods

The main aim of this study is to explore the issue: *to what extent can teachers orchestrate Casual Learn as part of their teaching practice in a manageable way?* The study is framed within an interpretative research paradigm, which does not pursue statistically-significant results, rather aiming to a deep understanding of the particularity of the concrete phenomena under study. During the evaluation design, we used an anticipatory data reduction process [5], using as its basis the $5+3$ aspects orchestration framework [6].

Four months before the case study took place, the authors of this paper gave a two-session seminar about Casual Learn to the teacher who participated. Then, the teacher freely created the learning design. During the enactment, we had an informal interview every week with the teacher ([WI]), so she reported the progress to us. Once the learning situation finished, we had a semi-structured interview with the teacher ([I]) and we collected some questionnaires from the teacher ([TQ]) and the students ([SQ]). We also collected the documents produced for the learning situation ([D]) and Casual Learn's logs ([L]).

---

[1] https://casuallearnapp.gsic.uva.es.

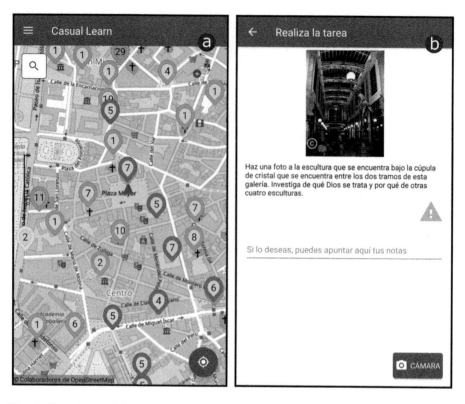

Fig. 1. Snapshots of the user interface of Casual Learn. a) view of the city center of Valladolid. b) a task description related to the "Pasaje Gutiérrez".

2.1 Research Context

This case study was carried out in a public secondary-education school located in a middle-class district of the city of Valladolid (Castile and Leon, Spain). The participants were a teacher of History with more than 20 years of teaching experience, and 89 students of the fourth grade of secondary education (15–16 years). The students belonged to four different classes. The case study was carried out in the course 2020/2021, when school trips and organized tourist visits were not allowed due to the restrictions related to the COVID-19 pandemic, although people could walk freely around the city of Valladolid, alone or in small groups.

The aim of the learning situation was to understand the rise of the bourgeoisie in the city of Valladolid. This topic had been explained by the teacher before the learning situation started. The learning situation was divided into two phases:

The first phase took 21 d. Each class was divided into four groups of four or five students. Each group was assigned a topic (culture, economy, politics, and society) and a set of four or five Cultural Heritage sites of Valladolid related to their topic (18 sites in total). The teacher provided each group with some basic bibliography that they were expected to extend. Then, learners should produce, for each Cultural Heritage site, an electronic document that contains a short description of the site, an extended description which may contain images and references, and a set of tasks to be done by their colleagues. Overall, 36 descriptions and 74 tasks were proposed by the students, reviewed by the teacher and published in Casual Learn.

The second phase took 16 d. 80 students used Casual Learn to carry out the tasks proposed by their classmates. They freely formed 23 groups between of three or four students each. In their evenings or weekends they had to visit the 18 Cultural Heritage sites proposed by the teacher. They also use Casual Learn to send their answers to the teacher via Microsoft Teams. Overall, they carried out 451 tasks in Casual Learn: 222 tasks proposed by a group; 199 proposed by another group; and 30 tasks previously existing in Casual Learn.

3 Results

This section reports the main findings regarding the orchestration of the learning situation, organized according to the dimensions of the 5 + 3 aspects orchestration framework [6]. Letters in brackets indicate the data sources analyzed for each dimension, as indicated in Sect. 2.

Design: the evaluation showed that Casual Learn enabled the teacher to implement an UL design to learn Cultural Heritage. This design included collaborative in- and out-classroom across physical and virtual spaces [WI]. It is noteworthy that Casual Learn is a technology that enabled the implementation of a learning design that alleviated the impact of the restrictions related to the COVID-19 pandemic [I].

Management: in this case study the teacher could manage the UL situation with almost no support from Casual Learn developers [WI]. During the first phase of the situation, she had to further scaffold students offering them more sources and motivating them to deepen their analysis [WI][I]. During the second phase of the situation, the students used Casual Learn without the need of further support [WI][I].

Awareness: Casual Learn allowed the teacher to be aware of her student's progress [I]. The integration of Casual Learn to Microsoft Teams was key to support this awareness [I][TQ].

Adaptation: the teacher and the students could adapt the learning process using Casual Learn [D]. The teacher published in Casual Learn the tasks proposed by two classes before the second phase of the situation started (see Fig. 1 for an example). Thus, she adapted the functionality of Casual Learn to the content of her course. Regarding the students, they took advantage of the hundreds of tasks available in Casual Learn and related to Cultural Heritage sites from Valladolid [L].

Theory: the pedagogical aims of this learning situation were not transformed, but enriched, by using Casual Learn. Casual Learn is an application that offers students outdoor learning opportunities and is well aligned to the school's promotion of competence-based learning [I].

Pragmatism: Casual Learn was used by a non-ICT expert teacher and her secondary-school students in an authentic collaborative learning situation. Indeed, it was perceived as an easy-to-use application by the teacher and by the students [TQ] [SQ]. The teacher also said that orchestrating this learning situation required a significant amount of work, especially during the enactment of its first phase [I].

Synergy: Casual Learn could be used together with Microsoft Teams, which is widely adopted by Spanish secondary schools [L]. This was key to integrate Casual Learn in the technological environment used in the classroom [I].

Roles of the Teacher and other Actors: the orchestration load was successfully shared between the teacher and the students. Indeed, during its second phase the students could carry out the learning tasks with Casual Learn without any explicit support or supervision from the teacher [I][L].

Acknowledgements. Authors would like to thank María Rosario Jaén Martín, the teacher that participated in this research, and her students from I.E.S. Pinar de la Rubia. This research has been partially funded by projects VA257P18 (Regional Government of Castile and Leon, ERDF), TIN2017-85179-C3-2-R (AEI, ERDF).

References

1. Cárdenas-Robledo, L., Peña-Ayala, A.: Ubiquitous learning: a systematic review. Telemat. Inform. **35**(5), 1097–1132 (2018)
2. Fermoso, A., Mateos, M., Beato, M.E., Berjón, R.: Open linked data and mobile devices as e-tourism tools. a practical approach to collaborative e-learning. Comput. Hum. Behav. **51**, 618–626 (2015)
3. Greene, J., Kisida, B., Bowen, D.: The educational value of field trips: taking students to an art museum improves critical thinking skills, and more. Educ. Next **14**(1), 78–86 (2014)
4. Hwang, G.J., Tsai, C.C.: Research trends in mobile and ubiquitous learning: a review of publications in selected journals from 2001 to 2010. Br. J. Educ. Technol. **42**(4), E65–E70 (2011)
5. Miles, M.B., Huberman, A.M.: Qualitative Data Analysis. An Expanded Sourcebook. SAGE Publications Inc., Thousand Oaks, California, USA (1994)
6. Prieto, L., Dlab, M., Gutiérrez, I., Abdulwahed, M., Balid, W.: Orchestrating technology enhanced learning: a literature review and conceptual framework. Int. J. Technol. Enhanc. Learn. **3**(6), 583–598 (2011)
7. Ruiz-Calleja, A., et al.: CasualLearn: a smart application to learn history of art. In: Alario-Hoyos, C., Rodríguez-Triana, M.J., Scheffel, M., Arnedillo-Sánchez, I., Dennerlein, S.M. (eds.) EC-TEL 2020. LNCS, vol. 12315, pp. 472–476. Springer, Cham (2020). https://doi.org/10.1007/978-3-030-57717-9_47
8. Ruotsalo, T., et al.: Smartmuseum: a mobile recommender system for the web of data. J. Web Semant. **20**, 50–67 (2013)

Bibliometric Analysis of the Last Ten Years of the European Conference on Technology-Enhanced Learning

Manuel J. Gomez[✉], José A. Ruipérez-Valiente, and Félix J. García Clemente

Faculty of Computer Science, University of Murcia, Murcia, Spain
manueljesus.gomezm@um.es

Abstract. Over the last decade, we have seen a large amount of research being performed in technology-enhanced learning. The European Conference on Technology-enhanced Learning (EC-TEL) is one of the conferences with the most extended trajectory in this area. The goal of this paper is to provide an overview of the last ten years of the conference. We collected all papers from the last ten years of the conference, along with the metadata, and used their keywords to find the most important ones across the papers. We also parsed papers' full text automatically, and used it to extract information about this year's conference topic. These results will shed some light on the latest trends and evolution of EC-TEL.

Keywords: Technology-enhanced learning · Bibliometrics · Natural language processing · Education

1 Introduction

The term technology-enhanced learning (TEL) is used to describe the application of information and communication technologies to teaching and learning [5]. Nowadays, technology is changing and improving year after year, and this development is also making a significant impact on educational environments. Despite there are still some limitations that contribute to the still-limited application of technology in education [2] (such as economic ones), research and interest in this area have been growing over the years. This increase is an excellent motivation to analyze the current trends in educational technology (EdTech) and see changes and new emerging patterns.

There are several approaches to do this type of analysis [6,9]: systematic reviews, scoping reviews, or even meta-reviews of multiple review papers, among others. Unfortunately, analyzing a large collection of papers is often very time-consuming, specially when we find large number of them as we do in this area. We propose a methodology to discover trends quickly and easily, and since the European Conference on Technology-enhanced Learning (EC-TEL) has become the primary educational technology conference in Europe and one of the world's leading conferences, we consider that this venue is very representative of the trends in this area.

Specifically, our analysis has focused on the following three main objectives: 1) Discover which are the main topics of the conference using paper keywords. 2) Discover the evolution of said topics over the last ten years of the conference. 3) Discover how many papers have tackled this year's conference theme on "Free, Safe and Sustainable World." The rest of the paper is organized as follows. Section 2 describes the methodology followed to conduct the research and Sect. 3 presents the results of the synthesis and analysis. Then, we finalize the paper with conclusions and future work in Sect. 4.

2 Methodology

To conduct the research, we divided our work in different stages. Next, we explain each part of the methodology in detail:

- **Data extraction.** The first step in our analysis was to get all the data necessary to begin the research. To download each paper in PDF, we used the Springer Link database [11]. On the other hand, we used two different databases to get each paper's metadata: Scopus [1] and Web of Science [10]. Although we did not find the metadata corresponding to the papers of the EC-TEL 2015 edition, we included these papers' metadata that we needed for our analysis manually. The final data collection contains a total of 447 documents and 1 905 keywords (4.26 average keywords).
- **PDF parsing.** In this stage, we parsed every PDF file into a plain text (TXT) file. To make that possible, we used *PdfToText* library, which parsed 100% of the papers with high fidelity.
- **Data cleaning & lemmatization.** We cleaned each paper's full text, along with the keywords, by removing, for example, unnecessary URLs, numbers, or additional space characters. Once the text is cleaned, we applied lemmatization (i.e., the process of converting a word to its base form) to every document and keyword using *pywsd* library.
- **NLP & keyword analysis.** To discover the main topics based on the papers' keywords, we inspected the data manually to merge similar keywords into a single one. That way, if we find, for example, "technology-enhanced learning" and "technology enhanced learning," both keywords are merged and their number of appearances are aggregated.

3 Results

3.1 Main Topics of EC-TEL Based on Keywords

After applying the proposed methodology in the previous Section, we calculated the top ten keywords proportion across the last ten years of EC-TEL. As we see in Fig. 1, the most frequent keywords appearing are "learn analytics" (2.99%), "collaborative learning" (2.67%) and "massive open online course" (2.36%).

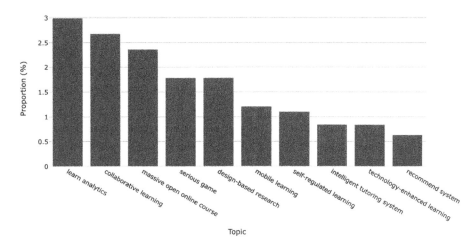

Fig. 1. Keyword distribution across all papers.

3.2 Evolution of Topics Across the Previous Ten Years

After reviewing keywords taking into account all ten years, we analyzed each year separately, calculating the proportion of each keyword in each year individually.

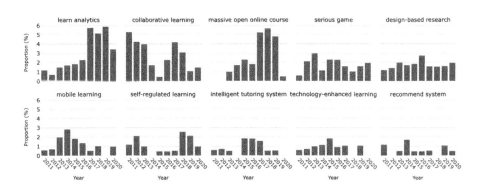

Fig. 2. Keyword distribution by year.

Figure 2 shows the evolution of each keyword's distribution over time. We see some keywords that have never been as trendy as others, but they keep appearing year after year. This is the case of "design-based research," which has a stable distribution almost every year. Moreover, we also see other keywords that have increased their frequency significantly, such as "learn analytics" (increasing from 1.17% in 2011 to a maximum of 5.88% in 2019). What we discover looking at Fig. 2 is that almost every keyword has lost frequency from 2019 to 2020, which possibly means that 2020 was a year with new trends, or maybe papers' topics are more diverse.

3.3 Evolution of This Year's Conference Topic on "Free, Safe and Sustainable World"

We searched the appearance of certain quotes: using the papers' full text, we searched for the quotes: "free world," "safe world," "sustainable world," and "sustainability"; then, we made a manual review of those papers found to check if they are really addressing any related area to this year's theme. All papers (a total of ten) resulting from our search matched the quote "sustainability", and none of them matched any other quote. We identified that all these papers addressed four main topics:

- **Economical sustainability.** We found one paper matching this topic, dealing with the economical issues of implementing technology in the classroom. Specifically, [4] created a multi-user simulation environment for LEGO robots, which are expensive and typically could not be used by students at home.
- **Technological sustainability.** We found a total of three papers in this topic, addressing some existing technological challenges in the area. For example, the work in [8] describes multi-tier architecture and data model to support the deployment of learning designs, which is sustainable and scalable.
- **Pedagogical sustainability.** We found two papers matching this topic. These papers propose new approaches to content generation issues over time. For example, the focus in [7] is on the construction, use, pedagogical potential, and long-term sustainability of certain web-based tools designed for teaching logic.
- **EdTech about sustainability.** We found four papers in this topic, including EdTech research where the tool developed (e.g., games, MOOCs) includes sustainability concepts. For example, authors in [3] discuss the design, implementation and evaluation of a pilot project that integrated inquiry-based learning with mobile game design, addressing topics such as energy consumption or sustainable development.

4 Conclusions and Future Work

This student presents a methodology to discover the latest trends in the last 10 years of the EC-TEL conference. Some of the most frequent keywords that we found are "learning analytics," and "massive open online course," which have gained popularity over time. Other keywords, like "collaborative learning," have also been very popular, but their popularity is decreasing over the years. We also analyzed how papers have addressed this year's conference theme on "Free, Safe and Sustainable World," finding that not many papers have tackled it in the past. However, we consider that this is an emergent topic that should be addressed in a world of ever-increasing technology development. It is important to adapt the future of learning to address the current global challenges and continue growing in a safe, free, and sustainable world.

This work has some limitations. First of all, we did not use the complete proceedings of EC-TEL since we excluded demo and poster papers from our analysis. With respect to the keyword analysis, we are limited by authors' keywords, expecting they cover all the possible topics addressed in each paper. However, usually, it is not like that. As part of our future work, we will be expanding this analysis to the conference's entire trajectory, including the 15 years of manuscripts. As we have also collected all the papers' metadata, including authors and also citations available in the full manuscript, we are working on a network analysis to establish relations between the different papers and authors across the conference trajectory. We expect our study to shed some light on the latest trends and evolution of EC-TEL.

References

1. Elsevier: About Scopus (2021). https://www.elsevier.com/es-es/solutions/scopus
2. Fabry, D.L., Higgs, J.R.: Barriers to the effective use of technology in education: current status. J. Educ. Comput. Res. **17**(4), 385–395 (1997)
3. Firssova, O., et al.: Mobile inquiry-based learning with sensor-data in the school: effects on student motivation. In: Rensing, C., de Freitas, S., Ley, T., Muñoz-Merino, P.J. (eds.) EC-TEL 2014. LNCS, vol. 8719, pp. 112–124. Springer, Cham (2014). https://doi.org/10.1007/978-3-319-11200-8_9
4. Kammer, T., Brauner, P., Leonhardt, T., Schroeder, U.: Simulating LEGO Mindstorms robots to facilitate teaching computer programming to school students. In: Kloos, C.D., Gillet, D., Crespo García, R.M., Wild, F., Wolpers, M. (eds.) EC-TEL 2011. LNCS, vol. 6964, pp. 196–209. Springer, Heidelberg (2011). https://doi.org/10.1007/978-3-642-23985-4_16
5. Kirkwood, A., Price, L.: Technology-enhanced learning and teaching in higher education: what is 'enhanced' and how do we know? a critical literature review. Learn. Media Technol. **39**(1), 6–36 (2014)
6. Noble, H., Smith, J.: Reviewing the literature: choosing a review design (2018)
7. Øhrstrøm, P., Sandborg-Petersen, U., Thorvaldsen, S., Ploug, T.: Teaching logic through web-based and gamified quizzing of formal arguments. In: Hernández-Leo, D., Ley, T., Klamma, R., Harrer, A. (eds.) EC-TEL 2013. LNCS, vol. 8095, pp. 410–423. Springer, Heidelberg (2013). https://doi.org/10.1007/978-3-642-40814-4_32
8. Prieto, L.P., Asensio-Pérez, J.I., Dimitriadis, Y., Gómez-Sánchez, E., Muñoz-Cristóbal, J.A.: GLUE!-PS: a multi-language architecture and data model to deploy TEL designs to multiple learning environments. In: Kloos, C.D., Gillet, D., Crespo García, R.M., Wild, F., Wolpers, M. (eds.) EC-TEL 2011. LNCS, vol. 6964, pp. 285–298. Springer, Heidelberg (2011). https://doi.org/10.1007/978-3-642-23985-4_23
9. Rickinson, M., May, H.: A comparative study of methodological approaches to reviewing literature. The Higher Education Academy, York Science Park, Heslington. Retrieved January 23, 2017 (2009)
10. Science, W.O.: Web of science (2021). https://apps.webofknowledge.com/
11. Springer: European conference on technology enhanced learning (2021). https://link.springer.com/conference/ectel

Interactive Screencasts as Learning Tools in Introductory Programming

Kristina Litherland(✉) [ID], Anders Kluge [ID], and Anders I. Mørch [ID]

Department of Education, University of Oslo, P.O. Box 1092, 0317 Blindern, Oslo, Norway
kristina.litherland@iped.uio.no

Abstract. The purpose of this study was to investigate how interactive screencasts enhance learning in computer science education. We employed a socio-cultural perspective on learning, understanding interactive screencasts as mediating tools in elective introductory programming courses taught in secondary education in Norway. In this qualitative study, we used an interactive screencasting tool that captures a voice track and screen activity as two separate but conceptually connected processes. Based on audio–visual recordings of classroom interactions and student-produced screencasts, we suggest understanding screencast recording as an extended part of the learning process, where the students' focus shift from technical development to collaborative knowledge development.

Keywords: Screencasts · Introductory programming · Design-based research

1 Introduction

In this study, we investigated the interactive screencast as a new and innovative method for teaching and learning introductory programming. Screencast is a synonym for screen recording, i.e. captured activities on a digital screen, often accompanied by a voice track. Screencasts in programming education have a wide range of uses, from directed instructional videos to students' recordings of their own knowledge development [3, 5]. We employed a socio-cultural perspective of learning; that is, we considered learning a mediated interaction via language (e.g. dialogue in small groups) and using digital as well as physical tools [7, 8].

In a survey of 27 empirical studies in teaching and learning programming, Lye and Koh [4] found that research in computer science (CS) education is focused on conceptual programming knowledge, such as selection (if-then-else) and repetition (loops), identifying a gap in the literature regarding students' programming practices. The authors recommended further studies of concrete (hands-on) programming practices, including the use of design-based (interventionist) research methods and students' verbal and on-screen interactions as data, which we did in this study. We asked the following research question: *How does the use of an integrated and interactive screencasting tool support and extend learning processes in programming education?*

Throughout the study, we used the web-based tool Scrimba, which includes a file directory, code editor, output window, recording tool, and playback functionality. When recording, Scrimba captures audio-visual activity (soundtrack and screen activity). Technically, a screencast in this tool is not a video, per se, but a set of recorded events and audio played in sequence with a reduced file size – approximately 1% of the size of an equivalent video file, increasing possible application areas. All the technical objects in the screencasts – such as text, program code and output – are interactive and modifiable, making Scrimba suitable for a wide range of different learning activities. In essence, watching screencasts, reading other peoples' code, and developing your own code and screencasts, are integrated activities within the same tool.

In the next section, we describe the method we applied in this study. In Sect. 3, we present two data extracts. Finally, in Sect. 4, we discuss our preliminary results, paving the way for future research.

2 Method

We framed the study using design-based research (DBR) [1], a research method for studying learning in authentic contexts through interventions that often involves various stakeholders. The project was a collaboration between the developers of the screencasting tool, six schools, researchers and an experienced reference teacher. Together, the team developed the classroom intervention, which we tested in six secondary schools, in the school years 8 to 13, over the course of two academic years. Data in this paper is from the second design iteration. We performed two iterations of the intervention. In this paper, we focus on Scrimba as a code editor compared to Scrimba for recording student-produced screencasts. Six teachers and 134 students participated in the project.

The dataset consisted of two different types of audio–visual recordings: video recordings of classroom activity (28 h) and screencasts produced by students and teachers (71 screencasts, in total 7 h). All the teachers and students (or their guardians) signed a written consent form to participate in the study. The first author translated all the transcripts from Norwegian into English.

We analysed the data using thematic analysis [2] and used a combination of deductive and inductive coding of the data, sometimes referred to as abductive thematic analysis [6]. We used an initial set of codes (existing theories) as initial categories, and then we let the "data speak for itself" within those categories (inductive coding). Next, we iterated between codes and data instances until a stable set of codes emerged. Due to the space restrictions of this paper, we present only two data excerpts representing the theme of verbal and technical development.

3 Data

The excerpts below are transcribed verbal dialogues where two students worked together on a pair-programming task to develop simple functionality for a virtual automated teller machine (ATM). The task included printing the value of the account balance and making functionality to "deposit" and "withdraw" money from the account (i.e. changing the balance variable based on input from the user). In Scrimba, we provided the students with a written description of the task, and a draft program that included a dummy form and incomplete JavaScript to use as a starting point for solving the task. The draft code included named (but incomplete) functions, with descriptions of what they should do.

The students in the two excerpts below encountered two problems when solving the task: default actions in forms and converting input values to the correct data types (numbers). In the following extract, the students identified the data type problem when they tried adding 789 to 20000, and got an output of 20000789. Student B had just suggested using the Number() function to solve the problem.

Table 1. Students working on the data types of input values.

Turn	Actor	Utterance	Action/comment/code
1.1	G	Yes, it's because of the numbers. It's not treating them as numbers, it just puts them one after the other.	Confirming that the code is not adding the numbers together correctly.
1.2	B	Then we either have to… We need to make… Deposit dot value… Balance dot value… or do I need…?	Discussing which of the that needs a changed data type.
1.3	G	No, it's a variable, you can't put value on it.	Referring to the balance variable not being an input field and therefore not having a value attribute.
1.4	B	Okay. If we put Number outside here then? How do you do that?	`$Number({saldo + inpInntak.value})`
1.5	G	I don't remember any of the Number stuff.	
1.6	B	I'll just try something. Yes, haha, oops.	B runs the code, laughs when he sees his code is output as pure text: $Number({saldo + inpInntak.value})
1.7	G	But isn't Number something you add when you define the variable?	B undoes the changes and tests again, reproducing the error from earlier: 20000 + 890 = 20000890.
1.8	B	Okay. Let balance equal Number (20000)	Reads out while typing: `let saldo = Number(20000);`

The Number() function, in layman's terms, converts values to numbers. G agreed with B about using this function, explaining that the program cannot process the values as numbers. However, even though the students identified the bug and its solution (using the Number() function), they struggled to implement it. They did not understand that the data type of the input value was incorrect, as demonstrated in turn 1.8 when B used Number() on the balance variable, which was already a number. After several minutes of troubleshooting, they called the teacher, who helped them use Number() on the correct value.

Later during the same class, the two students recorded the final moments of their four-minute screencast, explaining their virtual ATM code. G took the lead and talked about the depositMoney (settInnPenger) function they worked on in Table 1.

Table 2. Coding and developing knowledge while recording a screencast

Turn	Actor	Utterance	Action/comment/code
2.1	G	Then we update the global variable [balance/saldo]. Then we change... We don't need this?	G highlights part of the code `saldo= saldo + Number(inpInntak.value); info.innerHTML="Du har satt inn: ${inpInntak.value} og du (inpInntak.value)} igjen på saldoen" txtSaldo.innerHTML = saldo + Number(inpInntak.value);`
2.2	B	Yes. No, we don't. There, that's better.	G deletes the above highlighted code
2.3	G	Then we have to call the functions at the bottom. What is this actually used for?	G points to the depositMoney (settInnPenger) reference `skjemaUttak.onsubmit = taUtPenger; skjemaInntak.onsubmit = settInnPenger;`
2.4	B	It's like when you click the button, it runs [the function].	
2.5	G	It runs	G confirms B's statement.

In turn 2.1, mid-sentence, G noticed an error in the program that stemmed from their struggle with data types. B first ignored dismissed the error, but acknowledged it after a moment's thought. G deleted the highlighted code in turn 2.2. In turn 2.3, G shifted focus to the last two of the code, explaining how they invoked the deposit and withdrawal functions. G was unsure about the functions' invocation but B helped her by clarifying in simpler terms. In essence, her first understanding was correct.

4 Discussion

Scrimba allowed us to provide the students with a draft code in a simple and convenient way. Because of the available code, the students could move straight to the formalities of developing the JavaScript functions, focusing their attention on the problem at hand, and stimulating reading and reflecting on the framework (draft) on which they were building.

The whole task, including reading the assignment, receiving and reading the draft, code development, testing, presenting and recording, took place within the same tool. In fact, B and G never left Scrimba or opened any other window throughout the one-hour ATM task. This finding shows how lightweight tools can provide an integrated development environment usable in various learning activities.

The students continued working with the code during the screencast recording. In Table 2, we saw that not only was the technical object (the code) developed during the recording, but it also created a situation where G could ask her partner about a part of the code about which she was unsure. Changing the task allowed the students to view the code afresh so that they noticed new ways to develop both the code and their own understanding. While the development process seen in Table 1 was characterised by trial and error, it turned to a more focused learning process during the recording session in Table 2. The students did not test the code after editing it in turn 2.2, strengthening the claim that this was a different type of development compared to what we saw in Table 1. Recording the screencast created an environment in which the students could learn from each other [8], instead of focusing on making the program 'work'.

However, some recording issues are worth mentioning. The problems the students encountered in the development process (default actions and understanding data types) were either ignored or mentioned in passing while recording – giving the impression (consciously or not) that the students had no problems solving the task. For instance, the Number() function and the term 'data types' were never mentioned in the screencast, even though they spent a lot of time on this issue during initial development. This finding indicates that the students' collective understanding may have been underdeveloped in relation to the complexity of the program code. Therefore, the screencasts only provide an approximate account of the learning process. Instead, screencast recordings should be thought of as an extended part of the learning process, where the focus shifts from technical development to collaborative knowledge development and reflection [7].

The interactivity of the screencasting tool lied in the integration of the different stages of the task. The technical objects (codes) were interactive at the same level of abstraction regardless of the students' mode of working, including after the final recording of the screencast.

In future work, we continue exploring how interactive screencasts methodologically and pedagogically compare to researchers' observation in programming education.

References

1. Barab, S., Squire, K.: Design-based research: putting a stake in the ground. J. Learn. Sci. **13**(1), 1–14 (2004)
2. Braun, V., Clarke, V.: Thematic analysis. In: Cooper, H., Camic, P.M., Long, D.L., Panter, A.T., Rindskopf, D., Sher, K.J. (eds.) APA Handbook of Research Methods in Psychology, vol. 2, pp. 57–71. American Psychological Association (2012)
3. Kluge, A., Litherland, K.L., Borgen, P.H., Langslet, G.O.: Combining programming with audio explanations. In: Proceedings of the ICETC 2019, pp. 155–159. ACM, New York (2019)
4. Lye, S.Y., Koh, J.H.L.: Review on teaching and learning of computational thinking through programming: what is next for K-12? Comput. Hum. Behav. **41**, 51–61 (2014)
5. Powell, L.M.: Evaluating the effectiveness of self-created student screencasts as a tool to increase student learning outcomes in a hands-on computer programming course. Inf. Syst. Educ. J. **13**(5), 106 (2015)
6. Reichertz, J.: Induction, deduction, abduction. In: Flick, U. (ed.) The SAGE Handbook of Qualitative Data Analysis, pp. 123–135. SAGE Publications, London (2014)
7. Stahl, G.: Group Cognition: Computer Support for Building Collaborative Knowledge (Acting with Technology). The MIT Press, Cambridge (2006)
8. Vygotsky, L.S., Luria, A.R.: Tool and symbol in child development. In: Valsiner, J., van der Veer, R. (eds.) The Vygotsky Reader, pp. 99–175. Blackwell, Oxford (1994)

Teachers' Orchestration Needs During the Shift to Remote Learning

LuEttaMae Lawrence[1(✉)], Kenneth Holstein[1], Susan R. Berman[2], Stephen Fancsali[2], Bruce M. McLaren[1], Steven Ritter[2], and Vincent Aleven[1]

[1] Carnegie Mellon University, Pittsburgh, USA
{llawrenc,kjholste,bmclaren,aleven}@andrew.cmu.edu
[2] Carnegie Learning, Pittsburgh, USA
{sberman,sfancsali,sritter}@carnegielearning.com

Abstract. Transitioning from in-person to remote instruction has forced teachers to navigate unexpected constraints while providing meaningful learning experiences for their students. This transition has drastically changed how teachers orchestrate learning for their students. To explore these unique orchestration challenges, we used needs finding and validation activities to explore middle school teachers' emergent needs and constraints during the unplanned shift to remote instruction. Our findings highlight the need for informative, real-time tools, issues with workload and burnout, and concerns with students feeling disconnected. The contribution of this work includes insights from the early stages of our design process and reflections on how we might support teachers during remote learning and in navigating future emergency shifts.

Keywords: Participatory design · COVID-19 · K-12 teaching · Orchestration

1 Introduction and Background

The transition from in-person to remote instruction has drastically changed how teachers *orchestrate learning*, meaning their *ability to manage variables in learning environments* [1]. Without the physical and contextual indicators of the classroom, teachers have lost a primary channel of information about their students, creating challenges to their typical orchestration. This shift has introduced new variables, never considered part of a teachers' orchestration (e.g., students' internet access at home [2]). Throughout this paper, we use the terminology *remote instruction*, recognizing the context of crisis, specifically, *emergency online teaching during the pandemic*. By using this term, we acknowledge the differences between remote instruction during the pandemic and traditional online learning. Remote instruction was rushed, did not allow teachers to sufficiently plan, and caused stress and trauma for teachers [3].

While some of the orchestration challenges teachers are experiencing during the pandemic are new, many stem from existing inequities that have been exacerbated by the pandemic [4]. Centering teachers in the design of tools can reposition them as having power in addressing new and existing orchestration challenges. Previous research on orchestration tools have focused on in-person learning environments (e.g., [5–7]), yet there remains a need to investigate how existing and future tools work in remote contexts, to account for future emergencies (e.g., future pandemic or natural disasters) or accessibility for students who need to rapidly shift to remote instruction. Given the unique challenges of teacher orchestration amidst the COVID-19 pandemic and the potential future shifts to remote instruction, we ask *what are the unique orchestration challenges teachers face amidst the shift to remote instruction?*

2 Methods

2.1 Learning Context

We report on needs finding and concept validation activities with teachers who use Carnegie Learning's adaptive learning system called *MATHia* [8]. *MATHia* is an intelligent tutoring system (ITS) for middle and high school mathematics in which students learn math content through multi-step, complex problems. Within the *MATHia* system, the teacher has access to reports about the students' overall progress and a classroom orchestration tool called *LiveLab*. Designed for in-person classroom use, *LiveLab* directs teachers' attention to students who may need monitoring.

2.2 Participants

The participants were six middle school math teachers from six school districts across the United States. Three were teaching remotely and three were teaching in a hybrid model. These teachers had a range from four to thirty years of experience teaching. Five teachers used *MATHia* as a regular component of their teaching pre-COVID-19 and all were using it in their remote instruction.

2.3 Design and Procedures

We conducted six, hour-long sessions with one teacher. During sessions, we first conducted semi-structured interviews with open-ended questions to understand how teachers had adapted to remote instruction since the pandemic began and uncover emergent constraints when using *MATHia* in a remote setting. Second, we conducted a storyboard-based speed dating exercise [9]. We asked the teachers for feedback on storyboard concepts regarding how they identified students who need help, how they might receive this information, and what they needed to reach out to students.

2.4 Data Collection and Analysis

Sessions were held and recorded over a video platform, resulting in approximately six hours of video recording, which were transcribed for analysis. We analyzed the interviews using thematic analysis [10], allowing themes to emerge naturally regarding our research question rather than assigning predefined codes. This allowed us to evaluate the data considering the needs and challenges of orchestration learning during the pandemic rather than reproducing themes reported in the literature that do not reflect these new complexities. To create these themes, we used Affinity Diagramming [11], a design method for clustering and re-clustering quotes from interviews to identify emerging themes. The data used in the clustering were on-topic dialogue from interviews as individual quotes. Across these six interviews, we analyzed 242 quotes extracted from transcripts.

3 Results

To answer our research question, we extracted seven high-level themes, using the methods described above.

Learning Process: "I Wish I Could See What They're Doing." All teachers described frustration when it came to identifying what students needed or how they were doing. One teacher who taught remotely explained, *"I would definitely say that's one of my weaknesses right now is figuring out skills that students are struggling with. And then like working backwards and solidifying those skills, and helping them understand, I just can't see it."* Several teachers noted the value in being able to see students' actions like in-person instruction. Teachers described requesting screenshots or asking students to share their screens during meetings. Not all students engaged one-on-one with teachers. One fully remote teacher said, *"You know, there's always five kids that stick out in a class. And when you can't see these kids, how do you know? In a classroom, you can walk around. They can't avoid you. And I feel like they can avoid you right now."*

Real-Time: "I Want to Know As Soon As Possible." Teachers shared concerns that they could not identify and correct problems immediately as they could in-person. Not being able to pinpoint misconceptions quickly meant they could be missing moments of struggle until an assessment. Teachers also described missing the ability to quickly provide praise and support. One teacher remarked, *"Encouragement is a huge part of learning, saying, 'hey, you're moving in the right direction!'"* Identifying these moments to praise and reward students is hard during remote instruction.

Collaboration: "Use Each Other to Support Each Other." All teachers emphasized the importance of using group work during remote learning. They each had their own method of facilitating remote collaboration that was largely impacted by factors out of their control, including the technology their school offered, internet access, or class size. Some teachers described using virtual break-out rooms, a feature of video conferencing software, to facilitate small group work, while others explained their refusal to use such tools for issues such as bullying. One teacher felt without supervision online collaboration was not yet feasible for her classes. Even though this teacher described the benefits of using collaboration.

Technology Limitations: "It's Just Too Much!" All teachers faced limitations of technology including *students' technology management* and *internet access*. Even though many students were familiar with technology, the transition to managing multiple websites and learning platforms from home was challenging. One remote teacher described responses she got from a survey to ask how students were doing, *"I had the kids answer* a question, like what's going well and what's not. And a lot of them just said, 'It's just too much! It's Google classroom, it's Google forms, it's MATHia. We don't know where to go.' You know, and I don't have an answer for them."* All teachers touched on internet constraints during the interviews. Several reported most of their students had internet access, but every class had a few students who struggled to get access or had limitations due to rural locations. One teacher who saw her students two days a week in person explained, *"I mean. I haven't asked [about access] and I keep meaning to… I haven't asked them, but it's like I haven't asked because there is too many other things."* This comment represents issues around internet access but also workload.

Teacher Load: "I Have Two Classrooms Going All the Time." All participating teachers noted the high demands and exhaustion of teaching during the pandemic. There was a consensus about feelings of stress and burnout. A teacher who taught in a hybrid context depicted her increased teaching load, *"In reality, it's twice as much. I have two classrooms going all the time. Yeah, all the time! Two classrooms!"* She and the two other teachers with hybrid classes explained, managing a group of students in person and at home was overwhelming.

Teachers wanted information as soon as possible, but on their terms, to have agency over how best to allocate their time. They requested designs to customize the information they received and when and how it was delivered. There was excitement regarding designs that could support teachers. One teacher justified many of her choices as being in *"survival mode"* and strongly requested the designs discussed to be implemented soon as it was encouraging to discuss tools that could alleviate stress.

Transition to Remote: "We Can't Do This Every Day." One constraint that contributed to the high workload of teachers was the issue that lessons and tools were not designed for remote instruction, such as *LiveLab*. The teachers who used *LiveLab* before the start of the pandemic described how their interactions with the tool changed. One teacher who taught remotely explained, *"So I'm not using [LiveLab] too much this year so far simply because I don't know that they're all on at the same time nor can I see their screens at the same time."*

Student Interactions: "They are Disconnected." Teachers also acknowledged challenges regarding students, including *issues of engagement* and *communication*. One hybrid teacher, summarized her interactions with her students, *"We're four weeks into the school year, which means, you know, I've seen these kids and they ought to kind of be lightening up a little bit… It is almost sad. They are disconnected."* This theme of feeling disconnected resonated with many teachers, describing many barriers (e.g., distractions at home and disengaged students). Some teachers acknowledged positive components of communications; one remote teacher explained her school district provided time daily to work with her students, which resulted in positive interactions with many students (even though not all students were willing to meet). For other teachers, their communication varied by the tools supplied by their school districts and the students' willingness to engage.

4 Discussion and Conclusions

In this paper, we contribute insights from our initial design process regarding *challenges teachers have experienced during the transition to remote instruction*. We argue some of our findings have implications regarding how we might support teachers in remote learning and in navigating future emergency shifts to remote learning. Teachers expressed needs for real-time tools to provide additional details about *what students were doing and what they needed help with*, reiterating findings from previous studies [1, 5, 7]. These issues were exacerbated during remote learning by teachers' loss of ability to monitor students for valuable physical cues. Our findings also highlighted that *LiveLab*, developed specifically for in-person awareness and monitoring did not directly transfer to remote teaching, demonstrating a need to explore how orchestration tools might be designed to support shifts in different learning environments. These findings highlight important future work for designers of orchestration technology regarding *how technology might support teachers in future remote teaching contexts* and *how future tools might be developed to support seamless shifts between in-person and remote instruction?*

Acknowledgment. This work was supported in part by the Institution of Educational Sciences (IES; R305A180301). We thank all participating teachers and reviewers.

References

1. Dillenbourg. P., Prieto, L.P., Olsen, J.K.: Classroom orchestration. In: International Handbook of the Learning Sciences, pp. 180–190 (2018)
2. Skates, L., Chan, C.: Edtech's answer to remote learning burnout. Andreessen Horowitz (2020)
3. Hodges, C., Moore, S., Lockee, B., Trust, T., Bond, A.: Remote teaching and online learning. Educ. Rev. 1–15 (2020)
4. Jurow, A.S., Shea, M.: Learning in equity-oriented scale-making projects. J. Learn. Sci. **24**(2), 286–307 (2015)
5. Wise, A.F., Jung, Y.: Teaching with analytics: towards a situated model of instructional decision-making. J. Learn. Anal. **6**(2), 53–69 (2019)
6. Lawrence, L., Mercier, E.: Co-design of an orchestration tool: supporting engineering teaching assistants as they facilitate collaborative learning. Interact. Des. Archit. J. **42**, 111–130 (2019)
7. Holstein, K., McLaren, B.M., Aleven, V.: Co-designing a real-time classroom orchestration tool to support teacher–AI complementarity. J. Learn. Anal. **6**(2), 27–52 (2019)
8. Ritter, S., Anderson, J.R., Koedinger, K.R., Corbett, A.: Cognitive tutor: applied research in mathematics education. Psychon. Bull. Rev. **14**(2), 249–255 (2007)
9. Davidoff, S., Lee, M.K., Dey, A.K., Zimmerman, J.: Rapidly exploring application design through speed dating. In: Krumm, J., Abowd, G.D., Seneviratne, A., Strang, T. (eds.) UbiComp 2007. LNCS, vol. 4717, pp. 429–446. Springer, Heidelberg (2007). https://doi.org/10.1007/978-3-540-74853-3_25
10. Braun, V., Clarke, V.: Using thematic analysis in psychology. Qual. Res. Psychol. **4**, 77–101 (2006)
11. Martin, B., Hanington, B.: Universal Methods of Design: 100 Ways to Explore Complex Problems, Develop Innovative Strategies, and Deliver Effective Design Solutions (2012)

Designing a Pre-service Teacher Community Platform: A Focus on Participants' Motivations

Nicolas Felipe Gutiérrez-Páez(✉), Patricia Santos, Davinia Hernández-Leo, and Mar Carrió

Universitat Pompeu Fabra, 08005 Barcelona, Spain
{nicolas.gutierrez,patricia.santos,davinia.hernandez-leo,
mar.carrio}@upf.edu

Abstract. Online communities (OC) have several applications in the domain of education with a special focus on teacher professional development. The development of OC of teachers enables knowledge exchange, reflection on teacher practice, sharing of educational resources, and emotional support. Nevertheless, several barriers have been found to affect community members' participation such as their time constraints due to teachers' busy schedules, the community moderation and social support, and their peripheral participation. This research aims to better understand teachers' initial motivations to participate in such OCs, and how useful is this information to tackle and reduce the barriers that affect their participation. We present how a supporting platform for an OC of teachers is designed following a design-based research methodology within a pre-service science teacher master course to explore, share, and comment learning designs. We gathered information about 40 pre-service teachers' motivations to participate in the OC and their perceptions about the supporting platform. Results suggest that participants' main motivation is to gain knowledge and to use technologies to simplify designing and sharing of learning designs. In contrast, reputation is the least important motivation to participate in such an OC. These results provide valuable information to refine the designed platform as there is a relationship between participants' motivations and the perceived importance of the implemented features of the supporting platform. Further iterations will evaluate the refinements and the usefulness of the implemented features.

Keywords: Online communities · Teacher communities · Motivations · Learning design

1 Introduction

Online communities (OCs) have several applications in the domain of education with a special focus on teacher professional development [5]. The development of OC of teachers enables knowledge exchange, reflection on teacher practice, sharing of educational resources, and emotional support [7]. As in any type of OC, issues around community members' participation and motivations pose main challenges in OCs of teachers. For instance, teachers' willingness to participate is described as means of sharing information and creating repositories of shared resources, as a source of collegial support and emotional engagement and reflection [6]. However, several barriers have been found to affect community members' participation such as their time constraints due to teachers' busy schedules, the community moderation and social support, and their peripheral participation [6,7]. Furthermore, each OC requires different types of support according to members' pre-existing relationships, preferences, motivation, and curiosity to reveal meaning in the specific educational community [8]. This study aims to design a supporting platform to explore, share and discuss learning designs (LDs) in a pre-service teachers' community, while understanding participants motivations and the relationship with the perceived usefulness of the implemented features.

2 Methodology

This research follows design-based research methodology (Fig. 1), since it allows to adjust systematically and iteratively aspects of the designed platform so that each change works as an experimentation test environment, and generates theory and reusable design in real situations [11]. This paper presents the preliminary results of the first two phases and the first iteration of the third phase. Second iteration and the fourth phase are currently being performed and are out of the scope of this paper.

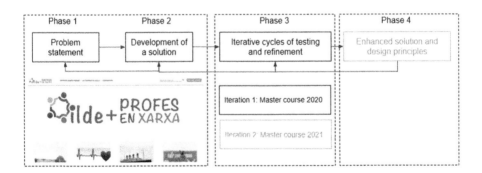

Fig. 1. Design-based research methodology diagram, based on [1].

In the first two phases, a minimum viable product (MVP) of the ILDE platform [2] was designed, called ILDE+. According to previous studies, teachers' motivations to participate in online communities include exploring ideas to gain knowledge and experience, improve the field of teaching, combating teacher isolation, curiosity and utilizing the advantages of online environments [3,4]. Thus, five main features were included in the MVP: it implements **a template** to help with the creation of new LDs and to gather metadata to **filter LDs** when exploring the available content in the community. It also allows users to add **comments** on LDs, as well as to **duplicate an LD** to further modify it, always keeping the authorship of the original design. Users can also **co-design resources** by sharing the authorship of a design. Besides, ILDE+ implements **community features** such as a like button, and design counters of views and comments. Users can also explore community members, and follow them to get information about their contributions within the community. This MVP version of the ILDE platform gathers the characteristics needed to support an OC of teachers [12].

In the third phase we propose iteration cycles to test and refine the MVP within a pre-service science teacher master course. In the first iteration, an introductory face-to-face activity was performed. First, participants filled a pre-questionnaire (N = 40) about their motivations to participate in OCs or platforms for sharing and exploring learning activities or didactic units. An adapted version of the motivational model used by Nov et al. [10] was used and six motivational factors were evaluated: collective motives (COM), reputation benefits (REP), social interaction benefits (SOI), enjoyment (FUN), the interest of acquiring knowledge Furthermore (KNO), and use of technology to simplify activities currently performed without the help of any tool (SIM). Then, participants used the ILDE+ platform to explore previously uploaded LDs for inspiration and then to share their own LDs. Afterwards, a focus group with all the 40 participants was conducted to know their perceptions about the platform and about the participation incentives that could be implemented, as well as to deeply discuss the positive and negative aspects of the platform. During the focus group, a researcher participated as an observer, taking field notes. After the activity, participants filled a post-questionnaire with open-ended questions about their perception of the platform and desired features (N = 30).

3 Preliminary Results

The analysis of the motivations to participate in an OC for sharing and exploring their educational activities designs (Fig. 2) showed that participants main motivation is to gain knowledge ($M_{KNO} = 4$, $Mo_{KNO} = 4$), followed by the use of technology to simplify activities currently performed without the help of any tool ($M_{SIM} = 3$, $Mo_{SIM} = 2$), which is in line with other with previous research [3,4]. In contrast, respondents have indicated that reputation ($M_{REP} = 2$, $Mo_{REP} = 2$) is the least important motivation to participate in such an OC. Nevertheless, previous research [9] indicates the importance of reputation systems in OCs, as reputation is highly associated with leadership and trust among community members.

During the focus group session, one of the discussed topics was the best way to display and recommend LDs for users. Participants acknowledged the

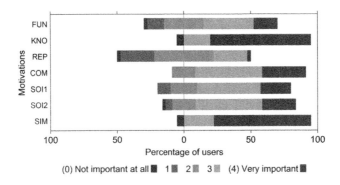

Fig. 2. Motivations to participate in an OC for didactic units and classroom activities design sharing.

importance of rankings as a way to explore the most useful designs and the best contributors, even when reputation is not a motivator for them. They also indicated that the template for uploading designs was too long and they did not fill it entirely, but they acknowledged the importance of the metadata collected through the template in order to explore and discover other users' LDs. Another important issue mentioned by participants is the quantity and quality of the available LDs. To complement this analysis, a content analysis was done with the open-ended answers using manual coding, and general topics were defined. Regarding the positive aspects, participants highlighted the simplicity of the platform and that it is easy to use (11 responses), as well as the ability to explore other teachers' ideas (6 responses) and the available filtering options (6 responses). As for the aspects to improve, users pointed out the limited number of available LDs during the training session. Regarding the desired features, even when users do not consider social interaction as the main motivator, they would like to have social network features such as forums or private chats to discuss and to contact directly with other members.

4 Conclusions and Future Work

Results of participants' perceived motivations offered valuable information to refine and enhance the ILDE+ platform. Since participants main motivation is to improve their skills and extend their knowledge (intrinsic motivation) through the exploration and sharing of LDs in an easy-to-use environment, the fields of the creation template were reduced to simplify the process. Additionally, a progress indicator was added to show each member how complete is a design (based on the template fields) to reduce the number of designs without any metadata and to provide an initial feedback to the users about the completeness of their own designs and about its usefulness within the community. Based on the feedback obtained from the focus group, the community features of the platform were refined, as social interaction is important for community members, and filters for exploring designs and members were added based on likes, comments, views and followers rankings. These community features were used to add a list of featured designs to the home section of the platform, which is automatically updated based on the comments, visualizations and likes each design has. These results are strongly connected to the context in which the analysis was conducted, making them difficult to generalize to other communities or platforms. For this reason, additional iteration cycles are being performed to collect data from other communities and platforms beyond pre-service teachers, as well as to understand how motivations relate with participants behavior and performance within the community, and the usefulness of the different incentives implemented.

Acknowledgments. This work has been partially funded by the EU Regional Development Fund and the National Research Agency of the Spanish Ministry of Science and Innovation under project grants TIN2017-85179-C3-3-R and PID2020-112584RB-C33. P. Santos acknowledges the support by the Spanish Ministry of Science and Innovation under the Ramon y Cajal programme. D. Hernández-Leo (Serra Húnter) acknowledges the support by ICREA under the ICREA Academia program.

References

1. Amiel, T., Reeves, T.C.: Design-based research and educational technology: rethinking technology and the research agenda. J. Educ. Technol. Soc. **11**(4), 29–40 (2008)
2. Hernández-Leo, D., et al.: An integrated environment for learning design. Front. ICT **5**, 9 (2018). https://doi.org/10.3389/fict.2018.00009
3. Hew, K.F., Hara, N.: Empirical study of motivators and barriers of teacher online knowledge sharing. Educ. Tech. Res. Dev. **55**(6), 573 (2007). https://doi.org/10.1007/s11423-007-9049-2
4. Hur, J.W., Brush, T.A.: Teacher participation in online communities. J. Res. Technol. Educ. **41**(3), 279–303 (2009). https://doi.org/10.1080/15391523.2009.10782532
5. Kirschner, P.A., Lai, K.: Online communities of practice in education. Technol. Pedagogy Educ. **16**(2), 127–131 (2007). https://doi.org/10.1080/14759390701406737
6. Lantz-Andersson, A., Lundin, M., Selwyn, N.: Twenty years of online teacher communities: a systematic review of formally-organized and informally-developed professional learning groups. Teach. Teach. Educ. **75**, 302–315 (2018). https://doi.org/10.1016/j.tate.2018.07.008
7. Maciá, M., García, I.: Informal online communities and networks as a source of teacher professional development: a review. Teach. Teach. Educ. **55**, 291–307 (2016). https://doi.org/10.1016/j.tate.2016.01.021
8. Michos, K., Hernández-Leo, D.: Supporting awareness in communities of learning design practice. Comput. Hum. Behav. **85**, 255–270 (2018). https://doi.org/10.1016/j.chb.2018.04.008
9. Muller, P.: Reputation, trust and the dynamics of leadership in communities of practice. J. Manag. Gov. **10**(4), 381–400 (2006). https://doi.org/10.1007/s10997-006-9007-0

10. Nov, O., Anderson, D., Arazy, O.: Volunteer computing: a model of the factors determining contribution to community-based scientific research. In: Proceedings of the 19th International Conference on World Wide Web, pp. 741–750 (2010). https://doi.org/10.1145/1772690.1772766
11. Reimann, P.: Design-based research. In: Markauskaite, L., Freebody, P., Irwin, J. (eds.) Methodological Choice and Design, vol. 9, pp. 37–50. Springer, Dordrecht (2011). https://doi.org/10.1007/978-90-481-8933-5_3
12. Wenger, E.C., Snyder, W.M.: Communities of practice: the organizational Frontier. Harv. Bus. Rev. **78**(1), 139–146 (2000)

Exploring Teachers' Needs for Guidance While Designing for Technology-Enhanced Learning with Digital Tools

Eleni Zalavra[1(✉)], Kyparisia Papanikolaou[2], Yannis Dimitriadis[3], and Cleo Sgouropoulou[1]

[1] University of West Attica, Athens, Greece
ezalavra@uniwa.gr
[2] School of Pedagogical and Technological Education, Athens, Greece
[3] Universidad de Valladolid, Valladolid, Spain

Abstract. Supporting teachers to represent their teaching ideas has attracted researchers' interest in developing digital learning design tools that provide some form of guidance around the design practice in a Technology-Enhanced Learning (TEL) environment. This paper reports on a study in a teacher education context utilising WebCollage as the learning design tool. The research focuses on teachers' needs on determining resources and technologies while designing for TEL. Our findings convey that teachers' needs converge towards a learning design tool providing flexibility to the designer to either (i) utilise a sound scaffolding mechanism incorporating a taxonomy that follows technology advancements or (ii) determine applying resources and technologies without providing any guidance. These findings may stimulate momentum for further attention to researchers involved with learning design tools' development.

Keywords: Learning design · Learning design tools · Technology-Enhanced Learning · Teacher needs · Teacher education

1 Introduction

Supporting teachers to represent their teaching ideas has attracted researchers' interest in developing various digital learning design tools [1–3]. Aiming to help teachers shift from an implicit, belief-based approach towards one more explicit and design-based approach, a key facet of all learning design tools is that they attempt to provide designers with some form of guidance and support around their design practice [4]. However, existing proposals regarding the form and degree of guidance are still inconclusive, as learning design tools also need to have sufficient flexibility to support creativity and accommodate teachers' personal design paths and styles [5, 6].

Focusing on the additional expectations of teachers applying Technology-Enhanced Learning (TEL) methods in their practice [7, 8], research should consider how learning design tools may guide teachers into knowing when, how and what learning technologies to embed in their learning designs. Such research should give voice to the teachers as the better we understand teachers' current practice, the more effectively learning design tools will support them [5, 9, 10]. However, studies on learning design tools have mostly taken on a specialist/researcher (as opposed to a teacher) perspective [2]. Previous research shows that significantly more attention has been paid to developing tools than establishing what teachers designing TEL activities actually need [10].

To this end, our research aims to allow teachers express directly their needs and preferences as TEL designers. We report on an exploratory study in teacher education following a convergent mixed-methods research methodology [12]. As part of broader research addressing several forms of guidance that digital tools may provide, this paper focuses on exploring teachers' needs for determining the resources and technologies incorporated in a learning design.

2 Methods

The study took place in the context of two courses offered in a postgraduate programme in teacher education. Participants were 30 teachers, 16 in-service and 14 pre-service. Their academic disciplines were from a broad spectrum of sciences such as informatics, mathematics, engineering, pedagogy, philosophy, sociology and physical education. The majority, 63%, had not used any learning design tool before the study, while 37% had. Each course involved teachers in a learning design project that include authoring a learning design collaboratively. Specifications that the learning designs had to meet were relevant to the courses' curriculum. The course "Digital Technologies in Distance Learning" required that the learning designs: (i) integrate technological resources with Web-based tools, (ii) follow specific principles for developing distance learning content and (iii) support personalised learning. The module "Collaborative Learning with Digital Technologies" required that the learning designs: (i) apply a collaborative learning technique and (ii) integrate technology with Web 2.0 tools to implement the collaborative technique.

We assigned participants to use the digital tool WebCollage [11] for authoring the designs as we opted to provide them with a design experience in a tool providing mixed guidance to designers. For example, WebCollage scaffolds organising collaborative learning by providing pedagogical patterns whilst, in the case of the resources and technologies utilised in a learning design, it supports a free-form definition.

We applied a convergent mixed-methods research methodology [12], collecting, analysing, and triangulating quantitative with qualitative data. We performed frequency analysis at the quantitative data and content analysis at the qualitative data. Our focus is grounding findings on teachers' experience based on the mixed-methods approach towards a deeper consideration rather than generalising based on quantitative results.

Utilising a survey questionnaire, we addressed several forms of guidance that digital tools may provide to teachers as TEL designers. In this paper, due to space limitations, we present participants' responses in two closed-ended questions as Likert-scaled statements and one open-ended question. As resources and technologies are core elements of TEL, through this data, we address the research question, *"How do teachers prefer determining the resources and technologies of a learning design?"*.

3 Results

We report the results of 27 valid survey questionnaires. Figure 1 includes the frequencies of the responses to the statements of the two closed-ended questions.

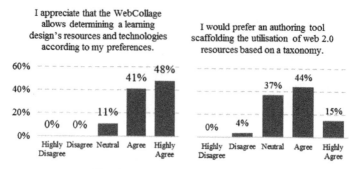

Fig. 1. Quantitative results (n = 27).

In the content analysis of the responses to the open-ended question asking participants to argue on their needs either by commenting on issues addressed in the closed-ended questions or suggesting others, we extracted two categories. One category provides a solid argument for preferring a learning design tool like WebCollage that does not scaffold technologies' determination: *"because such a mechanism will be obsolete due to technology advancements"*. The other category suggests a flexible approach providing designers with alternative options: *"According to the designer's preferences, either support him to utilise resources and especially Web 2.0 technologies or simply allow him to decide on his own"*.

The mixed-method analysis considers as quantitative findings that free determination of a design's resources and technologies is favoured; nevertheless, scaffolding based on a taxonomy also shows a remarkable preference. As qualitative findings, we consider that some participants stand against scaffolding the utilisation of resources and technologies while others suggest being flexible to the designers' preferences. The mixed-method interpretation conveys that participants' needs converge towards a learning design tool that provides flexibility to the designer to either (i) utilise a sound scaffolding mechanism incorporating a taxonomy that follows technology advancements or (ii) allow determining the utilisation of resources and technologies without providing any guidance.

4 Discussion and Conclusions

This paper describes a study in teacher education utilising a digital tool to address teachers' needs while designing for TEL. The research focuses on their needs to determine the appropriate resources and technologies for a learning design.

Our findings align with previous research asserting teachers' needs in between guidance and flexibility in structuring a learning design [3, 5] and sheds light on specifically the issue of designers determining the resources and technologies used in designing for learning. In our study, teachers seem open to a tool involving a sound scaffolding mechanism incorporating a taxonomy that follows technology advancements. For example, such a mechanism is the "Typology of Free Web-based Learning Technologies" [13], incorporating 226 technologies arranged into 40 types and 15 clusters. This typology updates the previous "Typology of Web 2.0 Learning Technologies" [14], aiming to support teachers' conceptualising and applying technologies. At the same time, teachers would like to freely apply their preferences, arguing that as technology advancements are soon rendering technologies obsolete, such a mechanism will inevitably not cover all their needs.

Although we conducted the study in the context of a postgraduate programme, the sample of participants, including both in-service and pre-service teachers from several disciplines, may infer findings for all teacher education types. Furthermore, the specifications that the learning designs developed had to meet, including distance learning, collaborative learning and personalised learning under the umbrella of TEL, allows exploring teachers' needs while designing for TEL within a broad spectrum of contemporary learning. This study's context also reports on a rich learning design experience that evolved around two learning design projects over a full academic semester rather than short training sessions and workshops reported in other studies [2, 5, 7] lasting between a few hours up to a couple of days. Consequently, we conclude that the findings of this study may stimulate momentum for further attention to researchers involved with learning design tools' development.

The limitations of this study refer to the small sample of participants, the limited insights provided by the open-ended question, and the utilisation of only one learning design tool [2, 3]. Although our study did not evaluate the tool per se, a future research design may provide participants with a richer design experience if more digital learning design tools are used. Also, it may yield ample insights if qualitative data include apart from open-ended questions and in-depth interviews.

Our future work involves investigating teachers' needs of a learning design's representation regarding other elements, such as the format, the contextualisation, the formalism, and the organisation [5, 6], to achieve an overall perspective of teachers' needs during the learning design process.

Acknowledgments. The authors acknowledge that the publication/registration fees were totally covered by the University of West Attica. The Universidad de Valladolid co-authors acknowledge funding of the European Regional Development Fund and the National Research Agency of the Spanish Ministry of Science, Innovation and Universities, under project grant TIN2017-85179-C3-2-R, and PID2020-112584RB-C32, the European Regional Development Fund and the Regional Government of Castile and Leon, under project grant VA257P18.

References

1. Celik, D., Magoulas, G.D.: A review, timeline, and categorization of learning design tools. In: Chiu, D.K.W., Marenzi, I., Nanni, U., Spaniol, M., Temperini, M. (eds.) ICWL 2016. LNCS, vol. 10013, pp. 3–13. Springer, Cham (2016). https://doi.org/10.1007/978-3-319-47440-3_1

2. Prieto, L.P., Tchounikine, P., Asensio-Pérez, J.I., Sobreira, P., Dimitriadis, Y.: Exploring teachers' perceptions on different CSCL script editing tools. Comput. Educ. **78** (2014). https://doi.org/10.1016/j.compedu.2014.07.002
3. Dagnino, F.M., Dimitriadis, Y.A., Pozzi, F., Asensio-Pérez, J.I., Rubia-Avi, B.: Exploring teachers' needs and the existing barriers to the adoption of Learning Design methods and tools: a literature survey. Br. J. Educ. Technol. **49** (2018). https://doi.org/10.1111/bjet.12695
4. Conole, G., Wills, S.: Representing learning designs - making design explicit and shareable. Educ. Media Int. **50** (2013). https://doi.org/10.1080/09523987.2013.777184
5. Pozzi, F., Asensio-Perez, J.I., Ceregini, A., Dagnino, F.M., Dimitriadis, Y., Earp, J.: Supporting and representing Learning Design with digital tools: in between guidance and flexibility. Technol. Pedagogy Educ. **29** (2020). https://doi.org/10.1080/1475939X.2020.1714708
6. Laurillard, D., et al.: A constructionist learning environment for teachers to model learning designs. J. Comput. Assist. Learn. **29** (2013). https://doi.org/10.1111/j.1365-2729.2011.00458.x
7. Albó, L., Hernández-Leo, D.: Identifying design principles for learning design tools: the case of edCrumble. In: Pammer-Schindler, V., Pérez-Sanagustín, M., Drachsler, H., Elferink, R., Scheffel, M. (eds.) EC-TEL 2018. LNCS, vol. 11082, pp. 406–411. Springer, Cham (2018). https://doi.org/10.1007/978-3-319-98572-5_31
8. Papanikolaou, K.A., Gouli, E, Makrh, K., Sofos, I., Tzelepi, M.: A peer evaluation tool of learning designs. In: Verbert, K., Sharples, M., Klobučar, T. (eds.) EC-TEL 2016. LNCS, vol. 9891, pp. 193–206. Springer, Cham (2016). https://doi.org/10.1007/978-3-319-45153-4_15
9. Bennett, S., Agostinho, S., Lockyer, L.: Technology tools to support learning design: Implications derived from an investigation of university teachers' design practices. Comput. Educ. **81** (2015). https://doi.org/10.1016/j.compedu.2014.10.016
10. Kali, Y., Goodyear, P., Markauskaite, L.: Researching design practices and design cognition: contexts, experiences and pedagogical knowledge-in-pieces. Learn. Media Technol. **36** (2011). https://doi.org/10.1080/17439884.2011.553621
11. Villasclaras-Fernández, E., Hernández-Leo, D., Asensio-Pérez, J.I., Dimitriadis, Y.: Web Collage: an implementation of support for assessment design in CSCL macro-scripts. Comput. Educ. **67** (2013). https://doi.org/10.1016/j.compedu.2013.03.002
12. Creswell, J.W., Plano Clark, V.L.: Designing and Conducting Mixed Methods Research. SAGE Publications Ltd., Thousand Oaks (2017)
13. Bower, M., Torrington, J.: Typology of free Web-based learning technologies. Educause (2020)
14. Bower, M.: Deriving a typology of Web 2.0 learning technologies. Br. J. Educ. Technol. **47** (2016). https://doi.org/10.1111/bjet.12344

Measuring and Predicting Students' Effort: A Study on the Feasibility of Cognitive Load Measures to Real-Life Scenarios

Barbara Moissa[✉], Geoffray Bonnin, and Anne Boyer

Loria, Nancy, France
{barbara.moissa,geoffray.bonnin,anne.boyer}@loria.fr

Abstract. Students' effort is often considered to be a key element in the learning process. As such, it can be a relevant element to integrate in learning analytics tools, such as dashboards, intelligent tutoring systems, adaptive hypermedia systems, and recommendation systems. A prerequisite to do so is to measure and predict it from learning data, which poses some challenges. We propose to rely on the cognitive load theory to infer the students' perceived effort using subjective, performance, behavioral and physiological data collected from 120 seventh grade students. We also estimate students' effort in future tasks using the data from previous tasks. Our results show a high relevance of interaction data to measure students' effort, especially when compared to physiological data. Moreover, we also found that using the data collected on previous tasks allows us to achieve slightly higher accuracy values than the data collected during the task execution. Finally, this approach also allowed us to predict students' perceived effort in future tasks, which, to the best of our knowledge, is one of the first attempts towards this goal.

Keywords: Learning analytics · Students' engagement · Students' effort · Cognitive load · Multimodal data

1 Introduction

Students' effort is often considered a vital determinant of educational success. As such, exploiting this construct to develop learning analytics tools – dashboards, adaptive hypermedia systems, recommendation systems, etc. – could help teachers to save time and improve the quality of their teaching practice. However, despite all the possible ways in which it can be exploited and all the interest it has attracted over the last decades, several challenges still need to be tackled to fully exploit its potential.

Students' effort has been defined in several different ways in the literature. Moreover, these effort definitions are often similar to engagement definitions. In this plethora of overlapping engagement and effort definitions, we believe the most interesting definition for our purposes is the one proposed by Rozo [9]. Effort is defined as a factor related to the actions taken to overcome a difficulty and is considered as an engagement component. This definition is interesting because it removes the ambiguity found in the literature by defining effort as a component of engagement, it links effort to a single task and implies engagement is a long-term construct.

The lack of a widely adopted definition further reflects on the way it is measured, posing the first challenge tackled in this paper. So far, effort has been mostly measured through subjective ratings provided by teachers or students [3], which is time consuming and cumbersome; or through objective measures, such as log data [2,10] and physiological data [2], which are taken over a long-time period (e.g., weeks, months) and do not allow measurements at the task level.

This issue might be overcome by relying on the cognitive load literature. The cognitive load (CL) is the amount of cognitive resources used during the execution of a task, and is considered by several researchers as being equivalent to the mental effort [6,8]. Several studies from this research area seek to identify CL measures, and can therefore contribute to the effort measurement. As examples of such studies we can cite the recent study from Herbig et al. [4], who used multiple regressors to measure students' perceived effort based on physiological data; and the one of Borys et al. [1], who classified students' exercises also using physiological data.

Such measurements might be further exploited to predict the effort in future tasks, which constitutes the second challenge tackled in this paper. To the best of our knowledge, there are only two works seeking to predict some form of students' effort in future tasks. One of these studies predicts whether students will present an effortful behavior or will try to guess the answers of an exercise [11], while the other uses log data to predict the students' cognitive load [5].

2 Measuring and Predicting Students' Effort

In order to measure and predict the student's effort, we used data collected from 120 students of five French schools [7]. From these 120 students, we were able to use the data of 102 students (we excluded the data from 18 participants because it was incomplete), from which 52 are boys and 50 are girls, all of them between 11 and 14 years old. The collected data contain behavioral data (the interaction with the learning environment), physiological data (heart rate, pupil diameter and eye gaze), performance data (grade of students for each exercise) and subjective data (perceived effort using a 7-point Likert scale). From the collected behavioral and physiological data, we derived two types of features: effort features, i.e., features at the scale of one single exercise, and engagement features, i.e., features based on all the exercises already solved by the students. To the best of our knowledge, such engagement features have never been used to infer effort at the task-level. For each student and in each exercise solved, we extracted 128 effort features and 411 engagement features[1].

Measuring the Effort. To study how one can measure how much effort students exerted during an activity using data collected with equipment adapted to real-life, we experimented with several standard classification, regression and ordinal regression models to infer the different level of perceived effort using the data described above. We found that the Extra Trees classifier had the best performance. We also experimented different combinations of features as input to train the models to see how different types of features contribute to the identification of the perceived effort ratings. These combinations were preprocessed in order to remove highly correlated features and were then used to train different models using a 5-fold cross validation process and a grid search to choose the best hyperparameters. We selected too baselines. The first is a dummy classifier that returns random values according to the class distribution. The second is the reproduction, to the best extent possible, of one of the models proposed by Borys et al. [1]. To allow a more direct comparison with their work we also mapped our 7 classes of perceived effort into 3 classes.

The results are shown in Table 1. The left part of the table shows the results when only the effort features are used and the right part when the engagement effort are used. Statistically significant differences with the first baseline[2] are marked by an asterisk (*), and with the second baseline by an octothorp (#).

In the left part of the table (effort features) one can see that all feature sets performed consistently better than chance and had a performance equal or better than the model proposed by Borys et al. [1] when used to classify the data into 7 classes, and comparable with the values obtained by Borys et al. [1] when classifying their data into three cognitive states. This suggests that the proposed measures enable a reliable identification of the amount of effort required from teenage students during English exercises. Furthermore, the model trained with interaction features is as accurate as the other models, which suggests that it might be possible to measure students' effort without resorting to any additional equipment, such as eye trackers and smartwatches, making it even more feasible to be used in real-life scenarios.

In the right part of the table (engagement features), one can see that most of the accuracy values are slightly higher than those obtained with effort features. Those differences are even statistically significant for the behavioral features. Especially, compared to the model of Borys et al. (left part of the table), the best values we obtained when using the engagement features (right part of the table) lead to an increase of 100% with 7 effort levels (0.19 against 0.40), and

---

[1] A full list of the extracted effort and engagement features can be seen here: https://bit.ly/2UUYfuc.

[2] All the statistical tests mentioned in this paper were done with the unpaired Student's T-test (for the parametric data) or the unpaired Mann-Whitney U test (for the non-parametric data) after checking for normality with the Shapiro-Wilk test. The null hypothesis was rejected when p-value < 0.05.

Table 1. Accuracy of the effort measurement models

	Effort features		Engagement features	
	1–7	1–3	1–7	1–3
Dummy	0.19	0.45	0.17	0.42
Borys et al. [1]	0.19	0.59		
Eye activity	0.35 *	0.63 * #	0.38 *	0.67 *
Interactions	0.36 * #	0.66 * #	0.40 *	0.66 *
Performance	0.29 *	0.60 *	0.37 *	0.67 *
Behavioral	0.34 *	0.62 *	0.40 *	0.67 *
Physiological	0.37 * #	0.65 * #	0.38 *	0.68 *
All	0.38 * #	0.66 * #	0.40 *	0.67 *
All + perceived effort			0.40 *	0.67 *

15% with 3 effort levels (0.59 against 0.68). These results suggest that the students' engagement has a better predictive power when it comes to the students' perceived effort. Finally, we also looked at the results obtained when the perceived effort ratings from the previous exercises were also used as input of the classifier (last line of the table). Surprisingly, also using the actual perceived effort values from the previous exercises did not lead to any increase in accuracy compared to when only the inferred effort measurements were used.

Predicting the Effort. To study how one can predict how much effort students will exert in an activity using data collected with equipment adapted to real-life scenarios, we trained models – following the same methodology used to train the previous models – to predict the students' effort in a future exercise (e.g., exercise 4) using the engagement features computed with data from the previous exercises (e.g., exercises 1, 2, and 3).

Table 2. Accuracy of the effort prediction models

Effort levels	1–7	1–3
Dummy	0.16	0.41
Perceived effort	0.38 *	0.61 *
Eye activity	0.39 *	0.64 *
Interactions	0.37 *	0.64 *
Performance	0.37 *	0.59 *
Behavioral	0.36 *	0.63 *
Physiological	0.38 *	0.63 *
All	0.38 *	0.64 *
All + perceived effort	0.37 *	0.64 *

We can see in Table 2 that all feature sets perform consistently better than chance and that the results are similar to the results obtained during the effort measurement (using the engagement features, otherwise they are slightly better). Interestingly, the interaction features are also able to predict students' effort, which allows the model to be exploited in virtual learning environments. Another interesting result is the possibility of exploiting such models without the need of any effort ratings, which are not always available in real-life scenarios.

3 Conclusion

The main goal of this paper was to measure and predict students' effort. We distinguished students' effort from students' engagement, and relied on the cognitive load theory to measure and predict students' effort. We extracted several effort-related and engagement-related features and trained several measurement and prediction models. All of the models performed consistently better than chance, and a few measurement models using effort features presented a better performance than our state-of-the-art baseline. Moreover, we found that interaction data alone can be used to achieve high accuracy measurement and prediction models, and that we do not need the previous explicit effort ratings in order to estimate its value for future tasks.

References

1. Borys, M., Plechawska-Wójcik, M., Wawrzyk, M., Wesołowska, K.: Classifying cognitive workload using eye activity and EEG features in arithmetic tasks. In: Damaševičius, R., Mikašytė, V. (eds.) ICIST 2017. CCIS, vol. 756, pp. 90–105. Springer, Cham (2017). https://doi.org/10.1007/978-3-319-67642-5_8
2. D'Mello, S., Dieterle, E., Duckworth, A.: Advanced, analytic, automated (AAA) measurement of engagement during learning. Educ. Psychol. **52**, 104–123 (2017)
3. Henrie, C.R., Halverson, L.R., Graham, C.R.: Measuring student engagement in technology-mediated learning: a review. Comput. Educ. **90**, 36–53 (2015)
4. Herbig, N., et al.: Investigating multi-modal measures for cognitive load detection in e-learning. In: Proceedings of UMAP. ACM (2020)
5. Kelleher, C., Hnin, W.: Predicting cognitive load in future code puzzles. In: Proceedings of CHI Conference on Human Factors in Computing Systems. ACM (2019)
6. Leppink, J.: Cognitive load theory: practical implications and an important challenge. J. Taibah Univ. Med. Sci. **12**, 385–391 (2017)
7. Moissa, B., Bonnin, G., Boyer, A.: Towards the exploitation of multimodal data to measure students' mental effort. In: Proceedings of ICALT. IEEE (2020)
8. Paas, F., Tuovinen, J.E., Tabbers, H., Van Gerven, P.W.M.: Cognitive load measurement as a means to advance cognitive load theory. Educ. Psychol. **38**, 36–71 (2003)
9. Rozo, R.C.: Suivi de l'engagement des apprenants lors de la construction de cartes mentales à partir de traces d'interaction. Ph.D. thesis, Université de Lyon (2019)
10. Scariot, A.P., Andrade, F.G., da Silva, J.M.C., Imran, H.: Students effort vs. outcome: analysis through Moodle logs. In: Proceedings of ICALT (2016)
11. Sharma, K., Papamitsiou, Z., Olsen, J.K., Giannakos, M.: Predicting learners' effortful behaviour in adaptive assessment using multimodal data. In: Proceedings of the LAK. ACM (2020)

Educawood: A Socio-semantic Annotation System for Environmental Education

Jimena Andrade-Hoz[1], Guillermo Vega-Gorgojo[1], Irene Ruano[2], Miguel L. Bote-Lorenzo[1], Juan I. Asensio-Pérez[1], Felipe Bravo[2], and Cristóbal Ordóñez[2]

[1] Group of Intelligent and Cooperative Systems, Universidad de Valladolid, Valladolid, Spain
jimena.andrade@alumnos.uva.es, {guiveg,migbot,juaase}@tel.uva.es
[2] Sustainable Forest Management Research Institute, Universidad de Valladolid, Valladolid, Spain
{irene,fbravo,a_cristo}@pvs.uva.es
https://www.gsic.uva.es, http://sostenible.palencia.uva.es

Abstract. Educawood is a socio-semantic annotation system intended for environmental learning in Secondary and Higher Education. It can be used to socially annotate trees and other ecosystem structures such as dead wood. Furthermore, Educawood allows the exploration of existing semantic datasets of land cover maps and forestry inventories as well as social tree annotations (all released as Linked Open Data). Teachers can browse these data to propose contextualized environmental education activities, e.g. finding and annotating singular trees. Students can go on a field trip and use Educawood with their mobile devices to submit tree annotations. Follow-up activities can exploit socially-created tree annotations, for example in virtual field trips.

Keywords: Environmental education · Forestry datasets · Linked Open Data · Semantic annotations · Virtual field trips

1 Introduction

Environmental education is critical to better understand Earth's ecosystems and promote more responsible attitudes towards the conservation and conscious and sustainable use of our planet. Multiple investigations suggest a deeper and better understanding of environmental science through active learning experiences grounded on real-life settings [2,3]. For example, field trips can be organized to identify tree species and analyze biodiversity; the impact of climate change can be assessed using biomass equations to estimate ecosystem carbon stocks grounded on forest data. To support such kinds of environmental learning activities we propose the software system Educawood.

Educawood can be used to support learning activities based on the social annotation of trees and other ecosystem structures; it also allows the exploration of the forestry information available in an area of interest. Educawood exploits existing semantic datasets of land cover maps and forestry inventories that were released as Linked Open Data for the Iberian peninsula in our previous work [1]. Teachers can check such information to propose contextualized activities for environmental education, e.g. finding a holm oak in a nearby dehesa and annotate it. Students can go on a field trip and perform the proposed activities, using Educawood with their mobile phones to annotate trees (locations, species, dendrologic measures, photos...) as required. These annotations are published as Linked Open Data and can thus be reused for performing new learning activities such as virtual field trips.

2 Activity Catalogue and Supported Annotations

We aim to support learning activities in environmental education such as the following:

A1. Find and annotate a typical tree of a patch
A2. Find and annotate a singular tree (rare species, big size...) of a patch
A3. Identify the species of an annotated tree by checking its images
A4. Given a tree annotated by other students, estimate how many trees like it are necessary to compensate car carbon emissions in a 1,000 km journey
A5. Follow a specific track and annotate all the dead wood you find
A6. Follow a specific track and annotate all the microhabitats (nests, cavities) you find

These activities have been proposed by forestry academics, requiring land cover maps and forestry inventories of the zone of interest. A land cover map such as the Spanish one provides information of the geometries and main species of homogeneous areas (called patches). A forestry inventory provides tree annotations of a territory using a sampling strategy, e.g. the Spanish inventory uses a grid of $1\,km^2$ cells. In our previous work we have proposed the tool Forest Explorer [4] for browsing those datasets.

Tree annotation is an important activity in the forestry domain and in environmental education. We have thus developed the Simple Tree Annotation ontology (STA –namespace `sta`). It supports typical tree annotations –namely, location, height, width, and species identification– plus image annotation and creator metadata. We borrow terms from WGS84 Geo[1] and Dublin Core[2] vocabularies when appropriate. Note that STA supports multiple and probably inconsistent annotations from multiple users –the ontology includes primary properties, e.g. `hasPrimaryPosition` that can be used for conflict resolution. We have finished a working (and tested) version of STA for tree annotation. A future release will support annotations of dead wood and microhabitats. Listing 1 includes a sample annotation of a tree in RDF with STA.

---

[1] https://www.w3.org/2003/01/geo/wgs84_pos.
[2] https://dublincore.org/specifications/dublin-core/dcmi-terms/.

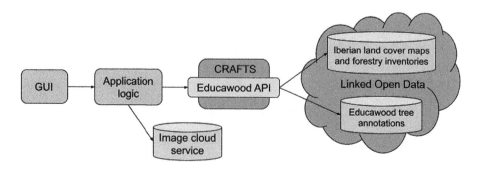

Fig. 1. Logical architecture of Educawood.

Listing 1. Annotation of a tree with a position and an image of its general view in RDF using Turtle syntax.

```
:tree0 a sta:Tree ;
   dc:creator :jimand ;
   sta:hasPositionAnnotation :posann0 ;
   sta:hasPrimaryPosition :posann0 ;
   sta:hasImageAnnotation :imgann0 .
:posann0 a sta:PositionAnnotation, sta:PrimaryPosition ;
   dc:creator :jimand ;
   geo:lat 41.012 ;
   geo:long -4.967 .
:imgann0 a sta:ImageAnnotation ;
   dc:creator :jimand ;
   sta:hasImage :alcornoque.jpg .
:alcornoque.jpg a sta:Image, sta:GeneralView .
```

3 Architecture of Educawood

Educawood is a socio-semantic system for the annotation of trees and other ecosystem structures. The logical architecture is graphically depicted in Fig. 1. Users access the system through the GUI; this component exposes an interactive map for exploring forestry data coming from land cover maps, forest inventories, and social tree annotations. The GUI also includes a form for creating annotations such as the one in Listing 1. User actions performed through the GUI are forwarded to the Application logic component that provides the system's core functionalities: user management, tree annotation, forestry data retrieval, and image upload (which relies on an external Image cloud service).

Tree annotations created with the system are stored in the Educawood tree annotations dataset. Iberian land cover maps and forestry inventories are also employed to retrieve forestry data from an area of interest. Since these sources are available as Linked Open Data, we use CRAFTS[3] (Configurable

---

[3] https://crafts.gsic.uva.es.

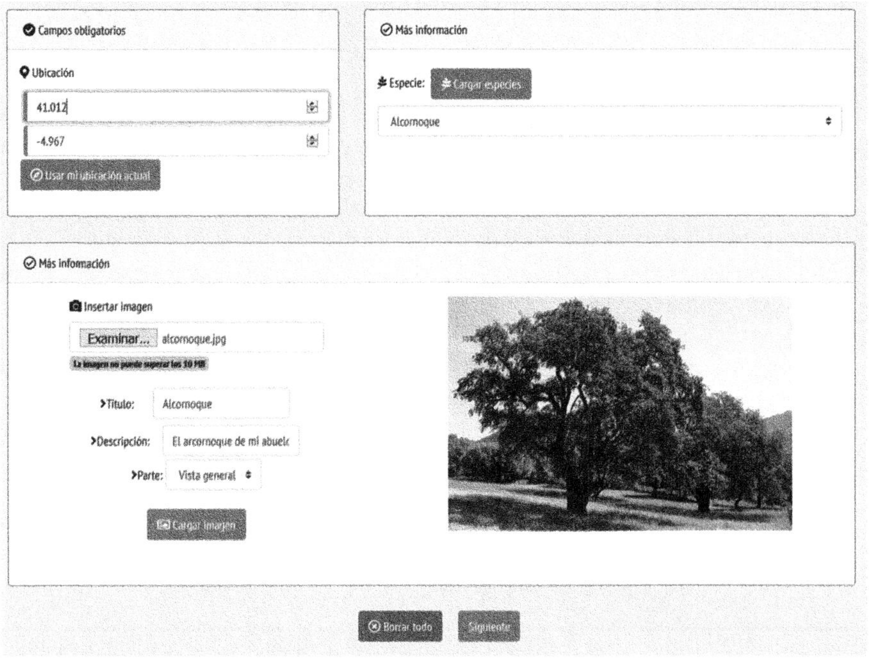

Fig. 2. Tree annotation example with Educawood corresponding to Listing 1.

RESTful APIs For Triple Stores). More specifically, the Educawood API exposes a regular RESTful API that greatly simplifies the access to the data sources –note that the alternative involves the usage of Semantic Web technologies such as SPARQL, OWL, and RDF.

We have developed a preliminary working prototype of Educawood. The source datasets are already deployed in distinct SPARQL endpoints, while the Educawood API is deployed at https://crafts.gsic.uva.es/apis/educawood. The Application logic is based on Express[4] –a popular Node.js web application framework. We have employed Angular[5] to develop the GUI. This prototype is web-based and can thus be used with any device with a modern web browser (to run the GUI –see Fig. 2). This facilitates the use of Educawood with mobiles in field trips, as well as with computers in the classroom or at home.

4 Sample Learning Scenario

Educawood is intended to be used in blended learning settings in Secondary and Higher Education. The proposed activities can be carried out in field trips, computer-mediated, and face-to-face classroom practices. We present below a learning scenario intended for a Nature Sciences course in Secondary school:

---

[4] https://expressjs.com/.
[5] https://angular.io/.

1. The teacher uses Educawood (or Forest Explorer) to prepare a field trip, finding a suitable patch with a mixture of Scots pines and Black pines with Holly trees in the under-story.
2. The teacher proposes several activities for their students: (i) identify singular trees (rare species, big size...), (ii) identify tree microhabitats (nests and cavities), and (iii) measure trees (diameter and height). Focusing on the target patch, students can search for common tree species of pines and distinguish between them, and look for Holly trees.
3. (Field trip) Students complete the proposed activities. They use Educawood with their mobile devices to annotate trees and tree microhabitats – see Fig. 2 for an annotation example with Educawood.
4. (Classroom) Students can estimate carbon stock of the measured trees by fractions (branches, stem, roots, and leaves) using appropriate equations in the classroom.
5. (Home) More follow-up activities like forest virtual visits[6] to identify main species and locate tree microhabitats that can lead to new annotations with Educawood. This can be used as a basis to gain insight on concepts like intertree competition, structural and specific diversity and sustainable management by guessing the trees to harvest in order to promote bioeconomy while enhancing diversity.

Acknowledgements. This research has been partially funded by projects VA257P18 (Regional Government of Castile and Leon, ERDF), TIN2017-85179-C3-2-R (AEI, ERDF), Cross-Forest (CEF 2017-EU-IA-0140), VirtualForests (Erasmus+ 2020-1-ES01-KA226-HE-095836) and 'Virtualización de aulas forestales ? Marteloscopes virtualization', UVA didactic innovation project (UVA-PID2020-015).

References

1. Baiget-Llompart, R., Vega-Gorgojo, G., Lerner-Cuzzi, M., Giménez-García, J.M., et al.: CROSS-FOREST, armonización y modelización de datos. Un proyecto transfronterizo de datos forestales abiertos de España y Portugal. MAPPING **28**(198), 38–44 (2019)
2. Cheng, S.C., Hwang, G.J., Chen, C.H.: From reflective observation to active learning: a mobile experiential learning approach for environmental science education. Br. J. Edu. Technol. **50**(5), 2251–2270 (2019)
3. Derevenskaia, O.: Active learning methods in environmental education of students. Procedia Soc. Behav. Sci. **131**, 101–104 (2014)
4. Vega-Gorgojo, G., Giménez-García, J.M., Ordóñez, C., Bravo, F.: Pioneering easy-to-use forestry data with forest explorer. Semant. Web (2021). http://www.semantic-web-journal.net/content/pioneering-easy-use-forestry-data-forest-explorer-1. Accepted for publication

---

[6] http://sostenible.palencia.uva.es/content/virtual-forest-tours.

Understanding the Well-Being Impact of a Computer-Supported Collaborative Learning Tool: The Case of PyramidApp

Eyad Hakami[✉], Davinia Hernández-Leo, and Ishari Amarasinghe

Universitat Pompeu Fabra, Barcelona, Spain
eyad.hakami01@estudiant.upf.edu, {davinia.hernandez-leo, ishari.amarasinghe}@upf.edu

Abstract. The global efforts toward evaluating the impact of the use of data-driven technologies on humans' well-being continue to establish societal guidelines for such systems to remain human-centric, serving humanity's values and safeguarding well-being. In this paper, we apply the first activity of IEEE P7010 recommended practice, a methodology and a set of metrics, to understand the well-being impact of a web-based tool (PyramidApp) that allows teachers to design and deploy Pyramid-pattern based collaborative learning activities in classroom learning scenarios. The tool's creators who are learning technology researchers (n = 2) and a sample of the tool's users and stakeholders who are undergraduate students (n = 11), master students (n = 14) and instructors (n = 2) are engaged in surveys and interviews to investigate the tool's well-being impact by reflecting on well-being indicators distributed to multiple well-being domains. The findings discuss possible impacts of the tool on the well-being domains of life satisfaction, affect, psychological state, community, education, government, human settlement and work. The creators also share views about the extent to which the use of IEEE P7010 increases their awareness of the intended and unintended impacts of their tool on well-being.

Keywords: Well-being · Computer-Supported Collaborative Learning · Ethics · Values

1 Introduction and Background

Given the rapid emergence of Information and Communication Technologies (ICT) and their increasing adoption by individuals and societies, personal and societal well-being are now inextricably linked with the state of our information environment and the digital technologies that mediate our interaction with it [1]. With the growing role of data analytics and Artificial Intelligence (AI) techniques in this digital space, the global efforts toward evaluating the different impacts of digital technologies continue to establish guidelines and metrics for such systems to remain human-centric, serving humanity's values and safeguarding well-being [e.g., 2, 3]. Well-being refers to what is directly or ultimately good for a person or population, and it is not limited to one dimension, but rather encompasses the full spectrum of personal, social, and environmental factors that enhance human life and on which human life depends [2]. The expression "digital well-being" is used to describe the impact of digital technologies on what it means to live a life that is good [1], including intended and unintended, positive and negative impacts on all well-being dimensions.

Computer-Supported Collaborative Learning (CSCL) is an interdisciplinary field of research that aims to investigate how learners engage in collaboration with the help of computers. Some of the well-known examples of CSCL scripts include Pyramid, Jigsaw, Think-Pair-Share (TPS), and Thinking Aloud Pair Problem Solving (TAPPS) [4]. Pyramid scripts integrate activities occurring at multiple social levels. First, learners will study a given problem individually to propose an initial solution. Learners then join in small groups and then increasingly larger groups to discuss their solutions, and to propose a shared solution to the given problem. In this study, a tool called PyramidApp that implements a particularization of the Pyramid pattern has been used to deploy CSCL activities [5]. The tool provides an activity authoring space, a teacher-facing dashboard and an activity enactment space for students. The teacher-facing dashboard not only provided a real-time overview of collaboration but also consisted of different controls, e.g., activity pause-resume, increasing time, and an alerting mechanism that informed critical moments of collaboration to the teachers to support their orchestration actions.

We engage samples of the creators, users and stakeholders of PyramidApp in the first activity of IEEE P7010-2020, a recommended practice to assess the well-being impact of autonomous and intelligent systems [3]. This activity is composed of 1) an internal analysis conducted by the tool's creators where they apply internal analysis techniques (e.g., brainstorming, hypothesizing, utilizing scenarios, etc.) and 2) surveys and interviews with the tools' users and stakeholders, to answer the following question: *What are the possible impacts of PyramidApp on learner and teacher well-being?*

2 Method

IEEE P7010 Well-being Impact Assessment (WIA) is an iterative process that aims at producing a well-being indicators dashboard and using it in the design, development, deployment and continual improvement of data-driven tools in order to help safeguard and improve human well-being [3]. This process consists of five activities: 1) Internal, user, and stakeholder analysis, 2) Well-being indicators dashboard creation, 3) Data collection plan and data collection, 4) Well-being data analysis and use of well-being indicators data, and 5) Iteration. The recommended practice provides a wide range of indicators drawn from well-being instruments already in use (i.e., scientifically valid) to be used to identify impacted well-being areas of a particular data-driven technology on the following domains of well-being: satisfaction with life, affect (feelings), psychological well-being, community, culture, education, economy, environment, government, health, human settlement, and work.

We apply the first activity of this approach with the objective of identifying well-being domains and indicators that can reflect possible impacts of PyramidApp on the well-being of its users and stakeholders (i.e., students and teachers). This activity consists of three tasks: initial analysis, user engagement, and stakeholder engagement. Task 1 is an internal analysis conducted by the tool's creators and involves forecasting, hypothesizing, projecting and utilizing scenarios to select well-being indicators that can reflect the impact of the tool and be used as principles of design during redesign and improvement processes. In the latter two tasks, user and stakeholder engagement, we seek to test the assumptions arriving from task 1.

Table 1. Well-being indicators selected by Sample 1 (creators)

Well-being domains	Well-being indicators	Impacted party		
		Students	Teachers	Society
Life satisfaction	Satisfaction with life as a whole	✓	✓	
Affect	Calm in a given time period	✓	✓	
	Stress level in a given time period	✓	✓	
Psychological well-being	Sense one is capable and good at what they do	✓	✓	
Community	Sense one sees oneself as part of a community	✓		
	Sense that if one were in trouble, they would have relatives or friends they can count on to help them whenever they need them, or not	✓		
	Satisfaction with relationships	✓	✓	
Education	Access to opportunities to learn	✓		
Government	Sense there is freedom of assembly, demonstration, and open public discussion	✓	✓	
Human settlements	Proportion of youth and adults with information and communications Technology (ICT) skills	✓	✓	✓
	Proportion of population covered by a mobile network, by technology			✓
	Access to internet at home			✓
	Having a computer at home			✓
Work	Sense that one gets support and help from co-workers	✓		

2.1 Participants and Procedures

The following samples were selected based on convenience sampling, and the interviewed students were selected to represent the different views coming from the survey.

Sample 1. Learning technologies researchers (n = 2) who have co-created PyramidApp and were presented to 134 well-being indicators distributed to 12 well-being domains in a survey manner allowing them to: 1) identify the system and its goals, users, and stakeholders 2) read the definitions and indicators of each well-being domain, and 3) select well-being indicators allocate them to the impacted party (Table 1). Then they were interviewed individually for 30 munities to reflect on the process.

Sample 2. Master students (n = 14) who took part in PyramidApp activities on five occasions. They responded twice to an 11-items Yes/No survey: a) after their last use of the tool immediately, and b) two weeks after their last use of the tool (Table 2). Two of them were interviewed individually for 15 min to provide in-depth answers.

Sample 3. Undergraduate students (n = 11) who took part in PyramidApp activities on five occasions. They responded to a 11-items Yes/No survey two weeks after their last use of the tool (Table 2). Three of them were interviewed to provide in-depth answers.

Sample 4. Instructors (n = 2) who applied PyramidApp activities on many occasions during the last two years. They were interviewed to discuss how the tool could impact their students' well-being and their own well-being as stakeholders of the tool.

3 Findings

As shown in (Table 1), PyramidApp's creators found the tool impactful on eight different well-being domains. These assumptions were well-aligned with the responses of the tool's users (i.e., students) on the 11-item survey (Table 2). The tool's stakeholder (i.e., teachers) also reported such an impact through their answers in the individual interviews. Students and teachers agreed that the time restrictions in PyramidApp activities can cause negative feelings like stress and anxiety, although they stated that it can be a positive level of stress that could encourage students to quickly generate ideas and be fully active during the learning process. On another hand, they reported that the positive feelings of satisfaction, capability and sense of belonging can be obtained due to the competences of freedom of discussion and collaboration, where students can seek and get help and support from each other. The students found the tool impactful on their learning too and reported that their knowledge about the topic under discussion were developed during the activity in a constructive way.

Table 2. Responses to the questionnaire by samples 2 and 3 (students)

Survey items based on Table 1	Sample 2(a) n = 14		Sample 2(b) n = 14		Sample 3 n = 11	
	Yes	No	Yes	No	Yes	No
I'm satisfied with the activity	86%	14%	100%	0%	100%	0%
I was calm during the activity	64%	36%	79%	21%	100%	0%
I was stressed during the activity	43%	57%	21%	79%	0%	100%
During the activity I felt that I was capable at what I'm doing	93%	7%	100%	0%	91%	9%
During the activity I felt that I'm part of a community	93%	7%	86%	14%	45%	55%
During the activity I felt that I belong to a community	43%	57%	64%	36%	45%	55%
During the activity I sense that if I was in trouble, I would have friends I can count on to get help whenever I need them	57%	43%	64%	36%	55%	45%
I'm satisfied with relationships I had with classmates and teacher during the activity	93%	7%	86%	14%	73%	27%
Activity has given me access to learning opportunities	100%	0%	86%	14%	82%	16%
Activity helped to improve my ICT skills	64%	36%	43%	57%	91%	9%
I think the activity has a freedom of assembly, demonstration, and open public discussion	86%	14%	93%	7%	100%	0%

4 Discussion and Future Work

The application of IEEEP7010 standard was considered by the creators of PyramidApp a good start-point toward including the different dimensions of well-being as additional requirements for the tool's evaluation and redesign processes. They found the well-being definitions and indicators provided by this standard rich and informative and that this activity has increased their awareness of the potential well-being impact of their tool and therefore their capacity to address them in the design lifecycle. Samples of the tool's users and stakeholders had views that were to a considerable extent well-aligned with the creators' ones regarding both positive and negative well-being impacts.

The continuation of this work includes identifying data sources to detect well-being issues to be used in creating a well-being dashboard that should be designed and continuously refined in a fashion where data over time is integrated to provide useful, timely and relevant well-being data based on the indicators selected in this phase. Such for monitoring, management and improvement of the tool to help safeguard well-being.

Yet, this approach can be restricted by practical challenges and faced by philosophical arguments that find it difficult to avoid negative impacts through better design of technology and urge to direct these efforts toward training users on healthy and positive use of technology. On the practical level, questions need to be addressed before moving forward include: What data sources are useful to measure students' senses of satisfaction, stress, capability and belonging in a computer-supported collaborative learning environment?

Acknowledgement. This work has been partially funded by the EU Regional Development Fund and the National Research Agency of the Spanish Ministry of Science and Innovation under project grants TIN2017-85179-C3-3-R, PID2020-112584RB-C33. D. Hernández-Leo (Serra Húnter) acknowledges the support by ICREA under the ICREA Academia program. E. Hakami acknowledges the grant by Jazan University, Saudi Arabia.

References

1. Burr, C., Taddeo, M., Floridi, L.: The ethics of digital well-being: a thematic review. Sci. Eng. Ethics **26**, 2313–2343 (2020). https://doi.org/10.1007/s11948-020-00175
2. IEEE Global Initiative on Ethics of Autonomous and Intelligent Systems: Ethically Aligned Design: A Vision for Prioritizing Human Well-being with Autonomous and Intelligent Systems, 1st edn. IEEE (2019)
3. IEEE: IEEE Recommended Practice for Assessing the Impact of Autonomous and Intelligent Systems on Human Well-Being. IEEE Std 7010-2020, pp.1–96 (2020). https://doi.org/10.1109/IEEESTD.2020.9084219
4. Hernández-Leo, D., Villasclaras-Fernandez, E.D., et al.: CSCL scripting patterns: hierarchical relationships and applicability. In: Proceedings of the 6th IEEE International Conference on Advanced Learning Technologies, pp. 388–392 (2006). https://doi.org/10.1109/ICALT.2006.1652452
5. Manathunga, K., Hernández-Leo, D.: Authoring and enactment of mobile pyramid-based collaborative learning activities. Br. J. Educ. Technol. **49**(2), 262–275 (2018)

Atelier – Tutor Moderated Comments in Programming Education

Ansgar Fehnker[(✉)], Angelika Mader, and Arthur Rump

University of Twente, P.O Box 217, 7500 AE Enschede, The Netherlands
ansgar.fehnker@utwente.nl

Abstract. In the programming course of our engineering design degree tutorials are the focal point of learning. This is especially so since we employ a tinkering based educational approach, in which students explore, from the very beginning, the material by self-defined projects. The assignment defines ingredients to use and sets expectations, but students are free to set their own design goals. In this setting tutorials are an important place of feedback and learning, and we developed an online platform that supports tutors during tutorials. This paper reports on the educational philosophy and underpinnings, and results from applying the tool in two first-year courses.

Keywords: Novice programmers · Online platform · Tutorials · Semi-automated feedback · Community of practice

1 Introduction

This paper presents *Atelier*, an online platform that supports tutoring in programming courses, emphasising collaboration and sharing[1]. It is built for the *Community of Practice* [1] of students, tutors, and lecturers involved in teaching programming, where personal feedback is a core element. *Atelier* is intended to support, but not replace personal tutoring.

The platform has been developed in the context of our bachelor programme *Creative Technology* (*CreaTe*), which is a multidisciplinary programme with a base in computer science and electrical engineering, a strong focus on design, and which includes elements of entrepreneurship. The programming courses of *CreaTe* require students to use concepts that were covered in the course, but they are free to define their own projects from the very beginning. We refer to this approach as *Tinkering* [5]. The student fully owns the problem; there is no example solution that students can work towards or that tutors can refer to.

In this setup, the focal point of learning programming is the tutorial, where students work on their projects, supported by a team of tutors and lecturers. Accordingly, individual feedback is a key element in this teaching approach. The

---

[1] The Atelier project is supported by SURF as part of its 2018 call on Open and Online Education.

Atelier platform provides tutors with automated feedback that is initially only visible to the tutors; feedback they can share and discuss with the student if they see it fit.

Tools that automatically provide feedback have been around since at least the 1970s. Keuning analysed 101 tools and found that the majority look at *knowledge of mistakes*, and there is less attention for the quality of the programs [4]. They found that testing is the most popular technique. Douce, Livingstone and Orwell [2] describe several generations of these tools, which require well-defined exercises with supplied test cases to function correctly. This is a very different setting from ours, as we mainly use open exercises. Keuning studied the use of static analysis tools similar to ours and found that novices often to not fix issues that such tools report, especially problems with design [4]. Keuning theorises that students may simply not know how to fix their code.

Our approach differs from many automated tools in literature with regards to two important aspects. We consciously chose not to use automated tools to replace tutor-student interaction, and we also do not use them for grading. They are used to assist tutors, during tutorials, to provide feedback that is more transparent and consistent. This gives rise to the research question whether warnings that are given to a student by a tool, differ in effectiveness from automated warnings that a tutor shares and follows up.

2 The *Atelier* platform

The aim of *Atelier* is to support the feedback process on student-defined projects in *CreaTe*. Tool support is primarily aimed at helping the tutor. *Atelier* uses two tools, *Zita* to highlight potential programming issues [3], and *Apollo* to estimate whether a student achieves certain learning outcomes [6]. Importantly, both tools are not included for marking, or to substitute tutor feedback, but are meant to aid the tutor.

Setting. The platform *Atelier* was developed for use during programming tutorials when students work on exercises that relate to topics covered by lectures. In line with the *tinkering* approach, students have to incorporate what they have learned in a self-defined project. The tutor should give the student feedback on their code verbally, and the online platform should not substitute this process, but complement it.

Usage Scenario. The primary usage scenario is illustrated in Fig. 1. The student shared the program with a tutor, e.g. via a QR code. During the exchange, the tutor can make notes and comment on the program or individual lines of code. The tutor is also presented with automated *Zita* comments which are initially only visible to the tutor. In this case, the tutor decided to make the comment visible and further elaborate on the warning. The student was able to reply, and the tutor involved another tutor in the discussion.

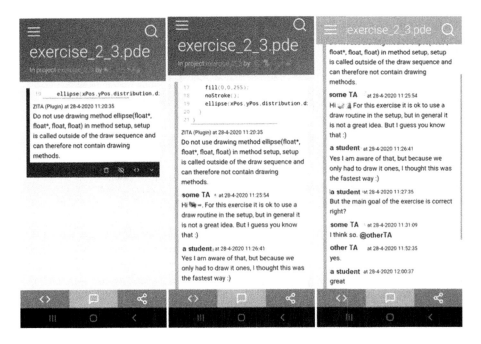

Fig. 1. An exchange from a tutorial, illustrating the main usage scenario. Names have been replaced by generic labels "a student", "some TA", and "other TA".

Implementation. *Atelier* is available as an open-source project on GitHub[2]. The two plugins we developed, *Zita* and *Apollo*, are available under the same GitHub organisation. These projects are not part of the main program, because they are specific to PROCESSING and to our courses.

3 Experience and Observations

Context. The first year of the *CreaTe* bachelor is organised in four modules. A module is an integrated study unit that has several components; for some of these modules this includes programming. *Atelier* was first deployed in module 4 of the first year, which includes an algorithms course.

The course started about a month into the first nationwide lockdown in the Netherlands in response to the COVID19 pandemic. To maintain the spirit of traditional tutorials we chose a synchronous form of teaching, with one main conference, a queuing system for help requests, and breakout rooms.

We used a similar setup for module 1 in the next academic year, for a new cohort of students. This module includes an introductory programming course, with 5 weeks of tutorials and lectures that cover the basics of programming, like variables, decisions and loops, up to objects, classes and arrays.

---

[2] See https://github.com/creativeprogrammingatelier/atelier.

Usage. Over the two modules we had 211 students and 43 tutors and lecturers use *Atelier*. Students shared in total 809 programs. Users could indicate whether we could use their data for research. This was permitted by 128 students and 33 tutors and lecturers. This left 499 student submissions for analysis, which are used in the remainder. Figure 2 shows that in the research data set, less than 33% of the students submitted 4 or more programs.

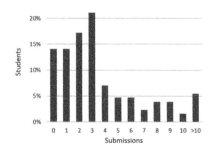

Fig. 2. Histogram of the number of submission per student.

Evaluation. The tools *Zita* and *Apollo* generated 3864 comments, of which 312 were made visible to students. This is a low percentage, and tutors indicated that this is in part because of the repetitive nature of *Zita* comments. For example, one submission received 95 warnings of the same type – a naming convention – but only 2 of them were made visible.

An interesting observation could be made with respect to the effectiveness of sharing *Zita* comments. We distinguish between comments that were shared with the student, and comments that were shared **and** followed up by an additional comment. To measure the effectiveness we define for each submission a window of future submissions and checked whether the same of the 35 *Zita* rules issued another warning within the window.

Figure 3 depicts the results for window sizes up to 5. The left figure shows, e.g., that 54% of the students avoids repeating a mistake relating to a shared warning in the next submission (window size 1). Unfortunately, this share decreases as the window size increases. Five submissions later 78% repeat the same mistake. Note, that the total numbers decline with increasing window size, since there will be fewer submissions by the same student for larger window sizes.

The right figure show that *Zita* comments that were followed up were somewhat more effective, even though that effect also waned with an increasing window size. Note, that the same mistake may be repeated for various reasons, for example because a student finds different ways to violate the same rule.

Threats to Validity. The module 4 course had only 8 weeks of lectures and tutorials, while the module 1 course had only 5 weeks of tutorials, for a different cohort. This means that we could only measure the use of a newly developed tool for a short period. The effect of feedback may change if students are exposed to it for a longer time, positively because of consistent messaging, or negatively because they get used to it.

When considering the effectiveness of tutor feedback, one also has to keep in mind that the student knows the person, and also knows that this person may assess them in the future. This is both a threat to the validity, but also a strength because it introduces a personal aspect into the process.

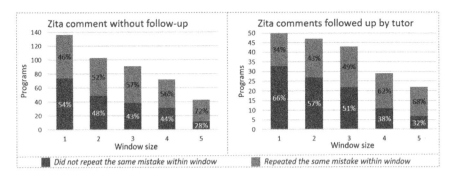

Fig. 3. Number and share of repeated mistakes, depending on whether a *Zita* comment was followed up or not.

4 Conclusions

For a bachelor programme which combines design with engineering approaches, and which has a very diverse student population, we use a teaching method for programming that emphasises creativity, ownership and individual solutions. Given these individual learning paths, providing good feedback is one of the key ingredients of the approach. This paper introduced the platform *Atelier* developed for this purpose, integrating the tool *Zita* for automated feedback. Tutors can give feedback on a program or on certain lines of code, and use automated feedback as a starting point for further discussion, which proved to be somewhat effective.

Currently, *Atelier* is still limited to working with projects created using PROCESSING. This limitation will stay in place while we work to improve the platform, but we are planning to remove these limitations and enable *Atelier* to be used with other programming languages at a later stage.

References

1. Coenders, M.: De Canon van het Leren, chap. Community of Practice - Etienne Wenger, pp. 126–136. Vakmedianet Management B.V. (2012)
2. Douce, C., Livingstone, D., Orwell, J.: Automatic test-based assessment of programming. J. Educ. Resour. Comput. **5**(3), 4-es (2005). https://doi.org/10.1145/1163405.1163409
3. Fehnker, A., de Man, R.: Detecting and addressing design smells in novice PROCESSING programs. In: McLaren, B.M., Reilly, R., Zvacek, S., Uhomoibhi, J. (eds.) CSEDU 2018. CCIS, vol. 1022, pp. 507–531. Springer, Cham (2019). https://doi.org/10.1007/978-3-030-21151-6_24
4. Keuning, H.: Automated feedback for learning code refactoring. Ph.D. thesis, Open Universiteit (2020)
5. Mader, A., Fehnker, A., Dertien, E.: Tinkering in informatics as teaching method. In: CSEDU 2020. Scitepress (2020). https://doi.org/10.5220/0009467304500457
6. Rump, A., Fehnker, A., Mader, A.: Automated assessment of learning objectives in programming assignments. In: Cristea, A.I., Troussas, C. (eds.) ITS 2021. LNCS, vol. 12677, pp. 299–309. Springer, Cham (2021). https://doi.org/10.1007/978-3-030-80421-3_33

Smart Groups: A Tool for Group Orchestration in Synchronous Hybrid Learning Environments

Adrián Carruana Martín[✉] [iD], Carlos Alario-Hoyos[✉] [iD], and Carlos Delgado Kloos[✉] [iD]

Universidad Carlos III de Madrid, Madrid, Spain
acarruan@inf.uc3m.es, {calario,cdk}@it.uc3m.es

Abstract. Smart Groups is a tool consisting of one mobile application for the teacher and another one for the student for group orchestration in synchronous hybrid learning environments, i.e. when there are both onsite and online students. The teacher application shows recommendations of Collaborative Learning Flow Patterns (CLFPs) when creating groups for collaborative learning, being the location of the student transparent to the teacher. Regarding group management, if the teacher selects a CLFP the change between the phases of the CLFP is done automatically or by following the steps indicated by the application. The application also serves for the communication between the teacher and students and for sharing resources (e.g., documents, external tools, webs...) with the whole class or with each group. The student application indicates the group the student belongs to. Moreover, if the student is in the classroom the application points to the location where the group members should gather, taking into account the current need for social distancing. The student can communicate with the group mates and the teacher through the application and have access to the additional resources provided by the teacher. Finally, both applications warn users that are in the physical location if their safety distance (1.5 m) with another user is not being respected for more than 10 s.

Keywords: Hybrid learning · Collaborative learning · Orchestration · Smart learning environment · Indoor positioning

1 Background

COVID-19 has changed the way classes are taught. More and more institutions have adopted synchronous hybrid learning environments where some students attend class online while others are onsite at the same time [1]. This presents new problems, especially in the area of group orchestration, including coordination, communication, and group management. Tools to support collaboration do not usually take into account that some members of the group may be online and others onsite. Another problem derived from COVID-19 is the need for social distancing when working in groups in the case of students who are in the same physical location. These problems need more accurate and real-time response technological solution.

2 Description of the Prototype

This paper presents two complementary mobile applications (apps) called Smart Groups. Smart Groups aims to solve the orchestration problems in synchronous hybrid learning environments. To do so, the applications connect to a server to obtain the necessary data such as teacher course information, or class information. Moreover, the teacher app provides the necessary tools to coordinate, manage and communicate with students and groups, as well as enriches the creation of groups with Collaborative Learning Flow Patterns (CLFPs) [2]. The student app allows them to know which group they belong to, have access to the necessary resources to work in groups, communicate with their group mates, and if they are in the classroom know the location to gather with the group members. Finally, both apps warn the users if they are not respecting the safety distance (1.5 m) currently required due to COVID-19.

2.1 Teacher App

The teacher logs in with the corporate account to obtain data on their courses and students. Once teachers have access, they can select the class they want to work on. In this class, they can see previous group configurations, either saved for later use or used previously. The teacher can choose one of these configurations or create a new one. The screen shown in Fig. 1a appears empty or filled in depending on whether the teacher selects a previous configuration or creates a new one.

In the group settings screen (Fig. 1a), the first parameter to set is the name of the new configuration. The second parameter is the selection of the characteristics of the task: whether it is possible to split it into smaller tasks, whether it has several topics and whether it has several possible solutions. The third parameter is the selection of the number of students per group at the beginning of the activity. Below this setting, there is a checkbox to indicate if the teacher wants the groups to change during the activity either in number or in members. The last parameter is the type of group to be created. If the application has access to the previous performance of students, a profile per student will be created. By having these profiles the application can organise the students in a homogeneous way (the members of the group have a similar profile), in a heterogeneous way (the members of the group have different profiles) or in a random way; this last option is the one that is chosen by default if there are no data on students' previous performance [3]. The teacher has in this last parameter the possibility to choose how these profiles are defined. Profile creation is typically associated with students watching videos and doing exercises related to the course; otherwise, this option would not be available. The teacher can choose

Fig. 1. (a) Group settings and (b) CLFPs recommendation

(a) Name, task characteristics, students per group and group type

(b) CLFPs: simple, jigsaw, pyramid and Think-Pair-Share

between taking into account only the videos (e.g., number of videos watched), only the exercises (the exercises done, how many attempts needed to do them correctly, how many finished incorrectly, etc.) or both. Afterwards, the teacher can save this configuration or execute it. As soon as the teacher executes one of the configurations, CLFPs will be recommended. The teacher can select the CLFP indicated (see Fig. 1b), another CLFP or the "simple" pattern. Once the teacher selects an option and accepts it, the groups created will be shown. These groups will be formed only with the students attending the class, either in person or online. Students attending the class will be identified because they have started their app.

Once the groups are created the teachers can interact with each group or with all of them at the same time. The options available are: "Change members", "Send resource", and "Chat". When the teacher wants to "Change members" there are three choices if a CLFP is selected. The first one will ask them if they want to move to the next phase automatically (i.e. the application will do it autonomously). In the second choice, the teachers will be shown the recommendations to follow to move to the next phase (i.e. the teachers will be guided to set up the groups according to the next phase of the CLFP but will have the possibility to ignore them). The last choice is to postpone the phase change and make other changes upon the teacher's request. The option "Send resource" allows the teachers to send a link from different categories. The first category is to send a link to a document (this document can be on the teachers' device, on Google Drive or an external link); another category is to send a link to a new chat room that can also be created for internal communication of the group or the communication with other groups; the third category allows the teachers to provide a link to a tool from the Google suite; finally, the teachers can add a link that does not fit into the other categories. The last option available to the teachers is "Chat". This chat room will show the links sent and the conversation that the teachers have with the students.

2.2 Student App

The students also need to log in with their corporate account so that the application can be linked to their courses and teachers. Once students access the application and a course, they can see the group they belong to; if the groups have not been created yet, they have to wait to be assigned to a group. Smart groups uses indoor positioning sensors via Bluetooth called Beacons to detect students attending class onsite. Onsite students receive a map of the classroom with the location to go to work in the group the students belong to. For this positioning, the distribution of the class is taken into account and the groups are separated as much as possible so that they do not disturb each other and the members of the group are kept at a safe distance due to COVID-19.

Once the students have been assigned to a group they will be able to access the different tools for group work. The first tool is the chat, which can be used to communicate with the other group members and the teacher. The student can also request the link to the chat room in case they prefer to access it from another device. Finally, the resources sections where students can see the materials shared by the type (document, chat room, tools and others).

3 Use Case

A situation of synchronous hybrid learning environments would be a course where part of the students attend face-to-face and others attend online. In each class, the teachers may not know which students attend online and which ones face-to-face. The teachers can carry out group tasks as part of their class. To do this, students attending the class log in to their app and wait for the teachers to create the groups. When the teachers want to start with the group activity, they open their app and select a configuration that they made beforehand. Before creating the groups, the application recommends using the Pyramid CLFP. The teachers decide to accept the recommendation. The groups are divided into groups of two, the students are notified, and those who are face-to-face will be told where to go in the classroom. The teachers specify via chat to all groups which is the first activity. When the teachers see it necessary, they change the groups for the next Pyramid phase. The teachers access the section for changing members, the app asks them if they want to do it automatically and the teachers can accept this suggestion. The app makes the relevant changes and notifies the affected students, and if they are in the classroom, it gives them the new location. For the next change of phase, the teachers decide that they will do it themselves following the recommendations given by the app. The teachers go group by group selecting students and moving them to other groups as told by the app following the role distribution. In one of these steps, the teachers decide not to make the change indicated by the app because they have seen a change in the student's attitude and believe that another group will be more favourable. During the activities, one group asks for a tutorial and the teachers send them a new chat room to meet after class. At the end of the class, the teachers can specify that the group work is finished or not to continue during the next class.

4 Future Agenda

So far, a Smart Groups pilot has been carried out for a preliminary evaluation. This evaluation was carried out with 100 users who used a mock-up of Smart Groups and filled in a questionnaire. From that set of 100, a selection of 10 teachers who were in synchronous hybrid learning environments was interviewed. The next steps to be taken will be the corrections indicated by the users in the preliminary evaluation. After these corrections, the incorporation of learning analytics for the analysis of motivation, student participation, and teacher attention will be considered. With this data, useful information will be shown to the teachers to improve their decision making and group orchestration. Finally, an evaluation will be carried out in a realistic environment to test the usefulness and usability of Smart Groups.

Acknowledgements. This work was supported in part by the FEDER/Ministerio de Ciencia, Innovación y Universidades–Agencia Estatal de Investigación, through the Smartlet Project under Grant TIN2017-85179-C3-1-R, and in part by the Madrid Regional Government through the e-Madrid-CM Project under Grant S2018/TCS-4307 and under the Multiannual Agreement with UC3M in the line of Excellence of University Professors (EPUC3M21), and in the context of the V PRICIT (Regional Programme of Research and Technological Innovation), a project which is co-funded by the European Structural Funds (FSE and FEDER). Partial support has also been received from the European Commission through Erasmus+ Capacity Building in the Field of Higher Education projects, more specifically through projects LALA, InnovaT and PROF-XXI (586120-EPP-1-2017-1-ES-EPPKA2-CBHE-JP), (598758-EPP-1-2018-1-AT-EPPKA2-CBHE-JP), (609767-EPP-1-2019-1-ES-EPPKA2-CBHE-JP). This publication reflects the views only of the authors and funders cannot be held responsible for any use which may be made of the information contained therein.

References

1. Raes, A., Detienne, L., Windey, I., Depaepe, F.: A systematic literature review on synchronous hybrid learning: gaps identified. Learn. Environ. Res. **23**(3), 269–290 (2019). https://doi.org/10.1007/s10984-019-09303-z
2. Hernández Leo, D., Asensio-Pérez, J.I., Dimitriadis, Y.: Computational representation of collaborative learning flow patterns using IMS learning design. J. Educ. Technol. Soc. **8**(4), 75–89 (2005). https://doi.org/10.2307/jeductechsoci.8.4.75
3. Rubio-Fernández, A., Muñoz-Merino, P.J., Kloos, C.D.: Analyzing the group formation process in intelligent tutoring systems. In: Coy, A., Hayashi, Y., Chang, M. (eds.) ITS 2019. LNCS, vol. 11528, pp. 34–39. Springer, Cham (2019). https://doi.org/10.1007/978-3-030-22244-4_5

Awareness Tools for Monitoring Socio-emotional Regulation During Collaboration in Settings Outside School Without Teacher Supervision

Mariano Velamazán[✉][iD], Patricia Santos[iD], and Davinia Hernández-Leo[iD]

Pompeu Fabra University, Barcelona, Spain
mariano.velamazan01@estudiant.upf.edu

Abstract. There are several awareness tools developed to research how to support different phases and modes of socio-emotional regulation of learning. Most of these tools have focused on only one mode of regulation (self-, co- or socially-shared) or on one phase (planning, monitoring or reflection) and have been tested in formal settings and at specific, researchers' predetermined, moments of collaboration (at the beginning, in the middle or at the end of collaboration). In this paper we extend previous research in this area to propose a new tool that could be more *naturally* integrated during the *whole* process of collaboration in the underexplored context of informal settings without teacher supervision. The tool presented introduces some features that aim at facilitating a better understanding of social and emotional interactions and regulation of learning. More precisely, the tool supports a communication flow during the monitoring phase of regulation and includes: a) the possibility to be used by a large number of groups of learners, b) awareness tools for monitoring self-, co- and socially-shared emotional regulation c) at any time needed *during* collaboration, and d) includes other affordances that should indirectly support a better asynchronous collaboration.

Keywords: Socio-emotional regulation · Computer supported collaborative learning · Group awareness

1 Theoretical Background

Agency [1, 2] and collaboration [3] are two of the most important capacities to be developed in education. But if emotional issues arise during collaboration, they can have a strong impact on the groups' performance [4]. Learners do not necessarily activate their regulatory skills to face these problems and being aware of them requires learning and experience [5]. This is more critical when students have little experience collaborating for school purposes and they do it without teacher supervision. Regulatory skills in individuals and in collaboration have been extensively studied. Modes and phases have been described in previous studies. Among all these processes, socio-emotional regulation and interactions have been the least studied [6]. Socio-emotional regulation in collaboration refers to the processes and strategies that students enact in order to consciously recognize, control and influence which emotions they experience and express while learning together [6].

We have analyzed previous research [7–11] and tools about social and emotional awareness and regulation. For example, Cernea and colleagues [12] tried to increase emotional awareness through a virtual agent that supported collaboration with the help of lightweight electroencephalographic portable devices. Since one of our goals is to promote young students' agency and awareness of their emotional state, instead of reading students' *brain waves*, we propose a tool in which students can choose to share their emotions with others. This approach is more similar to Molinari's et al. [13], who developed an Emotional Awareness Tool (EAT) which allowed sharing members self reported emotions. They concluded that it did not influence the perception of emotions of group members but the collaboration they tested was synchronous, members of the group talked to each other through microphone and the average age was 23. We believe that in these conditions, the EAT might not be so necessary. The tool we present addresses younger students that work asynchronously and have little collaboration experience for academic purposes. Bakhtiar et al. [14] used the COPES framework [15] to develop and test their Socio Emotional Sampling Tool, but this is a scripting tool (not an awareness tool, see next section) and was not used freely by students who were instructed to do so at the beginning, middle and end of the collaboration process. The same happened with the S-Reg Tool [9] and the EmAtool [11]. We conclude that more research is needed on three aspects: a) to understand socio-emotional regulation *during the whole process* of collaboration, b) include hedonic affordances [16], and c) following Järvenoja and colleagues [11], we plan to test this prototype in other real learning scenarios; in informal settings without teacher supervision.

2 Description of the Emotional and Motivational *Affordances* of the Prototype

The application presented here (Fig. 1 is the chat screen of it) is an asynchronous communication tool designed to be used during collaborative tasks by secondary school (13–16 year old) students. Each group has a set of activities (defined by the teacher) and for each activity a chat is created. Each chat is extended with the socio-emotional and motivational *awareness tools* that we present below.

Miller and Hadwin [8] presented the concept of *awareness tools* as complementary to *scripting tools* since those are considered less invasive to the natural flow of collaboration. Awareness tools can help students realize challenges that require action. Malmberg et al. [7] divided awareness in CSCL into cognitive and social group awareness. Our work focuses on the latest.

Members' Avatars Selection (Signing-Up And Profile Panels)
When students create their account in this prototype, they can choose an avatar from some predefined options (you can see one of the avatars at the top side of Fig. 2). This feature has been included for two reasons: a) providing *hedonic* affordances to the group [16] and b) facilitating young students to express and share their emotions in the conversations of the group [17] (Fig. 4).

Self-regulation: My *Emotions* Panel
This panel (Fig. 2) presents a list of epistemic, achievement and social emotions [18,

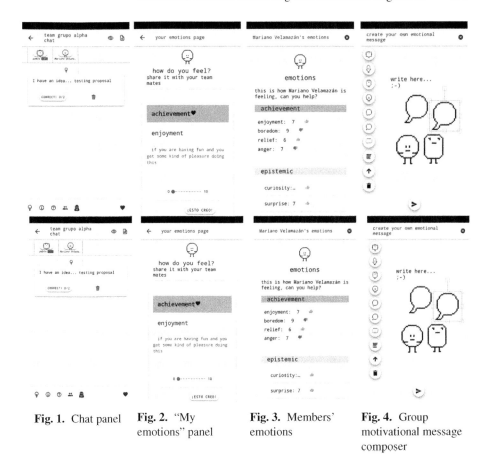

Fig. 1. Chat panel **Fig. 2.** "My emotions" panel **Fig. 3.** Members' emotions **Fig. 4.** Group motivational message composer

19]. Each one of these emotions is described and can be measured in a likert scale (0–10) to facilitate each member to be aware of their felt emotions *at any time* during collaboration.

Co-regulation: Members' Reported Emotions (Hedonic)

When members of the group have expressed and shared their emotions using the previously presented "*my emotions*" panel, the rest of the group can see their report clicking on those users' avatars (Fig. 3). If users report negative emotions or emotions with a negative *valence* [20] a red background with the number of negative emotions reported on the foreground is displayed (see the red badge at the top side of Fig. 1) to let the rest of the group be aware that there are members of the group that could benefit from some socio-emotional co-regulation.

Socially-Shared (and Co-)regulation

For socially-shared regulation we present below two awareness tools:

- *Emotional messages composer with avatars* (Fig. 3): In order to provide externalization of emotions and hedonic features [16] to facilitate collaboration, this panel lets members share motivational and emotional messages with the group making use of the avatars selected by each member. The messages can be chosen from a predesigned set of visual emotional-motivational messages or members can design their own message using the tool provided.
- *Anonymous messages*: The socially-shared emotional regulation feature is the possibility to send anonymous messages to the group. This feature has been designed to support members that are shy or afraid to express their ideas, problems or emotions with the rest of the group at any time during collaboration.

3 Preliminary Tests and Future Work

Previous versions of the current prototype were tested by two groups of students in order to base our design decisions on a user-centered design approach. Following that approach, the design of this new iteration was based on their feedback through a questionnaire and a face to face interview.

We are designing a new test with more groups that should answer our next research questions: Which are the most frequently reported emotions (by group members)? How often do the members check (or show interest in) other members' emotions? Do they take any actions? Does our application support the regulation of socio-emotional challenges? and if so, how?

We plan to test this prototype following a design based research approach with several iterations that should help us better understand what aspects of socio-emotional regulation are important in contexts without teacher supervision, and thus, improve the tool testing it during longer periods of time. Our ultimate goal is to check if our target students improve their regulatory skills during collaboration.

Acknowledgements. This work has been partially funded by FEDER, the National Research Agency of the Spanish Ministry of Science, Innovations and Universities TIN2017-85179-C3-3-R, PID2020-112584RB-C33. Davinia Hernández-Leo (Serra Húnter) acknowledges the support by ICREA under the ICREA Academia programme. Patricia Santos acknowledges the support by the Spanish Ministry of Science and Innovation under the Ramón y Cajal programme.

References

1. Scardamalia, M., Bereiter, C.: Higher levels of agency for children in knowledge building: a challenge for the design of new knowledge media. J. Learn. Sci. **1**(1), 37–68 (1991). https://doi.org/10.1207/s15327809jls0101_3
2. Tchounikine, P.: Learners' agency and CSCL technologies: towards an emancipatory perspective. Int. J. Comput.-Support. Collab. Learn. **14**(2), 237–250 (2019). https://doi.org/10.1007/s11412-019-09302-5
3. OECD, PISA 2015 Results (Volume V) (2017). https://www.oecd-ilibrary.org/content/publication/9789264285521-en

4. Barron, B.: When smart groups fail. J. Learn. Sci. **12**(3), 307–359 (2003). https://doi.org/10.1207/S15327809JLS1203_1
5. Järvelä, S., Gašević, D., Seppänen, T., Pechenizkiy, M., Kirschner, P.A.: Bridging learning sciences, machine learning and affective computing for understanding cognition and affect in collaborative learning. Br. J. Educ. Technol. (2020).https://doi.org/10.1111/bjet.12917
6. Järvenoja, H., Näykki, P., Törmänen, T.: Emotional regulation in collaborative learning: when do higher education students activate group level regulation in the face of challenges? Stud. High. Educ. **44**(10), 1747–1757 (2019). https://doi.org/10.1080/03075079.2019.1665318
7. Malmberg, J., Järvelä, S., Järvenoja, H., Panadero, E.: Promoting socially shared regulation of learning in CSCL: progress of socially shared regulation among high- and low-performing groups. Comput. Hum. Behav. **52**, 562–572 (2015). https://doi.org/10.1016/j.chb.2015.03.082
8. Miller, M., Hadwin, A.: Scripting and awareness tools for regulating collaborative learning: changing the landscape of support in CSCL. Comput. Hum. Behav. **52**, 573–588 (2015). https://doi.org/10.1016/j.chb.2015.01.050
9. Järvenoja, H., Järvelä, S., Malmberg, J.: Supporting groups' emotion and motivation regulation during collaborative learning. Learn. Instr., 101090 (2017). https://doi.org/10.1016/j.learninstruc.2017.11.004
10. Splichal, J.M., Oshima, J., Oshima, R.: Regulation of collaboration in project-based learning mediated by CSCL scripting reflection. Comput. Educ. **125**, 132–145 (2018). https://doi.org/10.1016/j.compedu.2018.06.003
11. Järvenoja, H., Malmberg, J., Järvelä, S., Näykki, P., Kontturi, H.: Investigating students' situation-specific emotional state and motivational goals during a learning project within one primary school classroom. Learn. Res. Pract. **5**(1), 4–23 (2018). https://doi.org/10.1080/23735082.2018.1554821
12. Cernea, D., Weber, C., Kerren, A., Ebert, A.: Group affective tone awareness and regulation through virtual agents. In: Proceeding of IVA 2014 Workshop on Affective Agents, Boston, MA, USA, 27–29 August 2014, pp. 9–16 (2014)
13. Molinari, G., Chanel, G., Betrancourt, M., Pun, T., Bozelle Giroud, C.: Emotion feedback during computer-mediated collaboration: effects on self-reported emotions and perceived interaction (2013)
14. Bakhtiar, A., Webster, E.A., Hadwin, A.F.: Regulation and socio-emotional interactions in a positive and a negative group climate. Metacogn. Learn. **13**(1), 57–90 (2017). https://doi.org/10.1007/s11409-017-9178-x
15. Winne, P.H., Hadwin, A.F.: The weave of motivation and self-regulated learning. In: Motivation and Self-regulated Learning, pp. 309–326. Routledge (2012)
16. Kreijns, K., Kirschner, P.A.: Extending the SIPS-model: a research framework for online collaborative learning. In: Pammer-Schindler, V., Pérez-Sanagustín, M., Drachsler, H., Elferink, R., Scheffel, M. (eds.) EC-TEL 2018. LNCS, vol. 11082, pp. 277–290. Springer, Cham (2018). https://doi.org/10.1007/978-3-319-98572-5_21
17. Avry, S., Molinari, G., Bétrancourt, M., Chanel, G.: Sharing emotions contributes to regulating collaborative intentions in group problem-solving. Front. Psychol. **11** (2020). https://doi.org/10.3389/fpsyg.2020.01160
18. Pekrun, R., Vogl, E., Muis, K.R., Sinatra, G.M.: Measuring emotions during epistemic activities: the epistemically-related emotion scales. Cogn. Emot. **31**(6), 1268–1276 (2017). https://doi.org/10.1080/02699931.2016.1204989
19. Vogl, E., Pekrun, R., Murayama, K., Loderer, K.: Surprised–curious–confused: epistemic emotions and knowledge exploration. Emotion **20**(4), 625–641 (2020). https://doi.org/10.1037/emo0000578
20. Pekrun, R.: The control-value theory of achievement emotions: assumptions, corollaries, and implications for educational research and practice. Educ. Psychol. Rev. **18**(4), 315–341 (2006)

Narrative Scripts Embedded in Social Media Towards Empowering Digital and Self-protection Skills

Davinia Hernández-Leo[1], Emily Theophilou[1], René Lobo[1], Roberto Sánchez-Reina[1], and Dimitri Ognibene[2]

[1] TIDE, ICT Department, Universitat Pompeu Fabra, Barcelona, Spain
`{davinia.hernandez-leo,emily.theophilou,rene.lobo, roberto.sanchez}@upf.edu`
[2] University of Milano Bicocca, Milan, Italy
`dimitri.ognibene@unimib.it`

Abstract. Social media has become an important part of adolescents' lives, with an increasing number of teenagers spending a great part of their time creating, sharing, and socializing with online content. Although the popularity of social media keeps growing, different studies identified threats and dangers that exist in such networks. From harmful content to negative behaviors, users can fall victim to negative social media phenomena that can affect their mental health and wellbeing. Several media literacy initiatives have been designed to promote social media awareness amongst the youth using traditional approaches to teaching about social media risks and threats. However, these approaches are limited in enabling deep reflection about the dangers behind their social media interactions and empowering their empathy, perspective-taking, critical thinking, digital and self-protection skills. This demo paper introduces a perspective in this context proposing the integration of educational opportunities within social media. The proposed approach is designed as a social media simulated learning platform where embedded learning activities follow a novel "narrative scripting" approach, in which Computer Supported Collaborative Learning script mechanisms are combined with counter-narratives strategies.

Keywords: Social media · Digital skills · Self-protection skills · CSCL scripts · Counter-narratives

1 Pedagogical and Technological Background

As digital media is more present in teens' lives, the use of Social Media (SM) sites leads as their favorite activity [1]. Yet, the existence of harmful content and toxic behaviors would make adolescents be exposed to dangers in the SM environment [2]. Recent studies suggest that most adolescents have had a negative experience in social media; nevertheless, only a few of them have asked for adults' advice or mediation [3]. Negative experiences in SM can affect adolescents' wellbeing [4]. Some of the potential harms of

SM exposure include its impact on self-esteem, eating attitudes, or depressive disorders. Moreover, some studies have connected its prolonged use to addictive behaviors and anxiety [5]. In response to that, different actions have taken place to reduce the impact of SM exposure. While the regulation of social media networks is still a debating issue in most countries, digital education has been foreseen as a more effective action [6]. Different media literacy initiatives have taken place in order to promote both digital skills and social media awareness (e.g. [7, 8]). Although educating about SM currently involves different issues, there is still the need to promote SM awareness; especially when interventions have centered on traditional methods such as the persuasive discourses based on fear and risks, in addition to the formal structure some of these have adopted within the school curricula [8].

The COURAGE project introduces a new perspective in this context proposing the integration of digital educational opportunities within social media [9]. This paper proposes an approach designed as a social media simulated learning platform where embedded learning activities follow a novel "narrative scripting" approach. Our proposed notion of "Narrative Scripts" (NS) borrows design elements from the Computer Supported Collaborative Learning field in combination with the use of narrative pedagogy strategies (see Table 1). When narrative scripts are applied to educate about social media, it leads

Table 1. Pedagogical strategies behind the formulation of "narrative scripts"

Narrative Scripts (NS)
Narrative – Storytelling: provides students with motivating, engaging, authentic scenarios suited to their personal experiences, making the content seem important and valuable [10]. Storytelling has been reported as an effective approach for helping students to generate new ideas and organize their knowledge, improving the students' comprehension of the learning content. After successfully completing challenging tasks, students who are actively involved in learning gain confidence and motivation
Narrative - Counter-narratives: The use of narratives within an educational content also enables having students exposed to contrasting or opposing views about certain concepts or realities. Having students exposed to counter-narratives [11] that challenge previously made assumptions can generate learning trough awareness about cognitive conflicts and bias and the need to organize and contextualize the phenomena behind the narratives
Scripting - Scaffolding: Structuring the learning method through small, manageable steps for students to complete across a learning path that is aligned with their previous knowledge and has been designed to lead them to expected learning outcomes [12]
Scripting - Structuring social interaction: CSCL scripts structure a collaborative learning flow (group formation, sequence of tasks, role rotation, etc.) to facilitate the triggering of desired social interactions leading to fruitful learning. Conversation with rich argumentation is one of these key social interactions as it promotes productive ways of thinking, conceptual change, and problem-solving. These can be achieved by pairing students with contrasting opinions to work on a task (ArgueGraph [13]), by distributing pieces of knowledge (Jigsaw [14]) or by confronting views thought a consensus-building process in collaborative social groupings (Pyramid [15]). In the case of narrative scripts, the conflicting perspectives leading to productive interactions are provided by the (counter-)narratives

to learning scenarios in which students are immersed in SM stories that expose them to counter-narratives - and conversations about counter-narratives - of biases, discrimination, or attitudes and behaviors in what (and how) is spread online. Such an approach can support learning by raising awareness through motivation, external thinking, empathy, responsibility, and perspective-taking, while at the same time develop digital and self-protection skills related to SM.

There are several CSCL tools that enable the design and implementation of collaboration scripts (see examples in the last row of Table 1). We propose an integration of CSCL script tools in SM platforms operationalized with stories framing missions to be solved through scripted sequences of tasks. A first prototype of NS educating about SM integrates the PyramidApp tool [15] into the PixelFed platform [16]. PixelFed is an open-source SM environment that reflects the features of a photo sharing social network. PyramidApp implements scripts based on the Pyramid collaborative learning flow pattern, which enables individuals to share their perspectives about a narrative and to contrast them through argumentation and consensus-building across incrementally larger groups [17]. The current platform consists of a frontend written in HTML, with the Javascript framework Vue.js, as well as a backend with a MySQL database supported in the Laravel PHP framework.

2 Description of the Prototype and Use Case

The prototype of NS embedded in SM is a responsive web-based application that works as an interactive learning environment. The implementation includes a full-fledged script focused on social media behaviors (Digital Self), with tasks involving free-roaming inside the platform, guided roaming following a (counter-)narrative, quizzes, minigames, or participating in structured group tasks (Fig. 1). Students are required to register to access the learning material. A classroom ID is also required to enable teachers to run synchronous activities and enable specific topics of interest to their class. Once the student is registered they can start using the platform to share and browse photos or videos. The NS are accessible through a learning progress page.

A *use case* illustrating the developed prototype is as follows: A high school teacher is worried about the digital footprint her students might be leaving behind them. She, therefore, initiates the Digital Self narrative script activity and shares a classroom ID with her students. The students use the ID and enter the chat in the SM platform where a fictional character initiates a conversation with them. The students can reply with predefined options or in some cases with open text, Likert scales, or checkboxes (Fig. 1a). The character narrates a story regarding employing influencers to promote the SM platform and shares information about them that it found online (e.g. photos, videos, reviews and posts the influencers might have posted some years ago) (Fig. 1b). The character prompts the students to reflect on the digital footprint the influencers might have left behind by asking them questions related to the information that was found online. The students reflect on three influencers. Each influencer has a different kind of digital footprint. Once the students go through all three influencers the script initiates a scripted collaborative activity (Fig. 1c), where the students have to individually reflect on how much social media knows about us and then collaboratively choose or propose a better answer. The activity then ends. The students should now have become more critical about the information they share online.

Fig. 1. Screenshots of (a) the chat interface where the NS take place embedded in the SM. The student can answer with predefined answers, free text, Likert scale, or checkboxes. (b) A task within the script referred to as the evidence folder. (c) A collaborative task with PyramidApp

3 Preliminary Results and Future Work

Before the development of the first version of the web-based prototype, we conducted a pilot study with 50 teenage students (20 females, 29 males, 1 did not specify) (Mage = 18.2, SD = 1.9). The purpose of the pilot studies was to evaluate the learning material and the activities' intrinsic motivation levels. The pilot studies were in the format of a virtual workshop. The students completed tasks with material based on the Digital Self script. In the end, a motivation questionnaire extracted from the intrinsic motivation inventory (IMI) [18] was used to measure their interest/enjoyment levels during the workshop. The results showed that students found the material interesting (5.06 - *average agreement of Interest/Enjoyment IMI scale w/1 = Not at all true; 7 = Very true*) and would recommend the provided material to younger teenagers (6.18 - *average agreement of the statement "I would recommend this material to younger teenagers" w/1 = Strongly disagree; 7 – Strongly agree*). Moreover, through the analysis of the results, we found it important to make changes related to guaranteeing the reinforcement of student's previous knowledge with concepts in which to base their reflection and argumentation and revisions to the clarity of the (counter-)narratives.

Teaching teenagers about SM risks and threats in a SM environment can enhance not only their knowledge/awareness about a problem but to sharpen their emotional skills, preventing toxic behaviors and unhealthy attitudes. In this vein, we aim to consolidate the research work testing the NS to assess the implication of social interaction, participation, motivation and learning gains. Forthcoming research also encompasses the implementation and testing of adaptive scripting strategies aligned with students' learning needs, e.g. by assigning learners to counter-narratives that can especially contrast with assumptions and prior knowledge.

Acknowledgments. This work has been partially funded by the Volkswagen Foundation (COURAGE project, no. 95567). TIDE-UPF also acknowledges he support by FEDER, the National Research Agency of the Spanish Ministry, TIN2017–85179-C3–3-R and by ICREA under the ICREA Academia programme (D. Hernández-Leo, Serra Hunter).

References

1. Rideout, V., Robb, M.B.: Social Media, Social Life: Teens Reveal Their Experiences. Common Sense Media, San Francisco, CA (2018)
2. Weinstein, E.: The social media see-saw: positive and negative influences on adolescents' affective well-being. New Media Soc. **20**(10), 3597–3623 (2018)
3. Redmiles, E. M., Bodford, J., Blackwell, L.: I just want to feel safe: a diary study of safety perceptions on social media. In: Proceedings of the International AAAI Conference on Web and Social Media, vol. 13, pp. 405–416 (2019)
4. O'Reilly, M.: Social media and adolescent mental health: the good, the bad and the ugly. J. Ment. Health **29**(2), 200–206 (2020)
5. Adelhardt, Z., Markus, S., Eberle, T.: Teenagers' reaction on the long-lasting separation from smartphones, anxiety and fear of missing out. In: Proceedings of the 9th International Conference on Social Media and Society, pp. 212–216 (2018)
6. Buckingham, D.: Defining digital literacy. In: Medienbildung in neuen Kulturräumen, pp. 59–71. VS Verlag für Sozialwissenschaften (2010)
7. McLean, S.A., et al.: A pilot evaluation of a social media literacy intervention to reduce risk factors for eating disorders. Int. J. Eat. Disord. **50**(7), 847–851 (2017)
8. Krutka, D., Manca, S., Galvin, S., et al.: Teaching "against" social media: confronting problems of profit in the curriculum. Teach. Coll. Rec. **121**(14), 1–19 (2019)
9. Ognibene, D., et al.: Challenging Social Media Threats using Collective Well-being Aware Recommendation Algorithms and an Educational Virtual Companion. arXiv preprint arXiv:2102.04211 (2021)
10. Hazel, P.: Toward a narrative pedagogy for interactive learning environments. Interact. Learn. Environ. **16**, 199–213 (2008)
11. Davies G, Ouellet M, Bouchard M: Toward a framework understanding of online programs for countering violent extremism. J. Deradicalization Spring **6**, 51–86 (2016)
12. Ludvigsen, S., Cress, U., Law, N., Rosé, C.P., Stahl, G.: Collaboration scripts and scaffolding. Int. J. Comput.-Support. Collab. Learn. **11**(4), 381–385 (2016). https://doi.org/10.1007/s11412-016-9247-1
13. Jermann P, Dillenbourg P.: An analysis of learner arguments in a collective learning environment. In: Proceedings of the 3rd Conference on CSCL, USA, pp. 265–273 (1999)
14. Aronson, E.: The Jigsaw Classroom. Sage, Thousand Oaks (1978)
15. Hernández-Leo, D., Martinez-Maldonado, R., Pardo, A., Muñoz-Cristóbal, J.A., Rodríguez-Triana, M.J.: Analytics for learning design: a layered framework and tools. Br. J. Educ. Technol. **51**(1), 139–152 (2019)
16. Pixelfed Homepage. https://pixelfed.org/. Accessed 15 April 2021
17. Ryan, R.M.: Control and information in the intrapersonal sphere: an extension of cognitive evaluation theory. J. Pers. Soc. Psychol. **43**(3), 450 (1982)
18. Ryan, R.M.: Control and information in the intrapersonal sphere: an extension of cognitive evaluation theory. J. Pers. Soc. Psychol. **43**, 450–461 (1982)

Conceptual Checks for Programming Teachers

Luca Chiodini[✉][iD], Matthias Hauswirth[iD], and Andrea Gallidabino[iD]

Software Institute, Università della Svizzera italiana, Lugano, Switzerland
{luca.chiodini,matthias.hauswirth,andrea.gallidabino}@usi.ch
https://luce.si.usi.ch/

Abstract. Learning to program and learning a new programming language is difficult because it requires learners to undergo conceptual change. Research on conceptual change has shown that instructors' awareness of their students' misconceptions can significantly affect learning outcomes. In this demo we present "conceptual checks", a web-based tool that allows instructors and teaching assistants of programming courses to quickly get an overview of the misconceptions that might come up at a given point in their course. Based on the idea of refutation texts, it asks users to assess the correctness of statements about programming language concepts. We implemented conceptual checks on top of progmiscon.org, an educational repository of programming language misconceptions observed in students learning to program. The inventory currently catalogues more than 200 misconceptions. This demonstration illustrates conceptual checks as an efficient and effective means for instructors to access the relevant information in the large body of misconceptions.

Keywords: Misconceptions · Programming languages · Refutation texts · Self assessment

1 Pedagogical and Technological Background

Conceptual Change. Based on constructivism, conceptual change theories have been applied to many fields in science education. The main observation is that learners always possess some prior knowledge, and thus learning does not always occur by accumulating facts, but by revisiting and changing wrong conceptions. For this reason, prior works have examined the role of *misconceptions* in the learning process, positing that learning occurs precisely by overcoming those wrong conceptions. This also justifies why learning (to program, in this case) is so difficult: students tend not to abandon their beliefs unless there are good reasons for doing so [5].

Refutation Texts. Two decades of research on the topic of refutation texts [7] have shown that, among text-based instruments, they stand out as a powerful mechanism to overcome (wrong) knowledge ingrained in learners. Showing one next to the other the "statement of a commonly held misconception, and an explicit refutation of that misconception with an emphasis on the currently accepted scientific explanation" [7] has been proven to be more effective than just stating the correct conception. According to studies, using a clear expository format should be preferred over a longer narrative description that can be perceived as less rigorous. A good refutation text should start by clearly stating the misconception, marking the transition with a "refutation cue" (e.g., "but this is wrong"), and finally presenting the correct conception. Textbooks, however, do not seem to employ them enough [7]. A variation on the theme that can more directly engage learners are the *conceptual change texts* [1]. Before presenting the correct conception, they actively involve the reader by asking to make a prediction, stimulating thinking before reading the scientifically correct fact. Going beyond text as a medium, *concept cartoons*, a visual version of refutation texts, have been used in science education since the early 1990s [3].

Conceptual Checks. In contrast to the existing kinds of refutation texts, the purpose of the idea of *conceptual checks* introduced in this paper is not the teaching per se, but the preparation of teachers. This different purpose has a significant impact on the wording of the texts: misconceptions' statements are written using expert terminology instead of using a vocabulary more accessible to novices. The resulting texts have then minimal ambiguity as they use proper domain-specific terminology. In the domain of programming languages, one has the advantage of being able to refer to their authoritative specifications.

progmiscon.org. As an effort to collect and properly document misconceptions about programming [4], we have built and we maintain progmiscon.org, a curated inventory of programming language misconceptions [2]. Besides a unique, memorable name, each misconception is characterized by an unambiguous statement that describes, entirely in terms of the syntax and the semantics of the relevant programming language, what is the wrong belief students hold (even though they might not express it in those very words). Moreover, misconceptions are accompanied with information about the possible origin (where it might come from) and common symptoms (artifacts produced by students who hold the misconception), with the goal of making educators aware of the rich body of wrong conceptions their students might develop in their journey of learning to program.

2 Conceptual Checks in progmiscon.org

Our inventory contains, due to its own nature, precise statements about the wrong conceptions novice learners have about how a certain language feature works. We have augmented this data with correct statements that contrast the incorrect ones and precisely describe what is the truly correct behavior, according to the authoritative programming language specification.

As an example, consider the Java misconception AssignmentCopiesObject. The statement which might be spoken by a student and describes the wrong conception is "assignment copies the object". Instead, the correct statement is "assignment copies the reference pointing to the object". By juxtaposing the two texts, one can easily obtain a refutation text such as "Some people believe that an *assignment copies the object*. That is not true: an *assignment copies the reference pointing to the object*".

However, we deemed that a list with just the refutation texts would probably not be appealing as a reading. Taking conceptual change texts one step further, we built an interactive system in which visitors are presented with both statements, the wrong and the correct one, and are challenged to make a choice and select the one they believe to be true for a specific programming language. Only after thinking and selecting one of the two claims, visitors can click a button to "solve the mystery" and check whether their prediction was correct or not.

We call this process *conceptual check* (see Fig. 1), as it can serve the purpose of self-assessing the knowledge of a programming language, or a subset of it, through the means of selecting what is true at a conceptual level.

Performing these checks on the whole body of misconceptions (which at the time of writing consists of more than 200 misconceptions) is unfeasible and also not very useful for revising. Instead, the checks can be conveniently configured so that they target a coherent set of misconceptions. In particular, one can select to do a check on misconceptions that pertain to a certain concept or a set of concepts, since all misconceptions are tagged with one or more concepts derived from the programming language field (e.g., Constructor, Expression, Type and many more); or a check on misconceptions that can be potentially induced by reading specific sections of a textbook, since they are also indexed by popular books used for teaching (only Java is supported at the moment).

3 Use Cases and Next Steps

Out of Scope. Asking novices to assess the correctness of conceptual statements such as "references can point to variables" can be problematic: novices do not just lack the expert terminology (e.g., the term "variable"), but for domains they are entirely unfamiliar with, they may not have any vocabulary at all (e.g., no word to denote the idea of a "variable"). Thus, when assessing the conceptual understanding of novices, conceptual questions are often too abstract and devoid of meaning, and there may be no rephrasing of the questions in the students' own words. To best assess novices, questions based on concrete examples and situations, like the kinds of questions used in concept inventories, are necessary. Thus conceptual checks are not targeted at students, but at teachers. Teachers, unlike their students, usually already possess the necessary domain vocabulary.

Teacher Training. Teachers are often confronted with students who struggle to grasp certain concepts. It has been shown that timely feedback is a key element for overcoming students' difficulties and wrong conceptions. It is even better if one could prevent those wrong conceptions from forming in the very first place, since once a knowledge element becomes familiar for a learner, it becomes difficult to replace it with the correct knowledge. For these reasons, pedagogical content knowledge includes knowledge about misconceptions [6]. When teachers

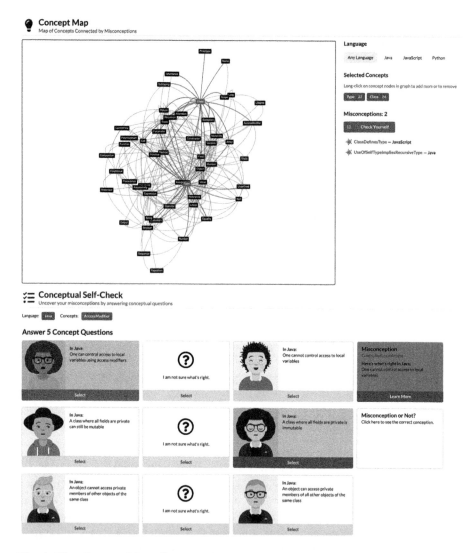

Fig. 1. The Concept Map allows teachers to configure a conceptual check by selecting a combination of concepts on which to be checked. The conceptual check then presents conceptual change text questions to the teachers. This provides them with an effective and efficient way to assess their own conceptual understanding and reminds them of the potential misconceptions students could hold about the chosen concepts.

know which misconceptions are likely to be developed, they can quickly recognize them and put in place a variety of strategies to deal with them, including devoting classroom time to address common issues, preparing or selecting extra material, and tailoring assignments. The explicit discussion of misconceptions during courses to train current or future teachers can thus be highly beneficial.

Instructor Preparation for a Lecture. Instructors benefit from remembering what misconceptions might pop up in a specific lecture of their course, as they can exploit tactics to challenge them or even anticipate them. When lectures are synchronized with a specific chapter of a book, instructors can take advantage of checks that focus exclusively on the contents of that chapter.

TA Preparation for a Course. Many universities employ students as teaching assistants (TAs) to help instructors in the courses they teach. Conceptual checks offer a quick and effective opportunity to revise the course material for being better prepared to answer students' questions and being able to remedy their incorrect understandings. Moreover, given external constraints, it can happen that students are assigned to courses outside their specific area of expertise (for example, a doctoral student whose research interests lie in machine learning could be needed in an undergraduate course in introductory programming). In such cases, learning about misconceptions is even more important.

We hope that this tool will further increase teacher's awareness of the multitude of programming language misconceptions that have been the subject of research studies in the last decades. The goal is that this increased awareness about specific misconceptions can then translate into improved teaching. We explicitly welcome suggestions and new contributors to progmiscon.org, to improve the quality and the quantity of conceptual checks, foster the community around it, and increase the value for educators all around the world.

References

1. Chambers, S.K., Andre, T.: Gender, prior knowledge, interest, and experience in electricity and conceptual change text manipulations in learning about direct current. J. Res. Sci. Teach. **34**(2), 107–123 (1997). https://doi.org/10.1002/(SICI)1098-2736(199702)34:2%3C107::AID-TEA2%3F3.0.CO%3C2-X
2. Chiodini, L., Moreno Santos, I., Gallidabino, A., Tafliovich, A., Santos, A.L., Hauswirth, M.: A curated inventory of programming language misconceptions. In: Proceedings of the 26th ACM Conference on Innovation and Technology in Computer Science Education, ITiCSE '21, vol. 1, pp. 380–386. Association for Computing Machinery, New York (2021). https://doi.org/10.1145/3430665.3456343
3. Keogh, B., Naylor, S.: Concept cartoons, teaching and learning in science: an evaluation. Int. J. Sci. Educ. **21**(4), 431–446 (1999). https://doi.org/10.1080/095006999290642
4. Qian, Y., Lehman, J.: Students' misconceptions and other difficulties in introductory programming: a literature review. ACM Trans. Comput. Educ. **18**(1), 1–24 (2017). https://doi.org/10.1145/3077618
5. Sawyer, R.K. (ed.): The Cambridge Handbook of the Learning Sciences. Cambridge Handbooks in Psychology, 2nd edn. Cambridge University Press, Cambridge (2014). https://doi.org/10.1017/CBO9781139519526
6. Shulman, L.S.: Those who understand: knowledge growth in teaching. Educ. Res. **15**(2), 4–14 (1986). https://doi.org/10.3102/0013189X015002004
7. Tippett, C.D.: Refutation text in science education: a review of two decades of research. Int. J. Sci. Math. Educ. **8**(6), 951–970 (2010). https://doi.org/10.1007/s10763-010-9203-x

Demonstration of SCARLETT: A Smart Learning Environment to Support Learners Across Formal and Informal Contexts

Sergio Serrano-Iglesias[✉], Eduardo Gómez-Sánchez,
Miguel L. Bote-Lorenzo, Juan I. Asensio-Pérez, Adolfo Ruiz-Calleja,
and Guillermo Vega-Gorgojo

GSIC-EMIC Research Group, Universidad de Valladolid, Valladolid, Spain
{sergio,adolfo}@gsic.uva.es, {edugom,migbot,juaase,guiveg}@tel.uva.es

Abstract. This demo paper presents SCARLETT, a Smart Learning Environment designed to track the evolution of learners across formal and informal contexts in order to provide personal support to learners. SCARLETT benefits from a variety of Technology Enhanced Learning systems and tools for collecting information about the students actions across physical and virtual spaces and, based on it, deploying and recommending personalized resources and activities to be performed in the students' current formal or informal context. To provide such support, the learning design plays a key role in how SCARLETT works, as it helps to coordinate the data collection, to model and characterize learners, and to deploy the resulting personalized resources and activities.

Keywords: Smart learning environments · Learning design · Formal learning · Informal learning · Across-spaces

1 Pedagogical and Technological Background

In recent years, the growth and diversity of learning systems and tools has fostered the appearance of Smart Learning Environments (SLEs). SLEs aim to provide personalized support to learners taking into account both their individual learning needs and context [8]. SLEs make a combined use of Virtual Learning Environments (VLEs), mobile devices and applications, and Internet of Things (IoT) devices so as to gather data about the interactions of learners and their current learning contexts across different physical and virtual spaces.

Some authors [1,2] consider SLEs an opportunity to connect formal and informal learning experiences across spaces. Compared to formal education, with learning situations carefully prepared by teachers based on specific learning objectives and topics according to the curriculum, informal learning experiences are driven by learners at any time, either intentionally or serendipitously, in a more unstructured manner [5]. The connection of both types of learning experiences can be beneficial for learners [3]. Learners can reflect on concepts discussed in formal education in appealing informal learning activities, while informal learning experiences can be extended and complemented with formal lectures for the provision of appropriate feedback that can help to settle the reflections. However, a limited number of contributions have explored this connection in SLEs [8], specially due to the combination of multiple learning environments from both formal and informal contexts supporting learning activities that happen in different physical and virtual spaces. This demonstration shows how SCARLETT addresses them in order to provide informal learning support to learners connected with the formal learning situation.

2 SCARLETT Overview

SCARLETT (Smart Context-Aware Recommendation of Learning Extensions in ubiquiTous seTtings) is an SLE designed to integrate third-party learning environments and tools (VLEs, mobile apps, IoT-enriched settings, *etc.*) with the goal of supporting students during learning situations that make use of physical and virtual spaces, enriching formal learning with suggestions for informal learning opportunities [6,7]. Its architecture is presented in Fig. 1. The support provided by SCARLETT is accomplished through (i) *sensing* and collecting data traces from the involved learning systems, including learners' actions and contextual information; (ii) *analyzing* this information in order to model and characterize the progression and participation of learners through the different activities, and to identify contextual conditions of the learning environments they are using; and (iii) *reacting* and providing suitable and personalized learning recommendations under the current context of learners.

To provide such support, the learning design (LD) of the situation plays a central role in how SCARLETT works. Through it, the instructional designer specifies the activities and resources that learners should perform, their associated learning goals and topics, and the learning environments and spaces learners are expected to participate in. This information helps SCARLETT to coordinate the collection of data, derivation of student model and assessment of the alignment of informal learning activities with the formal learning goals.

3 Use Case

Anna, a teacher of History of Art in a high school, has prepared a learning situation with the main goal to understand the influence of the Romanesque style in the architecture of the region. During three weeks, her students have to explore their city and identify examples of the main characteristics of the Romanesque style in local monuments. The LD comprises the following individual activities: an initial quiz about their prior knowledge on the Romanesque; an assignment about the identified monuments and characteristics; and its presentation to the rest of the class. Anna has deployed all these activities in Moodle, with additional resources like videos and web pages that may help her students. Moreover, Anna

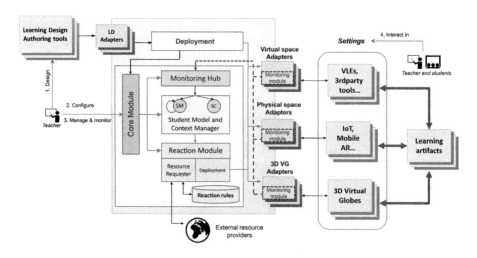

Fig. 1. SCARLETT architecture.

has encouraged them to install and use the CasualLearn application [4] in their mobile devices if they want to get recommendations of learning tasks to be carried out when visiting Romanesque buildings in their city.

Figure 2 represents the information flow to support this scenario. Anna makes SCARLETT import the learning design she deployed in Moodle, so that SCARLETT can obtain both the ids of the resources and activities in the different environments, and the ids of the learners participating. With this information, the `monitoring hub` of SCARLETT periodically tracks the actions of learners within the learning environments (flow 3 in Fig. 2). In the case of Christina, a student of Anna, she has regularly visited the available resources in Moodle, achieved a high score in the quiz, submitted in time her assignment and made use of CasualLearn while she explored the monuments. In comparison, Peter, another student of Anna, is not so interested in this topic and he has not participated that much in the activities, roughly passed the quiz and not submitted his assignment yet. However, he likes the tasks available in CasualLearn and he has spent some time doing them, even if they are not mandatory. All this information is collected by the monitoring hub, and stored in a database. The acquisition of the data is performed through different monitoring adapters, that convert the requests to the specific API of each platform and translate the incoming data into a common format within SCARLETT.

These traces are later processed in the `student model and context manager`. This module manages the instances of the student model (4), with variables devoted to track student progress associated to the learning goals specified in the LD (*e.g.*, knowledge of Romanesque), that evolve as action data is gathered and learning analytics are performed (*e.g.*, analysis of the grades in a quiz on Romanesque). In our case, the information previously collected shows the number of accesses to the complementary resources and the score obtained

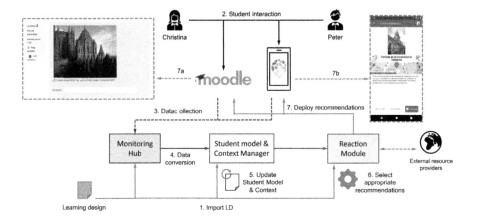

Fig. 2. Information flow of SCARLETT during the use case

in the quiz, among other. This information is used to update Christina's model, adding indicators about a high interest and knowledge level in Romanesque, while in Peter's model can be seen his low performance and lack of participation in the assignment.

Apart from the students' actions, the `monitoring hub` collects information related with the current context of the learners, which is processed by the `student model and context manager` to determine further information. Thanks to this data, combined with the student models and the LD, SCARLETT can deploy recommendations of resources and activities in the appropriate learning environment. This process is performed in the `reaction module`, conformed by a rule engine that checks the information contained in these three entities to select a suitable recommendation to make (6), consisting of some resource recovered from external providers, that is deployed in one of the involved learning environments (7). For example, given that Christina's student model reflects her high knowledge of Romanesque and the list of monuments visited with CasualLearn is known, the reaction module retrieves some videos and a medium difficulty quiz associated to those Romanesque buildings and deploys them in Moodle in her private space (7a). As for Peter, since he is using CasualLearn and he is "behind" on Romanesque, the reaction module retrieves an easy geolocalized task (like providing a picture of the gates of a church) and asks Peter to perform it in that very context (7b).

4 Prototype and Future Work

The current version of the prototype is able to read the LD created by instructors (using bricolage approach) in Moodle or Canvas. It then senses, through adaptors, the interactions with resources (quizzes, submissions, *etc.*) in these platforms, as well as CasualLearn mobile app, and transforms the data to an internal homogenous format. This is used to update the student context and model, through simple, but extensible, performance indicators. The reaction module is then triggered and can look for videos (in YouTube), pages (in Wikipedia) and quizzes (in CasualLearn SPARQL endpoint) and deploy them in Moodle, or send a link to the student through mail. In the near future, other resource providers and learning environments will be integrated, and more elaborated learning indicators implemented.

Acknowledgements. This research is partially funded by the Spanish State Research Agency (AEI) and the ERDF, under project grant TIN2017-85179-C3-2-R; and by the Regional Government of Castilla y León and the ERDF, under project grant VA257P18.

References

1. Gros, B.: The design of smart educational environments. Smart Learn. Environ. **3**(1), 1–11 (2016). https://doi.org/10.1186/s40561-016-0039-x
2. Kinshuk, Chen, N.S., Cheng, I.L., Chew, S.W.: Evolution is not enough: Revolutionizing current learning environments to smart learning environments. Int. J. Artif. Intell. Educ. **26**(2), 561–581 (2016). https://doi.org/10.1007/s40593-016-0108-x
3. Ley, T., et al.: Scaling informal learning at the workplace: a model and four designs from a large-scale design-based research effort. Br. J. Edu. Technol. **45**(6), 1036–1048 (2014)
4. Ruiz-Calleja, A., et al.: CasualLearn: a smart application to learn history of art. In: Alario-Hoyos, C., Rodríguez-Triana, M.J., Scheffel, M., Arnedillo-Sánchez, I., Dennerlein, S.M. (eds.) EC-TEL 2020. LNCS, vol. 12315, pp. 472–476. Springer, Cham (2020). https://doi.org/10.1007/978-3-030-57717-9_47
5. Schumacher, C.: Supporting informal workplace learning through analytics. In: Ifenthaler, D. (ed.) Digital Workplace Learning, pp. 43–61. Springer, Cham (2018). https://doi.org/10.1007/978-3-319-46215-8_4
6. Serrano-Iglesias, S., et al.: Personalizing the connection between formal and informal learning in smart learning environments. In: Proceedings of 'Hybrid Learning Spaces - Design, Data, Didactics' Workshop, pp. 47–52. CEUR Workshop Proceedings (2019)
7. Serrano-Iglesias, S., et al.: From informal to formal: connecting learning experiences in smart learning environments. In: Proceedings of 21th IEEE International Conference on Advanced Learning Technologies (ICALT 2021) (2021)
8. Tabuenca, B., et al.: Affordances and core functions of smart learning environments: a systematic literature review. IEEE Trans. Learn. Technol. **14**(2), 129–145 (2021)

The L2L System for Second Language Learning Using Visualised Zoom Calls Among Students

Aparajita Dey-Plissonneau[1], Hyowon Lee[2(✉)], Vincent Pradier[3], Michael Scriney[2(✉)], and Alan F. Smeaton[2(✉)]

[1] School of Applied Languages and Intercultural Studies, Dublin City University, Glasnevin, Dublin 9, Ireland
[2] Insight Centre for Data Analytics, Dublin City University, Glasnevin, Dublin 9, Ireland
Alan.Smeaton@DCU.ie
[3] PSL University (Paris Sciences et Lettres) 60, rue Mazarine, 75006 Paris, France

Abstract. An important part of second language learning is conversation which is best practised with speakers whose native language is the language being learned. We facilitate this by pairing students from different countries learning each others' native language. Mixed groups of students have Zoom calls, half in one language and half in the other, in order to practice and improve their conversation skills. We use Zoom video recordings with audio transcripts enabled which generates recognised speech from which we extract timestamped utterances and calculate and visualise conversation metrics on a dashboard. A timeline highlights each utterance, colour coded per student, with links to the video in a playback window. L2L was deployed for a semester and recorded almost 250 h of zoom meetings. The conversation metrics visualised on the dashboard are a beneficial asset for both students and lecturers.

Keywords: Second language learning · Dialogue metrics

1 Pedagogical/Technological Background

Virtual exchange programmes use technology to connect people from around the world for educational exchange. The emphasis is on international partnerships not only to build on content-knowledge but also to develop 21st century skills, global citizenship, intercultural understanding, empathy, and collaboration. This mission is fulfilled by a number of organisations [5].

In foreign language learning and teaching, such synchronous and asynchronous virtual exchanges are commonly referred to as telecollaboration [2].

The research was partly supported by Science Foundation Ireland under Grant Number SFI/12/RC/2289_P2, co-funded by the European Regional Development Fund.

Telecollaboration facilitates the development of linguistic and interactional competencies in the foreign language, intercultural understanding, and the capacity to negotiate and collaborate in multicultural work environments. It has been integrated in some form in foreign language pedagogy since the arrival of the internet. More recently, high quality videoconferencing as a telecollaboration tool has afforded language learners a fast-paced synchronous interaction with native speakers of the target language. In response to the current Covid-19 crisis, telecollaboration efforts have been catapulted with more training, mentoring, webinars, and pre-mobility partnerships.

Facilitated by technological progress, innovative learning activities, such as students reviewing recordings of their online interactions for learning and reflection, are gaining importance in language pedagogy in tertiary education [3]. While the potential of such telecollaboration-integrated curricula is huge, the possibilities of enhancing the telecollaboration experience by extending the affordances of videoconferencing is now needed. Challenges such as lack of confidence in speaking in a second language, sustaining student engagement, creating student-led experiences, and a sense of community, all need to be addressed. This paper introduces the L2L system developed to facilitate language students' engagement through concrete visualisation of their synchronous participation in Zoom calls with native speakers. This provides both students and lecturers with insightful feedback on the fast-paced synchronous interactions that take place while facilitating self- and peer-review in the post-session phase, thus making such fast-paced synchronous interactions pedagogically more meaningful.

2 Description of the Prototype

The L2L system is based on the infrastructure of Help-Me-Watch, a system to provide personalised summaries of live video lectures [4]. It makes use of Zoom's automatic audio transcription feature to analyse conversations and to prepare the review page for each Zoom meeting. Figure 1 shows how the system works from the participating students' point of view. The reader should refer to the numbering in the Figure.

Before a Zoom conversation session starts, one of the participating students needs to register the session by visiting the L2L web interface and filling in the email addresses of all students who will join the session (1), which generates an immediate confirmation and invitation email with a unique Zoom session code (2) needed later to review the session. Students then perform a Zoom-based conversation session with the Zoom cloud recording of the video and the audio transcript options enabled (3). Some time after the session ends, Zoom sends an automated email informing students/users of the availability of the cloud recording and other meta data including the audio transcript in VTT format. One of the students then copies/pastes the URLs for the cloud recording of the video and the audio transcript to the L2L system (4). Having received these, the L2L system analyses the session conversation by parsing the audio transcript text, calculating the characteristics of the session conversation in terms of turn-taking, utterances, volatility of dialogue, participation times of each student, etc.

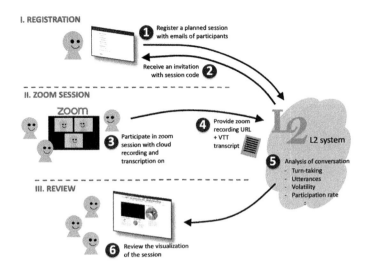

Fig. 1. Using the L2L system - overall flow

(5). The result of this analysis is then aligned with the cloud video recording of the session, and presented back to the students (6) as a web page. This setup is not straightforward but necessary in this version in order to anonymise students and secure the necessary data protection office and GDPR approval. Automation of this process and management by the system in forming and managing groups and meetings, is planned.

The review screen shown in Fig. 2 summarises the analysis of s Zoom meeting. On the top of the screen, a timeline visualises the start and end of every utterance made by each student during the session. Each participating student shows his/her name with a colour used throughout the graphics on the screen. The teacher or a student can click on any part of this timeline to immediately start playing the video in the window below from the clicked point onwards. Conversation flow is a chord chart which visually summarises the amount of dialogue from one person to one another, thus indicating who was talking to whom. A pie chart shows the total duration of each participant's talking. We also calculate conversational volatility, a measure usually applied to quantify the changing and dynamic nature of share prices on the stock market but when applied to conversational turn-taking it measures the dynamic nature of the dialogue.

3 Use Case to Demonstrate System Relevance

During March-April 2021, L2L was used in a telecollaborative project between Dublin City University, an English-speaking University with 63 students involved and Paris Sciences et Lettres, a French-speaking University with 45 students involved. The imbalance between the headcounts led us to organise groups into 45 Fr-Eng teams, 16 composed of three students (2 Eng and 1 Fr) and 29 composed

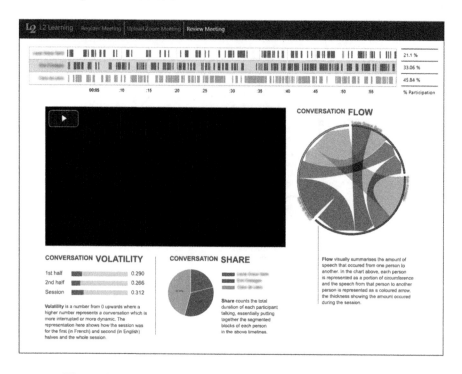

Fig. 2. Screenshot of review screen (student names are blurred)

of two students (1 Eng and 1 Fr). Some of the two-student teams were later turned into quadruplets, in order to train students in language interactions in the context of larger groups.

The 45 teams collaborated for seven weeks on tasks focused on developing their interaction skills in their target language, thanks to access to resources and guidance provided by questions framing their discussions. As per the definition of the project, the discussions were managed half in French and half in English, so as to benefit from the mastery of the language by the native speaker, as a help to improve the learner's skills. The topics of the tasks changed every week and dealt with international news events and professional development content. For instance the students exchanged on international issues such as statelessness or professional questions such as job search and workplace inequalities between men and women.

These frequent direct exchanges with native speakers of the target languages were opportunities for students to increase the quantity of input in a wider variety of accents, but also the amount of moments of interaction practice in their target language. It provided students with a unique environment in which they could face the difficulties of exchanging in a foreign language, in the reassuring context of a team whose members could help them develop their skills.

4 Results and Outcomes Achieved

The L2L system has been used for the analysis of almost 250 student Zoom meetings for second language learning. Student feedback on how the visualisations helped their reflection on meetings by allowing them to see overviews and replay specific parts, is described elsewhere [1] but we can summarise this by highlighting that 90% said L2L helped their conversational language learning and 77% said it helped their reflection.

At this point the system is operational and quite easy to use in terms of Zoom recordings and sharing Zoom cloud files but there were difficulties for some students in initially setting it up. These were mostly around configuring the correct Zoom settings and enabling the correct type of video recording and audio transcription on Zoom. Our instructions to students on the steps to achieve this were by necessity long in order to preserve their anonymity and for the future, subject to DPO approval, we intend to de-anonymise student identities and extend the visualisation dashboard to allow week-on-week progress for each student to be seen.

5 Future Agenda and Next Steps

L2L has been used for hundreds of hours of student meetings in an English-speaking country learning French, collaborating with students in a French-speaking country learning English. Following some initial teething problems with Zoom configurations, the system operates without problem. When Zoom generates an audio transcript of the spoken dialogue, it is configured to recognise English, so when the speakers speak French the actual transcribed text is unrecognisable. Because our system only uses the timing information (who speaks when, and for how long) this is not an issue for our analysis. This means that L2L can be used for any language pair and broadening the languages is one of our next steps.

References

1. Dey-Plissonneau, A., Pradier, V., Smeaton, A.F., Lee, H., Riaz, H., Scriney, M.: How visualising their participation rates with native speakers via video conferencing can help intermediate l2 learners improve their reflection on their language development? In: Proceedings of EuroCALL (2021)
2. Dooly Owenby, M.A., O'Dowd, R.: In This Together: Teachers' Experiences with Transnational. Peter Lang International Academic Publishers, Telecollaborative Language Learning Projects (2018)
3. Guichon, N., Cohen, C.: Enhancing L2 learners' noticing skills through self-confrontation with their own oral production performance. Cahiers de l'Apliut XXX I(3), 87–104 (2012)
4. Lee, H., Liu, M., Riaz, H., Rajasekaren, N., Scriney, M., Smeaton, A.F.: Attention based video summaries of live online zoom classes. In: AAAI-2021 Workshop on AI Education: "Imagining Post-COVID Education with AI" (TIPCE) (2021)
5. O'Dowd, R., O'Rourke, B.: New developments in virtual exchange in foreign language education. Lang. Learn. Technol. **23**(3), 1–7 (2019)

Usage-Based Summaries of Learning Videos

Hyowon Lee, Mingming Liu, Michael Scriney, and Alan F. Smeaton

Insight Centre for Data Analytics, Dublin City University, Dublin 9, Ireland
Alan.Smeaton@dcu.ie

Abstract. Much of the delivery of University education is now by synchronous or asynchronous video. For students, one of the challenges is managing the sheer volume of such video material as video presentations of taught material are difficult to abbreviate and summarise because they do not have highlights which stand out. Apart from video bookmarks there are no tools available to determine which parts of video content should be replayed at revision time or just before examinations. We have developed and deployed a digital library for managing video learning material which has many dozens of hours of short-form video content from a range of taught courses for hundreds of students at undergraduate level. Through a web browser we allow students to access and play these videos and we log their anonymised playback usage. From these logs we score to each segment of each video based on the amount of playback it receives from across all students, whether the segment has been re-wound and re-played in the same student session, whether the on-screen window is the window in focus on the student's desktop/laptop, and speed of playback. We also incorporate negative scoring if a video segment is skipped or fast-forward, and overarching all this we include a decay function based on recency of playback, so the most recent days of playback contribute more to the video segment scores. For each video in the library we present a usage-based graph which allows students to see which parts of each video attract the most playback from their peers, which helps them select material at revision time. Usage of the system is fully anonymised and GDPR-compliant.

Keywords: Video summaries · Video learning · Online learning

1 Pedagogical Background

University classes virtually conducted on Zoom or other online platforms as the result of COVID-19 have had an immediate impact on how students study and review what was delivered during the semester in preparation for semester-ending exams. For classes delivered synchronously (e.g. an online, live lecture

---

The research was partly supported by Science Foundation Ireland under Grant Number SFI/12/RC/2289_P2, co-funded by the European Regional Development Fund.

over Zoom), the recording of those sessions is useful and thus typically is made available on a learning management systems (LMS) for students to re-watch later on; for classes that use asynchronous video materials (e.g. a series of short video screencasts in which a lecturer may explain concepts), typically many short or long recorded videos become available for students to watch in their own time. Many university courses have been employing a mixture of these synchronous and asynchronous methods to compensate for the lack of the benefits of face-to-face class setting. Students' views on using such educational videos as the main source of learning has recently been studied [1] showing a mixture of benefits and fears.

Partly due to the inherent temporal nature of video medium that requires a viewer to "playback" in order to understand the contents, and partly due to the unedited and linear nature of lecture videos (unlike production videos featuring content-induced structure such as camera shots and scenes, chapters, and transitions), one consequence in the consumption of the video materials generated in this context is an increased burden to the students who face a large amount of unstructured lecture videos and screencasts at the time of reviewing: simply re-watching all video materials is not feasible, and yet there is no way to know what parts of the videos they should focus on. There are recent studies on tracking students' eye-gaze while watching a video lecture [4] or logging their level of attention during online classes [3], the knowledge of which could be used in suggesting the parts of videos that students should/could focus on in reviewing. This requires the capturing of the data at the time of watching/lecturing, an overhead on the front-end such as camera or other installed software to capture the eye-tracking/attention data.

The system described in this demonstration paper is a web-based video library of recorded video materials (both synchronous and asynchronous) as a result of running a remote online course at our university. By recording and analysing the detailed playback usage of each video including fast-forward, jumping forward while playing and re-playing over time by the student cohort, the system visualises and highlights which portions within each video have been found to be most important or most used by other students, thus offering clues during the re-watching/ revision process without requiring any manual intervention (e.g. lecturer indicating the parts of videos to watch).

2 Description of the Prototype

Our system generates a usage visualisation purely based on the playback-related interaction logs incurred by anonymised students, after the videos are made available for them for viewing on the course. The visualisation is a time-based graph aligned with the playback timeline of video content, where the height along the timeline indicates usage scores calculated using the strategy below. The playback-related interactions captured and factored in by the system include playing/pausing, seeking/skip forward (i.e. jumping from one point to another within a video), video playback window moving in/out of focus, and playback speed/rate.

Each video is divided into 1-second windows and each window starts with an initial score of 0 which is incremented every time any student plays or skips it. Every time any part of the video is played, that part will gain a score, thus over time as the usage increases the score in each second-by-second window on the timeline will increase. An important consideration is how much score gain each 1-second-window should receive from each of the playback-related interactions above, in order to result in a meaningful and useful indication when accumulated over time, in guiding students in their selective watching.

Our strategy and the rationale for calculating the score gain for each 1-second-window is summarised below:

- *Playback as part of "run through"*: As the most basic scoring strategy, the window gets **+1** when that portion is played. However, if the video playback window was not the window of focus on the student's screen when the student was playing it, then this increment is **+0.25** only (the student may be reading email or something else while half-listening to the video).
- *Replay as part of rewind within the same session* will gain **+2** score for each 1-second-window so it gets a cumulative +3: +1 from the initial playback and +2 from the replay). This assumes a replay is done with the playback window as the window in focus, as it would not be possible to select and replay if the window was not the focus.
- *Playback at 2× (double speed)* will gain **+0.6** and if the window is not the window of focus then it will be **+0.2** only because when the student is attending another window, the double-speed playback is too fast to properly comprehend.
- *Playback at 1.5×* will gain **+1.5**, and **+0.5** if the playback window is not the window of focus. In fact, a moderate acceleration of the video playback may potentially lead to increased students' learning performance. For instance, a recent study [2] shows that playing educational videos at 1.25× resulted in better outcomes (e.g. getting higher grades) than normal speed, while also testing for other speeds (0.75× and 1.75×).
- *Skip forward*: If a student skips forward from the current position at minute S0 by a segment of video then windows within 1-, 2-, and 3-minute segments directly following the segment S0 will get score adjustments as follows: S60: **-0.3**, S120: **-0.2**, and S180: **-0.1**. The rationale for this deduction is that the student must have had an idea what was coming up next, after S0, but anticipated it as being not interesting or useful thus less likely for other students to find it also interesting or useful.
- *Adjusting the score over time*: Overarching this scoring strategy is a **decay function** based on recency of playback, with the most recent days of playback interaction being more meaningful or useful than prior to that. The scores calculated by the above strategy are re-calculated from the interaction log each midnight. In this way the score increments (both + and −) as above are called our BaseIncrements = (+1.0, +0.25, +2, +0.6, +0.2, +1.5, +0.5, −0.3, −0.2, −0.1) and the system makes those the actual increments on day 0. Then on day 1 it makes those increments each multiplied by 1.1 before

adding, on day 2 the base increments multiplied by 1.2, and so on. The effect is that on day 10 we have a score for each 1-second window which has a 10-day linear decay function so that something played on day 9 has twice the value of something played on day 0 and by day 20 we have a score which has a 20-day linear decay with the "half-life" being 10 days. This continues indefinitely.

The scores for the 1-second windows are normalised within each video usage graph at display time making the visualisation less susceptible over time to any maligned attempt at artificially inflating scores by jumping to or repeatedly playing an obscure segment of video. Figure 1 shows a screenshot of the system.

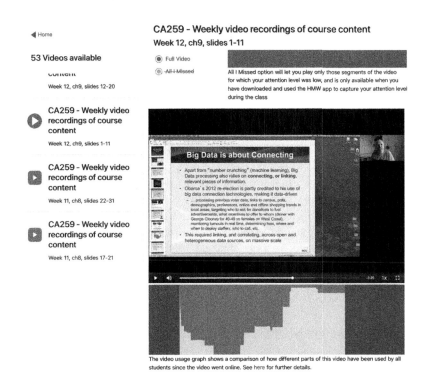

Fig. 1. Screenshot of system interface showing the user has 3:26 left to play at 1x speed of what appears as a 10-minute video from week 12, Chapter 9, slides 1 to 11 of course CA259. The yellow graph under the video playback window indicates the section the user is about to play has had highest usage rating based on previous video playback from the class whereas the part of the video at about the 1/3 mark has near zero usage.

3 Use Case and Results Achieved

The system has been deployed in our university and we use as an example, an undergraduate-level course during the Spring semester 2021, with a class size of 131 students. This has 11 synchronous class recordings of about 1 h and 20 min each and 53 asynchronous short-form video screencasts of about 10 min each, amounting to approximately 23 and a half hours of playable video content. Since the semester started, students have been using the system, actively playing and re-playing the video contents as part of their studies thus feeding into the playback usage analysis which, in turn, helps guide the portions of each video for them to watch.

At the time of submission, the system is being used extensively by students with 2,900 h of video streamed across 434 distinct sessions. On average per-session each student watched 1.5 videos and spent 6.7 min (404.8 s) viewing materials. As a percentage of a video viewed per-session each student on average viewed 35% with a standard deviation of 0.4. However as the semester is incomplete at the time of submission, and we expect a large increase in usage as we get closer to end-of-semester examinations, it is too early to draw any further conclusions from this usage.

4 Future Work

Since this is the first time the system has operated for the full duration of a semester, we are learning from the usage data and how to leverage it. We plan to fine-tune the scoring strategy based on the gained insights as well as diversifying to a greater range of interaction logs (e.g. playback volume). The timeline visualisation will be further refined to more effectively convey the usage data. More formal usability testing with students will also take place. Further validation on the effectiveness of our system by using semantic feedback from both students and lecturers on video content will also be part of our future work.

References

1. Krieter, P., Viertel, M., Breiter, A.: We know what you did last semester: learners' perspectives on screen recordings as a long-term data source for learning analytics. In: Alario-Hoyos, C., Rodríguez-Triana, M.J., Scheffel, M., Arnedillo-Sánchez, I., Dennerlein, S.M. (eds.) EC-TEL 2020. LNCS, vol. 12315, pp. 187–199. Springer, Cham (2020). https://doi.org/10.1007/978-3-030-57717-9_14
2. Lang, D., Chen, G., Mirzaei, K., Paepcke, A.: Is faster better? A study of video playback speed. In: Proceedings of the Tenth International Conference on Learning Analytics & Knowledge, LAK20, pp. 260–269. Association for Computing Machinery (2020). https://doi.org/10.1145/3375462.3375466
3. Lee, H., Liu, M., Riaz, H., Rajasekaren, N., Scriney, M., Smeaton, A.: Attention based video summaries of live online Zoom classes. In: Proceedings of the 35th AAAI Conference on Artificial Intelligence, Workshop on Imagining Post-COVID Education with Artificial Intelligence, 9 February (2021)
4. Srivastava, N., et al.: Are you with me? Measurement of learners' video-watching attention with eye tracking. In: LAK21: 11th International Learning Analytics and Knowledge Conference, LAK21, pp. 88–98. Association for Computing Machinery (2021). https://doi.org/10.1145/3448139.3448148

Including Students' Voices in the Design of Blended Learning Lesson Plans

Laia Albó[1(✉)], Nayia Stylianidou[2], Xenofon Chalatsis[3], Max Dieckmann[1], and Davinia Hernández-Leo[1]

[1] Universitat Pompeu Fabra, Barcelona, Spain
laia.albo@upf.edu
[2] European University Cyprus, Nicosia, Cyprus
[3] Athens Lifelong Learning Institute, Athens, Greece

Abstract. Voice inclusive pedagogy urges teachers to consider how they will act to incorporate children's voices within their teaching practice. In blended learning environments, students' views in technology-enhanced classrooms are a useful source of information that is often not utilised to its full potential. This demonstration paper presents an authoring tool that facilitates the co-design of blended learning lesson plans between teachers and students. The platform supports teachers to collect students' voices to define the main components of a lesson plan. It has integrated an inquiry feature to gather students' feedback during the design process throughout the definition of the learning objectives, the activities and tools, and the procedures for reflection and assessment.

Keywords: Voice inclusive pedagogy · Blended learning · Learning design · Authoring tools · Co-design · Lesson planning · Students' voices

1 Pedagogical Background

The adoption of the UN Convention on the Rights of the Child in 1989, Article 12 [1] clearly states children's right to express their opinion for issues that concern them. Regarding educational environments and learning settings, students' voice is of utmost importance as it is linked to their increased active participation in learning. Additionally, it can contribute to dealing with practises of exclusion [2]. If students' voices are not heard, it can lead to a culture of silence [3], as children lose the right to their own voice. In line with the above, the pedagogical framework called voice inclusive pedagogy (VIP) urges teachers to consider how they will act to incorporate children's voices within their teaching practices [4]. In blended learning environments, students' views in technology-enhanced classrooms are a useful source of information that is often not utilised to its full disposal [5]. Engaging with the philosophy of VIP in digital and blended contexts creates opportunities to understand, identify, incorporate, and implement students' preferences in their learning to fully realise the potential of digital spaces in education [6].

Our approach to address the above-mentioned challenge is linking the philosophy and educational practices related to students' voices with the design of dialectical-synergic blended lesson plans (DSBLP). These lesson plans involve the participation and collaboration of teachers and students in the mutual design of the lesson, leading to a more inclusive education environment. Generally, co-design, or collaborative design, is rooted in the tradition of participatory design [7]. It is therefore a learning synergy in which teachers and students share ideas and experiences to design innovative solutions. The main element of co-design is to enable creative and generative collaboration [8] which, in the case of the collaboration between students and teachers, multiple benefits can be achieved [9].

In this work we present a lesson planning tool that has been specifically designed to support teachers to create DSBLPs. By using the tool, teachers and students can take all the necessary steps together by exchanging ideas, opinions, and feedback to achieve a final lesson plan. Therefore, the roles of the teacher and the student to a great extent coincide. They both need to create, design, provide feedback and amend accordingly, express their views openly and equally, think critically about different aspects of the lesson plan (such as the sequence of activities), test different approaches for the same issue, democratically decide and finalise items, justify proposals and suggestions, respect others' opinions and views, and monitor the design process mutually. The aspect which differentiates the teacher's role is that (s)he is responsible for setting the lesson's overarching learning goal based on the overall curriculum and verifying that the produced DSBLP is in accordance with it, while leaving space for creativity and personal expression on the part of the students.

2 Technological Background

Learning design authoring tools support teachers in creating learning activity plans, including description of tasks, supporting resources and tools and expected learning outcomes [10]. Although there are several learning design tools available, only a few of them provide co-design features [11–13] and they have been essentially oriented towards supporting co-design between teachers [14]. Our tool has been built upon the Ldshake [11] and the Ld-feedback [15] tools. Although the connection between the design tool and the feedback app was already explored in the past [15], in the current tool we are extending this connection to all the steps of the lesson plan and improving the integration between them. The current platform is realized as a website and - as is common for this type of application - consists of a frontend written in HTML, JavaScript and Jquery, as well as a backend with a MySQL database and PHP code. The feedback app is embedded directly into the DSBLP template, encouraging interaction and co-design with the students in all stages of the design process.

3 Description of the Prototype

The design platform has three main components (see the top menu in Fig. 1): tools and tips; collaborative lesson plans; and feedback app. The *Tools and tips* menu offers a catalogue of digital tools to be used by teachers and students in the classroom. The main objective of the catalogue is to provide information and tips on how to create, use and make more accessible the digital technologies that teachers might use in their classrooms. There are nine categories of tools: wikis; blogs; discussion forums; webcasting; e-portfolios; online survey and quizzes; virtual reality; augmented reality; and other technologies. Teachers and students can openly access the catalogue to help facilitate the creation of the DSBLPs.

Fig. 1. Screen capture of the lesson plan editor interface.

The menu *Collaborative lesson plans* is the space where teachers can co-create their lesson plans and it requires to sign in with a Google account. The Create button, in the second line menu, opens the lesson plan editor (see Fig. 1). The *Lesson plans* menu allows teachers to explore other teachers' lesson plans within the platform. Moreover, the *Community* menu shows the list of the teachers' profiles within the community. Returning to the *Create* menu and the lesson plan editor (Fig. 1), on the left side of the editor appears the profile picture of the teacher as well as an image that can be uploaded for representing the lesson within the platform. In the main area, the editor invites teachers to specify the title for the lesson plan, provide a short description of the lesson, and select the educational levels, educational areas, and the digital competences related to the lesson plan. The template has three text areas to co-design the three main parts of the lesson plan: the learning objectives, the sequence of activities and tools, and the assessment tools and pedagogical strategies for promoting reflection. Next to each text area there is a discussion button that opens a pop-up window (Fig. 2) for discussing each part of the lesson plan with the students. The pop-up window contains two tabs. The *Feedback App* tab allows teachers to use the web-based application to collect students' views (left figure). A default template with closed and/or open questions for the students is available depending on each step e.g., the default template for discussing the learning objectives only includes an open question (Fig. 2, left). Teachers can edit and adapt the default questions depending on their needs. Once they have agreed with the questions to ask, they can press the start button (Fig. 2, left) and the app generates a unique five-digit code. Teachers can share the code with the students to allow them to express their views anonymously (the feedback app does not require any sign in by students). The button *View results* (Fig. 2, left) shows the aggregated results of the rating questions and the list of the open responses, depending on the case. The responses collected are linked to the specific co-design step within the specific lesson plan. The *Other* tab allows teachers to report information collected by other means e.g., oral inquiry (right figure). Back in the main window, there is also a *Feedback* tab (see the blue tab called Feedback in Fig. 1, next to the Lesson plan tab) which has the same functionality as the discuss buttons and pop-up windows but is mainly aimed to collect students' general feedback after the implementation of the lesson plan.

Fig. 2. Pop-up window that is activated with the discussion buttons.

Finally, the menu *Feedback App* is the interface to be used by the students. By sharing the link to this section of the platform, students can find the place to insert the code created by the teacher. When inserting the code, they can access the feedback app questions prepared for the co-design process. Once they have submitted the answers, students can view the aggregated results submitted by the rest of the students in the class. The interface follows a responsive design to allow students accessing the feedback app through any device. The platform can be accessed at https://ildeplus.upf.edu/BLENDI/.

4 Use Case, Preliminary Results and Future Work

The platform is being developed within the context of a research project titled "BLENDI – Blended Learning for Inclusion" that aims to support teachers in designing more inclusive blended learning practices. It involves five countries across Europe and each partner works locally with at least one (up to three, depending on the country) primary and/or secondary schools. In order to get teachers and students' opinions and to validate the initial requirements for the platform, each partner has carried out a research comprised of questionnaires and focus group discussions with their teachers and students. An initial version of the platform was shown during the focus group discussions and, despite the results being currently analysed, the initial insights have been promising. Both teachers and students have shown their positive interest in using the platform and have acknowledged some of the potential DSBLPs' benefits commented in the first section. The multilingual platform will be piloted in the schools across the five countries in the next months.

Acknowledgements. The authors would like to thank all members of the BLENDI project for their contributions in shaping the platform. This work has been partially funded by the EU Regional Development Fund, the National Research Agency of the Spanish Ministry of Science and Innovation and Erasmus+, under project grants TIN2017-85179-C3-3-R, PID2020-112584RB-C33, 2019-1-FI01-KA201-060881. D. Hernández-Leo (Serra Húnter) acknowledges the support by ICREA under the ICREA Academia programme.

References

1. United Nations Convention on the Rights of the Child. https://www.ohchr.org/en/professionalinterest/pages/crc.aspx
2. Taylor, C., Robinson, C.: Student voice: theorising power and participation. Pedagog. Cult. Soc. **17**(2), 161–175 (2009)
3. Freire, P.: The Politics of Education: Culture, Power, and Liberation. Greenwood Publishing Group, Westport (1985)
4. Sargeant, J., Gillett-Swan, J.K.: Empowering the disempowered through voice-inclusive practice: children's views on adult-centric educational provision. Eur. Educ. Res. J. **14**(2), 177–191 (2015)
5. Levin, T., Wadmany, R.: Listening to students' voices on learning with information technologies in a rich technology-based classroom. J. Educ. Comput. Res. **34**(3), 281–317 (2006)
6. Gillett-Swan, J.K., Sargeant, J.: Voice inclusive practice, digital literacy and children's participatory rights. Child. Soc. **32**(1), 38–49 (2018)
7. Kvan, T.: Collaborative design: what is it? Autom. Constr. **9**(4), 409–415 (2000)
8. Simoff, S.J., Maher, M.L.: Analysing participation in collaborative design environments. Des. Stud. **21**(2), 119–144 (2000)
9. Garcia, I., Barberà, E., Noguera, I.: empowering students by co-designing expanded learning scenarios. In: European Distance and E-Learning Network (EDEN) Conference Proceedings, pp. 483–492 (2015)
10. Pozzi, F., Asensio-Perez, J.I., Ceregini, A., Dagnino, F.M., Dimitriadis, Y., Earp, J.: Supporting and representing learning design with digital tools: in between guidance and flexibility. Technol. Pedagog. Educ. **29**(1), 109–128 (2020)
11. Hernández-Leo, D., Moreno, P., Chacón, J., Blat, J.: LdShake support for team-based learning design. Comput. Hum. Behav. **37**, 402–412 (2014)
12. Nicolaescu, P., Rosenstengel, M., Derntl, M., Klamma, R., Jarke, M.: Near real-time collaborative modeling for view-based web information systems engineering. Inf. Syst. **74**, 23–39 (2018)
13. Hernández-Leo, D., et al.: An integrated environment for learning design. Front. ICT **5**, 9 (2018)
14. Martinez-Maldonado, R., et al.: Supporting collaborative design activity in a multi-user digital design ecology. Comput. Hum. Behav. **71**, 327–342 (2017)
15. Michos, K., Fernández, A., Hernández-Leo, D., Calvo, R.: Ld-feedback app: connecting learning designs with students' and teachers' perceived experiences. In: Lavoué, É., Drachsler, H., Verbert, K., Broisin, J., Pérez-Sanagustín, M. (eds.) Data Driven Approaches in Digital Education. EC-TEL 2017. Lecture Notes in Computer Science, vol. 10474, pp. 509–512. Springer, Cham (2017). https://doi.org/10.1007/978-3-319-66610-5_51

EvaWeb: A Web App for Simulating the Evacuation of Buildings with a Grid Automaton

André Greubel[✉][iD], Hans-Stefan Siller[iD], and Martin Hennecke

University of Wuerzburg, Würzburg, Germany
andre.greubel@uni-wuerzburg.de

Abstract. In this Demo-Paper, we present EvaWeb, a Web Application for simulating the evacuation of buildings with a grid automaton. It is designed to support learning in the domain of mathematical modelling based on real-world problems. EvaWeb allows for 1) creating scenarios consisting of floor plans and persons within the environment, 2) loading and storing these scenarios to a text string, 3) automatically executing these scenarios, and 4) configuring the aesthetics and algorithms used during the execution. EvaWeb can be used online for free at https://evadid.it/eva2.

Keywords: Simulation · Building evacuation · Mathematical modelling

1 Introduction

Mathematical education is often associated with increasing skills that are considered useful in modern life [4]. But unfortunately, mathematical education ofen times focuses on teaching small, inner-mathematical abilities and students frequently solve mathematical problems with no regard to aspects of the real world [2]. A common countermeasure is the inclusion of real-world problems into the classroom. This has the additional benefit that the problem itself, as well as its solution are motivating for students. However, meaningful real-world problems also tend to be complex and requires students to spend a lot of time while solving them. To keep the motivation high, pre-structuring and regular, visual feedback are desirable for such a problem-solving process.

In this demo paper, we present EvaWeb, a web application designed to support mathematical modelling in classroom. It enables the simulation of the evacuation of buildings with a grid automaton. This domain was chosen because building evacuations are an established area in which mathematical modelling can be taught (cf. [5]) and where comprehensive technology can be applied (cf. [3]) for automatizing calculations, as well as a visualization of the model, its intermediate states, and results. The goal of EvaWeb is to enable students to work on

---

This research was supported by Deutsche Telekom Stiftung.

interesting, real-world problems, while keeping the focus of the learning process on mathematical modeling and mathematical evaluation, rather than dry calculations.

2 Overview over EvaWeb

EvaWeb is a tool for simulating the evacuation of buildings via a grid automaton.

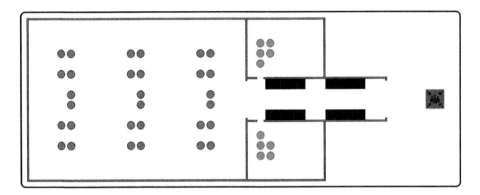

Fig. 1. Example of a scenario depicting a sports hall. The sports hall consists of a large gym area, as well as two dressing rooms. 30 blue and 10 red persons are trying to flee through a hallway, narrowed by four lockers, to the exit. (Color figure online)

2.1 Core Functionality

EvaWeb provides the following core functionalities:

1. **Scenario Editor:** Build Scenarios by placing objects in a grid.
2. **Scenario Manager:** Load and store scenarios to a text.
3. **Scenario Player:** Automatically execute scenarios.

In the following section, we will describe each of these functionalities in more details.

Scenario Editor. Foremost, the Scenario Editor enables the creation of new scenarios. In this mode, an overview of all available tiles is shown on the right side. These tiles include walls, obstacles, objects, and safe zones.

After selection of a tile on the overview, it is possible to place that tile by clicking on a space on the main map. By default, all tiles in the scenario are empty. Selecting a different tile and placing it at the same position as a prior tile will overwrite this tile.

Additionally, it is possible to place sprites like persons or decorative object (that do not interact with their environment) via the same method. However, sprites will only overwrite other sprite and tiles will only overwrite other tiles. Hence, it is possible that a grid space contains both: a tile, and a sprite.

Using the controls above the tiles and sprites, it is possible to extend or shrink the size of the building.

Scenario Management. The Scenario Manager enables loading, storing, and inserting scenarios via two buttons.

When clicking on *Store Scenario to Textbox*, a text representing this scenario is inserted into a textbox in the control area. This text is formatted as "<spritemap>:<tiles>: <sprites>", where <spritemap> is the ID of the sprite map used for the tiles and sprites, <tiles> is the BASE64-encoded, compressed building plan of all tiles, and <sprites> is the BASE64-encoded, compressed information about the sprites in the scenario. The text can then be copied out of the textbox and used as is suitable (e.g., stored to a text file, or transmitted via e-mail).[1]

Afterwards, it can be inserted into the textbox again and loaded using the *Load Scenario from Textbox* button. Additional buttons enable the user to load multiple pre-defined scenarios (including the sports hall depicted in Fig. 1).

Once a scenario String is loaded in the textbox, it is also possible to insert it in the currently loaded scenario. This is done by first hovering over the main map, during which the scenario (after insertion) is pre-shown. With clicking on the Tile, the tiles are inserted. This enables scenario creators to speed up the creation process by re-using certain configuration of tiles (e.g., by inserting multiple rooms with the same layout into a bigger building).

Scenario Player. The Scenario Player enables the automatic execution of a scenario. After execution, all persons try to get to one of the safe locations using the algorithm described in Sect. 2.2. After execution, the results are shown immediately. Most notably, these include:

- **Simulation Steps:** The number of simulation steps until every person arrived at a save location
- **Simulation Micro Steps:** The total number of steps person took in this simulation

As well as the configuration (like algorithms) used to execute the scenario.

Furthermore, the Simulation Player also enables the visualization of the simulation. Most notably, it is possible to:

- Execute the simulation manually step-by-step or microstep-by-microstep.
- Show the direction each person will be moving to if going to the next step. This direction is shown as an arrow in the circle depicting the person.
- Show the path a person will take to the goal. This path is shown when hovering over a person.
- Jump to the beginning or end of the simulation.

---

[1] The text of the sports hall in Fig. 1 consists of 469 characters. This is less than one character for each of the 688 (=13*43) tiles and 40 sprites in the same scenario.

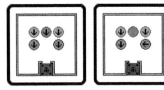 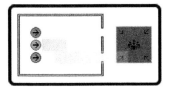

(a) On the left, black moves first and all persons head down. On the right, black is the last one to move. As going left or right would increase the distance to the nearest goal from 3 to 4 (An increase of more than 30%), black chooses not to move at all.

(b) Path highlighting: The arrows highlight the next step a person takes; the yellow overlay highlights the full path the red person takes.

Fig. 2. Snapshots of three simulations using the default16 spritemap, and the Threshold Accepting strategy ($y = 30\%$, Neumann neighbours) for execution. (Color figure online)

2.2 Evacuation Algorithms

EvaWeb is able to utilize two different algorithms, each of which can be further configured.

Basic Algorithm. The basic algorithms for the evacuation is:
```
unmoved_persons = get_all_persons()
do:
    shuffle(unmoved_persons)
    for every person in unmoved_persons:
        desired_choices = person.decide_movement()
        if desired_choices is not empty:
            selected = min(acceptable_option)
            unmoved_persons.remove(person)
while(at least one person moved)
```

Where min(acceptable_options) selects one (random) movement option that minimizes the distance to the nearest goal. This, and the shuffling in line two, can lead to randomized results (c.f. Fig. 2). The configurable algorithms are derived by further specifying the strategy used in decide_movement().

Strategy 1 (Hillclimbing): In this strategy, each person will only move to a neighbouring tile, if that tile decrease the distance to the nearest safe zone.

Strategy 2 (Threshold Accepting): In this strategy, derived from [1], persons will move to a neighbouring tile, if the minimal distance to any goal after movement is at most $y\%$ greater than the current distance to the nearest goal.

Differences Between the Strategies. Both strategies lead to realistic movements in most scenarios. However, the Threshold Accepting strategy has a "bias for movement" and "incentives" people to switch their goal if the shortest path to the nearest goal is blocked by other people. Hence, it leads to more realistic movements if a scenario makes it likely that there is a jam before the nearest goal. However, using only a single goal, the hillclimbing algorithm leads to more realistic movements as persons are less likely to side-track unnecessarily.

2.3 Configuration

In the Configuration, it is possible to select the algorithm that should be used for execution. The standard algorithm used is the Threshold Accepting algorithm. However, as of right now, it is only possible to select the algorithm itself. It is not (yet) possible to select the parameters used for this algorithm. For example, the Threshold Accepting algorithms is executed with a default value of $y = 30\%$ (that lead to lead to realistic movements for all test scenarios during development).

Additionally, it is possible to define when two grid tiles are neighbours. In the standard configuration, the *Neumann-Neighboruhood* is used: In this neighoburhood, every cell has 4 neighbours (top, right, bottom, left). Alternatively, the *Moore-Neigbhourhood* can be used. In this neighbourhood, every cell has four additional neighours (top-right, bottom-right, bottom-left, top-left).

Lastly, it is also possible to configure the aesthetics and size of the tiles and sprites with different sprite maps.

2.4 Implementation Details

EvaWeb is written in Scala and cross-compiled with ScalaJS to a Javascript file. The repository containing the source code is linked on the homepage. As of the time of submission, the source code consists of around 6500 non-empty lines of code (5700 lines of which are Scala code).

3 Future Work

In this demo paper, we presented EvaWeb, a web application for simulating the evacuation of buildings. As a next step, we want to develop teaching material suitable to teach mathematical modelling for 16-year-olds with EvaWeb. This material will include both the provision of the pre-build buildings, as well as exercise sheets for teachers.

References

1. Dueck, G., Scheuer, T.: Threshold accepting: a general purpose optimization algorithm appearing superior to simulated annealing. J. Comput. Phys. **90**(1), 161–175 (1990)

2. Greer, B.: Modelling reality in mathematics classrooms: the case of word problems. Learn. Instr. **7**(4), 293–307 (1997)
3. Greubel, A., Siller, H.-S., Hennecke, M.: Teaching simulation literacy with evacuations. In: Alario-Hoyos, C., Rodríguez-Triana, M.J., Scheffel, M., Arnedillo-Sánchez, I., Dennerlein, S.M. (eds.) EC-TEL 2020. LNCS, vol. 12315, pp. 200–214. Springer, Cham (2020). https://doi.org/10.1007/978-3-030-57717-9_15
4. Jang, H.: Identifying 21st century STEM competencies using workplace data. J. Sci. Educ. Technol. **25**(2), 284–301 (2016). https://doi.org/10.1007/s10956-015-9593-1
5. Ruzika, S., Siller, H.-S., Bracke, M.: Evakuierungsszenarien in Modellierungswochen – ein interessantes und spannendes Thema für den Mathematikunterricht. In: Humenberger, H., Bracke, M. (eds.) Neue Materialien für einen realitätsbezogenen Mathematikunterricht 3. RM, pp. 181–190. Springer, Wiesbaden (2017). https://doi.org/10.1007/978-3-658-11902-7_14

Self-tracking Time-On-Task: Web-Based Weekly Timesheets for Higher Education Students

Isabel Hilliger[1(✉)], Constanza Miranda[1,2], Gregory Schuit[2], and Mar Pérez-Sanagustín[1,3]

[1] Pontificia Universidad Católica de Chile, Santiago, Chile
ihillige@ing.puc.cl
[2] Johns Hopkins University, Baltimore, MD, USA
constanzamiranda@jhu.edu, gkschuit@uc.cl
[3] Université Paul Sabatier, Toulouse, France
mar.perez-sanagustin@irit.fr

Abstract. Due to the transition to online education, higher education students require more support to self-regulate their learning and their time management. This paper presents a work-in-progress conducted to design and implement web-based weekly timesheets to collect students' self-reports of time-on-task regarding different course activities. During the second semester of 2020, 5,221 students received the web-based weekly timesheets, and 3,131 voluntarily self-reported time-on-task throughout 16 weeks. At the end of the semester, a questionnaire was applied to evaluate the perceived usability and usefulness of this web-based application. This questionnaire was voluntarily answered by 1,200 students; 92% perceived that the timesheets were easy to use and 75% that it was useful for monitoring their academic workload. In their comments, students reveal that the tool allowed them to become aware of the number of hours spent outside of class time. Considering their suggestions, future work involves incorporating a student-facing dashboard in this web-based application.

Keywords: Self-regulated learning · Time-on-task · Higher education

1 Pedagogical and Technological Background

Time management is one of the factors associated with self-regulated learning that impacts students' academic success [1, 2]. According to Lay and Schouwenberg [3], time management can be defined as clusters of behavioral skills that are important in the organization of course load and self-study, such as awareness of time and task planning [1]. Previous studies indicate that good time management skills help students achieve learning outcomes, along with allowing them to buffer stress [4]. Further studies also suggest that poor time management skills increase the academic stress towards the end of the course, making it difficult for students to perform as expected [4].

Over the past year, time management has become even more critical to higher education. During the COVID-19 pandemic, two thirds of higher education institutions have continued its activities by using distance learning [5], and the majority implemented what researchers call 'emergency online education'. Online learning environments demand greater self-regulatory skills than traditional face-to-face education because the lack of face-to-face interactions between instructors and classmates diminishes extrinsic accountability [2]. Besides, the use of asynchronous learning activities requires students to make more decisions about when to do work [2].

Causal evidence demonstrates that effective time management is positively related to academic outcomes in Massive Open Online Courses (MOOCs) [6, 7], but these results are not necessarily generalizable to students in traditional college courses [2]. Some researchers have proposed to estimate time-on-task by using student log-files obtained from Learning Management Systems (LMS), along with technological scaffolding interventions to develop time management skills in blended and online for-credit courses [2, 8]. However, there are several issues associated to the use of this type of data, such as handling time spans between learning sessions and outliers within trace data [9, 10].

Our approach to overcome the abovementioned problem was to adapt a paper-based timesheet to encourage students to self-report time-on-task on a weekly basis. This timesheet was based on previous work of Hägman, Honda and Yang [11] and adapted to follow geographically distributed teams of undergraduate engineer-designers [12]. Considering that weekly timesheets have been used in many professional scenarios — such as programming and consulting— a web-based application was developed to scale the application of weekly timesheets to a larger number of courses. Thus, this paper describes the proposed web-based application, along with presenting the outcomes of having used it in 134 course sections during the second semester of 2020.

2 Description of the Web-Based Application and its Use Cases

The web-based weekly timesheets consist of a monolithic web application that was developed in Ruby under the Ruby on Rails framework (https://rubyonrails.org/) according to a Model-View-Controller design pattern (see Fig. 1). This web-based application runs inside a Docker container (https://docs.docker.com/compose/rails/), using a PostgreSQL database (postgresql.org). It uses Git for version control, and the source code is stored in a Bitbucket repository.

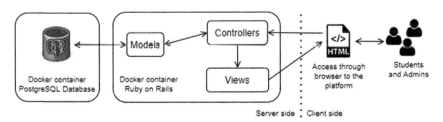

Fig. 1. Architecture of the web-based weekly timesheets

The purpose of using web-based weekly timesheets is twofold. First, it makes the students aware of their weekly workload inside and outside the class because they are encouraged to estimate the hours spent on specific tasks — including class-attendance and self-study activities. Secondly, the data provided allows managers and teaching faculty to visualize the perceived academic workload in real time and to contrast it with academic credit [13]. Along with this purpose, the web-based weekly timesheets have two main users: students and system admins (people who are responsible for the upkeep and the configuration of the web-based application). To apply these web-based weekly timesheets throughout an academic period, a system admin needs to carry out the following tasks before the period starts:

- Enter the starting date and the number of weeks in which the timesheets will be applied
- Upload the course numbers in which the timesheets will be applied
- Upload the list of students who are currently enrolled in these courses
- Configure the types of academic tasks that will be included in each timesheet (see Table 1)

Table 1. Tasks included in web-based weekly timesheets according to the type of course

Type of course	Academic activities included in the timesheet
Traditional	Lecture, Teaching Assistantship Sessions, Self-study
Project-based	Lecture, Project Work, Teaching Assistantship Sessions, Self-study
Labs	Lecture, Lab activities, Teaching Assistantship Sessions, Self-study
Capstone	Lecture, Capstone Project, Teaching Assistantship Sessions, Self-study

Note: Before the academic period starts, teaching staff can suggest other types of courses to include other type of academic activities in the corresponding timesheets

Once the system admins conduct these tasks, and the starting date is reached, students start receiving a weekly email with the URL to the web-based weekly timesheets. Then, students can authenticate themselves in the web-based application (using their university credentials) and self-report the number of hours that they have spent in specific academic tasks in each one of their courses over the past week (https://youtu.be/pyo2C9q2Da0) or opt out of the process indicating that they do not want to continue receiving the weekly emails. Once students declare the number of weeks, the system admins can download all the data that was collected for each course to report it to managers and faculty members.

3 Results and Outcomes Achieved

During the second semester of 2020, 5.221 students — who were enrolled in 134 course sections —were invited to participate in web-based weekly timesheets, and 3,131 voluntarily self-reported time-on-task throughout 16 weeks. In 76 out of the 134 course sections, bonus points were offered to those students who answered at least 80% of the surveys (only applicable for those students who have already approved the course). Throughout the semester, the rate of response ranged from 81% (2,542 out of 3,131 students in the second week) to 36% (1,147 out of 3,131 students in the sixteenth week) and teaching staff were provided with a dashboard to visualize student self-reports of time-on-task that enabled them to redesign subject activities for reducing workload [13].

After the academic period ended, an online survey was applied to the students who self-reported time-on-task, and 39% of them decided to voluntarily answer it (1,200 out of 3,113). In order to assess perceived usefulness and ease-of-use, the survey included a 5-point Likert scale based on prior work of Ali et al. [14] (see Fig. 2), along with the following check-box question: *Which of the following reasons explains your participation in the web-based weekly timesheets? Check all that apply* (see Fig. 3). Besides, a text box was included to allow students to make comments or suggestions at the end of the survey, and the inductive coding of its responses reveal that most students value weekly reminders to fill weekly timesheets and extra incentives to hold them accountable, such as bonus points. Still, they suggest including a dashboard, so they can analyze their academic workload weekly, monthly, and on a semester basis.

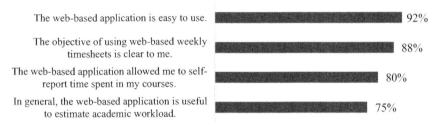

Fig. 2. Percentage of students who agreed or strongly agreed with the questionnaire items related to the perceived usefulness and ease of use of the web-based application (N = 1,200)

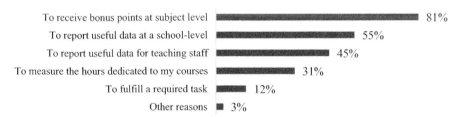

Fig. 3. Distribution of the percentage of students according to the reasons why they decided to self-report time-on-task throughout the web-based weekly timesheets (N = 1,200)

4 Future Work

Considering that many institutions are seeking simple, low-cost, scalable interventions aimed at improving time management [2], further research is required to develop this type of skills among students. In these lines, we are currently working in the integration of the web-based weekly timesheets into the institutional LMS. In addition to the dashboard that we already created to provide teaching staff with information about the perceived peaks of academic workload throughout the semester [13], we expect to provide students with visualizations that contrast their self-reported time-on-task with the one estimated by means of student log files.

References

1. Adams, R.V., Blair, E.: Impact of time management behaviors on undergraduate engineering students' performance. SAGE Open **9**(1), 2158244018824506 (2019). https://doi.org/10.1177/2158244018824506
2. Baker, R., Evans, B., Li, Q., Cung, B.: Does inducing students to schedule lecture watching in online classes improve their academic performance? An experimental analysis of a time management intervention. Res. High Educ. **60**(4), 521–552 (2019)
3. Lay, C.H., Schouwenburg, H.C.: Trait procrastination, time management, and academic behavior. J. Soc. Behav. Pers. **8**(4), 647–662 (1993)
4. Scherer, S., Talley, C.P., Fife, J.E.: How personal factors influence academic behavior and GPA in African American STEM students. SAGE Open **7**(2), 215824401770468 (2017). https://doi.org/10.1177/2158244017704686
5. IAU: The Impact of Covid-19 on Higher Education around the World (2020)
6. Kizilcec, R.F., Pérez-Sanagustín, M., Maldonado, J.J.: Recommending self-regulated learning strategies does not improve performance in a MOOC. In: L@S 2016 - Proceedings of the 3rd 2016 ACM Conference on Learning Scale, pp. 101–104 (2016). https://doi.org/10.1145/2876034.2893378
7. Baker, R., Evans, B., Dee, T.: A randomized experiment testing the efficacy of a scheduling nudge in a massive open online course (MOOC). AERA Open **2**(4), 233285841667400 (2016). https://doi.org/10.1177/2332858416674007
8. Pérez-Sanagustín, M., et al.: A MOOC-based flipped experience: scaffolding SRL strategies improves learners' time management and engagement. Comput. Appl. Eng. Educ. **29**(4), 750–768 (2021). https://doi.org/10.1002/cae.22337
9. Nguyen, Q.: Rethinking time-on-task estimation with outlier detection accounting for individual, time, and task differences. In: ACM International Conference Proceeding Series, 2020, pp. 376–381 (2020). https://doi.org/10.1145/3375462.3375538
10. Kovanovic, V., Gašević, D., Dawson, S., Joksimovic, S., Baker, R.: Does time-on-task estimation matter? Implications on validity of learning analytics findings. J. Learn. Anal. **2**(3), 81–110 (2016). https://doi.org/10.18608/jla.2015.23.6
11. Häggman, A., Honda, T., Yang, M.C.: The influence of timing in exploratory prototyping and other activities in design projects (2013). https://doi.org/10.1115/DETC2013-12700
12. Hilliger, I., Miranda, C., Celis, S., Pérez-Sanagustín, M.: Evaluating usage of an analytics tool to support continuous curriculum improvement. In: European Conference on Technology Enhanced Learning, 2019, vol. 2437, pp. 1–14 (2019). http://ceur-ws.org/Vol-2437/paper5.pdf
13. Hilliger, I., Miranda, C., Schuit, G., Duarte, F., Anselmo, M., Parra, D.: Evaluating a learning analytics dashboard to visualize student self-reports of time-on-task: a case study in a Latin American University. In: Proceedings of the 11th International Conference on Learning Analytics and Knowledge, 2021, pp. 592–598 (2021). https://doi.org/10.1145/3448139.3448203
14. Ali, L., Asadi, M., Gašević, D., Jovanović, J., Hatala, M.: Factors influencing beliefs for adoption of a learning analytics tool: an empirical study. Comput. Educ. **62**, 130–148 (2013)

Author Index

Afzaal, Muhammad 16
Alario-Hoyos, Carlos 384
Albó, Laia 419
Aleven, Vincent 207, 260, 347
Alonso-Prieto, Víctor 332
Amarasinghe, Ishari 373
Andrade, Pamela 315
Andrade-Hoz, Jimena 368
Andriamiseza, Rialy 245
Aristeidou, Maria 110
Asensio-Pérez, Juan I. 163, 332, 368, 404

Barzola, Valeria 310
Ben Soussia, Amal 193
Bennacer, Ibtissem 320
Berman, Susan R. 347
Bhatt, Sohum Mandar 300
Bongard, Leonard 289
Bonnin, Geoffray 363
Bote-Lorenzo, Miguel L. 332, 368, 404
Bothorel, Cecile 82
Bouchet, François 221
Boyer, Anne 193, 363
Bravo, Felipe 368
Brender, Jérôme 67
Brisson, Laurent 82
Broisin, Julien 245
Bruno, Barbara 67
Buraha, Tetiana 137
Buzzi, Marina 37
Buzzi, Maria Claudia 37

Carrió, Mar 352
Carron, Thibault 221
Carruana Martín, Adrián 384
Chalatsis, Xenofon 419
Charbey, Raphaël 82
Chessel-Lazzarotto, Frédérique 67
Chiodini, Luca 399
Chung, Cheng-Yu 149
Clemente, Félix J. García 337
Cukurova, Mutlu 163

Daniel, Morgane 221
De Bie, Lien 300
De Laet, Tinne 52
Delgado Kloos, Carlos 384
Dennerlein, Sebastian 1
Dey-Plissonneau, Aparajita 409
Di Mitri, Daniele 137
Dieckmann, Max 419
Dimitriadis, Yannis 163, 358
Divitini, Monica 178
Djelil, Fahima 82

Echeverria, Vanessa 260, 310
El-Hamamsy, Laila 67

Fancsali, Stephen 347
Fehnker, Ansgar 379
Fendt, Marvin 235
Fessl, Angela 1

Gallidabino, Andrea 399
García-Zarza, Pablo 332
Gilliot, Jean-Marie 82
Gomez, Manuel J. 337
Gómez-Sánchez, Eduardo 404
Greubel, André 424
Guo, Boyuan 260
Gutiérrez-Páez, Nicolas Felipe 352

Hakami, Eyad 373
Hauswirth, Matthias 399
Heidmets, Mati 28
Heintz, Matthias 315
Henderikx, Maartje 305
Hennecke, Martin 424
Hernández-Leo, Davinia 352, 373, 389, 394, 419
Hilliger, Isabel 430
Holstein, Kenneth 347
Hsiao, I-Han 149, 326

Iksal, Sébastien 320

Author Index

Jost, Patrick 178

Kluge, Anders 342
Kreijns, Karel 305

Law, Effie Lai-Chong 315
Lawrence, LuEttaMae 260, 347
Lee, Hyowon 409, 414
Leoste, Janika 28
Ley, Tobias 28
Li, Xiu 16
Litherland, Kristina 342
Liu, Mingming 414
Lobo, René 394
López-Pernas, Sonsoles 122

Macías, Julio 310
Mader, Angelika 379
Maitz, Katharina 1
McLaren, Bruce M. 347
Michel, Christine 96
Miranda, Constanza 430
Moissa, Barbara 363
Mondada, Francesco 67
Mørch, Anders I. 342

Nagashima, Tomohiro 207
Nistor, Nicolae 235
Nouri, Jalal 16

Ognibene, Dimitri 394
Ordóñez, Cristóbal 368
Pammer-Schindler, Viktoria 1

Papanikolaou, Kyparisia 358
Paredes, Yancy Vance 326
Parmentier, Jean-François 245
Pedro, Luís 295
Pérez-Sanagustín, Mar 430
Pichardo, Harlyn 310
Pierrot, Laëtitia 96
Pishtari, Gerti 275
Pradier, Vincent 409
Prieto, Luis P. 275

Ritter, Steven 347
Rodríguez-Triana, María Jesús 275
Roussanaly, Azim 193
Ruano, Irene 368

Ruffieux, Philippe 82
Ruipérez-Valiente, José A. 337
Ruiz-Calleja, Adolfo 332, 404
Rummel, Nikol 260
Rump, Arthur 379

Sánchez-Reina, Roberto 394
Santos, Carlos 295
Santos, Patricia 352, 389
Saqr, Mohammed 122
Scheers, Hanne 52
Scheibenzuber, Christian 235
Schiffner, Daniel 137
Schneider, Jan 137
Schuit, Gregory 430
Scriney, Michael 409, 414
Senette, Caterina 37
Sergent, Thomas 221
Serrano-Iglesias, Sergio 332, 404
Sgouropoulou, Cleo 358
Siller, Hans-Stefan 424
Silvestre, Franck 245
Smeaton, Alan F. 409, 414
Sobrino, Sara Lorena Villagrá 332
Solari-Landa, Melina 96
Sousa, Lorena 295
Stepanova, Jelena 28
Steuer, Tim 289
Stylianidou, Nayia 419
Suraworachet, Wannapon 163

Theophilou, Emily 394
Trujillo, Amaury 37

Uhlig, Jan 289

Van Den Noortgate, Wim 300
Vega-Gorgojo, Guillermo 368, 404
Velamazán, Mariano 389
Venant, Rémi 320
Villa-Torrano, Cristina 163

Weegar, Rebecka 16
Wu, Yongchao 16

Xu, Kate M. 305

Yadav, Gautam 207
Yang, Kexin Bella 260

Zalavra, Eleni 358
Zambrano, Dick 310
Zhou, Qi 163

Zia, Aayesha 16
Zimmer, Gianluca 289
Zufferey, Jessica Dehler 67

Printed by Printforce, the Netherlands